Contents

Items listed in green at the end of each chapter relate to tables available on the web only. Data relating to other items are also available on the website, including alternative time periods. All are accessible from the Regional Trends on-line publication www.statistics.gov.uk/regionaltrends39

Carshalton College

00015038

R 314.2

national
STATISTICS

Regional Trends

No. 39

2006 edition

Learning Centre   iE
Carshalton College
Nightingale Road   Y SM5 2EJ
Carshalton, SM5 2EJ   Statistics
Tel: 020 8544 4344
Return on or before the last date stamped below.

LEARNING CENTRE
CARSHALTON COLLEGE
02/07

palgrave
macmillan

© Crown copyright 2006

Published with the permission of the Controller of Her Majesty's Stationery Office (HMSO)

You may re-use this publication (excluding logos) free of charge in any format for research, private study or internal circulation within an organisation. You must re-use it accurately and not use it in a misleading context. The material must be acknowledged as Crown copyright and you must give the title of the source publication. Where we have identified any third party copyright material you will need to obtain permission from the copyright holders concerned.

This publication is also available at the National Statistics website: **www.statistics.gov.uk**

For any other use of this material please apply for a Click-Use Licence for core material at **www.opsi.gov.uk/click-use/system/online/pLogin.asp** or by writing to:

Office of Public Sector Information
Information Policy Team
St Clements House
2-16 Colegate
Norwich NR3 1BQ

Fax: 01603 723000
E-mail: hmsolicensing@cabinet-office.x.gsi.gov.uk

First published 2006 by
PALGRAVE MACMILLAN
Houndmills, Basingstoke, Hampshire RG21 6XS and
175 Fifth Avenue, New York, NY 10010, USA
Companies and representatives throughout the world.

PALGRAVE MACMILLAN is the global academic imprint of the Palgrave Macmillan division of St. Martin's Press, LLC and of Palgrave Macmillan Ltd. Macmillan® is a registered trademark in the United States, United Kingdom and other countries. Palgrave is a registered trademark in the European Union and other countries.

ISBN 1-4039-9071-9
ISSN 0261-1783

This book is printed on paper suitable for recycling and made from fully managed and sustained forest sources.

A catalogue record for this book is available from the British Library.

10   9   8   7   6   5   4   3   2   1
15 14 13 12 11 10 09 08 07 06

Printed and bound in Great Britain by Hobbs the Printers Ltd, Totton, Hampshire.

A National Statistics publication

National Statistics are produced to high professional standards set out in the National Statistics Code of Practice. They are produced free from political influence.

About the Office for National Statistics

The Office for National Statistics (ONS) is the government agency responsible for compiling, analysing and disseminating economic, social and demographic statistics about the United Kingdom. It also administers the statutory registration of births, marriages and deaths in England and Wales.

The Director of ONS is also the National Statistician and the Registrar General for England and Wales.

Contact points

For enquiries about this publication, contact the Editor.

E-mail: regional.trends@ons.gov.uk

For general enquiries, contact the National Statistics Customer Contact Centre.

Tel: 0845 601 3034 (minicom: 01633 812399)
E-mail: info@statistics.gsi.gov.uk
Fax: 01633 652747
Post: Room 1015, Government Buildings, Cardiff Road, Newport NP10 8XG

You can also find National Statistics on the Internet at: **www.statistics.gov.uk**

Introduction

Regional Trends, published by the Office for National Statistics, exists to paint a statistical picture of areas within the United Kingdom to assist in understanding the complex relationships between locations and the people who live there. The information aids decision making at national, local and European level. This volume brings together data from a wide range of sources, both from within government and outside, to provide an insight into the countries and regions of the United Kingdom.

Interest in local information and regional diversity continues to grow, as does the wealth of data available at various geographic levels. Similarly, the range of customers for this type of information widens and Regional Trends must evolve to meet these requirements. We continue to develop our products – Regional Trends and associated datasets – to reflect these changing priorities, new policies and data improvements.

Since the last edition we have investigated the most appropriate ways of responding to customer needs and changing situations by conducting a review of our publication portfolio. As a result, we are putting in place a more integrated set of products which will provide an authoritative reference source while allowing more flexibility in terms of format and frequency of updating. Regional Trends will remain one of the central pillars for delivering information, but will be linked to an electronic hub to provide access to a much wider range of information.

We are shifting the emphasis of Regional Trends to give more importance to analysis and interpretation, while still providing a balanced overview of the major topic areas. Datasets that underpin the analysis are being made available via the National Statistics website (www.statistics.gov.uk). The new approach also allows datasets to be updated more frequently and include data for longer, or alternative, time periods. An improved on-line version of Regional Trends will give access to Excel versions of the tables (or data behind maps and charts), as well as PDF versions of the chapters.

Statistics will be accompanied by more analysis and commentary, including research into new data sources and statistical tools to aid understanding of what makes one area different from, or similar to, another. We aim to provide evidence for discussion or to help elucidate questions such as how the characteristics of an area can be used to inform policies, or ways in which these can be implemented to benefit the majority of people. In this edition we outline how the National Statistics classification of output areas can be used to profile areas, look at the ethnic mix in different areas with various levels of deprivation and examine the factors influencing regional economic performance.

A new web page has been set up to complement Regional Trends and to provide a gateway to other regional and sub-regional information. This Regional Snapshot web page will provide access to a wide range of data, maps and articles, including key local authority data. A first version was launched in September 2005 at www.statistics.gov.uk/regionalsnapshot. This will be enlarged and updated to include information previously available through our Region in Figures series. The Regional Snapshot will allow greater flexibility in updating the information and provide access to a wider selection of contextual material for the reader.

Presentation of high quality and relevant information as outlined above is only part of the Regional Statistics Framework that is being developed jointly across the Government Statistical Service (GSS). Other elements that will in due course impact on the availability of relevant statistics are processes to identify regional users' needs, the identification of key statistics that need to be made available on a comparable basis across the UK and in the longer term the development of new statistical sources.

Regional Trends is designed to help address general questions posed by users of sub-national statistics who require statistics that can examine for example:

i. the latest figures for a particular topic for a defined area

ii. the relationship between areas (for example neighbouring or similar areas) in terms of these statistics

iii. deeper spatial relationships between statistics and the underlying geography of areas

iv. multiple relationships between statistics on different topics across the social/economic spectrum including environmental information.

The intention of Regional Trends as a 'flagship' publication is to enable readers to see the big picture emerging from such perspectives. The publication will not necessarily contain all the information and analysis, but will help point users to relevant sources, and it is here in particular that the developments in the regional web pages will be relevant.

Coverage and definitions

A section of Notes and Definitions provides details of coverage to assist in analysing and interpreting the information; additional data are also included in some instances. There is also a section on maps showing the geographic boundaries applicable to various datasets. This publication includes maps and notes that support information available via the website. Because of variations in coverage and definitions, some care may be needed when comparing data from more than one source. Readers are encouraged to consult the Notes and Definitions, footnotes to the tables and other references provided.

Where possible we have included data for the enlarged European Union which came into being in May 2004. Comparative data for the previous 15 Member States have been retained for this volume.

Availability of electronic data

The contents of Regional Trends 39 will be available free of charge via the National Statistics web site, both in PDF format and as downloadable Excel files. An on-line publication based on the individual topic areas will be available (www.statistics.gov.uk/regionaltrends39), which together with the Regional Snapshot web page (www.statistics.gov.uk/regionalsnapshot) will provide easy access to a wider range of data than before. Previous editions of Regional Trends are also available from the Virtual Bookshelf area of the National Statistics site (www.statistics.gov.uk).

Further information

Regional and sub-regional statistics can be found in a range of other GSS publications, statistical bulletins and regular press releases. Much of the information relating to population, households and the labour market presented in Regional Trends can be found on Nomis®, the on-line database run by Durham University under contract to the Office for National Statistics (ONS). It contains government statistics down to the smallest available geographic area, which might be unpublished elsewhere.

Neighbourhood Statistics also delivers a wealth of data relating to more local areas. More information about the service can be found on the Neighbourhood Statistics web pages at www.statistics.gov.uk/neighbourhood

In addition, data for Wales are published on the National Assembly for Wales website (www.wales.gov.uk), data for Scotland are published on the Scottish Executive website (www.scotland.gov.uk), and data for Northern Ireland are published on the Northern Ireland Office website, (www.northernireland.gov.uk). Details of these sources, and others, are available on the National Statistics website (www.statistics.gov.uk).

Summary

Regional Trends provides a unique description of the regions and countries of the United Kingdom. It covers a wide range of demographic, social, industrial and economic statistics, taking a look at most aspects of life. The book falls broadly into four sections: articles outlining research and development of new datasets, regional profiles (Chapter 1), comparisons across the European Union (Chapter 2) and the main topic areas (Chapters 3 to 13). In support of these chapters there are comprehensive sections on Geography and Notes and Definitions. To make comparison between regions easy, information is given in clear tables, with footnotes highlighting differences in coverage where appropriate.

Regional statistics are essential for a wide range of people including policy makers and planners in both the public and private sectors, marketing professionals, researchers, students and teachers, journalists, and anyone with a general interest in regional information. *Regional Trends 39* brings together data from diverse sources and, for some topics, is the only publication where data for the whole of the United Kingdom are available in one place. Wherever data for the component parts of the United Kingdom are sufficiently comparable, figures have been aggregated to give a national average or total.

Given the wide subject content as well as the geographic dimension, it is not possible to provide a simple summary of what the statistics show. The following paragraphs set out some of the highlights of this volume.

Convergence of economic prosperity

One of the major developments over the last few years in respect of Government policies relating to the parts of the United Kingdom and the regions within England has been the aim to reduce the economic divergence between the different parts of the UK. This has been measured through the statistics of regional gross value added (GVA). Chapter 12 of this volume sets out the latest figures on this topic and shows how the divergence between regions has stabilised even though major differences in the level of prosperity continue to exist. The article *Analysing Differences in Regional Economic Performance* provides a further examination of the variations between regions, showing how the differences in prosperity can be divided into components, taking account in particular, of information about hours worked.

The perception of relative regional performance can change considerably according to the measure of productivity chosen. For example, GVA per hour worked is considered a more appropriate measure of productivity since it takes into account the mix of part-time and full-time workers.

The more detailed analysis also shows the importance of differences within, rather than simply between regions: for example, that the areas of Bedfordshire and Hertfordshire in the East of England and Berkshire, Buckinghamshire and Oxfordshire in the South East are more productive in terms of GVA per hour worked than Inner London.

Differences between types of areas

Within the UK, local areas each have characteristics that may be similar to, or at variance with, others in the region or elsewhere. These characteristics allow the local areas to be grouped in various ways. These groupings or classifications are powerful tools to aid understanding of the areas, and are examined in the article *Profiling Areas using the Output Area Classification*.

Different types of locality can show wider variation than that exhibited between regions. For example a population 'churning effect' (a high proportion of population moving into and out of an area) can be identified in one of the classification groups, found in larger concentrations in cities, regardless of region.

Area classifications are used widely by the public sector and private sector to target policies and marketing campaigns. The Output Area Classification featured in this article has a multitude of potential uses from aiding decisions about strategies or policies down to understanding the area in which the user lives.

Analysis of deprivation

Deprivation is an important issue and analyses have been developed to respond to the policy drive to reduce the difference between the poorer and wealthier areas of the UK. Improved information at a local level to support these analyses is essential so that resources can be targeted as accurately as possible. One tool developed to measure deprivation at a local level was the 2004 Indices of Multiple Deprivation. These indices measured deprivation in very small areas (on average 1,500 people per area) using a variety of indicators covering several topics such as employment, health service provision and housing. The article *Deprivation and Ethnicity in England: A Regional Perspective* uses a combination of data from the 2004 Indices of Multiple Deprivation and the 2001 Census to analyse the population mix of different types of areas.

Improving understanding of the characteristics of people and their areas can assist in addressing the complex issues of deprivation, a key objective for Government policies.

Ethnicity data from the 2001 Census is used to illustrate how the proportion of different ethnic groups varies considerably between the regions of England, and between local areas with different levels of deprivation. This is a new way of analysing ethnicity data and adds value to the interpretation of the geographic distribution of ethnic groups across the regions of the UK. It was found that some ethnic groups were more likely to live in local areas that have been classed as among the more deprived in England. For example, the Bangladeshi and Pakistani groups were the most likely to live in deprived areas, making up four times the proportion of the population in the most deprived local areas that they did for England as a whole.

Diversity within and between regions

While it is true that regional diversity exists, there is often evidence of greater differences within the regions. For example in the North West, Eden has a population density of 24 people per square kilometre compared with over 4,000 people in the same size area in Blackpool. (Table 1.7)

The average house price in Macclesfield was over £230,000, two and half times the average in Blackburn with Darwen, at £85,000 in 2004, whereas average dwelling prices varied between £115,000 in the North East and £126,000 in the North West. (Tables 1.4 and 1.8)

Gross weekly average earnings for males in London reached £575 in April 2005, but their female counterparts earned over £90 per week less at £483. In other areas of the UK, earnings for both males and females were lower, with £410 per week in Northern Ireland being the lowest for males and £328 in the North East the lowest for females. (Tables 1.45 and 1.25)

Over the last three years, earnings have continued to increase in all regions, with the increase averaging almost 10 per cent for males and 12.5 per cent for females since April 2002. The greatest increases were for females in Northern Ireland (18.6 per cent) and Scotland and the North East (16.5 per cent each).

Although London continued to have the highest gross value added (GVA) per head of over £22,200 in 2004, there was a slight narrowing of the range compared with the UK average. In 2004 London was 32 per cent above the average with the North East 20 per cent below. The East of England and South East were the only other regions with GVA per head above the national average, by 9 and 16 per cent respectively. (Table 12.1)

Housing costs in London were considerably higher than elsewhere, £20 per week above the national average. Household expenditure per person was highest in the South East at £204 per week, with London £10 below this. Between 13 and 16 per cent of household expenditure went on transport in each area, the largest single item, ranging from £47 to over £61 per week. (Table 8.11)

Wales, the North East and North West each spent 15 per cent of total household expenditure on recreation and culture each week, more than £50 per week in each case. All regions, with the exception of London, spent more on recreation and culture than they did on housing. (Table 8.11)

Cohabiting was highest in the South East and South West, each with over 30 per cent of non-married people aged between 16 and 59 living together. The proportion was lowest in Northern Ireland at 13 per cent. (Figure 3.15)

Between 1981 and 2003 the greatest growth in the number of households was in the East and South West, each increased by 30 per cent to 2.3 million and 2.1 million respectively. The South East had the highest number of households, 3.4 million in 2003, and also the highest projected growth of 20 per cent to just over 4 million by 2021. (Table 3.16)

Are we getting greener?

Despite more new cars being registered, there was a slight decrease in the distance each person travelled by car in Great Britain between 2002/03 and 2003/04. The South East had the largest decrease of 242 miles between the two years (4 per cent reduction). Four regions showed slight increases in this period, ranging from the North West (21 miles) to Wales (243 miles). (Tables 10.1 and 10.5)

People in Wales and the East Midlands walked further in 2003/04 than the previous year, an additional 10 and 11 miles respectively. In Scotland and the North East there were reductions of 13 and 10 miles respectively in average distances walked. Residents of the East Midlands cycled further, increasing the distance they pedalled by almost one-third to 49 miles per person in 2004. Only people in the West Midlands and the South East reduced the distance cycled, by 14 per cent and 15 per cent respectively.

Air travel has increased substantially over the last few years, the largest increase being at Stansted Airport in the East where there was a four-fold increase between 1998 and 2004 to over 17 million scheduled international passengers. The regional airports of Edinburgh, Bristol and East Midlands have more than doubled their international passenger numbers over the same time period. (Table 10.16)

Overall, the amount of waste reduced slightly by 0.6 kg per household per week between 2002/03 and 2003/04, although the amount produced in Wales increased across the four-year period from 22.8 kg in 2000/01 to 24.1 kg per household in 2003/04. Households in the North West and the East each reduced their production of waste by 0.8 kg between 2002/03 and 2003/04.

Recycling has increased in all regions over the last three years: on average about 18 per cent of household waste in England and Wales was recycled in 2003/04. The North East recycled the lowest amount of household waste, only 12 per cent in 2003/04, compared with 23 per cent in the East and South East. The amount of paper and card recycled increased by 19 per cent between 2002/03 and 2003/04 overall for England. (Tables 11.14 and 11.15)

Is life improving?

Standards achieved in GCSE or Scottish equivalent examinations continued to increase throughout the UK over the last few years, with 54 per cent of pupils achieving 5 or more grade A*-C GCSEs (or equivalent) in 2003/04. Fewer than 5 per cent of pupils did not obtain a graded qualification. Northern Ireland with 60 per cent, Scotland with just over and the South East just under 58 per cent, had the largest proportion of pupils achieving these higher grades.(Table 4.4)

For English, 65 per cent of females achieved a GCSE grade A*-C (or equivalent) compared with 50 per cent of males. In modern languages females were also more successful, 45 per cent compared with the males' rate of 30 per cent. However, in mathematics the difference in achievement between females and males narrowed to 2.8 percentage points. (Web: ET3)

Death rates continue to decline in all areas and in 2003 were 10.3 per 1,000 population for the UK overall. The rates were lowest in London (7.8) and Northern Ireland (8.5) compared with 11.6 and 11.5 per 1,000 population in Scotland and Wales respectively. Cancer accounted for over one-quarter of each region's mortality rate in 2003.

Heart disease is also a major cause of death, with more than 200 male deaths per 100,000 population in the North East, North West, Wales and Scotland during 2003.

Female deaths from heart disease were somewhat lower, ranging from 134 in the South East to 193 in Scotland. (Tables 3.7, 3.11 and 7.4)

The number of recorded criminal offences reduced by 7 per cent for Great Britain between 2003/04 and 2004/05. All regions except Scotland showed reductions in the number of offences, ranging from just over 1 per cent in the South East to nearly 14 per cent in Yorkshire and the Humber. Burglary was down by over 17 per cent overall, and in northern regions of England and the Midlands the reduction in rates was around 20 per cent. Yorkshire and the Humber again showed the most improvement of 28 per cent between the two years. (Table 9.1)

Geography

Regional boundaries

The United Kingdom comprises Great Britain and Northern Ireland; Great Britain consists of England, Wales and Scotland. The Isle of Man and the Channel Islands are not part of the United Kingdom. The Scilly Isles are included as part of Cornwall throughout.

The statistical regions of the United Kingdom comprise the Government Office Regions for England, plus Wales, Scotland and Northern Ireland. The local government administrative structure provides the main framework for breaking down the regions into smaller areas. A map of the statistical regions of the United Kingdom can be found in the Regional Profiles chapter. Details of other key boundaries for the UK are given towards the back of the volume in the section on Maps.

Nomenclature for Territorial Units (NUTS)

Some data are presented using the European Nomenclature for Territorial Units (NUTS) area classification, primarily economic data in Chapters 12 and 13 and also in Chapter 2. Further information on the NUTS classification is contained in the Notes and Definitions.

Sub-regional geography

The sub-regional information relates mainly to local authorities and reflects the complete implementation of the local government reorganisation that happened between 1 April 1995 and 1 April 1998. In a few chapters other sub-regional geography may be used, for example Strategic Health Authorities in Chapter 7.

Summary information for the local authorities can be found in the Regional Profiles (Chapter 1); however, more detailed data at this level of geography will be found on www.statistics.gov.uk/regionalsnapshot

Data for local authorities are presented firstly by unitary authorities (UAs) listed in alphabetical order, followed by counties subdivided into local authority districts (LAD), again listed alphabetically.

Full details of the local government reorganisation and the NUTS area classification are given in the *Gazetteer of Old and New Geographies of the United Kingdom* available from the National Statistics website www.statistics.gov.uk/geography/changing_geog.asp

Acknowledgements

The editors would like to thank the following people for their help in producing this book:

Production Manager: Rukshinda Jahangir

Authors and
Production Team:

Robert Adams	Michael Jacobs	Dev Virdee
Linda Alderslade	Daniela New	Sharan Virdee
Judy Chan	Richard Seymour	Susan Williams
Janette Conquest	Sujata Talukdar	Iain Wilson
Peter Culver	Jonathan Tinsley	Mark Yeomans

Maps: Alistair Dent   Deborah Rhodes

Data collection: Core Table Unit

Contributors

The editors, authors and production team wish to thank all their colleagues in the ONS, contributing government departments and other organisations for their generous support and helpful comments, without whose help this publication would not be possible.

Data providers

Cadw
Central Services Agency, Northern Ireland
Centre for Ecology and Hydrology
Centre for Infections
Civil Aviation Authority
Department for:
   Culture, Media and Sport
   Education and Skills
   Employment & Learning, Northern Ireland
   Environment, Food and Rural Affairs
   Social Development in Northern Ireland
   Transport
   Work and Pensions
Department of:
   Agriculture and Rural Development for Northern Ireland
   Economic Development, Northern Ireland
   Education, Northern Ireland
   Enterprise, Trade and Investment, Northern Ireland
   Health
   Health, Social Services and Public Safety, Northern Ireland
   the Environment in Northern Ireland
   Trade and Industry
   English Heritage
   Environment Agency
   Environment and Heritage Service, Northern Ireland
Eurostat
Forest Service
Forestry Commission
General Register Office for Scotland

Health and Social Care Information Centre
Her Majesty's Inspectorate of Constabulary
Higher Education Statistics Agency
Historic Scotland
HM Revenue and Customs
Home Office
Institute of Child Health
Irish Central Statistical Office
Land Registry
Loughborough University
Met Office
National Assembly for Wales
National Health Service, Scotland
National Tourist Boards
Northern Ireland Court Service
Northern Ireland Office
Northern Ireland Statistics and Research Agency
Office of the Deputy Prime Minister
OFWAT
Ordnance Survey
Police Service of Northern Ireland
Scottish Centre for Infection and Environmental Health
Scottish Environment Protection Agency
Scottish Executive
Scottish Executive Education Department
Scottish Executive Justice Department
Scottish Executive Rural Affairs Department
Small Business Service
UK Trade and Investment

Analysing Differences in Regional Economic Performance

By Daniela New and Dev Virdee

Key points

- There are significant and persistent differences in economic performance both between and within the regions of the United Kingdom.

- Spatial differences in the UK appear large in comparison with those observed in other EU Member States and in the United States, as recently reported in the OECD report *Regions at a Glance* (2005).

- Differences in productivity, participation rates in the labour market and commuting patterns explain most of the regional differences in GVA (gross value added) per head.

- The perception of relative regional performance can change considerably according to the measure of productivity that is chosen. GVA per hour worked is considered a more appropriate measure of productivity since it takes into account the mix of part-time and full-time workers.

- If GVA per hour worked is used as the measure of productivity, the performance gap between regions reduces compared with other measures. In particular, the North East, which appears to be considerably below the UK average in terms of GVA per head (21 per cent below), is close to the average in terms of GVA per hour worked (1 per cent below).

- At sub-regional level (NUTS 2 level), there are areas (Bedfordshire and Hertfordshire in the East of England and Berkshire, Buckinghamshire and Oxfordshire in the South East) that seem to be more productive, in terms of GVA per hour worked, than Inner London. These areas are good examples of clever exploitation of untapped resources (infrastructure), specialisation in high value added sectors and high investment in research.

Introduction

It is well known that there are significant and persistent differences in economic performance, both between and within the regions of the United Kingdom. Moreover, spatial differences in the UK appear large in comparison with those observed in other EU Member States and in the USA.[a] These regional disparities, measured as differences in gross value added (GVA) per capita (per head), have been well documented recently in the OECD (Organisation for Economic Co-operation and Development) *Regions at a Glance* report and, previously, in the report *Productivity in the UK: 3 – The regional dimension* (HM Treasury, November 2001). The Treasury has recognised that underlying these regional economic differentials there are a number of different factors[1] and, according to this view, has identified five key drivers of economic growth to help the weakest regions to raise their productivity – skills, investment, innovation, enterprise and competition.

This article presents an analysis of the determinants of regional economic performance, aiming to identify the components that are more likely to explain the differences in GVA per capita between the regions.[2] This objective is pursued using a common framework, consistent with previous OECD work, which also allows the possibility of international comparisons.

For this analysis, it has been necessary to address various issues regarding the data and sources in order to select the best available data to fit the purposes. In particular, in respect of labour market data, it has been necessary to investigate and compare the different sources and variable definitions in order to be able to analyse the productivity issues in more detail. Particular focus has been on the differences in the composition of full-time and part-time workers in the regional labour markets, introducing an indicator of GVA per hour worked at the sub-regional level. This work has been done consistently for all the regions and countries of the UK, aiming to ensure comparability of the analysis, even though some of the data for Scotland and Northern Ireland may have come from different sources than those for England and Wales.

The main results of the work show how differences in productivity, in commuting flows and in participation in the

---

1   *HM Treasury has recognised that differences in GDP per capita are a function of regional variations in productivity and employment (in terms of demographics, labour market participation rates, etc).*

2   *The term region refers to the EU statistical geographical NUTS 1 level; the analysis also extends to the NUTS 2 and NUTS 3 levels.*

labour market, are important factors in explaining the variations in GVA per capita between UK regions. Moreover, they show that different measures of productivity can give a different picture of the regional economic performances. In particular, if the GVA per hour worked is used as the preferred measure of productivity instead of the GVA per capita or GVA per job, the gap between regions is lower.

Methodological overview

The OECD Directorate for Public Governance and Territorial Development has recently produced a document in which differences from the national averages in regional GVA per capita have been decomposed into six components: sector specialisation, average labour productivity, employment rates, age structure of population, activity rates and commuting rates.

Each of these components can be interpreted as an indicator of the determinants of economic performance at the regional level. These components can be grouped into two types of resources: natural endowments and untapped resources. Natural endowments are characteristics of a region that cannot be changed or can only be changed in the long run, such as geographic location, natural resources, urban or rural type, and demographics. The untapped resources are resources that could be more efficiently used and allocated to generate a higher level of GVA, e.g. transportation, general infrastructures, tourism-oriented facilities, labour market institutions and regulation, human and social capital.

On the basis of this decomposition, each region can be analysed to determine the components that explain the

largest proportions of the difference in GVA per capita, and policy makers can see the significance of individual factors on the economic performance of particular regions. The main determinants of differences in GVA per capita from the UK average are: **productivity**, **employment rate**, **commuting rate** and **activity rate** (please see definitions in Annex 2 and Formula 1 in Annex 1).

The measurement of productivity is very important as it is one of the main components of the economic performance of a region or a country. Different measures can tell a different story about the economy. Average labour productivity, as measured by GVA per worker or GVA per job, does not take into account the possible mix of part-time and full-time workers, which can vary by region. GVA per worker can therefore give a biased view of the productivity of a region, since it does not take account of the actual hours worked, and is therefore not considered to be the best measure of the effective performance of the labour force. In particular, with the current structure of the labour market (increasing home-working, part-time work and job-share availability), the GVA per hour worked is considered a more appropriate measure of productivity. Indicators of both GVA per hour worked and hours worked per job have therefore been developed for this analysis to give a more detailed picture of what lies underneath differences in productivity.

The GVA per hour worked indicator is computed using the **total workforce hours worked** data as the denominator. These data are extracted from the Labour Force Survey (LFS), and based on published data.[d] Figure A1.1 shows a comparison of three different measures of productivity, showing the

Figure **A1.1** Indicators comparison: GVA per capita, GVA per job and GVA per hour worked 2001

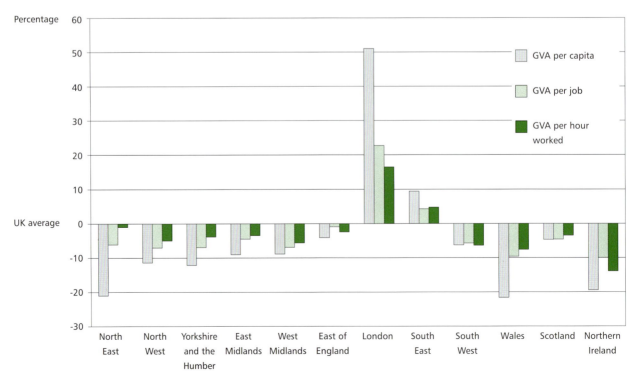

differences between each UK region and the UK average for the relevant indicator. It is quite clear how any judgement of a particular region's economic performance can change according to the indicator used.

Data on total actual hours worked, a different series, are however available from the Labour Force Survey at regional, unitary authority and local authority district (UA/LAD) level. Up to now, data on the preferred measure of workforce hours worked has only been available at regional (NUTS 1) level. The workforce hours worked series includes methodological changes designed to remove a previous bias towards full-time workers, and is therefore considered a more appropriate denominator for GVA per hour worked.

For the purpose of the analysis reported in this article, when looking at sub-regional economies, it was considered necessary to maintain consistency between the different geographical levels. It was therefore decided to pro-rate and constrain the NUTS 2 and NUTS 3[3] total hours worked series to the relevant NUTS 1 total for workforce hours worked.

Results

As mentioned above, different measures of productivity can tell a very different story about the regions' economic performances. In the same way, similar productivity levels may translate into very different outcomes in terms of GVA[e] per

capita for various reasons, including differences in the labour market and in the demographics of the population. In general, regional differences in GVA per head are greater than those in labour productivity (Figure A1.1). This work is an attempt[4] to show how the different components of GVA per capita are affecting these different performances; a corollary of this analysis is to show how the relevant factors impact at sub-regional level, and show in this way the variety of sub-national economies.

Figure A1.2 shows the main factors explaining the differences in GVA per capita for the NUTS 1 regions compared with the UK average. A large part of differences in GVA per capita can be explained by differences in labour productivity. If we consider the GVA per job measure the regions that lead in terms of GVA per capita, London (51 per cent above the UK average) and the South East (9 per cent above), are also lead-ing in terms of labour productivity (respectively 23 and 4 per cent above the UK average). However, labour productivity can vary when differences in the structure of the labour markets are taken into account (analysing the amount of hours worked).

The regions of the UK have been experiencing relatively low unemployment over the last few years and therefore **employment rate** is not particularly significant in explaining the regional differences from the UK average. The regions with the highest employment rates are the same in 2004 as they were in 2001 and in 1997, namely, the East of England,

Figure **A1.2** Main factors explaining regional differences in GVA per capita from UK average

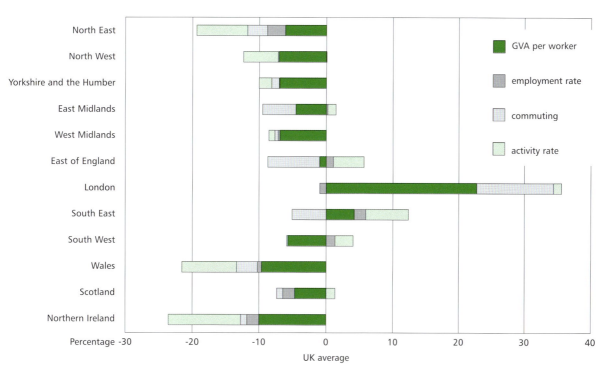

---

3   Since there were no data available for Northern Ireland at NUTS 3 level it was decided to multiply the average hours worked of Northern Ireland by the number of workforce jobs in the NUTS 3 sub-regions of Northern Ireland.

4   Since the analysis is based on different sources and variables, there is a residual from the average differences in GVA per head that is not explained. On average, 80 per cent of the differences are explained by the four main components, i.e. productivity (including an indicator GVA per hour worked), commuting, activity and employment rate.

South East and South West. If we consider the years between 1997 and 2001, most regions except Northern Ireland experienced increases in the rates of employment. In 2004 some of the UK NUTS 2 regions (Dorset and Somerset, and North Yorkshire) are among the regions with the lowest unemployment rate in the 25 countries of the EU[f] (2.4 per cent and 2.7 per cent respectively). However, it is worth noting that there are local areas suffering from high unemployment rates, and some of these areas have been recently identified in the report *Local Area Labour Market: Statistical indicators*, September 2005, published by ONS. This report also highlights how there can be a wide variation in local labour markets. London, for example, had in 2004 the highest average unemployment rate (7.1 per cent), but a closer look at its constituent boroughs showed enormous variation, from 12.6 per cent unemployment for Tower Hamlets to 2.6 per cent for Havering.

Activity rate is the percentage of the population in a region that is active or participating in the labour force. Compared with the employment rate, activity rate seems much more significant in explaining the regional differences in GVA per capita (please see Map A1.3 for activity rate at NUTS level 3). In particular, some of the regions that seem to be lagging behind have relatively low activity rates. Northern Ireland, Wales and the North East appear to be the most affected by particularly low rates of participation. The number of people in the labour force depends on several factors, including the demographic composition of the population. In this sense, we are observing different natural endowments in the regions, which cannot be changed, except in the long run. Almost all the regions with GVA per head higher than the UK average have high rates of participation in the labour force. The only exceptions are Inner London with high GVA per head, but low activity rate; the converse is evident in Highlands and Islands (Scotland) with GVA per head lower than the UK average whereas the activity rate is above average. Both exceptions can be explained: the age structure of the population and the concentration of disadvantaged groups within the Inner London resident population can explain the London exception, while resource and natural endowments play a relevant role in the case of this Scottish area.

At NUTS 3 level, most of the large cities seem to have a common characteristic: high GVA per capita but low activity rate. Belfast, Glasgow, Leicester and Birmingham are some examples of cities with GVA per capita higher than the UK average and participation rates below the average. In the case of cities, the high inflow of commuters has a large upward effect on the GVA per capita of the area, since the commuters are not included in the denominator, which is resident population.

Commuting effects are particularly important in determining GVA per head on a workplace basis. As may seem obvious, the highest rates of inward commuting were seen in the areas classified as predominantly urban, and commuters are likely to contribute to inflate the indicator (GVA per head) of the areas.

Inner London is of course the most striking example, with the highest level of inward commuting of all the UK areas. In particular, Inner London West has more than one and a half times the number of workers on a workplace basis as on a residence basis. Other cities such as Nottingham, Leicester, Belfast, Glasgow and Bristol follow a similar pattern, although to a lesser degree. Rural areas, in particular in Scotland (Lochaber, Skye and Lochalsh and Argyll and the Islands, or Inverness and Nairn and Moray, Badenoch and Strathspey) or in Yorkshire and the Humber (East Riding of Yorkshire, intermediate area) suffer the largest outflows of workers. Please see Map A1.4 for commuting flows at NUTS 3 level.

GVA per hour worked

As stated above, the perception of relative regional performance can change considerably according to the measure of productivity that is used.

Figure A1.5 reproduces the GVA per capita decomposition seen in Figure A1.2, but replacing the GVA per job by the GVA per hour worked as a measure of productivity and adding the hours worked per job, as a measure of work patterns.

It is evident that the differences between regions of GVA per hour worked, the preferred measure of productivity, seem much less striking than GVA per worker seen in Figure A1.2. The leading regions as always are London and the South East but their productivity advantages relative to other areas are reduced. The data for the North East region is of particular interest. According to the GVA per hour worked indicator, the North East is not much below average in terms of productivity, most of this difference from the UK average being explained by a negative hours worked ratio. The gap is also significantly smaller for Yorkshire and the Humber, followed by the North West and Wales.

The differences in terms of productivity (GVA per hour worked) within the regions are also of considerable interest. At the NUTS 2 level, the sub-regions of Berkshire, Buckinghamshire and Oxfordshire, and Bedfordshire and Hertfordshire appear to be the most productive in terms of GVA per hour worked, 20 per cent above the UK average against the 19 per cent of Inner London. Both areas have the advantages and disadvantages of being very close to London, which is the administrative and economic centre of the country. They both have an outward flow of workers commuting to London, where they are employed, which negatively affects the GVA on a workplace basis (even though this means that these areas have very high levels of income). On the other hand, both areas appear to have exploited this proximity to the heart of UK economic activity to their advantage.

Bedfordshire and Hertfordshire seems to be a good example of clever exploitation of untapped resources. Infrastructure such as Luton airport, situated on the southern border of the county of Bedfordshire and close to Hertfordshire, has become an important element in the economy of the area.

Map **A1.3**   Activity rate compared with the national average in the UK (NUTS level 3)

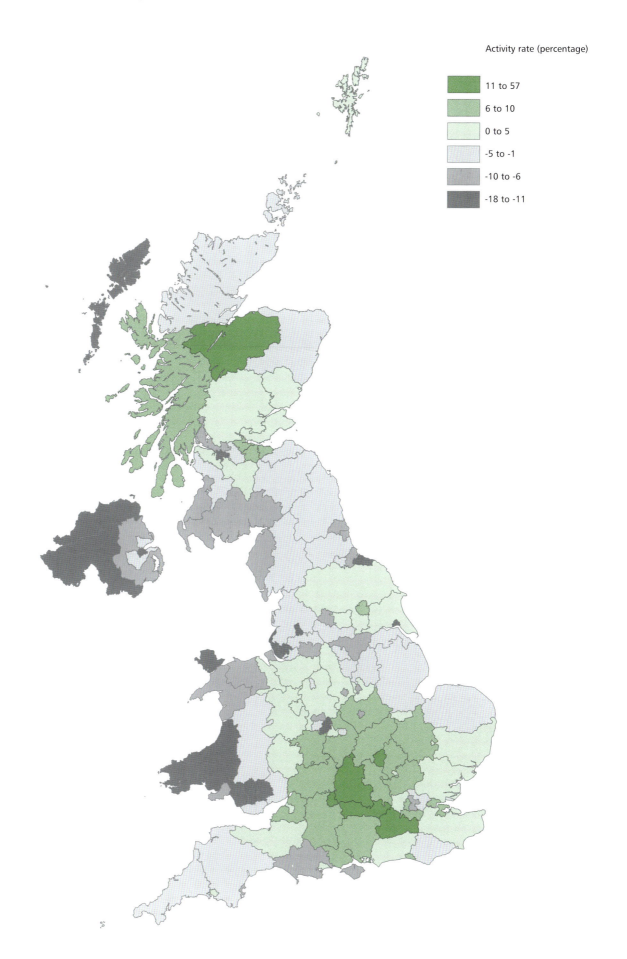

Activity rate (percentage)

- 11 to 57
- 6 to 10
- 0 to 5
- -5 to -1
- -10 to -6
- -18 to -11

Map **A1.4**   Net commuting flows within the UK (NUTS level 3)

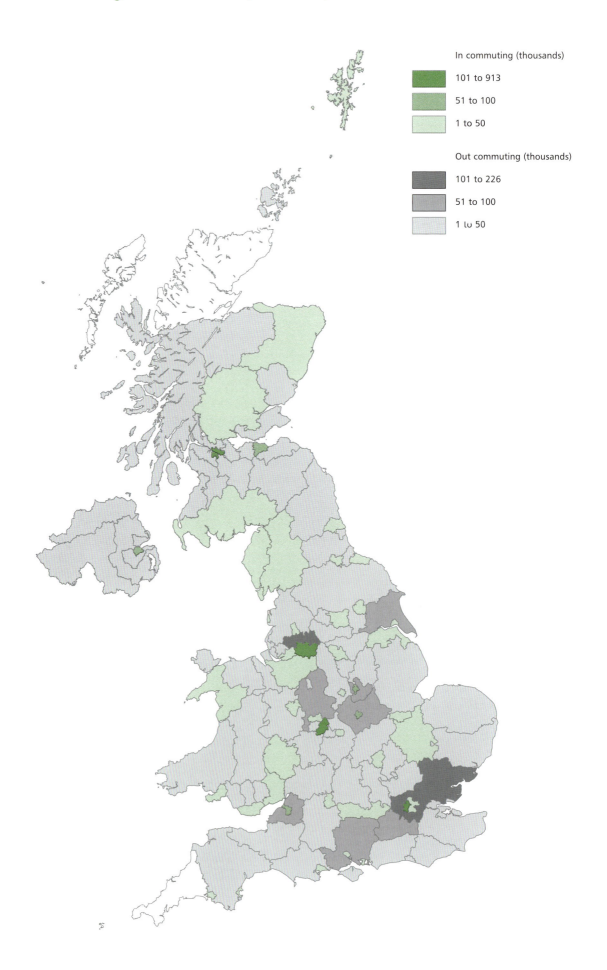

In commuting (thousands)

101 to 913

51 to 100

1 to 50

Out commuting (thousands)

101 to 226

51 to 100

1 to 50

Figure A1.5 Main factors explaining regional differences in GVA per capita from UK average, including GVA per hour worked as indicator of productivity

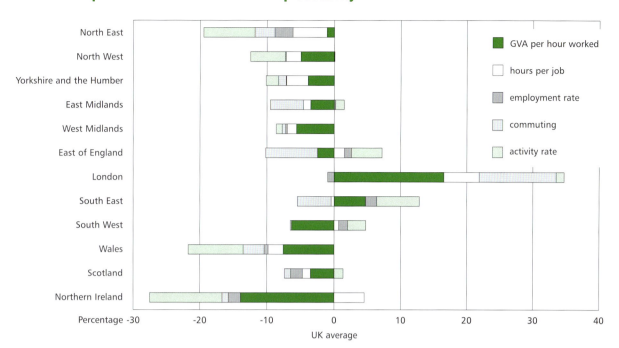

Luton is the seventh largest airport in the UK, considered as one of the London airports, and a very important international transit point, especially for charter flights. In 2001, 6.5 million passengers used Luton airport, with the revolution of low-cost airlines having had a significant impact on numbers.

Sectoral specialisation of an area is also an important part of the explanation for variations in the average levels of productivity. Major employers in Bedfordshire are the electronics, light and precision industries. The area is also a major centre of research and experimental development in natural sciences and engineering. Similarly, sectors such as biotechnology and pharmaceuticals, electronics and IT were, and still are, contributing significantly to the economy of Hertfordshire. The existence of such highly productive industries in the area contributes to the high overall productivity level for Bedfordshire and Hertfordshire.

Berkshire, Buckinghamshire and Oxfordshire has been one of the most successful areas in attracting key industrial sectors. Computing, telecommunications, pharmaceuticals and business and financial services are among the most important industries of the area. This area has witnessed strong economic growth in the past few years, which has created pressure for more skilled employees. More than 30 per cent of people of working age who are economically active have at least a higher degree.

Availability of excellent transport links in the South East is also a factor: the region has 12 motorways including the M25 (London orbital motorway), and two of the world's busiest airports – Heathrow and Gatwick. The M4, which runs through the Thames Valley, is the main link from London to Wales and the west of England.

As shown in Figure A1.6, the East and the South East have in

recent years been the regions with the highest level of total expenditure in research and development in the UK. In particular, in 2001, Bedfordshire and Hertfordshire in the East and Berkshire, Buckinghamshire and Oxfordshire in the South East were the areas with the highest investment in research and development in the business sector (see Figure A1.7).

It is also important to recognise the importance that foreign direct investment has in determining the productivity of this area. Berkshire, Buckinghamshire and Oxfordshire has proved to be a highly attractive location for inward investment, which is known to be a source of increased productivity, through knowledge spillovers and increased competition. IBM, Nokia, Vodafone and American Express are just some of the international companies located in the South East, as well as Microsoft, Sun Microsystems, Sony, Ericsson and Pfizer.

At NUTS 3 level it is interesting to note that there are areas that are below the UK average in terms of GVA per capita but above the average in terms of productivity, i.e. GVA per hour worked. Their poor performance in terms of GVA on a workplace basis is mainly due to a negative hours ratio (they work fewer hours per job) and to negative commuting rates, which mean that these areas normally experience substantial outflows of commuters. These areas include: South Nottinghamshire in the East Midlands, Sefton and East Merseyside in the North West, East Riding of Yorkshire, North Lanarkshire in South Western Scotland, Sunderland in the North East, and Medway in the South East.

Conclusions

In the UK, differences within regions are as important as those between regions. The aim of this article has been to identify

Figure **A1.6** Total investment in Research and Development as percentage of GVA for UK regions

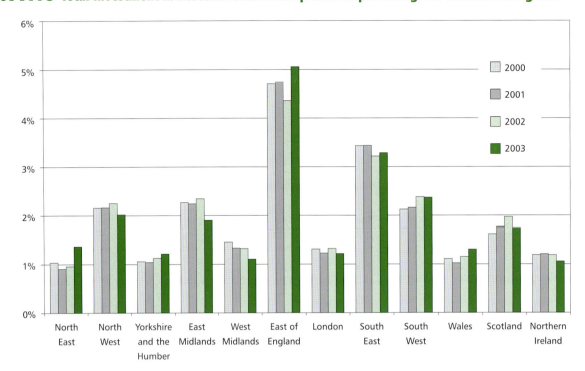

the components that are more likely to determine such differences.

Different measures of productivity can tell a very different story about the regions' economic performance. However, similar productivity levels may translate into very different outcomes in terms of GVA per capita due to various factors, including differences in the labour market and in the demographics of the population. In this article it has been shown that the differences in productivity, together with the commuting effect, are important factors in explaining the differences in GVA per capita. This work also shows how differently the regions and local areas can be seen if we change our perspective. In particular, if we take into account the GVA per hour worked as a measure of productivity, instead of GVA per capita or GVA per job, the gaps between regions seem to be smaller and, in some cases, even the ranking is different.

References

a. See Chart 1.2 HM Treasury report 2001 *Productivity in the UK: 3 – The Regional Dimension* and, more recently, an article in the *Financial Times* 6 October 2005.

b. *People and jobs: comparing sources of employment data* by Helen Ganson, Labour Market Trends, January 2002, ONS.

c. Data for ABI1 (number of employee jobs) have been supplied by Regional Accounts at NUTS 2 and NUTS 3 level. These data may differ from the data published on the NOMIS website due to adjustments made to take into account data outliers or implausible data.

d. Total Workforce Hours series is published as Table B33 of Labour Market Trends, although this is available only for NUTS 1 regions.

e. Figures on GVA per capita are supplied by ONS, Regional Account Division, which produces estimates of Workplace Based Nominal Gross Value Added (GVA). Data utilised in this report were released in December 2004.

f. As reported by Eurostat in the recent *Statistics in Focus*, March 2005.

General background

- *Identifying the Determinants of Regional Performances*, Vincenzo Spiezia, 2004, OECD

- *Labour Productivity Measures from the Annual Business Inquiry*, Chris Daffin and Eunice Lau. Economic Trends No. 589, Dec. 2002, ONS

- *Introducing new and improved labour productivity data*, Chris Daffin, Economic Trends No.570, May 2001, ONS

- *Regional labour market performance*, Craig Lindsay, Labour Market Trends, May 2002, ONS

- *Hours worked: a comparison of estimates from the Labour Force Survey and New Earnings Survey*, Richard D. Williams, Labour Market Trends, August 2002, ONS

- *Regional Growth*, Frontier Economics, September 2004

- *International comparisons of productivity – an update and developments*, Chris Drew, Craig Richardson and Prabhat Vaze, Economic Trends No.570, May 2001, ONS

Figure **A1.7** Investment in Research and Development in the Business Sector, for UK NUTS 2 areas, 2001

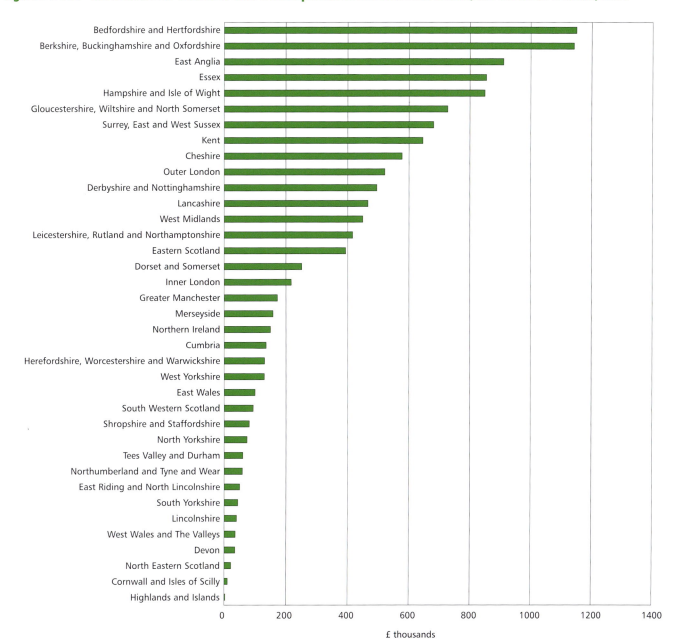

£ thousands

- *UK official productivity estimates: review of methodology*, Matthew Barnes and Mark Williams, Economic Trends No.610, September 2004

- *Revisions to workforce jobs and comparison with the Labour Force Survey jobs*, Ian Richardson, Labour Market Trends, February 2003

- *Working Hours, Productivity, Participation and Unemployment: Accounting for differences in regional performance*, a report from David Harvie, Bruce Philp and Gary Slater of the Political Economy Research Unit, Dept of Economics and Politics, Nottingham Trent University for the Nottinghamshire Research Observatory, April 2003

- *Local Area Labour Markets: statistical indicators September 2005*, ONS. Weblink: www.statistics.gov.uk/statbase/Product.asp?vlnk=14160

- *Portrait of the Regions*, Eurostat 2005

- *Regions at a Glance*, OECD 2005

Annex 1

GVA per capita (in logarithms) in region i can be written as:

$$\frac{GVA_i}{P_i} = \frac{GVA_i}{EW_i} + \frac{EW_i}{LFW_i} + \frac{LFW_i}{LFR_i} + \frac{LFR_i}{P_i} \qquad \text{Formula 1}$$

GVA per capita | Productiv-ity (GVA per job) | employ-ment rate | commut-ing effect | activity rate

where P, EW, LFW and LFR stand, respectively, for population, employment at the workplace, labour force at the workplace and labour force at the place of residence.

If the GVA per hour worked indicator is added, dividing the GVA per employee into GVA per hour worked (new productivity measure) and in hours worked per employee, Formula 1 shown above can be rewritten as:

$$\frac{GVA_i}{P_i} = \frac{GVA_i}{HW_i} + \frac{HW_i}{EW_i} + \frac{EW_i}{LFW_i} + \frac{LFW_i}{LFR_i} + \frac{LFR_i}{P_i}$$

Formula 2

where HW = hours worked.

Annex 2

Data sources and variable definitions:

Labour Force Survey (LFS) is a survey of households. The sample of 60,000 households is interviewed each quarter, with each household staying in the survey for one year. Five interviews are carried out at three-month intervals. A sample of addresses is drawn from Consignia's (which was at the time of the 2001 survey the Royal Mail's operating name) small users address file in Great Britain and the Valuation and Land Agency Register in Northern Ireland.

Commuting flows: Data on commuting were extracted using the LFS data on people in employment on a residence basis and on a workplace basis. LFS normally covers data on a residence basis but it also asks for the postcode of the respondents' workplace. These data may have a certain degree of error in the location of the place of work, since not everyone is aware of the postcode of where they work. However, this information is then aggregated at local authority level and at this level the error is likely to be less significant. Since the analysis is based on the NUTS classification, to allow for international comparisons, the data were transformed from unitary authority or local administrative units level 1 into what was previously know as NUTS 4 level and from here were summed up to NUTS 3, 2 and 1.

This procedure had some difficulties: in fact, while it was relatively easy to find a common code to link unitary authority and NUTS 4 geographical units for England and Wales,

there were problems regarding Scotland and Northern Ireland.

In Scotland, there is not a clear link between UA/LAD and what were the NUTS 4 geographical units. Data have been therefore allocated to the Scottish NUTS 4 (equivalent) geographies in proportion to the number of UAs included and with percentages proxied by the amount of population in each of them.

Regarding Northern Ireland, data on Employment at Workplace were available only at NUTS 1 and NUTS 2 level (which coincide). At NUTS 3 level data were extracted from the Northern Ireland Census 2001 (table UV 079). The difference in the total is not significant so this breakdown may be considered a faithful approximation of the LFS data.

Finding suitable data on people in employment at their place of work was one of the key issues of this research. Workplace-based data on employment are normally extracted from part 1 of the Annual Business Inquiry (ABI1).

Annual Business Inquiry is based on a random survey of 78,000 employers in the UK and covers mainly employees. The sample of businesses for inclusion in ABI is drawn from the Interdepartmental Business Register (IDBR), which is a register of those businesses with a VAT or PAYE record. This means that jobs that are not in the IDBR are omitted; examples of these are jobs in private households, jobs in non-UK organisations (such as embassies) and all of the hidden economy (jobs in which may be counted in the LFS if the respondents report them). The difference between people in employment at their place of work as computed by LFS and ABI is, taking account of known differences in coverage, just over 1 million. This is in line with a previous analysis made by ONS and reported in an article in *Labour Market Trends*, January 2002.[b]

ABI data[c] are known to be more informative about the productivity effects in general, but ONS advises that the workforce jobs series should be used in examining breakdown by industry. However it was thought that the data from LFS could be more informative about the commuting effects, since the same source would be used as for the residence-based data.

Profiling Areas using the Output Area Classification

By Susan Williams and Andrew Botterill

Introduction

Area classifications group together geographic areas according to key characteristics that are common to areas within the grouping. Classifications are used widely by the public and private sectors for understanding and analysing area-based data to identify issues and formulate strategies to resolve problems with a geographic perspective.

The purpose of this article is to introduce the Output Area Classification which was published on the National Statistics website[1] in August 2005.

Background

Over the past few years, Government policy has focused on increasing the prosperity and bridging the disparities for all areas of the United Kingdom – the nine Government Office Regions in England plus Wales, Scotland and Northern Ireland (referred to as 'regions' in the rest of this article).

Diversity exists both within and between these regions and, in order to assess and construct tailored solutions for the different challenges sub-UK areas face, there has been an increasing demand for small area information. The resulting growth in this information has led to the development and application of modelling techniques to analyse and interpret geographically referenced datasets. One such technique is the application of area classifications.

The National Statistics Area Classification provides area classifications at four different geographic levels – there is an area classification for health areas, local authorities, wards and at output area[2] level. All of these area classifications group together sub-UK areas in which the population exhibits similar characteristics according to 2001 Census data.[3] The statistical technique used to create the area classifications is known as **cluster analysis.**[4]

Structure of the Output Area Classification (OAC)

Output Areas are small areas of approximately 125 households designed specifically for the 2001 Census. These are the geographical unit used to create the Output Area Classification (OAC).

Following a similar structure to the other National Statistics Area Classifications the OAC has been constructed as a three-layered hierarchy of clusters. The three layers are:

> **Supergroups**: Seven main clusters or Supergroups. Any Output Area in the UK is classified as belonging to one of these seven types of Supergroup.

> **Groups**: Each Supergroup consists of between two and four constituent Groups. There are 21 Groups across all the Supergroups.

> **Subgroups**: Each Group consists of between two and four Subgroups. There are 52 Subgroups in total.

For example, Supergroup 1 breaks down first into three Groups and then further into eight Subgroups as follows:

Supergroup	Group	Subgroup
1	1a	1a1, 1a2,1a3
	1b	1b1, 1b2
	1c	1c1, 1c2, 1c3

This structure allows the classification to be used to analyse data in different ways. Using the classification at Supergroup level can give an overall perspective and help to analyse particularly sparse datasets. Analysis with Groups and Subgroups can provide more detail.

---

1   www.statistics.gov.uk/about/methodology_by_theme/area_classification

2   *Output Areas are built up from postcode units using an approach which renders them particularly suitable for statistical analysis (www.statistics.gov.uk/geography/census_geog.asp). Output Areas are the smallest geography for which Census data are published, and to complement this information other datasets have been developed and have been made available at this level of geography. Similar principles were used in the construction of data zones for Scotland and Northern Ireland output areas.*

3   *The National Statistics Area Classification uses data from each of the 2001 Censuses – England and Wales, Scotland and Northern Ireland. The resulting area classifications are UK-wide and facilitate comparative analyses between the separate countries.*

4   *Cluster analysis is a general term that describes a number of methods that are used by statisticians and analysts to explore data and identify groupings or clusters within data. These groups are created using three ideals:*

- *the difference between all members of a particular cluster/group will be as small as possible, while*
- *the difference between the groups themselves will be as large as possible, and*
- *the groups/clusters are reasonable and meaningful.*

Cluster summaries

Cluster summaries use a radar map or spider diagram to show information about a particular cluster within the classification. Figure A2.1 shows the cluster summary for Supergroup 7. The summary describes the socio-demographic make-up of the output areas in this Supergroup at the time of the 2001 Census. It holds information on all the Census variables used in the cluster analysis and how they compare with the UK average.

The radar map shows the 42 Census variables used to create the OAC. There are three circles embedded within each other. The circle midway between the outer and inner circles represents the average value of each variable across the UK.[5] The inner and outer circles represent values that are 50 per cent less and 50 per cent more than the UK value respectively. The profile of Supergroup 7 is overlaid onto the chart and shows the difference of each variable from the UK average. Variables having values between the inner and middle circles (i.e. below the UK mean) are found in lower proportions than average within Supergroup 7 areas. Variables having values between the middle and outer circles are found in higher proportions.

Cluster summaries (radar maps) have been created for each Supergroup, Group and Subgroup within the OAC. These can be found on the National Statistics website[1] under 'Output Areas, Cluster Summaries'.

The summary shows that within areas classified as Supergroup 7 the proportion of detached housing is far below the national average. Conversely the proportions of flats, renting and people taking public transport to work are far above the national average. Compared with the UK, there is a greater proportion of people having been born abroad as well as a higher proportion of people from minority ethnic groups.

Characteristics of the Supergroups

The information contained in the cluster summary for each Supergroup highlights the following characteristics.[6]

Supergroup 1

These areas are found all across the UK with high concentrations in the North East, South Wales, and cities around Scotland and Midlands. Overall, 16.7 per cent of the UK population live in Supergroup 1 areas.

Variables with proportions far above the UK average	*Variables with proportions far below the UK average*
Terraced housing	Higher education qualifications
Public renting	Flats

Supergroup 2

These areas show in high concentrations within city areas, especially London. Across the UK, 6.1 per cent of the population live in Supergroup 2 areas.

Variables with proportions far above the UK average	*Variables with proportions far below the UK average*
Single person households (not pensioner)	Detached housing
Private rents	Households with non-dependent children age 5 to 14
Flats	
Higher education qualifications	
People born outside the UK	

Supergroup 3

Supergroup 3 areas can be found all across the UK, especially in more rural areas. Overall, 12.5 per cent of the UK population live in Supergroup 3 areas.

Variables with proportions far above the UK average	*Variables with proportions far below the UK average*
Detached housing	Public transport to work
Homeworkers	Population density
People working in agriculture	Flats
Two or more car households	

Supergroup 4

Supergroup 4 areas represent the most common area type in the UK, with 23.1 per cent of the UK population living in such areas.

Variables with proportions far above the UK average	*Variables with proportions far below the UK average*
Detached housing	Public renting
Two or more car households	Private renting
	Terraced housing
	Flats
	No central heating

Supergroup 5

These areas are to be found around cities, and Scotland especially has a high concentration of this area type. Across the UK, 10.9 per cent of the population live in Supergroup 5 areas.

Variables with proportions far above the UK average	*Variables with proportions far below the UK average*
Public renting	Detached housing
Flats	Two or more car households
	Higher education qualifications

---

5 Most variables are represented as proportions except for the variables 'average household size' and 'average number of rooms per household'.

6 The cluster summaries also highlight variables that are very close to the UK average.

Figure **A2.1** Supergroup 7

The members of this Supergroup can be found concentrated around major cities of England, in particular London and Birmingham. The Supergroup comprises two groups, 7a (three Subgroups) and 7b (two Subgroups). There are 67 wards across the UK that have all their Output Areas classified in this Supergroup including 60 in London, four in the West Midlands, two in the North West and one in the South East. Within this Supergroup:

The variables with proportions far above the national average are[3]

- Rent (private)

- Public transport to work

- Rent (public)

- All flats

- Born outside the UK

- Indian, Pakistani or Bangladeshi

- Black African, Black Caribbean or Other Black

The variable with a proportion far below the national average is[1]

- Detached housing

The variables with proportions close to the national average are[2]

- Routine/semi-routine occupation

- Work from home

- Health and social work employment

- Wholesale/retail trade employment

The radar chart below shows range-standardised difference from the UK mean. Positive values show an above average level of the population and negative values show a below average level.

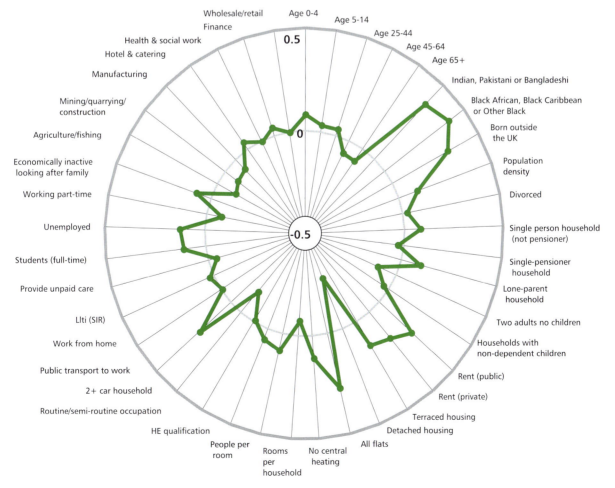

1   For a variable to be 'far below average' it must have a difference of more than 0.15 below the UK mean.

2   For a variable to be 'close to the average' it must have a difference of no more than 0.015 either below or above the UK mean.

3   For a variable to be 'far above average' it must have a difference of more than 0.15 above the UK mean.

Supergroup 6

Supergroup 6 areas are to be found throughout the UK. Overall, 19.3 per cent of the UK population live in Supergroup 6 areas.

Variables with proportions far above the UK average	Variables with proportions far below the UK average
Terraced housing	Public renting

Supergroup 7

These areas are to be found in concentrations around major cities such as London and Birmingham. Supergroup 7 areas have 11.5 per cent of the UK population residing in them.

Variables with proportions far above the UK average	Variables with proportions far below the UK average
Minority ethnic population	Detached housing
People born abroad	
Flats	
Public renting	
Private renting	
Use of public transport to work	

Mapping the classification

The geographic distribution of the Output Area Classification can be more easily visualised using a map. Map A2.3 shows the distribution of the seven Supergroups within the London Government Office Region.

London contains output areas that are classified to each of the Supergroups. Generally, high concentrations of Supergroup 7 areas are seen throughout London, with Supergroup 2 areas found in concentration in central and south west London. Supergroups 4, 5 and 6 are found around the periphery of London while Supergroup 1 features less prominently and mainly in certain pockets in the East End.

Similar maps showing the location of the Supergroups within the other regions are available via www.statistics.gov.uk/regionalsnapshot

The distribution of the Supergroups across the UK

Every household in the UK is located within a specific output area. Under the classification each output area can be categorised as a certain Supergroup, Group and Subgroup. Therefore, using census data, it is possible to calculate the population living within similarly classified areas across a larger geography such as the UK and each of its regions.

Table A2.2 shows the proportion of each region's population living within each of the seven Supergroups at the time of the 2001 Census.

The table shows that the population living in output areas categorised as each Supergroup is to be found in differing proportions across the UK. The table also shows that each region has a different population distribution compared with the UK as a whole. The North East and Northern Ireland have been selected to highlight this and the different characteristics.

Table A2.2   Population living within Supergroups 1 to 7, 2001

Percentages and thousands

	Percentage of individuals in each Supergroup							Total population (thousands) (=100%)	Percentage of UK population within region
	1	2	3	4	5	6	7		
United Kingdom	16.7	6.1	12.5	23.1	10.9	19.3	11.5	58,789	100.0
North East	34.4	3.0	4.9	23.8	16.4	15.0	2.6	2,515	4.3
North West	19.7	3.3	7.2	26.3	13.0	24.0	6.5	6,730	11.4
Yorkshire and the Humber	21.2	3.3	10.6	22.5	11.4	23.2	7.7	4,965	8.4
East Midlands	19.2	2.3	17.6	30.6	7.7	16.3	6.3	4,172	7.1
West Midlands	18.7	2.4	11.5	24.9	10.9	17.4	14.3	5,267	9.0
East	15.3	4.0	18.0	27.4	9.2	21.7	4.3	5,388	9.2
London	2.7	18.1	0.1	8.4	2.2	10.7	57.8	7,172	12.2
South East	12.0	6.9	13.1	28.9	8.1	27.0	4.0	8,001	13.6
South West	13.3	5.6	25.4	19.8	8.3	26.3	1.2	4,928	8.4
England	15.6	6.2	11.7	23.3	9.1	20.6	13.5	49,139	83.6
Wales	25.6	2.7	20.3	19.4	10.5	19.8	1.6	2,903	4.9
Scotland	18.9	9.4	10.4	21.7	29.4	9.8	0.6	5,062	8.6
Northern Ireland	27.2	1.3	26.8	26.8	9.9	7.9	0.1	1,685	2.9

Map **A2.3**   The distribution of the Supergroups within London

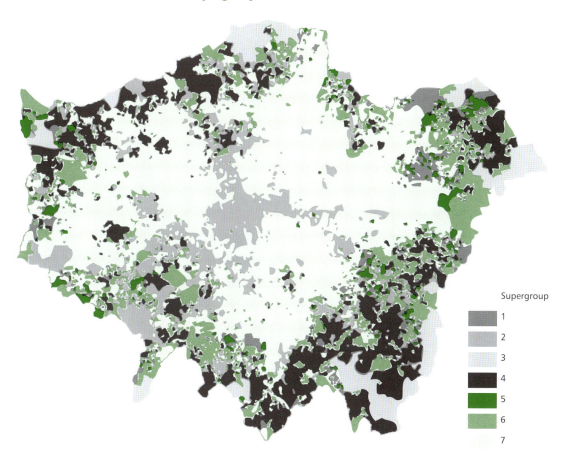

Supergroup

	1
	2
	3
	4
	5
	6
	7

North East

Figure A2.4 shows that at the time of the 2001 Census, 34.4 per cent of the population within the North East lived in areas classified as Supergroup 1 whereas only 16.7 per cent of the total UK population did so. The summary of characteristics on Supergroup 1 shows that these areas have higher proportions of terraced housing, public renting, lone family households and unemployment than the UK average. The population living in these areas had fewer higher education qualifications and a lower minority ethnic proportion than the UK in general.

Conversely, only 2.6 per cent of the North East population lived in Supergroup 7 areas compared with 11.5 per cent of the whole UK population. Supergroup 7 areas have higher than average proportions of minority ethnic groups and people born outside the UK. These areas also have more flats and rental properties and a propensity for the resident population to use public transport to travel to work.

Northern Ireland

Similarly for Northern Ireland, a high proportion (27.2 per cent) of its population were living in Supergroup 1 areas and a very low proportion of the population (0.1 per cent) were living in Supergroup 7 areas[7] (see Figure A2.5). However, Northern Ireland most markedly differs from the North East by

having a large percentage of its population (26.8 per cent) living in areas classified as Supergroup 3.

Supergroup 3 areas contain more detached housing and fewer flats than the UK average. There is a greater proportion of homeworkers and people working in agriculture than for the UK as a whole. The population density is lower than average and there is a greater proportion of households with two or more cars – leading to a reduced reliance on public transport to get to work. High proportions of Supergroup 3 can be found in more rural areas.

Similar charts for each region will be available via www.statistics.gov.uk/regionalsnapshot. These charts illustrate that no region contains an identical population mix to the UK overall, or indeed to any other region.

Area-based analysis

Area-based analysis is growing in popularity in both the public and private sectors, and the use of area classifications is becoming more widespread. Analysis using area classifications can produce valuable insights by its ability to identify and summarise patterns in large datasets of geographically referenced data. However, as with many other analytical

---

7   There are very few Output Areas classified as Supergroup 7 in Northern Ireland, which means that only a small number of people will be residing in them.

Figure **A2.4** Percentage of population in the North East living in each Supergroup

Percentage of population within each Supergroup

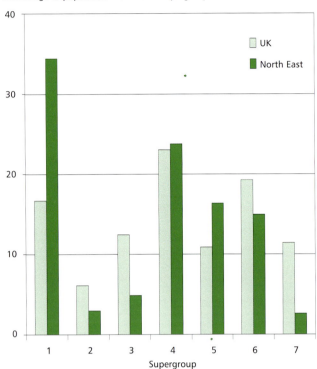

Figure **A2.5** Percentage of population living in each Supergroup in Northern Ireland, 2001

Percentage of population within each Supergroup

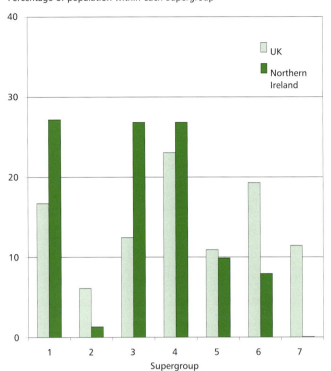

techniques, insights drawn from analyses at larger geographies such as the whole UK can differ from similar analyses at smaller geographies such as for each country and region. The following example on migration flows shows some types of analysis which are possible using the Output Area Classification, and highlights the increased detail discovered by using the OAC at Group and Subgroup level.

Migration data example

Understanding migration flows is important to all the regions of the UK, as changing profiles of population demographics can have a large impact on the regional economy. Infrastructure such as housing, schools, hospitals and transport links needs to be planned for well in advance. For example, planning is already well developed within the Thames Gateway for the anticipated population increase relating to the regeneration strategy to create 180 thousand jobs by 2016, and build capacity to meet the needs of the 2012 Olympics.

Using migration data from the 2001 Census,[8] Figure A2.6 shows the net rate of migration for similarly classified areas. It shows the proportion of the population resident at the time of the Census who moved into and from areas classified as Supergroup 1 to 7[9] in the 12 months prior to the Census (i.e. April 2000 to April 2001). Care is needed when interpreting

this simple migration model as it does not capture the outward migration of people who left the UK during this time. Such data could not be captured with the Census and there are no reliable estimates of this effect reported at Output Area level. The omission of migrants out of the UK means that the rate of outward migration has been underestimated and consequently the net rate of growth overestimated. The official estimate for total UK outward migration during the year 2001 is 308 thousand, and further modelling of the migration data would be required to allocate this to individual Output Areas and Supergroups.

Across the UK we can see that the total resident population classified to each Supergroup showed an increase (the overall UK population increase using this model is 1.5 per cent). This is partly explained by the omission of emigrants from the UK, but it is also known that the UK population has been found to be increasing with the arrival of immigrants from outside the UK.

Ignoring for sake of example the underestimation effect of outward migration, the model shows us that although all Groups experienced an increase in their population, areas classified as Supergroup 2 have grown the most, with a net increase of 7.1 per cent across the UK. The summary on Supergroup 2 areas tells us that these areas are concentrated within the city centres of the UK, and so the analysis supports the view that people are moving in greater numbers into the cities.

8   Origin/Destination statistics at Output Area level. Census table MG301.

9   The total of out-migrants from an area is the sum of migrants who moved within the area plus the migrants who moved to elsewhere in the UK. The total of in-migrants is the sum of movers into an area from elsewhere in the UK plus movers in from outside the UK plus movers in who had no fixed address in the previous year plus movers who moved within the area.

Figure **A2.6** **Simplified migration model: people moving in the 12 months prior to the 2001 Census**

Percentage of 2001 population

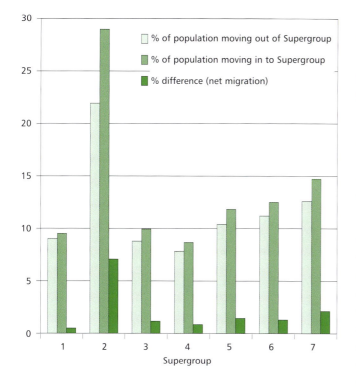

We can also see that the numbers of people moving from and to Supergroup 2 areas is strikingly high compared with the other Supergroups (almost 30 per cent of the population in Supergroup 2 areas moved in the year prior to the Census). This gives evidence in support of a large population 'churning' effect which could give these areas a fast-paced and more transient feel.

Migration effects at the Group and Subgroup level

Analysis using the Supergroups of the OAC has given an overview of the migration patterns across the UK. Reporting similar aggregate out-migration rates by OAC Group level gives more detail on these migration effects and even shows that not all area types experienced growth.

Supergroup 2 areas can be further classified as being one of two Groups, 2a and 2b. The analysis at Group level shows that these two Groups have different 'population churn' and net growth rates. Overall, Supergroup 2 areas had a net growth in population of 7.1 per cent; however the results at Group level show that Group 2a had a growth rate of 9.8 per cent whilst Group 2b only increased by 5.5 per cent. The cluster summaries for Groups 2a and 2b show that although they both bear a similar profile to that for Supergroup 2, there are some more extreme variables within Group 2a. Group 2a areas contain higher than average proportions of people aged between 25 and 44 and low proportions of people older or younger than this range. There is a high

Figure **A2.7** **Migration flows in and out of areas classified as Supergroup 2 for each region of the UK**

Percentage

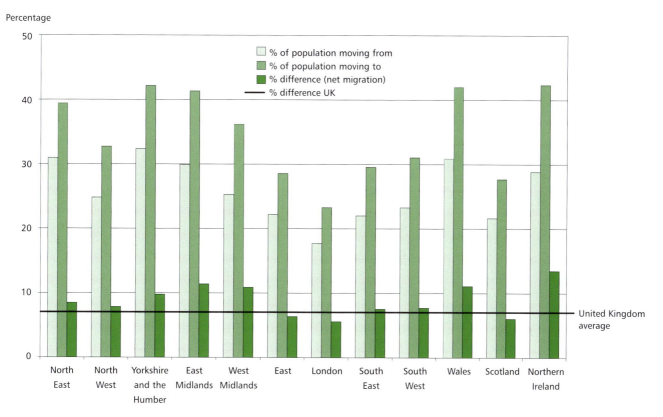

proportion of people working in the finance sector and higher than average usage of public transport to work. The proportion of detached housing and terraced housing is extremely low whilst the proportion of flats is extremely high.

Taking this analysis still further, areas classified as Subgroup 2a1 experienced a net growth of 11.1 per cent, with over 40 per cent of the population moving into these areas in the preceding 12 months, while Subgroup 2b1 areas only increased by 4.4 per cent and correspondingly had an inward migration rate of just under 20 per cent.

Analysis at the Group level gives enough detail to show that not all area types experienced growth. Group 4c areas actually had a slight overall reduction of 0.1 per cent in population at the time of the Census compared with the previous year. Given that outward migration from the UK has not been captured, the total reduction in population could be greater than that indicated.

How does geography fit in?

We have shown that output areas classified as Supergroup 2 have experienced the greatest rates of inward migration. Examination of the distribution of this Supergroup shows that it is present in high concentrations in city centres, especially in London. We might therefore suppose that London is experiencing the greatest rate of net inward migration of all

the regions. Figure A2.7 shows the migration flows into and out of Supergroup 2 areas in each region.

Figure A2.7 shows that the net inward migration rate for London Supergroup 2 areas is only 5.6 per cent compared with the UK figure of 7.1 per cent. All the other regions of the UK had a higher net inward migration rate. Northern Ireland Supergroup 2 areas grew the most, with a net population increase of 13.5 per cent. This figure also shows that the inward and outward migration rates (churn effect) for Supergroup 2 output areas within all other regions is higher than in London.

Conclusions

This classification is a powerful analytical tool which ONS has made available for wider use.[1] The area classification, along with the other geographic classifications, enables many types of analyses of Census data and helps to understand the characteristics of the people within different types of areas.

Area classifications are used widely by the public sector and private sector as being an effective means of targeting policies and marketing campaigns. The classification has a multitude of potential uses which range from aiding decisions about strategies or policies down to understanding the area in which you live.

Deprivation and Ethnicity in England: A Regional Perspective

By Jonathan Tinsley and Michael Jacobs

Key points

- The ethnic mix of population in small areas can be provided from Census data. Analysing these using results from the Index of Multiple Deprivation gives differing patterns across regions of England.

- Some ethnic groups are more likely to live in areas which are more deprived. Bangladeshi and Pakistani groups make up a four times higher proportion of the population in the most deprived local areas than of England as a whole.

- Black African and Black Caribbean groups make up approximately two and a half times as high a proportion of the population in the most deprived local areas as for England as a whole.

- London had the highest proportions of all minority groups, but for a number of these there was a different pattern across deprivation levels than for other regions.

Summary

This article uses a definition of local area deprivation developed by the Office of the Deputy Prime Minister to present a new way of describing variations in the mix of ethnic groups in England using 2001 Census data. Ethnic breakdowns by local area deprivation score within each region were analysed and compared with the proportion of the population of England, or national baseline, made up by each ethnic group.

It was found that some ethnic groups were more likely to live in local areas that have been classed as among the more deprived in England. The Bangladeshi and Pakistani groups were the most likely to live in deprived areas, making up four times as high a proportion of the population in the most deprived local areas as they did for England as a whole. For the Black African and Black Caribbean groups, this figure was approximately two and a half times as high a proportion of the population in the most deprived local areas than for England as a whole.

London was the region with the highest proportions of all minority groups, but a number of these groups showed different patterns across deprivation scores than other regions.

This analysis can be used as a starting point to identify regions where patterns in the relative proportions of a particular ethnic group were different across local areas with different levels of deprivation.

Introduction

The 2001 Census included a question on ethnicity. Analysis by small areas is possible with Census data and a regional picture of ethnicity can be produced. This article describes how deprived areas are spread within each English region, and then looks at how different ethnic groups are spread over England by region and by levels of deprivation.

Measurement of local deprivation

In recent years, local area deprivation in England has been measured through the Indices of Multiple Deprivation (IMD). The IMD take account of different types of deprivation such as health, employment and housing. Relevant indicators in these subject areas like levels of disability, unemployment and overcrowding are combined to assign a deprivation score to each local area. These scores are then ordered, ranging from the most deprived area in England, with an IMD score of 1, to the least deprived with the highest score.[1]

For the analysis in this article, the 2004 IMD for England have been used to define the level of deprivation in an area and the 2001 Census has provided details of the ethnic mix. The 2004 IMD were produced for a new small area geography – 'Lower Layer Super Output Areas'. These areas were designed using the 2001 Census to each contain similar numbers of people and to be as homogeneous as possible.[2] This analysis is therefore based on data at this level, referred to as local areas for the rest of this article.

In order to look at how deprivation is spread across the regions of England, the local areas were ranked according to their deprivation scores. The areas were then divided into ten equally sized groups, each making up 10 per cent of the total in England. These groups are called deciles and will be referred to as such throughout this article. Figure A3.1 shows how the spread of deprivation is different in each region. For example, more than 20 per cent of the North East's local areas are among those in the most deprived decile in England. On the other hand, less than 3 per cent of local areas in the South East are in this decile.

Deprivation and ethnicity

The following analysis compares the ethnic composition of local areas according to the Census with the distribution of deprivation across the different regions of England.

The proportion of each ethnic group in the population of England as a whole has been used as a baseline for this analysis. The proportion of each group within local areas in each decile is then compared with this baseline to show whether the group was present in relatively high or low proportions across different levels of deprivation. The same process was also completed for each region. This revealed regions where a particular group was present in large proportions in general, as well as how the relative size of the group varied across different levels of deprivation within that region. This was compared with that group's situation for England as a whole.

This analysis allows the identification and examination of where ethnic groups are present in higher or lower proportions than the national baseline for that group. However, it does not compare the sizes of the different groups relative to each other, as the levels in different groups may be different. To illustrate this, in 2001 in England as a

whole, 2.1 per cent of the population were Indian and 0.6 per cent Bangladeshi. If Bangladeshis made up 1.2 per cent of the population in a region, this would be double their national baseline. However, this would still be a lower proportion of the population than if the Indian group was present at its baseline level of 2.1 per cent.

The following sections of this article look at individual ethnic groups. Figures A3.2 to A3.9 show how the proportions of each ethnic group[3] varied across different levels of deprivation in England as a whole, and within selected English Regions.[4] In the charts, the national baseline proportion for each group has been set to 100.

Aslan Indian group

Figure A3.2 shows how proportions of the Indian group varied across different levels of deprivation in England, and selected English regions.

England:

- There was a tendency for Indians to live in more deprived areas, with proportions larger than the national baseline living in the most deprived 50 per cent of local areas.

- There was a steady increase in proportions of Indians in the more deprived deciles.

- This was true except for local areas in the most deprived decile, where proportions were only just above baseline.

Regionally:

- London had the largest proportions of Indians compared with baseline but the pattern across different levels of deprivation was not the same as nationally. Most Indians lived in areas with medium deprivation scores, not in the most or least deprived 30 per cent.

- In the West Midlands (where proportions of the Indian group were generally lower than in London) the highest proportions were in the most deprived local areas. Here, the proportion of Indians in local areas in the most deprived decile was over two and a half times the national baseline, and was higher than in London.

- The South East and Yorkshire and the Humber illustrate regions where the Indian group was present in proportions below the national baseline.

- These regions also show different patterns across levels of

---

1　A fuller explanation of this classification can be found at http://neighbourhood.statistics.gov.uk/dissemination/

2　A fuller explanation of output area geography can be found at http://www.statistics.gov.uk/geography/soa.asp

3　Of the 16 ethnic categories presented in the 2001 Census, the 'Other' categories have been excluded as residual groups representing relatively few people. The 'Mixed' categories have also been excluded. The mixed categories were White mixed with either Asian, Black Caribbean or Black African. Again, these groups represent relatively few people, Mixed White and Black Caribbean and Mixed White and Black African show very similar results to the Black Caribbean and Black African groups, and the Mixed White and Asian group shows results very similar to the Indian group.

4　It was not possible to show all regions for reasons of space. Regions with different patterns from England as a whole or each other were chosen, using the same regions throughout to allow comparability as far as possible. The North East and South West were generally excluded as they had very low proportions of most groups. The West and East Midlands often showed similar patterns and the West Midlands was used throughout. Yorkshire and the Humber and the North West generally showed similar patterns and the former has been analysed throughout.

Figure **A3.1** **Percentage of each region made up of areas within each decile across England of the 2004 IMD**

Percent

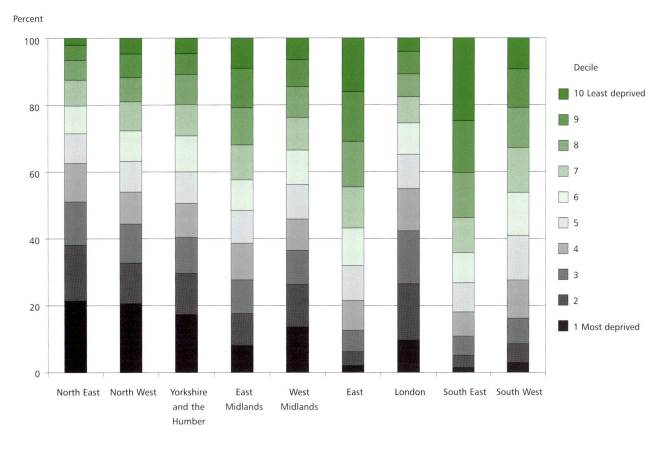

Figure **A3.2** **Relative proportions of the Indian ethnic group compared with baseline proportions (100), by region and deprivation decile**

Relative proportion

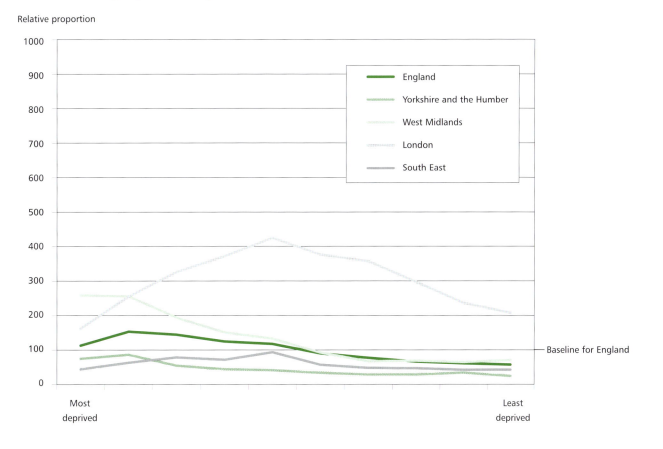

deprivation. In the South East, proportions were higher in local areas with medium deprivation scores but in Yorkshire and the Humber, proportions were highest in the most deprived 20 per cent of areas.

Asian Pakistani group

Figure A3.3 shows how proportions of the Pakistani group varied across different levels of deprivation in England, and selected English regions.

England:

- There was a strong tendency for proportions of the Pakistani group to be higher in more deprived local areas, and proportions were above the national baseline living in the most deprived 30 per cent of areas.

Regionally:

- In the West Midlands and Yorkshire and the Humber, proportions of the Pakistani group were higher than nationally, but only in the most deprived deciles.

- At the most extreme, the proportion of Pakistanis in local areas in the most deprived decile in the West Midlands was almost nine times the baseline for England.

- Different patterns were seen in London and the South East. Here, the Pakistani group made up more of the population

in moderately deprived local areas but then tailed off to relatively low proportions in the most deprived decile.

- Apart from London, the Pakistani group was present in proportions far below the national baseline in the least deprived 40 per cent of areas.

Asian Bangladeshi group

Figure A3.4 shows how proportions of the Bangladeshi group varied across different levels of deprivation in England, and selected English regions. The graph has been rescaled in this instance due to the large proportions in the most deprived areas of London (over 17 times the national baseline).

England:

- The variation in proportions of the Bangladeshi group across areas with different levels of deprivation was very similar to the Pakistani group, with above average representation in the most deprived local areas.

Regionally:

- Bangladeshis made up a far greater proportion of the population in London than in other regions.

- The variation across areas with different levels of deprivation within each region followed patterns similar to

Figure A3.3 Relative proportions of the Pakistani ethnic group compared with baseline proportions (100), by region and deprivation decile

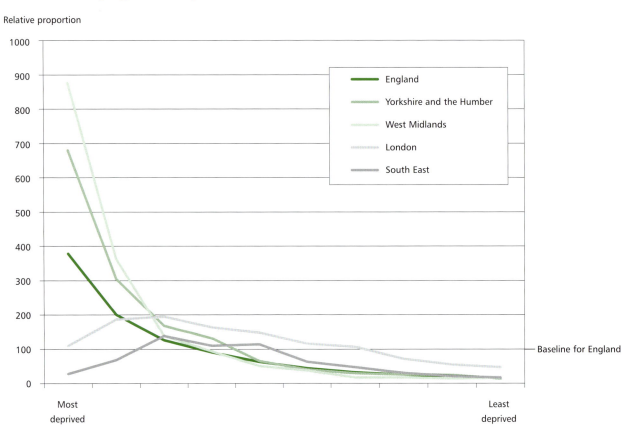

Relative proportion

Figure A3.4 **Relative proportions of the Bangladeshi ethnic group compared with baseline proportions (100), by region and deprivation decile**

Relative proportion

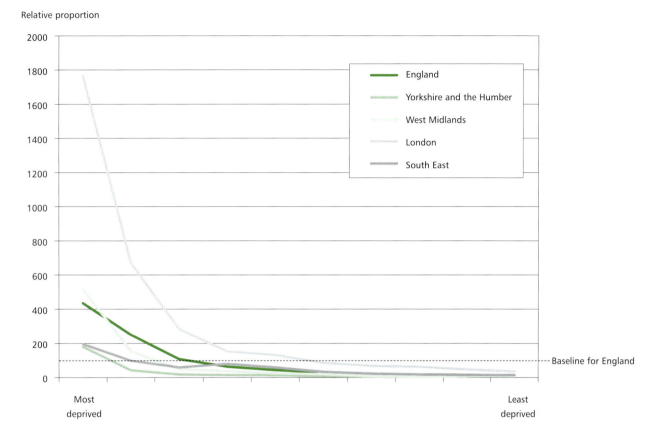

England, with Bangladeshis making up greater proportions of the population in the most deprived local areas.

- This variation was seen in London and the South East as well as other regions. This differs from the Pakistani group where different patterns across different levels of deprivation were seen in these two regions.

- Bangladeshis made up well below baseline proportions of the population in the least deprived 60 per cent of local areas in all regions except London, and even here, the discrepancy within London between these areas and the most deprived was very large.

Black African group

Figure A3.5 shows how proportions of the Black African group varied across different levels of deprivation in England, and selected English regions.

England:

- The Black African group made up a greater proportion of the population in the most deprived 40 per cent of local areas than nationally, with a peak in the second decile where proportions were more than two and half times the baseline.

Regionally:

- Compared with nationally, the Black African group made

up large proportions of the population in London, where the pattern across different levels of deprivation was more pronounced than for England as a whole.

- The proportion of Black African people living in local areas in the most deprived decile in London was just over 13 times larger than the national baseline.

- In both the South East and the West Midlands, proportions of the Black African group were below the baseline for England. Within each region, the proportion of the population made up by this group was at its largest in the more deprived local areas, but still below the national baseline.

- Apart from in London, the Black African group made up very small proportions of the population in the least deprived 40 per cent of local areas.

Black Caribbean group

Figure A3.6 shows how proportions of the Black Caribbean group varied across different levels of deprivation in England, and selected English regions.

England:

- The patterns for the proportion of the population made up by the Black Caribbean group compared with baseline were very similar to the Black African group across regions, and between areas with different levels of deprivation.

Figure **A3.5** **Relative proportions of the Black African ethnic group compared with baseline proportions (100), by region[1] and deprivation decile**

Relative proportion

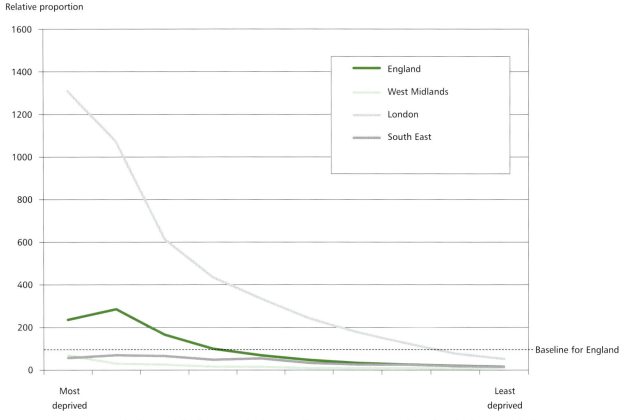

1   Yorkshire and the Humber has been excluded for presentational purposes because patterns were similar to those for the West Midlands.

Figure **A3.6** **Relative proportions of the Black Caribbean ethnic group compared with baseline proportions (100), by region and deprivation decile**

Relative proportion

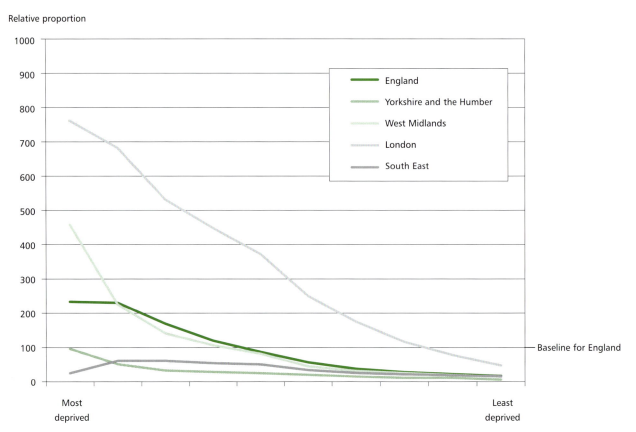

Regionally:

- In London, the proportion of the population made up of the Black Caribbean group was largest in local areas in the most deprived decile, with proportions well over seven times the baseline.

- The main difference from the Black African group was in the West Midlands, where the Black Caribbean group made up a far greater proportion of the population than in England as a whole. Within the West Midlands, proportions were highest in the most deprived local areas – well over four times the national baseline.

Chinese group

Figure A3.7 shows how proportions of the Chinese group varied across different levels of deprivation in England, and selected English regions.

England:

- The proportion of the population made up of the Chinese group was similar across local areas at all levels of deprivation.

Regionally:

- In London, the proportion of the population made up of the Chinese group was approximately two and half times the national baseline. Within London, the lowest

proportions were seen in local areas in the least deprived decile.

- Two examples of other regions are shown. In both the West Midlands and Yorkshire and the Humber, the Chinese group made up less of the population than nationally. Both regions showed limited variation across areas with different levels of deprivation, although proportions were highest in the least deprived local areas where they were close to the national baseline.

White Irish group

Figure A3.8 shows how proportions of the White Irish group varied across different levels of deprivation in England, and selected English regions.

England:

- The proportion of the population made up by the White Irish group varied very little across local areas at all levels of deprivation. Proportions were slightly higher than nationally in the most deprived 50 per cent of local areas, and slightly lower in the least deprived 50 per cent of areas.

Regionally:

- In London, in the most deprived 50 per cent of local areas, the White Irish group made up approximately two and half

Figure A3.7 **Relative proportions of the Chinese ethnic group compared with baseline proportions (100), by region[1] and deprivation decile**

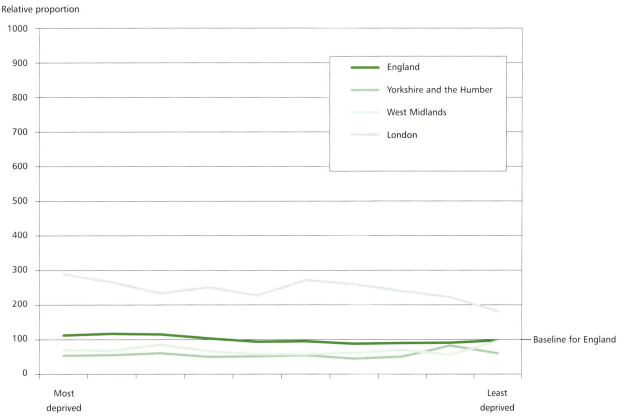

1 The South East has been excluded for presentational purposes because patterns were similar to those for the West Midlands.

Figure A3.8 Relative proportions of the White Irish ethnic group compared with baseline proportions (100), by region and deprivation decile

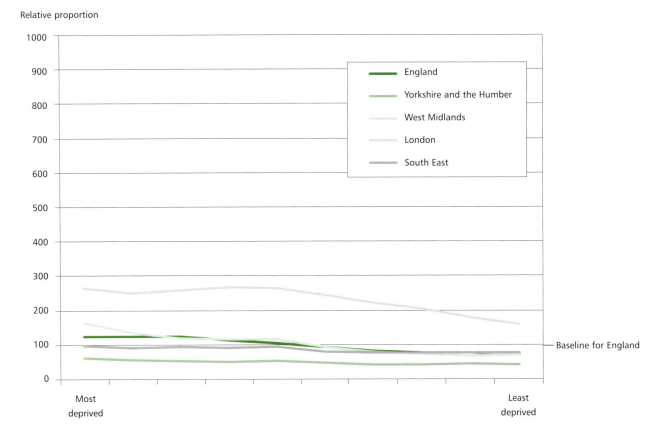

Relative proportion

times as much of the population as for England as a whole.

- Proportions of the White Irish group were lower in the less deprived local areas of London, but still above the national baseline.

- In the West Midlands, proportions of the White Irish group were similar to nationally, with similar patterns across local areas with different levels of deprivation.

- In the South East and Yorkshire and the Humber, the White Irish group made up a smaller proportion of the population than nationally.

- Within these regions, the White Irish group made up slightly higher proportions of the population in the more deprived local areas.

White British group

Figure A3.9 shows how proportions of the White British group varied across different levels of deprivation in England, and selected English regions. The graph has been rescaled due to the significantly different patterns seen for this group. This is because in England, the White British group is in the majority and made up approximately 87 per cent of the population in 2001. As this was set as a baseline, there was little potential for large values, even in areas where the White British group made up 100 per cent of the population.

England:

- The White British group made up more of the population in the least deprived 50 per cent of areas than in England as a whole. The largest departure from baseline was in the most deprived local areas, where proportions were less than 90 per cent of baseline.

Regionally:

- The White British group made up the smallest proportion of the population in London compared with other regions. This is intuitively clear because where other groups are found in large numbers, as in London, proportions of this group will be relatively low.

- In the most deprived areas of London, the White British group made up less than half the proportion of the population that it did nationally.

- The West Midlands and Yorkshire and the Humber showed similar patterns across different levels of deprivation, with lower proportions of the White British group in the more deprived local areas. However, these regions generally had higher proportions of the White British group in the population overall.

- In the South East, and particularly the North East, the White British group made up above-average proportions of the population.

Figure **A3.9** **Relative proportions of the White British ethnic group compared with baseline proportions (100), by region and deprivation decile**

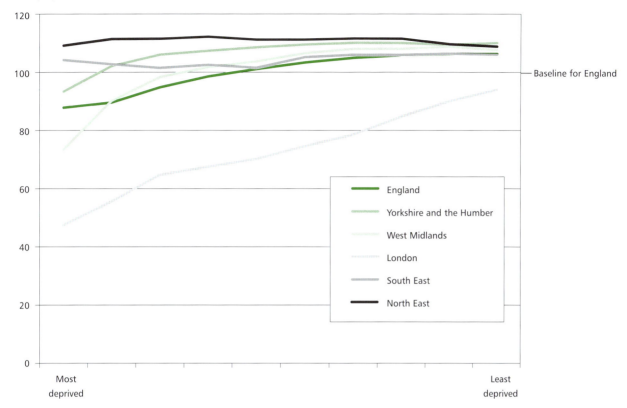

Relative proportion

Legend:
- England
- Yorkshire and the Humber
- West Midlands
- London
- South East
- North East

Baseline for England

Most deprived — Least deprived

Summary

The analyses above show how the different ethnic groups were spread regionally, and across different levels of deprivation, in 2001. Patterns for the White British group basically mirrored a composite of the patterns seen for the other groups – that is, where large proportions of minority groups were present, proportions of the majority group were relatively low.

London was the region with the highest proportions of all minority groups, but for a number of groups showed different patterns across deprivation scores than other regions. This was particularly true for the Pakistani group, and to a lesser extent the Indian group. Proportions of the population made up by the Pakistani group were often very high in the most deprived areas of other regions, but not in London. For example, the Pakistani group was at about the national baseline level in local areas in the most deprived decile in London, compared with nine times baseline in the West Midlands. The Indian group showed the highest proportions for areas in the fifth decile in London, but higher proportions in the more deprived deciles nationally.

The Bangladeshi and Pakistani groups were the most likely to live in deprived areas on a national basis, making up four times as much of the population in the most deprived local

areas as they did for England as a whole. For the two Black groups, this figure was approximately two and a half times their national baselines. The Indian, Chinese and White Irish groups made up approximately the same proportion of the population in the most deprived areas as they did for England as a whole. By contrast with these patterns for other groups, the proportion of the most deprived areas made up by the White British group was only 90 per cent of the baseline proportion for this group.

In general, a far greater proportion of minority groups live in urban areas, and these are more likely to contain deprived local areas. This is part of the explanation why proportions of the White British group are higher in the less deprived areas, and minority groups are higher in more deprived areas. This pattern is not however a general one and varies across regions and ethnic groups. For example the Indian and Pakistani groups in London have a different pattern of relative proportions across areas with different levels of deprivation than in the national picture.

In terms of overall population, all groups except the White British group grew between 1991 and 2001.[5] Whether through natural growth or through immigration, social and family links will mean growth tends to occur in areas where members of that group are already present in relatively high

5   See A Guide to Comparing 1991 and 2001 Census Ethnic Group Data (released 31 March 2006 on the ONS website).

proportions.[6] As discussed, these areas may be in inner city areas and among the most deprived in England – for example, the growth of the Bangladeshi population in Tower Hamlets in London. This area is quite deprived but has a large Bangladeshi community which in turn may give rise to growth in this group in this area. However, the accessibility of the surrounding areas of lower deprivation may mitigate the level of hardship and social exclusion experienced by those living in a deprived area. For example, access to services and employment opportunities in nearby areas of lower deprivation will be easier from deprived areas in London than from similar areas elsewhere because of the available transport infrastructure.

Nationally, certain groups have a tendency to show high or low rates for some of the indicators included in the IMD. For example, the Bangladeshi group suffers from high levels of unemployment and long-term disability,[7] and the IMD takes into account unemployment and incapacity among its

indicators. As such, large numbers of a particular group suffering such disadvantages may have as much to do with a local area being classed as deprived as the area itself affecting their quality of life. On the other hand, indicators such as distance to the nearest GP are included and these apply to all population groups in the locality. Care should therefore be taken in considering what the causative factors may be for the associations seen between ethnic groups and deprivation.

This article has used a definition of local area deprivation to present a new way of describing variations in the mix of ethnic groups across the regions of England. This analysis can be used as a starting point to identify regions where patterns in the relative proportions of a particular ethnic group were different across local areas with different levels of deprivation. As has been shown, patterns in London were often different from other regions for many groups. London is the region where the proportion of the population made up by most minority groups is highest.

---

6   Rees P and Phillips D (1996) 'Geographical spread: the national picture', in Ratcliffe P (ed) Social Geography and Ethnicity in Britain: Geographical spread, spatial concentration and internal migration (London: HMSO), 23-110.

7   More information and evidence for this statement can be found at http://www.statistics.gov.uk/CCI/nugget.asp?ID=1089&Pos=1&ColRank=2&Rank=768

Chapter 1 **Regional Profiles**

Statistical regions[1] of the United Kingdom

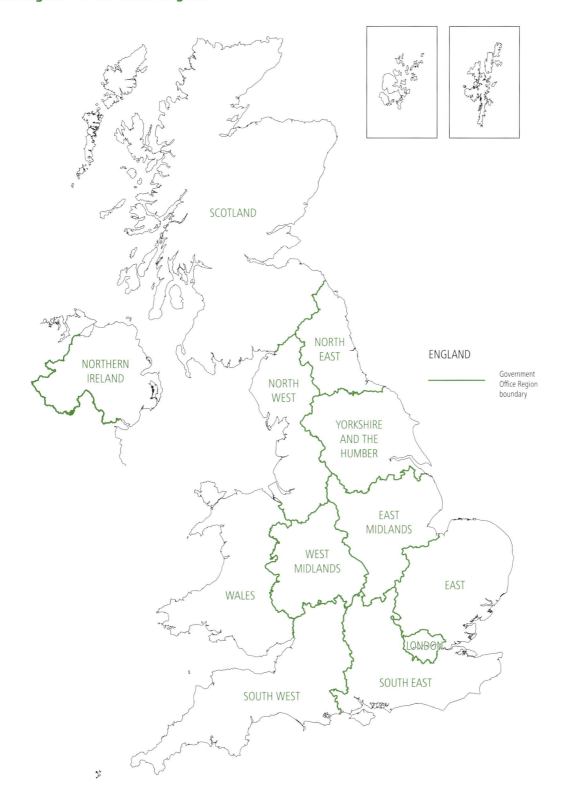

SCOTLAND

NORTHERN
IRELAND

NORTH
EAST

NORTH
WEST

YORKSHIRE
AND THE
HUMBER

ENGLAND

Government
Office Region
boundary

EAST
MIDLANDS

WEST
MIDLANDS

WALES

EAST

LONDON

SOUTH EAST

SOUTH WEST

1 *For the purposes of statistical analyses, the United Kingdom has been divided into 12 'statistical regions'.*

North East

In 2004, the North East had a population of 2.5 million. The resident population of the North East increased by six thousand between mid-2003 and mid-2004. However, in the 23 years between 1981 and 2004 the population of the North East decreased by 3.6 per cent, according to the mid-year population estimates. The greatest percentage change in population between 1981 and 2004 at local authority level was a decrease of 8.4 per cent in Middlesbrough. (Tables 3.1 and 3.8)

In 2004, the infant mortality rate in the North East was lower than the UK average (4.9 and 5.1 deaths of infants under one year of age per 1,000 live births respectively). (Table 7.2)

The North East had 10.5 per cent of maintained primary school classes with more than 30 pupils compared with 12 per cent in Great Britain as a whole in 2004/05. (Table 4.2)

In 2003/04, 80 per cent of 16-year-olds in the North East were in post-compulsory education or government-supported training, just above the England rate of 79 per cent. (Table 4.7)

The proportion of people of working age qualified to GCE A level/equivalent or higher in the North East was around 46 per cent in spring 2005 compared with a UK average of 50 per cent. In 2004 the proportion of full-time first degree graduates studying in the North East who subsequently gained employment in the UK was below the UK national average. (Tables 4.9 and 4.10)

In spring 2005 the employment rate in North East for males of working age was 72 per cent, the lowest of the countries and regions of the UK. (Table 5.1)

In the North East, 31 per cent of households have lived continuously in their homes for over 20 years, and between 2001/02 and 2002/03, this proportion increased by 6 percentage points, which was the highest of all regions and countries. (Table 6.5)

The average price for a terraced house in England was £140,000. This was almost 60 per cent higher than in the North East for the same type of dwelling at around £89,000. (Table 6.7)

In April 2005, gross weekly earnings for full-time employees on adult rates in the North East were £423.50 for males and £328.40 for females, 10 and 12 per cent below the UK levels respectively. These figures are median values so half of the males (or females) earned above these amounts and half earned below. (Table 1.1)

The North East has the highest percentage of cars less than three years old (38 per cent) and the lowest percentage of cars more than six years old (35 per cent) (Table T1)

The North East was one of only two regions that showed increases in the number of fatal or serious accidents on major roads, with a 3 per cent rise between 2002 and 2004. (Table 10.14)

In the North East, manufacturing accounted for almost 20 per cent of GVA in 2003, compared with 16 per cent for the UK. Agriculture, hunting, forestry and fishing accounted for 0.6 per cent of GVA compared with just over 1 per cent in the UK overall. (Table 12.5)

GVA per head in the North East was £13,400 in 2004 which was 20 per cent below the GVA for the UK at £17,300 per head. (Table 12.1)

Table **1.1**   Key statistics for the North East

	North East	United Kingdom[1]		North East	United Kingdom[1]
Population, 2004[2] (thousands)	2,545	59,835	Gross value added, 2004 (£ billion)	34.2	1005.4
Percentage aged under 16[2]	18.9	19.5	Gross value added per head index, 2004 (UK=100)	79.9	100
Percentage pension age and over[2]	19.4	18.6	Total business sites,[5] March 2004 (thousands)	76.7	2,573.1
Standardised Mortality Ratio (UK=100), 2003	110	100	Average dwelling price,[1] 2004 (£)	121,853	183,449
Infant mortality rate,[3] 2004	4.9	5.1			
Percentage of pupils achieving 5 or more grades A*-C at GCSE level or equivalent, 2003/04[1]	49.7	54.2	Motor cars currently licensed,[1,6] 2003 (thousands)	948	26,240
			Fatal and serious accidents on roads,[1] 2004 (rates per 100,000 population)	41.1	51.1
Economic activity rate,[4] spring 2005 (percentages)	75.1	78.5			
Employment rate,[4] spring 2005 (percentages)	69.7	74.4	Recorded crime rate,[1] 2004/05 (recorded offences per 100,000 population)	10,168	10,508
Unemployment rate,[4] spring 2005 (percentages)	6.4	4.7			
Median gross weekly earnings: males in full-time employment, April 2005 (£)	423.5	471.5	Average gross weekly household income, 2001/02 to 2003/04[7] (£)	458	554
Median gross weekly earnings: females in full-time employment, April 2005 (£)	328.4	371.8	Average weekly household expenditure, 2001/02 to 2003/04[7] (£)	335.70	406.20
			Households in receipt of Tax Credits,[1] 2003/04 (percentages)	16	15

1 Figures relate to the United Kingdom except for GCSE results and average dwelling prices (covering England); currently licensed motor cars, fatal and serious accidents and Tax Credits (Great Britain), and recorded crime rate (England and Wales).
2 Population figures for 2004 are mid-year population estimates. Pension age is men aged 65 or over and women aged 60 or over.
3 Deaths of infants under one year of age per 1,000 live births.
4 Seasonally adjusted data for people of working age, men aged 16 to 64 and women aged 16 to 59.
5 Registered for VAT and/or PAYE local unit basis, e.g. an individual factory or shop.
6 Totals for the United Kingdom include vehicles where the country of the registered vehicle is unknown, that are under disposal or from countries unknown within Great Britain.
7 Data combined from the 2001/02, 2002/03 and 2003/04 Expenditure and Food Surveys.

Map **1.2**   Population density: by local or unitary authority, 2004

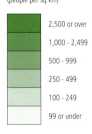

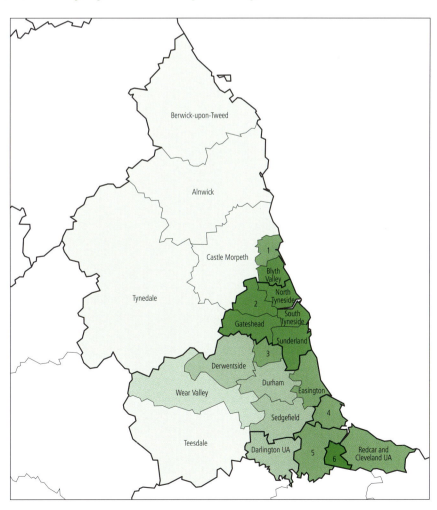

Population density, 2004 (people per sq km)

- 2,500 or over
- 1,000 - 2,499
- 500 - 999
- 250 - 499
- 100 - 249
- 99 or under

1 Wansbeck
2 Newcastle upon Tyne
3 Chester-le-Street
4 Hartlepool UA
5 Stockton-on-Tees UA
6 Middlesbrough UA

Table 1.3   Local authority[1] population and vital statistics: North East, 2004

	Area (sq km)	People per sq km	Population (thous) Total	Total population percentage change 1981-2004	Percentage of population: aged under 5	of pension age[2] or over	Total fertility rate (TFR)[3]	Standardised Mortality Ratio (UK=100) (SMR)[4]	Live birth rate per 1,000 population	Death rate per 1,000 population	Infant mortality rate[5]
United Kingdom	242,515	247	59,835	6.2	5.7	18.6	1.77	100	12.0	9.7	5.3
England	130,281	385	50,094	7.0	5.7	18.5	1.78	99	12.1	9.6	5.3
North East	8,573	297	2,545	-3.5	5.3	19.4	1.71	114	10.9	11.0	4.9
Darlington UA	197	499	99	0.0	5.8	19.7	2.08	115	12.7	11.8	4.2
Hartlepool UA	94	960	90	-5.1	5.9	19.0	1.95	127	11.9	11.4	6.6
Middlesbrough UA	54	2,560	138	-8.4	6.1	17.4	1.99	126	13.4	10.7	5.6
Redcar and Cleveland UA	245	568	139	-7.8	5.3	20.5	1.86	106	10.9	10.5	6.9
Stockton-on-Tees UA	204	913	186	7.1	5.6	17.3	1.75	114	11.4	9.5	5.2
Durham County	2,226	223	497	-2.9	5.0	19.8	1.74	113	10.8	10.9	4.7
Chester-le-Street	68	787	53	2.8	5.1	19.5	1.69	120	10.1	10.9	5.6
Derwentside	271	317	86	-2.8	5.2	20.5	1.77	110	10.5	11.4	3.4
Durham	187	486	91	-2.9	4.4	17.1	1.39	101	8.9	8.7	3.8
Easington	145	642	93	-8.5	5.2	20.3	1.97	120	11.9	11.5	6.5
Sedgefield	217	404	88	-6.1	5.3	19.7	2.01	111	11.9	10.4	5.1
Teesdale	836	30	25	-0.3	4.2	22.8	1.98	98	9.3	11.3	0.0
Wear Valley	503	123	62	-3.8	5.4	20.8	2.12	123	11.8	13.2	4.7
Northumberland	5,013	62	311	3.9	4.9	21.1	1.75	108	9.5	11.4	3.1
Alnwick	1,080	30	32	10.4	4.7	23.5	1.80	105	8.8	12.6	3.6
Berwick-upon-Tweed	972	27	26	0.5	4.1	26.5	1.41	87	6.7	11.7	10.0
Blyth Valley	70	1,157	81	5.0	5.4	17.8	1.68	122	10.6	10.8	4.6
Castle Morpeth	618	81	50	-0.1	4.4	22.9	1.71	97	8.0	11.0	0.0
Tynedale	2,206	27	60	10.6	4.9	21.5	1.91	104	9.4	11.4	1.9
Wansbeck	67	922	62	-1.7	5.4	20.3	1.84	122	10.9	12.1	1.5
Tyne and Wear (Met County)	540	2,010	1,086	-6.1	5.2	19.3	1.59	115	10.8	11.1	4.9
Gateshead	142	1,344	191	-10.4	5.4	20.3	1.74	115	11.1	11.4	5.9
Newcastle upon Tyne	113	2,375	270	-5.2	5.2	17.8	1.43	109	10.8	10.4	4.5
North Tyneside	82	2,315	191	-4.0	5.3	20.5	1.82	114	11.3	11.9	3.3
South Tyneside	64	2,352	152	-6.4	5.0	20.6	1.67	119	10.2	12.2	3.3
Sunderland	137	2,056	283	-5.2	5.1	18.6	1.58	120	10.5	10.4	6.6

1 Local government structure as at 1 April 1998. See Notes and Definitions.
2 Pension age is 65 or over for men and 60 or over for women.
3 The total fertility rate (TFR) is the average number of children who would be born to a woman if the current pattern of fertility persisted throughout her child-bearing years.
4 The Standardised Mortality Ratio (SMR) takes account of the age structure of the population. Data are based on occurrences.
5 Data are based on occurrences.

Source: Office for National Statistics

Table 1.4   Local authority[1] housing, households and labour market: North East

	Economic activity[2] rate 2004-2005 (percentages)	Claimant[3] unemployment March 2005 (thousands)	Percentage claiming over 12 months, computerised claims only[4] March 2005	Lone parents[5] as a percentage of all households, spring 2005	Housing completions[6] by private enterprise 2004	Average dwelling price[7] 2004 (£ thousands)	Percentage change in dwelling price 2003 to 2004	Local authority average weekly rent per dwelling[8] (£), April 2005 (provisional)
United Kingdom	78.2	882.3	14.0	7.2				
England	78.5	717.3	13.8	7.2	129,544	181	13.8	55.11
North East	74.5	48.1	11.5	8.1	5,469	115	22.1	45.38
Darlington UA	71.1	1.8	9.2	6.7	387	119	26.3	45.94
Hartlepool UA	73.5	2.2	12.4	4.1	221	79	7.3	..
Middlesbrough UA	73.9	4.0	17.0	14.4	101	88	27.9	..
Redcar and Cleveland UA	76.7	2.9	15.1	10.8	334	100	19.9	..
Stockton-on-Tees UA	80.7	3.4	13.2	6.8	393	120	21.7	49.34
Durham	73.6	6.5	5.9	8.6	1,856	104	27.5	45.74
Chester-le-Street	72.5	0.6	5.4	5.3	9	118	26.6	44.88
Derwentside	78.9	1.2	3.8	4.8	322	104	30.5	46.58
Durham	68.5	0.9	7.6	7.8	192	138	25.8	46.22
Easington	71.2	1.2	6.2	13.3	332	83	30.0	45.45
Sedgefield	70.8	1.4	4.4	9.0	248	84	22.0	46.06
Teesdale	81.5	0.2	5.2	11.2	51	152	32.3	46.12
Wear Valley	79.5	1.1	8.8	9.4	315	101	30.3	44.48
Northumberland	75.8	4.7	11.6	5.6	595	141	22.4	42.44
Alnwick	76.6	0.4	11.8	2.7	85	173	23.4	44.75
Berwick-upon-Tweed	78.9	0.4	9.0	2.7	1	145	30.0	46.33
Blyth Valley	76.9	1.5	10.7	6.9	71	104	24.0	40.80
Castle Morpeth	78.2	0.5	13.0	5.3	76	215	22.3	47.02
Tynedale	71.6	0.6	13.3	9.5	151	182	18.0	..
Wansbeck	75.1	1.4	11.9	3.6	151	91	18.4	40.36
Tyne and Wear (Met County)	73.7	22.6	11.4	8.2	1,969	122	20.9	45.27
Gateshead	74.3	3.6	11.9	9.7	681	113	20.3	47.12
Newcastle upon Tyne	73.1	5.4	12.7	8.5	125	147	18.1	45.07
North Tyneside	75.7	3.8	11.7	7.5	330	127	24.5	44.88
South Tyneside	74.7	4.4	13.1	5.7	207	108	25.9	43.74
Sunderland	71.9	5.4	8.2	9.0	548	108	21.1	..

1 Local government structure as at 1 April 1998. See Notes and Definitions.
2 For those of working age. See Notes and Definitions for Chapter 5.
3 Counts of claimants of unemployment-related benefits at March 2005. See Notes and Definitions for Chapter 5.
4 People who have been claiming unemployment-related benefits for more than 12 months (computerised claims only), as a percentage of total computerised claimants in March 2005.
5 Lone parents with at least one dependent child.
6 District figures do not always add to county totals. See Notes and Definitions for Chapter 6.
7 Excludes those bought at non-market prices. Sales below £1,000 and above £20 million are excluded from these figures. Averages are based on four quarters of the year.
8 Some local authorities have no housing stock following large-scale voluntary transfers (..) to Registered Social Landlords (RSLs), so the average rent is no longer applicable.

Source: Office for National Statistics; Office of the Deputy Prime Minister

North West

In 2004, the North West had a population of 6.8 million. The population of the North West increased by 23 thousand between mid-2003 and mid-2004. This followed a population decrease of 1.6 per cent in the 23 years between 1981 and 2004, according to the mid-year population estimates. The largest percentage change was in Warrington with almost 14 per cent increase. (Table 3.1 and Map 1.49)

Between 1976 and 2003 the number of marriages in the North West decreased by 19,300, which is almost a quarter of the decrease for England of 83,400. (Table 3.14)

In 2004, the infant mortality rate in the North West was higher than the UK average (5.4 and 5.1 deaths of infants under one year of age per 1,000 live births respectively). (Table 7.2)

The North West had nearly 15 per cent of its maintained primary school classes with more than 30 pupils compared with 12 per cent in Great Britain as a whole in 2004/05. (Table 4.2)

In 2003/04, 79 per cent of 16-year-olds in the North West were in post-compulsory education or government-supported training, the same proportion as England. (Table 4.7)

The proportion of people of working age qualified to GCE A level/equivalent or higher in the North West was 48 per cent in spring 2005, compared with a UK average of almost 50 per cent. In 2004, almost two-thirds of full-time first degree graduates studying in the North West subsequently gained employment in the UK, which was 5 per cent above the UK average. (Tables 4.10 and 4.9)

In spring 2005, the employment rate in the North West was 73 per cent for people of working age which was slightly lower than the UK average of 74 per cent. (Table 5.1)

In April 2005, gross weekly earnings for full-time employees on adult rates in the North West were £450.00 for males and £351.60 for females, each approximately 5 per cent below the UK levels. These figures are median values so half of the males (or females) earned above these amounts and half earned below. (Table 1.5)

The largest proportion of manufacturing GVA came from the North West with £18.4 billion which accounted one-fifth of the total GVA for that region. In the North West, manufacturing accounted for 19 per cent of GVA in 2003, compared with 15 per cent for the UK as a whole. Agriculture, hunting, forestry and fishing accounted for 0.8 per cent of GVA compared with just over 1 per cent in the UK overall. (Table 12.5)

GVA per head in the North West in 2004 was around £14,900 which was 11 per cent lower than the UK figure of £17,300 per head. (Table 12.1)

The North West had the highest percentage increase of 19 per cent in the value of detached houses, with a rise of nearly £39,000 between 2003 and 2004. The region had the second highest percentage increase for all dwellings of 17.5 per cent compared with the rate for England of 11.2 per cent. (Table 6.7)

In 2004/05, the North West had almost 3,500 household offences recorded by the police per 10,000 households which was the highest of all regions and countries. This was 16 per cent higher than the rate for England of 3,000. (Table 9.2)

In 2003, total turnover from manufacturing businesses for the UK reached almost £439 billion and the North West accounted for 13 per cent of this with £59 billion. (Table 13.4)

Table **1.5**   **Key statistics for the North West**

	North West	United Kingdom[1]		North West	United Kingdom[1]
Population, 2004[2] (thousands)	6,827	59,835	Gross value added, 2004 (£ billion)	102.0	1,005.4
Percentage aged under 16[2]	19.8	19.5	Gross value added per head index, 2004 (UK=100)	88.9	100
Percentage pension age and over[2]	18.7	18.6	Total business sites,[5] March 2004 (thousands)	257.9	2,573.1
Standardised Mortality Ratio (UK=100), 2003	109	100	Average dwelling price,[1] 2004 (£)	132,543	183,449
Infant mortality rate,[3] 2004	5.4	5.1			
Percentage of pupils achieving 5 or more grades A*-C at GCSE level or equivalent, 2003/04[1]	52.0	54.2	Motor cars currently licensed,[1,6] 2003 (thousands)	2,942	26,240
			Fatal and serious accidents on roads,[1] 2004 (rates per 100,000 population)	49.7	51.1
Economic activity rate,[4] spring 2005 (percentages)	76.8	78.5			
Employment rate,[4] spring 2005 (percentages)	72.9	74.4	Recorded crime rate,[1] 2004/05 (recorded offences per 100,000 population)	11,464	10,508
Unemployment rate,[4] spring 2005 (percentages)	4.3	4.7			
Median gross weekly earnings: males in full-time employment, April 2005 (£)	450.0	471.5	Average gross weekly household income, 2001/02 to 2003/04[7] (£)	489	554
Median gross weekly earnings: females in full-time employment, April 2005 (£)	351.6	371.8	Average weekly household expenditure, 2001/02 to 2003/04[7] (£)	383.60	406.20
			Households in receipt of Tax Credits,[1] 2003/04 (percentages)	17	15

1 Figures relate to the United Kingdom except for GCSE results and average dwelling prices (covering England); currently licensed motor cars, fatal and serious accidents and Tax Credits (Great Britain), and recorded crime rate (England and Wales).
2 Population figures for 2004 are mid-year population estimates. Pension age is men aged 65 or over and women aged 60 or over.
3 Deaths of infants under one year of age per 1,000 live births.
4 Seasonally adjusted data for people of working age, men aged 16 to 64 and women aged 16 to 59.
5 Registered for VAT and/or PAYE local unit basis, e.g. an individual factory or shop.
6 Totals for the United Kingdom include vehicles where the country of the registered vehicle is unknown, that are under disposal or from countries unknown within Great Britain.
7 Data combined from the 2001/02, 2002/03 and 2003/04 Expenditure and Food Surveys.

Map **1.6**   **Population density: by local or unitary authority, 2004**

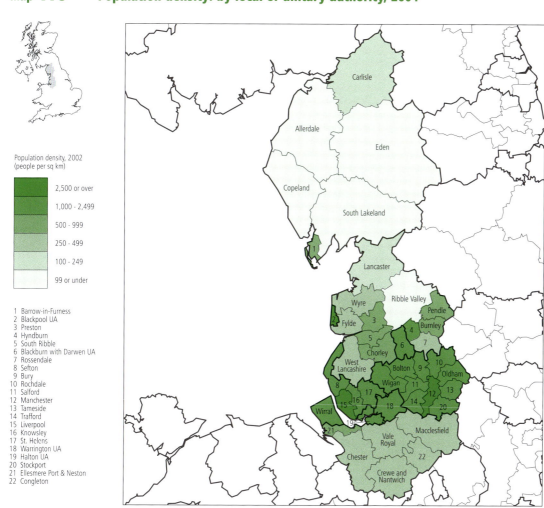

Population density, 2002
(people per sq km)

- 2,500 or over
- 1,000 - 2,499
- 500 - 999
- 250 - 499
- 100 - 249
- 99 or under

1 Barrow-in-Furness
2 Blackpool UA
3 Preston
4 Hyndburn
5 South Ribble
6 Blackburn with Darwen UA
7 Rossendale
8 Sefton
9 Bury
10 Rochdale
11 Salford
12 Manchester
13 Tameside
14 Trafford
15 Liverpool
16 Knowsley
17 St. Helens
18 Warrington UA
19 Halton UA
20 Stockport
21 Ellesmere Port & Neston
22 Congleton

Table 1.7 Local authority[1] population and vital statistics: North West, 2004

	Area (sq km)	People per sq km	Population (thous) Total	Total population percentage change 1981-2004	Percentage of population: aged under 5	Percentage of population: of pension age[2] or over	Total fertility rate (TFR)[3]	Standardised Mortality Ratio (UK=100) (SMR)[4]	Live birth rate per 1,000 population	Death rate per 1,000 population	Infant mortality rate[5]
United Kingdom	242,515	247	59,835	6.2	5.7	18.6	1.77	100	12.0	9.7	5.3
England	130,281	385	50,094	7.0	5.7	18.5	1.78	99	12.1	9.6	5.3
North West	14,106	484	6,827	-1.6	5.6	18.7	1.81	111	11.9	10.5	5.9
Blackburn with Darwen UA	137	1,023	140	-1.6	7.4	15.1	2.32	120	15.6	9.4	7.0
Blackpool UA	35	4,086	143	-4.3	5.2	22.2	2.03	118	11.8	13.7	7.1
Halton UA	79	1,504	119	-3.8	6.0	16.1	1.94	127	13.0	10.0	5.5
Warrington UA	181	1,073	194	13.8	5.8	17.4	1.83	104	11.0	9.0	7.7
Cheshire County	2,083	326	680	6.3	5.3	20.2	1.75	99	10.7	10.1	5.2
Chester	448	266	119	1.8	5.1	20.6	1.60	98	10.8	10.4	8.0
Congleton	211	435	92	14.7	5.1	19.9	1.59	97	9.5	9.7	1.1
Crewe and Nantwich	430	263	113	15.0	5.6	19.4	1.94	109	11.6	10.7	4.1
Ellesmere Port and Neston	88	915	81	-2.1	5.3	20.1	1.79	101	10.6	9.7	6.0
Macclesfield	525	287	150	0.4	5.1	21.7	1.71	93	10.3	10.5	5.5
Vale Royal	380	328	125	11.6	5.5	18.9	1.94	99	11.5	9.5	5.4
Cumbria	6,768	73	495	2.8	4.9	21.8	1.76	103	9.9	11.4	5.8
Allerdale	1,242	77	95	-0.4	4.8	21.7	1.67	103	9.3	11.2	3.3
Barrow-in-Furness	78	904	71	-4.0	5.3	20.3	1.97	112	11.2	11.7	6.8
Carlisle	1,040	100	104	2.5	5.0	20.7	1.76	105	11.1	11.1	5.5
Copeland	732	96	71	-3.2	5.0	19.7	1.70	112	9.8	10.8	10.1
Eden	2,142	24	52	20.2	4.7	22.2	1.75	97	9.4	10.9	4.3
South Lakeland	1,534	67	103	8.4	4.4	25.2	1.70	95	8.5	12.4	5.5
Greater Manchester (Met County)	1,276	1,990	2,539	-3.0	5.9	17.2	1.84	115	13.0	10.2	6.1
Bolton	140	1,894	265	1.0	6.1	17.5	1.95	116	12.8	10.5	6.3
Bury	99	1,831	182	2.8	5.9	17.6	1.98	113	12.7	10.1	4.1
Manchester	116	3,778	437	-4.8	6.1	14.1	1.70	122	15.1	9.5	6.5
Oldham	142	1,534	218	-1.4	6.9	17.0	2.28	117	14.6	10.2	6.5
Rochdale	158	1,306	207	-0.8	6.3	16.7	2.06	121	13.4	10.3	7.4
Salford	97	2,226	216	-13.2	5.6	18.2	1.78	124	12.6	11.7	6.1
Stockport	126	2,238	282	-3.6	5.4	19.7	1.77	97	11.2	9.7	6.8
Tameside	103	2,072	214	-2.2	5.7	17.7	1.88	117	12.2	10.6	7.2
Trafford	106	2,006	213	-4.6	5.8	18.7	1.80	98	12.2	9.5	4.4
Wigan	188	1,623	305	-0.5	5.6	17.6	1.83	123	11.9	10.4	4.4
Lancashire County	2,903	397	1,152	5.3	5.4	19.6	1.84	107	11.4	10.7	6.3
Burnley	111	796	88	-5.0	5.9	17.9	2.07	122	13.1	11.4	11.9
Chorley	203	508	103	11.7	5.5	17.3	1.95	113	12.1	9.9	3.6
Fylde	166	458	76	9.9	4.3	25.9	1.59	99	7.9	13.5	5.3
Hyndburn	73	1,119	82	2.8	6.4	17.8	2.16	109	13.5	9.9	6.2
Lancaster	576	237	137	9.2	4.9	20.3	1.49	102	9.7	11.1	8.3
Pendle	169	527	89	3.4	6.2	17.9	2.11	104	13.0	9.9	10.8
Preston	142	920	131	3.6	5.8	16.7	1.81	112	13.4	9.6	10.1
Ribble Valley	583	97	57	5.0	5.1	20.5	1.71	100	9.2	10.4	2.0
Rossendale	138	477	66	1.4	5.7	17.0	2.05	116	12.4	10.1	2.8
South Ribble	113	934	106	9.0	5.3	19.0	1.84	95	11.3	8.9	2.7
West Lancashire	347	315	109	1.5	5.4	19.5	1.82	112	10.8	10.5	4.4
Wyre	283	387	109	10.1	4.6	25.9	1.81	104	9.3	13.4	1.0
Merseyside (Met County)	645	2,118	1,366	-10.3	5.4	19.4	1.68	115	11.1	11.0	4.8
Knowsley	86	1,732	150	-13.7	6.0	17.6	1.95	125	12.7	10.0	2.9
Liverpool	112	3,974	445	-14.0	5.3	17.0	1.48	129	11.3	11.0	4.7
St. Helens	136	1,296	177	-7.4	5.4	19.0	1.80	104	9.7	11.6	7.1
Sefton	153	1,840	282	-6.1	4.9	22.3	1.71	112	11.2	10.1	3.6
Wirral	157	1,993	313	-8.1	5.5	21.2	1.93	106	11.2	11.7	5.7

1 Local government structure as at 1 April 1998. See Notes and Definitions.
2 Pension age is 65 or over for men and 60 or over for women.
3 The total fertility rate (TFR) is the average number of children who would be born to a woman if the current pattern of fertility persisted throughout her child-bearing years.
4 The Standardised Mortality Ratio (SMR) takes account of the age structure of the population. Data are based on occurrences.
5 Data are based on occurrences.

Source: Office for National Statistics

Table 1.8   Local authority[1] housing, households and labour market: North West

	Economic activity[2] rate 2004-2005 (percentages)	Claimant[3] unemployment March 2005 (thousands)	Percentage claiming over 12 months, computerised claims only[4] March 2005	Lone parents[5] as a percentage of all households, spring 2005	Housing completions[6] by private enterprise 2004	Average dwelling price[7] 2004 (£ thousands)	Percentage change in dwelling price 2003 to 2004	Local authority average weekly rent per dwelling[8] (£), April 2005 (provisional)
United Kingdom	78.2	882.3	14.0	7.2				
England	78.5	717.3	13.8	7.2	129,544	181	13.8	55.11
North West	76.2	102.5	12.1	8.7	16,550	126	21.0	48.86
Blackburn with Darwen UA	72.5	2.3	6.7	10.4	342	85	26.5	..
Blackpool UA	77.1	2.8	7.7	18.3	139	103	27.5	49.72
Halton UA	74.2	2.2	11.3	5.4	728	118	22.6	50.16
Warrington UA	78.2	1.6	6.8	5.4	513	159	16.9	49.81
Cheshire County	79.2	5.2	7.3	6.0	3,261	180	16.5	49.15
Chester	82.7	1.0	8.8	2.9	293	188	20.8	..
Congleton	86.2	0.5	4.6	3.7	243	167	13.4	..
Crewe and Nantwich	76.0	0.9	8.5	12.9	585	149	16.5	..
Ellesmere Port and Neston	74.1	0.8	6.2	6.9	98	151	21.1	44.54
Macclesfield	75.2	0.9	7.3	6.8	296	231	15.0	54.35
Vale Royal	81.1	1.0	6.8	3.4	359	163	18.0	..
Cumbria	82.1	5.6	9.8	5.8	1,071	131	22.0	52.23
Allerdale	80.7	1.2	9.1	3.1	163	124	21.7	..
Barrow-in-Furness	82.1	1.3	8.5	3.8	107	77	27.3	50.44
Carlisle	80.6	1.3	9.1	6.0	366	119	26.7	..
Copeland	84.1	1.2	15.6	12.4	149	99	34.2	..
Eden	87.5	0.2	4.5	6.8	132	178	23.9	..
South Lakeland	80.6	0.5	5.1	4.7	154	196	21.0	53.82
Greater Manchester (Met County)	75.5	38.7	9.7	9.9	5,668	122	21.9	48.73
Bolton	79.0	4.0	5.0	9.0	575	107	30.3	44.93
Bury	76.8	2.0	4.1	12.8	400	121	21.2	49.85
Manchester	63.0	10.7	11.8	14.9	1,714	112	18.4	52.51
Oldham	74.0	3.3	6.6	10.3	268	94	26.2	44.48
Rochdale	72.1	3.4	9.1	8.4	141	105	27.9	46.38
Salford	79.8	3.5	12.6	10.3	742	112	28.3	50.75
Stockport	83.6	2.4	8.8	5.7	270	162	16.9	45.16
Tameside	79.6	2.9	11.4	10.2	285	103	21.1	..
Trafford	78.8	2.2	8.5	8.7	671	202	18.3	..
Wigan	75.5	4.4	11.5	8.1	850	105	22.8	47.85
Lancashire County	77.1	12.5	9.3	6.7	3,672	118	19.6	47.28
Burnley	71.2	1.0	4.6	8.8	132	56	8.8	..
Chorley	75.3	0.9	7.9	8.4	385	140	21.3	45.26
Fylde	74.3	0.4	10.9	3.5	316	171	22.5	..
Hyndburn	76.2	1.1	5.2	5.1	163	72	32.8	46.73
Lancaster	77.6	1.7	12.3	2.9	494	127	26.2	49.05
Pendle	76.2	1.0	3.4	11.4	158	74	17.6	45.27
Preston	70.3	2.2	11.1	8.9	215	116	24.0	49.27
Ribble Valley	79.6	0.2	4.5	7.6	226	191	28.3	45.75
Rossendale	79.5	0.7	6.6	7.0	208	107	26.9	46.49
South Ribble	86.6	0.8	8.5	7.2	269	140	22.1	..
West Lancashire	83.3	1.7	14.2	3.4	256	157	20.8	47.31
Wyre	74.0	0.9	10.8	9.0	343	140	16.3	..
Merseyside (Met County)	73.2	31.7	18.6	10.1	2,878	119	24.4	49.75
Knowsley	72.1	3.6	16.9	14.7	398	109	32.3	..
Liverpool	67.7	14.9	23.8	12.5	888	104	25.8	49.27
St. Helens	77.0	2.8	14.3	9.1	441	112	27.2	..
Sefton	77.4	4.4	17.3	6.4	423	140	19.4	50.48
Wirral	75.5	6.0	9.5	8.1	486	130	24.5	..

1 Local government structure as at 1 April 1998. See Notes and Definitions.

2 For those of working age. See Notes and Definitions for Chapter 5.

3 Counts of claimants of unemployment-related benefits at March 2005. See Notes and Definitions for Chapter 5.

4 People who have been claiming unemployment-related benefits for more than 12 months (computerised claims only), as a percentage of total computerised claimants in March 2005.

5 Lone parents with at least one dependent child.

6 District figures do not always add to county totals. See Notes and Definitions for Chapter 6.

7 Excludes those bought at non-market prices. Sales below £1,000 and above £20 million are excluded from these figures. Averages are based on four quarters of the year.

8 Some local authorities have no housing stock following large scale voluntary transfers (..) to Registered Social Landlords (RSLs), so the average rent is no longer applicable.

Source: Office for National Statistics; Office of the Deputy Prime Minister

Yorkshire and the Humber

In 2004, Yorkshire and the Humber had a population of 5 million. The resident population of the region increased by 30 thousand between mid-2003 and mid-2004. The population of Yorkshire and the Humber also increased by over 2 per cent in the 23 years between 1981 and 2004, according to the mid-year population estimates. The largest percentage increase was in East Riding of Yorkshire with almost 20 per cent. (Table 3.1 and Map 1.49)

In 2004, the Infant Mortality rate in Yorkshire and the Humber was higher than the UK rate (5.5 and 5.1 deaths of infants under one year of age per 1,000 live births respectively). (Table 7.2)

Yorkshire and the Humber had the second highest proportion (15 per cent) of maintained primary school classes with more than 30 pupils compared with 12 per cent in Great Britain as a whole in 2004/05. (Table 4.2)

In 2003/04, 76 per cent of 16-year-olds in Yorkshire and the Humber were in some form of post-compulsory education or government-supported training. This was below the England rate of 79 per cent. (Table 4.7)

The proportion of people of working age qualified to GCE A level/equivalent or higher in Yorkshire and the Humber was around 46 per cent in spring 2005. In 2004 the proportion of full-time first degree graduates studying in Yorkshire and the Humber who subsequently gained employment in the UK was above the UK average. (Tables 4.9 and 4.10)

In spring 2005 the employment rate in Yorkshire and the Humber (for people of working age), was almost 74 per cent, which was similar to the UK rate overall. (Table 5.1)

In April 2005, gross weekly earnings for full-time employees on adult rates in Yorkshire and the Humber were £438.70 for males and £335.50 for females, 7 and 10 per cent below the UK levels respectively. These figures are median values so half of the males (or females) earned above these amounts and half earned below. (Table 1.9)

Yorkshire and the Humber had the highest rate for recorded offences of burglary of 1,740 per 100,000 population in 2004/05. (Table 9.1)

Yorkshire and the Humber had the greatest area of national parks at 315 thousand hectares (21 per cent of the region's land area) in 2005. (Table 11.13)

In Yorkshire and the Humber, manufacturing accounted for almost 20 per cent of GVA in 2003, compared with just over 15 per cent for the UK as a whole. Agriculture, hunting, forestry and fishing accounted for 1.2 per cent of GVA compared with 1.1 per cent in the UK overall. (Table 12.5)

GVA per head in Yorkshire and the Humber in 2004 was just over £14,900, compared with £17,300 for the UK as a whole. (Table 12.1)

In March 2004, 31 per cent of businesses in Yorkshire and the Humber were in the areas of distribution, hotels and catering or repairs industries; this was higher than the UK average of 28 per cent. (Table 13.3)

Over one-quarter of the 5.2 million pigs in the UK were in Yorkshire and the Humber in 2004. (Table 13.14)

Table **1.9**   Key statistics for Yorkshire and the Humber

	Yorkshire and the Humber	United Kingdom[1]		Yorkshire and the Humber	United Kingdom[1]
Population, 2004[2] (thousands)	5,039	59,835	Gross value added, 2004 (£ billion)	75.2	1,005.4
Percentage aged under 16[2]	19.6	19.5	Gross value added per head index, 2004 (UK=100)	88.8	100
Percentage pension age and over[2]	18.8	18.6	Total business sites,[5] March 2004 (thousands)	192.1	2,573.1
Standardised Mortality Ratio (UK=100), 2003	102	100	Average dwelling price,[1] 2004 (£)	133,801	183,449
Infant mortality rate,[3] 2004	5.5	5.1			
Percentage of pupils achieving 5 or more grades A*-C at GCSE level or equivalent, 2003/04[1]	48.3	54.2	Motor cars currently licensed,[1,6] 2003 (thousands)	2,039	26,240
			Fatal and serious accidents on roads,[1] 2004 (rates per 100,000 population)	59.5	51.1
Economic activity rate,[4] spring 2005 (percentages)	78.1	78.5			
Employment rate,[4] spring 2005 (percentages)	73.8	74.4	Recorded crime rate,[1] 2004/05 (recorded offences per 100,000 population)	11,776	10,508
Unemployment rate,[4] spring 2005 (percentages)	5.1	4.7			
Median gross weekly earnings: males in full-time employment, April 2005 (£)	438.7	471.5	Average gross weekly household income, 2001/02 to 2003/04[7] (£)	474	554
Median gross weekly earnings: females in full-time employment, April 2005 (£)	335.5	371.8	Average weekly household expenditure, 2001/02 to 2003/04[7] (£)	363.70	406.20
			Households in receipt of Tax Credits,[1] 2003/04 (percentages)	17	15

1 Figures relate to the United Kingdom except for GCSE results and average dwelling prices (covering England); currently licensed motor cars, fatal and serious accidents and Tax Credits (Great Britain), and recorded crime rate (England and Wales).
2 Population figures for 2004 are mid-year population estimates. Pension age is men aged 65 or over and women aged 60 or over.
3 Deaths of infants under one year of age per 1,000 live births.
4 Seasonally adjusted data for people of working age, men aged 16 to 64 and women aged 16 to 59.
5 Registered for VAT and/or PAYE local unit basis, e.g. an individual factory or shop.
6 Totals for the United Kingdom include vehicles where the country of the registered vehicle is unknown, that are under disposal or from countries unknown within Great Britain.
7 Data combined from the 2001/02, 2002/03 and 2003/04 Expenditure and Food Surveys.

Map **1.10**   Population density: by local or unitary authority, 2004

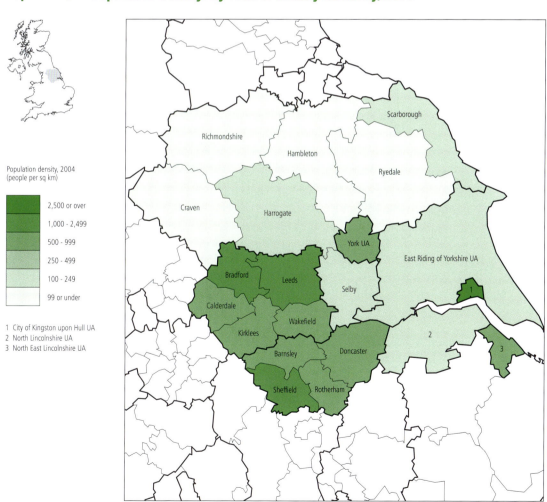

Population density, 2004
(people per sq km)

- 2,500 or over
- 1,000 - 2,499
- 500 - 999
- 250 - 499
- 100 - 249
- 99 or under

1 City of Kingston upon Hull UA
2 North Lincolnshire UA
3 North East Lincolnshire UA

Table **1.11** Local authority[1] population and vital statistics: Yorkshire and the Humber, 2004

	Area (sq km)	People per sq km	Population (thous) Total	Total population percentage change 1981-2004	Percentage of population: aged under 5	of pension age[2] or over	Total fertility rate (TFR)[3]	Standardised Mortality Ratio (UK=100) (SMR)[4]	Live birth rate per 1,000 population	Death rate per 1,000 population	Infant mortality rate[5]
United Kingdom	242,515	247	59,835	6.2	5.7	18.6	1.77	100	12.0	9.7	5.3
England	130,281	385	50,094	7.0	5.7	18.5	1.78	99	12.1	9.6	5.3
Yorkshire and the Humber	15,408	327	5,039	2.4	5.6	18.8	1.82	105	11.9	10.2	5.7
East Riding of Yorkshire UA	2,408	135	325	19.6	4.8	22.2	1.78	99	9.3	11.1	4.8
Kingston upon Hull, City of UA	71	3,479	249	-9.2	5.5	17.1	1.79	116	12.9	10.2	6.4
North East Lincolnshire UA	192	822	158	-2.2	5.6	19.6	2.03	107	12.0	10.7	4.6
North Lincolnshire UA	846	185	157	3.6	5.5	20.1	1.93	102	10.8	10.2	4.9
York UA	272	680	185	11.8	4.8	19.5	1.45	93	10.5	9.5	3.3
North Yorkshire County	8,038	72	580	13.4	5.0	21.7	1.83	94	9.9	10.7	1.9
Craven	1,177	46	54	13.1	4.5	23.9	1.70	85	8.2	11.1	2.3
Hambleton	1,311	65	85	13.3	4.9	21.8	1.90	87	9.6	9.4	2.3
Harrogate	1,308	118	154	12.8	5.1	20.7	1.71	95	10.3	10.5	3.3
Richmondshire	1,319	38	51	16.5	6.0	17.9	1.81	92	10.7	8.4	1.8
Ryedale	1,507	34	52	18.4	4.5	24.2	1.83	92	9.1	11.6	0.0
Scarborough	817	131	107	4.7	4.6	25.2	2.02	103	10.1	13.7	0.9
Selby	599	129	77	24.0	5.3	18.0	1.80	96	10.2	8.9	1.3
South Yorkshire (Met County)	1,552	824	1,278	-3.0	5.5	18.9	1.78	109	11.8	10.5	5.6
Barnsley	329	672	221	-2.3	5.4	19.0	1.88	118	11.4	11.2	5.8
Doncaster	568	509	289	-0.6	5.7	19.3	2.00	113	11.9	10.7	4.9
Rotherham	287	881	252	-0.3	5.7	18.6	1.88	112	11.6	10.5	6.3
Sheffield	368	1,403	516	-5.7	5.4	18.7	1.68	101	11.9	10.1	5.6
West Yorkshire (Met County)	2,029	1,039	2,108	2.0	6.1	17.4	1.86	106	13.1	9.7	6.9
Bradford	366	1,313	481	3.6	7.3	16.3	2.20	113	16.0	9.7	8.7
Calderdale	364	534	194	0.8	6.0	18.1	2.07	105	12.7	10.2	6.8
Kirklees	409	962	393	4.2	6.3	17.1	2.04	108	13.7	9.7	8.0
Leeds	552	1,304	720	0.3	5.4	17.6	1.55	99	11.7	9.3	5.4
Wakefield	339	944	320	1.7	5.5	18.3	1.82	112	11.5	10.3	4.8

1 Local government structure as at 1 April 1998. See Notes and Definitions.
2 Pension age is 65 or over for men and 60 or over for women.
3 The total fertility rate (TFR) is the average number of children who would be born to a woman if the current pattern of fertility persisted throughout her child-bearing years.
4 The Standardised Mortality Ratio (SMR) takes account of the age structure of the population. Data are based on occurrences.
5 Data are based on occurrences.

Source: Office for National Statistics

Table **1.12**   Local authority[1] housing, households and labour market: Yorkshire and the Humber

	Economic activity[2] rate 2004-2005 (percentages)	Claimant[3] unemployment March 2005 (thousands)	Percentage claiming over 12 months, computerised claims only[4] March 2005	Lone parents[5] as a percentage of all households, spring 2005	Housing completions[6] by private enterprise 2004	Average dwelling price[7] 2004 (£ thousands)	Percentage change in dwelling price 2003 to 2004	Local authority average weekly rent per dwelling[8] (£), April 2005 (provisional)
United Kingdom	78.2	882.3	14.0	7.2				
England	78.5	717.3	13.8	7.2	129,544	181	13.8	55.11
Yorkshire and the Humber	77.7	77.5	10.7	7.3	13,629	128	20.6	46.25
East Riding of Yorkshire UA	75.0	3.8	11.6	4.6	1,285	145	23.3	48.53
Kingston upon Hull, City of UA	71.7	7.9	12.1	6.4	319	66	15.9	49.22
North East Lincolnshire UA	74.2	4.0	10.9	9.8	503	93	25.9	..
North Lincolnshire UA	75.3	2.2	9.8	9.6	517	115	25.2	45.58
York UA	82.2	1.7	8.7	4.7	396	172	14.8	51.98
North Yorkshire County	85.2	4.6	12.3	5.0	1,714	186	20.4	52.29
Craven	85.0	0.3	7.9	3.2	161	176	17.8	..
Hambleton	89.7	0.5	13.8	4.6	123	208	20.7	..
Harrogate	87.3	0.9	11.3	3.9	311	221	14.4	55.63
Richmondshire	79.1	0.3	10.7	5.8	24	178	28.6	51.05
Ryedale	88.9	0.3	15.7	8.5	109	196	20.5	..
Scarborough	83.0	1.6	14.7	5.7	220	144	28.0	..
Selby	81.2	0.7	7.8	4.9	298	165	14.7	48.87
South Yorkshire (Met County)	76.0	20.7	11.8	8.6	3,294	115	24.1	44.37
Barnsley	76.9	3.0	6.4	6.5	758	103	30.6	43.97
Doncaster	78.3	5.2	10.8	9.9	546	109	28.2	44.48
Rotherham	74.8	3.9	10.5	8.4	778	106	22.3	42.44
Sheffield	75.1	8.6	14.8	8.9	736	129	20.5	45.29
West Yorkshire (Met County)	77.9	32.5	9.4	7.4	5,951	124	19.5	46.42
Bradford	73.6	8.3	10.7	9.0	979	109	23.1	..
Calderdale	81.9	2.6	6.1	7.1	487	115	22.9	..
Kirklees	78.1	5.0	5.5	8.4	670	120	21.0	48.78
Leeds	79.2	12.2	11.5	6.2	2,851	142	16.0	45.50
Wakefield	78.5	4.5	8.0	6.8	964	119	20.0	..

1 Local government structure as at 1 April 1998. See Notes and Definitions.
2 For those of working age. See Notes and Definitions for Chapter 5.
3 Counts of claimants of unemployment-related benefits at March 2005. See Notes and Definitions for Chapter 5.
4 People who have been claiming unemployment-related benefits for more than 12 months (computerised claims only), as a percentage of total computerised claimants in March 2005.
5 Lone parents with at least one dependent child.
6 District figures do not always add to county totals. See Notes and Definitions for Chapter 6.
7 Excludes those bought at non-market prices. Sales below £1,000 and above £20 million are excluded from these figures. Averages are based on four quarters of the year.
8 Some local authorities have no housing stock following large scale voluntary transfers (..) to Registered Social Landlords (RSLs), so the average rent is no longer applicable.

Source: Office for National Statistics; Office of the Deputy Prime Minister

East Midlands

In 2004, the East Midlands had a population of 4.3 million. The population increased by 11 per cent in the 23 years between 1981 and 2004, according to the mid-year population estimates. The greatest change was in South Northamptonshire with an increase of nearly one-third (30.5 per cent) between these years. Nottingham Unitary Authority was the only UA to show a slight decline of just over 1 per cent during the same time period. (Table 3.1 and Map 1.49)

In 2004, the infant mortality rate in the East Midlands was 5.1 deaths of infants under one year of age per 1,000 live births, the same as the UK rate. (Table 7.2)

In East Midlands, 83.7 per cent of women aged between 25 and 64 years were screened for cervical cancer, above the proportion for the UK at 80.6 per cent in the year ending March 2004. Screening for breast cancer was also above the UK average, 79.7 per cent of the target age group between 53 and 64 years in the East Midlands, compared with a UK figure of 74.4 per cent. (Table 7.6)

The East Midlands had the highest proportion (around 16 per cent) of maintained primary school classes with more than 30 pupils, compared with 12 per cent of schools in Great Britain as a whole in 2004/05. (Table 4.2)

In 2003/04, 77 per cent of 16-year-olds in the East Midlands were in post-compulsory education or government-supported training. This was slightly below the rate for England of 79 per cent. (Table 4.7)

The proportion of people of working age qualified to GCE A level/equivalent or higher in the East Midlands was around 49 per cent in spring 2005, 1 percentage point below the UK average. In 2004 the proportion of full-time first degree graduates studying in the East Midlands who subsequently gained employment in the UK was above the UK average. (Tables 4.9 and 4.10)

In spring 2005 the employment rate in the East Midlands was 76 per cent for people of working age, compared with 74 per cent in the UK overall. (Table 5.1)

In April 2005, gross weekly earnings for full-time employees on adult rates in the East Midlands were £455.30 for males and £343.40 for females, 3 and 8 per cent below the UK levels respectively. These figures are median values so half of the males (or females) earned above these amounts and half earned below. (Table 1.13)

In March 2005, there were 9,437 police officers in East Midlands, making it one of the smallest forces in the UK. Just under one in five ordinary police officers were women and 3.4 per cent of officers were from minority ethnic groups. (Table 9.6)

In the East Midlands, manufacturing accounted for 22 per cent of the region's gross value added (GVA) in 2003, compared with 15 per cent for the UK as a whole. Agriculture, hunting, forestry and fishing accounted for 1.6 per cent of GVA compared with 1.0 per cent in the UK overall. (Table 12.5)

In March 2003, one-tenth of businesses in the East Midlands were in the mining, quarrying, energy, water supply and manufacturing sectors; this was slightly higher than the UK average. (Table 12.5)

Table **1.13** Key statistics for the East Midlands

	East Midlands	United Kingdom[1]		East Midlands	United Kingdom[1]
Population, 2004[2] (thousands)	4,280	59,835	Gross value added, 2004 (£ billion)	65.8	1,005.4
Percentage aged under 16[2]	19.4	19.5	Gross value added per head index, 2004 (UK=100)	91.5	100
Percentage pension age and over[2]	18.9	18.6	Total business sites,[5] March 2004 (thousands)	175.6	2,573.1
Standardised Mortality Ratio (UK=100), 2003	100	100	Average dwelling price,[1] 2004 (£)	152,247	183,449
Infant mortality rate,[3] 2004	5.1	5.1			
Percentage of pupils achieving 5 or more grades A*-C at GCSE level or equivalent, 2003/04[1]	52.4	54.2	Motor cars currently licensed,[1,6] 2003 (thousands)	1,965	26,240
			Fatal and serious accidents on roads,[1] 2004 (rates per 100,000 population)	57.7	51.1
Economic activity rate,[4] spring 2005 (percentages)	79.7	78.5			
Employment rate,[4] spring 2005 (percentages)	76.0	74.4	Recorded crime rate,[1] 2004/05 (recorded offences per 100,000 population)	10,733	10,508
Unemployment rate,[4] spring 2005 (percentages)	4.1	4.7			
Median gross weekly earnings: males in full-time employment, April 2005 (£)	455.3	471.5	Average gross weekly household income, 2001/02 to 2003/04[7] (£)	532	554
Median gross weekly earnings: females in full-time employment, April 2005 (£)	343.4	371.8	Average weekly household expenditure, 2001/02 to 2003/04[7] (£)	391.10	406.20
			Households in receipt of Tax Credits,[1] 2003/04 (percentages)	16	15

1 Figures relate to the United Kingdom except for GCSE results and average dwelling prices (covering England); currently licensed motor cars, fatal and serious accidents and Tax Credits (Great Britain), and recorded crime rate (England and Wales).
2 Population figures for 2004 are mid-year population estimates. Pension age is men aged 65 or over and women aged 60 or over.
3 Deaths of infants under one year of age per 1,000 live births.
4 Seasonally adjusted data for people of working age, men aged 16 to 64 and women aged 16 to 59.
5 Registered for VAT and/or PAYE local unit basis, e.g. an individual factory or shop.
6 Totals for the United Kingdom include vehicles where the country of the registered vehicle is unknown, that are under disposal or from countries unknown within Great Britain.
7 Data combined from the 2001/02, 2002/03 and 2003/04 Expenditure and Food Surveys.

Map **1.14** Population density: by local or unitary authority, 2004

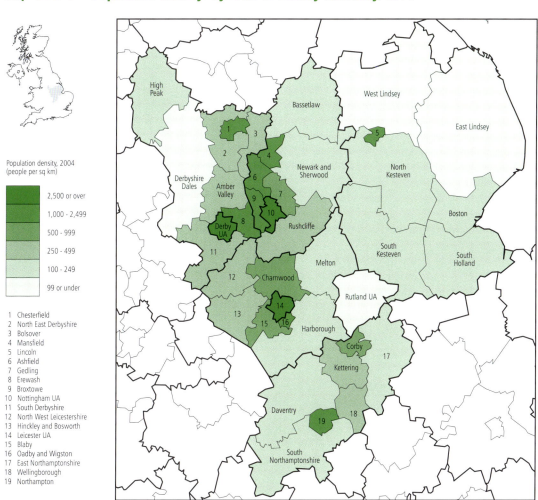

Population density, 2004
(people per sq km)

- 2,500 or over
- 1,000 - 2,499
- 500 - 999
- 250 - 499
- 100 - 249
- 99 or under

1 Chesterfield
2 North East Derbyshire
3 Bolsover
4 Mansfield
5 Lincoln
6 Ashfield
7 Gedling
8 Erewash
9 Broxtowe
10 Nottingham UA
11 South Derbyshire
12 North West Leicestershire
13 Hinckley and Bosworth
14 Leicester UA
15 Blaby
16 Oadby and Wigston
17 East Northamptonshire
18 Wellingborough
19 Northampton

Table 1.15 Local authority[1] population and vital statistics: East Midlands, 2004

	Area (sq km)	People per sq km	Population (thous) Total	Total population percentage change 1981-2004	Percentage of population: aged under 5	Percentage of population: of pension age[2] or over	Total fertility rate (TFR)[3]	Standardised Mortality Ratio (UK=100) (SMR)[4]	Live birth rate per 1,000 population	Death rate per 1,000 population	Infant mortality rate[5]
United Kingdom	242,515	247	59,835	6.2	5.7	18.6	1.77	100	12.0	9.7	5.3
England	130,281	385	50,094	7.0	5.7	18.5	1.78	99	12.1	9.6	5.3
East Midlands	15,607	274	4,280	11.1	5.5	18.9	1.76	101	11.3	9.8	5.9
Derby UA	78	2,996	234	7.5	6.0	18.2	1.81	98	12.8	9.4	6.5
Leicester UA	73	3,889	285	0.7	6.9	14.9	1.94	112	15.9	9.3	7.1
Nottingham UA	75	3,687	275	-1.1	5.5	15.3	1.53	112	12.8	9.2	9.0
Rutland UA	382	96	37	10.7	4.8	20.4	3.35	80	9.3	8.2	3.2
Derbyshire County	2,547	293	746	7.0	5.2	19.9	1.76	102	10.4	10.5	4.7
Amber Valley	265	445	118	8.0	5.2	19.7	1.68	100	10.0	10.4	4.4
Bolsover	160	457	73	3.1	5.3	20.1	1.91	113	11.2	11.7	5.1
Chesterfield	66	1,511	100	1.8	5.1	20.4	1.75	101	10.6	10.7	4.8
Derbyshire Dales	792	88	70	3.0	4.6	23.0	1.72	92	8.4	11.0	4.8
Erewash	110	1,003	110	6.0	5.3	19.0	1.77	103	11.3	10.1	7.0
High Peak	539	168	91	9.8	5.3	18.5	1.77	98	10.5	9.7	3.5
North East Derbyshire	276	353	97	1.4	4.6	21.9	1.70	105	9.2	11.3	3.5
South Derbyshire	338	256	87	26.4	5.8	16.9	1.83	105	11.6	9.2	4.1
Leicestershire County	2,083	300	624	15.0	5.4	18.9	1.72	95	10.6	9.1	5.3
Blaby	130	702	92	18.6	5.5	18.9	1.79	86	11.0	7.9	3.0
Charnwood	279	564	158	12.4	5.1	17.6	1.56	98	10.3	8.9	9.4
Harborough	592	135	80	29.9	5.7	19.0	1.80	90	10.4	8.8	2.3
Hinckley and Bosworth	297	344	102	16.1	5.4	19.4	1.82	96	10.9	9.6	6.7
Melton	481	100	48	11.0	5.3	19.7	1.77	95	10.1	9.7	2.1
North West Leicestershire	279	316	88	11.5	5.9	18.8	1.95	99	11.8	9.7	5.7
Oadby and Wigston	24	2,386	56	5.7	4.6	20.8	1.59	97	8.7	9.9	2.0
Lincolnshire	5,921	114	674	21.8	4.8	22.5	1.73	100	9.6	11.3	7.5
Boston	362	160	58	10.2	5.0	23.2	2.10	102	11.1	12.0	14.7
East Lindsey	1,760	77	136	29.1	4.2	26.8	1.80	103	8.2	13.4	10.4
Lincoln	36	2,425	87	13.1	5.4	17.4	1.58	104	11.9	9.9	7.5
North Kesteven	922	109	101	25.3	4.9	22.0	1.60	103	9.1	11.1	6.5
South Holland	742	109	81	29.5	4.8	25.4	1.76	103	9.1	12.8	1.4
South Kesteven	943	136	128	29.7	5.2	20.1	1.78	90	10.0	9.3	8.1
West Lindsey	1,156	73	84	8.1	4.8	21.8	1.76	100	8.9	10.8	4.2
Northamptonshire	2,364	274	647	21.5	6.1	16.9	1.71	99	12.3	8.8	6.3
Corby	80	663	53	1.2	6.0	17.3	2.06	114	12.4	9.1	7.0
Daventry	663	114	75	29.9	5.9	16.5	1.85	100	10.8	8.3	4.8
East Northamptonshire	510	158	81	29.3	5.9	17.6	1.97	103	11.6	9.8	7.5
Kettering	233	365	85	19.3	6.2	17.9	2.01	100	13.0	9.8	3.7
Northampton	81	2,412	195	22.6	6.1	16.0	1.80	100	13.2	8.6	7.5
South Northamptonshire	634	133	84	30.5	6.1	16.6	1.91	86	11.3	7.4	4.3
Wellingborough	163	449	73	13.2	6.0	17.9	2.04	97	12.2	8.9	7.0
Nottinghamshire County	2,085	364	760	6.1	5.2	19.6	1.72	100	10.7	9.9	3.9
Ashfield	110	1,036	113	6.4	5.5	18.8	1.82	115	11.6	10.9	3.9
Bassetlaw	638	173	110	7.2	5.1	19.6	1.82	109	10.3	10.7	4.6
Broxtowe	80	1,357	109	4.3	4.7	19.5	1.40	92	9.3	9.1	3.9
Gedling	120	927	111	2.8	5.0	20.3	1.64	92	10.2	9.6	1.9
Mansfield	77	1,287	99	-1.3	5.3	19.4	1.93	104	12.0	10.1	8.4
Newark and Sherwood	651	169	110	9.2	5.4	20.5	1.92	96	11.0	10.0	3.7
Rushcliffe	409	262	107	15.2	5.3	19.2	1.63	91	10.5	9.2	0.9

1 Local government structure as at 1 April 1998. See Notes and Definitions.
2 Pension age is 65 or over for men and 60 or over for women.
3 The total fertility rate (TFR) is the average number of children who would be born to a woman if the current pattern of fertility persisted throughout her child-bearing years.
4 The Standardised Mortality Ratio (SMR) takes account of the age structure of the population. Data are based on occurrences.
5 Data are based on occurrences.

Source: Office for National Statistics

Table **1.16** Local authority¹ housing, households and labour market: East Midlands

	Economic activity² rate 2004-2005 (percentages)	Claimant³ unemployment March 2005 (thousands)	Percentage claiming over 12 months, computerised claims only⁴ March 2005	Lone parents⁵ as a percentage of all households, spring 2005	Housing completions⁶ by private enterprise 2004	Average dwelling price⁷ 2004 (£ thousands)	Percentage change in dwelling price 2003 to 2004	Local authority average weekly rent per dwelling⁸ (£), April 2005 (provisional)
United Kingdom	78.2	882.3	14.0	7.2				
England	78.5	717.3	13.8	7.2	129,544	181	13.8	55.11
East Midlands	79.2	55.7	13.4	6.6	13,760	145	15.3	48.02
Derby UA	73.3	4.3	16.0	6.9	330	130	23.5	46.86
Leicester UA	66.4	8.5	21.3	9.6	804	127	20.1	47.23
Nottingham UA	69.6	6.7	16.0	9.0	712	119	13.2	46.15
Rutland UA	89.9	0.1	4.9	5.9	106	220	9.6	52.98
Derbyshire County	82.3	8.7	13.3	6.2	1,959	139	18.9	46.64
Amber Valley	84.4	1.3	12.6	6.9	196	135	19.0	..
Bolsover	75.7	1.2	13.1	10.7	225	98	23.3	44.82
Chesterfield	77.0	1.9	15.1	7.6	375	117	21.3	45.69
Derbyshire Dales	89.4	0.4	14.2	3.9	84	215	23.8	..
Erewash	85.3	1.3	12.4	5.7	17	126	15.9	..
High Peak	80.0	0.9	10.0	6.6	125	158	19.2	50.26
North East Derbyshire	75.5	1.2	17.4	3.2	143	136	17.9	45.98
South Derbyshire	92.1	0.6	8.0	4.5	308	149	11.5	49.77
Leicestershire County	82.9	4.9	13.1	6.4	2,955	166	12.8	47.53
Blaby	80.1	0.6	17.2	3.7	132	159	12.8	47.05
Charnwood	86.8	1.6	12.6	7.9	578	164	16.4	45.71
Harborough	86.3	0.4	8.8	6.7	217	205	7.8	53.82
Hinckley and Bosworth	83.1	0.8	13.7	6.3	522	156	13.5	47.27
Melton	79.1	0.3	9.6	4.1	153	172	10.1	48.41
North West Leicestershire	81.7	0.7	10.0	5.3	51	156	15.1	47.01
Oadby and Wigston	77.9	0.5	17.5	10.5	113	156	12.9	47.67
Lincolnshire	79.0	7.1	6.0	3.9	3,340	141	16.9	47.19
Boston	83.3	0.6	2.3	3.6	405	123	16.8	..
East Lindsey	73.9	1.7	4.0	3.1	489	138	19.8	..
Lincoln	70.0	1.4	7.5	9.1	366	119	20.1	45.27
North Kesteven	80.9	0.6	8.0	3.1	548	148	13.7	47.91
South Holland	83.3	0.7	6.0	3.7	550	139	12.1	46.48
South Kesteven	81.8	1.0	5.6	3.3	621	163	16.0	49.61
West Lindsey	83.5	1.0	8.8	2.5	361	142	22.3	..
Northamptonshire	84.4	7.1	11.5	6.5	2,509	155	10.0	53.67
Corby	84.1	1.0	10.2	12.1	380	112	17.6	49.24
Daventry	82.9	0.5	12.3	2.8	218	189	6.8	52.17
East Northamptonshire	82.6	0.7	10.9	4.0	397	162	9.1	..
Kettering	82.1	0.9	11.7	7.8	224	143	11.9	49.26
Northampton	82.9	2.7	13.6	9.6	404	145	12.4	57.75
South Northamptonshire	94.2	0.4	8.2	4.1	501	209	6.0	57.26
Wellingborough	84.3	0.9	8.0	3.1	90	136	11.7	50.22
Nottinghamshire County	78.6	8.2	9.7	7.7	2,997	141	16.3	47.33
Ashfield	77.1	1.6	9.6	6.1	458	110	22.9	47.99
Bassetlaw	80.9	1.4	7.9	3.9	168	128	16.9	50.85
Broxtowe	79.9	1.1	11.4	5.7	98	146	14.7	44.93
Gedling	75.2	1.1	14.0	9.2	324	141	9.0	45.72
Mansfield	76.2	1.5	6.9	14.0	292	107	26.0	45.76
Newark and Sherwood	82.5	1.0	6.7	9.2	584	155	16.2	46.89
Rushcliffe	78.1	0.6	15.3	5.6	202	206	12.4	..

1 Local government structure as at 1 April 1998. See Notes and Definitions.
2 For those of working age. See Notes and Definitions for Chapter 5.
3 Counts of claimants of unemployment-related benefits at March 2005. See Notes and Definitions for Chapter 5.
4 People who have been claiming unemployment-related benefits for more than 12 months (computerised claims only), as a percentage of total computerised claimants in March 2005.
5 Lone parents with at least one dependent child.
6 District figures do not always add to county totals. See Notes and Definitions for Chapter 6.
7 Excludes those bought at non-market prices. Sales below £1,000 and above £20 million are excluded from these figures. Averages are based on four quarters of the year.
8 Some local authorities have no housing stock following large-scale voluntary transfers (..) to Registered Social Landlords (RSLs), so the average rent is no longer applicable.

Source: Office for National Statistics; Office of the Deputy Prime Minister

West Midlands

In 2004, the West Midlands had a population of 5.3 million. The resident population of the region increased by 14 thousand between mid-2003 and mid-2004. (Table 3.1)

The population of the West Midlands increased by 2.8 per cent in the 23 years between 1981 and 2004, according to the mid-year population estimates. The largest percentage increase was in Telford and Wrekin at 28.3 per cent. (Map 1.49)

In 2004, the infant mortality rate in the West Midlands was higher than the UK average (6.8 and 5.1 deaths of infants under one year of age per 1,000 live births respectively). (Table 7.2)

The West Midlands had just over 12 per cent of its maintained primary school classes with more than 30 pupils, slightly above the proportion for Great Britain as a whole in 2004/05. (Table 4.2)

In 2003/04, 78 per cent of 16-year-olds in the West Midlands were in post-compulsory education or government-supported training. This was close to the England rate of 79 per cent. (Table 4.7)

The proportion of people of working age qualified to GCE A level/equivalent or higher in the West Midlands was around 46 per cent in spring 2005, compared with a UK average of 50 per cent. In 2004 the proportion of full-time first degree graduates studying in the West Midlands who subsequently gained employment in the UK was just above the UK national average. (Tables 4.9 and 4.10)

In spring 2005, the employment rate in the West Midlands was 75 per cent of people of working age, which was slightly higher than the UK overall. (Table 5.1)

In April 2005, gross weekly earnings for full-time employees on adult rates in the West Midlands were £444.10 for males and £345.50 for females, 6 and 7 per cent below the UK levels respectively. These figures are median values so half of the males (or females) earned above these amounts and half earned below. (Table 1.17)

In March 2005 more than one-fifth (24 per cent) of ordinary police officers in the West Midlands were women, a higher rate than elsewhere in the UK. (Table 9.6)

In 2003 the West Midlands had the lowest number of noise offences relating to motor vehicles. (Table 11.8)

In the West Midlands, manufacturing accounted for 19 per cent of GVA in 2003, compared with 15 per cent for the UK as a whole. Agriculture, hunting, forestry and fishing accounted for 1.2 per cent of GVA compared with just over 1 per cent in the UK overall. (Table 12.5)

GVA per head in the West Midlands in 2004 was £15,300, compared with £17,300 for the UK as a whole. (Table 12.6)

In March 2004, 29 per cent of businesses in the West Midlands were in the areas of distribution, hotels and catering or repairs industries, slightly higher than the UK average of 28 per cent. (Table 13.3)

Table **1.17** Key statistics for West Midlands

	West Midlands	United Kingdom[1]		West Midlands	United Kingdom[1]
Population, 2004[2] (thousands)	5,334	59,835	Gross value added, 2004 (£ billion)	81.7	1,005.4
Percentage aged under 16[2]	20.1	19.5	Gross value added per head index, 2004 (UK=100)	91.2	100
Percentage pension age and over[2]	18.9	18.6	Total business sites,[5] March 2004 (thousands)	213.3	2,573.1
Standardised Mortality Ratio (UK=100), 2003	102	100	Average dwelling price,[1] 2004 (£)	157,219	183,449
Infant mortality rate,[3] 2004	6.8	5.1			
Percentage of pupils achieving 5 or more grades	52.0	54.2	Motor cars currently licensed,[1,6] 2003 (thousands)	2,612	26,240
A*-C at GCSE level or equivalent, 2003/04[1]			Fatal and serious accidents on roads,[1] 2004 (rates per 100,000 population)	46.8	51.1
Economic activity rate,[4] spring 2005 (percentages)	78.4	78.5			
Employment rate,[4] spring 2005 (percentages)	74.6	74.4	Recorded crime rate,[1] 2004/05 (recorded offences	10,024	10,508
Unemployment rate,[4] spring 2005 (percentages)	4.4	4.7	per 100,000 population)		
Median gross weekly earnings: males in full-time employment, April 2005 (£)	444.1	471.5	Average gross weekly household income, 2001/02 to 2003/04[7] (£)	505	554
Median gross weekly earnings: females in full-time employment, April 2005 (£)	345.5	371.8	Average weekly household expenditure, 2001/02 to 2003/04[7] (£)	375.60	406.20
			Households in receipt of Tax Credits,[1] 2003/04 (percentages)	16	15

1 Figures relate to the United Kingdom except for GCSE results and average dwelling prices (covering England); currently licensed motor cars, fatal and serious accidents and Tax Credits (Great Britain), and recorded crime rate (England and Wales).
2 Population figures for 2004 are mid-year population estimates. Pension age is men aged 65 or over and women aged 60 or over.
3 Deaths of infants under one year of age per 1,000 live births.
4 Seasonally adjusted data for people of working age, men aged 16 to 64 and women aged 16 to 59.
5 Registered for VAT and/or PAYE local unit basis, e.g. an individual factory or shop.
6 Totals for the United Kingdom include vehicles where the country of the registered vehicle is unknown, that are under disposal or from countries unknown within Great Britain.
7 Data combined from the 2001/02, 2002/03 and 2003/04 Expenditure and Food Surveys.

Map **1.18** Population density: by local or unitary authority, 2004

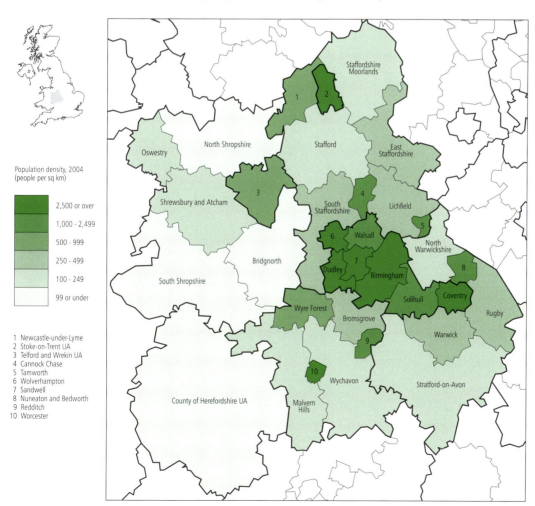

Population density, 2004 (people per sq km)

- 2,500 or over
- 1,000 - 2,499
- 500 - 999
- 250 - 499
- 100 - 249
- 99 or under

1 Newcastle-under-Lyme
2 Stoke-on-Trent UA
3 Telford and Wrekin UA
4 Cannock Chase
5 Tamworth
6 Wolverhampton
7 Sandwell
8 Nuneaton and Bedworth
9 Redditch
10 Worcester

Table **1.19**   Local authority[1] population and vital statistics: West Midlands, 2004

	Area (sq km)	People per sq km	Population (thous) Total	Total population percentage change 1981-2004	Percentage of population: aged under 5	of pension age[2] or over	Total fertility rate (TFR)[3]	Standardised Mortality Ratio (UK=100) (SMR)[4]	Live birth rate per 1,000 population	Death rate per 1,000 population	Infant mortality rate[5]
United Kingdom	242,515	247	59,835	6.2	5.7	18.6	1.77	100	12.0	9.7	5.3
England	130,281	385	50,094	7.0	5.7	18.5	1.78	99	12.1	9.6	5.3
West Midlands	12,998	410	5,334	2.8	5.8	18.9	1.91	103	12.4	9.9	7.4
Herefordshire, County of UA	2,180	82	178	19.0	4.9	23.1	1.81	91	9.5	10.6	3.0
Stoke-on-Trent UA	93	2,547	238	-5.7	5.8	18.8	2.02	119	13.6	11.4	9.4
Telford and Wrekin UA	290	555	161	28.3	6.2	15.6	1.97	107	13.0	8.3	3.7
Shropshire County	3,197	90	288	12.8	4.9	22.0	1.80	95	9.6	10.6	6.7
Bridgnorth	633	84	53	4.8	4.5	21.6	1.61	100	8.2	10.6	4.1
North Shropshire	679	86	59	14.5	5.2	21.5	1.91	98	10.1	10.6	12.0
Oswestry	256	151	39	22.2	5.0	21.2	1.79	93	9.9	10.0	7.9
Shrewsbury and Atcham	602	159	96	9.1	5.1	20.9	1.80	96	10.2	10.3	5.9
South Shropshire	1,027	41	42	22.7	4.6	26.5	1.95	89	8.8	11.6	2.8
Staffordshire County	2,620	310	813	6.1	5.2	19.5	1.80	104	10.6	9.9	7.0
Cannock Chase	79	1,177	93	9.0	5.7	17.1	1.83	108	11.7	8.9	5.5
East Staffordshire	387	274	106	10.1	5.9	18.7	2.06	107	12.1	9.9	7.4
Lichfield	331	286	95	6.2	5.2	20.2	1.74	108	9.6	10.5	11.4
Newcastle-under-Lyme	211	583	123	2.1	5.0	20.1	1.63	100	10.4	10.1	5.8
South Staffordshire	407	258	105	9.4	4.5	20.9	1.74	103	8.9	10.2	5.8
Stafford	598	205	123	4.5	4.9	20.7	1.78	96	10.2	10.1	6.9
Staffordshire Moorlands	576	164	94	-1.6	4.7	21.6	1.70	107	9.1	11.3	3.6
Tamworth	31	2,395	74	13.3	6.2	14.6	1.98	105	13.2	7.4	9.3
Warwickshire	1,975	266	526	10.1	5.3	19.2	1.70	100	11.0	9.9	5.6
North Warwickshire	284	218	62	3.3	5.0	18.7	1.73	108	10.3	9.9	10.3
Nuneaton and Bedworth	79	1,523	120	5.6	5.7	18.1	1.97	112	12.4	10.0	5.1
Rugby	351	257	90	3.1	5.8	19.0	1.89	100	11.6	10.0	5.1
Stratford-on-Avon	978	119	117	16.1	5.1	21.9	1.73	95	10.0	10.6	4.8
Warwick	283	482	136	18.2	5.1	18.1	1.41	91	10.5	9.0	5.0
West Midlands (Met County)	902	2,861	2,579	-3.9	6.4	18.0	2.00	105	13.9	9.7	8.4
Birmingham	268	3,706	992	-3.6	7.1	16.2	2.08	106	15.8	9.2	11.0
Coventry	99	3,084	304	-4.7	5.9	17.5	1.84	104	13.1	9.6	6.6
Dudley	98	3,108	305	1.1	5.6	20.2	1.88	104	11.5	10.2	4.5
Sandwell	86	3,339	286	-7.7	6.4	18.7	2.13	115	14.4	10.9	7.8
Solihull	178	1,124	200	0.9	5.3	20.1	1.73	87	9.9	8.8	2.9
Walsall	104	2,432	253	-5.4	6.4	19.6	2.18	105	13.5	9.9	6.6
Wolverhampton	69	3,443	239	-7.3	5.9	19.3	1.88	107	12.8	10.6	8.2
Worcestershire County	1,741	317	552	15.4	5.3	19.9	1.80	97	10.8	10.0	5.4
Bromsgrove	217	418	91	14.0	5.0	20.8	1.80	104	9.9	11.1	5.9
Malvern Hills	577	129	74	9.3	4.6	24.5	1.79	96	8.3	12.6	0.0
Redditch	54	1,462	79	17.2	6.1	15.0	2.01	101	13.8	8.1	9.4
Worcester	33	2,812	94	21.3	6.1	17.0	1.74	100	13.0	8.8	5.0
Wychavon	664	175	116	23.1	5.2	21.3	1.78	86	10.0	9.3	3.4
Wyre Forest	195	502	98	7.0	4.9	20.8	1.71	101	10.1	10.6	7.1

1 Local government structure as at 1 April 1998. See Notes and Definitions.
2 Pension age is 65 or over for men and 60 or over for women.
3 The total fertility rate (TFR) is the average number of children who would be born to a woman if the current pattern of fertility persisted throughout her child-bearing years.
4 The Standardised Mortality Ratio (SMR) takes account of the age structure of the population. Data are based on occurrences.
5 Data are based on occurrences.

Source: Office for National Statistics

Table **1.20** Local authority[1] housing, households and labour market: West Midlands

	Economic activity[2] rate 2004-2005 (percentages)	Claimant[3] unemployment March 2005 (thousands)	Percentage claiming over 12 months, computerised claims only[4] March 2005	Lone parents[5] as a percentage of all households, spring 2005	Housing completions[6] by private enterprise 2004	Average dwelling price[7] 2004 (£ thousands)	Percentage change in dwelling price 2003 to 2004	Local authority average weekly rent per dwelling[8] (£), April 2005 (provisional)
United Kingdom	78.2	882.3	14.0	7.2				
England	78.5	717.3	13.8	7.2	129,544	181	13.8	55.11
West Midlands	78.0	89.1	15.8	7.4	12,559	151	15.3	51.32
Herefordshire, County of UA	84.9	1.5	6.8	3.8	486	191	17.4	..
Stoke-on-Trent UA	72.6	4.1	7.4	9.4	450	81	30.0	46.91
Telford and Wrekin UA	83.4	1.8	8.0	6.6	685	135	18.5	..
Shropshire County	84.8	2.1	9.9	3.8	1,228	178	16.2	50.10
Bridgnorth	82.3	0.3	10.2	1.9	38	194	6.7	52.50
North Shropshire	90.9	0.4	11.2	2.7	141	178	19.2	48.90
Oswestry	81.1	0.4	10.5	5.2	112	162	24.3	48.60
Shrewsbury and Atcham	82.5	0.8	9.7	5.2	91	167	16.9	..
South Shropshire	91.0	0.3	7.3	2.6	143	204	19.4	..
Staffordshire County	81.5	7.6	9.1	6.1	2,713	150	16.5	50.51
Cannock Chase	81.1	1.1	9.5	9.9	321	122	12.8	51.44
East Staffordshire	79.8	0.9	4.7	3.8	242	140	18.0	..
Lichfield	86.5	0.8	12.3	5.6	566	197	13.9	..
Newcastle-under-Lyme	79.8	1.0	9.6	5.0	221	122	20.8	..
South Staffordshire	91.0	0.9	11.4	2.5	140	180	10.0	..
Stafford	76.5	1.2	11.1	11.1	374	163	18.6	47.82
Staffordshire Moorlands	86.2	0.7	9.2	5.4	214	144	26.0	..
Tamworth	71.9	1.0	5.3	4.2	113	138	17.5	52.58
Warwickshire	79.5	4.6	13.5	5.1	2,098	187	14.7	52.09
North Warwickshire	75.1	0.6	11.4	4.9	70	156	21.8	50.71
Nuneaton and Bedworth	79.7	1.4	12.2	7.0	474	123	14.8	48.66
Rugby	76.7	0.9	15.8	8.6	332	170	20.8	52.07
Stratford-on-Avon	84.1	0.7	13.0	0.9	559	243	9.3	..
Warwick	79.6	1.0	14.7	5.2	574	212	10.2	56.57
West Midlands (Met County)	74.4	61.8	18.6	9.0	4,564	138	14.4	51.89
Birmingham	71.3	30.7	24.2	9.6	1,393	141	11.8	52.23
Coventry	77.4	5.6	14.2	9.2	438	123	15.5	..
Dudley	78.2	5.3	17.0	5.5	276	131	15.3	51.44
Sandwell	71.8	6.9	14.8	11.5	874	112	16.7	54.61
Solihull	82.8	2.1	12.0	5.6	422	217	11.9	52.80
Walsall	74.4	5.1	9.4	10.4	598	128	16.7	..
Wolverhampton	74.2	6.2	10.3	9.7	327	116	19.7	47.45
Worcestershire County	83.6	5.5	9.5	7.1	1,956	185	13.4	52.10
Bromsgrove	86.5	0.9	10.1	7.6	368	211	10.7	..
Malvern Hills	86.7	0.4	5.7	6.5	90	224	12.1	..
Redditch	82.2	1.1	9.6	9.8	347	153	14.6	52.10
Worcester	81.3	1.1	11.0	8.5	75	160	13.1	..
Wychavon	86.9	0.8	10.8	4.2	364	214	14.5	..
Wyre Forest	78.0	1.0	7.7	6.4	146	159	14.5	..

1 Local government structure as at 1 April 1998. See Notes and Definitions.
2 For those of working age. See Notes and Definitions for Chapter 5.
3 Counts of claimants of unemployment-related benefits at March 2005. See Notes and Definitions for Chapter 5.
4 People who have been claiming unemployment-related benefits for more than 12 months (computerised claims only), as a percentage of total computerised claimants in March 2005.
5 Lone parents with at least one dependent child.
6 District figures do not always add to county totals. See Notes and Definitions for Chapter 6.
7 Excludes those bought at non-market prices. Sales below £1,000 and above £20 million are excluded from these figures. Averages are based on four quarters of the year.
8 Some local authorities have no housing stock following large-scale voluntary transfers (..) to Registered Social Landlords (RSLs), so the average rent is no longer applicable.

Source: Office for National Statistics; Office of the Deputy Prime Minister

East of England

In 2004, the East had a population of 5.5 million. The resident population of the region increased by 28 thousand between mid-2003 and mid-2004. The population of the East increased by 13.1 per cent in the 23 years between 1981 and 2004, according to the mid-year population estimates. The largest percentage change over this period was a 27.1 per cent increase in Cambridgeshire. (Tables 3.1 and 1.49)

In 2004, the infant mortality rate in the East was lower than the UK rate (4.2 and 5.1 deaths of infants under one year of age per 1,000 live births respectively). (Table 7.2)

The proportion of maintained primary school classes in the East with more than 30 pupils was similar to the proportion in Great Britain as a whole in 2004/05 at nearly 12 per cent. (Table 4.2)

The proportion of people of working age qualified to GCE A level/equivalent or higher in the East was around 48 per cent in spring 2005, slightly below the UK average. In 2004 the proportion of full-time first degree graduates studying in the East who subsequently gained employment in the UK was the lowest of any region. The proportion of full-time first degree graduates that went on to further study was the highest in the UK. (Tables 4.9 and 4.10)

In spring 2005, the employment rate in the East was 78.6 per cent of people of working age. This was among the highest employment rates of the countries and regions of the UK. (Table 5.1)

In April 2005, gross weekly earnings for full-time employees on adult rates in the East were £500.00 for males and £375.70 for females, 6 and 1 per cent above the UK levels respectively. These figures are median values so half of the males (or females) earned above these amounts and half earned below. (Table 1.21)

Household income for the East at £594 per week was one of the highest figures in the UK for the period 2001 to 2004. (Table 8.1)

The East had one of the UK's highest levels of household internet access, 48 per cent, in the period 2001 to 2004. (Figure 8.15)

The distance each person travelled in the East, in 2003-2004, was 7,791 miles,15 per cent greater than the average for Great Britain. (Table 10.5)

Gross value added (GVA) per head in the East was £18,300 in 2004, which was 9 per cent higher than the GVA per head for the UK as a whole. (Table 12.1)

In the East, manufacturing accounted for 13 per cent of gross value added in 2003, compared with 15 per cent for the UK as a whole. Agriculture, hunting, forestry and fishing accounted for 1.4 per cent of GVA compared with just over 1 per cent in the UK overall. (Table 12.5)

In 2003, businesses in the East were responsible for one-quarter of UK businesses expenditure on research and development. (Table 13.6)

In 2004, the East had the highest area utilised for wheat production, 26 per cent of the UK total. Also agricultural holdings in the East, in June 2004, contained 15 per cent of the total UK poultry population. (Tables 13.13 and 13.14)

Table **1.21** Key statistics for the East of England

	East	United Kingdom[1]		East	United Kingdom[1]
Population, 2004[2] (thousands)	5,491	59,835	Gross value added, 2004 (£ billion)	100.3	1,005.4
Percentage aged under 16[2]	19.6	19.5	Gross value added per head index, 2004 (UK=100)	108.7	100
Percentage pension age and over[2]	19.4	18.6	Total business sites,[5] March 2004 (thousands)	251.6	2,573.1
Standardised Mortality Ratio (UK=100), 2003	92	100	Average dwelling price,[1] 2004 (£)	196,763	183,449
Infant mortality rate,[3] 2004	4.2	5.1			
Percentage of pupils achieving 5 or more grades A*-C at GCSE level or equivalent, 2003/04[1]	56.4	54.2	Motor cars currently licensed,[1,6] 2003 (thousands)	2,711	26,240
			Fatal and serious accidents on roads,[1] 2004 (rates per 100,000 population)	60.1	51.1
Economic activity rate,[4] spring 2005 (percentages)	81.8	78.5			
Employment rate,[4] spring 2005 (percentages)	78.6	74.4	Recorded crime rate,[1] 2004/05 (recorded offences per 100,000 population)	8,822	10,508
Unemployment rate,[4] spring 2005 (percentages)	3.7	4.7			
Median gross weekly earnings: males in full-time employment, April 2005 (£)	500.0	471.5	Average gross weekly household income, 2001/02 to 2003/04[7] (£)	594	554
Median gross weekly earnings: females in full-time employment, April 2005 (£)	375.7	371.8	Average weekly household expenditure, 2001/02 to 2003/04[7] (£)	431.20	406.20
			Households in receipt of Tax Credits,[1] 2003/04 (percentages)	14	15

1 Figures relate to the United Kingdom except for GCSE results and average dwelling prices (covering England); currently licensed motor cars, fatal and serious accidents and Tax Credits (Great Britain), and recorded crime rate (England and Wales).
2 Population figures for 2004 are mid-year population estimates. Pension age is men aged 65 or over and women aged 60 or over.
3 Deaths of infants under one year of age per 1,000 live births.
4 Seasonally adjusted data for people of working age, men aged 16 to 64 and women aged 16 to 59.
5 Registered for VAT and/or PAYE local unit basis, e.g. an individual factory or shop.
6 Totals for the United Kingdom include vehicles where the country of the registered vehicle is unknown, that are under disposal or from countries unknown within Great Britain.
7 Data combined from the 2001/02, 2002/03 and 2003/04 Expenditure and Food Surveys.

Map **1.22** Population density: by local or unitary authority, 2004

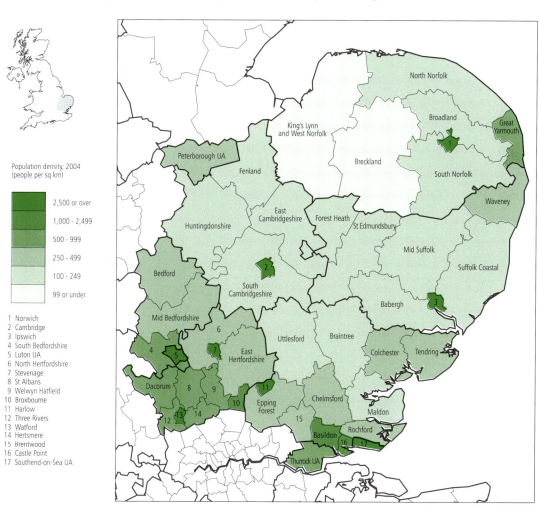

Population density, 2004 (people per sq km)

- 2,500 or over
- 1,000 - 2,499
- 500 - 999
- 250 - 499
- 100 - 249
- 99 or under

1 Norwich
2 Cambridge
3 Ipswich
4 South Bedfordshire
5 Luton UA
6 North Hertfordshire
7 Stevenage
8 St Albans
9 Welwyn Hatfield
10 Broxbourne
11 Harlow
12 Three Rivers
13 Watford
14 Hertsmere
15 Brentwood
16 Castle Point
17 Southend-on-Sea UA

Table **1.23** Local authority[1] population and vital statistics: East, 2004

	Area (sq km)	People per sq km	Population (thous) Total	Total population percentage change 1981-2004	Percentage of population: aged under 5	Percentage of population: of pension age[2] or over	Total fertility rate (TFR)[3]	Standardised Mortality Ratio (UK=100) (SMR)[4]	Live birth rate per 1,000 population	Death rate per 1,000 population	Infant mortality rate[5]
United Kingdom	242,515	247	59,835	6.2	5.7	18.6	1.77	100	12.0	9.7	5.3
England	130,281	385	50,094	7.0	5.7	18.5	1.78	99	12.1	9.6	5.3
East	19,110	287	5,491	13.1	5.7	19.4	1.83	94	11.7	9.6	4.5
Luton UA	43	4,244	184	11.6	7.4	14.5	2.34	110	17.3	8.0	4.2
Peterborough UA	343	463	159	18.9	6.6	16.4	2.20	99	15.1	8.3	8.6
Southend-on-Sea UA	42	3,821	160	1.3	5.8	21.5	1.96	100	12.2	12.2	5.2
Thurrock UA	163	892	146	14.4	6.6	15.4	1.93	102	14.2	8.0	6.1
Bedfordshire County	1,192	329	392	13.6	6.0	16.9	1.82	97	12.1	8.5	5.4
Bedford	476	317	151	13.2	5.9	17.5	1.80	97	12.4	9.0	7.8
Mid Bedfordshire	503	253	127	21.6	6.1	16.0	1.69	93	11.4	7.6	2.1
South Bedfordshire	213	536	114	6.4	6.1	17.1	1.99	103	12.6	8.7	5.9
Cambridgeshire County	3,046	190	579	27.1	5.6	17.5	1.54	91	10.8	8.4	4.6
Cambridge	41	2,911	119	17.3	4.4	13.8	1.19	92	10.0	7.6	6.5
East Cambridgeshire	651	118	77	42.5	6.0	19.4	1.83	88	11.5	8.6	5.5
Fenland	546	159	87	30.4	5.4	22.7	1.76	99	9.5	11.3	2.1
Huntingdonshire	906	178	162	29.1	6.0	16.3	1.78	91	11.3	7.6	5.5
South Cambridgeshire	902	150	135	24.0	5.9	17.7	1.75	86	11.4	8.1	3.3
Essex County	3,465	384	1,330	11.1	5.6	20.0	1.82	94	11.2	9.7	4.5
Basildon	110	1,514	167	9.2	6.4	17.7	1.97	103	13.4	9.0	3.2
Braintree	612	223	136	20.9	6.1	17.8	1.90	95	11.7	9.1	5.2
Brentwood	153	459	70	-3.2	5.3	21.3	1.73	86	10.4	9.6	8.5
Castle Point	45	1,927	87	0.0	5.0	21.8	1.85	97	9.7	10.1	3.6
Chelmsford	339	472	160	14.5	5.6	17.7	1.68	88	11.2	8.0	3.4
Colchester	329	488	161	15.7	5.5	17.6	1.68	93	11.6	8.7	3.5
Epping Forest	339	358	121	4.5	5.8	19.8	1.81	100	11.8	10.3	6.4
Harlow	31	2,538	78	-2.6	6.5	17.3	2.02	90	14.4	7.5	7.3
Maldon	359	168	60	24.9	5.4	19.6	1.78	102	9.9	10.1	1.7
Rochford	169	466	79	7.3	5.2	21.4	1.77	86	10.0	9.1	3.9
Tendring	338	419	142	24.0	4.6	30.1	1.92	94	8.5	15.0	4.9
Uttlesford	641	110	70	13.1	5.5	18.5	1.77	92	9.9	9.1	4.2
Hertfordshire	1,643	634	1,041	7.4	6.1	17.7	1.81	95	12.5	8.9	3.3
Broxbourne	51	1,674	86	7.8	5.9	18.2	1.90	98	12.7	8.5	2.9
Dacorum	212	650	138	5.5	6.0	17.9	1.76	92	11.4	8.7	6.0
East Hertfordshire	476	275	131	19.1	6.0	16.5	1.63	94	11.7	8.0	1.9
Hertsmere	101	922	93	3.5	5.9	18.8	1.84	102	12.3	10.7	2.8
North Hertfordshire	375	320	120	10.4	6.0	18.7	1.87	95	12.4	9.6	2.1
St. Albans	161	820	132	5.5	6.6	17.1	1.84	97	13.2	8.8	1.1
Stevenage	26	3,042	79	5.8	6.4	16.4	1.99	94	13.8	7.7	6.5
Three Rivers	89	945	84	3.6	5.9	19.1	1.86	86	11.9	9.0	2.1
Watford	21	3,703	79	6.4	6.2	15.3	1.84	106	14.6	8.8	4.5
Welwyn Hatfield	130	761	99	4.6	5.8	19.3	1.72	90	11.6	9.3	4.6
Norfolk	5,371	152	817	16.2	4.9	23.5	1.75	92	10.0	11.2	4.6
Breckland	1,305	96	125	29.6	5.1	22.9	1.74	93	9.8	11.0	3.4
Broadland	552	218	121	22.9	5.0	23.1	1.75	93	9.5	11.0	6.1
Great Yarmouth	174	531	92	13.5	5.1	23.2	2.01	102	10.8	12.2	5.0
King's Lynn and West Norfolk	1,429	97	139	14.0	5.1	25.1	2.03	93	10.5	11.7	4.4
North Norfolk	964	104	100	19.8	4.0	30.0	1.84	88	8.0	13.6	2.6
Norwich	39	3,202	125	-0.9	4.9	18.0	1.49	90	12.2	9.3	5.1
South Norfolk	908	126	114	20.0	5.0	23.0	1.74	85	9.0	10.1	4.9
Suffolk	3,801	180	684	13.7	5.5	21.6	1.94	93	11.1	10.5	3.7
Babergh	594	143	85	14.5	5.3	22.2	1.99	92	10.3	10.7	1.2
Forest Heath	378	159	60	14.1	7.2	16.5	1.87	93	14.3	8.1	1.3
Ipswich	39	2,979	117	-2.2	5.9	18.8	2.01	100	13.8	10.3	5.2
Mid Suffolk	871	102	89	25.2	5.3	21.1	2.10	89	10.9	9.8	2.4
St. Edmundsbury	657	153	101	15.3	5.6	20.1	1.85	94	11.1	9.7	7.0
Suffolk Coastal	892	132	118	21.9	4.8	24.6	1.80	87	8.7	11.4	2.9
Waveney	370	309	114	14.2	5.1	25.3	1.93	93	10.0	12.3	3.4

1 Local government structure as at 1 April 1998. See Notes and Definitions.
2 Pension age is 65 or over for men and 60 or over for women.
3 The total fertility rate (TFR) is the average number of children who would be born to a woman if the current pattern of fertility persisted throughout her child-bearing years.
4 The Standardised Mortality Ratio (SMR) takes account of the age structure of the population. Data are based on occurrences.
5 Data are based on occurrences.

Source: Office for National Statistics

Table 1.24 Local authority[1] housing, households and labour market: East

	Economic activity[2] rate 2004-2005 (percentages)	Claimant[3] unemployment March 2005 (thousands)	Percentage claiming over 12 months, computerised claims only[4] March 2005	Lone parents[5] as a percentage of all households, spring 2005	Housing completions[6] by private enterprise 2004	Average dwelling price[7] 2004 (£ thousands)	Percentage change in dwelling price 2003 to 2004	Local authority average weekly rent per dwelling[8] (£), April 2005 (provisional)
United Kingdom	78.2	882.3	14.0	7.2				
England	78.5	717.3	13.8	7.2	129,544	181	13.8	55.11
East	81.6	60.8	11.4	5.5	16,799	190	10.4	57.53
Luton UA	70.1	3.6	11.4	8.0	138	143	10.9	57.59
Peterborough UA	81.4	2.6	8.4	8.2	666	135	16.7	..
Southend-on-Sea UA	83.1	2.7	10.3	6.9	134	166	11.1	54.40
Thurrock UA	78.2	2.3	10.2	7.0	819	162	9.0	59.14
Bedfordshire County	83.5	4.2	10.9	6.8	1,522	182	8.6	63.38
Bedford	83.7	2.1	12.9	10.4	407	172	10.8	..
Mid Bedfordshire	87.6	0.8	10.6	4.6	683	199	6.8	..
South Bedfordshire	78.2	1.2	7.5	4.1	294	174	9.1	63.38
Cambridgeshire County	83.7	4.6	10.1	4.4	3,071	187	8.3	59.33
Cambridge	75.7	1.2	13.5	6.5	410	232	3.5	60.69
East Cambridgeshire	90.2	0.6	10.4	2.6	512	182	6.8	..
Fenland	77.5	1.0	8.3	2.1	543	134	13.0	53.68
Huntingdonshire	86.0	1.1	7.6	6.7	323	172	7.8	..
South Cambridgeshire	87.7	0.7	10.5	2.8	477	233	10.9	61.26
Essex County	81.4	12.6	10.2	6.2	4,882	203	9.7	58.66
Basildon	81.6	2.2	9.0	10.0	294	178	9.4	58.16
Braintree	83.7	1.2	10.4	5.7	541	191	9.4	58.71
Brentwood	80.3	0.4	8.0	4.7	219	274	6.9	62.77
Castle Point	77.9	0.7	9.4	3.9	73	183	8.0	62.93
Chelmsford	84.4	1.3	13.5	3.5	719	214	6.9	..
Colchester	75.8	1.5	7.9	5.9	1,095	181	13.7	54.79
Epping Forest	82.3	1.1	12.7	11.8	223	280	5.3	61.67
Harlow	88.0	1.2	8.1	6.4	59	164	12.0	59.19
Maldon	83.4	0.4	13.6	6.2	117	214	12.0	..
Rochford	87.8	0.5	5.9	7.7	191	210	9.9	56.69
Tendring	72.9	1.7	12.3	3.9	145	158	13.3	51.90
Uttlesford	83.9	0.3	8.6	4.6	264	269	12.2	63.25
Hertfordshire	83.2	9.2	9.8	5.0	2,604	243	7.1	63.66
Broxbourne	76.6	1.0	12.4	7.8	147	211	6.0	67.31
Dacorum	86.2	1.4	9.2	3.9	613	243	6.2	62.28
East Hertfordshire	86.1	0.7	9.8	6.4	190	251	7.3	..
Hertsmere	76.8	0.9	11.8	5.4	102	275	4.6	..
North Hertfordshire	83.4	1.0	9.6	1.5	161	219	8.3	..
St. Albans	84.7	0.8	5.3	4.1	205	300	5.0	65.17
Stevenage	87.3	1.0	12.2	7.7	50	162	9.5	63.18
Three Rivers	80.5	0.6	7.3	5.9	109	298	11.1	66.18
Watford	84.8	1.0	8.7	6.6	269	205	7.7	64.10
Welwyn Hatfield	80.8	0.9	10.2	4.3	642	244	8.5	62.17
Norfolk	79.9	11.5	13.2	4.8	2,472	159	13.1	48.36
Breckland	82.5	1.3	7.1	3.1	616	155	12.9	..
Broadland	83.8	0.9	11.8	4.7	242	170	10.0	..
Great Yarmouth	76.5	2.9	16.2	9.0	178	128	18.2	45.54
King's Lynn and West Norfolk	82.1	1.7	7.6	5.6	493	157	14.4	50.69
North Norfolk	70.9	1.0	13.6	3.8	306	175	13.2	49.33
Norwich	77.2	2.9	16.8	4.1	395	142	11.6	48.18
South Norfolk	84.1	0.8	12.5	3.6	204	185	12.4	..
Suffolk	82.1	7.5	14.8	4.8	2,248	172	15.0	52.88
Babergh	86.8	0.6	13.5	6.2	197	191	7.9	57.78
Forest Heath	81.9	0.4	5.0		54	162	21.0	..
Ipswich	82.2	2.2	16.8	7.6	356	142	17.8	52.18
Mid Suffolk	80.4	0.5	12.8	6.0	309	188	12.2	53.68
St. Edmundsbury	85.4	0.8	10.8	5.6	441	182	13.3	..
Suffolk Coastal	79.5	0.7	12.4	3.0	533	200	15.7	..
Waveney	79.9	2.2	17.4	3.2	358	141	15.0	49.81

1 Local government structure as at 1 April 1998. See Notes and Definitions.
2 For those of working age. See Notes and Definitions for Chapter 5.
3 Counts of claimants of unemployment-related benefits at March 2005. See Notes and Definitions for Chapter 5.
4 People who have been claiming unemployment-related benefits for more than 12 months (computerised claims only), as a percentage of total computerised claimants in March 2005.
5 Lone parents with at least one dependent child.
6 District figures do not always add to county totals. See Notes and Definitions for Chapter 6.
7 Excludes those bought at non-market prices. Sales below £1,000 and above £20 million are excluded from these figures. Averages are based on four quarters of the year.
8 Some local authorities have no housing stock following large-scale voluntary transfers (..) to Registered Social Landlords (RSLs), so the average rent is no longer applicable.

Source: Office for National Statistics; Office of the Deputy Prime Minister

London

In 2004, London had a population of 7.4 million. The resident population of the region increased by 41.3 thousand between mid-2003 and mid-2004. The population of London increased by 9.2 per cent in the 23 years between 1981 and 2004, according to the mid-year population estimates. (Table 3.1)

In 2004, the infant mortality rate in London was 5.2, slightly higher than the UK rate of 5.1 deaths of infants under one year of age per 1,000 live births. (Table 7.2)

London has the highest rate of tuberculosis (TB) notifications, 34.8 per 100,000 population in 2004 (Table 7.3)

London had the third lowest percentage (nearly 7.0 per cent) of maintained primary school classes with more than 30 pupils, compared with 12 per cent in Great Britain as a whole in 2004/05. However, London had the highest average primary school class size, 26.8. (Table 4.2)

In 2003/04, 82 per cent of 16-year-olds in London were in some form of post-compulsory education or government-supported training. This compared with an England rate of 79 per cent. (Table 4.7)

In spring 2005 the employment rate in London (for people of working age), at 69 per cent, was among the lowest of the countries and regions of the UK. (Table 5.1)

In April 2005, gross weekly earnings for full-time employees on adult rates in the London were £574.80 for males and £482.90 for females, 22 and 30 per cent above the UK levels respectively. These figures are median values so half of the males (or females) earned above these amounts and half earned below. (Table 1.25)

In London, 37 per cent of households had an average gross weekly income of £750 or more, which was the highest proportion of any region. London also had the highest percentage of individuals (47 per cent) with an income liable to income tax assessment of £20,000 or more. (Tables 8.2 and 8.5)

In 2004 overseas residents made 13.4 million trips to London and spent £6.4 billion in 90.2 million nights. (Table 8.17)

In 2003 and 2004 London's road casualties decreased by nearly 4,000. Between 2002 and 2004 fatal and serious accidents on all roads fell in London by 1,319 (25 per cent). (Tables 10.15 and 10.14)

London had the greatest proportion of previously developed land changing to residential use (90 per cent), with the highest proportion of such land being previously vacant or derelict (43 per cent). (Table 11.11)

In London, manufacturing accounted for 9 per cent of GVA in 2003, compared with 15 per cent for the UK as a whole. Agriculture, hunting, forestry and fishing accounted for 0.03 per cent of GVA, the smallest regional contribution, compared with 1.1 per cent in the UK overall. (Table 12.5)

The GVA per head index for London in 2004 was 132.2 (Index UK = 100). The largest regional GVA by industry contributor in 2003 was London, which produced £159 billion of GVA, with over a third of this generated by real estate, renting and business activities. (Tables 12.1 and 12.5)

London was the only region where the value of trade to the EU was less than the value going outside the EU. (Table 13.5)

Table **1.25**   Key statistics for London

	London	United Kingdom[1]		London	United Kingdom[1]
Population, 2004[2] (thousands)	7,429	59,835	Gross value added, 2004 (£ billion)	165.0	1,005.4
Percentage aged under 16[2]	19.4	19.5	Gross value added per head index, 2004 (UK=100)	132.2	100
Percentage pension age and over[2]	13.9	18.6	Total business sites,[5] March 2004 (thousands)	383.1	2,573.1
Standardised Mortality Ratio (UK=100), 2003	97	100	Average dwelling price,[1] 2004 (£)	274,860	183,449
Infant mortality rate,[3] 2004	5.2	5.1			
Percentage of pupils achieving 5 or more grades A*-C at GCSE level or equivalent, 2003/04[1]	54.4	54.2	Motor cars currently licensed,[1,6] 2003 (thousands)	2,480	26,240
			Fatal and serious accidents on roads,[1] 2004 (rates per 100,000 population)	52.1	51.1
Economic activity rate,[4] spring 2005 (percentages)	74.8	78.5			
Employment rate,[4] spring 2005 (percentages)	69.3	74.4	Recorded crime rate,[1] 2004/05 (recorded offences per 100,000 population)	13,858	10,508
Unemployment rate,[4] spring 2005 (percentages)	6.9	4.7			
Median gross weekly earnings: males in full-time employment, April 2005 (£)	574.8	471.5	Average gross weekly household income, 2001/02 to 2003/04[7] (£)	740	554
Median gross weekly earnings: females in full-time employment, April 2005 (£)	482.9	371.8	Average weekly household expenditure, 2001/02 to 2003/04[7] (£)	485.50	406.20
			Households in receipt of Tax Credits,[1] 2003/04 (percentages)	9	15

1 Figures relate to the United Kingdom except for GCSE results and average dwelling prices (covering England); currently licensed motor cars, fatal and serious accidents and Tax Credits (Great Britain), and recorded crime rate (England and Wales).
2 Population figures for 2004 are mid-year population estimates. Pension age is men aged 65 or over and women aged 60 or over.
3 Deaths of infants under one year of age per 1,000 live births.
4 Seasonally adjusted data for people of working age, men aged 16 to 64 and women aged 16 to 59.
5 Registered for VAT and/or PAYE local unit basis, e.g. an individual factory or shop.
6 Totals for the United Kingdom include vehicles where the country of the registered vehicle is unknown, that are under disposal or from countries unknown within Great Britain.
7 Data combined from the 2001/02, 2002/03 and 2003/04 Expenditure and Food Surveys.

Map **1.26**   Population density: by local or unitary authority, 2004

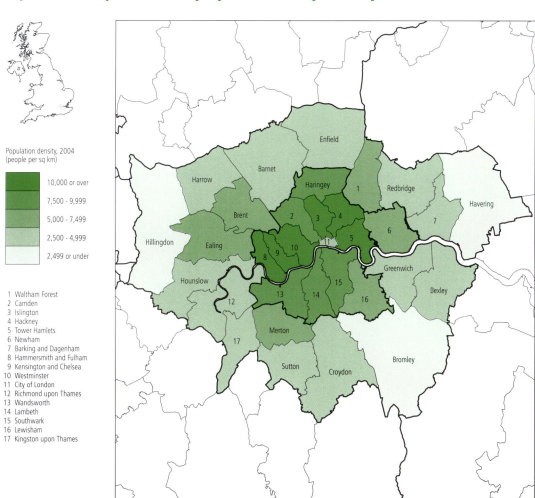

Population density, 2004
(people per sq km)

- 10,000 or over
- 7,500 - 9,999
- 5,000 - 7,499
- 2,500 - 4,999
- 2,499 or under

1 Waltham Forest
2 Camden
3 Islington
4 Hackney
5 Tower Hamlets
6 Newham
7 Barking and Dagenham
8 Hammersmith and Fulham
9 Kensington and Chelsea
10 Westminster
11 City of London
12 Richmond upon Thames
13 Wandsworth
14 Lambeth
15 Southwark
16 Lewisham
17 Kingston upon Thames

Table **1.27**   Local authority[1] population and vital statistics: London, 2004

	Area (sq km)	People per sq km	Population (thous) Total	Total population percentage change 1981-2004	Percentage of population: aged under 5	of pension age[2] or over	Total fertility rate (TFR)[3]	Standardised Mortality Ratio (UK=100) (SMR)[4]	Live birth rate per 1,000 population[5]	Death rate per 1,000 population	Infant mortality rate[6]
United Kingdom	242,515	247	59,835	6.2	5.7	18.6	1.77	100	12.0	9.7	5.3
England	130,281	385	50,094	7.0	5.7	18.5	1.78	99	12.1	9.6	5.3
London[6]	1,572	4,726	7,429	9.2	6.5	13.9	1.76	96	15.3	7.3	5.4
Inner London	319	9,180	2,931	14.9	6.7	11.4	1.69	100	16.6	6.3	6.2
Camden	22	9,959	217	21.2	5.9	11.4	1.36	101	14.0	6.6	4.4
City of London	3	2,969	9	29.4	3.2	13.3	..	67	..	5.5	0.0
Hammersmith and Fulham	16	10,776	177	17.7	5.9	11.6	1.46	87	14.8	5.6	5.1
Kensington and Chelsea	12	15,174	184	30.4	5.6	13.6	1.18	67	12.0	5.1	3.6
Wandsworth	34	8,070	277	5.4	6.3	11.6	1.43	98	15.7	6.6	3.7
Westminster	21	10,709	230	22.1	5.1	12.7	1.15	82	11.9	5.8	2.9
Hackney[7]	19	10,861	207	11.8	8.3	10.5	2.20	103	20.5	5.9	7.0
Haringey	30	7,581	224	8.4	7.1	11.0	1.97	104	17.9	6.0	9.5
Islington	15	12,105	180	8.8	6.0	11.4	1.48	117	14.9	7.0	7.9
Lambeth	27	9,996	268	6.5	6.8	10.4	1.90	110	17.7	6.2	7.1
Lewisham	35	7,027	247	4.0	6.9	12.3	1.89	111	16.5	7.7	5.1
Newham	36	6,838	248	16.9	8.4	10.0	2.39	113	20.9	6.2	7.3
Southwark	29	8,826	255	16.4	6.9	11.7	1.91	100	17.5	6.4	9.2
Tower Hamlets	20	10,589	209	44.6	7.8	9.8	1.88	110	19.5	5.7	4.8
Outer London	1,253	3,591	4,498	5.7	6.4	15.6	1.84	94	14.5	8.0	4.7
Barking and Dagenham	36	4,560	165	2.0	7.3	15.5	2.18	107	16.7	9.2	5.0
Bexley	61	3,625	220	1.0	5.9	18.5	1.86	92	12.3	8.9	6.1
Enfield	81	3,464	280	7.3	6.7	15.7	2.02	96	15.1	8.1	7.6
Greenwich	47	4,767	226	5.4	7.0	13.9	1.91	106	16.5	8.4	6.1
Havering	112	2,004	225	-7.0	5.3	20.4	1.83	96	11.4	9.9	2.5
Redbridge	56	4,384	247	11.5	6.4	15.5	1.89	94	14.1	8.1	5.3
Waltham Forest	39	5,715	222	2.1	7.2	13.1	2.12	110	17.8	7.9	4.5
Bromley	150	1,992	299	0.0	5.9	19.3	1.71	88	12.0	9.2	4.7
Croydon	87	3,932	340	6.1	6.3	14.7	1.86	97	14.3	7.8	4.4
Kingston upon Thames	37	4,076	152	12.9	5.9	14.5	1.63	87	13.4	7.5	2.2
Merton	38	5,112	192	14.7	6.3	14.3	1.70	85	14.7	6.9	6.2
Sutton	44	4,049	178	4.3	5.9	16.8	1.74	92	12.5	8.6	4.0
Barnet	87	3,767	327	10.7	6.4	16.0	1.69	87	13.7	7.9	4.2
Brent	43	6,193	268	7.9	6.5	13.7	1.88	89	16.2	6.1	4.3
Ealing	56	5,460	303	6.3	6.4	13.3	1.85	95	15.7	6.8	4.2
Harrow	50	4,198	212	6.0	5.9	16.6	1.83	85	13.6	7.8	5.6
Hillingdon	116	2,150	249	6.5	6.4	15.7	1.80	99	14.0	8.4	3.0
Hounslow	56	3,793	212	5.7	6.8	13.2	2.07	109	17.1	7.6	5.1
Richmond upon Thames	57	3,183	183	10.9	6.6	14.6	1.59	86	14.1	7.5	3.1

1 Local government structure as at 1 April 1998. See Notes and Definitions.
2 Pension age is 65 or over for men and 60 or over for women.
3 The total fertility rate (TFR) is the average number of children who would be born to a woman if the current pattern of fertility persisted throughout her child-bearing years.
4 The Standardised Mortality Ratio (SMR) takes account of the age structure of the population. Data are based on occurrences.
5 To protect confidentiality all births and maternities for the City of London LB have been included with those for Hackney LB.
6 Data are based on occurrences.
7 Hackney and City of London data for TFR only

Source: Office for National Statistics

Table **1.28** Local authority[1] housing, households and labour market: London

	Economic activity[2] rate 2004-2005 (percentages)	Claimant[3] unemployment March 2005 (thousands)	Percentage claiming over 12 months, computerised claims only[4] March 2005	Lone parents[5] as a percentage of all households, spring 2005	Housing completions[6] by private enterprise 2004	Average dwelling price[7] 2004 (£ thousands)	Percentage change in dwelling price 2003 to 2004	Local authority average weekly rent per dwelling[8] (£), April 2005 (provisional)
United Kingdom	78.2	882.3	14.0	7.2				
England	78.5	717.3	13.8	7.2	129,544	181	13.8	55.11
London[6]	74.4	164.2	18.7	9.7	15,088	276	9.5	69.37
Inner London	69.4	84.3	21.5	11.6		328	8.8	69.81
Camden	67.7	5.6	22.3	8.4	104	414	6.8	71.84
City of London	78.5	0.1	19.8		213	314	-3.5	71.16
Hammersmith and Fulham	78.1	4.0	17.8	8.5	91	384	8.8	71.23
Kensington and Chelsea	75.6	2.5	20.1	7.0	423	715	6.2	76.46
Wandsworth	77.1	5.3	18.8	9.4	526	337	11.8	87.02
Westminster	68.8	4.0	19.4	5.8	786	508	9.3	87.12
Hackney	61.4	7.7	18.0	14.3	254	237	7.3	65.00
Haringey	70.9	7.7	23.8	12.9	49	260	9.4	68.46
Islington	67.2	5.8	23.4	14.2	119	321	8.4	70.38
Lambeth	69.2	10.0	20.9	11.5	227	254	6.5	70.76
Lewisham	76.9	7.5	19.5	17.8	406	199	7.6	64.47
Newham	59.5	7.3	15.0	10.3	968	191	8.0	60.49
Southwark	70.2	9.1	29.6	12.8	568	253	5.5	64.68
Tower Hamlets	60.2	7.7	25.2	10.4	1,675	260	10.3	70.14
Outer London	77.8	79.9	15.8	8.5		243	9.0	68.69
Barking and Dagenham	70.0	3.8	12.7	8.6	191	164	12.6	62.95
Bexley	80.0	2.9	13.6	8.2	687	189	7.9	..
Enfield	77.7	6.1	16.3	13.9	353	220	6.7	68.98
Greenwich	74.5	6.0	15.2	13.1	710	210	8.1	67.43
Havering	79.4	2.5	12.2	3.5	283	209	7.9	54.91
Redbridge	76.0	4.1	11.8	5.8	404	234	10.3	71.79
Waltham Forest	72.8	6.5	20.0	12.8	82	195	8.8	72.08
Bromley	85.0	4.0	16.3	7.4	287	261	9.4	..
Croydon	83.6	6.3	12.4	8.5	235	210	6.6	70.47
Kingston upon Thames	77.0	1.7	14.4	5.2	377	268	9.3	74.83
Merton	80.8	3.0	14.8	4.7	109	281	13.3	66.08
Sutton	85.9	2.2	16.3	6.8	192	213	8.2	65.35
Barnet	74.1	5.2	16.4	7.0	806	311	8.9	67.86
Brent	71.8	8.0	25.8	9.9	322	250	7.4	79.87
Ealing	75.2	5.9	14.6	9.5	511	262	9.2	69.01
Harrow	80.2	3.1	14.1	6.8	218	272	6.2	77.36
Hillingdon	77.7	3.8	13.7	9.0	296	225	6.4	78.07
Hounslow	74.8	3.3	9.3	13.8	689	248	5.9	67.46
Richmond upon Thames	80.1	1.7	17.6	5.1	356	385	10.4	..

1 Local government structure as at 1 April 1998. See Notes and Definitions.
2 For those of working age. See Notes and Definitions for Chapter 5.
3 Counts of claimants of unemployment-related benefits at March 2005. See Notes and Definitions for Chapter 5.
4 People who have been claiming unemployment-related benefits for more than 12 months (computerised claims only), as a percentage of total computerised claimants in March 2005.
5 Lone parents with at least one dependent child.
6 District figures do not always add to county totals. See Notes and Definitions for Chapter 6.
7 Excludes those bought at non-market prices. Sales below £1,000 and above £20 million are excluded from these figures. Averages are based on four quarters of the year.
8 Some local authorities have no housing stock following large-scale voluntary transfers (..) to Registered Social Landlords (RSLs), so the average rent is no longer applicable.

Source: Office for National Statistics; Office of the Deputy Prime Minister

South East

In 2004, the South East had a population of 8.1 million. The resident population of the South East increased by 30 thousand between mid-2003 and mid-2004. The region showed an increase of 12 per cent in the 23 years between 1981 and 2004, according to the mid-year population estimates. (Table 3.1)

In 2004, the infant mortality rate in the South East was the lowest in the UK at 3.9, compared with the UK average of 5.1 deaths of infants under one year of age per 1,000 live births. (Table 7.2)

In 2003/04, 81 per cent of 16-year-olds in the South East were in post-compulsory education or government-supported training. This was similar to the average for England of 79 per cent. (Table 4.7)

The proportion of people of working age qualified to GCE A level/equivalent or higher in the South East was around 54 per cent in spring 2005, compared with a UK average of 50 per cent. In 2004, three-fifths of full-time first degree graduates studying in the South East subsequently gained employment in the UK, which was just below the UK national average. (Table 4.9 and 4.10)

In spring 2005, the employment rate in the South East was 79 per cent for people of working age, one of the highest of the countries and regions of the UK, which had an overall rate of 74 per cent. (Table 5.1)

There were nearly 3.5 million dwellings in the South East in 2004, the highest number in the UK. Dwellings had increased in number by 8.7 per cent over ten years compared with the overall UK increase of 7.5 per cent since 1994. (Table 6.1)

The proportion of non-married people aged 16 to 59 who were cohabiting was highest in the South East (jointly with the South West) at 30 per cent. (Table 3.15)

In April 2005, gross weekly earnings for full-time employees on adult rates in the South East were £521.20 for males and £392.90 for females, 11 and 6 per cent above the UK levels respectively. These figures are median values so half of the males (or females) earned above these amounts and half earned below. (Table 1.29)

Gross value added (GVA) per head of population in the South East in 2004 was £19,500, 16 per cent higher than the UK average of £17,300. (Table 12.1)

In the South East, manufacturing accounted for less than 12 per cent of GVA in 2003, compared with 15 per cent for the UK as a whole. Agriculture, hunting, forestry and fishing accounted for 0.7 per cent of GVA compared with slightly over 1.0 per cent in the UK overall. (Table 12.5)

In March 2004, a quarter of businesses in the South East were in the distribution, hotels and catering or repairs sectors; this was the lowest proportion in the UK. (Table 13.3)

Table **1.29** Key statistics for the South East

	South East	United Kingdom[1]		South East	United Kingdom[1]
Population, 2004[2] (thousands)	8,110	59,835	Gross value added, 2004 (£ billion)	158.2	1,005.4
Percentage aged under 16[2]	19.5	19.5	Gross value added per head index, 2004 (UK=100)	116.1	100
Percentage pension age and over[2]	19.1	18.6	Total business sites,[5] March 2004 (thousands)	390.9	2,573.1
Standardised Mortality Ratio (UK=100), 2003	91	100	Average dwelling price,[1] 2004 (£)	228,296	183,449
Infant mortality rate,[3] 2004	3.9	5.1			
Percentage of pupils achieving 5 or more grades A*-C at GCSE level or equivalent, 2003/04[1]	57.7	54.2	Motor cars currently licensed,[1,6] 2003 (thousands)	4,162	26,240
			Fatal and serious accidents on roads,[1] 2004 (rates per 100,000 population)	49.8	51.1
Economic activity rate,[4] spring 2005 (percentages)	81.9	78.5			
Employment rate,[4] spring 2005 (percentages)	78.6	74.4	Recorded crime rate,[1] 2004/05 (recorded offences per 100,000 population)	8,983	10,508
Unemployment rate,[4] spring 2005 (percentages)	3.7	4.7			
Median gross weekly earnings: males in full-time employment, April 2005 (£)	521.2	471.5	Average gross weekly household income, 2001/02 to 2003/04[7] (£)	658	554
Median gross weekly earnings: females in full-time employment, April 2005 (£)	392.9	371.8	Average weekly household expenditure, 2001/02 to 2003/04[7] (£)	473.40	406.20
			Households in receipt of Tax Credits,[1] 2003/04 (percentages)	12	15

1 Figures relate to the United Kingdom except for GCSE results and average dwelling prices (covering England); currently licensed motor cars, fatal and serious accidents and Tax Credits (Great Britain), and recorded crime rate (England and Wales).
2 Population figures for 2004 are mid-year population estimates. Pension age is men aged 65 or over and women aged 60 or over.
3 Deaths of infants under one year of age per 1,000 live births.
4 Seasonally adjusted data for people of working age, men aged 16 to 64 and women aged 16 to 59.
5 Registered for VAT and/or PAYE local unit basis, e.g. an individual factory or shop.
6 Totals for the United Kingdom include vehicles where the country of the registered vehicle is unknown, that are under disposal or from countries unknown within Great Britain.
7 Data combined from the 2001/02, 2002/03 and 2003/04 Expenditure and Food Surveys.

Map **1.30** Population density: by local or unitary authority, 2004

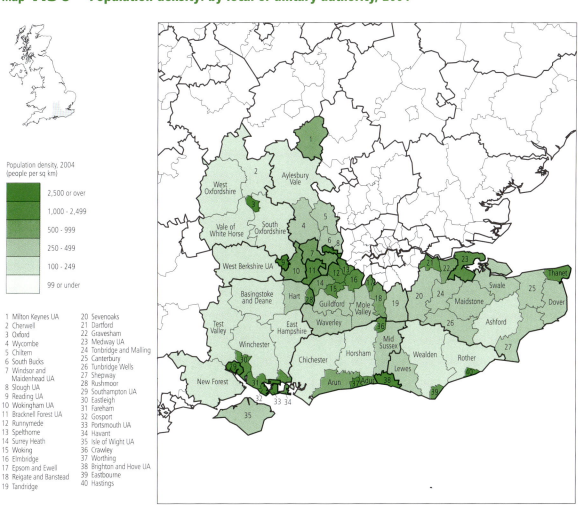

Population density, 2004 (people per sq km)

- 2,500 or over
- 1,000 - 2,499
- 500 - 999
- 250 - 499
- 100 - 249
- 99 or under

1 Milton Keynes UA
2 Cherwell
3 Oxford
4 Wycombe
5 Chiltern
6 South Bucks
7 Windsor and Maidenhead UA
8 Slough UA
9 Reading UA
10 Wokingham UA
11 Bracknell Forest UA
12 Runnymede
13 Spelthorne
14 Surrey Heath
15 Woking
16 Elmbridge
17 Epsom and Ewell
18 Reigate and Banstead
19 Tandridge

20 Sevenoaks
21 Dartford
22 Gravesham
23 Medway UA
24 Tonbridge and Malling
25 Canterbury
26 Tunbridge Wells
27 Shepway
28 Rushmoor
29 Southampton UA
30 Eastleigh
31 Fareham
32 Gosport
33 Portsmouth UA
34 Havant
35 Isle of Wight UA
36 Crawley
37 Worthing
38 Brighton and Hove UA
39 Eastbourne
40 Hastings

Table **1.31** Local authority[1] population and vital statistics: South East, 2004

	Area (sq km)	People per sq km	Population (thous) Total	Total population percentage change 1981-2004	Percentage of population: aged under 5	of pension age[2] or over	Total fertility rate (TFR)[3]	Standardised Mortality Ratio (UK=100) (SMR)[4]	Live birth rate per 1,000 population	Death rate per 1,000 population	Infant mortality rate[5]
United Kingdom	242,515	247	59,835	6.2	5.7	18.6	1.77	100	5.3	9.7	5.3
England	130,281	385	50,094	7.0	5.7	18.5	1.78	99	5.3	9.6	5.1
South East	19,069	425	8,110	12.0	5.6	19.1	1.77	92	4.2	9.5	3.9
Bracknell Forest UA	109	1,009	110	30.3	6.3	13.3	1.76	91	2.1	6.4	1.4
Brighton and Hove UA	83	3,047	252	6.2	5.2	17.3	1.35	93	5.3	9.6	7.2
Isle of Wight UA	380	364	138	17.2	4.4	25.4	1.70	89	2.7	12.2	4.2
Medway UA	192	1,307	251	4.5	6.2	15.4	1.85	105	6.4	8.2	7.3
Milton Keynes UA	309	702	217	72.1	6.7	12.3	2.06	110	8.0	7.2	4.7
Portsmouth UA	40	4,683	189	-1.5	5.5	16.8	1.56	102	3.6	9.7	5.2
Reading UA	40	3,565	144	4.8	6.0	14.3	1.72	99	6.5	7.8	6.6
Slough UA	33	3,615	118	16.7	7.1	13.4	2.14	106	5.0	7.6	3.4
Southampton UA	50	4,438	221	5.4	5.2	16.0	1.45	95	1.6	8.6	1.9
West Berkshire UA	704	206	145	18.1	6.0	16.3	1.83	87	4.6	7.3	4.7
Windsor and Maidenhead UA	197	696	137	0.9	5.9	17.8	1.70	95	3.6	8.9	3.1
Wokingham UA	179	851	152	30.2	5.8	15.2	1.72	83	5.4	6.4	1.1
Buckinghamshire County	1,565	306	479	8.1	6.1	17.8	1.86	88	4.5	8.2	3.9
Aylesbury Vale	903	185	167	24.6	6.3	15.9	1.85	95	4.0	7.9	3.4
Chiltern	196	454	89	-1.7	5.8	20.5	1.89	84	2.1	8.8	3.2
South Bucks	141	444	63	3.0	5.6	20.7	1.80	90	3.2	9.8	-
Wycombe	325	492	160	1.5	6.4	17.2	1.89	85	6.5	7.6	5.9
East Sussex County	1,709	291	497	16.1	5.0	25.9	1.93	91	4.8	13.3	4.8
Eastbourne	44	2,085	92	18.8	5.0	26.9	1.83	92	4.0	14.6	3.0
Hastings	30	2,846	85	11.8	5.6	20.4	1.99	106	4.2	12.3	10.1
Lewes	292	320	93	18.3	5.1	26.0	1.95	82	3.5	11.8	7.9
Rother	509	169	86	12.1	4.2	32.1	1.92	94	7.7	16.9	-
Wealden	833	169	141	18.4	5.1	24.8	1.95	88	5.3	11.8	2.3
Hampshire County	3,679	341	1,253	15.4	5.5	19.5	1.79	90	3.5	9.1	3.2
Basingstoke and Deane	634	245	155	17.8	6.2	15.3	1.78	95	3.2	7.5	1.6
East Hampshire	514	215	111	20.7	5.5	19.3	1.84	91	1.8	9.3	-
Eastleigh	80	1,454	116	24.8	5.4	18.0	1.75	95	2.5	8.9	1.5
Fareham	74	1,464	109	22.1	5.2	21.2	1.79	85	4.7	9.0	0.9
Gosport	25	3,046	77	-1.1	5.7	19.3	1.86	101	5.7	10.0	7.4
Hart	215	403	87	24.0	6.1	16.1	1.80	83	2.1	6.8	3.9
Havant	55	2,090	116	0.0	5.2	22.8	2.03	93	5.7	10.5	3.2
New Forest	753	228	172	18.1	4.6	26.5	1.80	82	2.0	11.7	3.9
Rushmoor	39	2,275	89	2.1	6.2	14.1	1.73	94	6.8	7.0	6.8
Test Valley	628	178	112	21.6	5.6	18.4	1.81	93	4.4	9.0	3.3
Winchester	661	168	111	19.4	5.2	19.8	1.62	88	0.9	9.6	4.4
Kent County	3,544	384	1,359	9.2	5.6	20.0	1.84	97	4.9	10.2	3.7
Ashford	581	186	108	23.9	6.4	18.8	1.99	88	3.8	8.7	3.1
Canterbury	309	459	142	15.9	4.9	21.3	1.48	100	2.9	11.9	6.8
Dartford	73	1,190	87	6.6	6.1	17.0	1.90	113	4.5	9.8	2.6
Dover	315	337	106	2.6	5.1	22.0	1.88	96	5.8	11.1	2.8
Gravesham	99	959	95	-0.6	5.7	18.5	1.89	98	3.7	8.9	4.5
Maidstone	393	362	143	9.0	5.8	18.7	1.76	97	4.1	9.4	1.9
Sevenoaks	369	299	110	0.4	5.6	20.6	1.84	85	0.0	9.0	1.7
Shepway	357	278	99	15.0	5.1	23.1	1.93	96	6.0	12.0	5.8
Swale	373	338	126	14.6	6.0	18.1	1.95	105	6.3	9.6	4.0
Thanet	103	1,238	128	5.0	5.2	24.4	1.98	104	9.6	13.9	2.9
Tonbridge and Malling	240	462	111	13.3	6.2	18.2	1.95	86	7.2	7.9	2.2
Tunbridge Wells	331	319	106	7.0	5.8	18.8	1.86	94	4.1	9.6	7.5

(continued...)

1 Local government structure as at 1 April 1998. See Notes and Definitions.
2 Pension age is 65 or over for men and 60 or over for women.
3 The total fertility rate (TFR) is the average number of children who would be born to a woman if the current pattern of fertility persisted throughout her child-bearing years.
4 The Standardised Mortality Ratio (SMR) takes account of the age structure of the population. Data are based on occurrences.
5 Data are based on occurrences.

Source: Office for National Statistics

Table **1.31**   Local authority[1] population and vital statistics: South East, 2004 *(continued)*

	Area (sq km)	People per sq km	Population (thous) Total	Total population percentage change 1981-2004	Percentage of population: aged under 5	of pension age[2] or over	Total fertility rate (TFR)[3]	Standardised Mortality Ratio (UK=100) (SMR)[4]	Live birth rate per 1,000 population	Death rate per 1,000 population	Infant mortality rate[5]
United Kingdom	242,515	247	59,835	6.2	5.7	18.6	1.77	100	5.3	9.7	5.3
England	130,281	385	50,094	7.0	5.7	18.5	1.78	99	5.3	9.6	5.1
South East	19,069	425	8,110	12.0	5.6	19.1	1.77	92	4.2	9.5	3.9
Oxfordshire	2,605	238	620	14.4	5.7	17.1	1.71	89	3.7	8.2	4.3
Cherwell	589	227	134	22.3	6.3	16.4	2.01	93	3.5	8.0	4.4
Oxford	46	3,182	145	11.3	4.9	13.5	1.38	92	4.2	7.4	3.5
South Oxfordshire	679	189	128	9.2	6.1	18.8	1.94	88	2.6	8.7	5.0
Vale of White Horse	578	201	116	12.3	5.7	18.8	1.94	83	3.8	8.1	6.5
West Oxfordshire	714	136	97	18.7	5.8	19.5	1.92	87	4.6	9.0	1.8
Surrey	1,663	642	1,067	5.6	5.7	19.1	1.71	87	2.4	9.1	2.8
Elmbridge	95	1,341	128	13.4	6.1	18.3	1.70	83	2.0	8.6	3.9
Epsom and Ewell	34	1,997	68	-1.9	5.8	19.4	1.72	79	0.0	8.5	1.3
Guildford	271	483	131	4.6	5.3	17.6	1.62	82	2.1	7.8	2.0
Mole Valley	258	313	81	4.4	5.3	22.5	1.69	89	3.7	10.7	1.3
Reigate and Banstead	129	983	127	8.4	6.1	18.7	1.81	101	1.9	10.5	1.3
Runnymede	78	1,006	79	7.9	5.1	18.7	1.46	90	1.1	9.2	5.9
Spelthorne	45	1,969	88	-2.9	5.5	20.2	1.76	90	1.9	9.1	5.8
Surrey Heath	95	853	81	6.7	6.1	17.1	1.90	90	2.2	7.7	-
Tandridge	248	319	79	4.4	5.7	20.2	1.85	84	3.5	9.2	-
Waverley	345	337	116	3.9	5.7	20.8	1.82	86	4.7	10.0	3.9
Woking	64	1,408	90	9.2	6.2	17.1	1.76	88	2.5	8.1	4.3
West Sussex	1,991	383	762	14.0	5.3	23.2	1.87	92	10.8	11.8	4.7
Adur	42	1,418	59	1.1	5.2	24.7	1.97	94	10.5	12.7	5.1
Arun	221	654	144	21.7	4.7	29.3	1.92	93	9.3	15.3	3.2
Chichester	786	138	109	10.1	4.6	26.3	1.76	90	9.3	12.7	7.3
Crawley	45	2,194	99	20.2	6.3	16.6	1.89	83	13.9	7.4	3.0
Horsham	530	235	125	24.3	5.6	19.9	1.81	87	10.4	9.3	2.3
Mid Sussex	334	384	128	9.2	5.7	19.6	1.86	91	11.4	9.7	7.8
Worthing	32	3,015	98	5.9	5.4	25.2	1.90	99	11.3	15.5	4.7

1 Local government structure as at 1 April 1998. See Notes and Definitions.
2 Pension age is 65 or over for men and 60 or over for women.
3 The total fertility rate (TFR) is the average number of children who would be born to a woman if the current pattern of fertility persisted throughout her child-bearing years.
4 The Standardised Mortality Ratio (SMR) takes account of the age structure of the population. Data are based on occurrences.
5 Data are based on occurrences.

Source: Office for National Statistics

Table **1.32**   Local authority[1] housing, households and labour market: South East

	Economic activity[2] rate 2004-2005 (percentages)	Claimant[3] unemployment March 2005 (thousands)	Percentage claiming over 12 months, computerised claims only[4] March 2005	Lone parents[5] as a percentage of all households, spring 2005	Housing completions[6] by private enterprise 2004	Average dwelling price[7] 2004 (£ thousands)	Percentage change in dwelling price 2003 to 2004	Local authority average weekly rent per dwelling[8] (£), April 2005 (provisional)
United Kingdom	78.2	882.3	14.0	7.2				
England	78.5	717.3	13.8	7.2	129,544	181	13.8	55.11
South East	81.6	74.2	12.7	5.4	21,018	223	9.5	61.69
Bracknell Forest UA	82.7	0.8	16.1	3.6	156	211	1.0	67.93
Brighton and Hove UA	78.7	5.1	24.2	3.5	132	206	7.9	55.28
Isle of Wight UA	72.6	1.8	9.2	4.9	467	174	16.6	..
Medway UA	81.5	3.7	8.1	5.8	459	150	12.0	56.47
Milton Keynes UA	81.9	2.7	14.1	8.7	820	172	10.5	64.04
Portsmouth UA	78.5	2.6	6.6	5.4	434	153	10.9	57.53
Reading UA	78.9	2.0	18.4	6.4	417	190	5.5	72.60
Slough UA	86.3	2.1	24.6	6.3	239	179	10.1	64.48
Southampton UA	66.7	3.0	5.8	7.4	537	161	9.6	52.90
West Berkshire UA	87.4	0.7	14.1	5.9	249	245	7.2	..
Windsor and Maidenhead UA	83.1	1.0	25.9	3.3	316	328	6.8	..
Wokingham UA	86.2	0.8	14.4	6.3	359	265	7.0	65.50
Buckinghamshire County	82.9	3.7	18.5	5.7	2,156	279	8.1	66.44
Aylesbury Vale	86.5	1.1	14.2	4.5	793	222	11.1	64.26
Chiltern	80.6	0.6	9.8	5.2	117	382	12.5	..
South Bucks	72.3	0.3	26.9	6.9	91	408	4.8	..
Wycombe	83.5	1.7	22.5	6.9	254	257	4.8	69.00
East Sussex County	77.5	5.4	17.5	6.8	1,189	196	10.0	55.39
Eastbourne	74.3	1.4	18.5	8.9	540	174	7.8	54.47
Hastings	70.7	1.7	19.0	11.2	90	142	16.0	..
Lewes	80.3	0.8	16.0	8.7	139	213	12.9	59.94
Rother	80.4	0.8	17.0	6.2	128	204	8.3	..
Wealden	81.2	0.7	14.8	1.9	160	241	7.1	51.78
Hampshire County	84.7	7.9	7.1	6.0	4,964	224	9.2	60.88
Basingstoke and Deane	84.8	1.0	11.6	6.8	575	216	7.5	..
East Hampshire	83.2	0.6	10.2	6.7	330	255	5.8	..
Eastleigh	81.1	0.7	4.8	7.9	395	202	10.3	..
Fareham	86.2	0.7	6.0	3.3	212	207	10.9	58.35
Gosport	87.1	0.6	1.6	10.5	405	153	10.9	50.94
Hart	89.7	0.4	8.9	5.6	402	267	9.2	..
Havant	83.9	1.3	6.8	4.8	122	184	12.3	..
New Forest	81.1	0.8	6.8	5.4	426	247	12.2	66.51
Rushmoor	88.0	0.7	7.5	10.4	108	181	6.4	..
Test Valley	84.1	0.5	5.6	5.0	436	231	5.8	..
Winchester	86.7	0.6	7.9	1.7	418	292	9.8	62.90
Kent County	80.9	15.3	8.6	5.4	4,204	198	12.9	58.52
Ashford	86.6	0.9	2.9	3.9	652	197	10.3	60.77
Canterbury	78.7	1.4	9.5	6.3	448	195	13.4	60.25
Dartford	80.0	1.0	10.0	6.2	558	184	4.8	61.18
Dover	78.3	1.6	6.9	8.6	90	163	18.9	59.94
Gravesham	81.1	1.5	8.2	7.0	134	177	11.6	55.78
Maidstone	82.8	1.1	7.7	3.4	423	203	8.7	..
Sevenoaks	79.1	0.7	11.9	4.1	136	300	10.0	..
Shepway	77.8	1.6	9.5	6.9	402	170	14.5	54.56
Swale	76.8	1.7	6.0	4.3	343	163	13.6	..
Thanet	81.5	2.5	11.7	6.0	48	148	13.7	55.55
Tonbridge and Malling	84.1	0.8	7.3	3.3	307	243	13.8	..
Tunbridge Wells	83.9	0.7	8.1	5.5	100	266	11.5	..

(continued...)

1 Local government structure as at 1 April 1998. See Notes and Definitions.
2 For those of working age. See Notes and Definitions for Chapter 5.
3 Counts of claimants of unemployment-related benefits at March 2005. See Notes and Definitions for Chapter 5.
4 People who have been claiming unemployment-related benefits for more than 12 months (computerised claims only), as a percentage of total computerised claimants in March 2005.
5 Lone parents with at least one dependent child.
6 District figures do not always add to county totals. See Notes and Definitions for Chapter 6.
7 Excludes those bought at non-market prices. Sales below £1,000 and above £20 million are excluded from these figures. Averages are based on four quarters of the year.
8 Some local authorities have no housing stock following large-scale voluntary transfers (..) to Registered Social Landlords (RSLs), so the average rent is no longer applicable.

Source: Office for National Statistics; Office of the Deputy Prime Minister

Table **1.32** Local authority[1] housing, households and labour market: South East *(continued)*

	Economic activity[2] rate 2004-2005 (percentages)	Claimant[3] unemployment March 2005 (thousands)	Percentage claiming over 12 months, computerised claims only[4] March 2005	Lone parents[5] as a percentage of all households, spring 2005	Housing completions[6] by private enterprise 2004	Average dwelling price[7] 2004 (£ thousands)	Percentage change in dwelling price 2003 to 2004	Local authority average weekly rent per dwelling[8] (£), April 2005 (provisional)
United Kingdom	78.2	882.3	14.0	7.2				
England	78.5	717.3	13.8	7.2	129,544	181	13.8	55.11
South East	81.6	74.2	12.7	5.4	21,018	223	9.5	61.69
Oxfordshire	82.3	4.1	13.7	3.9	1,484	243	7.3	64.05
Cherwell	86.9	0.9	12.9	4.4	391	202	8.8	..
Oxford	73.1	1.7	15.7	3.0	350	269	7.9	64.05
South Oxfordshire	79.2	0.7	15.4	4.0	146	271	5.6	..
Vale of White Horse	88.4	0.5	9.1	1.5	202	240	5.1	..
West Oxfordshire	87.6	0.4	9.9	6.9	395	245	8.6	..
Surrey	82.6	6.1	11.2	3.9	2,787	299	8.5	70.09
Elmbridge	84.7	0.7	9.0	3.7	383	411	12.3	..
Epsom and Ewell	82.1	0.4	9.1	3.7	131	281	14.3	..
Guildford	84.6	0.8	17.9	3.2	293	295	8.7	72.92
Mole Valley	75.6	0.3	11.3	2.9	119	315	8.8	63.10
Reigate and Banstead	82.3	0.7	5.7	2.3	377	275	9.1	..
Runnymede	77.6	0.5	13.0	3.1	190	273	5.2	70.57
Spelthorne	79.7	0.8	10.9	9.4	427	225	3.6	..
Surrey Heath	85.5	0.4	9.3	2.8	160	282	4.3	..
Tandridge	82.8	0.4	7.9	4.1	206	298	7.4	61.27
Waverley	82.6	0.6	15.3	3.1	92	318	5.7	76.86
Woking	88.0	0.6	11.3	6.0	394	262	4.8	69.21
West Sussex	82.2	5.4	14.0	5.3	2,038	220	8.8	64.18
Adur	83.1	0.5	19.7	3.2	52	182	12.0	58.64
Arun	73.9	1.1	12.8	3.0	369	199	8.3	60.51
Chichester	83.6	0.8	15.2	5.4	343	277	7.4	..
Crawley	82.3	1.0	11.8	8.8	64	180	10.0	67.50
Horsham	85.9	0.7	16.5	3.3	446	260	10.7	..
Mid Sussex	86.7	0.7	9.8	5.9	486	244	5.3	..
Worthing	80.4	0.7	15.4	8.2	103	183	8.6	..

1 Local government structure as at 1 April 1998. See Notes and Definitions.
2 For those of working age. See Notes and Definitions for Chapter 5.
3 Counts of claimants of unemployment-related benefits at March 2005. See Notes and Definitions for Chapter 5.
4 People who have been claiming unemployment-related benefits for more than 12 months (computerised claims only), as a percentage of total computerised claimants in March 2005.
5 Lone parents with at least one dependent child.
6 District figures do not always add to county totals. See Notes and Definitions for Chapter 6.
7 Excludes those bought at non-market prices. Sales below £1,000 and above £20 million are excluded from these figures. Averages are based on four quarters of the year.
8 Some local authorities have no housing stock following large scale voluntary transfers (..) to Registered Social Landlords (RSLs), so the average rent is no longer applicable.

Source: Office for National Statistics; Office of the Deputy Prime Minister

South West

In 2004, the South West had a population of 5 million. The resident population of the region decreased by 39 thousand between mid-2003 and mid-2004. The population of the South West increased by 14.9 per cent in the 23 years between 1981 and 2004, according to the mid-year population estimates. (Tables 3.1 and 3.8)

Dorset was the local authority within the South West with the highest proportion of people of retirement age (27.1 per cent in 2004). The South West overall also had the largest percentage of households (34 per cent) receiving pensions. Households had the highest proportion of income from investments (5 per cent) with a further 9 per cent from annuities and pensions.

Over one-fifth (21 per cent) of workers are employed part-time. This reflects the nature of the population and labour market in that area. (Tables 3.5, 8.7, 8.1, 5.3)

In 2004, the infant mortality rate in the South West was lower than the UK rate (4.7 and 5.1 deaths of infants under one year of age per 1,000 live births respectively). (Table 7.2)

The South West had the third highest proportion (nearly 15 per cent) of maintained primary school classes with more than 30 pupils compared with 12 per cent in Great Britain as a whole in 2004/05. (Table 4.2)

In 2003/04, 81 per cent of 16-year-olds in the South West were in some form of post-compulsory education or government-supported training. This was similar to the England rate of 79 per cent. (Table 4.7)

The proportion of people of working age qualified to GCE A level/equivalent or higher in the South West was around 51 per cent in spring 2005. In 2004 the proportion of full-time first degree graduates studying in the South West who subsequently gained employment in the UK was slightly above the UK average of 60 per cent. (Tables 4.10 and 4.9)

In spring 2005 the employment rate in the South West (for people of working age) was the highest in the UK at 79 per cent (Table 5.1)

In April 2005, gross weekly earnings for full-time employees on adult rates in the South West were £453.00 for males and £343.70 for females, 4 and 8 per cent below the UK levels respectively. These figures are median values so half of the males (or females) earned above these amounts and half earned below. (Table 1.33)

The GVA per head was £15,600 in the South West, 92.9 per cent of the UK figure in 2004. (Table 12.1)

In the South West, manufacturing accounted for 15 per cent of GVA in 2003, the same as the UK as a whole. Agriculture, hunting, forestry and fishing accounted for nearly 2 per cent of GVA, almost double the proportion for the UK overall. (Table 12.5)

In March 2004, 28 per cent of businesses in the South West were in the areas of distribution, hotels and catering or repairs; this was slightly higher than the UK average. (Table 13.3)

UK residents made 20 million trips and spent £4 billion visiting the South West, the most popular United Kingdom destination in 2004. The South West was the only region where expenditure increased. (Table 8.18)

Table **1.33** Key statistics for the South West

	South West	United Kingdom[1]		South West	United Kingdom[1]
Population, 2004[2] (thousands)	5,038	59,835	Gross value added, 2004 (£ billion)	78.7	1,005.4
Percentage aged under 16[2]	18.4	19.5	Gross value added per head index, 2004 (UK=100)	92.9	100
Percentage pension age and over[2]	21.7	18.6	Total business sites,[5] March 2004 (thousands)	240.8	2,573.1
Standardised Mortality Ratio (UK=100), 2003	91	100	Average dwelling price,[1] 2004 (£)	198,769	183,449
Infant mortality rate,[3] 2004	4.7	5.1			
Percentage of pupils achieving 5 or more grades	56.6	54.2	Motor cars currently licensed,[1,6] 2003 (thousands)	2,523	26,240
A*-C at GCSE level or equivalent, 2003/04[1]			Fatal and serious accidents on roads,[1] 2004 (rates per 100,000 population)	44.3	51.1
Economic activity rate,[4] spring 2005 (percentages)	82.1	78.5			
Employment rate,[4] spring 2005 (percentages)	78.9	74.4	Recorded crime rate,[1] 2004/05 (recorded offences	8,914	10,508
Unemployment rate,[4] spring 2005 (percentages)	3.3	4.7	per 100,000 population)		
Median gross weekly earnings: males in full-time employment, April 2005 (£)	453.0	471.5	Average gross weekly household income, 2001/02 to 2003/04[7] (£)	517	554
Median gross weekly earnings: females in full-time employment, April 2005 (£)	343.7	371.8	Average weekly household expenditure, 2001/02 to 2003/04[7] (£)	390.10	406.20
			Households in receipt of Tax Credits,[1] 2003/04 (percentages)	15	15

1 Figures relate to the United Kingdom except for GCSE results and average dwelling prices (covering England); currently licensed motor cars, fatal and serious accidents and Tax Credits (Great Britain), and recorded crime rate (England and Wales).
2 Population figures for 2004 are mid-year population estimates. Pension age is men aged 65 or over and women aged 60 or over.
3 Deaths of infants under one year of age per 1,000 live births.
4 Seasonally adjusted data for people of working age, men aged 16 to 64 and women aged 16 to 59.
5 Registered for VAT and/or PAYE local unit basis, e.g. an individual factory or shop.
6 Totals for the United Kingdom include vehicles where the country of the registered vehicle is unknown, that are under disposal or from countries unknown within Great Britain.
7 Data combined from the 2001/02, 2002/03 and 2003/04 Expenditure and Food Surveys.

Map **1.34** Population density: by local or unitary authority, 2004

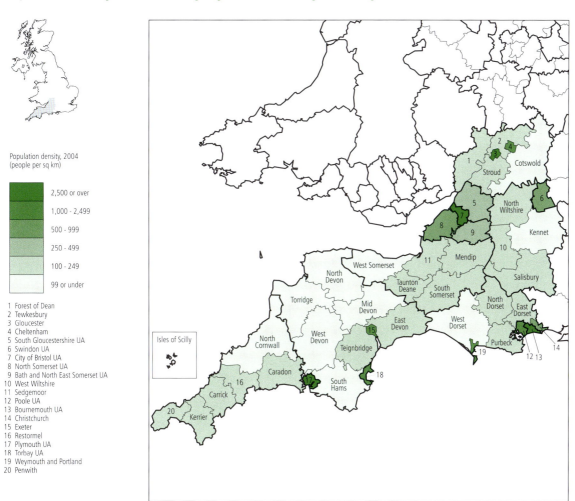

Population density, 2004 (people per sq km)

- 2,500 or over
- 1,000 - 2,499
- 500 - 999
- 250 - 499
- 100 - 249
- 99 or under

1 Forest of Dean
2 Tewkesbury
3 Gloucester
4 Cheltenham
5 South Gloucestershire UA
6 Swindon UA
7 City of Bristol UA
8 North Somerset UA
9 Bath and North East Somerset UA
10 West Wiltshire
11 Sedgemoor
12 Poole UA
13 Bournemouth UA
14 Christchurch
15 Exeter
16 Restormel
17 Plymouth UA
18 Torbay UA
19 Weymouth and Portland
20 Penwith

Table **1.35**   Local authority[1] population and vital statistics: South West, 2004

	Area (sq km)	People per sq km	Population (thous) Total	Total population percentage change 1981-2004	Percentage of population: aged under 5	Percentage of population: of pension age[2] or over	Total fertility rate (TFR)[3]	Standardised Mortality Ratio (UK=100) (SMR)[4]	Live birth rate per 1,000 population[5]	Death rate per 1,000 population	Infant mortality rate[6]
United Kingdom	242,515	247	59,835	6.2	5.7	18.6	1.77	100	12.0	9.7	5.3
England	130,281	385	50,094	7.0	5.7	18.5	1.78	99	11.5	9.6	5.3
South West	23,837	211	5,038	14.9	5.1	21.7	1.74	91	10.4	10.5	4.1
Bath and North East Somerset UA	346	498	172	6.6	4.9	20.4	1.45	89	9.4	9.9	3.7
Bournemouth UA	46	3,541	164	14.0	4.6	22.6	1.40	91	10.0	12.3	3.1
Bristol, City of UA	110	3,594	394	-1.8	5.7	16.3	1.63	99	13.4	9.0	5.0
North Somerset UA	374	516	193	18.5	5.3	22.6	1.94	91	10.6	11.2	6.8
Plymouth UA	80	3,063	244	-3.5	5.2	18.5	1.70	104	11.4	10.2	6.2
Poole UA	65	2,116	137	13.9	5.0	23.7	1.91	90	11.2	11.7	2.7
South Gloucestershire UA	497	498	248	21.8	5.7	17.9	1.81	83	11.7	7.4	3.1
Swindon UA	230	792	182	20.2	6.1	16.3	1.89	100	13.0	8.3	5.1
Torbay UA	63	2,107	133	17.1	4.7	25.9	1.89	93	9.8	13.6	6.3
Cornwall and the Isles of Scilly	3,563	145	518	21.3	4.8	23.5	1.74	91	9.2	11.3	4.3
Caradon	664	123	82	21.0	4.6	22.9	1.84	91	8.9	10.8	2.9
Carrick	458	197	90	19.0	4.5	24.4	1.54	83	8.8	11.1	6.3
Kerrier	474	202	96	14.3	5.1	22.6	1.87	91	9.9	10.6	3.2
North Cornwall	1,195	70	84	29.1	4.8	24.5	1.75	90	8.8	11.5	6.6
Penwith[5]	304	211	64	18.7	4.5	24.9	1.63	100	8.2	13.2	2.0
Restormel	452	221	100	27.2	5.1	22.6	1.83	96	10.3	11.3	4.2
Isles of Scilly	16	132	2	9.2	5.0	21.6	..	103	..	12.2	0.0
Devon County	6,564	110	725	20.9	4.7	24.2	1.74	89	9.2	11.6	2.6
East Devon	814	158	129	19.5	4.2	30.3	1.76	85	7.8	14.4	1.0
Exeter	47	2,450	115	14.5	4.7	17.9	1.30	96	9.9	9.6	4.5
Mid Devon	913	79	72	23.4	5.4	21.9	1.99	88	10.3	10.1	1.3
North Devon	1,086	83	90	14.8	5.0	23.8	2.17	96	10.6	12.0	7.1
South Hams	886	93	82	23.6	4.4	24.4	1.90	84	8.5	10.9	4.3
Teignbridge	674	184	124	29.3	4.7	25.2	1.81	88	9.0	12.0	0.0
Torridge	984	63	62	27.3	4.6	24.6	1.91	94	8.7	11.9	0.0
West Devon	1,160	43	50	17.4	4.6	23.8	2.26	84	9.6	10.5	2.4
Dorset County	2,542	157	400	19.3	4.5	27.1	1.85	80	8.5	11.5	3.6
Christchurch	50	894	45	16.9	4.1	33.2	1.97	75	8.5	13.6	2.7
East Dorset	354	241	85	23.6	4.3	29.7	1.75	72	7.3	11.2	2.9
North Dorset	609	106	65	32.0	4.7	23.3	1.99	81	9.7	9.8	3.7
Purbeck	404	111	45	11.3	4.3	25.4	1.65	85	8.2	11.3	0.0
West Dorset	1,081	88	95	19.1	4.4	28.3	1.87	84	8.1	12.5	5.1
Weymouth and Portland	42	1,542	64	11.0	4.8	22.7	1.86	89	9.7	11.0	4.9
Gloucestershire	2,653	216	573	13.1	5.4	20.4	1.74	94	10.5	10.2	4.6
Cheltenham	47	2,378	111	7.9	5.1	19.6	1.50	85	10.6	9.4	6.9
Cotswold	1,165	71	83	17.5	5.0	23.0	1.67	90	9.2	11.1	2.7
Forest of Dean	527	153	81	10.2	5.3	21.1	1.86	99	9.8	10.5	3.7
Gloucester	41	2,734	111	10.5	6.1	17.7	1.99	107	13.0	9.9	7.6
Stroud	461	238	110	13.9	5.4	20.8	1.75	92	9.7	10.3	0.9
Tewkesbury	414	189	78	23.1	5.3	21.4	1.77	91	10.3	10.1	3.8
Somerset	3,451	149	513	19.0	5.1	22.7	1.85	89	9.9	10.7	3.9
Mendip	739	144	107	18.8	5.3	20.3	1.94	93	10.7	10.2	5.5
Sedgemoor	564	193	109	21.2	5.0	22.4	1.85	90	9.6	10.5	5.5
South Somerset	959	162	155	16.5	5.1	23.0	1.87	88	9.9	10.7	1.9
Taunton Deane	462	229	106	20.0	5.1	22.0	1.76	91	10.3	10.8	3.6
West Somerset	725	49	36	20.9	3.9	30.8	1.95	80	7.8	13.2	3.7
Wiltshire County	3,255	137	445	18.5	5.8	19.6	1.88	91	11.0	9.3	3.2
Kennet	967	79	77	13.8	5.8	18.9	1.99	92	10.8	9.2	0.0
North Wiltshire	768	167	128	22.2	6.0	17.6	1.82	91	11.2	8.3	4.6
Salisbury	1,004	116	116	13.2	5.3	21.3	1.82	91	10.6	10.2	2.5
West Wiltshire	517	239	124	23.2	5.9	20.4	1.93	90	11.2	9.6	4.3

1 Local government structure as at 1 April 1998. See Notes and Definitions.
2 Pension age is 65 or over for men and 60 or over for women.
3 The total fertility rate (TFR) is the average number of children who would be born to a woman if the current pattern of fertility persisted throughout her child-bearing years.
4 The Standardised Mortality Ratio (SMR) takes account of the age structure of the population. Data are based on occurrences.
5 To protect confidentiality all births and maternities for the Isles of Scilly have been included with those for Penwith.
6 Data are based on occurrences.

Source: Office for National Statistics

Table **1.36** Local authority[1] housing, households and labour market: South West

	Economic activity[2] rate 2004-2005 (percentages)	Claimant[3] unemployment March 2005 (thousands)	Percentage claiming over 12 months, computerised claims only[4] March 2005	Lone parents[5] as a percentage of all households, spring 2005	Housing completions[6] by private enterprise 2004	Average dwelling price[7] 2004 (£ thousands)	Percentage change in dwelling price 2003 to 2004	Local authority average weekly rent per dwelling[8] (£), April 2005 (provisional)
United Kingdom	78.2	882.3	14.0	7.2				
England	78.5	717.3	13.8	7.2	129,544	181	13.8	55.11
South West	81.7	45.2	9.4	5.8	14,672	192	12.8	52.00
Bath and North East Somerset UA	86.5	1.0	7.7	4.2	178	235	8.6	..
Bournemouth UA	71.6	1.8	9.1	3.2	772	193	9.3	53.60
Bristol, City of UA	78.0	5.7	11.5	7.3	472	171	8.3	48.87
North Somerset UA	81.7	1.2	5.5	7.8	945	183	13.0	59.72
Plymouth UA	78.3	3.7	11.5	8.0	331	133	21.6	45.84
Poole UA	77.1	0.8	6.7	5.0	344	236	11.0	55.57
South Gloucestershire UA	87.6	1.4	10.9	5.5	364	178	11.1	55.76
Swindon UA	87.6	2.4	10.5	4.6	960	154	6.2	51.91
Torbay UA	74.9	1.8	11.3	4.4	320	166	17.3	..
Cornwall and the Isles of Scilly	78.1	6.2	8.8	6.3	1,708	193	17.8	49.87
Caradon	75.2	0.7	7.0	4.7	358	170	17.3	48.21
Carrick	78.8	1.2	8.6	6.1	354	222	17.7	51.56
Kerrier	78.1	1.1	8.7	11.7	189	178	18.5	..
North Cornwall	75.8	0.9	11.3	6.5	296	208	20.7	49.63
Penwith	83.2	0.9	10.2	4.5	119	202	17.3	..
Restormel	78.1	1.4	7.5	4.3	199	180	16.4	..
Isles of Scilly	-	0.0	0.0	-	5	280	-2.4	53.64
Devon County	79.6	5.7	9.3	6.0	2,808	205	15.8	50.54
East Devon	76.5	0.7	6.7	6.2	365	223	14.3	50.14
Exeter	86.2	1.1	11.4	8.7	134	179	16.4	48.20
Mid Devon	83.0	0.4	9.1	6.8	443	193	14.4	52.67
North Devon	82.0	1.0	11.0	5.8	145	198	21.3	..
South Hams	76.0	0.5	5.6	1.1	79	243	13.9	..
Teignbridge	81.6	0.9	5.2	5.9	504	196	14.8	..
Torridge	65.7	0.8	13.7	9.4	282	185	18.7	54.63
West Devon	76.4	0.3	9.5	3.6	205	208	13.1	..
Dorset County	82.9	2.2	5.5	6.0	2,589	222	10.7	..
Christchurch	85.3	0.3	3.8	7.6	82	236	11.3	..
East Dorset	86.3	0.3	9.1	4.1	86	258	9.8	..
North Dorset	77.8	0.3	7.0	8.2	516	212	11.1	..
Purbeck	85.8	0.2	5.4	5.6	76	225	14.0	..
West Dorset	82.1	0.4	2.2	2.9	510	227	11.1	..
Weymouth and Portland	81.4	0.7	6.0	11.4	97	172	9.6	..
Gloucestershire	84.0	5.4	11.7	5.8	1,415	194	12.1	56.64
Cheltenham	81.2	1.3	15.3	7.2	415	200	12.8	60.34
Cotswold	86.7	0.4	10.9	4.3	126	269	6.3	..
Forest of Dean	82.0	0.7	7.5		109	175	13.7	..
Gloucester	82.6	1.6	12.7	5.9	443	142	13.5	53.64
Stroud	87.2	0.9	8.2	9.2	236	206	13.2	55.95
Tewkesbury	85.0	0.5	12.0	5.1	86	195	10.9	..
Somerset	83.7	3.7	7.0	4.6	1,624	184	14.9	51.48
Mendip	85.5	0.8	8.9	5.4	283	188	13.4	..
Sedgemoor	84.8	0.9	6.8	4.1	375	173	19.9	51.13
South Somerset	82.6	1.0	5.3	2.5	482	188	15.7	..
Taunton Deane	88.7	0.7	8.0	8.0	340	182	11.8	51.71
West Somerset	59.2	0.3	6.1	3.1	119	197	9.0	..
Wiltshire County	86.8	2.2	3.6	5.9	2,483	207	10.2	64.44
Kennet	89.7	0.5	5.4	6.4	233	231	6.9	..
North Wiltshire	83.6	0.6	4.9	7.2	331	209	10.5	..
Salisbury	86.2	0.4	2.3	4.3	248	230	8.9	64.44
West Wiltshire	89.1	0.7	2.1	5.8	660	180	13.5	..

1 Local government structure as at 1 April 1998. See Notes and Definitions.
2 For those of working age. See Notes and Definitions for Chapter 5.
3 Counts of claimants of unemployment-related benefits at March 2005. See Notes and Definitions for Chapter 5.
4 People who have been claiming unemployment-related benefits for more than 12 months (computerised claims only), as a percentage of total computerised claimants in March 2005.
5 Lone parents with at least one dependent child.
6 District figures do not always add to county totals. See Notes and Definitions for Chapter 6.
7 Excludes those bought at non-market prices. Sales below £1,000 and above £20 million are excluded from these figures. Averages are based on four quarters of the year.
8 Some local authorities have no housing stock following large-scale voluntary transfers (..) to Registered Social Landlords (RSLs), so the average rent is no longer applicable.

Source: Office for National Statistics; Office of the Deputy Prime Minister

Wales

In 2004, Wales had a population of just under 3 million. The resident population of the region increased by nearly 15 thousand between mid-2003 and mid-2004. The population of Wales increased by 4.9 per cent in the 23 years between 1981 and 2004, according to the mid-year population estimates. The largest change was an increase of 27.6 per cent in Ceredigion. (Table 3.1 and Map 1.49)

In 2004, the infant mortality rate in Wales was equal to the UK rate of 5.1 deaths of infants under one year of age per 1,000 live births. (Table 7.2)

Wales had the lowest proportion (just over 5 per cent) of maintained primary school classes with more than 30 pupils compared with 12 per cent in Great Britain as a whole in 2004/05. (Table 4.2)

In 2003/04, 81 per cent of 16-year-olds in Wales were in some form of post-compulsory education or government-supported training. This was similar to the average for England of 79 per cent. (Table 4.7)

The proportion of people of working age qualified to GCE A level/equivalent or higher in Wales was around 46 per cent in spring 2005, compared to a UK average of 50 per cent. In 2004 the proportion of full-time first degree graduates studying in Wales who subsequently gained employment in the UK was below the UK national average. (Tables 4.9 and 4.10)

In spring 2005, the employment rate in Wales was 71 per cent for people of working age, which was below the UK overall rate of 74 per cent. (Table 5.1)

In April 2005, gross weekly earnings for full-time employees on adult rates in Wales were £433.20 for males and £337.00 for females, 8 and 9 per cent below the UK levels respectively. These figures are median values so half of the males (or females) earned above these amounts and half earned below. (Table 1.37)

Dwelling prices in Wales increased by 22.4 per cent between 2003 and 2004; this was the largest percentage change of any region. (Table 6.7)

In Wales, manufacturing accounted for 19 per cent of gross value added (GVA) in 2003, compared with 15 per cent for the UK as a whole. Agriculture, hunting, forestry and fishing accounted for 1.6 per cent of GVA compared with just over 1 per cent in the UK overall. (Table 12.5)

GVA per head in Wales in 2004 was £13,300 compared with £17,300 for the UK as a whole. (Table 12.1)

In March 2003, 29 per cent of businesses in Wales were in the areas of distribution, hotels and catering or repairs; this was slightly higher than the UK average of 28 per cent. (Table 13.3)

In 2004, Wales maintained the same number of business deregistrations as in 2003, of 28 per 10,000 adult population. (Table 13.8)

Wales had the highest net capital expenditure per employee in 2003 of £5,023 compared with the overall UK figure of £3,755 per employee. (Table 13.4)

Table **1.37** Key statistics for Wales

	Wales	United Kingdom[1]		Wales	United Kingdom[1]
Population, 2004[2] (thousands)	2,953	59,835	Gross value added, 2004 (£ billion)	39.2	1,005.4
Percentage aged under 16[2]	19.4	19.5	Gross value added per head index, 2004 (UK=100)	79.1	100
Percentage pension age and over[2]	20.4	18.6	Total business sites,[5] March 2004 (thousands)	116.7	2,573.1
Standardised Mortality Ratio (UK=100), 2003	103	100	Average dwelling price,[1] 2004 (£)	138,859	183,449
Infant mortality rate,[3] 2004	5.1	5.1			
Percentage of pupils achieving 5 or more grades A*-C at GCSE level or equivalent, 2003/04[1]	51.4	54.2	Motor cars currently licensed,[1,6] 2003 (thousands)	1,305	26,240
			Fatal and serious accidents on roads,[1] 2004 (rates per 100,000 population)	44.1	51.1
Economic activity rate,[4] spring 2005 (percentages)	74.6	78.5			
Employment rate,[4] spring 2005 (percentages)	70.8	74.4	Recorded crime rate,[1] 2004/05 (recorded offences per 100,000 population)	9,110	10,508
Unemployment rate,[4] spring 2005 (percentages)	4.5	4.7			
Median gross weekly earnings: males in full-time employment, April 2005 (£)	433.2	471.5	Average gross weekly household income, 2001/02 to 2003/04[7] (£)	461	554
Median gross weekly earnings: females in full-time employment, April 2005 (£)	337.0	371.8	Average weekly household expenditure, 2001/02 to 2003/04[7] (£)	348.60	406.20
			Households in receipt of Tax Credits,[1] 2003/04 (percentages)	17	15

1 Figures relate to the United Kingdom except for GCSE results and average dwelling prices (covering England); currently licensed motor cars, fatal and serious accidents and Tax Credits (Great Britain), and recorded crime rate (England and Wales).
2 Population figures for 2004 are mid-year population estimates. Pension age is men aged 65 or over and women aged 60 or over.
3 Deaths of infants under one year of age per 1,000 live births.
4 Seasonally adjusted data for people of working age, men aged 16 to 64 and women aged 16 to 59.
5 Registered for VAT and/or PAYE local unit basis, e.g. an individual factory or shop.
6 Totals for the United Kingdom include vehicles where the country of the registered vehicle is unknown, that are under disposal or from countries unknown within Great Britain.
7 Data combined from the 2001/02, 2002/03 and 2003/04 Expenditure and Food Surveys.

Map **1.38** Population density: by unitary authority, 2004

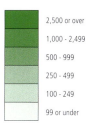

Population density, 2004 (people per sq km)

- 2,500 or over
- 1,000 - 2,499
- 500 - 999
- 250 - 499
- 100 - 249
- 99 or under

1 Swansea UA
2 Neath Port Talbot UA
3 Bridgend UA
4 Rhondda, Cynon, Taff UA
5 Merthyr Tydfil UA
6 Caerphilly UA
7 Blaenau Gwent UA
8 Torfaen UA
9 The Vale of Glamorgan UA
10 Newport UA

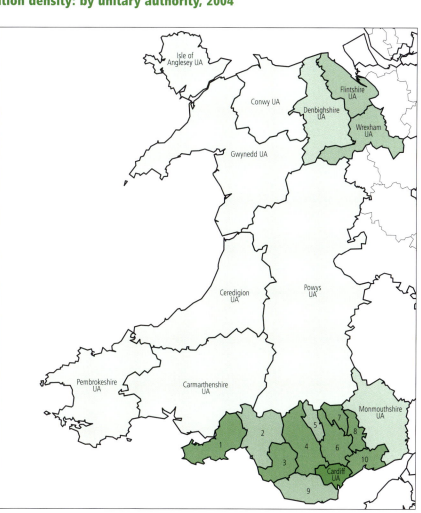

Table **1.39** Unitary authority[1] population and vital statistics: Wales, 2004

	Area (sq km)	People per sq km	Population (thous) Total	Total population percentage change 1981-2004	Percentage of population: aged under 5	of pension age[2] or over	Total fertility rate (TFR)[3]	Standardised Mortality Ratio (UK=100) (SMR)[4]	Live birth rate per 1,000 population	Death rate per 1,000 population	Infant mortality rate[5]
United Kingdom	242,515	247	59,835	6.2	5.7	18.6	1.77	100	12.0	9.6	5.3
Wales	20,732	142	2,953	4.9	5.4	20.4	1.77	105	10.9	10.9	4.3
Isle of Anglesey	711	97	69	1.0	5.1	22.8	1.79	95	9.6	10.9	2.9
Gwynedd	2,535	47	118	5.6	5.4	22.5	1.70	103	10.1	11.8	5.2
Conwy	1,126	99	112	12.9	4.8	26.5	1.92	98	9.6	13.7	5.7
Denbighshire	837	114	96	12.7	5.1	23.4	1.90	101	10.2	12.7	4.2
Flintshire	438	343	150	8.3	5.5	18.4	1.86	104	11.5	9.6	5.6
Wrexham	504	258	130	7.6	5.6	18.8	1.82	107	11.6	10.4	2.1
Powys	5,181	25	131	16.5	4.9	23.6	1.88	93	9.3	11.2	4.3
Ceredigion	1,792	44	78	27.6	4.1	21.9	1.42	94	7.9	10.7	4.9
Pembrokeshire	1,589	74	117	9.2	5.3	23.1	1.93	99	10.1	11.3	4.3
Carmarthenshire	2,394	74	178	7.6	5.2	22.7	1.84	112	10.2	13.0	2.8
Swansea	378	597	226	-1.6	5.4	21.0	1.77	102	11.1	11.2	2.1
Neath Port Talbot	441	308	136	-4.9	5.2	21.2	1.92	111	11.0	12.1	3.7
Bridgend	251	520	130	2.7	5.7	19.8	1.95	113	11.6	11.1	5.4
The Vale of Glamorgan	331	370	122	8.7	5.5	19.8	1.73	100	10.3	10.3	8.4
Cardiff	139	2,281	317	10.4	5.5	16.1	1.47	102	11.7	8.8	5.1
Rhondda, Cynon, Taff	424	547	232	-2.8	5.6	19.1	1.83	115	11.8	11.1	4.5
Merthyr Tydfil	111	497	55	-9.0	5.5	19.2	1.98	128	11.8	12.0	4.7
Caerphilly	278	615	171	-0.6	6.0	18.3	1.99	120	12.4	10.9	3.0
Blaenau Gwent	109	634	69	-9.0	5.2	20.1	1.84	121	10.8	12.3	5.8
Torfaen	126	720	90	-0.3	5.3	20.0	1.93	106	11.3	10.5	7.8
Monmouthshire	849	103	87	13.9	5.1	21.7	1.94	93	10.0	10.3	1.1
Newport	190	732	140	5.3	6.0	18.8	2.01	104	12.5	9.9	2.9

1 Local government structure as at 1 April 1998. See Notes and Definitions.
2 Pension age is 65 or over for men and 60 or over for women.
3 The total fertility rate (TFR) is the average number of children who would be born to a woman if the current pattern of fertility persisted throughout her child-bearing years.
4 The Standardised Mortality Ratio (SMR) takes account of the age structure of the population. Data are based on occurrences.
5 Data are based on occurrences.

Source: Office for National Statistics

Table **1.40** Unitary authority[1] housing, households and labour market: Wales

	Economic activity[2] rate 2004-2005 (percentages)	Claimant[3] unemployment March 2005 (thousands)	Percentage claiming over 12 months, computerised claims only[4] March 2005	Lone parents[5] as a percentage of all households, spring 2005	Housing completions[6] by private enterprise 2004	Average dwelling price[7] 2004 (£ thousands)	Percentage change in dwelling price 2003 to 2004	Local authority average weekly rent per dwelling[8] (£), April 2005 (provisional)
United Kingdom	78.2	882.3	14.0	7.2				
Wales	74.2	42.2	12.5	7.0	7,850	129	24.4	47.99
Isle of Anglesey	70.0	1.4	29.2	-	154	136	35.9	45.11
Gwynedd	73.4	1.8	20.6	7.3	114	128	26.4	46.45
Conwy	72.1	1.3	14.5	10.4	206	146	26.0	46.19
Denbighshire	82.6	1.1	13.8	4.3	276	125	24.6	44.93
Flintshire	79.8	1.6	13.6	5.4	110	131	21.4	48.22
Wrexham	73.2	1.4	8.4	8.3	373	134	21.8	44.51
Powys	82.6	1.2	13.7	7.0	416	153	22.1	45.56
Ceredigion	66.1	0.6	8.0	6.5	267	153	26.6	50.66
Pembrokeshire	74.3	1.8	12.7	5.7	268	144	24.1	44.92
Carmarthenshire	77.3	2.0	11.1	4.7	395	119	32.0	46.07
Swansea	69.3	3.4	10.4	10.8	551	127	32.7	47.85
Neath Port Talbot	74.9	2.2	8.6	11.5	250	89	33.9	46.38
Bridgend	72.5	1.9	8.2	5.2	469	116	28.3	..
The Vale of Glamorgan	79.3	1.7	9.9	3.8	475	163	18.6	55.98
Cardiff	77.1	4.9	11.7	7.5	1,733	160	13.7	53.93
Rhondda, Cynon, Taff	74.1	3.6	8.7	8.6	730	88	28.9	42.94
Merthyr Tydfil	62.1	1.1	17.5	6.5	92	69	25.5	..
Caerphilly	70.5	3.0	15.1	6.6	183	102	26.9	50.26
Blaenau Gwent	56.2	1.7	18.4	6.4	26	69	47.9	44.44
Torfaen	73.1	1.2	7.7	10.1	97	111	22.2	51.87
Monmouthshire	74.1	0.8	9.9	3.3	388	186	15.0	53.26
Newport	76.3	2.3	11.5	4.0	277	135	24.2	50.96

1 Local government structure as at 1 April 1998. See Notes and Definitions.
2 For those of working age. See Notes and Definitions for Chapter 5.
3 Counts of claimants of unemployment-related benefits at March 2005. See Notes and Definitions for Chapter 5.
4 People who have been claiming unemployment-related benefits for more than 12 months (computerised claims only), as a percentage of total computerised claimants in March 2005.
5 Lone parents with at least one dependent child.
6 District figures do not always add to county totals. See Notes and Definitions for Chapter 6.
7 Excludes those bought at non-market prices. Sales below £1,000 and above £20 million are excluded from these figures. Averages are based on four quarters of the year.
8 Some local authorities have no housing stock following large-scale voluntary transfers (..) to Registered Social Landlords (RSLs), so the average rent is no longer applicable.

Source: Office for National Statistics; Office of the Deputy Prime Minister

Scotland

Scotland had a population of 5.1 million in 2004. The resident population of the country increased by 21 thousand between mid-2003 and mid-2004. The population of Scotland decreased by 2 per cent in the 23 years between 1981 and 2004, according to the mid-year population estimates. The largest percentage increase was 23 per cent in Aberdeenshire and the largest decrease was 19 per cent in Glasgow City. This compares with an overall increase of 6 per cent in the United Kingdom. (Tables 1.49 and 3.1)

Scotland had the lowest proportion of under-16-year-olds at 18 per cent in 2004. Edinburgh had the lowest proportion of any local authority at 16 per cent. (Table 3.4)

In 2004, the infant mortality rate in Scotland was lower than the UK rate (4.9 and 5.1 deaths of infants under one year of age per 1,000 live births respectively). (Table 7.2)

In 2003, Scotland had the highest Standardised Mortality Ratio, at 116, for all areas of the UK. (Table 3.11)

Scotland had the highest proportion of one-person households in 2004, 32 per cent compared with 29 per cent for the UK. (Table 3.17)

Scotland had one of the lowest proportions (nearly 8 per cent) of maintained primary school classes with more than 30 pupils, compared with 12 per cent in Great Britain as a whole in 2004/05. (Table 4.2)

The proportion of people of working age qualified to GCE A level/equivalent or higher in Scotland was the highest in the UK at 59 per cent in spring 2005. In 2004 the proportion of full-time first degree graduates studying in Scotland who subsequently gained employment in the UK was 59 per cent, just below the UK national average. (Tables 4.9 and 4.10)

In spring 2005 the employment rate in Scotland (for people of working age), at 75 per cent, was just above the UK average of 74 per cent. (Table 5.1)

In April 2005, gross weekly earnings for full-time employees on adult rates in Scotland were £447.80 for males and £362.10 for females, 5 and 3 per cent below the UK levels respectively. These figures are median values so half of the males (or females) earned above these amounts and half earned below. (Table 1.41)

In the three-year period 2001/02 to 2003/04, children in Scotland spent an average of just under £16 a week, the highest in the UK. The next highest was £11.50 in the North West. (Table 8.10)

In the ten-year period 1994 to 2003, the percentage of women holding driving licences increased more in Scotland than in any other region. It grew by 12 percentage points from 46 to 58 per cent compared with the Great Britain increase of 7 percentage points from 54 to 61 per cent. (Table 10.3)

GVA per head in 2004 for Scotland was £16,200 compared with £17,300 for the UK as a whole. (Table 12.1)

In Scotland, manufacturing accounted for 15 per cent of GVA in 2003, the same as the UK as a whole. Agriculture, hunting, forestry and fishing accounted for 2 per cent of GVA, double the proportion for the UK overall. (Table 12.5)

In March 2004, 11 per cent of businesses in Scotland were in the areas of agriculture, hunting, forestry and food; this was the second highest figure in the UK. (Table 13.3)

Table **1.41** Key statistics for Scotland

	Scotland	United Kingdom[1]		Scotland	United Kingdom[1]
Population, 2004[2] (thousands)	5,078	59,835	Gross value added, 2004 (£ billion)	82.0	1,005.4
Percentage aged under 16[2]	18.4	19.5	Gross value added per head index, 2004 (UK=100)	96.2	100
Percentage pension age and over[2]	19.1	18.6	Total business sites,[5] March 2004 (thousands)	196.1	2,573.1
Standardised Mortality Ratio (UK=100), 2003	116	100			
Infant mortality rate,[3] 2004	4.9	5.1	Motor cars currently licensed,[1,6] 2003 (thousands)	2,031	26,240
Percentage of pupils achieving 5 or more grades A*-C at GCSE level or equivalent, 2003/04[1]	58.4	54.2	Fatal and serious accidents on roads,[1] 2004 (rates per 100,000 population)	51.0	51.1
Economic activity rate,[4] spring 2005 (percentages)	79.8	78.5	Recorded crime rate,[1] 2004/05 (recorded offences per 100,000 population)	8,627	10,508
Employment rate,[4] spring 2005 (percentages)	74.6	74.4			
Unemployment rate,[4] spring 2005 (percentages)	5.9	4.7			
			Average gross weekly household income, 2001/02 to 2003/04[7] (£)	500	554
Median gross weekly earnings: males in full-time employment, April 2005 (£)	447.8	471.5	Average weekly household expenditure, 2001/02 to 2003/04[7] (£)	370.30	406.20
Median gross weekly earnings: females in full-time employment, April 2005 (£)	362.1	371.8	Households in receipt of Tax Credits,[1] 2003/04 (percentages)	15	15

1 Figures relate to the United Kingdom except for GCSE results (covering England); currently licensed motor cars, fatal and serious accidents and Tax Credits (Great Britain), and recorded crime rate (England and Wales).
2 Population figures for 2004 are mid-year population estimates. Pension age is men aged 65 or over and women aged 60 or over.
3 Deaths of infants under one year of age per 1,000 live births.
4 Seasonally adjusted data for people of working age, men aged 16 to 64 and women aged 16 to 59.
5 Registered for VAT and/or PAYE local unit basis, e.g. an individual factory or shop.
6 Totals for the United Kingdom include vehicles where the country of the registered vehicle is unknown, that are under disposal or from countries unknown within Great Britain.
7 Data combined from the 2001/02, 2002/03 and 2003/04 Expenditure and Food Surveys.

Map **1.42** Population density: by council area, 2004

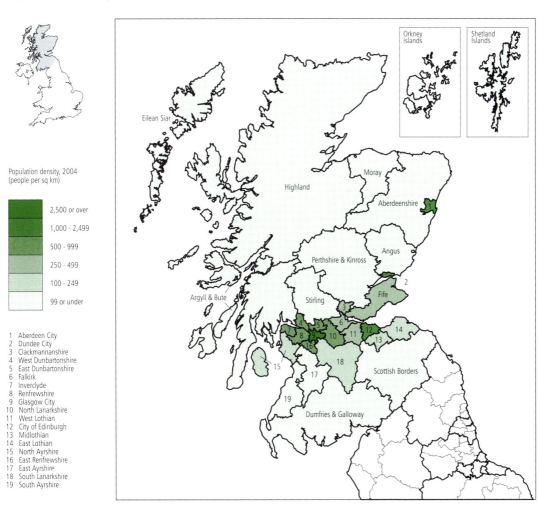

Population density, 2004
(people per sq km)

- 2,500 or over
- 1,000 - 2,499
- 500 - 999
- 250 - 499
- 100 - 249
- 99 or under

1 Aberdeen City
2 Dundee City
3 Clackmannanshire
4 West Dunbartonshire
5 East Dunbartonshire
6 Falkirk
7 Inverclyde
8 Renfrewshire
9 Glasgow City
10 North Lanarkshire
11 West Lothian
12 City of Edinburgh
13 Midlothian
14 East Lothian
15 North Ayrshire
16 East Renfrewshire
17 East Ayrshire
18 South Lanarkshire
19 South Ayrshire

Table **1.43** Council area[1] population and vital statistics: Scotland, 2004

	Area (sq km)	People per sq km	Population (thous) Total	Total population percentage change 1981-2004	Percentage of population: aged under 5	of pension age[2] or over	Total fertility rate (TFR)[3]	Standardised Mortality Ratio (UK=100) (SMR)[4]	Live birth rate per 1,000 population	Death rate per 1,000 population	Infant mortality rate[5]
United Kingdom	242,515	247	59,835	6.2	5.7	18.6	1.77	100	12.0	10.2	5.3
Scotland	77,925	65	5,078	-2.0	5.2	19.1	1.60	116	10.6	11.5	5.1
Aberdeen City	186	1,095	203	-4.3	4.6	18.3	1.38	108	10.2	10.7	6.0
Aberdeenshire	6,313	37	233	23.3	5.5	17.7	1.82	98	10.3	9.2	4.2
Angus	2,182	50	109	2.8	5.2	21.8	1.84	106	9.9	12.2	4.6
Argyll & Bute	6,909	13	91	0.3	4.5	22.8	1.87	106	8.8	12.6	1.4
Clackmannanshire	159	304	48	0.0	5.3	18.0	1.72	113	10.4	10.3	8.5
Dumfries & Galloway	6,426	23	148	1.7	4.6	23.7	1.94	107	9.7	12.9	3.8
Dundee City	60	2,371	142	-16.3	4.9	20.7	1.53	120	10.8	13.2	6.5
East Ayrshire	1,262	95	120	-6.0	5.2	19.4	1.74	129	10.6	12.8	4.0
East Dunbartonshire	175	610	107	-2.9	4.8	19.9	1.50	95	8.3	9.4	4.2
East Lothian	679	135	92	13.5	5.5	20.5	1.83	109	10.4	11.9	3.1
East Renfrewshire	174	516	90	11.7	5.5	19.4	1.86	104	10.5	10.6	4.5
Edinburgh, City of	264	1,720	454	1.7	4.6	17.4	1.21	103	10.1	10.1	5.5
Eilean Siar	3,071	9	26	-16.8	4.9	23.3	1.58	124	8.5	15.7	0.0
Falkirk	297	496	147	1.6	5.5	18.5	1.78	120	11.8	11.2	5.0
Fife	1,325	268	355	3.8	5.3	19.4	1.68	108	10.5	11.1	4.4
Glasgow City	175	3,292	578	-18.9	5.2	17.3	1.39	143	11.4	13.3	5.2
Highland	25,659	8	211	8.4	5.1	20.5	1.90	108	10.3	11.4	1.9
Inverclyde	160	514	82	-18.5	5.0	19.9	1.76	130	10.9	13.5	9.6
Midlothian	354	225	80	-4.7	5.6	18.5	1.84	111	11.1	10.3	1.2
Moray	2,238	39	88	5.1	5.0	20.0	1.82	108	9.7	10.9	6.1
North Ayrshire	885	154	136	-0.9	5.2	20.1	1.71	118	10.3	12.0	6.5
North Lanarkshire	470	687	323	-5.5	5.8	17.0	1.80	132	12.4	11.1	8.8
Orkney Islands	990	20	20	1.7	4.5	21.0	1.71	94	8.8	10.6	5.8
Perth & Kinross	5,286	26	138	12.9	5.0	22.3	1.73	101	9.3	11.9	3.1
Renfrewshire	261	653	171	-7.8	5.3	18.7	1.70	130	11.0	12.3	7.3
Scottish Borders	4,732	23	109	7.9	5.1	22.4	1.79	110	9.6	13.0	7.6
Shetland Islands	1,466	15	22	-16.7	5.7	17.6	1.81	107	10.5	10.3	15.9
South Ayrshire	1,222	92	112	-1.2	4.6	23.0	1.66	109	9.2	13.2	3.0
South Lanarkshire	1,772	172	305	-1.5	5.3	18.6	1.69	119	11.0	11.0	4.2
Stirling	2,187	39	86	7.6	5.4	19.0	1.66	107	10.8	10.6	3.5
West Dunbartonshire	159	579	92	-13.1	5.2	18.7	1.63	134	10.9	13.0	6.1
West Lothian	427	381	163	17.0	6.2	14.8	1.85	131	12.6	9.5	2.0

1 Local government structure as at 1 April 1998. See Notes and Definitions.
2 Pension age is 65 or over for men and 60 or over for women.
3 The total fertility rate (TFR) is the average number of children who would be born to a woman if the current pattern of fertility persisted throughout her child-bearing years.
4 The Standardised Mortality Ratio (SMR) takes account of the age structure of the population. Data are based on occurrences.
5 Data are based on occurrences.

Source: Office for National Statistics

Table 1.44 Council area[1] housing, households and labour market: Scotland

	Economic activity[2] rate 2004-2005 (percentages)	Claimant[3] unemployment March 2005 (thousands)	Percentage claiming over 12 months, computerised claims only[4] March 2005	Lone parents[5] as a percentage of all households, spring 2005	Housing completions[6] by private enterprise 2004	Average dwelling price[7] 2004 (£ thousands)	Percentage change in dwelling price 2003 to 2004	Local authority average weekly rent per dwelling[8] (£), April 2005 (provisional)
United Kingdom	78.2	882.3	14.0	7.2				
Scotland	79.3	93.6	14.0	7.3	21,637	109	16.0	42.32
Aberdeen City	80.8	2.6	10.7	5.3	831	96	10.9	42.67
Aberdeenshire	85.1	1.9	10.7	4.8	1,532	107	12.1	40.33
Angus	78.3	1.9	14.5	4.3	338	92	13.4	37.33
Argyll & Bute	82.4	1.5	21.1	1.2	327	110	21.1	44.19
Clackmannanshire	78.5	1.0	14.9	3.4	400	89	23.3	40.19
Dumfries & Galloway	81.3	2.3	14.0	3.2	623	102	25.2	..
Dundee City	80.2	3.9	15.2	11.7	330	78	13.4	44.72
East Ayrshire	78.5	3.3	13.3	8.4	246	80	16.8	41.93
East Dunbartonshire	78.6	1.1	13.6	4.4	247	146	18.5	44.79
East Lothian	85.4	1.0	13.7	8.6	425	145	16.2	36.25
East Renfrewshire	83.6	0.8	12.5	5.6	94	159	18.9	42.74
Edinburgh, City of	78.7	7.1	11.8	6.0	2,958	162	13.3	49.44
Eilean Siar	91.9	0.6	20.2	12.3	79	64	25.7	45.61
Falkirk	83.7	2.8	12.1	6.4	1,038	90	21.0	42.68
Fife	80.3	7.9	16.3	8.3	1,551	96	14.2	41.44
Glasgow City	71.5	16.0	18.6	12.6	2,545	109	15.7	..
Highland	83.9	3.4	10.8	4.6	627	105	20.6	47.42
Inverclyde	76.8	2.5	12.0	6.3	284	98	22.7	52.80
Midlothian	83.6	1.1	13.3	8.7	102	120	13.1	33.77
Moray	72.7	1.2	8.9	3.3	388	87	12.4	34.34
North Ayrshire	77.7	3.8	12.9	8.0	451	82	18.6	38.60
North Lanarkshire	80.9	6.4	10.7	11.4	1,198	79	16.1	42.49
Orkney Islands	83.7	0.2	18.1	3.3	56	75	20.8	39.82
Perth & Kinross	85.8	1.6	11.2	3.7	726	117	13.1	37.59
Renfrewshire	77.7	3.3	14.8	6.3	451	92	17.7	46.78
Scottish Borders	79.7	1.1	9.6	4.6	461	122	14.3	..
Shetland Islands	95.4	0.3	17.7		91	71	17.9	50.75
South Ayrshire	74.6	2.2	13.0	10.3	367	103	11.5	39.84
South Lanarkshire	78.7	4.8	11.9	8.2	1,589	97	18.0	42.08
Stirling	78.0	1.1	14.8	3.4	183	136	14.2	39.27
West Dunbartonshire	76.5	2.6	14.8	10.6	228	81	19.8	42.18
West Lothian	78.2	2.5	8.9	6.5	871	104	16.7	46.70

1 Local government structure as at 1 April 1998. See Notes and Definitions.
2 For those of working age. See Notes and Definitions for Chapter 5.
3 Counts of claimants of unemployment-related benefits at March 2005. See Notes and Definitions for Chapter 5.
4 People who have been claiming unemployment-related benefits for more than 12 months (computerised claims only), as a percentage of total computerised claimants in March 2005.
5 Lone parents with at least one dependent child.
6 District figures do not always add to county totals. See Notes and Definitions for Chapter 6.
7 Excludes those bought at non-market prices. Sales below £1,000 and above £20 million are excluded from these figures. Averages are based on four quarters of the year.
8 Some local authorities have no housing stock following large-scale voluntary transfers (..) to Registered Social Landlords (RSLs), so the average rent is no longer applicable.

Source: Office for National Statistics; Office of the Deputy Prime Minister

Northern Ireland

In 2004, Northern Ireland had a population of 1.7 million. The resident population of the country increased by 7.7 thousand between mid-2003 and mid-2004. The population of Northern Ireland increased by 11 per cent in the 23 years between 1981 and 2004, according to the mid-year population estimates. The largest percentage increase was 46 per cent in Banbridge, the only decrease was 15 per cent in Belfast. This compared with an overall increase of 6 per cent in the United Kingdom. (Tables 1.49 and 3.1)

Newry and Mourne had the highest proportion (25 per cent) of residents aged under 16 in the UK in 2004. (Map 3 4)

Cohabitation amongst non-married people aged 16 to 59 was lowest in Northern Ireland; half the Great Britain proportion of 26 per cent. (Chart 3.15)

Northern Ireland had the lowest proportion (3 per cent) of maintained primary school classes with more than 30 pupils compared with 12 per cent in Great Britain as a whole in 2004/05. (Table 4.2)

The proportion of people of working age qualified to GCE A level/equivalent or higher in Northern Ireland was 46 per cent in spring 2005, compared with the average for the UK of just under 50 per cent. In 2004 the proportion of full-time first degree graduates studying in Northern Ireland who subsequently gained employment in the UK was 58 per cent. Both these figures are just below the UK national average. (Tables 4.9 and 4.10)

The employment rate in spring 2005 for Northern Ireland (for people of working age) was the lowest in the UK at 68 per cent. (Table 5.1)

In April 2005, gross weekly earnings for full-time employees on adult rates in Northern Ireland were £409.50 for males and £355.80 for females, 13 and 4 per cent below the UK levels respectively. These figures are median values so half of the males (or females) earned above these amounts and half earned below. (Table 1.45)

Between 2003 and 2004 Northern Ireland had the highest percentage of households in receipt of child benefit, 36 per cent. (Table 8.8)

GVA per head in 2004 for Northern Ireland was £13,500 compared with £17,300 for the UK as a whole. Although Northern Ireland had the third lowest GVA per head at 80 per cent of the UK average, it was one of only three areas whose GVA per head has increased in relation to the UK average over the ten years to 2004. (Table 12.1)

In Northern Ireland, manufacturing accounted for 17 per cent of GVA in 2003, compared with 15 per cent for the UK as a whole. Agriculture, hunting, forestry and fishing accounted for 2 per cent of GVA compared with 1.0 per cent in the UK overall. (Table 12.5)

In March 2004, 22 per cent of businesses in Northern Ireland were in the areas of agriculture, hunting, forestry and food; this was the highest figure in the UK. Conversely, 13 per cent of businesses were in financial intermediation, real estate renting and business activities, the lowest percentage in the UK. (Table 13.3)

Table 1.45 Key statistics for Northern Ireland

	Northern Ireland	United Kingdom[1]		Northern Ireland	United Kingdom[1]
Population, 2004[2] (thousands)	1,710	59,835	Gross value added, 2004 (£ billion)	23.1	1,005.4
Percentage aged under 16[2]	*22.4*	*19.5*	Gross value added per head index, 2004 (UK=100)	80.2	100
Percentage pension age and over[2]	*16.1*	*18.6*	Total business sites,[5] March 2004 (thousands)	78.3	2,573.1
Standardised Mortality Ratio (UK=100), 2003	100	100			
Infant mortality rate,[3] 2004	5.5	5.1	Recorded crime rate,[1] 2004/05 (recorded offences	6,907	10,508
Percentage of pupils achieving 5 or more grades A*-C at GCSE level or equivalent, 2003/04[1]	59.5	54.2	per 100,000 population)		
			Average gross weekly household income, 2001/02	461	554
Economic activity rate,[4] spring 2005 (percentages)	*71.9*	*78.5*	to 2003/04[6] (£)		
Employment rate,[4] spring 2005 (percentages)	*68.0*	*74.4*	Average weekly household expenditure, 2001/02 to	393.00	406.20
Unemployment rate,[4] spring 2005 (percentages)	*4.7*	*4.7*	2003/04[6] (£)		
Median gross weekly earnings: males in full-time employment, April 2005 (£)	409.5	471.5			
Median gross weekly earnings: females in full-time employment, April 2005 (£)	355.8	371.8			

1 Figures relate to the United Kingdom except for GCSE results (covering England) and recorded crime rate (England and Wales).
2 Population figures for 2004 are mid-year population estimates. Pension age is men aged 65 or over and women aged 60 or over.
3 Deaths of infants under one year of age per 1,000 live births.
4 Seasonally adjusted data for people of working age, men aged 16 to 64 and women aged 16 to 59.
5 Registered for VAT and/or PAYE local unit basis, e.g. an individual factory or shop.
6 Data combined from the 2001/02, 2002/03 and 2003/04 Expenditure and Food Surveys.

Map 1.46 Population density: by board and district, 2004

Population density, 2004
(people per sq km)

- 2,500 or over
- 1,000 - 2,499
- 500 - 999
- 250 - 499
- 100 - 249
- 99 or under

1 Newtownabbey
2 Carrickfergus
3 Belfast
4 North Down
5 Castlereagh

Table **1.47** District[1] population and vital statistics: Northern Ireland, 2004

	Area (sq km)	People per sq km	Population (thous) Total	Total population percentage change 1981-2004	Percentage of population: aged under 5	of pension age[2] or over	Total fertility rate (TFR)[3]	Standardised Mortality Ratio (UK=100) (SMR)[4]	Live birth rate per 1,000 population	Death rate per 1,000 population	Infant mortality rate[5]
United Kingdom	242,515	247	59,835	6.2	5.7	18.6	1.77	100	12.0	10.2	5.3
Northern Ireland	13,576	126	1,710	10.8	6.4	16.1	1.87	100	13.0	8.5	5.2
Eastern	1,751	379	664	3.6	5.9	17.4					
Ards	380	196	75	28.7	5.8	17.5	2.19	92	11.6	8.7	4.5
Belfast	110	2,445	269	-15.0	5.9	17.8	1.67	110	12.7	10.6	7.1
Castlereagh	85	774	66	8.0	5.6	19.6	1.64	94	10.8	9.6	4.1
Down	649	103	67	24.1	6.5	15.5	2.07	98	13.4	8.2	5.9
Lisburn	447	247	110	29.4	6.5	14.8	1.90	103	13.3	7.8	4.4
North Down	81	958	78	16.0	5.4	19.5	1.81	88	10.9	9.8	1.2
Northern	4,093	107	436	15.7	6.3	16.5					
Antrim	421	118	50	8.2	7.2	13.8	2.19	105	15.2	7.4	5.6
Ballymena	630	95	60	9.1	6.3	17.9	1.97	95	13.1	8.8	4.1
Ballymoney	416	68	28	23.0	6.6	16.6	2.11	78	14.0	6.6	2.9
Carrickfergus	81	478	39	34.9	6.0	16.5	1.69	97	11.3	8.1	6.6
Coleraine	486	116	57	20.6	5.8	18.1	1.82	86	11.9	8.0	3.2
Cookstown	514	65	34	18.5	6.7	14.2	2.13	85	14.9	6.4	0.0
Larne	336	92	31	6.2	5.5	18.2	1.64	106	10.2	10.0	8.7
Magherafelt	564	73	41	26.2	7.1	13.7	1.99	96	14.3	7.0	7.1
Moyle	494	33	16	13.6	5.9	17.8	1.94	95	12.1	8.9	5.1
Newtownabbey	151	532	80	10.8	6.1	17.5	1.87	100	13.0	8.8	3.1
Southern	3,075	105	321	17.1	7.0	14.9					
Armagh	671	82	55	11.2	6.8	15.5	1.89	89	13.3	7.0	5.2
Banbridge	451	97	44	45.5	6.9	15.0	1.88	97	13.3	7.7	4.7
Craigavon	282	295	83	13.1	6.5	15.4	2.07	100	14.1	7.9	11.9
Dungannon	772	64	49	12.3	7.0	15.0	2.30	100	15.9	7.9	4.6
Newry and Mourne	898	101	90	16.5	7.5	14.0	2.22	105	15.6	7.5	3.9
Western	4,658	62	289	15.2	6.8	13.8					
Derry	381	281	107	18.6	7.2	12.5	1.88	116	13.9	7.2	5.6
Fermanagh	1,699	35	59	13.8	6.2	16.4	1.82	101	11.7	9.1	8.3
Limavady	586	58	34	24.5	6.9	12.4	1.72	95	12.5	6.1	2.1
Omagh	1,130	44	50	11.8	6.8	13.8	1.81	100	12.9	7.4	0.0
Strabane	862	45	39	6.4	6.6	14.5	1.82	116	12.5	8.4	5.9

1 Local government structure as at 1 April 1998. See Notes and Definitions.
2 Pension age is 65 or over for men and 60 or over for women.
3 The total fertility rate (TFR) is the average number of children who would be born to a woman if the current pattern of fertility persisted throughout her child-bearing years.
4 The Standardised Mortality Ratio (SMR) takes account of the age structure of the population. Data are based on occurrences.
5 Data are based on occurrences.

Source: Office for National Statistics

Table **1.48** **District[1] housing, households and labour market: Northern Ireland**

	Economic activity[2] rate 2002-2003 (percentages)	Claimant[3] unemployment March 2005 (thousands)	Percentage claiming over 12 months, computerised claims only[4] April 2004-March 2005	Housing starts by private enterprise, 2004-2005	Average dwelling price[5] 2004 (£ thousands)	Percentage change new dwelling price 2003 to 2004
United Kingdom	78.2	882.3	14.0	7.2		
Northern Ireland	72.1	29.2	22.4	13,199	115	9.2
Eastern		12.0	23.0			
Ards	69.7	1.1	22.5	530	123	3.8
Belfast	65.1	7.0	24.7	969	123	0.7
Castlereagh	83.9	0.5	13.3	149	144	3.4
Down	77.2	1.0	21.4	552	122	4.6
Lisburn	72.0	1.4	21.6	974	147	-2.9
North Down	75.4	1.0	20.4	557	171	10.6
Northern		6.0	19.7			
Antrim	81.8	0.5	16.9	505	122	6.0
Ballymena	78.3	0.7	17.7	396	131	16.9
Ballymoney	69.8	0.4	17.8	395	94	17.7
Carrickfergus	80.0	0.6	18.0	111	124	13.4
Coleraine	76.5	1.3	22.6	429	128	16.8
Cookstown	77.9	0.4	17.0	395	95	8.5
Larne	81.8	0.5	20.9	219	90	7.9
Magherafelt	66.4	0.3	20.4	376	112	38.0
Moyle	72.8	0.3	25.2	175	109	8.6
Newtownabbey	84.3	1.0	19.3	600	120	0.2
Southern		4.2	22.4			
Armagh	72.5	0.8	26.5	552	100	13.3
Banbridge	72.1	0.4	18.6	585	110	-0.2
Craigavon	67.9	1.0	13.1	1,034	105	15.3
Dungannon	69.9	0.6	20.5	627	97	20.2
Newry and Mourne	71.3	1.4	28.6	678	105	5.2
Western		7.0	23.4			
Derry	60.1	3.4	21.8	545	108	22.6
Fermanagh	73.6	1.1	31.2	647	91	11.2
Limavady	72.8	0.7	19.6	298	97	13.3
Omagh	70.2	0.8	20.6	488	92	14.8
Strabane	68.2	1.1	25.1	413	83	16.6

1 Local government structure as at 1 April 1998. See Notes and Definitions.
2 For those of working age. See Notes and Definitions for Chapter 5.
3 Counts of claimants of unemployment-related benefits at March 2005. See Notes and Definitions for Chapter 5.
4 People who have been claiming unemployment-related benefits for more than 12 months (computerised claims only), as a percentage of total computerised claimants in March 2005.
5 Excludes those bought at non-market prices. Sales below £1,000 and above £20 million are excluded from these figures. Averages are based on four quarters of the year.

Source: Office for National Statistics; Office of the Deputy Prime Minister; Department of Enterprise, Trade and Investment, Northern Ireland; Department for
    Social Development, Northern Ireland

Map **1.49**   Population change, 1981 to 2004

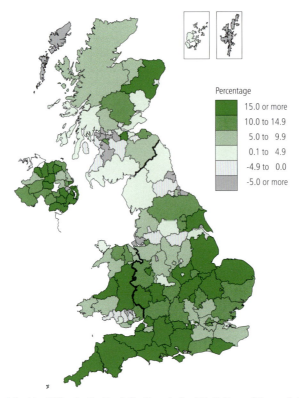

Percentage

- 15.0 or more
- 10.0 to 14.9
- 5.0 to 9.9
- 0.1 to 4.9
- -4.9 to 0.0
- -5.0 or more

Source: Office for National Statistics; General Register Office for Scotland; Northern Ireland Statistics and Research Agency

Map **1.50**   Projected population change,¹ 2005 to 2011

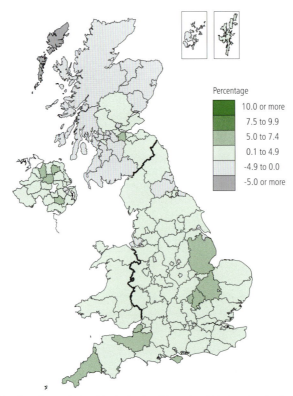

Percentage

- 10.0 or more
- 7.5 to 9.9
- 5.0 to 7.4
- 0.1 to 4.9
- -4.9 to 0.0
- -5.0 or more

1 *2003-based sub-national population projections have been calculated for England and for Wales; 2004-based projections have been calculated for Scotland and the Northern Ireland total only; 2002-based sub-national population projections have been calculated for remainder of Northern Ireland. See Notes and Definitions.*

Source: Office for National Statistics; General Register Office for Scotland; Northern Ireland Statistics and Research Agency

Chapter 2 **European Union**

From the EU15 to the EU25

Since 2004, the European Union has consisted of 25 Member States. The ten Accession States that joined in May 2004 were: Cyprus, the Czech Republic, Estonia, Hungary, Lithuania, Latvia, Malta, Poland, Slovakia and Slovenia. Together these new Member States had a total population of just over 74 million in 2002. Apart from the islands of Cyprus and Malta, the Accession States are located along the eastern edge of the European Union, ranging from the Mediterranean to the Baltic Sea.

Data relating to the 25 countries of the European Union (EU25) and the former 15 Member States (EU15) are not available for every topic in Tables 2.1 to 2.4; alternative time periods may be supplied where possible. Differences in definition may also exist and care should be taken when interpreting the data. The inclusion of 10 new states obviously affects comparisons with totals and averages previously published.

Boundary changes have also taken place for some regions in Italy. Please consult the NUTS level 1 map on page 85 for details of all areas covered.

Population and population density

The total population of the EU25 was over 450 million in 2002. Germany remained the largest country in the expanded European Union, with a population of 82 million. Of the new Accession States, Poland was the most populated with 38 million. The ten new states together form about 16 per cent of the total population of the EU25. The smallest country in the enlarged EU is Malta, with a population under 400 thousand. (Table 2.1)

Brussels in Belgium was the most densely populated region of the European Union with more than 6,100 people per sq. km in 2002. London in the United Kingdom (UK) with over 4,600 people per sq. km was the second most densely populated, followed by Berlin in Germany with 3,800 people per sq. km. The Netherlands was the most densely populated country in the European Union, with 477 people per sq. km in 2002; nearly 30 times higher than Finland (the least densely populated) with just 17 people in the equivalent area.

More recent population density figures for the UK can be found in Map 3.3 of the Population and Migration chapter.

In terms of the age structure of the population, Cyprus had the highest proportion of people aged under 15 years of all EU25 countries with 21.9 per cent in 2001. The Noroeste region in Spain had the lowest percentage (11.6 per cent) of young people under 15. Conversely, this region also had one of the highest proportions (20.1 per cent) of residents aged 65 or over; Centro, also in Spain, had the highest proportion of residents aged 65 or over with 20.4 per cent in 2001. Many regions, particularly in Germany, Greece, Italy, Portugal and Spain, had higher proportions of people aged 65 or over than those under 15. The largest differences were in Noroeste (Spain) and Nord Est (Italy) where the proportions of older people were 8.5 and 7.1 percentage points more than those under 15 in their region. In Cyprus and Eire the balance was the other way in 2001, with the proportion of under 15 years 10 percentage points more than those aged 65 and over. (Table 2.1)

Vital statistics

Of the 11 countries where birth rates were lower than death rates in 2002, eight were new Accession States. The region with the highest birth rate was Ile de France with 15.6 births per 1,000 population in 2001. The third highest birth rate was in London with 14.5 births per 1,000 population; this compared with the lowest rate in the UK, which was in the South West with 9.9 births per 1,000 population in 2001. The lowest birth rate overall was 6.8 per 1,000 population in Sachsen-Anhalt (Germany).

Canarias in Spain had the lowest death rate at 6.5 per 1,000 population. The highest rate was more than twice this in Latvia, with 13.9 deaths per 1,000 population; the rate in Estonia was also high at 13.5. Within the United Kingdom, Wales had the highest death rate at 11.4 per 1,000 population. (Table 2.1)

Infant mortality is an important indicator of welfare in a country. The highest rate of deaths for infants under 1 year of age was in the Wschodni region of Poland, with an average of 31.1 infant deaths for every 1,000 births. Hungary and Poland were the only countries that had regions with rates above 20 per 1,000 births. Previously, the highest infant mortality in EU15 countries was in Greece and Ireland, with 5.9 infant deaths per 1,000 births each in 2000. Bremen in Germany had the lowest infant mortality rate for a region (3.1 per 1,000 births, using 1999 figures). The lowest overall rate for a country was Sweden with 3.4 per 1,000 births. (Table 2.1)

Dependency

The dependency rate gives a measure of the number of people to be supported by the economy of an area, and is expressed as the total number of people over the age of 15, for every 100 people who are economically active. South East England (UK) and Oost-Nederland (Netherlands) had the lowest dependency rates for any EU25 region, both with 152 people for every 100 who were economically active (2003 figures). The overall rate for the UK was 160 and the highest level of dependency in the UK was in the North East region with 175 people for every 100 economically active residents. Isole in Italy had the highest dependency rate overall with 229. Belgium, Greece, Hungary, Italy, Malta and Spain all had regions where the rates were greater than 200. Greece recorded the highest rate for a country, with 205 people for every 100 who were economically active. The lowest dependency rate for a country was Denmark, with 153 people for every 100 economically active people. (Table 2.2)

Doctors

Italy was the country with the highest provision of physicians or doctors in 2003, with 6.3 for every 1,000 members of its population. However, Brussels in Belgium, with 7 doctors per 1,000 people, was the region with the highest rate of any EU25 country. Apart from Poland, which had the lowest availability of doctors nationally (2.3 per 1,000 people), the Accession States were similar to EU15 countries in provision of doctors. The lowest provision of doctors across the EU25 was in Northern Ireland, with 1.6 per 1,000 people. (Table 2.2)

Transport

Road transport remains vital for transferring goods across the EU regions. Unfortunately, figures for the EU25 are currently unavailable, so the figures for motorways presented here are for the EU15 countries in 2002, as previously published in RT38. The figures show that 'motorway density', the length of motorways in kilometres (km) for every 1,000 sq. km of land area, varied dramatically across the EU15 around an average figure of 16 km per 1,000 sq. km. The Netherlands had 68 km of motorway for every 1,000 sq. km; a rate more than 30 times higher than the lowest observed rates in Finland, Greece and Ireland with 2 km per 1,000 sq. km. The UK had 14 km of motorway per 1,000 sq. km; close to the EU15 average of 16. London had the highest concentration in the UK with a motorway density of 44 km, followed by North West England with 41 km per 1,000 sq. km. At the other end of the scale within the UK, Scotland had 5 km of motorway per 1000 sq. km. (Table 2.2)

Car ownership

Again figures are not available for the Accession States and the figures presented are for 2002. Of the EU15 countries, Luxembourg had the highest rate of car ownership at 586 cars per 1,000 population. This was just over twice the lowest national rate, for Greece, at 252 cars per 1,000 population. The UK had comparatively low rates of ownership with 403 cars per 1,000 making it joint fifth lowest in the EU15 with Finland. In the UK the rate was highest in South East with 472 cars per 1,000 population. The North East of England had the lowest rate of car ownership (327 per 1,000 population) followed by London (330 cars per 1,000 population). (Table 2.2)

Unemployment

The overall unemployment rate for the EU25 in 2003 was 9.1 per cent, one percentage point higher than that for the EU15 countries. Poland had the highest rate for a country at 19.6 per cent. With almost one-quarter (24.1 per cent) unemployed the region of Poludniowo-Zachodni in Poland had the highest rate in the EU25, over three times higher than the highest rate in the UK (London with 7 per cent unemployment). Of the EU25 countries, four regions in Poland and Germany had unemployment rates over 20 per cent. Luxembourg and the Netherlands had the joint lowest unemployment rate for a country, with 3.7 per cent out of work. (Table 2.3)

'Long-term unemployment' is a measure of those unemployed for 12 months or more, expressed as a proportion of all those unemployed. Slovakia had the highest rate for a country in 2003, where 65.2 per cent of the unemployed were classified as long-term unemployed. The UK had relatively low figures. The South West and South East regions had the second lowest rates in EU25 at 15.4 per cent, after Aland in Finland with 4.1 per cent. Even the highest rate for the UK, 41.4 per cent in Northern Ireland, was below that of many EU regions. Rates of long-term unemployment were above 50 per cent in 26 areas across six countries. (Table 2.3)

Employment

Although the services sector remained the largest employer of people in all EU25 states, many new Member States still had a large number of workers in agriculture and industry. The UK had the lowest proportion of workers in agriculture (1.3 per cent) and the third highest proportion of workers in the services sector (75.2 per cent) in the EU25. Wschodni (Poland) had the lowest proportion employed in the services sector (43.9 per cent) and the highest proportion in agriculture (33.4 per cent). At the country level, Poland had the highest proportion of employees working in agriculture at 18.4 per cent, and three regions of Greece employed more than one in five of their workforce in this sector.

Generally, the proportions of the workforce employed in industry were higher in the Accession States than in the EU15 countries. The Czech Republic employed the highest proportion (39.6 per cent) in industry in 2003. The countries of Slovakia, Slovenia and Hungary all had more than one in three workers in industry, and certain regions in France, Germany, Italy and Spain showed similar rates. In the UK, industrial employment was highest in the East Midlands (29.6 per cent in 2003), compared with an average of just under one in four for the UK overall. (Table 2.3)

GDP

Gross Domestic Product (GDP) figures for 2002 showed that many regions of the Accession States had less than half the purchasing power of the EU25 average. All the Accession States had GDP below the new EU25 average, the lowest being Latvia with 39 per cent of EU25, when calculated as GDP per head. Brussels in Belgium remained the 'richest' region at more than twice the EU25 standard. Most economies relied on services for the bulk of their GDP/output. However, Kentriki Ellada in Greece had the highest proportion derived from agriculture at 11.4 per cent, and two other regions out of the four in Greece relied on agriculture for more than 10 per cent of their economic prosperity. (Table 2.3)

Land use and agricultural statistics

Wide disparities in figures between countries reflect differences in climate and terrain, and in the degree of intensification of agricultural processes. Despite having the smallest proportion of its workers employed in agriculture, the UK had the largest proportion of its total land area devoted to agriculture in the EU25 (67.8 per cent, 2001 figures). Nearly 40 per cent of the UK agricultural land was used as arable. (Table 2.4)

The Netherlands had the highest yield for wheat (8.7 tonnes per hectare) and Belgium had the highest yield for barley (6.6 tonnes per hectare). Both countries had less than 5 per cent of their workforce employed in agriculture. (Table 2.3) Conversely, the lowest yields for these two cereal crops, 0.9 and 1.1 tonnes per hectare respectively, were in Portugal, where one in eight of the workforce were employed in agriculture. (Table 2.4)

Greece, Portugal, and the UK all had a higher density of sheep on their agricultural land in 2003 than other livestock such as cattle or pigs; in Greece the ratio was five to one. The highest concentration of pigs was in Zuid-Nederland (Netherlands), with a rate of about 17,500 pigs per 1,000 hectares of utilised agricultural land. This was 15 times higher than the highest density in the UK, which was in Yorkshire and the Humber. (Table 2.4)

NUTS level 1 areas in the European Union[1]

NETHERLANDS
1 Noord-Nederland
2 Oost-Nederland
3 Zuid-Nederland
4 West-Nederland

BELGIUM
5 Vlaams Gewest
6 Région Wallonne
7 Région de Bruxelles-Capitale / Brussels Hoofdstedelijk Gewest

8 **LUXEMBOURG**

GERMANY
9 Saarland
10 Rheinland-Pfalz
11 Baden-Württemberg
12 Mecklenburg-Vorpommern
13 Hamburg
14 Schleswig-Holstein

HUNGARY
15 Kozep-Magyarorszag

☐ non-EU countries

Região Autónoma dos Açores (Portugal)

Região Autónoma da Madeira (Portugal)

Ceuta y Melilla (Spain-Sur)

Spanish North Africa

Canarias (Spain)

MALTA

1 NUTS (Nomenclature of Units for Territorial Statistics) is a hierachical classfication of areas that provides a breakdown of the EU's economic territory. See Notes and Definitions.

Table **2.1**   Population and vital statistics, 2002

| | Area (sq km) | Popu- lation (thousands)[1] | People per sq km | Percentage of population[2] | | Births (per 1,000 population)[3] | Deaths (per 1,000 population)[3,4] | Infant mortality (per 1,000 births)[3,4,5] |
				Aged under 15	Aged 65 and over[2]			
EUR 25	..	**453,757**	..	..	..	..	..	..
EUR 15	**3,154,127**	**377,882**	**120**	..	..	**10.7**	**9.9**	..
Austria	**83,859**	**8,053**	**96**	*16.5*	*15.5*	**9.7**	**9.5**	**4.8**
Ostösterreich	23,554	3,379	144	*15.6*	*16.2*	9.7	10.6	5.2
Südösterreich	25,921	1,742	67	*16.1*	*16.5*	8.8	9.7	3.9
Westösterreich	34,384	2,933	85	*17.9*	*14.2*	10.3	8.1	4.9
Belgium	**30,518**	**10,333**	**339**	*17.5*	*16.9*	**10.8**	**10.2**	**4.8**
Bruxelles-Brussels	161	985	6,104	*18.1*	*16.4*	14.1	10.4	5.4
Vlaams Gewest	13,512	5,984	443	*16.9*	*17.1*	10.0	9.7	4.8
Région Wallonne	16,844	3,363	200	*18.5*	*16.8*	11.2	11.1	4.7
Cyprus	..	**710**	..	*21.9*	*11.5*	**11.6**	**6.9**	..
Czech Republic	**78,860**	**10,201**	**129**	*16.1*	*13.9*	**9.1**	**10.6**	**4.1**
Denmark	**43,094**	**5,374**	**125**	*18.7*	*14.8*	**11.9**	**10.9**	**5.3**
Estonia	**45,228**	**1,359**	**30**	*17.5*	*15.3*	**9.6**	**13.5**	**8.4**
Finland	**304,529**	**5,201**	**17**	*18.0*	*15.1*	**10.8**	**9.4**	**3.8**
Manner-Suomi	303,003	5,175	17	*18.0*	*15.1*	10.8	9.4	3.8
Åland	1,527	26	17	*18.5*	*16.4*	11.6	7.7	3.9
France	**543,965**	**59,489**	**109**	*18.8*	*16.2*	**13.0**	**8.9**	**4.2**
Île de France	12,012	11,107	925	*19.8*	*12.1*	15.6	6.7	4.7
Bassin Parisien	145,645	10,501	72	*19.2*	*16.5*	12.5	9.6	4.3
Nord - Pas-de-Calais	12,414	4,014	323	*21.2*	*13.9*	14.2	8.9	5.8
Est	48,030	5,217	109	*19.0*	*15.1*	12.4	8.6	5.4
Ouest	85,099	7,933	93	*18.4*	*17.8*	12.4	9.7	3.9
Sud-Ouest	103,599	6,315	61	*16.6*	*19.6*	11.0	10.5	4.2
Centre-Est	69,711	7,104	102	*18.9*	*15.9*	12.7	8.6	3.9
Méditerranée	67,455	7,298	108	*17.8*	*18.7*	11.9	9.9	4.6
Germany	**357,020**	**82,482**	**231**	*15.4*	*16.9*	**9.4**	**10.3**	**4.5**
Baden-Württemberg	35,751	10,631	297	*16.6*	*16.0*	10.3	9.3	4.3
Bayern	70,548	12,358	175	*16.3*	*16.4*	10.2	9.9	4.2
Berlin	891	3,390	3,803	*13.3*	*14.8*	8.8	10.3	4.4
Brandenburg	29,477	2,586	88	*13.1*	*15.9*	6.9	10.0	3.4
Bremen	404	660	1,633	*13.9*	*18.6*	9.2	11.5	3.1
Hamburg	755	1,727	2,287	*13.5*	*17.0*	9.4	10.9	4.5
Hessen	21,114	6,085	288	*15.4*	*16.7*	9.8	10.1	4.5
Mecklenburg-Vorpommern	23,172	1,752	76	*13.4*	*15.6*	7.0	9.7	4.9
Niedersachsen	47,614	7,970	167	*16.5*	*17.1*	10.2	10.5	5.3
Nordrhein-Westfalen	34,080	18,063	530	*16.2*	*17.2*	9.8	10.5	4.8
Rheinland-Pfalz	19,847	4,052	204	*16.2*	*17.6*	9.5	10.6	4.6
Saarland	2,570	1,065	415	*14.7*	*18.6*	8.3	11.9	5.6
Sachsen	18,413	4,366	237	*12.2*	*18.9*	7.0	11.3	4.2
Sachsen-Anhalt	20,447	2,565	125	*12.5*	*17.9*	6.8	11.3	3.9
Schleswig-Holstein	15,765	2,810	178	*16.1*	*17.0*	9.9	10.9	3.5
Thüringen	16,172	2,402	149	*12.5*	*17.2*	6.9	10.8	5.2
Greece	**131,626**	**10,988**	**84**	*15.3*	*17.1*	**9.4**	**9.5**	**5.9**
Voreia Ellada	56,457	3,535	63	*15.6*	*16.7*	9.6	9.4	6.3
Kentriki Ellada	53,902	2,439	45	*14.2*	*19.2*	8.3	10.7	6.6
Attiki	3,808	3,910	1,027	*15.3*	*15.8*	9.7	8.7	5.3
Nisia Aigaiou, Kriti	17,458	1,103	63	*17.0*	*17.5*	10.4	9.5	5.5
Hungary	**93,029**	**10,159**	**109**	*16.5*	*15.2*	**9.5**	**13.1**	..
Közép-Magyarország	6,918	2,827	409	*14.6*	*16.0*	9.3	13.0	9.3
Dunántúl	36,614	3,112	85	*16.3*	*14.8*	9.0	12.7	28.2
Alföld és Észak	49,497	4,220	85	*17.7*	*15.0*	9.9	13.3	26.8
Ireland	**70,273**	**3,917**	**56**	*21.3*	*11.2*	**15.1**	**7.8**	**5.9**

Table **2.1**   Population and vital statistics, 2002 *(continued)*

| | Area (sq km) | Popu-lation (thousands)[1] | People per sq km | Percentage of population[2] | | Births (per 1,000 population)[3] | Deaths (per 1,000 population)[3,4] | Infant mortality (per 1,000 births)[3,4,5] |
				Aged under 15	Aged 65 and over[2]			
Italy	**301,333**	**57,158**	**190**	*14.4*	*18.1*	**9.2**	**9.5**	..
Nord Ovest	57,944	14,985	259	*12.5*	*19.2*	8.7	10.1	7.0
Nord Est	61,976	10,694	173	*12.6*	*19.7*	9.0	10.1	6.8
Centro	58,346	10,946	188	*13.0*	*19.7*	8.5	10.0	8.8
Sud	73,275	13,929	190	*17.6*	*15.5*	10.3	8.2	14.8
Isole	49,793	6,603	133	*17.0*	*16.1*	9.7	8.7	10.2
Latvia	**64,589**	**2,339**	**36**	*17.0*	*15.4*	**8.6**	**13.9**	..
Lithuania	**65,300**	**3,469**	**53**	*19.3*	*14.1*	**8.7**	**11.8**	..
Luxembourg	**2,586**	**446**	**173**	*18.9*	*13.9*	**12.4**	**8.4**	**5.0**
Malta	..	**396**	..	*19.5*	*12.5*	..	..	..
Netherlands	**33,873**	**16,149**	**477**	*18.6*	*13.6*	**12.5**	**8.8**	**5.1**
Noord-Nederland	8,347	1,690	202	*18.2*	*14.7*	12.0	9.5	5.7
Oost-Nederland	9,741	3,399	349	*19.7*	*13.2*	13.2	8.5	5.2
West-Nederland	8,693	7,522	865	*18.5*	*13.6*	12.8	8.8	4.9
Zuid-Nederland	7,093	3,538	499	*18.2*	*13.6*	11.5	8.7	5.4
Poland	**312,685**	**38,232**	**122**	..	..	**9.3**	**9.4**	..
Centralny	53,817	7,737	144	..	..	8.9	10.6	14.9
Poludniowy	27,438	7,975	291	..	..	9.0	9.1	17.5
Wschodni	74,892	6,809	91	..	..	9.6	9.7	31.1
Pólnocno-Zachodni	66,712	6,060	91	..	..	9.6	8.9	25.4
Poludniowo-Zachodni	29,360	3,972	135	..	..	8.3	9.3	15.6
Pólnocny	60,466	5,679	94	..	..	10.1	8.6	23.9
Portugal	**91,906**	**10,368**	**113**	*16.0*	*16.4*	**11.0**	**10.2**	**5.5**
Continent	88,797	9,889	111	*15.8*	*16.6*	10.9	10.2	5.3
Açores	2,330	238	102	*21.4*	*12.6*	12.9	11.2	8.1
Madeira	779	241	309	*19.0*	*13.3*	12.9	11.1	8.1
Slovakia	**49,035**	**5,379**	**110**	*19.0*	*11.4*	**9.5**	**9.6**	**8.6**
Slovenia	**20,273**	**1,996**	**98**	*15.6*	*14.3*	**8.8**	**9.4**	**4.9**
Spain	**504,790**	**41,314**	**82**	*14.6*	*17.0*	**10.1**	**8.9**	**4.3**
Noroeste	45,297	4,295	95	*11.6*	*20.1*	7.1	10.7	3.7
Noreste	70,366	4,135	59	*12.5*	*19.0*	8.9	9.4	4.1
Comunidad de Madrid	7,995	5,500	688	*14.4*	*15.7*	11.5	7.2	4.1
Centro	215,025	5,292	25	*14.2*	*20.4*	8.4	10.0	4.2
Este	60,249	11,531	191	*14.4*	*16.9*	10.6	9.1	3.6
Sur	98,616	8,760	89	*17.5*	*14.3*	11.4	8.2	5.3
Canarias	7,242	1,801	237	*16.6*	*12.1*	10.6	6.5	6.4
Sweden	**410,934**	**8,925**	**22**	*18.3*	*17.2*	**10.7**	**10.6**	**3.4**
United Kingdom[6]	**243,820**	**59,322**	**243**	..	..	**11.4**	**10.2**	**5.6**
North East	8,612	2,538	295	*18.1*	*16.6*	10.3	11.2	6.5
North West	14,165	6,784	479	*18.9*	*16.0*	11.2	11.1	6.2
Yorkshire and the Humber	15,566	4,993	321	*18.8*	*16.2*	11.2	10.4	7.3
East Midlands	15,627	4,223	270	*18.5*	*16.1*	10.7	10.2	5.4
West Midlands	13,004	5,304	408	*19.1*	*16.0*	11.5	10.2	6.8
East	19,120	5,422	284	*18.7*	*16.6*	11.1	9.9	4.4
London	1,584	7,371	4,654	*18.5*	*12.1*	14.5	8.1	5.4
South East	19,111	8,044	421	*18.5*	*16.4*	11.1	9.9	4.4
South West	23,971	4,968	207	*17.6*	*18.7*	9.9	11.0	4.7
Wales	20,768	2,923	141	*18.6*	*17.4*	10.5	11.4	5.3
Scotland	78,132	5,055	65	*17.6*	*16.1*	10.4	11.3	5.7
Northern Ireland	14,160	1,697	120	*21.6*	*13.4*	13.0	8.6	5.1

1 Data are for 2001 for EUR 15.
2 Data are for 2001, estimates for numbers over 70 for Austria, Belgium, Denmark, Finland, Germany, Ireland, Lithuania, Netherlands, Portugal, Spain and Sweden. Data for 2000 used for France and Italy. Data for 1999 used for Greece.
3 Data are for 2001 for Cyprus, Finland, France, Ireland, Italy, Luxembourg and the United Kingdom, 1999 for EU15 and Germany.
4 Deaths are by date of occurrence and not date of registration.
5 Data for 2000, data for Germany are for 1999.
6 Government Office Regions for the United Kingdom equal NUTS 1 regions for the European Union. See Notes and Definitions.

Source: Eurostat

Table 2.2   Social statistics

	Dependency rate[1] 2003	Proportion of 16 to 18-year-olds in education or training (percentages) 2003[2,3]	Number of physicians or doctors per 1,000 population, 2003	Deaths and people injured in road traffic accidents per 10,000 population 2001[4,5,6]	Transport 2002	
					Length of motorways (km per 1,000 sq km)	Private cars per 1,000 population
EU25	177	..	..	..	..	..
EU15	176	..	..	..	16	..
Austria	169	83	3.3	72	20	496
Ostösterreich	169	83	3.8	56	18	475
Südösterreich	177	83	3.1	81	21	534
Westösterreich	163	83	2.8	84	19	496
Belgium	193	97	4.5	..	57	449
Bruxelles-Brussels	195	..	7.0		70	502
Vlaams Gewest	188	..	3.6	..	63	457
Région Wallonne	201	..	4.1	..	51	420
Cyprus	158	67	2.6	..	..	..
Czech Republic	169	96	3.9	..	..	
Denmark	153	87	3.7	..	22	347
Estonia	170	90	3.1	..	..	..
Finland	164	94	3.1	17	2	403
Manner-Suomi	164	94	3.1	17	2	403
Åland	171	90	2.4	15	-	527
France	179	90	3.5	28	18	490
Île de France	165	91	4.3	31	50	452
Bassin Parisien	177	88	2.7	26	19	501
Nord - Pas-de-Calais	189	87	3.0	17	48	426
Est	177	89	3.1	24	20	504
Ouest	176	93	2.9	21	10	492
Sud-Ouest	184	91	3.6	30	11	517
Centre-Est	179	90	3.3	25	22	505
Méditerranée	199	89	4.0	38	18	521
Germany	174	92	3.4	61	33	516
Baden-Württemberg	167	92	3.4	56	29	540
Bayern	166	92	3.6	73	32	553
Berlin	171	94	4.6	53	77	352
Brandenburg	166	84	2.8	66	27	507
Bremen	186	90	4.5	61	146	429
Hamburg	170	97	4.7	71	109	440
Hessen	173	93	3.4	61	45	556
Mecklenburg-Vorpommern	170	88	3.2	70	15	477
Niedersachsen	181	91	3.0	66	28	532
Nordrhein-Westfalen	185	100	3.4	52	64	504
Rheinland-Pfalz	178	86	3.2	62	42	549
Saarland	197	100	3.7	64	92	558
Sachsen	173	89	3.0	56	25	492
Sachsen-Anhalt	172	85	3.0	59	16	479
Schleswig-Holstein	172	86	3.4	66	31	526
Thüringen	172	86	3.0	62	18	499
Greece	205	77	4.4	25	2	252
Voreia Ellada	208	..	3.8	19	1	195
Kentriki Ellada	214	..	3.3	24	3	128
Attiki	199	..	5.8	35	18	416
Nisia Aigaiou, Kriti	201	..	3.7	17	-	208
Hungary	201	85	3.8	..	..	..
Közép-Magyarország	190	94	5.6	..	..	..
Dunántúl	193	83	..	..	..	..
Alföld és Észak	217	81	..	..	..	..
Ireland	166	88	2.6	28	2	339
Italy	203	81	6.3	..	21	535
Nord Ovest	191	76	..	..	36	554
Nord Est	187	81	..	..	22	545
Centro	201	90	..	..	16	561
Sud	226	78	..	..	14	442
Isole	229	75	..	..	..	..

Table 2.2　　Social statistics *(continued)*

	Dependency rate[1] 2003	Proportion of 16 to 18-year-olds in education or training (percentages) 2003[2,3]	Number of physicians or doctors per 1,000 population, 2003	Deaths and people injured in road traffic accidents per 10,000 population 2001[4,5,6]	Transport 2002	
					Length of motorways (km per 1,000 sq km)	Private cars per 1,000 population
Latvia	**174**	**89**	**2.8**	..	..	..
Lithuania	**172**	**94**	**4.0**	..	..	..
Luxembourg	**182**	**79**	**2.5**	**28**	**49**	**586**
Malta	**200**	**63**	**3.1**	..	..	..
Netherlands	**155**	**86**	**3.2**	..	**68**	**401**
Noord-Nederland	161	..	3.2	..	39	388
Oost-Nederland	152	..	2.7	..	63	403
West-Nederland	154	..	3.7	..	87	389
Zuid-Nederland	156	..	2.5	..	84	433
Poland	**183**	**91**	**2.3**	..	..	..
Centralny	177	91	..	..	..	..
Poludniowy	189	91	..	..	..	..
Wschodni	180	91	..	..	..	..
Pólnocno-Zachodni	181	92	..	..	..	..
Poludniowo-Zachodni	191	90	..	..	..	..
Pólnocny	183	90	..	..	..	..
Portugal	**161**	**73**	**3.3**	..	**18**	**430**
Continent	160	..	3.3	..	19	510
Açores	181	..	1.7	..	-	..
Madeira	170	..	2.0	..	-	..
Slovakia	**166**	..	**3.3**	..	..	..
Slovenia	**177**	**94**	..	..	..	..
Spain	**184**	**80**	**3.3**	**38**	**19**	**425**
Noroeste	196	83	3.0	36	24	397
Noreste	185	89	4.4	40	17	392
Comunidad de Madrid	179	87	3.2	36	69	527
Centro	200	84	3.0	40	12	364
Este	173	75	3.5	46	32	469
Sur	191	76	2.9	31	23	365
Canarias	175	79	3.2	22	28	477
Sweden	**161**	**96**	**2.7**	**26**	**4**	**527**
United Kingdom[7]	**160**	**73**	..	**54**	**14**	**403**
North East	175	71		47	8	327
North West	164	65	1.9	59	41	391
Yorkshire and the Humber	162	68	4.3	59	21	368
East Midlands	159	69	..	54	12	415
West Midlands	162	68	1.8	53	28	435
East	154	63	..	54	14	460
London	156	72	2.6	57	44	330
South East	152	66	1.8	53	34	472
South West	159	68	1.9	51	13	468
Wales	170	35	2.1	50	6	397
Scotland	160	44	2.7	39	5	356
Northern Ireland	169	36	1.6	71	..	..

1 Dependency rate shown expresses the number of people aged 15 and over, for every 100 people aged 15 and over who are economically active.
2 Participation rates are calculated by dividing the number of pupils aged 16 to 18 years enrolled in a region by the resident population aged 16 to 18 years in that region. Some young people may be resident in one region and in education in another; this interregional movement may influence the results. Eurostat's estimates.
3 Data for the regions of Austria are based on 1999. Data for Denmark, Ireland, Greece, Luxembourg, the Netherlands, Portugal, Sweden and the United Kingdom are for 2000. Data for Finland are based on 2000 and its regions are from 2001.
4 Data for Austria and the UK are for 2002.
5 Provisional data for Greece.
6 Data for the Netherlands are based on the number killed in 2002.
7 Government Office Regions for the United Kingdom equals NUTS 1 regions for the European Union. See Notes and Definitions.

Source: Eurostat

Table **2.3**   Economic statistics,[1] 2003

	People in employment (thousands)	Percentage employment in[2]			Unemployment rate (percentages)	Long-term unemployed[1] as a percentage of all unemployed (percentages)	Gross domestic product per head (PPS)[3] EUR 25=100, 2002	Estimates[4] of the percentage of GVA in 2002 derived from:		
		Agriculture	Industry	Services				Agriculture	Industry	Services
EU25	**193,221**	..	..	..	*9.1*	*45.0*	**100.0**	*2.1*	*26.7*	*71.2*
EU15	**164,413**	..	..	..	*8.1*	*41.8*	**109.4**	*2.0*	*26.5*	*71.5*
Austria	**3,736**	*5.6*	*29.3*	*65.1*	*4.2*	*28.7*	**120.8**	*2.0*	*30.3*	*67.6*
Ostösterreich	1,562	*4.8*	*24.8*	*70.3*	*5.6*	*35.2*	130.7	*1.8*	*24.1*	*74.1*
Südösterreich	782	*7.7*	*32.8*	*59.5*	*3.7*	*24.8*	101.7	*3.1*	*35.2*	*61.7*
Westösterreich	1,392	*5.2*	*32.3*	*62.5*	*3.0*	*17.5*	120.7	*1.8*	*35.7*	*62.5*
Belgium	**4,070**	*1.8*	*24.8*	*73.4*	*8.2*	*45.4*	**116.8**	*1.2*	*25.6*	*73.2*
Bruxelles-Brussels	352	*0.1*	*11.0*	*88.8*	*15.6*	*51.0*	234.5	*0.0*	*12.1*	*87.9*
Vlaams Gewest	2,500	*1.8*	*27.7*	*70.5*	*5.7*	*34.9*	115.6	*1.5*	*30.3*	*68.1*
Région Wallonne	1,218	*2.2*	*23.0*	*74.8*	*10.8*	*53.6*	84.3	*1.5*	*25.2*	*73.3*
Cyprus	**327**	*5.2*	*22.9*	*71.9*	*4.1*	*23.9*	**82.9**	*3.9*	*19.4*	*76.7*
Czech Republic	**4,701**	*4.5*	*39.6*	*55.8*	*7.8*	*48.8*	**67.6**	*3.1*	*37.9*	*59.0*
Denmark	**2,707**	*3.2*	*23.8*	*72.9*	*5.4*	*20.4*	**122.5**	*2.4*	*25.5*	*72.2*
Estonia	**594**	*6.2*	*32.5*	*61.3*	*10.0*	*45.9*	**46.6**	*4.9*	*27.6*	*67.5*
Finland	**2,365**	*5.1*	*26.2*	*68.3*	*9.0*	*25.2*	**113.8**	*3.5*	*31.1*	*65.4*
Manner-Suomi	2,351	*5.1*	*26.3*	*68.3*	*9.1*	*25.2*	113.6	*3.5*	*31.2*	*65.2*
Åland	14	*4.3*	*15.2*	*80.4*	*2.6*	*4.1*	154.9	*4.3*	*14.6*	*81.1*
France	**24,584**	*4.2*	*24.4*	*69.0*	*9.3*	*41.1*	**113.0**	*2.6*	*24.7*	*72.7*
Île de France	4,716	*0.4*	*16.6*	*82.3*	*9.2*	*41.6*	176.0	*0.2*	*17.1*	*82.7*
Bassin Parisien	4,431	*5.3*	*29.0*	*65.2*	*8.2*	*39.4*	99.9	*4.7*	*31.2*	*64.1*
Nord - Pas-de-Calais	1,522	*2.8*	*28.3*	*68.6*	*12.5*	*43.9*	90.5	*2.2*	*30.4*	*67.5*
Est	2,135	*2.2*	*33.1*	*64.3*	*8.3*	*33.5*	101.1	*2.2*	*32.6*	*65.1*
Ouest	3,591	*7.2*	*26.4*	*66.0*	*7.6*	*35.9*	98.0	*5.2*	*27.8*	*67.0*
Sud-Ouest	2,486	*8.4*	*22.7*	*68.4*	*8.9*	*41.1*	100.0	*4.7*	*24.2*	*71.1*
Centre-Est	2,792	*4.0*	*30.4*	*64.9*	*7.5*	*32.0*	110.7	*1.8*	*31.1*	*67.1*
Méditerranée	2,450	*4.4*	*17.5*	*77.6*	*10.8*	*45.0*	97.8	*2.9*	*18.8*	*78.3*
Germany	**35,927**	*2.4*	*31.4*	*66.2*	*9.7*	*50.0*	**108.7**	*1.1*	*28.8*	*70.1*
Baden-Württemberg	4,957	*2.0*	*39.2*	*58.8*	*5.6*	*41.5*	124.9	*0.8*	*37.7*	*61.5*
Bayern	5,823	*3.3*	*34.7*	*62.0*	*6.2*	*36.6*	126.3	*1.2*	*30.4*	*68.4*
Berlin	1,414	*0.6*	*18.4*	*81.0*	*17.5*	*50.2*	96.6	*0.2*	*17.4*	*82.4*
Brandenburg	1,102	*4.0*	*26.7*	*69.3*	*18.0*	*58.4*	73.4	*2.5*	*24.8*	*72.7*
Bremen	270	*0.7*	*25.8*	*73.6*	*11.1*	*54.0*	149.6	*0.2*	*29.4*	*70.3*
Hamburg	783	*0.8*	*19.5*	*79.6*	*9.4*	*44.7*	187.8	*0.2*	*18.7*	*81.2*
Hessen	2,727	*1.4*	*29.3*	*69.4*	*7.1*	*46.1*	134.1	*0.5*	*24.5*	*75.0*
Mecklenburg-Vorpommern	717	*5.7*	*23.0*	*71.3*	*20.1*	*57.6*	72.0	*3.9*	*19.1*	*76.9*
Niedersachsen	3,368	*3.8*	*30.5*	*65.7*	*8.4*	*53.9*	96.3	*2.4*	*30.8*	*66.8*
Nordrhein-Westfalen	7,475	*1.5*	*31.1*	*67.4*	*8.7*	*46.0*	109.1	*0.7*	*27.6*	*71.7*
Rheinland-Pfalz	1,792	*2.3*	*31.1*	*66.6*	*6.3*	*46.5*	96.2	*1.4*	*32.1*	*66.5*
Saarland	422	*1.7*	*30.4*	*67.9*	*8.1*	*49.5*	103.3	*0.3*	*31.3*	*68.4*
Sachsen	1,793	*2.5*	*32.2*	*65.3*	*17.6*	*58.5*	73.3	*1.4*	*27.7*	*70.9*
Sachsen-Anhalt	1,031	*3.7*	*30.2*	*66.0*	*19.6*	*63.6*	71.9	*2.4*	*26.6*	*71.0*
Schleswig-Holstein	1,238	*3.4*	*23.2*	*73.4*	*8.7*	*45.9*	99.0	*1.9*	*22.2*	*75.9*
Thüringen	1,016	*2.8*	*34.5*	*62.7*	*16.1*	*55.0*	72.7	*2.0*	*29.0*	*69.1*
Greece	**4,274**	*15.4*	*22.6*	*62.0*	*9.3*	*55.0*	**77.6**	*7.1*	*22.3*	*70.6*
Voreia Ellada	1,345	*22.4*	*23.6*	*54.0*	*10.6*	*57.1*	72.7	*10.9*	*22.4*	*66.7*
Kentriki Ellada	941	*26.7*	*20.5*	*52.8*	*9.0*	*58.9*	75.9	*11.4*	*27.8*	*60.8*
Attiki	1,554	*0.9*	*24.1*	*75.0*	*8.7*	*56.9*	82.3	*0.6*	*21.8*	*77.6*
Nisia Aigaiou, Kriti	434	*20.8*	*18.7*	*60.6*	*8.0*	*30.4*	80.2	*10.4*	*12.2*	*77.4*
Hungary	**3,922**	*5.3*	*33.4*	*61.3*	*5.9*	*41.1*	**58.6**	*3.7*	*30.2*	*66.1*
Közép-Magyarország	1,206	*1.6*	*26.0*	*72.4*	*4.0*	*46.3*	96.0	*0.9*	*23.0*	*76.1*
Dunántúl	1,260	*5.9*	*38.8*	*55.2*	*5.6*	*37.5*	51.8	*5.1*	*39.6*	*55.3*
Alföld és Észak	1,456	*8.0*	*34.8*	*57.2*	*7.6*	*41.1*	38.5	*6.9*	*33.0*	*60.2*
Ireland	**1,797**	*6.5*	*27.6*	*65.5*	*4.8*	*32.3*	**132.7**	*2.7*	*41.6*	*55.7*

Table **2.3** Economic statistics,[1] 2003 *(continued)*

	People in employment (thousands)	Percentage employment in[2]			Unemploy-ment rate (percentages)	Long-term unemployed[1] as a percent-age of all unemployed (percentages)	Gross domes-tic product per head (PPS)[3] EUR 25=100, 2002	Estimates[4] of the percentage of GVA in 2002 derived from:		
		Agriculture	Industry	Services				Agriculture	Industry	Services
Italy	**22,054**	*4.9*	*31.8*	*63.3*	*8.7*	*58.1*	*109.0*	*2.6*	*27.1*	*70.3*
Nord Ovest	6,573	2.7	37.6	59.6	4.2	40.8	134.6	1.7	31.5	66.8
Nord Est	4,785	4.7	37.1	58.2	3.2	22.5	130.1	3.0	31.7	65.3
Centro	4,494	3.3	27.7	69.0	6.5	56.8	119.5	1.8	23.1	75.1
Sud	4,249	8.5	25.8	65.6	17.0	67.3	73.8	4.3	21.3	74.4
Isole	1,954	8.2	21.8	70.0	19.2	64.5	74.0	3.7	17.6	78.7
Latvia	**1,007**	*13.7*	*27.0*	*59.3*	*10.5*	*41.4*	*39.0*	*4.6*	*22.6*	*72.8*
Lithuania	**1,433**	*17.9*	*28.1*	*53.9*	*12.4*	*48.0*	*42.4*	*7.0*	*29.9*	*63.1*
Luxembourg	**188**	*..*	*19.3*	*78.1*	*3.7*	*24.9*	*212.7*	*0.6*	*16.8*	*82.6*
Malta	**148**	*2.2*	*29.9*	*67.9*	*7.6*	*41.5*	*73.2*	*2.5*	*27.0*	*70.5*
Netherlands	**8,121**	*3.0*	*20.8*	*76.2*	*3.7*	*27.7*	*122.1*	*2.5*	*24.9*	*72.6*
Noord-Nederland	817	4.1	23.8	72.1	4.3	31.7	112.4	3.9	35.4	60.8
Oost-Nederland	1,722	3.6	22.7	73.7	3.5	26.0	103.1	2.9	26.4	70.7
West-Nederland	3,811	2.5	16.2	81.3	3.7	27.8	135.6	2.2	18.7	79.1
Zuid-Nederland	1,771	3.3	27.4	69.2	3.7	27.2	116.3	2.2	30.9	66.9
Poland	**13,617**	*18.4*	*28.6*	*53.0*	*19.6*	*56.0*	*45.6*	*3.1*	*29.7*	*67.2*
Centralny	2,957	18.5	24.4	57.0	17.6	62.2	60.0	2.7	26.0	71.4
Poludniowy	2,745	12.4	34.4	53.1	19.3	60.3	46.1	1.3	34.8	63.9
Wschodni	2,577	33.4	22.6	43.9	17.4	57.1	33.4	4.5	27.7	67.8
Pólnocno-Zachodni	2,204	15.1	30.9	54.0	20.6	46.1	45.3	4.5	29.7	65.8
Poludniowo-Zachodni	1,215	11.7	32.5	55.8	24.1	53.4	44.7	3.1	32.4	64.5
Pólnocny	1,919	14.7	29.5	55.8	21.9	54.4	41.2	3.7	29.4	66.9
Portugal	**5,118**	*12.5*	*32.3*	*55.2*	*6.3*	*35.0*	*76.7*	*3.6*	*27.3*	*69.1*
Continent	4,904	12.6	32.5	54.9	6.4	35.1	76.8	3.5	27.8	68.7
Açores	102	12.8	28.2	59.0	2.9	27.8	63.1	9.8	17.1	73.0
Madeira	112	9.5	26.6	63.8	3.4	31.7	89.6	2.8	17.1	80.2
Slovakia	**2,162**	*5.8*	*38.3*	*55.8*	*17.6*	*65.2*	*51.3*	*4.5*	*31.3*	*64.3*
Slovenia	**897**	*8.4*	*37.5*	*53.4*	*6.7*	*52.9*	*75.3*	*3.1*	*35.4*	*61.4*
Spain	**16,695**	*5.6*	*30.6*	*63.8*	*11.3*	*34.1*	*94.6*	*3.2*	*28.5*	*68.3*
Noroeste	1,705	10.4	31.3	58.3	12.1	43.0	78.3	4.7	31.3	64.0
Noreste	1,747	3.7	36.9	59.4	7.7	34.5	112.3	2.9	36.0	61.1
Comunidad de Madrid	2,352	0.6	23.8	75.6	7.2	35.5	126.7	0.2	22.6	77.2
Centro	1,978	10.0	30.7	59.3	11.9	33.4	78.5	7.3	29.5	63.2
Este	5,035	2.9	35.7	61.4	9.8	32.5	104.7	1.8	31.7	66.5
Sur	3,107	9.8	26.0	64.1	17.3	32.4	72.6	6.4	23.6	70.0
Canarias	771	4.6	20.4	74.9	11.4	32.1	89.0	1.9	19.4	78.6
Sweden	**4,314**	*2.5*	*22.5*	*74.9*	*5.7*	*17.7*	*114.8*	*1.8*	*27.5*	*70.6*
United Kingdom[5]	**28,696**	*1.3*	*23.3*	*75.2*	*5.0*	*21.6*	*117.8*	*0.9*	*23.0*	*73.9*
North East	1,103	1.1	26.8	71.9	6.4	22.8	90.9	0.6	30.3	69.1
North West	3,193	0.7	24.6	74.6	4.9	23.5	103.3	0.7	28.1	71.2
Yorkshire and the Humber	2,378	1.0	25.7	73.1	5.0	25.8	103.1	1.1	29.3	69.6
East Midlands	2,049	1.5	29.6	68.6	4.4	22.2	103.4	1.5	30.9	67.6
West Midlands	2,480	1.3	29.3	69.0	5.7	20.4	104.5	1.1	28.9	70.0
East	2,767	1.6	22.8	75.5	3.9	17.1	110.2	1.4	24.7	73.9
London	3,580	0.2	14.5	85.1	7.0	23.7	189.3	0.0	12.4	87.6
South East	4,170	1.1	21.1	77.7	3.8	15.4	128.0	0.7	20.3	79.0
South West	2,476	1.8	22.5	75.7	3.4	15.4	108.9	1.7	24.5	73.8
Wales	1,335	2.7	24.8	72.4	4.7	16.0	90.2	1.4	29.5	69.1
Scotland	2,424	1.8	22.9	75.1	5.8	22.5	112.3	1.6	26.2	72.2
Northern Ireland	740	3.7	26.6	69.1	5.6	41.4	92.6	2.2	27.5	70.3

1 See Notes and Definitions.
2 Data for the Netherlands are for 2002.
3 Purchasing Power Standard. See Notes and Definitions.
4 Total GVA data for United Kingdom includes extra-regio but this extra-regio data could not be allocated to the three sectors (agriculture, industry and services).
5 Government Office Regions for the United Kingdom equal NUTS 1 regions for the European Union. See Notes and Definitions.

Source: Eurostat; Office for National Statistics

Table 2.4　Agricultural statistics, 2003

	Agricultural land as a percentage of total land area[1]	Arable land as a percentage of agricultural land[2]	Average yield per hectare (ha)		Livestock per 1,000 hectares of utilised agricultural land[2]		
			Wheat 100kg/ha	Barley 100kg/ha	All cattle	All sheep and lambs	All pigs
EU25	..	..	**48**	**41**	..	..	..
EU15	..	..	**53**	**44**	..	..	..
Austria	*40.2*	*40.9*	44	42	608	96	962
Ostösterreich	*48.4*	*75.0*	41	39	429	59	883
Südösterreich	*31.5*	*25.7*	51	44	652	119	1,260
Westösterreich	*41.2*	*22.1*	56	48	727	114	853
Belgium	*45.6*	*59.8*	85	66	1,996	105	4,697
Bruxelles-Brussels	*1.2*	*100.0*	..	..	1,500	0	0
Vlaams Gewest	*46.8*	*67.3*	88	69	2.222	146	9,781
Region Wallonne	*45.1*	*53.6*	83	65	1,807	70	462
Cyprus	*14.7*	*63.8*	22	25	434	1,945	3,589
Czech Republic	*46.5*	*75.1*	41	38	389	28	902
Denmark	*61.3*	*92.6*	71	53	636	40	4,910
Estonia	*15.4*	*78.1*	22	19	372	45	486
Finland	*6.6*	*98.5*	35	32	435	..	621
Manner-Suomi	*6.6*	*98.8*	35	32	436	..	626
Åland	*12.4*	*68.5*	39	35	369	..	21
France	*53.7*	*61.8*	62	56	651	304	517
Île de France	*48.7*	*95.7*	67	60	57	22	19
Bassin Parisien	*64.1*	*71.4*	66	59	562	104	176
Nord - Pas-de-Calais	*68.7*	*77.4*	88	78	790	80	638
Est	*46.5*	*54.3*	54	54	756	163	145
Ouest	*68.5*	*78.0*	64	56	926	192	1,822
Sud-Ouest	*48.4*	*56.1*	46	39	637	743	237
Centre-Est	*45.2*	*35.9*	43	40	783	358	213
Méditerranée	*33.2*	*22.6*	31	31	146	660	53
Germany	*47.7*	*69.5*	65	51	802	125	1,548
Baden-Württemberg	*41.0*	*57.6*	59	51	784	..	1,585
Bayern	*46.2*	*64.4*	58	46	1,151	..	1,141
Berlin	*2.1*	*66.7*	..	..	222	..	56
Brandenburg	*45.6*	*77.6*	39	30	462	..	579
Bremen	*21.0*	*18.0*	..	..	1,270	..	56
Hamburg	*18.5*	*39.4*	..	..	518	..	102
Hessen	*36.3*	*63.2*	70	52	661	..	1,073
Mecklenburg-Vorpommern	*58.6*	*79.6*	64	54	419	..	510
Niedersachsen	*55.1*	*69.4*	73	55	1,016	..	2,977
Nordrhein-Westfalen	*44.0*	*70.7*	80	62	930	..	4,108
Rheinland-Pfalz	*35.7*	*55.3*	60	48	581	..	482
Saarland	*30.9*	*48.8*	54	45	757	..	268
Sachsen	*50.1*	*79.1*	49	43	571	..	702
Sachsen-Anhalt	*57.3*	*85.7*	64	52	312	..	702
Schleswig-Holstein	*64.8*	*61.6*	86	75	1,215	..	1,400
Thüringen	*49.6*	*77.6*	61	51	462	..	895
Greece	*29.5*	*56.7*	21	21	157	2,273	263
Voreia Ellada	*33.0*	*81.7*	23	27	237	1,578	226
Kentriki Ellada	*25.5*	*41.6*	21	21	96	2,750	355
Attiki	*33.5*	*10.4*	13	13	38	965	92
Nisia Aigaiou, Kriti	*29.9*	*18.2*	13	13	63	3,837	198
Hungary	*63.0*	*77.0*	26	24	126	221	838
Közép-Magyarország	*53.3*	*76.8*	18	16	135	181	560
Dunántúl	*59.6*	*80.3*	30	28	144	122	873
Alföld és Észak	*66.9*	*74.9*	25	21	113	289	848
Ireland	*62.2*	*27.1*	83	65	1,424	1,110	396
Italy	*49.0*	*51.6*	27	33	440	538	620
Nord Ovest	*38.8*	*53.0*	46	49	1,185	80	2,275
Nord Est	*43.8*	*60.8*	52	44	729	64	940
Centro	*43.2*	*60.5*	29	31	206	663	273
Sud	*56.5*	*51.1*	20	26	180	388	125
Isole	*63.3*	*36.4*	22	17	189	1,371	89

Table **2.4**   **Agricultural statistics, 2003** *(continued)*

	Agricultural land as a percentage of total land area[1]	Arable land as a percentage of agricultural land[2]	Average yield per hectare (ha)		Livestock per 1,000 hectares of utilised agricultural land[2]		
			Wheat 100kg/ha	Barley 100kg/ha	All cattle	All sheep and lambs	All pigs
Latvia	24.5	60.5	28	19	240	25	281
Lithuania	38.8	59.1	36	29	321	7	418
Luxembourg	49.2	48.1	61	54	1,453	59	597
Malta	34.2	86.3	..	..	1,662	1,377	6,769
Netherlands	51.5	56.5	87	63	1,954	616	5,804
Noord-Nederland	59.9	50.3	83	64	1,678	663	957
Oost-Nederland	50.1	50.0	88	57	2,667	429	6,719
West-Nederland	46.6	54.7	91	72	1,280	1,003	1,266
Zuid-Nederland	49.9	77.8	83	60	2,152	329	17,486
Poland	51.7	78.2	34	28	326	20	1,140
Centralny	57.8	76.4	30	26	431	11	1,123
Poludniowy	44.8	69.5	32	31	327	82	752
Wschodni	51.8	74.7	30	29	381	17	770
Pólnocno-Zachodni	49.7	82.6	31	24	265	18	1,663
Poludniowo-Zachodni	54.6	84.8	39	33	154	10	798
Pólnocny	50.2	80.0	38	27	307	18	1,399
Portugal	41.5	39.6	9	11	364	880	590
Continent	41.3	40.8	9	11	318	914	592
Açores	60.9	8.8	..	0	1,550	21	430
Madeira	7.8	43.4	13	0	656	984	3,443
Slovakia	45.6	61.7	30	30	265	146	645
Slovenia	25.1	33.8	34	29	883	208	1,219
Spain	49.8	52.1	28	28	260	933	955
Noroeste	31.8	25.9	31	18	1,256	336	644
Noreste	50.5	56.4	23	33	163	1,207	1,259
Comunidad de Madrid	43.1	46.4	28	27	250	450	46
Centro	56.2	61.0	30	27	208	1,047	548
Este	37.1	40.6	38	27	356	881	3,378
Sur	55.1	42.2	29	17	137	712	808
Canarias	11.0	21.2	10	10	288	835	810
Sweden	7.6	85.3	56	42	513	143	608
United Kingdom	67.8	38.7	78	59	641	1,497	295
North East	66.4	36.1	81	60	542	2,377	132
North West	62.4	24.0	71	51	1,110	2,333	178
Yorkshire and the Humber	68.4	58.7	82	62	555	1,411	1,161
East Midlands	75.8	73.8	75	59	452	753	364
West Midlands	70.3	54.2	77	57	863	1,849	239
East	71.4	86.1	79	61	167	180	781
London	7.9	54.7	0	0	..	..	..
South East	57.3	63.2	78	59	466	920	271
South West	72.7	43.7	74	54	1,058	1,382	263
Wales	67.0	13.6	74	53	894	4,621	32
Scotland	67.1	18.4	83	61	370	1,077	92
Northern Ireland	74.2	18.2	72	49	1,538	1,378	380

1 Data for Greece are for 2002. Data for Germany and the UK are for 2001.
2 Data for Greece are for 2002.

Source: Eurostat

Chapter 3 **Population and Migration**

Resident population

In the 23 years from 1981 to 2004 the UK population increased from 56.4 million to 59.8 million. Between 1991 and 2004 the highest percentage growth for the male resident population was in London (11.4 per cent), and it was in the East (7.1 per cent) for females. The North East showed the greatest percentage decline for males and females (1.3 and 1.9 per cent respectively). During the same period, the highest percentage growth in total resident population was 8.8 per cent in London and the greatest decrease was 1.6 per cent in the North East. Overall, in the UK growth was 4.2 per cent for all people, with the male population growing by 4.9 per cent and the female population growing by 3.5 per cent. (Table 3.1)

In the UK overall 28.6 per cent of residents were aged between 25 and 44 years in 2004. London had the highest regional proportion of residents between these ages with 36.5 per cent and Wales had the lowest at 25.9 per cent.

There were more females (30.6 million) than males (29.3 million) in total in the UK, with the greatest difference of 834 thousand in the 80 and over age group. For age bands below 20 years males outnumbered females by about 5 per cent in each band, falling to under 2 per cent between 20 to 24 years. In the 25 to 44 year band females outnumber males by just over 1 per cent and the gap widens as age increases. (Table 3.2)

Population density

In 2004, the London Borough of Kensington and Chelsea was the most densely populated local authority area in the UK at 15,174 people per square kilometre. At the other end of the scale, several Scottish Council areas had very low population densities, with Highland and Eilean Siar having the lowest at 8 and 9 people per sq. km respectively and the Scottish Borders at 23 people per sq. km. Eden in the North West is only slightly above this with 24 people per sq. km.

Outside Greater London, Portsmouth Unitary Authority in the South East had the highest population density of 4,683 people per sq. km, higher than Barking and Dagenham (Outer London) at 4,560 people per sq. km. (Map 3.3 and Regional Profile Tables)

Population by age

Northern Ireland had a higher proportion of residents who were under 16 than the average for the UK in 2004. North Down was the only Northern Ireland district council area to have below the UK average proportion of residents aged under 16 living in the area, with 18.9 per cent compared with 19.5 per cent for the UK overall. Conversely Newry and Mourne, also in Northern Ireland, had the highest proportion of its population aged under 16 years with 25.4 per cent. The City of Edinburgh had the lowest proportion of under-16-year-olds in the UK at 15.6 per cent in 2004. (Map 3.4)

Dorset in the South West of England had the highest proportion of pensioners (males aged 65 or over or females aged 60 or over), 27.1 per cent in 2004, whereas Inner London had the lowest proportion, less then half this amount at 11.4 per cent. (Map 3.5)

Socio-economic classification

In summer 2005, the largest single category of workers in the UK was employed in lower managerial and professional occupations. The South East had the highest percentage in this category at 24.7 per cent and Northern Ireland the lowest at 19.2 per cent. London and the South East, each with 14.2 per cent, had the highest proportion engaged in higher managerial and professional occupations. The North East and Northern Ireland shared the lowest proportion at 7.1 per cent for this category.

With 11.8 per cent the East Midlands had the highest percentage of workers in routine occupations and London the lowest at 6.3 per cent in 2005. Almost one-quarter of the workforce in Northern Ireland were long-term unemployed or had never worked, which was the highest proportion of any area in the UK. By comparison, the East had the lowest proportion of long-term unemployed workers at 14 per cent. (Web: PM1)

Ethnic groups

In 2001, London had the highest proportion (28.8 per cent) of non-white resident population in England and Wales. This was more than ten times the proportion in Wales which had the lowest proportion, 2.1 per cent, of non-white residents. The Indian ethnic group formed the highest non-white category in London with 6.1 per cent of the population. (Table 3.6)

Population change

The South West had the highest population growth of any region, 14.9 per cent between 1981 and 2004, and the North East had the greatest decline at 3.5 per cent. Over the same 23-year period, Milton Keynes in the South East region was the local authority with the greatest population growth, increasing by 72.1 per cent, and Glasgow in Scotland showed the largest decline in population at 18.9 per cent. (Map 1.49)

Population projections estimate that Milton Keynes will continue to grow by a further 6.8 per cent between 2005 and 2011, which is the highest projected population growth rate. Eilean Siar in Scotland is projected to have the largest decrease of 6.2 per cent over the same period based on the latest population estimates and projections. (Map 1.50)

Conceptions and birth rates

In 2003, London had the highest rate of live births at 14.9 per 1,000 population and the South West had the lowest (10.3 per 1,000 population). The highest death rates were in Scotland, Wales and the North East with 11.6, 11.5 and 11.3 per 1,000 population respectively, and the lowest death rate was in London at 7.8. The combination of high birth rate and low death rate mean that London had the highest rate of natural change in 2003 in the UK at 7.1 per 1,000 population. In contrast, the natural change in Scotland showed a decline 1.2 per 1,000 population in 2003. Both birth and death rates have declined overall since 1981. (Table 3.7)

Between mid-2003 and mid-2004, births (707.1 thousand) were higher than deaths (603.1 thousand) giving a UK net natural increase of 104 thousand. This was reversed for the North East (-1.1), South West (-3.1), Wales (-1.3) and Scotland (-4.0). The net migration and other changes (6.8 thousand) minus the net natural change (-1.1 thousand) gave the North East the lowest total change (5.7 thousand). London's resident population in 2003 was 7.39 million, rising to 7.43 million in 2004, and it had the greatest increase of all regions by 41 thousand. The North East increased the least, by 6 thousand, up to 2.55 million in 2004. (Table 3.8)

The North East had the highest rate of conceptions to women aged under 18, of 52.1 per 1,000 population in 2003, although this was lower than in 1999 (55.3 per 1,000 population). The South East had the lowest rate for conceptions to the under 18s for both years (33.1 in 2003 and 35.9 per 1,000 population in 1999). Over the same period, conceptions in total increased slightly in London (by 0.3 per 1,000 population), while all other areas decreased.

Yorkshire and the Humber had the highest proportion of conceptions leading to maternities for women aged under 18 (61.1 per cent in 2003) and London had the lowest (41.3 per cent). This corresponded to the number of abortions being the highest in London (58.7 per cent) and lowest in Yorkshire and the Humber (38.9 per cent).

The United Kingdom's Total Fertility Rate (TFR) dropped in 2004 to 1.77 per cent from the 1981 rate of 1.82. Total Fertility Rates are a guide to how many children might be born to each woman if her current fertility was maintained throughout her childbearing years. Northern Ireland had the highest TFR for 1981 and 1991 (2.60 and 2.16 respectively), but was replaced by the West Midlands with a TFR of 1.91 in 2004, while Scotland had the lowest rate of 1.60 for the same year.

The numbers of live births for 1981, 1991 and 2004 show similar patterns, whereby the highest birth rates occur to women between the ages of 25 to 34 and the lowest are at 40 and over. The highest birth rate in 1981 occurred to women aged 25 to 29 in Northern Ireland with 172 per 1,000 women. In 2004, the highest rate was 112 per 1,000 women aged 25 to 29 in the West Midlands, and London had the lowest rate for that age group at 79. However, for women of all ages London with 63 per 1,000 women had the highest rate and Scotland the lowest (51). For London, the South East, Northern Ireland and the East the highest birth rates were to women aged 30 to 34 in 2004. (Tables 3.9 and 3.10)

Death rates

The Standard Mortality Ratio (SMR) for both males and females in 2003 was highest in Scotland (116) and lowest in the South East and South West, each at 91. Standardised ratios make allowance for the differing age structure of the population. The lowest number of deaths in all areas occurred for males and females aged 5 to 15 years, whereas the highest number of deaths, unsurprisingly, was in the 85 and over age group. For this oldest age band, Scotland had the highest rate with 182.9 and London the lowest at 165.6 per 1,000 population.

The incidence of death for children under one year is higher than for age groups 1 through to 54 years of age. More deaths occurred for men than for women in all age groups. (Table 3.11)

Migration

The inflow of migrants was highest to the South East (223 thousand in 2004). Northern Ireland had the lowest number of migrants moving in (12 thousand) and moving out (10 thousand). For the same year, London's inflow was 155 thousand and outflow 260 thousand giving a net decrease of 105 thousand. Also in 1991, 1996 and 2001, London lost the highest number of people and the highest number of people moved into the South East. In 1991, 1996 and 2001, more people migrated into the United Kingdom than left.

In 2004, the most popular areas of destination for migrants within the UK after the South East were London (155 thousand), the East (146 thousand) and the South West (139 thousand). (Tables 3.12 and 3.13)

Marriage and cohabiting

Fewer marriages took place in Northern Ireland than elsewhere in the UK (7.8 thousand in 2003). The highest number of marriages took place in the South East (44.5 thousand). Both these figures represent around 1 per cent of the resident population aged between 20 and 60 years. The number of marriages solemnised in the UK in 1976 was 406 thousand; this had declined by almost 96 thousand to 310 thousand in 2003, a reduction of nearly 24 per cent. This pattern is evident in all other areas, with the number of marriages declining the most in the North East by over 40 per cent, and the South West declining the least by 6 per cent. (Table 3.14)

Cohabitation amongst non-married people aged 16 to 59 was the lowest in Northern Ireland (13 per cent) between 2000 and 2003. The South East and the South West shared the highest proportion at 30 per cent. Cohabitation for all other regions varied between 20 (Scotland) and 28 per cent (Yorkshire and the Humber). (Table 3.15)

Although household numbers increased for all regions between 1981 and 2003, the North East consistently had the lowest household numbers and projections and the South East the highest. The South East, with 2.64 million in 1981, increased the most by 0.76 million to 3.4 million in 2003. The North East increased the least by 0.11 million, a rise from 0.98 million in 1981 to 1.09 million in 2003. The pattern is repeated for household projections with the South East expected to reach 4.06 million by 2021 and the North East 1.17 million. (Table 3.16)

Households and marital status

The South East had the highest number of households (3.4 million in 2004) but the lowest proportions of lone parent households with dependent children (5.4 per cent) and with non-dependent children (2.5 per cent). Northern Ireland (667 thousand) had the lowest number of households and the highest proportion of married/cohabiting couples with dependent children (24.4 per cent), whereas Scotland had the lowest (19.3 per cent).

One-person households were most common in Scotland where they amounted to almost one-third (32.4 per cent) and were lowest in East Midlands (26.7 per cent). London had the highest proportion of households with two or more unrelated adults (6.1 per cent), a lone parent with dependent children (9.7 per cent) and households with two or more families (2.0 per cent.). (Table 3.17)

Table **3.1**   **Resident population[1]: by sex**

Thousands and percentages

	Population (thousands)				Total population growth (percentages)		
	1981	1991[2]	2001[3]	2004	1981 to 1991[2]	1991[2] to 2001[3]	1991[2] to 2004
Males							
United Kingdom	27,411.6	27,909.0	28,832.4	29,271.0	1.8	3.2	4.9
North East	1,283.1	1,253.7	1,232.1	1,237.4	-2.3	-1.7	-1.3
North West	3,357.6	3,311.4	3,288.5	3,325.0	-1.4	-0.7	0.4
Yorkshire and the Humber	2,395.0	2,398.5	2,421.0	2,459.9	0.1	0.8	2.6
East Midlands	1,894.8	1,968.4	2,061.0	2,108.9	3.9	4.6	7.1
West Midlands	2,555.6	2,563.9	2,588.8	2,620.2	0.3	1.0	2.2
East	2,386.0	2,511.3	2,647.7	2,696.3	5.3	5.4	7.4
London	3,277.3	3,296.4	3,597.1	3,673.4	0.6	9.1	11.4
South East	3,527.2	3,717.4	3,924.0	3,973.9	5.4	5.5	6.9
South West	2,118.5	2,269.6	2,405.5	2,458.9	7.1	5.9	8.3
England	22,795.0	23,290.6	24,165.6	24,553.9	2.2	3.7	5.4
Wales	1,365.1	1,390.7	1,408.7	1,434.3	1.9	1.2	3.1
Scotland	2,494.9	2,444.5	2,433.7	2,446.2	-2.0	-0.4	0.1
Northern Ireland	756.6	783.2	824.4	836.5	3.5	5.3	6.8
Females							
United Kingdom	28,945.9	29,529.7	30,281.1	30,564.0	2.0	2.4	3.5
North East	1,353.1	1,333.3	1,308.0	1,307.7	-1.5	-1.9	-1.9
North West	3,582.7	3,531.7	3,484.5	3,502.2	-1.4	-1.3	-0.8
Yorkshire and the Humber	2,523.5	2,537.6	2,555.6	2,578.9	0.6	0.6	1.6
East Midlands	1,957.9	2,043.0	2,128.6	2,170.8	4.3	4.0	6.3
West Midlands	2,631.1	2,665.8	2,692.0	2,713.8	1.3	1.0	1.8
East	2,469.0	2,609.8	2,752.8	2,795.0	5.7	5.5	7.1
London	3,527.7	3,532.9	3,725.3	3,755.8	0.1	5.0	6.3
South East	3,715.8	3,911.8	4,099.5	4,136.3	5.3	4.8	5.7
South West	2,264.9	2,418.6	2,537.9	2,579.3	6.8	4.8	6.6
England	24,025.8	24,584.4	25,284.2	25,539.8	2.3	2.7	3.9
Wales	1,448.4	1,482.3	1,501.6	1,518.2	2.3	1.2	2.4
Scotland	2,685.3	2,638.8	2,630.5	2,632.2	-1.7	-0.3	-0.3
Northern Ireland	786.3	824.1	864.9	873.8	4.8	4.9	6.0
All People							
United Kingdom	56,357.5	57,438.7	59,113.5	59,834.9	1.9	2.8	4.2
North East	2,636.2	2,587.0	2,540.1	2,545.1	-1.9	-1.8	-1.6
North West	6,940.3	6,843.0	6,773.0	6,827.2	-1.4	-1.0	-0.2
Yorkshire and the Humber	4,918.5	4,936.1	4,976.6	5,038.8	0.4	0.7	2.1
East Midlands	3,852.7	4,011.4	4,189.6	4,279.7	4.1	4.3	6.7
West Midlands	5,186.6	5,229.7	5,280.7	5,334.0	0.8	1.0	2.0
East	4,855.0	5,121.1	5,400.5	5,491.3	5.5	5.5	7.2
London	6,805.0	6,829.3	7,322.4	7,429.2	0.4	7.0	8.8
South East	7,243.1	7,629.2	8,023.4	8,110.2	5.3	5.1	6.3
South West	4,383.4	4,688.2	4,943.4	5,038.2	7.0	5.3	7.5
England	46,820.8	47,875.0	49,449.7	50,093.8	2.3	3.2	4.6
Wales	2,813.5	2,873.0	2,910.2	2,952.5	2.1	1.2	2.8
Scotland	5,180.2	5,083.3	5,064.2	5,078.4	-1.9	-0.4	-0.1
Northern Ireland	1,543.0	1,607.3	1,689.3	1,710.3	4.2	5.1	6.4

1 The estimated resident population of an area includes all people who usually live there, whatever their nationality. Members of HM and US armed forces in England and Wales are included on a residential basis wherever possible. HM forces stationed outside England and Wales are not included. Students are taken to be resident at their term-time address.
2 The mid-1991 population estimates for England and Wales shown in this table have been revised in the light of the results of the 2001 Census.
3 The mid-2001 population estimates for UK, England and Wales have been revised in the light of the Local Authority Population Studies.

Source: Office for National Statistics; General Register Office for Scotland; Northern Ireland Statistics and Research Agency

Table 3.2 Resident population[1]: by age and sex, 2004

Thousands and percentages

	0 to 4	5 to 15	16 to 19	20 to 24	25 to 44	45 to 59	60 to 64	65 to 79	80 and over	All ages
Males (thousands)										
United Kingdom	1,736.3	4,233.5	1,616.8	1,916.2	8,506.7	5,694.4	1,475.9	3,202.2	888.9	29,271.0
North East	68.8	177.4	72.1	85.9	333.3	254.5	63.3	146.4	35.7	1,237.4
North West	195.9	496.4	190.8	217.5	928.4	657.5	173.0	370.0	95.3	3,325.0
Yorkshire and the Humber	144.7	361.4	142.4	173.0	681.0	485.3	125.3	273.1	73.7	2,459.9
East Midlands	120.2	305.4	116.8	138.9	587.9	423.6	112.3	237.9	65.9	2,108.9
West Midlands	158.8	389.9	148.3	170.1	732.2	509.2	139.0	294.2	78.4	2,620.2
East	161.3	390.9	139.6	157.5	766.0	539.4	140.2	311.9	89.6	2,696.3
London	246.3	490.4	189.2	259.7	1,388.5	588.8	130.6	293.5	86.4	3,673.4
South East	235.0	579.6	214.0	244.9	1,131.3	795.4	201.8	438.7	133.4	3,973.9
South West	132.8	345.2	132.0	151.6	652.8	497.7	139.8	310.4	96.7	2,458.9
England	1,463.8	3,536.4	1,345.1	1,599.1	7,201.4	4,751.6	1,225.3	2,676.1	755.2	24,553.9
Wales	81.9	212.2	81.5	93.4	372.8	288.8	81.8	173.7	48.1	1,434.3
Scotland	134.5	344.2	135.4	164.3	694.5	503.3	129.5	274.4	66.3	2,446.2
Northern Ireland	56.1	140.6	54.8	59.4	238.0	150.8	39.4	78.0	19.3	836.5
Females (thousands)										
United Kingdom	1,652.7	4,023.7	1,524.4	1,883.6	8,622.7	5,823.0	1,545.0	3,765.7	1,723.2	30,564.0
North East	65.1	168.7	69.1	84.5	349.4	258.4	66.3	174.9	71.4	1,307.7
North West	186.4	471.3	184.1	220.2	957.8	668.6	179.8	440.3	193.8	3,502.2
Yorkshire and the Humber	138.6	346.1	135.3	168.6	699.7	491.5	129.1	324.4	145.7	2,578.9
East Midlands	113.6	287.8	110.0	132.0	595.6	425.3	114.4	270.6	121.4	2,170.8
West Midlands	151.7	371.6	139.7	166.7	737.0	512.1	143.1	339.8	152.1	2,713.8
East	153.0	373.0	131.7	151.1	771.3	549.5	145.6	354.1	165.8	2,795.0
London	236.9	469.2	176.5	277.5	1,323.9	618.6	144.4	347.5	161.3	3,755.8
South East	222.7	546.1	197.8	234.4	1,149.1	807.7	209.9	511.1	257.5	4,136.3
South West	126.0	327.1	122.0	137.5	665.0	517.2	145.1	357.1	182.2	2,579.3
England	1,393.9	3,360.7	1,266.2	1,572.6	7,248.8	4,848.9	1,277.7	3,119.8	1,451.2	25,539.8
Wales	77.2	201.2	77.4	92.7	390.6	298.7	84.5	202.1	93.8	1,518.2
Scotland	128.6	328.1	129.0	161.1	736.9	521.5	141.0	346.3	139.5	2,632.2
Northern Ireland	53.0	133.6	51.7	57.2	246.5	154.0	41.8	97.4	38.7	873.8
All people (percentages)										
United Kingdom	5.7	13.8	5.2	6.4	28.6	19.2	5.0	11.6	4.4	100.0
North East	5.3	13.6	5.5	6.7	26.8	20.2	5.1	12.6	4.2	100.0
North West	5.6	14.2	5.5	6.4	27.6	19.4	5.2	11.9	4.2	100.0
Yorkshire and the Humber	5.6	14.0	5.5	6.8	27.4	19.4	5.0	11.9	4.4	100.0
East Midlands	5.5	13.9	5.3	6.3	27.7	19.8	5.3	11.9	4.4	100.0
West Midlands	5.8	14.3	5.4	6.3	27.5	19.1	5.3	11.9	4.3	100.0
East	5.7	13.9	4.9	5.6	28.0	19.8	5.2	12.1	4.6	100.0
London	6.5	12.9	4.9	7.2	36.5	16.3	3.7	8.6	3.3	100.0
South East	5.6	13.9	5.1	5.9	28.1	19.8	5.1	11.7	4.8	100.0
South West	5.1	13.3	5.0	5.7	26.2	20.1	5.7	13.2	5.5	100.0
England	5.7	13.8	5.2	6.3	28.8	19.2	5.0	11.6	4.4	100.0
Wales	5.4	14.0	5.4	6.3	25.9	19.9	5.6	12.7	4.8	100.0
Scotland	5.2	13.2	5.2	6.4	28.2	20.2	5.3	12.2	4.1	100.0
Northern Ireland	6.4	16.0	6.2	6.8	28.3	17.8	4.7	10.3	3.4	100.0

1. The estimated resident population of an area includes all people who usually live there, whatever their nationality. Members of HM and US armed forces in England and Wales are included on a residential basis wherever possible. HM forces stationed outside England and Wales are not included. Students are taken to be resident at their term-time address.

Source: Office for National Statistics; General Register Office for Scotland; Northern Ireland Statistics and Research Agency

Map **3.3**   **Population density,¹ 2004**

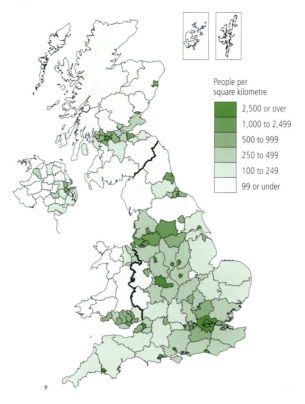

People per
square kilometre

2,500 or over
1,000 to 2,499
500 to 999
250 to 499
100 to 249
99 or under

1 See Notes and Definitions.

Source: Office for National Statistics; General Register Office for Scotland; Northern Ireland Statistics and Research Agency

Map **3.4**   **Population under 16,¹ 2004**

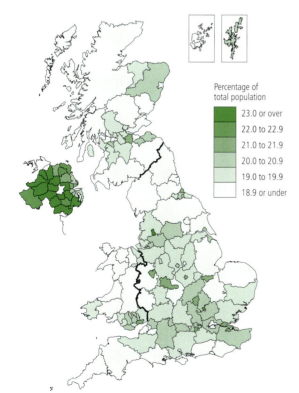

Percentage of
total population

23.0 or over
22.0 to 22.9
21.0 to 21.9
20.0 to 20.9
19.0 to 19.9
18.9 or under

1 See Notes and Definitions.

Source: Office for National Statistics; General Register Office for Scotland;
Northern Ireland Statistics and Research Agency

Map **3.5**   **Population of retirement age,¹ 2004**

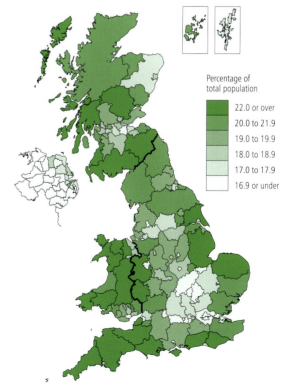

Percentage of
total population

22.0 or over
20.0 to 21.9
19.0 to 19.9
18.0 to 18.9
17.0 to 17.9
16.9 or under

1 Men aged 65 or over, women aged 60 or over as a percentage of the total
population in area. See Notes and Definitions.

Source: Office for National Statistics; General Register Office for
Scotland; Northern Ireland Statistics and Research Agency

Table **3.6**   Resident population: by ethnic group, 2001[1]

Percentages and thousands

	England and Wales	North East	North West	Yorkshire and the Humber	East Midlands	West Midlands	East	London	South East	South West	England	Wales
All people (thousands) (=100%)	52,042	2,515	6,730	4,965	4,172	5,267	5,388	7,172	8,001	4,928	49,139	2,903
White	91.3	97.6	94.4	93.5	93.5	88.7	95.1	71.2	95.1	97.7	90.9	97.9
White British	87.5	96.4	92.2	91.7	91.3	86.2	91.4	59.8	91.3	95.4	87.0	96.0
White Irish[2]	1.2	0.3	1.2	0.7	0.9	1.4	1.1	3.1	1.0	0.7	1.3	0.6
Other White	2.6	0.8	1.1	1.2	1.4	1.2	2.5	8.3	2.8	1.6	2.7	1.3
Non-White	8.7	2.4	5.6	6.5	6.5	11.3	4.9	28.8	4.9	2.3	9.1	2.1
Mixed												
Mixed White and Black Caribbean	0.5	0.1	0.3	0.4	0.5	0.8	0.4	1.0	0.3	0.3	0.5	0.2
White and Black African	0.2	0.1	0.1	0.1	0.1	0.1	0.1	0.5	0.1	0.1	0.2	0.1
White and Asian	0.4	0.2	0.3	0.3	0.3	0.3	0.3	0.8	0.4	0.2	0.4	0.2
Other Mixed	0.3	0.1	0.2	0.2	0.2	0.2	0.3	0.9	0.3	0.2	0.3	0.1
Asian or Asian British												
Indian	2.0	0.4	1.1	1.0	2.9	3.4	0.9	6.1	1.1	0.3	2.1	0.3
Pakistani	1.4	0.6	1.7	2.9	0.7	2.9	0.7	2.0	0.7	0.1	1.4	0.3
Bangladeshi	0.5	0.2	0.4	0.2	0.2	0.6	0.3	2.1	0.2	0.1	0.6	0.2
Other Asian	0.5	0.1	0.2	0.2	0.3	0.4	0.2	1.9	0.3	0.1	0.5	0.1
Black or Black British												
Caribbean	1.1	0.0	0.3	0.4	0.6	1.6	0.5	4.8	0.3	0.3	1.1	0.1
African	0.9	0.1	0.2	0.2	0.2	0.2	0.3	5.3	0.3	0.1	1.0	0.1
Other Black	0.2	0.0	0.1	0.1	0.1	0.2	0.1	0.8	0.1	0.0	0.2	0.0
Chinese	0.4	0.2	0.4	0.2	0.3	0.3	0.4	1.1	0.4	0.3	0.4	0.2
Other	0.4	0.2	0.2	0.2	0.2	0.3	0.3	1.6	0.4	0.2	0.4	0.2

1 Ethnic categories used are based on the 2001 Census and are different from those used in previous editions of Regional Trends. They are therefore not comparable with previous years. See Notes and Definitions.
2 Northern Ireland figures for White category include White Irish traveller.

Source: Office for National Statistics; General Register Office for Scotland; Northern Ireland Statistics and Research Agency

Table **3.7**   Live births, deaths and natural change in population

Thousands and rates

	Thousands					Rates per 1,000 population				
	1981	1986	1991	1996	2003	1981	1986	1991	1996	2003
Live births[1,2]										
United Kingdom	730.8	755.0	792.3	733.2	695.5	13.0	13.3	13.8	12.6	11.7
North East	34.2	34.7	34.9	30.1	27.0	13.0	13.3	13.4	11.7	10.6
North West	90.4	93.4	97.5	85.0	77.8	13.0	13.6	14.2	12.5	11.4
Yorkshire and the Humber	62.6	65.3	68.6	62.0	57.9	12.7	13.3	13.8	12.5	11.6
East Midlands	49.2	50.3	54.0	49.4	46.9	12.8	12.8	13.4	12.0	11.0
West Midlands	67.5	70.4	74.2	67.5	63.7	13.0	13.5	14.1	12.8	12.0
East	62.6	64.4	68.4	64.6	62.7	12.9	12.8	13.3	12.3	11.5
London	92.4	97.7	105.8	105.4	110.4	13.6	14.4	15.5	15.3	14.9
South East	89.0	92.9	99.8	95.3	91.8	12.3	12.4	13.0	12.2	11.4
South West	50.4	54.5	57.6	54.8	51.5	11.5	12.0	12.2	11.4	10.3
England	598.2	623.6	660.8	614.2	589.9	12.8	13.2	13.7	12.7	11.8
Wales	35.8	37.0	38.1	34.9	31.4	12.7	13.1	13.2	12.1	10.7
Scotland	69.1	65.8	67.0	59.3	52.4	13.3	12.8	13.1	11.6	10.4
Northern Ireland	27.2	28.0	26.0	24.4	21.6	17.6	17.8	16.2	14.7	12.7
Deaths[3]										
United Kingdom	658.0	660.7	646.2	638.9	612.1	11.7	11.6	11.2	11.0	10.3
North East	32.1	32.0	31.8	30.2	28.7	12.2	12.3	12.2	11.7	11.3
North West	86.6	85.5	82.7	79.5	74.9	12.5	12.5	12.0	11.7	11.0
Yorkshire and the Humber	59.1	58.9	57.3	55.4	52.6	12.0	12.0	11.5	11.2	10.5
East Midlands	42.8	43.5	43.9	43.9	44.0	11.1	11.1	10.9	10.7	10.3
West Midlands	56.4	57.7	57.0	56.1	55.6	10.9	11.1	10.8	10.7	10.4
East	50.7	52.4	53.3	53.8	54.2	10.4	10.5	10.3	10.3	9.9
London	77.6	73.9	68.9	65.4	58.0	11.4	10.9	10.1	9.4	7.8
South East	81.3	84.2	83.0	83.7	80.3	11.2	11.2	10.8	10.7	9.9
South West	54.4	56.4	56.2	55.9	55.9	12.4	12.4	11.9	11.7	11.2
England	541.0	544.5	534.0	524.0	504.1	11.6	11.5	11.1	10.8	10.1
Wales	35.0	34.7	34.1	34.6	33.8	12.4	12.3	11.8	12.0	11.5
Scotland	63.8	63.5	61.0	60.7	58.5	12.3	12.4	12.0	11.9	11.6
Northern Ireland	16.3	16.1	15.1	15.2	14.5	10.5	10.2	9.4	9.2	8.5
Natural change										
United Kingdom	72.8	94.3	146.1	94.3	83.4	1.3	1.7	2.6	1.6	1.4
North East	2.1	2.7	3.1	-0.1	-1.7	0.8	1.0	1.2	0.0	-0.7
North West	3.8	7.9	14.8	5.5	2.9	0.5	1.1	2.2	0.8	0.4
Yorkshire and the Humber	3.5	6.4	11.3	6.6	5.3	0.7	1.3	2.3	1.3	1.1
East Midlands	6.4	6.8	10.1	5.5	2.9	1.7	1.7	2.5	1.3	0.7
West Midlands	11.1	12.7	17.2	11.4	8.1	2.1	2.4	3.3	2.1	1.6
East	11.9	12.0	15.1	10.8	8.5	2.5	2.3	3.0	2.0	1.6
London	14.8	23.8	36.9	40.0	52.4	2.2	3.5	5.4	5.9	7.1
South East	7.7	8.7	16.8	11.6	11.5	1.1	1.2	2.2	1.5	1.5
South West	-4.0	-1.9	1.4	-1.1	-4.4	-0.9	-0.4	0.3	-0.3	-0.9
England	57.2	79.1	126.8	90.2	85.8	1.2	1.7	2.6	1.9	1.7
Wales	0.8	2.3	4.0	0.3	-2.4	0.3	0.8	1.4	0.1	-0.8
Scotland	5.3	2.3	6.0	-1.4	-6.1	1.0	0.4	1.1	-0.3	-1.2
Northern Ireland	10.9	11.9	10.9	9.2	7.1	7.1	7.6	6.8	5.5	4.2

1 Based on the usual area of residence of the mother. The United Kingdom figures have been calculated on all births registered in the United Kingdom including births to mothers usually resident outside the United Kingdom apart from the non-residents of Northern Ireland.
2 The total figure for United Kingdom does not include the total for 'Elsewhere' in England and Wales (i.e. 218 babies born in England and Wales in the year 2003 where the mother's usual area of residence is 'Elsewhere'.
3 Based on the usual area of residence of the deceased. The figures for the United Kingdom have been calculated on all deaths registered in the United Kingdom including deaths of persons usually resident outside the United Kingdom.

Source: Office for National Statistics; General Register Office for Scotland; Northern Ireland Statistics and Research Agency

Table **3.8**   **Components of population change, mid-2003 to mid-2004**

Thousands

	Resident population mid-2003	Births	Deaths	Net natural change[1]	Net migration and other changes[2,3,4]	Total change	Resident population mid-2004
United Kingdom	59,553.8	707.1	603.1	104.0	177.2	281.2	59,834.9
North East	2,539.4	27.6	28.7	-1.1	6.8	5.7	2,545.1
North West	6,804.5	79.5	74.2	5.2	17.4	22.6	6,827.2
Yorkshire and the Humber	5,009.3	59.3	52.8	6.5	23.0	29.5	5,038.8
East Midlands	4,252.3	47.9	43.2	4.7	22.7	27.4	4,279.7
West Midlands	5,319.9	64.9	54.7	10.2	3.9	14.1	5,334.0
East	5,462.9	63.8	53.8	10.0	18.4	20.4	5,491.3
London	7,387.9	111.7	56.5	55.2	-13.8	41.4	7,429.2
South East	8,080.3	93.3	79.2	14.1	15.9	30.0	8,110.2
South West	4,999.3	51.8	54.9	-3.1	42.0	38.9	5,038.2
England	49,855.7	599.8	497.9	101.8	136.2	238.0	50,093.8
Wales	2,938.0	31.7	33.0	-1.3	15.8	14.5	2,952.5
Scotland	5,057.4	53.6	57.6	-4.0	25.0	21.0	5,078.4
Northern Ireland	1,702.6	22.0	14.6	7.4	0.3	7.7	1,710.3

1 Net natural change refers to the excess of births over deaths.
2 Net migration and other changes includes changes in the population due to internal migration and civilian international migration. It also includes changes in sub-groups of the population such as armed forces. It can be derived by subtracting Net natural change from Total change.
3 For Scotland, net migration includes internal migration, civilian international migration, movements to/from armed forces and an adjustment for a recurring unattributable population change based on the 2001 Census which is assumed to be unmeasured migration. Other changes includes an adjustment for number of home and foreign armed forces and a prisoner adjustment.
4 Other changes principally includes changes in the number of armed forces stationed in Northern Ireland.

Source: Office for National Statistics; General Register Office for Scotland; Northern Ireland Statistics and Research Agency

Table **3.9**   **Conceptions[1,2] to women aged under 18[3]: by outcome**

	1999[4]				2003[5]			
	Percentage of conceptions				Percentage of conceptions			
	Leading to maternities	Leading to abortions	Total number	Rate per 1,000 population[3]	Leading to maternities	Leading to abortions	Total number	Rate per 1,000 population[3]
England and Wales	57.0	43.0	42,028	45.1	54.3	45.7	42,162	42.3
North East	63.1	36.9	2,666	55.3	58.5	41.5	2,613	52.1
North West	60.1	39.9	6,283	48.8	58.1	41.9	6,159	45.0
Yorkshire and the Humber	60.9	39.1	4,617	51.0	61.1	38.9	4,589	46.8
East Midlands	59.8	40.2	3,219	43.5	57.7	42.3	3,320	41.1
West Midlands	59.4	40.6	4,838	49.3	56.3	43.7	4,960	47.2
East	54.0	46.0	3,420	36.4	53.8	46.2	3,374	33.3
London	46.7	53.3	5,975	50.5	41.3	58.7	6,467	50.8
South East	54.4	45.6	5,058	35.9	51.7	48.3	4,932	33.1
South West	53.9	46.1	3,171	37.5	53.4	46.6	3,139	34.1
England	56.5	43.5	39,247	44.8	53.9	46.1	39,553	42.1
Wales	63.9	36.1	2,781	51.1	60.5	39.5	2,609	45.7

1 Conception statistics are derived from numbers of registered births and registered abortions. They do not include spontaneous miscarriages and illegal abortions. See Notes and Definitions.
2 Based on place of usual residence.
3 The rates for women aged under 18 are based on the population of women aged 15 to 17.
4 Rates have been calculated using the revised population estimates published on 7 October 2004.
5 Rates have been calculated using the 2003 mid-year population estimates released on 9 September 2004.

Source: Office for National Statistics

Table **3.10**   Age-specific birth rates[1]

Rates

	Live births per 1,000 women in age groups[2]							TFR[3]
	Under 20	20 to 24	25 to 29	30 to 34	35 to 39	40 and over	All ages	
1981								
United Kingdom	28	107	130	70	22	5	62	1.82
North East	34	114	128	60	18	4	62	1.79
North West	35	114	130	65	21	5	63	1.85
Yorkshire and the Humber	31	117	128	59	18	6	62	1.80
East Midlands	30	113	127	63	19	4	61	1.79
West Midlands	32	108	133	69	20	7	62	1.84
East	22	110	138	70	20	4	61	1.82
London	29	83	114	80	31	6	62	1.71
South East	20	97	138	73	23	4	59	1.77
South West	24	103	131	63	18	3	57	1.71
England	28	104	129	69	22	5	61	1.78
Wales	30	121	127	67	21	6	63	1.86
Scotland	31	112	131	66	21	4	63	1.84
Northern Ireland	27	135	172	117	52	13	86	2.60
1991								
United Kingdom	33	89	120	87	32	5	64	1.82
North East	44	102	120	72	23	4	63	1.81
North West	42	101	124	84	29	5	67	1.93
Yorkshire and the Humber	41	99	122	78	26	4	64	1.84
East Midlands	34	95	126	81	26	4	63	1.81
West Midlands	39	102	126	84	31	5	67	1.92
East	24	86	129	91	31	4	62	1.82
London	29	69	97	96	47	10	64	1.72
South East	23	78	122	95	35	5	61	1.79
South West	25	84	125	87	30	5	60	1.77
England	33	89	119	88	32	5	64	1.81
Wales	39	103	127	77	27	5	64	1.88
Scotland	33	82	117	78	27	4	60	1.69
Northern Ireland	29	97	146	105	46	10	75	2.16
2004								
United Kingdom	27	72	98	99	49	10	58	1.77
North East	34	78	101	83	37	7	54	1.71
North West	30	79	104	96	43	8	58	1.81
Yorkshire and the Humber	33	81	107	95	40	8	58	1.82
East Midlands	27	72	106	95	43	8	56	1.76
West Midlands	31	86	112	99	45	9	61	1.91
East	21	73	105	106	50	10	59	1.83
London	25	65	79	101	65	18	63	1.76
South East	21	61	96	109	54	12	57	1.77
South West	22	65	101	99	48	10	55	1.74
England	27	72	98	100	49	11	58	1.78
Wales	32	78	105	90	38	8	56	1.77
Scotland	26	62	89	90	43	8	51	1.60
Northern Ireland	23	63	110	113	56	9	61	1.87

1 Based on the usual area of residence of the mother. See Notes and Definitions for details of the inclusion or exclusion of births to non-resident mothers in the individual countries and regions of England.
2 The rates for women aged under 20, 40 and over and all ages are based upon the population of women aged 15 to 19, 40 to 44 and 15 to 44 respectively. See Notes and Definitions.
3 The total fertility rate (TFR) is the average number of children who would be born to a woman if the current pattern of fertility persisted throughout her child-bearing years. Previously known as total period fertility. See Notes and Definitions.

*Source: **Office for National Statistics; General Register Office for Scotland; Northern Ireland Statistics and Research Agency***

Table **3.11** Age-specific death rates: by sex, 2003[1]

Rates and Standardised Mortality Ratios

	Deaths per 1,000 population for specific age groups											SMR[3] (UK = 100)
	Under 1[2]	1 to 4	5 to 15	16 to 24	25 to 34	35 to 44	45 to 54	55 to 64	65 to 74	75 to 84	85 and over	
Males												
United Kingdom	5.7	0.3	0.1	0.7	1.0	1.7	3.9	9.9	27.0	73.6	191.9	100
North East	5.1	0.2	0.1	0.7	1.2	1.7	4.1	11.4	31.3	82.9	197.4	111
North West	6.5	0.3	0.2	0.7	1.1	1.9	4.5	11.1	30.0	79.1	197.4	109
Yorkshire and the Humber	6.1	0.3	0.2	0.7	1.2	1.7	3.9	10.0	27.0	76.7	192.6	102
East Midlands	6.4	0.3	0.2	0.7	0.9	1.6	3.5	9.3	26.5	75.8	194.5	100
West Midlands	7.9	0.3	0.1	0.8	1.1	1.8	3.9	10.2	27.6	75.6	194.0	103
East	4.7	0.2	0.1	0.7	0.9	1.2	3.1	8.2	22.8	67.1	192.8	90
London	5.7	0.2	0.2	0.6	0.7	1.7	4.2	10.6	27.0	70.7	174.0	97
South East	4.7	0.2	0.1	0.6	0.8	1.4	3.4	8.1	23.3	66.4	186.9	89
South West	4.5	0.1	0.1	0.6	0.9	1.4	3.4	8.0	22.8	66.7	189.0	89
England	5.7	0.2	0.1	0.7	0.9	1.6	3.8	9.5	26.1	72.4	190.0	98
Wales	4.7	0.2	0.1	0.9	1.4	1.7	4.2	10.0	28.2	77.0	198.2	104
Scotland	5.4	0.3	0.2	1.0	1.5	2.3	4.9	13.3	33.2	83.1	206.9	119
Northern Ireland	6.6	0.2	0.2	0.8	0.8	1.6	3.5	9.7	28.9	73.6	196.5	101
Females												
United Kingdom	4.8	0.2	0.1	0.3	0.5	1.0	2.6	6.1	17.1	51.8	166.5	100
North East	4.2	0.1	0.1	0.3	0.5	1.0	3.0	7.1	19.3	58.0	173.4	109
North West	5.4	0.2	0.1	0.3	0.5	1.1	2.9	6.8	19.1	57.0	175.0	109
Yorkshire and the Humber	5.5	0.4	0.1	0.3	0.5	1.0	2.3	6.2	17.5	53.6	163.7	101
East Midlands	5.5	0.3	0.1	0.3	0.4	0.9	2.5	6.0	16.9	51.9	166.6	100
West Midlands	6.6	0.3	0.1	0.3	0.4	0.9	2.6	6.0	17.1	53.7	167.7	101
East	4.2	0.2	0.1	0.2	0.5	0.8	2.4	5.2	14.8	48.3	164.5	94
London	5.1	0.2	0.1	0.3	0.4	1.0	2.5	5.8	16.9	49.3	162.0	97
South East	3.8	0.2	0.1	0.3	0.4	0.9	2.2	5.2	14.7	47.1	161.6	92
South West	3.5	0.2	0.1	0.3	0.4	0.9	2.3	5.0	14.5	46.1	163.0	92
England	4.9	0.2	0.1	0.3	0.4	0.9	2.5	5.8	16.6	51.1	165.7	98
Wales	3.5	0.2	0.1	0.3	0.5	1.0	2.7	6.7	17.9	53.0	168.0	103
Scotland	4.7	0.2	0.1	0.4	0.5	1.2	3.1	8.1	21.0	57.8	174.2	113
Northern Ireland	3.9	0.2	0.1	0.2	0.4	1.0	2.5	5.9	17.2	50.9	164.2	99
All people												
United Kingdom	5.3	0.2	0.1	0.5	0.7	1.3	3.2	8.0	21.8	60.6	173.7	100
North East	4.7	0.1	0.1	0.5	0.9	1.3	3.6	9.2	24.9	67.9	179.9	110
North West	5.9	0.3	0.1	0.5	0.8	1.5	3.7	8.9	24.2	65.7	181.0	109
Yorkshire and the Humber	5.8	0.4	0.2	0.5	0.9	1.3	3.1	8.1	21.9	62.9	171.6	102
East Midlands	5.9	0.3	0.2	0.5	0.7	1.3	3.0	7.6	21.5	61.9	174.7	100
West Midlands	7.3	0.3	0.1	0.5	0.7	1.4	3.3	8.1	22.1	62.6	175.2	102
East	4.5	0.2	0.1	0.5	0.7	1.0	2.7	6.7	18.6	56.1	172.8	92
London	5.4	0.2	0.2	0.4	0.5	1.3	3.3	8.1	21.7	57.9	165.6	97
South East	4.3	0.2	0.1	0.4	0.6	1.1	2.8	6.6	18.8	54.9	168.9	91
South West	4.0	0.2	0.1	0.4	0.7	1.1	2.9	6.5	18.5	54.5	170.7	91
England	5.3	0.2	0.1	0.5	0.7	1.3	3.1	7.6	21.1	59.7	172.6	98
Wales	4.1	0.2	0.1	0.6	0.9	1.4	3.5	8.3	22.8	62.7	176.4	103
Scotland	5.1	0.3	0.2	0.7	1.0	1.7	3.9	10.6	26.5	67.5	182.9	116
Northern Ireland	5.3	0.2	0.2	0.5	0.6	1.3	3.0	7.8	22.5	59.7	173.1	100

1 Based on the usual area of residence of the deceased. See Notes and Definitions for details of the inclusion or exclusion of deaths of non-resident persons in the individual countries and regions of England. The UK figures have been calculated on all deaths registered in the UK in 2003, i.e. including deaths of persons usually resident outside the UK.
2 Deaths of infants under one year of age per 1,000 live births.
3 Standardised Mortality Ratio (SMR) is the ratio of observed deaths to those expected by applying a standard death rate to the regional population. See Notes and Definitions.

Source: Office for National Statistics; General Register Office for Scotland; Northern Ireland Statistics and Research Agency

Table **3.12** Migration

Thousands

	Inflow				Outflow			
	1991	1996	2001	2004	1991	1996	2001	2004
Inter-regional migration[1]								
North East	40	39	40	41	41	45	43	39
North West	96	105	106	105	105	114	110	104
Yorkshire and the Humber	85	91	96	98	85	98	96	92
East Midlands	90	102	115	112	81	94	96	97
West Midlands	83	91	95	95	88	101	102	101
East	122	139	147	146	113	121	127	128
London	149	168	160	155	202	213	244	260
South East	198	228	224	223	185	199	216	208
South West	121	139	143	139	99	110	111	108
England	96	111	104	97	112	105	120	122
Wales	51	55	60	60	47	53	51	49
Scotland	56	47	56	57	47	54	50	45
Northern Ireland	12	11	13	12	9	12	11	10
International migration[2,3]								
United Kingdom	328	318	480	..	285	264	308	..
North East	7	3	11	..	4	5	6	..
North West	18	18	34	..	22	21	23	..
Yorkshire and the Humber	22	14	27	..	17	12	19	..
East Midlands	14	14	15	..	9	11	13	..
West Midlands	16	25	39	..	21	20	17	..
East	28	25	27	..	25	16	30	..
London	116	127	199	..	84	72	95	..
South East	53	46	65	..	43	56	50	..
South West	21	18	25	..	22	16	20	..
England	294	291	443	..	245	230	271	..
Wales	10	8	14	..	8	8	9	..
Scotland	21	16	20	..	27	22	24	..
Northern Ireland	4	3	3	..	5	4	4	..

1 Based on patients re-registering with NHS doctors in other parts of the United Kingdom. See Notes and Definitions.
2 Based mainly on data from the International Passenger Survey (IPS). Includes adjustments for (a) those whose intended length of stay changes so that their migrant status changes; (b) asylum seekers and their dependants not identified by the IPS; and (c) flows between the UK and the Republic of Ireland.
3 A consistent methodology (based primarily on the IPS) has been used to derive international migration estimates for the constituent countries of the UK and Government Office Regions within England. This methodology is currently under review as part of the National Statistics Quality Review of International Migration. Given the small sample size of the IPS for Scotland and Northern Ireland residents, adjustment of these estimates using data from administrative records is currently made for the purposes of population estimation in Scotland and Northern Ireland.

Source: National Health Service Central Register and International Passenger Survey, Office for National Statistics; General Register Office for Scotland; Northern Ireland Statistics and Research Agency; Home Office; Irish Central Statistical Office

Table 3.13 Inter-regional movements,[1] 2004

Thousands

					Area of origin								
	United Kingdom	England	North East	North West	York- shire and the Humber	East Mid- lands	West Mid- lands	East	London	South East	South West	Wales	Scot- land	Nor- thern Ireland
Area of destination														
United Kingdom[2]	.	122	39	104	92	97	101	128	260	208	108	49	45	10
England	97	.	34	83	83	89	87	118	244	188	92	47	41	8
North East	41	35	.	6	9	3	2	3	5	5	2	1	4	1
North West	105	88	6	.	18	9	13	8	14	13	8	8	7	2
Yorkshire and the Humber	98	90	9	18	.	16	8	9	12	12	6	3	4	1
East Midlands	112	105	3	10	17	.	16	19	14	19	7	3	3	1
West Midlands	95	84	2	12	7	14	.	8	13	15	12	8	3	1
East	146	138	3	7	7	13	7	.	67	26	9	3	4	1
London	155	143	4	12	10	10	11	28	.	52	15	5	7	1
South East	223	209	4	11	9	14	13	29	96	.	33	7	6	1
South West	139	124	2	9	6	8	16	14	24	45	.	10	4	1
Wales	60	58	1	11	3	3	10	4	6	10	11	.	2	0
Scotland	57	53	4	8	6	4	4	5	8	9	5	2	.	2
Northern Ireland	12	10	0	2	1	1	1	1	2	1	1	0	2	.

1 Based on patients re-registering with NHS doctors in other parts of the United Kingdom. See Notes and Definitions.
2 Total number of people moving from other parts of the United Kingdom.

Source: National Health Service Central Register, Office for National Statistics; General Register Office for Scotland; Northern Ireland Statistics and Research Agency

Table 3.14 Marriages[1,2]

Thousands

	1976	1986	2003
United Kingdom	406.0	393.9	310.0
North East	20.1	17.6	11.3
North West	50.3	46.3	31.0
Yorkshire and the Humber	36.3	35.2	23.9
East Midlands	26.7	27.4	21.3
West Midlands	36.6	35.2	25.3
East	32.2	34.7	28.8
London	58.4	47.5	41.4
South East	48.5	52.0	44.5
South West	30.1	32.5	28.3
England	339.0	328.4	255.6
Wales	19.5	19.5	14.5
Scotland	37.5	35.8	32.2
Northern Ireland	9.9	10.2	7.8

1 Marriages solemnised outside the United Kingdom are not included.
2 Region of occurrence of marriage.

Source: Office for National Statistics; General Register Office for Scotland; Northern Ireland Statistics and Research Agency

Figure 3.15 Percentage of non-married people aged 16 to 59 cohabiting, 2001/02-2002/03

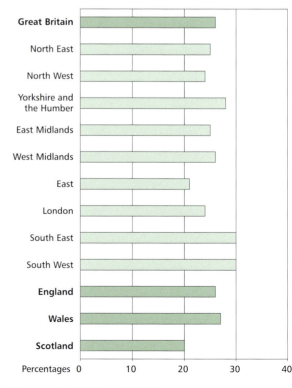

1 Combined data from the 2001/02 and 2002/03 surveys.

Source: General Household Survey, Office for National Statistics

Table **3.16** Household numbers and projections

Millions

	Household numbers[1]									Household projections[2]			
	1981	1991	1997	1998	1999	2000	2001	2002	2003	2006	2011	2016	2021
Great Britain	20.18	22.39	23.69	23.90	24.12	24.38	24.17	24.36	..	25.29	26.20	..	..
North East	0.98	1.05	1.08	1.09	1.09	1.09	1.08	1.09	1.09	1.12	1.14	1.15	1.17
North West	2.55	2.72	2.83	2.84	2.85	2.87	2.83	2.85	2.87	2.93	3.00	3.06	3.11
Yorkshire and the Humber	1.83	1.99	2.09	2.10	2.11	2.12	2.09	2.10	2.12	2.20	2.26	2.32	2.37
East Midlands	1.41	1.60	1.70	1.72	1.73	1.75	1.74	1.76	1.78	1.83	1.90	1.97	2.03
West Midlands	1.86	2.04	2.14	2.16	2.17	2.18	2.16	2.17	2.19	2.24	2.30	2.35	2.40
East	1.76	2.04	2.20	2.22	2.25	2.28	2.26	2.28	2.30	2.39	2.49	2.60	2.70
London	2.64	2.84	3.03	3.06	3.12	3.19	3.18	3.21	3.24	3.25	3.38	3.52	3.65
South East	2.64	3.03	3.27	3.30	3.35	3.38	3.35	3.37	3.40	3.57	3.74	3.91	4.06
South West	1.64	1.90	2.03	2.05	2.08	2.10	2.10	2.12	2.14	2.21	2.32	2.42	2.52
England	17.31	19.21	20.36	20.54	20.74	20.97	20.78	20.94	21.11	21.73	22.52	23.31	24.00
Wales	1.02	1.13	1.18	1.19	1.19	1.20	1.19	1.20	1.21	1.24	1.28	1.31	1.34
Scotland[2]	1.85	2.05	2.15	2.17	2.19	2.20	2.20	2.22	..	2.31	2.41	..	..

1 Estimates for England and Wales for 2001, 2002 and 2003 are based on mid-year population estimates which take into account 2001 census results. Estimates for 1982 onwards were subject to revision following revisions to population estimates, hence the apparent fall in numbers of households compared with those initially published.
2 Figures for 2006 onwards for England and Wales are 1996-based projections and do not take account of 2001 Census data. These are due for revision in February 2006. Figures for 2002 and onwards for Scotland are 2000 based projections.

Source: Office of the Deputy Prime Minister; National Assembly for Wales and Scottish Executive

Table **3.17** Households: by type, spring 2005

Percentages and thousands

	Types of households (percentages)								Total house- holds (=100%) (thou- sands)
			Married/cohabiting couple			Lone parent			
	One person	Two or more un- related adults	With dependent children	With non- dependent children only	With no children	With dependent children	With non- dependent children only	Two or more families[1]	
United Kingdom	28.7	3.0	21.9	6.3	28.8	7.2	3.1	1.1	24,834
North East	30.9	2.3	21.0	6.4	27.0	8.1	3.5	0.9	1,079
North West	29.1	2.2	22.7	6.3	26.9	8.7	3.3	0.9	2,802
Yorkshire and the Humber	29.4	2.8	20.6	5.4	30.6	7.3	2.8	1.1	2,136
East Midlands	26.7	2.5	22.2	7.0	31.1	6.6	2.9	0.9	1,749
West Midlands	27.1	2.2	23.2	7.3	28.5	7.4	3.1	1.1	2,156
East	26.8	2.3	22.7	7.0	31.6	5.5	3.0	1.0	2,287
London	29.3	6.1	21.6	5.3	22.6	9.7	3.4	2.0	2,946
South East	28.9	2.8	22.9	5.7	30.8	5.4	2.5	1.0	3,428
South West	27.5	2.9	20.9	6.0	33.2	5.8	2.7	1.0	2,127
England	28.4	3.0	22.1	6.2	29.0	7.2	3.0	1.1	20,711
Wales	27.3	2.9	22.3	6.3	29.6	7.0	3.5	1.0	1,217
Scotland	32.4	2.4	19.3	6.5	28.0	7.3	3.3	0.7	2,239
Northern Ireland	27.2	2.8	24.4	7.9	23.7	8.8	4.4	0.8	667

1 For some regions, sample sizes can be too small to provide a reliable estimate. See Notes and Definitions for further details.

Source: Labour Force Survey Household Datasets, Office for National Statistics; Department of Economic Development, Northern Ireland

Chapter 4 **Education and Training**

Pupils and teachers

Nearly ten million pupils attended United Kingdom schools in 2004/05. They were taught by 565 thousand teachers, giving a pupil to teacher ratio of 17.4. Public sector primary schools had 21.8 pupils per teacher while in public sector secondary schools the ratio was 16.2 pupils per teacher. In non-maintained schools the ratio was lower at 9.3 pupils per teacher.

Within the United Kingdom, Scotland had the lowest public sector ratios, at 17.6 pupils per teacher in primary schools and 12.7 in secondary schools. Northern Ireland also had lower ratios than the rest of the UK, with 20 pupils per teacher in primary schools and 14.3 in secondary schools. The ratios for English primary schools ranged from 21.7 in the North East to 22.9 in the East Midlands. For secondary schools the range of ratios was from 16.1 in the North West to 17.5 in the East. (Table 4.1)

Early years education

Nearly all three- and four-year-olds in England were receiving early years education in January 2005. Some double-counting from children attending more than one provider creates the impression that over 100 per cent of children in most English regions are in education. Participation rates were at their lowest in Northern Ireland where 73 per cent of three- and four-year-olds were in education.

Within the United Kingdom 65 per cent of three- and four-year-old children were taught in schools and 35 per cent by private and voluntary providers. The highest rate of education in schools, 86 per cent, was in the North East. The South West had the highest rate of voluntary and private sector provision at 60 per cent. (Web: ET1)

Class sizes

Very few Key Stage 1 classes (under 7 years) of primary school children had more than 30 pupils in 2004/05. For older (Key Stage 2) primary school children, the average class sizes were only slightly higher (average of 26.9 pupils, compared with 25.4 pupils for Key Stage 1).

However, the percentage of Key Stage 2 classes with more than 30 pupils showed considerable variability. Wales had only 4.1 per cent of classes above this size, while the comparable figure for England was 21.3 per cent. London class sizes were significantly lower than the other English regions, with only 9.8 per cent of classes having more than 30 pupils.

There was little variability between the regions of England and Wales in the average class size of secondary schools. Classes ranged from an average of 20.7 pupils in Wales to 21.8 pupils in the East Midlands, the East, London and the South West. The percentage of classes with over 30 pupils varied from 5.9 per cent in London to 10.0 per cent in the South West. (Table 4.2)

Free school meals

Nearly one in six children (17.7 per cent of pupils) in the UK maintained nursery and primary schools were known to be eligible for free school meals. Free school meals were actually taken by 14.5 per cent of pupils in these schools. Within the United Kingdom there was a considerable variation in the percentage of pupils eligible for free school meals. The South East, South West, East and East Midlands were below the UK average, ranging from 10.6 to 13 per cent. Eligibility exceeded 20 per cent of pupils in Scotland, Northern Ireland, the North West and the North East, and was highest in London at 26.6 per cent.

In maintained secondary schools, 14.8 per cent of the pupils in the UK were known to be eligible for free school meals. The distribution of eligibility was similar to that for nursery and primary schools. London had the highest proportion of eligible pupils, at 24 per cent, and the South East had the lowest at 8.5 per cent. (Web: ET2)

Pupil absence

The level of absence was higher in English secondary schools than in English primary schools; 8.1 per cent compared with 5.5 per cent in 2003/04. The secondary schools figure breaks down to 6.9 per cent authorised and 1.1 per cent unauthorised absence. Comparative primary school absence figures were 5.1 and 0.4 per cent respectively.

Unauthorised absences in primary schools were highest in London at 0.7 per cent. In secondary schools the highest level of unauthorised absence, 1.5 per cent, was in Yorkshire and the Humber.

The overall level of absence fell between 2003/04 and 2002/03. Authorised absence fell in all English regions. There was, however, a slight increase in unauthorised absence from secondary schools in England. (Table 4.3)

Examination achievements

In 2003/04, 54 per cent of pupils in the United Kingdom achieved five or more grades A*-C in GCSE examinations (or Scottish equivalent examinations) in their last year of compulsory education. Only 4 per cent of pupils did not obtain a graded qualification. Almost three-fifths of pupils in Northern Ireland achieved 5 or more A*-C grades; this was the highest proportion of any area. Scotland and the South East were the next highest.

Throughout the UK a markedly higher proportion of females, 59 per cent, achieved this level of qualification compared to 49 per cent of males. In the GCSE for English 65 per cent of females achieved a grade A*-C (or equivalent) compared with 50 per cent of males. In 'any modern language' females were again more successful, 45 per cent achieving the higher grades compared with 30 per cent of males. However, for mathematics and 'any science' the difference in achievement between females and males narrowed to 3 per cent. (Tables 4.4 and ET3)

Key Stage Assessments

Pupils are assessed formally at the ages of 7, 11 and 14 by a mixture of teacher assessments and by national tests in the core subjects of English, mathematics and science (and in Welsh in Welsh-speaking schools in Wales), though the method of assessment varies between subjects and countries. Northern Ireland has its own common curriculum, which is similar, but not identical, to the National Curriculum in England and Wales

At Key Stage 1 (age 7) the proportion of pupils reaching or exceeding the expected standard in English, mathematics and science showed little variation (from 82 to 91 per cent) in the English regions and Wales. A higher proportion of pupils in Northern Ireland (age 8), 95 per cent, reached or exceeded the standard in English and mathematics. Key stage 2 (age 11) results for England, Wales and Northern

Ireland showed a similar pattern but at a lower level; 71 to 86 per cent. The main difference between Key Stages 1 and 2 was that Northern Ireland figures for Key Stage 2 mathematics were in the same range as those for England and Wales. Results at Key Stage 3 (age 14) again revealed little variation across countries and regions. London had the lowest or equal lowest proportions of pupils reaching or exceeding standards at each of the three Key Stages. (Table 4.6)

Post-compulsory education

There was little variation between the regions in England and Wales in the proportion of 16-year-olds participating in post-compulsory education and Government-supported training, ranging from 76 per cent in Yorkshire and the Humber to 82 per cent in London in 2003/04. Comparative data are not available for Scotland and Northern Ireland. A similar pattern was seen for 17-year-olds where the proportions varied between 65 in Yorkshire and the Humber and 72 per cent in London.

Within the United Kingdom there was considerable variation in the balance between school and full-time further education for 16- and 17-year-olds. In Scotland 60 per cent of 16-year-olds studied at school with 15 per cent in full-time further education. In Northern Ireland 53 per cent of 16-year-olds studied at school with 25 per cent in full-time further education. For both England and Wales there was a much closer balance between school and full-time further education. (Table 4.7)

Further education

Just under two and a half million students from the UK were engaged in further education in England in 2003/04. Of these, around 30 per cent were involved at each of levels 1, 2 and 3 of courses leading to NVQ/GNVQ or equivalent academic qualifications. A further 5 per cent of further education students were studying at levels 4 or 5 and higher education courses. The remaining 7 per cent of students were taking 'other' courses.

The largest number of further education students were studying in London and the North West. London had the highest proportion, 18 per cent, of students studying 'other' courses. Yorkshire and the Humber with 7 per cent and the North West with 6 per cent had the highest proportions involved in levels 4, 5 and higher education. London had the lowest proportion studying at this level, 3 per cent. (Web: ET4)

Higher education

There were large variations in the proportions of the two million United Kingdom higher education students who studied in their area of domicile in 2003/4. At one extreme, 94 per cent of students living in Scotland studied in Scotland. Less than half this proportion, 44 per cent, living in the East of England studied in the East. However, a further 34 per cent of students living in the East studied in regions adjacent to the East. For a region surrounded by other regions, London, at 70 per cent, had a high proportion of resident students. The highest number of higher education students were domiciled in London, 14 per cent of the UK total. (Table 4.8)

Graduate destinations

In 2004, 60 per cent of the 188 thousand first degree graduates found employment in the United Kingdom. The North West had the highest proportion of students finding UK employment at 65 per cent, while the lowest proportion was 54 per cent of students from the East. However, the East had the highest level of graduates undertaking further study at 23 per cent. Northern Ireland had the highest level of graduates obtaining overseas employment at 5 per cent.

Of the graduates believed to be unemployed, the highest level was in London at 8 per cent in 2004. The lowest level was 5 per cent in Northern Ireland. Northern Ireland had the lowest level of graduates combining employment and further study at 7 per cent. The West Midlands had the highest level at 10 per cent. (Table 4.9)

Qualifications

In 2005, London had the highest proportion of any working population, 26 per cent, with a highest qualification at degree level or equivalent, compared with 18 per cent for the UK as a whole. The North East had the lowest proportion of its working age population qualified to degree level or equivalent at 12 per cent.

Scotland had the working population with the highest proportion of higher education qualifications below degree level as their highest qualification, at 13 per cent. This was also the case where GCE A level or equivalent was the highest qualification, at 29 per cent.

Northern Ireland had the highest proportion of its working age population with no qualifications, at 24 per cent. The lowest percentage with no qualifications was the South East at 10 per cent.

Two-thirds of 19-year-olds in England were qualified to at least NVQ level 2 in 2005. The proportion qualified varied between 63 per cent in each of Yorkshire and the Humber and the East Midlands and 72 per cent in the South East. In all regions a higher proportion of 19-year-old females were qualified to NVQ level 2.

In respect of economically active adults, 72 per cent were qualified to at least NVQ level 2 in 2005. This rate fell to 51 per cent for those qualified to at least NVQ level 3. A higher proportion of economically active male adults had achieved these qualifications than of female adults, in all regions. (Tables 4.10 and 4.11)

Training

Females of working age in the United Kingdom received more job-related training than males of working age in 2005 (19 per cent and 14 per cent respectively). The highest proportion of females receiving job-related training was in the East Midlands at 21 per cent. For males the highest proportion receiving job-related training was in the North East at 16 per cent.

Of the 283 thousand young people undertaking work-based learning in England and Wales in 2000/01 (the latest date for which data on outcomes are available), 52 per cent gained full qualifications. The proportion gaining full qualifications was highest in the South West at 57 per cent and lowest in Wales at 46 per cent. Six months after leaving learning 79 per cent of young people in the South East and South West were in employment. The highest proportions of leavers who were unemployed after six months were in Wales at 17 per cent and the North East at 16 per cent.

Of the 118 thousand adults undertaking work-based Learning in England and Wales in 2000/01, 41 per cent gained full qualifications. The proportion gaining full qualifications was highest in the East at 48 per cent and lowest in London at 34 per cent. Six months after leaving learning 49 per cent of adults in the South East and 48 per cent in Wales were in employment. The highest proportions of adult leavers who were unemployed after six months were in Yorkshire and the Humber at 53 per cent and the North East at 52 per cent. (Tables 4.12 and ET5)

Table 4.1 Pupils and teachers:[1] by type of school, 2004/05[2]

Thousands and numbers

	Public sector schools				Non-maintained schools[4,5]	All special schools	All schools
	Nursery schools	Primary schools[3]	Secondary schools	Pupil Referral units			
Pupils[6] (thousands)							
United Kingdom	101.9	4,896.6	4,001.9	..	638.1	106.4	9,759.4
North East	2.0	204.9	176.9	0.8	18.0	5.7	408.2
North West	3.6	587.2	468.5	2.4	56.2	13.9	1,131.7
Yorkshire and the Humber	1.9	430.5	348.5	1.4	34.0	7.6	823.8
East Midlands	1.4	353.2	295.8	1.5	38.1	6.0	695.9
West Midlands	3.3	460.1	377.3	1.2	45.6	11.8	899.3
East	2.1	431.8	388.1	1.3	63.8	8.8	895.9
London	5.1	600.7	422.7	3.3	137.1	11.7	1,180.6
South East	2.3	620.6	512.4	1.3	144.3	16.7	1,297.5
South West	1.3	380.3	325.8	1.3	61.6	7.1	777.4
England	22.9	4,069.2	3,315.8	14.5	598.5	89.4	8,110.3
Wales	1.3	259.3	214.6	..	9.7	3.8	488.7
Scotland[7]	72.7	398.1	318.1	.	29.1	8.5	826.5
Northern Ireland	5.0	170.0	153.4	.	0.8	4.7	333.9
Teachers[6] (thousands)							
United Kingdom	3.8	224.2	246.6	..	68.4	18.2	564.8
North East	0.1	9.4	10.9	0.2	1.6	0.9	23.2
North West	0.2	26.3	29.1	0.5	5.3	2.3	63.8
Yorkshire and the Humber	0.1	19.0	21.1	0.3	3.4	1.2	45.1
East Midlands	0.1	15.4	17.5	0.3	3.8	0.9	37.9
West Midlands	0.2	20.5	22.8	0.4	4.8	1.9	50.6
East	0.1	19.1	22.2	0.4	6.9	1.3	50.0
London	0.3	26.3	25.6	0.6	14.0	2.0	68.9
South East	0.2	27.7	29.6	0.4	17.4	2.7	77.9
South West	0.1	16.9	19.2	0.4	7.1	1.2	44.9
England	1.4	180.6	198.1	3.6	64.3	14.4	462.4
Wales	0.1	12.5	12.8	..	1.1	0.6	27.1
Scotland[7]	2.2	22.6	25.0	.	3.0	2.3	55.0
Northern Ireland	0.2	8.5	10.7	.	0.1	0.8	20.3
Pupils per teacher[6] (numbers)							
United Kingdom	26.5	21.8	16.2	..	9.3	5.9	17.4
North East	18.4	21.7	16.2	4.4	11.0	6.4	17.6
North West	16.3	22.3	16.1	4.7	10.7	5.9	17.8
Yorkshire and the Humber	16.9	22.6	16.5	4.6	10.1	6.1	18.2
East Midlands	15.9	22.9	16.9	5.8	10.0	6.4	18.3
West Midlands	18.9	22.5	16.5	2.9	9.5	6.4	17.8
East	15.9	22.7	17.5	3.0	9.2	6.8	17.9
London	15.7	22.8	16.5	5.2	9.8	5.9	17.1
South East	14.7	22.4	17.3	3.0	8.3	6.3	16.7
South West	16.7	22.5	16.9	3.1	8.7	5.9	17.3
England	16.5	22.5	16.7	4.0	9.3	6.2	17.5
Wales[8]	16.8	20.7	16.7	..	9.1	6.3	18.0
Scotland[7]	33.3	17.6	12.7	.	9.8	3.7	15.0
Northern Ireland[9]	25.7	20.0	14.3	.	8.4	5.8	16.5

1 Qualified teachers only in England and Wales. See Notes and Definitions.
2 Provisional.
3 For Northern Ireland, figures include the preparatory departments of grammar schools.
4 Excluding special schools.
5 Includes direct grant nursery schools, city technology colleges and city academies in England.
6 Full-time equivalents.
7 For Scotland nursery schools, full-time equivalent data are not available so full headcounts are used.
8 Pupils per teacher data for all schools excludes pupil referral units as information on teachers is not collected for Wales.
9 The 'All schools' pupil/teacher ratio in this table includes data for independent schools, but is more usually reported for grant-aided schools only in figures published by the Northern Ireland Department of Education.

Source: Department for Education and Skills; National Assembly for Wales; Scottish Executive; Northern Ireland Department of Education

Table **4.2**   Class sizes for all classes,[1] 2004/05

Numbers and percentages

| | Primary schools | | | | | | Secondary schools | |
| | Key Stage 1[2] | | Key Stage 2[2] | | All primary schools[3] | | | |
	Average number in class	Percentage of classes with 31 or more pupils	Average number in class	Percentage of classes with 31 or more pupils	Average number in class	Percentage of classes with 31 or more pupils	Average number in class	Percentage of classes with 31 or more pupils
Great Britain	25.4	1.9	26.9	19.5	25.9	11.8	21.7	..
North East	24.5	1.8	26.2	17.5	25.0	10.5	21.7	8.0
North West	25.2	1.8	27.3	25.1	26.0	14.5	21.6	8.8
Yorkshire and the Humber	25.5	2.7	27.4	23.5	26.4	15.1	21.6	7.5
East Midlands	25.0	2.4	27.5	26.8	26.1	16.2	21.8	7.7
West Midlands	25.7	1.9	27.3	20.8	26.1	12.4	21.6	8.3
East	25.6	2.3	27.4	19.8	26.3	11.9	21.8	7.6
London	26.9	1.4	27.2	9.8	26.8	6.6	21.8	5.9
South East	25.9	1.9	27.4	23.6	26.5	13.9	21.7	7.6
South West	25.6	1.6	27.4	25.6	26.2	14.7	21.8	10.0
England	25.7	1.9	27.3	21.3	26.2	12.8	21.7	7.9
Wales	24.3	2.3	25.0	4.1	24.2	5.1	20.7	9.2
Scotland[2]	23.3	0.9	24.8	13.6	23.8	7.7	..	..
Northern Ireland	22.9	1.9	23.8	6.0	23.0	3.6	..	..

1 Maintained schools only. Figures relate to all classes, not just those taught by one teacher. In Northern Ireland a class is defined as a group of pupils normally under the control of one teacher.
2 In Scotland primary P1-P3 is interpreted to be Key Stage 1 and P4-P7, Key Stage 2.
3 For all countries, pupils in composite classes which overlap Key Stage 1 and Key Stage 2 are included in the 'All primary schools' total, but are excluded from all other categories.
Source: Department for Education and Skills; National Assembly for Wales; Scottish Executive; Northern Ireland Department of Education

Table **4.3**   Pupil absence[1] from maintained primary and secondary schools

Percentages[1]

| | 2002/03 | | | | 2003/04 | | | |
| | Primary schools | | Secondary schools | | Primary schools | | Secondary schools | |
	Authorised	Unauthorised	Authorised	Unauthorised	Authorised	Unauthorised	Authorised	Unauthorised
England	5.38	0.43	7.21	1.07	5.08	0.41	6.92	1.14
North East	5.68	0.24	7.72	0.84	5.38	0.24	7.50	0.98
North West	5.20	0.39	7.39	1.07	5.04	0.40	7.28	1.16
Yorkshire and the Humber	5.34	0.45	7.35	1.47	4.98	0.41	6.92	1.49
East Midlands	5.35	0.40	7.07	1.27	5.03	0.38	6.83	1.39
West Midlands	5.71	0.38	7.24	0.98	5.28	0.37	6.86	1.00
East	5.37	0.38	7.10	0.87	5.11	0.36	6.85	0.95
London	5.58	0.79	6.92	1.34	5.20	0.74	6.51	1.32
South East	5.17	0.34	7.01	0.93	4.84	0.33	6.80	0.99
South West	5.27	0.32	7.38	0.81	5.06	0.32	7.01	0.94

1 Number of half-day sessions missed as a percentage of total possible pupil sessions. See Notes and Definitions.
Source: Department for Education and Skills

Table **4.4**   **Examination achievements:[1] by sex, 2003/04**

	Pupils in their last year of compulsory education[1]					Percentage of candidates[1,3,4] achieving:			Average GCE/VCE A/AS level point scores[1,7]
	Percentage achieving GCSE[2] or Scottish National Qualifications (NQs)[1]				Total (=100%) (thousands)				
	5 or more grades A*-C	1-4 grades A*-C	Grades D-G only[5]	No graded results		1 A level[6]	2 or more A levels	3 or more A levels	
Males									
United Kingdom	49.2	23.1	22.4	5.3	392.6	..	..	..	..
North East	44.9	22.3	26.7	6.1	17.2	8.3	88.7	67.1	238.7
North West	47.2	23.3	24.1	5.5	47.7	6.4	91.2	73.6	263.9
Yorkshire and the Humber	43.4	22.9	27.5	6.2	33.6	6.2	91.2	71.6	260.1
East Midlands	47.8	21.7	25.6	4.9	28.5	7.0	90.8	73.9	261.5
West Midlands	46.7	22.5	25.9	4.9	36.5	7.4	89.1	68.8	250.4
East	51.1	22.3	22.7	3.9	36.0	6.4	91.6	72.4	260.1
London	49.5	23.0	22.1	5.4	42.1	7.6	88.7	66.3	247.0
South East	52.9	21.1	21.9	4.1	52.9	6.5	91.3	74.5	267.4
South West	51.5	22.3	21.7	4.5	32.8	6.7	91.4	73.3	261.8
England	48.8	22.4	23.9	5.0	327.4	6.8	90.6	71.6	258.4
Wales	46.2	24.7	20.1	9.0	20.0	5.5	93.6	67.9	..
Scotland	53.9	29.5	10.9	5.7	32.2	..	..	..	..
Northern Ireland	53.1	24.7	17.0	5.2	12.9	3.2	90.6	79.8	..
Females									
United Kingdom	59.3	22.2	15.0	3.4	379.4	..	..	..	..
North East	54.6	22.2	19.5	3.7	16.8	5.6	92.8	73.8	260.9
North West	56.9	22.8	16.6	3.6	46.5	4.7	93.7	77.7	285.1
Yorkshire and the Humber	53.4	22.6	20.0	4.0	32.8	5.8	92.9	76.4	281.4
East Midlands	57.2	21.8	17.8	3.2	27.0	4.6	94.1	78.9	280.9
West Midlands	57.6	22.4	17.0	3.1	34.7	5.7	92.3	74.1	271.1
East	61.9	21.0	14.4	2.7	34.7	4.5	94.2	78.6	282.7
London	59.4	22.7	14.3	3.6	41.6	6.7	90.9	70.6	257.7
South East	62.7	20.7	13.9	2.7	50.6	4.3	94.5	79.7	290.6
South West	61.8	21.1	13.9	3.1	31.4	4.7	94.1	77.8	285.6
England	58.8	21.9	16.0	3.3	316.2	5.1	93.3	76.5	278.6
Wales	56.9	22.9	14.4	5.8	19.2	3.4	95.9	74.2	..
Scotland	63.0	25.4	7.4	4.2	31.2	..	..	..	..
Northern Ireland	66.0	21.2	10.4	2.5	12.8	2.6	93.0	83.3	..
All pupils/students									
United Kingdom	54.2	22.7	18.8	4.4	772.0	..	..	..	..
North East	49.7	22.2	23.2	4.9	34.0	6.9	90.9	70.7	250.6
North West	52.0	23.0	20.4	4.6	94.2	5.5	92.6	75.8	275.4
Yorkshire and the Humber	48.3	22.8	23.8	5.1	66.5	6.0	92.1	74.2	271.6
East Midlands	52.4	21.7	21.8	4.1	55.5	5.7	92.5	76.5	271.8
West Midlands	52.0	22.4	21.5	4.0	71.2	6.5	90.8	71.6	261.5
East	56.4	21.7	18.6	3.3	70.8	5.4	92.9	75.6	271.9
London	54.4	22.8	18.2	4.5	83.7	7.1	89.9	68.6	252.8
South East	57.7	20.9	18.0	3.4	103.5	5.3	93.0	77.2	279.5
South West	56.6	21.7	17.9	3.8	64.2	5.6	92.9	75.7	274.7
England	53.7	22.1	20.0	4.1	643.6	5.9	92.0	74.2	269.2
Wales	51.4	23.8	17.3	7.4	39.2	4.3	94.9	71.4	..
Scotland	58.4	27.5	9.2	4.9	63.5	..	..	..	..
Northern Ireland	59.5	22.9	13.7	3.8	25.7	2.8	92.0	81.8	..

1 See Notes and Definitions.
2 Figures for England and Wales include GNVQ equivalents. The England figures for 2003/4 include the wider range of pre-16 qualifications.
3 In schools and further education colleges in England and Scotland, and schools only in Wales and Northern Ireland. Figures for Scotland, however, exclude special schools as it is not possible to identify pupils in their final year of compulsory schooling
4 Including Vocational Certificates of Education (VCE) and equivalent in England, Wales and Northern Ireland.
5 No grades above D and at least one in the D-G range. Figures for Wales, England and the English regions include those pupils with only one GCSE short course. England figures for 2003/4 also include pupils who achieved any pass.
6 Including those with 1.5 A levels.
7 The average point scores for England are based on all schools and FE sector colleges, whereas those for the English regions are based on LEA maintained schools, city technology colleges (CTCs) and FE sector colleges only.

Source: Department for Education and Skills; National Assembly for Wales; Scottish Executive; Northern Ireland Department of Education

Map **4.5**   **Pupils[1] achieving 5 or more Grades A*-C at GCSE/Standard Grades 1-3 (or equivalent), 2003/04[2]**

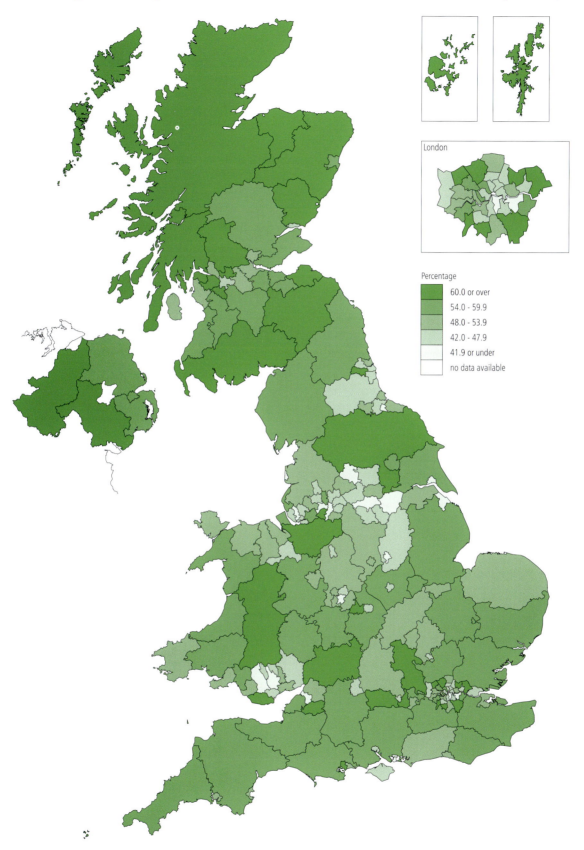

London

Percentage

- 60.0 or over
- 54.0 - 59.9
- 48.0 - 53.9
- 42.0 - 47.9
- 41.9 or under
- no data available

1 Pupils in their last year of compulsory schooling. Figures for England and Wales relate to maintained schools only, while figures for Scotland and Northern Ireland are
   for all schools.
2 Figures are presented by Local Education Authority in England, by unitary authority in Wales and Scotland and by Education and Library Board in Northern Ireland.

Source: Department for Education and Skills; Scottish Executive; National Assembly for Wales; Northern Ireland Department of Education

Table 4.6 Pupils reaching or exceeding expected standards:[1] by Key Stage Teacher Assessment, summer 2004[2]

Percentages

	Key Stage 1[3]			Key Stage 2[4]			Key Stage 3[5]		
	English	Mathematics	Science	English	Mathematics	Science	English	Mathematics	Science
England[6]	85	89	90	74	75	82	69	74	71
North East	85	89	90	73	76	83	68	72	67
North West	85	89	89	75	76	83	70	74	70
Yorkshire and the Humber	85	89	89	71	73	80	68	72	68
East Midlands	86	90	91	73	74	82	68	75	71
West Midlands	84	88	88	72	73	81	68	71	69
East	86	90	91	74	75	83	71	76	74
London	82	87	87	71	73	79	66	71	65
South East	86	90	91	75	76	84	72	77	75
South West	85	89	90	74	75	84	72	77	75
Wales	83	87	89	77	78	86	67	71	72
Northern Ireland[2,7]	95	95	..	74	77	..	74	72	72

1 For information about the National Curriculum in England and Wales and the common curriculum in Northern Ireland, see Notes and Definitions.
2 Data for Northern Ireland refer to 2003.
3 Percentage of pupils achieving level 2 or above at Key Stage 1.
4 Percentage of pupils achieving level 4 or above at Key Stage 2.
5 Percentage of pupils achieving level 5 or above at Key Stage 3.
6 Includes non-LEA maintained schools. These are not included in the regional figures.
7 In Northern Ireland Key Stage 1, pupils are assessed at the age of 8. Pupils are not assessed in science at Key Stages 1 and 2.

Source: Department for Education and Skills; National Assembly for Wales; Northern Ireland Department of Education

Table 4.7 16- and 17-year-olds participating in post-compulsory education and government-supported training, 2003/04[1]

Percentages[2]

	16-year-olds					17-year-olds				
		In further education[3]		Government-supported training (GST)[5]	All in full-time education and GST[6]		In further education[3]		Government-supported training (GST)[5]	All in full-time education and GST[6]
	At school[4]	Full-time	Part-time			At school[4]	Full-time	Part-time		
United Kingdom	38	34	..	..	..	29	30	..	..	..
North East	29	39	5	12	80	21	31	6	14	67
North West	24	44	4	10	79	20	36	5	11	68
Yorkshire and the Humber	30	36	6	10	76	24	30	7	11	65
East Midlands	38	31	5	8	77	30	26	6	10	67
West Midlands	32	38	5	8	78	26	31	7	9	66
East	40	34	4	6	79	33	27	5	8	69
London	43	35	4	3	82	34	33	5	5	72
South East	39	37	4	4	81	32	31	5	7	70
South West	39	35	4	6	81	32	30	5	10	71
England	35	37	4	7	79	28	31	6	9	69
Wales	40	33	7	8	81	30	28	8	11	69
Scotland[7]	60	15	21	..	..	26	18	21	..	..
Northern Ireland[8]	53	25	15	..	..	44	27	15	..	..

1 Provisional. Data for Wales refer to 2002/03.
2 As a percentage of the estimated 16- and 17-year-old population respectively.
3 Including sixth form colleges in England and a small element of further education in higher education institutions in England, Wales and Scotland.
4 For Scotland, includes both publicly funded and independent (non-maintained) primary, secondary and special schools. For publicly funded pupils, age is as at 31 March 2004, whereas for independent school pupils age is as at 31 December 2004.
5 For Scotland, reliable estimates of numbers in government-supported training are not available due to small sample sizes.
6 Figures for England exclude overlap between full-time education and government-supported training.
7 The estimates of 16-year-olds at school exclude those pupils who leave school in the winter term at the minimum statutory school-leaving age.
8 Participation in part-time FE should not be aggregated with full-time FE or schools activity due to an unquantified overlap of these activities.

Source: Department for Education and Skills; National Assembly for Wales; Scottish Executive; Northern Ireland Department of Education

Table 4.8 Home-domiciled higher education students:[1] by area of study and domicile, 2003/04[2]

Percentages and thousands

	Area of study												All students (=100%) (thousands)
	North East	North West	York-shire and the Humber	East Mid-lands	West Mid-lands	East	London	South East	South West	Wales	Scot-land	North-ern Ireland	
Area of domicile													
United Kingdom[3]	4.8	11.8	9.2	7.3	8.4	5.5	15.0	10.2	7.2	5.7	11.9	2.9	1,977.0
North East	74.4	5.2	8.9	2.6	1.4	0.9	1.5	1.3	0.7	0.5	2.5	0.1	80.1
North West	2.7	72.4	9.2	3.1	3.6	1.1	1.9	1.8	1.1	1.7	1.5	-	222.5
Yorkshire and the Humber	6.1	8.3	66.6	7.4	2.7	1.4	2.1	1.8	1.1	0.9	1.5	0.1	143.3
East Midlands	2.4	6.2	14.1	52.7	8.4	3.4	3.9	3.7	2.5	1.6	1.0	-	117.9
West Midlands	1.2	6.6	5.0	8.6	61.9	1.4	3.2	3.4	4.1	3.8	0.9	-	160.4
East	1.8	3.3	5.6	9.8	4.6	43.7	14.8	9.3	4.1	1.7	1.2	0.1	149.4
London	0.9	2.1	2.4	3.1	2.7	5.1	69.7	9.2	2.7	1.0	1.1	-	283.3
South East	1.5	2.8	3.5	5.4	4.0	4.1	16.5	49.2	8.6	2.9	1.4	-	240.0
South West	1.0	2.8	2.6	3.5	4.5	2.1	5.7	11.9	58.3	6.5	1.1	0.1	145.1
England[3]	5.8	14.1	11.2	8.9	10.2	6.7	18.5	12.4	8.6	2.3	1.3	0.1	1,580.4
Wales[2]	0.6	5.9	2.2	2.0	3.2	0.8	2.4	3.0	5.4	73.8	0.6	-	102.3
Scotland[2]	0.8	1.0	0.7	0.4	0.5	0.4	0.7	0.6	0.4	0.4	94.1	0.1	222.4
Northern Ireland	1.4	4.3	1.0	0.9	0.8	0.8	1.6	1.1	0.6	0.8	7.7	79.1	71.8

1 Including higher education students in further education institutions for England, Wales, Scotland and Northern Ireland. Excluding Open University students. These data are not comparable with figures prior to those shown in Regional Trends 35. See Notes and Definitions.
2 Provisional. Includes 2002/03 further education institution data for Wales and for Scotland.
3 Including students from the Channel Islands and Isle of Man and students whose region of domicile was unknown or unclassified.

Source: Department for Education and Skills; Higher Education Statistics Agency; National Assembly for Wales; Scottish Executive; Northern Ireland Department for Employment and Learning

Table 4.9 Destination of full-time first degree graduates, 2004[1]

Percentages and thousands

	UK employment only	Overseas employment	Combination of employment and study	Further study only	Believed unemployed	Not available for employment	Other known destinations[2]	Total of known destinations (thousands)
Area of study								
United Kingdom	60.3	2.4	8.7	16.1	6.5	5.0	1.0	187.9
North East	56.7	2.3	9.5	19.3	6.0	5.3	1.0	10.0
North West	65.3	1.5	8.4	13.6	5.9	4.4	1.0	21.4
Yorkshire and the Humber	61.7	2.5	7.8	15.7	5.7	5.4	1.2	19.0
East Midlands	63.1	2.0	7.8	14.2	6.6	5.3	1.0	16.7
West Midlands	60.5	2.1	10.1	14.5	6.8	4.8	1.1	14.0
East	53.8	2.7	9.0	22.7	6.9	4.1	0.8	9.5
London	59.7	2.2	8.9	15.4	7.8	4.9	1.2	25.1
South East	60.0	2.4	8.9	15.7	6.9	5.2	0.9	22.0
South West	60.6	2.6	9.0	14.3	6.6	6.1	0.8	15.2
England	60.8	2.2	8.7	15.6	6.6	5.1	1.0	153.0
Wales	57.8	2.7	9.9	17.6	6.4	4.7	0.9	11.4
Scotland	58.7	3.4	7.9	17.9	6.2	4.8	1.0	18.0
Northern Ireland	58.2	5.0	7.1	19.8	5.3	4.1	0.5	5.5

1 Home and EU students graduating from higher education institutions in 2004, with known destinations only. In addition there were 45,100 graduates with unknown destinations. Excludes non-EU overseas domiciled students.
2 Including students not in study who were looking for employment, further study or training.

Source: Department for Education and Skills; Higher Education Statistics Agency

Table **4.10** Population of working age:[1] by highest qualification,[2] spring 2005

Percentages

	Degree or equivalent	Higher education qualifications[3]	GCE A level or equivalent[4]	GCSE grades A*-C or equivalent	Other qualifications	No qualifications
United Kingdom	17.6	8.4	23.6	22.9	12.5	14.1
North East	12.4	8.2	25.3	25.4	13.0	15.2
North West	14.8	8.9	24.4	24.9	10.5	15.5
Yorkshire and the Humber	14.5	7.2	24.0	24.3	14.1	15.3
East Midlands	14.9	8.1	25.6	22.3	13.3	14.8
West Midlands	14.8	8.2	22.9	24.5	11.9	16.6
East	17.5	7.5	23.4	25.7	12.7	12.6
London	26.1	5.9	17.2	17.1	18.5	14.2
South East	20.5	8.7	24.4	23.9	11.8	10.0
South West	16.6	9.6	25.2	25.1	12.2	10.5
England	17.9	8.0	23.2	23.3	13.2	13.6
Wales	15.1	8.9	21.8	25.3	10.7	17.2
Scotland	17.6	12.8	29.0	17.9	8.4	13.8
Northern Ireland	15.0	8.0	23.4	21.9	6.3	24.2

1 Males aged 16 to 64 and females aged 16 to 59.
2 For information on equivalent level qualifications see Notes and Definitions.
3 Below degree level.
4 Includes recognised trade apprenticeship.

Source: Department for Education and Skills, from the Labour Force Survey

Table **4.11** Progress towards achieving National Targets[1] for England for young people and adults,[2] 2005

Percentages and thousands

	Young people			Adults						
	19-year-olds[3] qualified to at least NVQ level 2[4]			Adults qualified to at least NVQ level 2			Number of adults achieving NVQ level 2	Adults qualified to at least NVQ level 3		
	All	Males	Females	All	Males	Females	All	All	Males	Females
Region of residence										
North East	64	63	66	72	73	71	798	48	51	45
North West	64	60	68	73	74	72	2,217	51	54	48
Yorkshire and the Humber	63	61	66	70	72	68	1,607	48	49	45
East Midlands	63	58	68	71	72	69	1,409	50	51	49
West Midlands	64	59	69	70	71	69	1,702	48	49	47
East	69	65	72	70	72	68	1,846	48	51	45
London	65	60	70	72	73	72	2,559	55	55	54
South East	72	69	74	75	76	73	2,934	54	57	51
South West	70	67	73	73	75	71	1,723	52	55	48
England	67	62	72	72	73	71	16,796	51	53	49

1 These targets have superseded the former 2002 National Learning Targets. See Notes and Definitions for details of the targets.
2 Males aged 18 to 64 and females aged 18 to 59 in employment or actively seeking employment.
3 Those aged 19 in 2004.
4 Figures used to measure this target are from matched administrative data, replacing the previous Labour Force Survey (LFS) measure (see Statistical First Release 05/2005, on the DfES Research and Statistics Gateway), and are therefore not directly comparable with figures for 2004 and previous years.

Source: Department for Education and Skills

Table 4.12 Employees of working age[1] receiving job-related training:[2] by sex, spring 2005

Percentages

	Males[3]				Females[4]			
	On-the-job training only	Off-the-job training only	Both on- and off-the-job training	Any job-related training	On-the-job training only	Off-the-job training only	Both on- and off-the-job training	Any job-related training
United Kingdom	4.9	6.5	2.7	14.2	6.2	8.6	3.4	18.3
North East	5.7	7.4	3.1	16.2	8.0	8.1	4.2	20.3
North West	5.1	6.6	2.8	14.6	5.6	8.5	4.1	18.2
Yorkshire and the Humber	5.1	6.5	3.4	15.0	6.0	8.4	3.7	18.0
East Midlands	5.4	4.9	3.4	13.8	7.4	9.8	3.7	20.9
West Midlands	5.6	7.1	1.8	14.5	5.8	7.6	3.3	16.7
East	4.5	5.6	3.0	13.1	6.1	8.9	3.6	18.6
London	4.6	6.7	1.9	13.2	5.7	7.1	3.0	15.8
South East	4.7	7.4	2.8	14.8	5.7	10.4	3.2	19.2
South West	5.0	6.6	2.7	14.2	6.7	9.1	3.1	18.9
England	5.0	6.6	2.7	14.3	6.1	8.7	3.5	18.3
Wales	4.8	7.5	2.7	15.0	7.3	9.5	3.6	20.4
Scotland	4.7	6.0	2.7	13.4	6.6	7.7	3.5	17.9
Northern Ireland[5]	4.3	3.9	2.7	10.8	4.8	6.6	1.4	12.8

1 Males aged 16 to 64 and females aged 16 to 59.
2 Job-related education or training received in the four weeks before interview.
3 As a percentage of male employees of working age.
4 As a percentage of female employees of working age.
5 Estimates for 'both on and off-the-job training' are based on small sample sizes. They are subject to a higher degree of sampling variability and should therefore be treated with caution.

Source: Department for Education and Skills; Labour Force Survey, Office for National Statistics

Chapter 5 **Labour Market**

Labour force

The size of the labour force increased slightly in the United Kingdom between 2001 and 2005, rising by 516 thousand to 27.1 million people. Against this overall rise there was a reduction of 22 thousand in the number of males between 2001 and 2002. In every region there were more males employed than females, ranging from 11 per cent more in the North East to 25 per cent more in London.

The largest regional increase in female employment between 2001 and 2002 was in the North East, rising by 2.5 percentage points to 66 per cent. Wales showed a much smaller increase of 1.1 percentage points in male employment during the same period, but many regions showed decreases in rates.

Between 2002 and 2003, Northern Ireland showed a rise in male employment of 3.7 percentage points. Female employment in Wales rose from 63 per cent to 70 per cent during the same period.

Between 2003 and 2004 Northern Ireland had the largest decrease in male employment, 4.8 percentage points to 72 per cent, and there were only four regions showing an increase in rate. Female employment in the North East rose by 3 percentage points compared with the overall UK increase of 0.1.

Male employment in the West Midlands showed an increase of 1.8 percentage points between 2004 and 2005, compared with a decrease of 4.3 percentage points in Wales. The majority of the regions showed an increase in female employment, with the largest increase being in Northern Ireland of 0.9 percentage points to 62 per cent. Northern Ireland also showed an increased employment rate of 1.4 for all person employment compared with a decrease 1.6 percentage points in Wales.

Male employment over the last five years peaked in 2001 with a rate of 79 per cent for the UK, whereas for females the highest overall rate was 70 per cent in 2005. The employment rate for all people was highest in the South West at 79 per cent in 2005; 4.5 percentage points above the UK average. The South East and East also had rates in excess of 78 per cent. Northern Ireland, London and the North East had the lowest employment rates with 68, 69 and 70 per cent respectively. (Table 5.1)

The South West and the East had the highest economic activity rates of 82 per cent in spring 2005, only marginally higher than the South East. Apart from Northern Ireland (71 per cent) and Wales (74 per cent), London and the North East had the lowest activity rates of any region in 2005 at 75 per cent each.

The proportion of economically active people has declined slightly in London over the last two years from just over 75 per cent in 2003. Wales and the North West have also shown declines in both years, whereas other regions have shown increases. Looking back over the ten years since spring 1995, activity rates in London showed a reduction of 1.7 percentage points compared with an increase of 2.3 percentage points in Scotland.

Between 2004 and 2005 the percentage of employees in full-time work has increased in most areas by an average of 0.4 percentage points. However there were reductions of 0.9 percentage points in Wales, 0.7 in East Midlands and 0.6 points in London. (Table 5.3)

In most regions there are only slightly fewer employee jobs for females than for males. However, in the South West there were 26 thousand more female jobs in 2004. Northern Ireland and Scotland also had more jobs for females than males, with 19 and 7 thousand more respectively, in 2004.

The number of self-employed males was on average one-fifth of the number of employee jobs in each region, rising to 27 per cent in Northern Ireland in 2004. Self-employed women accounted for less than half the number of self-employed males in each region. Northern Ireland had the lowest number of self-employed females with 20 thousand in 2004 – only 22 per cent of the number of self-employed males. The North West was the only region where the number of females self-employed had continued to grow in the last three years, to 112 thousand in 2004. (Table 5.4)

Part-time working, flexible working and second jobs

The percentages of women who worked part-time were considerably higher than for men in spring 2005. In every region except London, the proportion of females in part-time work was at least four times the proportion of males, while in London this ratio was less than three. Northern Ireland had the lowest percentage of male workers who were part-time with 7 per cent, whereas 38 per cent of females in the province worked part-time. The South West had the highest percentage of part-time workers for both sexes (12 per cent for men and 50 per cent for women). (Figure 5.6)

The major reason given by both sexes for working part-time was that they did not want a full-time job, although the percentages of people with this reason were much higher for females than for males across all regions in spring 2005. The second most common reason for working part-time was student status, although the percentages were much higher for males than females in this category (32 per cent of males compared with 12 per cent of females in the UK overall).

The lowest percentage of females who were unable to find a full-time job was in the East (3.7 per cent). By contrast, one in ten females in Wales were working part-time because they could not find a full-time job, and this was the highest proportion in spring 2005. The South East had the lowest proportion of males (11 per cent) who were working part-time because they were unable to find a full-time job; half the rate of London. (Table 5.7)

The South West is a region where over one-fifth (21 per cent) of workers are employed part-time. The high proportion of part-timers reflects the nature of the population and labour market in that area. (Table 5.3)

The North East had the highest proportion of employees with flexible working patterns for both males and female in spring 2005 (22 per cent and 34 per cent respectively). This contrasted with the East Midlands, which had the lowest proportion of male employees at 14 per cent, and Northern Ireland, which had the lowest proportion at 25 per cent of female employees with flexible working patterns. (Figure 5.8)

Over one million people in the UK had a second job in spring 2005. As might be expected, the proportions were higher for females than males, ranging from 6.3 per cent of females in South West to 3.3 per cent in Northern Ireland. By comparison, 3.7 per cent of males in the South West had a second job, with the lowest proportion of 2.3 per cent being in the East Midlands. (Table 5.9)

Disputes

After a dip in 2003, the number of working days lost to labour disputes rose again to a UK average of 34 days per 1,000 employees in 2004. Within this overall position, Scotland had by far the highest rate of 160 days, with next highest being

Northern Ireland with 99 days per 1,000 employees. The fewest number of days lost to disputes in 2004 was in the East of England where only 11 days were lost per 1,000 employees. (Table 5.11)

Median earnings

The highest gross weekly earnings were for males in the financial intermediation sector in April 2005, amounting to £670 per week for the UK overall. In London earnings reached over £1,000 per week, with Wales having the lowest earnings in this sector at £409 for males and £299 for females. These are median values which give a truer reflection of typical values as the effects of very high or very low earners are minimised. A median value is one in which 50 per cent of a given population is below this value and 50 per cent are above.

In previous editions of Regional Trends, means have been quoted as the measure of average. To aid comparison, both means and medians have been included for the all industry totals on Table 5.12. The industry breakdown uses median values. The regional analysis in this table is based on where people work and is therefore different from figures shown in the Regional Profiles, which reflect where people live.

In each industry sector males earn considerably more than females, although the size of the gap is narrower, averaging £50 per week, in hotels and restaurants, where the earnings were lowest. In 2005, earnings in the hotel and restaurant sector were on average £296 per week for males and £245 for females; 60 per cent of the all-industry average. (Table 5.12)

Average earnings continued to rise in all areas between 2002 and 2005. In Northern Ireland average earnings as measured by median values have increased the most for females (£56 per week); this represents more than one-sixth of the 2002 median value. The greatest increase for males was seen in London at £58 per week, although this is a much lower percentage rise than some other regions.

In 2005, median values show that male full-time employees continue to earn more than their full-time female equivalents in every region and country within the UK. The East and South East had the largest differences (of £124.30 and £128.30 per week respectively) in median earnings between the sexes and Scotland and Northern Ireland showed the least difference (£85.70 and £53.70 respectively).

Over the last three years the differential between males and females remained virtually unchanged at the UK level, with a mean difference of over £130 per week. Even when using a median measure (which is less impacted by extremely high salaries) the difference overall is almost £100 per week. The gap has narrowed in some areas but widened on both measures in London and Yorkshire and the Humber.

Average differences between males and females in London and the South East were more than £170 per week in 2005.

Female full-time employees in the East Midlands also earned a similar amount to those in the West Midlands in 2005 (£343.40 compared with £345.50 per week). However male full-time employees earn more in the East Midlands (£455.30 compared with £444.10 per week in the West Midlands). (Key Statistics in Regional Profiles and LM1)

Unemployment

London had the highest unemployment rate for the last three years with 6.8 per cent in 2003, 6.6 per cent in 2004 and 6.9 per cent in 2005. Prior to this period the North East was the region with the highest rates. The South West had the lowest rate in each of the last three years, culminating in 3.3 per cent in spring 2005.

In all areas unemployment was highest in the 16- to 24-year-old age group. In London 18.9 per cent of this age group were unemployed, and the North East (16.2 per cent) and Scotland (13.9 per cent) had the next highest rates of youth unemployment. For some regions unemployment covering 16- to 24-year-olds was as much as three times the rate for the 25 to 34 age group. (Tables 5.13 and 5.17)

Northern Ireland and London had the highest proportion of males unemployed for two years or more. In each area, males unemployed for this length of time contributed more than 1 percentage point to the overall rates of 5.5 per cent in Northern Ireland and 7.2 per cent in London.

In all regions short-term unemployment of less than six months contributed the most to the overall unemployment rate for both males and females. Males unemployed for less than six months ranged from 1.7 per cent in Northern Ireland to 3.8 per cent in London and Yorkshire and the Humber. For females the range was slightly narrower; from 2.1 per cent in Northern Ireland to 3.7 per cent in the North East. (Table 5.18)

London had the highest unemployment rate in spring 2005 for people with a degree or equivalent qualification at 3.6 per cent, followed by the North East at 3.3 per cent. London also had the highest unemployment percentage rates for people with higher education qualifications below degree level, GCE A levels or equivalent and GCSE grades A*-C or equivalent (5.1, 5.8 and 10.0 per cent respectively). Each of these was well above the UK rates of 2.8, 3.4 and 5.7 per cent respectively. London also had, at 13.6 per cent, the highest percentage of unemployed who had no qualifications. (Table 5.19)

Table 5.1 Labour force and employment rates[1]

Thousands and percentages

	Labour force (thousands)					Employment rates[2] (percentages)				
	2001	2002	2003	2004	2005	2001	2002	2003	2004	2005
Males										
United Kingdom	14,524	14,502	14,635	14,700	14,702	79.1	78.6	78.9	78.9	78.6
North East	565	547	560	554	560	72.2	69.9	71.9	71.2	71.9
North West	1,584	1,558	1,617	1,611	1,601	76.1	74.8	77.1	76.6	76.0
Yorkshire and the Humber	1,182	1,196	1,218	1,232	1,222	76.7	77.2	78.0	78.6	77.7
East Midlands	1,056	1,069	1,069	1,073	1,068	80.4	80.8	80.9	80.9	80.2
West Midlands	1,298	1,307	1,293	1,287	1,318	79.1	79.3	78.4	77.9	79.7
East	1,426	1,420	1,408	1,412	1,422	84.8	84.2	83.6	83.5	83.7
London	1,800	1,814	1,836	1,879	1,857	77.3	76.7	75.9	76.7	75.1
South East	2,133	2,121	2,091	2,104	2,111	85.4	84.8	83.6	83.6	83.3
South West	1,239	1,234	1,234	1,248	1,260	82.7	82.0	81.8	82.3	82.5
England	12,285	12,267	12,328	12,400	12,418	79.9	79.4	79.4	79.5	79.2
Wales	638	650	664	690	654	72.1	73.2	74.5	77.1	72.8
Scotland	1,218	1,203	1,238	1,228	1,235	76.5	75.5	77.7	77.1	77.6
Northern Ireland	383	381	404	382	395	73.6	72.6	76.3	71.5	73.4
Females										
United Kingdom	12,065	12,170	12,256	12,315	12,405	69.3	69.5	69.7	69.8	70.0
North East	473	493	474	497	504	63.8	66.3	63.5	66.5	67.5
North West	1,363	1,361	1,376	1,381	1,386	69.0	68.5	69.2	69.5	69.6
Yorkshire and the Humber	1,004	989	1,014	1,024	1,024	69.1	67.6	69.2	69.7	69.6
East Midlands	856	881	876	905	898	70.0	71.4	70.3	72.2	71.5
West Midlands	1,044	1,049	1,060	1,067	1,065	68.4	68.2	68.8	69.1	69.1
East	1,158	1,155	1,166	1,194	1,189	73.8	73.3	72.9	73.9	73.3
London	1,487	1,509	1,468	1,467	1,477	64.4	64.5	63.5	63.4	63.1
South East	1,743	1,755	1,777	1,744	1,782	74.4	74.6	74.6	72.5	73.6
South West	1,039	1,059	1,057	1,060	1,081	74.3	75.3	74.3	74.0	75.1
England	10,167	10,250	10,267	10,339	10,405	69.9	70.0	69.8	70.0	70.2
Wales	530	532	596	573	585	63.3	62.9	70.3	67.4	68.7
Scotland	1,070	1,079	1,081	1,091	1,096	69.9	70.4	70.6	71.2	71.6
Northern Ireland	298	308	312	312	318	59.9	61.6	61.9	61.5	62.4
All people										
United Kingdom	26,590	26,671	26,891	27,016	27,106	74.3	74.1	74.4	74.5	74.4
North East	1,038	1,040	1,034	1,051	1,063	68.1	68.2	67.8	68.9	69.7
North West	2,948	2,919	2,993	2,992	2,987	72.7	71.7	73.3	73.1	72.9
Yorkshire and the Humber	2,187	2,185	2,232	2,256	2,246	73.0	72.5	73.7	74.3	73.8
East Midlands	1,912	1,951	1,945	1,977	1,965	75.4	76.2	75.7	76.7	76.0
West Midlands	2,342	2,356	2,353	2,354	2,383	73.9	73.9	73.8	73.7	74.6
East	2,584	2,575	2,574	2,606	2,611	79.5	78.9	78.4	78.8	78.6
London	3,288	3,323	3,304	3,347	3,334	70.9	70.6	69.8	70.2	69.3
South East	3,876	3,876	3,869	3,848	3,892	80.1	79.8	79.2	78.2	78.6
South West	2,278	2,293	2,291	2,308	2,341	78.6	78.7	78.2	78.3	78.9
England	22,452	22,518	22,595	22,739	22,823	75.1	74.8	74.8	74.9	74.8
Wales	1,169	1,182	1,260	1,263	1,239	67.8	68.2	72.4	72.4	70.8
Scotland	2,288	2,282	2,320	2,320	2,331	73.3	73.0	74.2	74.2	74.6
Northern Ireland	681	690	716	694	713	66.9	67.2	69.3	66.6	68.0

1 The data in this table have been reweighted to reflect revised 2001 Census population data and are from the Labour Force Survey spring quarter (not seasonally adjusted).
2 Total in employment as a percentage of all people of working age (males 16 to 64) and females (16 to 59) in each region.

Source: Office for National Statistics; General Register Office for Scotland; Northern Ireland Statistics and Research Agency

Table **5.2** Labour force:[1] by age, spring 2005

Percentages and thousands

	Percentage[2] aged:					
	16 to 24	25 to 34	35 to 44	Males 45 to 64/ females 45 to 59	Males 65 or over/ females 60 or over	All ages (=100%) (thousands)
United Kingdom	15.0	21.7	25.9	33.8	3.6	29,517
North East	17.6	20.3	25.8	34.2	2.1	1,161
North West	15.7	21.7	26.1	33.1	3.5	3,234
Yorkshire and the Humber	16.1	20.5	26.3	34.2	2.9	2,437
East Midlands	15.5	20.3	25.9	34.8	3.5	2,124
West Midlands	15.1	20.8	25.8	34.5	3.8	2,590
East	14.2	21.3	25.5	34.8	4.2	2,829
London	12.9	27.8	26.8	29.5	3.1	3,693
South East	14.4	21.1	25.4	34.6	4.5	4,231
South West	14.4	20.0	24.7	36.1	4.8	2,543
England	14.8	21.9	25.8	33.8	3.7	24,843
Wales	15.9	20.1	25.6	34.9	3.5	1,345
Scotland	16.2	20.2	26.1	34.3	3.2	2,558
Northern Ireland	16.0	24.2	26.3	30.4	3.0	772

1 The labour force includes those in employment and unemployment. Not seasonally adjusted. See Notes and Definitions.
2 The percentage figures in this table are based on data that have not been adjusted to take account of the Census 2001 population estimates. However, the totals figures in the final column have been adjusted in line with the Census population estimates.

Source: Labour Force Survey, Office for National Statistics

Table **5.3** Economic activity,[1] spring 2005

Percentages and thousands

	In employment							All of working age[3] (=100%) (thousands)
	Employees							
	Full- time	Part- time	Self- employed	Total[2]	Unemployed	Economically active	Economically inactive	
United Kingdom	49.5	17.4	9.8	77.3	4.7	78.2	21.9	36,422
North East	47.7	17.2	5.6	71.3	6.4	74.5	25.5	1,525
North West	49.9	17.0	8.4	75.6	4.3	76.2	23.8	4,098
Yorkshire and the Humber	48.7	18.8	8.0	76.1	5.1	77.7	22.3	3,044
East Midlands	50.0	18.0	10.4	78.8	4.1	79.3	20.8	2,587
West Midlands	49.8	18.3	9.0	77.6	4.4	78.0	22.0	3,196
East	52.5	18.5	10.5	82.0	3.7	81.7	18.4	3,323
London	47.7	12.1	11.2	71.6	6.9	74.6	25.6	4,811
South East	50.5	19.3	12.0	82.4	3.7	81.6	18.4	4,953
South West	48.9	21.3	11.9	83.0	3.3	81.7	18.3	2,965
England	49.6	17.6	10.0	77.8	4.6	78.5	21.6	30,502
Wales	46.7	17.3	8.8	73.5	4.5	74.2	25.8	1,749
Scotland	52.0	17.3	7.4	77.2	5.9	79.3	20.7	3,123
Northern Ireland	44.3	13.3	11.3	70.3	4.7	71.4	28.6	1,048

1 For people of working age. Not seasonally adjusted. See Notes and Definitions.
2 Includes those on government-supported employment and training schemes and unpaid family workers.
3 Based on the population of working age in private households, student halls of residence and NHS accommodation.

Source: Labour Force Survey, Office for National Statistics

127

Table **5.4**   Employee jobs and self-employment jobs:[1] by sex

Thousands

| | Employee jobs | | | | | | Self-employment jobs[2] | | | | | |
| | Males | | | Females | | | Males | | | Females | | |
	2002	2003	2004	2002	2003	2004	2002	2003	2004	2002	2003	2004
United Kingdom	13,131	13,185	13,381	12,882	12,933	12,885	2,612	2,799	2,785	1,020	1,108	1,060
North East	501	503	508	491	495	495	71	84	80	23	24	23
North West	1,473	1,503	1,522	1,464	1,463	1,461	258	274	265	89	98	112
Yorkshire and the Humber	1,026	1,084	1,123	1,069	1,057	1,040	188	201	209	72	73	68
East Midlands	883	897	878	886	865	864	178	180	188	62	77	68
West Midlands	1,178	1,188	1,198	1,134	1,121	1,112	194	221	223	78	71	81
East	1,138	1,161	1,182	1,121	1,150	1,159	290	309	299	111	114	113
London	2,078	2,039	2,081	1,839	1,847	1,842	354	412	393	153	186	155
South East	1,833	1,810	1,811	1,805	1,790	1,782	424	435	451	176	190	188
South West	1,067	1,029	1,065	1,030	1,093	1,091	262	261	272	115	127	117
England	11,178	11,218	11,367	10,839	10,879	10,845	2,221	2,376	2,379	880	961	926
Wales	537	543	554	556	562	554	122	134	126	52	55	48
Scotland	1,091	1,097	1,128	1,148	1,148	1,135	187	199	190	70	72	66
Northern Ireland	325	327	332	339	344	351	82	90	90	18	20	20

1 At September each year. See Notes and Definitions.
2 With or without employees.

Source: *Short-term Employment and Labour Force Surveys; Office for National Statistics; Quarterly Employment and Labour Force Surveys; Department of Economic Development, Northern Ireland*

Table **5.5**   Economic activity rates:[1] by sex

Percentages

| | Males | | | | Females | | | | All people | | | |
	2002	2003	2004	2005	2002	2003	2004	2005	2002	2003	2004	2005
United Kingdom	83.9	84.1	83.6	83.4	73.0	73.0	73.2	73.4	78.6	78.7	78.6	78.5
North East	76.6	78.4	77.0	78.3	70.3	67.3	69.7	71.8	73.5	73.0	73.4	75.1
North West	80.4	82.3	81.0	80.6	71.9	72.1	72.6	72.7	76.3	77.4	77.0	76.8
Yorkshire and the Humber	82.8	83.9	82.7	83.2	71.3	72.5	73.1	72.6	77.2	78.4	78.1	78.1
East Midlands	85.1	85.1	84.8	84.4	74.6	73.5	75.7	74.6	80.0	79.5	80.4	79.7
West Midlands	84.6	84.2	83.5	84.0	72.4	72.4	73.0	72.3	78.8	78.5	78.5	78.4
East	87.9	87.4	87.5	87.4	75.7	76.0	76.9	75.8	82.0	81.9	82.4	81.8
London	83.7	82.6	83.0	81.7	68.8	67.8	68.0	67.4	76.5	75.4	75.7	74.8
South East	88.8	87.6	87.3	86.9	77.5	77.0	75.4	76.5	83.3	82.5	81.6	81.9
South West	86.1	85.9	85.8	85.9	77.9	77.2	76.8	78.1	82.1	81.7	81.5	82.1
England	84.5	84.5	84.1	83.8	73.4	73.1	73.4	73.4	79.2	79.0	78.9	78.8
Wales	78.8	79.5	80.8	77.2	67.3	73.1	71.8	71.9	73.2	76.4	76.4	74.6
Scotland	82.2	83.2	83.3	83.4	75.3	74.8	75.4	76.2	78.8	79.1	79.4	79.8
Northern Ireland	77.9	81.4	76.8	78.6	64.8	65.1	63.3	64.9	71.5	73.5	70.2	71.9

1 At spring of each year, seasonally adjusted. Based on the population of working age in private households, student halls of residence and NHS accommodation. See Notes and Definitions.

Source: *Labour Force Survey, Office for National Statistics*

Figure 5.6 Part-time[1] working:[2] by sex, spring 2005

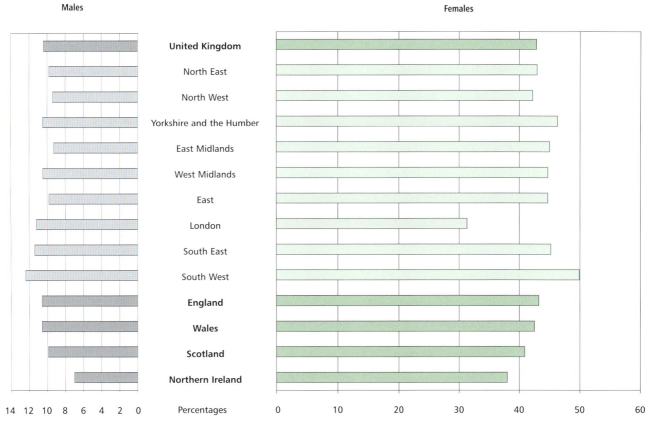

Males

Females

14 12 10 8 6 4 2 0   Percentages   0   10   20   30   40   50   60

1 Part-time workers as a percentage of all in employment (employees and the self-employed only). Based on respondents' own definition of part-time.
2 These data are not seasonally adjusted.

Source: Labour Force Survey, Office for National Statistics

Table 5.7 Reasons given for working part-time,[1] spring 2005

Percentages and thousands

	Males				Females			
	Did not want a full-time job	Could not find a full-time job	Student or at school	All part-time workers[2,3] (=100%) (thousands)	Did not want a full-time job	Could not find a full-time job	Student or at school	All part-time workers[2,3] (=100%) (thousands)
United Kingdom	48.8	14.4	32.3	1,562	80.5	6.1	11.6	5,564
North East	42.6	18.3	33.4	55	78.5	7.9	11.8	221
North West	53.0	11.8	29.4	152	78.8	6.9	12.6	613
Yorkshire and the Humber	46.1	12.3	36.8	129	80.3	5.7	11.7	494
East Midlands	48.3	14.2	31.3	101	82.8	6.4	10.0	423
West Midlands	50.1	14.4	31.1	141	81.6	6.4	10.8	501
East	56.9	12.8	27.2	143	84.8	3.7	9.6	557
London	41.4	21.3	33.9	209	75.6	8.5	14.6	482
South East	50.9	10.7	33.0	248	81.2	4.4	12.6	854
South West	54.7	11.2	29.9	161	83.5	3.9	10.2	569
England	49.7	13.9	31.8	1,340	81.0	5.7	11.6	4,715
Wales	47.6	19.4	28.6	70	77.0	10.9	11.4	259
Scotland	41.9	16.2	39.4	125	78.2	7.9	12.7	466
Northern Ireland	42.7	19.7	32.6	28	79.5	6.6	10.0	124

1 Based on respondents' own definition of part-time.
2 Employees and the self-employed only.
3 Includes people who said they worked part-time because they were ill or disabled. Hence percentages shown do not add to 100 per cent.

Source: Labour Force Survey, Office for National Statistics

Figure **5.8**   Employees with flexible working patterns:[1] by sex, spring 2005

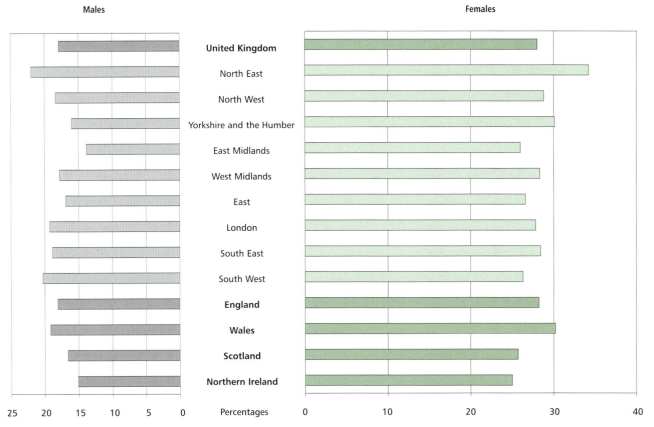

1 Includes those on flexi-time, annualised hours, term-time working, job sharing, nine day fortnight, four and a half day week and zero hours contract (not contracted to work a set number of hours but paid for the actual number of hours worked). Data are not seasonally adjusted.

Source: Labour Force Survey, Office for National Statistics

Table **5.9**   People in employment with a second job:[1] by sex, spring 2005

Thousands and percentages

	People with a second job (thousands)			As a percentage of all in employment		
	Males	Females	All people	Males	Females	All people
United Kingdom	469	622	1,090	3.1	4.7	3.8
North East	15	20	35	2.6	3.8	3.2
North West	41	65	106	2.4	4.4	3.4
Yorkshire and the Humber	35	50	84	2.8	4.6	3.6
East Midlands	26	44	71	2.3	4.6	3.4
West Midlands	37	45	82	2.7	4.0	3.3
East	49	63	112	3.3	5.1	4.1
London	66	60	126	3.4	3.8	3.6
South East	73	101	174	3.3	5.4	4.3
South West	49	72	120	3.7	6.3	4.8
England	391	520	910	3.0	4.7	3.8
Wales	23	28	51	3.4	4.5	3.9
Scotland	42	63	105	3.3	5.5	4.3
Northern Ireland	13	11	24	3.2	3.3	3.3

1 Not seasonally adjusted. Employees and self-employed.

Source: Labour Force Survey, Office for National Statistics

Table 5.10 **Average usual weekly hours¹ of work of full-time employees: by occupational group,²
spring 2005**

Hours

	Managers & senior officials	Professional occupations	Associate professional & technical	Administrative & secretarial	Skilled trades occupations	Personal service occupations	Sales & customer service occupations	Process, plant & machine operatives	Elementary occupations	All occupations³
United Kingdom	45.5	44.5	41.6	38.6	43.6	38.9	39.5	44.9	42.1	42.7
North East	44.0	44.5	40.8	38.6	42.9	39.0	38.7	45.7	41.9	42.1
North West	45.0	43.7	41.0	38.3	43.1	39.5	39.1	43.9	41.4	42.0
Yorkshire and the Humber	45.0	44.6	41.4	38.5	43.6	37.3	38.6	45.5	42.7	42.6
East Midlands	46.3	45.4	41.1	39.0	44.3	39.2	39.5	44.8	42.0	43.2
West Midlands	45.2	45.2	41.5	38.6	43.2	39.2	38.9	44.6	42.7	42.7
East	45.2	44.6	41.8	38.9	44.7	38.7	39.8	46.1	42.4	43.0
London	46.2	44.4	42.3	38.9	43.2	38.2	40.9	43.9	42.3	42.9
South East	45.9	45.3	42.4	38.7	43.9	40.3	40.4	45.3	42.5	43.3
South West	45.3	45.2	41.5	38.7	43.3	40.1	39.6	44.1	41.5	42.6
England	45.5	44.7	41.7	38.7	43.6	39.1	39.6	44.8	42.2	42.8
Wales	45.7	44.1	40.3	38.6	42.7	38.6	38.5	44.2	42.1	42.1
Scotland	45.2	43.4	41.6	37.9	44.6	38.0	38.6	46.4	42.1	42.4
Northern Ireland	43.3	42.2	40.6	38.7	41.7	37.4	38.8	44.2	40.4	41.1

1 Includes paid and unpaid overtime and excludes meal breaks. The analysis also excludes those who did not state the number of hours they worked.
2 Uses the new Standard Occupational Classification (SOC) 2000 for major occupation group in main job. This replaces the SOC 90 classification. Further information on the new occupational classification can be obtained from the Labour Force Survey web page.
3 Includes those who did not specify their occupation.

Source: Labour Force Survey, Office for National Statistics

Table 5.11 **Working days lost due to labour disputes**

Days lost per 1,000 employees

	2000	2001	2002	2003	2004
United Kingdom¹	20	20	51	19	34
North East	6	12	119	2	33
North West	20	32	76	10	19
Yorkshire and the Humber	4	24	44	8	37
East Midlands	5	8	50	6	20
West Midlands	20	33	41	8	23
East	6	11	26	4	11
London	7	24	60	51	18
South East	4	4	36	6	16
South West	1	8	32	7	13
England	8	17	54	11	21
Wales	6	17	74	9	28
Scotland	136	29	54	39	160
Northern Ireland	33	1	34	101	99

1 Regional rates are based on data for stoppages that exclude widespread disputes that cannot be allocated to a specific region. These are included in the United Kingdom figures only. See Notes and Definitions.

Source: Office for National Statistics

Table 5.12 Median[1] and average weekly earnings:[2] by industry[3] and sex, April 2005

£ per week

| | Whole economy (average) | | | Whole economy (median) | | | Median | | | |
| | | | | | | | Agriculture, hunting and forestry | | Manufacturing | |
	Males	Females	All people	Males	Females	All people	Males	Females	Males	Females
United Kingdom	569.0	436.1	517.0	471.5	371.8	431.2	334.9	256.1	460.0	336.0
North East	494.6	390.0	452.2	424.2	330.6	385.5	..	..	443.7	310.0
North West	525.6	409.4	479.5	446.7	350.0	407.2	286.9	234.4	463.6	335.8
Yorkshire and the Humber	508.1	400.6	467.2	435.2	339.8	399.3	335.2	225.1	435.1	308.8
East Midlands	512.5	392.4	469.4	450.0	334.8	406.7	385.6	..	455.6	306.7
West Midlands	520.5	400.3	475.5	440.8	345.0	402.5	316.6	..	436.0	306.7
East	565.6	417.9	512.1	476.8	356.7	428.7	344.9	230.0	476.1	355.4
London	789.5	567.1	697.6	619.9	491.8	555.8	294.0	..	571.9	480.8
South East	596.0	446.0	539.0	497.3	383.3	450.0	345.0	284.8	511.8	376.9
South West	518.0	401.0	473.1	443.8	340.2	401.0	336.4	..	450.6	325.2
England	579.7	440.7	526.1	478.9	374.3	436.3	..	..	..	..
Wales	491.5	398.4	454.4	425.7	334.8	389.9	..	..	444.8	322.0
Scotland	522.9	423.8	479.6	446.0	361.0	409.6	339.4	279.1	442.4	300.3
Northern Ireland	487.1	402.3	452.2	409.5	355.8	387.0	..	..	..	..

| | Median | | | | | | | | |
| | Mining and quarrying | | Electricity, gas and water supply | | | Construction | | Hotel and restaurants | |
	Males	Females	Males	Females		Males	Females	Males	Females
United Kingdom	523.4	404.0	566.5	415.4		479.1	345.2	295.8	245.4
North East	616.9	..	564.7	339.5		421.2	..	294.2	238.8
North West	..	..	..	..		458.3	316.7	280.0	244.5
Yorkshire and the Humber	603.6	..	639.7	484.0		460.0	340.8	295.9	231.6
East Midlands	528.9	..	534.8	324.5		495.4	306.2	287.3	222.2
West Midlands	611.4	..	506.8	..		479.1	340.3	308.7	241.2
East	..	..	509.8	344.9		507.4	357.6	300.0	259.9
London	..	..	630.1	..		642.3	433.2	348.1	291.8
South East	..	..	577.6	..		500.0	385.7	291.5	255.3
South West	422.7	..	551.9	..		442.0	301.9	263.3	237.1
England	..	..	..	..		..	..	..	..
Wales	..	..	..	359.6		423.0	301.7	270.3	228.9
Scotland	602.2	441.7	571.3	427.6		462.2	333.8	261.3	237.6
Northern Ireland	..	..	..	..		..	..	..	..

1 Median values are less affected by extremes of earnings at either ends of the scale, with half the workers earning above the stated amount and half below.
2 Median and average gross weekly earnings are workplace based. Data relate to full-time employees on adult rates whose pay for the survey pay-period was not affected by absence. See Notes and Definitions.
3 Classification is based on Standard Industrial Classification 2003.

Source: Annual Survey of Hours and Earnings, Office for National Statistics; Department of Enterprise, Trade and Investment, Northern Ireland

Table **5.12** Median[1] and average weekly earnings:[2] by industry[3] and sex, April 2005 *(continued)*

£ per week

| | Median | | | | | | | |
| | Wholesale and retail trade[4] | | Transport, storage and communication | | Financial intermediation | | Real estate, renting and business activities | |
	Males	Females	Males	Females	Males	Females	Males	Females
United Kingdom	383.3	281.4	453.7	372.3	670.0	389.2	533.6	388.1
North East	325.2	256.3	400.7	327.9	449.1	328.6	410.8	303.7
North West	364.4	282.5	420.4	319.3	537.9	352.8	474.8	335.4
Yorkshire and the Humber	365.0	259.7	399.1	341.5	536.8	361.6	429.9	311.6
East Midlands	383.3	279.4	435.0	342.0	528.1	346.1	494.0	322.5
West Midlands	383.3	263.9	393.5	368.1	571.2	341.8	450.0	345.0
East	396.4	287.5	484.5	356.0	582.1	345.0	539.7	364.1
London	437.5	349.4	555.1	481.0	1,034.9	604.6	689.9	528.7
South East	424.4	309.2	463.3	421.9	552.4	370.4	607.2	408.1
South West	360.2	270.4	429.0	331.2	554.6	366.2	506.0	334.4
England	..	..	..	..	..	..	..	..
Wales	333.5	253.9	423.8	370.9	408.7	298.8	381.2	321.1
Scotland	354.2	248.3	421.1	366.2	555.1	350.6	484.5	335.4
Northern Ireland	..	..	..	..	..	..	..	..

| | Median | | | | | | | |
| | Public administration and defence | | Education | | Health and social work | | Other community, Social and personal service activities | |
	Males	Females	Males	Females	Males	Females	Males	Females
United Kingdom	539.8	395.3	528.4	454.1	508.5	394.5	417.3	343.3
North East	403.6	330.7	497.6	403.2	480.3	353.3	348.5	242.2
North West	506.6	370.3	525.3	438.0	491.1	381.4	381.8	311.7
Yorkshire and the Humber	511.8	383.8	501.3	426.6	522.9	365.7	365.2	277.7
East Midlands	498.2	388.6	523.0	434.6	445.6	359.5	391.4	283.1
West Midlands	542.6	368.0	507.7	436.2	494.5	386.7	386.5	297.1
East	510.5	387.3	519.7	427.2	479.7	389.0	401.6	321.9
London	649.5	499.7	620.5	526.4	614.1	478.9	536.6	490.9
South East	521.1	397.4	560.6	442.0	485.5	393.1	426.8	328.6
South West	502.5	365.3	522.4	432.6	491.7	368.8	383.9	306.5
England	..	..	..	..	..	..	..	..
Wales	507.9	333.7	492.1	423.7	475.8	380.6	369.4	279.4
Scotland	539.8	394.8	484.3	464.2	482.6	400.0	356.5	307.5
Northern Ireland	..	..	..	..	..	..	..	..

1 Median values are less affected by extremes of earnings at either ends of the scale, with half the workers earning above the stated amount and half below.
2 Median and average gross weekly earnings are workplace based. Data relate to full-time employees on adult rates whose pay for the survey pay-period was not affected by absence. See Notes and Definitions.
3 Classification is based on Standard Industrial Classification 2003.
4 Also includes repair of motor vehicles, motorcycles and personal and household goods.

Source: Annual Survey of Hours and Earnings, Office for National Statistics; Department of Enterprise, Trade and Investment, Northern Ireland

133

Table **5.13** Unemployment rates[1]

Percentages

	Spring quarter of each year				
	2001	2002	2003	2004	2005
United Kingdom	4.8	5.2	4.9	4.7	4.7
North East	7.4	6.8	6.7	5.5	6.4
North West	5.1	5.4	4.8	4.4	4.3
Yorkshire and the Humber	5.0	5.4	5.4	4.4	5.1
East Midlands	5.0	4.2	4.1	4.1	4.1
West Midlands	5.1	5.5	5.6	5.5	4.4
East	3.6	3.5	4.0	4.0	3.7
London	6.0	6.7	6.8	6.6	6.9
South East	3.0	4.0	3.8	3.8	3.7
South West	3.5	3.6	3.7	3.3	3.3
England	4.6	4.9	4.9	4.6	4.6
Wales	5.8	6.0	4.5	4.7	4.5
Scotland	5.8	6.8	5.5	6.0	5.9
Northern Ireland	6.3	5.5	5.4	4.8	4.7

1 For those people of working age. Not seasonally adjusted. The data in this table
   are reweighted based on the mid-2003 population estimates.

Source: Labour Force Survey, Office for National Statistics

Table **5.14** Claimant count rates[1]

Percentages

	March each year				
	1998	2002	2003	2004	2005
United Kingdom	3.8	2.6	2.6	2.4	2.2
North East	5.5	3.8	3.5	3.0	2.9
North West	4.0	2.9	2.7	2.4	2.3
Yorkshire and the Humber	4.5	2.9	2.8	2.5	2.3
East Midlands	3.2	2.3	2.2	2.1	1.9
West Midlands	3.9	2.9	2.9	2.8	2.6
East	3.2	1.7	1.7	1.7	1.7
London	3.9	3.4	3.5	3.3	3.3
South East	3.2	1.4	1.5	1.5	1.4
South West	3.9	1.7	1.6	1.4	1.4
England	3.7	2.5	2.5	2.3	2.2
Wales	4.1	2.7	2.6	2.3	2.2
Scotland	4.3	3.3	3.1	3.0	2.7
Northern Ireland	5.8	3.6	3.3	3.1	2.8

1 Claimant count rates are calculated by expressing the number of claimants as a
   percentage of the estimated total workforce. Claimants are people receiving
   unemployment related benefits such as Jobseeker's Allowance (JSA) and National
   Insurance Credits. See Notes and Definitions.

Source: Office for National Statistics

Map **5.15**   Claimant count rate:[1] by county or unitary authority,[2] March 2005

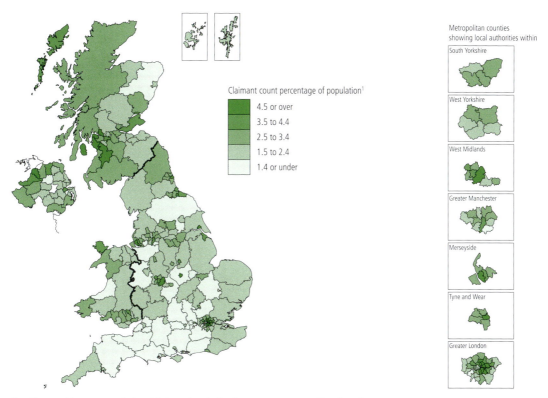

Claimant count percentage of population[1]

- 4.5 or over
- 3.5 to 4.4
- 2.5 to 3.4
- 1.5 to 2.4
- 1.4 or under

Metropolitan counties
showing local authorities within

South Yorkshire

West Yorkshire

West Midlands

Greater Manchester

Merseyside

Tyne and Wear

Greater London

1 Percentages of resident working-age population claiming Jobseeker's Allowance. Not seasonally adjusted.
2 Counties or unitary authorities in England, unitary authorities in Wales, council areas in Scotland and district council areas in Northern Ireland, with the exception of
   Greater London and the metropolitan areas where local authorities are used.

Source: Office for National Statistics

Map **5.16**   Percentage claiming for more than 12 months:[1] by local authority,[2] March 2005

Metropolitan counties
showing local authorities within

South Yorkshire

West Yorkshire

West Midlands

Greater Manchester

Merseyside

Tyne and Wear

Greater London

Long-term claimant count proportion[1]
(percentage)

- 20.0 or over
- 16.0 to 19.9
- 12.0 to 15.9
- 8.0 to 11.9
- 7.9 or under

1 People who have been claiming for more than 12 months (computerised claims only), as a percentage of total computerised claimants in each area.
2 Counties or unitary authorities in England, unitary authorities in Wales, council areas in Scotland and district council areas in Northern Ireland, with the exception of
   Greater London and the metropolitan areas where local authorities are used.

Source: Office for National Statistics

Table **5.17** Unemployment rates:[1] by age, spring 2005

Percentages and thousands

	Percentage of the economically active who were unemployed and aged:				All unemployed of working age (thousands)
	16 to 24	25 to 34	35 to 49	Males 50 to 64, females 50 to 59	
United Kingdom	11.8	4.4	3.1	2.9	1,335
North East	16.2	4.8	3.9	4.5	73
North West	10.6	3.6	2.8	3.1	134
Yorkshire and the Humber	13.6	4.4	3.6	2.0	120
East Midlands	9.8	3.8	2.9	2.4	84
West Midlands	10.3	4.8	2.5	3.1	109
East	8.6	4.1	2.6	2.1	101
London	18.9	6.2	4.5	4.5	246
South East	8.8	3.5	2.6	2.4	148
South West	8.3	3.3	2.1	2.4	81
England	11.5	4.3	3.0	2.9	1,096
Wales	13.3	4.2	2.4	2.2	58
Scotland	13.9	5.7	4.1	3.2	145
Northern Ireland	12.2	3.5	3.3	2.9	36

1 The data in this table are reweighted based on the mid-2003 population estimates. Not seasonally adjusted.

Source: Labour Force Survey, Office for National Statistics

Table **5.18** Contributions to ILO unemployment rates:[1] by duration and sex, spring 2005

Percentages and thousands

	Males						Females					
	Percentage unemployed					Total ILO unemployed (thousands)	Percentage unemployed					Total ILO unemployed (thousands)
	Less than 6 months	6 months and up to 12 months	1 year and up to 2 years	2 years and over	Total unemployment rate		Less than 6 months	6 months and up to 12 months	1 year and up to 2 years	2 years and over	Total unemployment rate	
United Kingdom	2.9	0.9	0.7	0.6	5.0	792	2.8	0.6	0.4	0.3	4.1	557
North East	3.7	1.5	1.2	0.8	7.2	44	3.7	0.9	0.7	0.3	5.6	31
North West	2.4	0.9	0.8	0.4	4.5	78	2.7	0.6	0.3	0.2	3.8	57
Yorkshire and the Humber	3.8	1.0	0.7	0.6	6.1	80	2.8	0.6	0.2	-	3.6	40
East Midlands	2.4	0.6	0.6	0.7	4.4	50	2.6	0.4	0.5	0.1	3.6	35
West Midlands	2.6	0.8	0.5	0.6	4.5	64	2.6	0.6	0.6	0.2	3.9	45
East	2.7	0.5	0.4	0.3	3.9	60	2.4	0.5	0.3	0.1	3.3	43
London	3.8	1.4	1.0	1.1	7.2	147	3.6	1.0	0.8	0.7	6.0	100
South East	2.3	0.6	0.3	0.4	3.6	81	2.6	0.5	0.3	0.1	3.5	69
South West	2.3	0.4	0.3	0.4	3.3	45	2.5	0.2	0.3	0.2	3.1	37
England	2.9	0.8	0.6	0.6	4.9	649	2.8	0.6	0.4	0.2	4.0	459
Wales	2.7	0.9	0.9	0.7	5.1	36	2.8	0.4	0.2	0.2	3.6	23
Scotland	3.4	1.1	0.9	0.8	6.2	84	3.5	0.7	0.5	0.5	5.2	63
Northern Ireland	1.7	1.0	1.2	1.6	5.5	23	2.1	0.3	0.5	0.6	3.5	12

1 For those aged 16 and over. Not seasonally adjusted. See Notes and Definitions.

Source: Labour Force Survey, Office for National Statistics

Table **5.19**   Unemployment:[1] by highest qualification, spring 2005

Percentages and thousands

	Degree or equivalent	Higher education qualification[2]	GCE A level or equivalent[3]	GCSE grades A*-C or equivalent	Other qualifications	No qualifications	Total[4] (=100%) (thousands)
United Kingdom	2.4	2.8	3.4	5.7	6.7	9.5	1,335
North East	3.3	2.9	4.9	7.3	10.7	11.1	73
North West	1.5	2.9	3.4	5.4	6.7	7.6	134
Yorkshire and the Humber	2.1	1.9	3.9	5.1	7.8	11.9	120
East Midlands	1.5	1.5	2.6	4.2	7.9	9.6	84
West Midlands	2.6	3.8	2.1	5.2	5.6	8.9	109
East	1.7	3.0	2.5	5.0	3.9	8.1	101
London	3.6	5.1	5.8	10.0	8.0	13.6	246
South East	2.4	2.1	2.7	4.8	5.0	6.7	148
South West	1.9	1.3	2.7	4.0	4.6	7.1	81
England	2.4	2.7	3.3	5.5	6.5	9.4	1,096
Wales	2.8	2.7	3.2	5.5	5.6	7.7	58
Scotland	2.6	3.6	4.2	8.8	10.5	11.7	145
Northern Ireland	1.5	1.4	3.6	5.6	7.3	9.4	36

1 Males aged 16 to 64 and females aged 16 to 59.
2 Below degree level.
3 Includes recognised trade apprenticeships.
4 Includes those who did not state their qualifications.

Source: Labour Force Survey, Office for National Statistics

Map **5.20**   Jobs density: by local authority, 2003

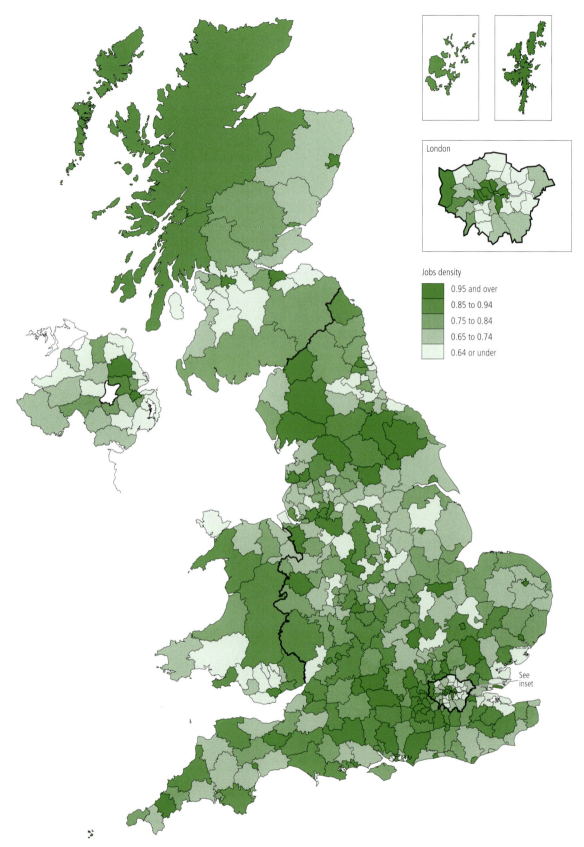

Jobs density

- 0.95 and over
- 0.85 to 0.94
- 0.75 to 0.84
- 0.65 to 0.74
- 0.64 or under

London

See inset

Source: Office for National Statistics; Department of Enterprise, Trade and Development

Chapter 6 **Housing**

Stock of dwellings

There were over three million dwellings in the South East in 2004 and this region has consistently had the highest number in the UK since 1992. Over the ten years between 1994 and 2004 the largest increase in stock of dwellings was 11.5 per cent, in Northern Ireland, and the South West also showed a rise of more than 10 per cent. The North East showed the least growth over the same period, with about one-third of these increases. (Table 6.1)

Housebuilding

Private enterprises constructed the vast majority of new houses in the UK, making up 89 per cent of the total in 2004/05. Of this 183 thousand total, 138 thousand were built in England; an increase of more than 10 per cent on the 2002/03 figures. Between 1994/95 and 2004/05 the number of houses built by Registered Social Landlords (RSLs) changed very little in most areas with the exception of London (up by 1,800), the North West (down by 400) and Yorkshire and the Humber (down by 200) over the ten-year period. (Table 6.2)

Tenure of dwellings

Three-quarters of homes in the East Midlands, East and South East were 'owner-occupied' in 2004, and the highest proportion was in Northern Ireland at 77 per cent. This compared to just under three-fifths (60 per cent) in London, the region with the lowest proportion of owner-occupation.

There was little change over time in many regions in the proportions of households with different types of tenure. The proportion of owner-occupation continued to grow slightly between 2003 and 2004 in most regions, and remained constant at 75 per cent and 74 per cent in the South East and South West respectively. The majority of regions recorded small reductions in the proportion of households renting from local authorities. An increase of 2 per cent in the latest figures for 'rented from private owners' in South West was recorded, and was the largest increase of any sector from 2003 to 2004. (Table 6.3)

Type of dwelling

Semi-detached houses accounted for just under one-third of the stock overall in the UK in 2002/03. In the majority of regions this type of dwelling was the most common. Northern Ireland had the highest proportion of detached dwellings at 37 per cent compared with 25 per cent semi-detached. In the South East and East of England the proportions of detached and semi-detached dwellings were very similar, each around 30 per cent. The proportion of detached houses in the East had grown by 2 percentage points since 2001/02 to 31 per cent. London had by far the lowest percentage of detached houses, with only 5 per cent, less than one-quarter the average for England.

The North East had the highest proportion (36 per cent) of terraced houses in 2002/03, and the North West, Yorkshire and the Humber, Northern Ireland and London also each had more than 30 per cent of this type of house. By contrast, between 2001/02 and 2002/03 the North East showed a considerable increase of 11 per cent in the percentage of semi-detached houses, with a corresponding reduction in the proportion of terraced houses. The largest reduction (of 4 per cent) in semi-detached homes was seen in the South West.

East Midlands had the lowest proportion of purpose-built flats or maisonettes in the UK at 6 per cent in 2002/03, a reduction of 3 percentage points compared to 2001/02 figures. The proportion of purpose-built flats or maisonettes in London decreased by 7 percentage points, but still accounted for a little under a third of the total dwellings in the capital. Scotland had the highest percentage of purpose-built flats or maisonettes with 33 per cent in 2002/03. (Table 6.4)

Length of time at current address

Across the UK as a whole, about one-quarter of households had, in 2002/03, been at their current address for 20 years or more, while in the North East and Northern Ireland this proportion was as high as 31 per cent. Another quarter of households had stayed in their homes for less than 5 years. Between 2001/02 and 2002/03, the proportion staying put in the North East increased by 6 percentage points, which is higher than other regions and countries. (Table 6.5)

Satisfaction with their area

Over three-quarters of the people interviewed were 'very or fairly satisfied' with where they lived in 2003/04, rising to over 90 per cent of householders in the South West and Scotland. Households in the southern regions showed the greatest reductions from 2002/03 to 2003/04 in the proportion who categorised themselves as 'very satisfied'. London showed the largest reduction in very satisfied households of 4 per cent, and there was a smaller reduction of 1.5 per cent in the South East. The exceptions to this tendency were households in Yorkshire and the Humber and the North East where being 'very satisfied with area' was up by nearly 6 per cent and just over 3 per cent respectively. (Web: H2)

Selected housing costs of owner-occupiers

Mortgage payments in 2003/04 showed reductions compared with 2002/03 for all regions except the South East and South West. Yorkshire and the Humber, the West Midlands and London each showed reductions of £5 per week. Only in the East Midlands did mortgage payments increase by £2 per week. The largest reduction was in Wales where the saving on mortgage payments amounted to £6 per week in 2003/04. This compared with 2002/03, when mortgage payers in Yorkshire and the Humber were saving a total of £13 per week. (Table 6.6)

Average dwelling prices

London continued to be the most expensive place to buy a property, regardless of the type of dwelling, with prices averaging £275,000 in 2004, although the percentage increase from 2003 of 6 per cent was the lowest of any region. Increases in Wales averaged 22 per cent over all types of property. The northern regions (North East, North West and Yorkshire and the Humber) each showed increases of between 17 and 18 per cent compared with 2003. The increases from 2003 to 2004 were lower than from 2002 to 2003 in all areas.

Detached houses were the most expensive type in each region, ranging from £204,000 in Wales and £215,000 in the North East to £561,000 in London in 2004. The cost of a flat or maisonette in London was on average greater than a detached house in Wales, the North East, East Midlands or Yorkshire and the Humber. The cost of terraced houses in London only rose by just over £10,000 between 2003 and 2004, the smallest value monetary increase in any sector or region. London also saw the largest increase in prices of detached houses at over £52,000. (Table 6.7)

Mortgage advances, and income and age of borrowers

The average age of first-time buyers throughout the UK reduced by one or two years to 33 in 2004 compared with 2003. First-time buyers' average recorded income rose in every region and country to reach just over £32,000 for the UK. The biggest regional increase was London at just over £5,000, followed by the East Midlands and West Midlands at around £4,000 each.

Among previous owner-occupiers, the largest increases in average income were seen in London and Wales at £4,000 and £3,000 respectively. At almost half London's figure, the average increases of previous owner-occupiers in the North East, North West and Yorkshire and the Humber increased by approximately £2,000. (Table 6.8)

Average weekly rents

The cost of renting from the private sector increased considerably from 2002/03 to 2003/04, by almost one-quarter to £121 per week for the UK as a whole. The East saw the largest rise of £28 per week, closely followed by Yorkshire and the Humber and London at £27 per week, all far in excess of the rate of inflation. The smallest increase of £3 per week was in the West Midlands and was equivalent to less than 4 per cent.

Rents charged by local authorities and registered social landlords remained consistent with an average rise of around £2 per week across the regions from 2002/03 to 2003/04. The exceptions were London and the South East where a £6 rise was observed. For local authority rents this represented a growth of over 8 per cent in London and 10 per cent in the South East. (Table 6.9)

Dwellings in council tax bands

In 2004/05, council tax bands A to D covered over 80 per cent of all dwellings in England and ranged from less than 70 per cent of dwellings in London to over 90 per cent in the North East. A quarter of the dwellings located in the South East region are in Bands A and B. In London, the higher council tax bands E to H accounted for 31 per cent of the dwellings, compared with fewer than 7 per cent in the North East. London was the only region to have more than 1 per cent of dwellings in band H, the highest band. (Table 6.10)

County Court mortgage possession orders

Between 2002 and 2003, 'actions entered' for mortgage possession orders increased by 10 per cent to 62.7 thousand for England. A further rise of nearly 11 thousand was seen in 2004.

The 2004 figures showed that Wales recorded 200 fewer 'suspended orders' than in 2003, although the 'actions entered' and 'orders made' remained at the same level when compared to 2003. The North West is the only region maintaining the same level of 'orders made'. The other eight regions showed increases ranging from just over 6 per cent in Yorkshire and the Humber to 40 per cent in the South West. An increase in orders made also occurred in Northern Ireland. The increase in England in total was 3.6 thousand compared with 2003; over half of these were in London, the South East and the South West combined. (Table 6.11)

Homelessness

The South West was the only region where the total number of homeless households reduced between 2002/03 and 2003/04, down by 12 per cent to 11,230 households. The number of homeless households increased by more than one thousand during the same period in five regions: Wales (2,170 households), the North East (1,430), Scotland (1,560), and the East Midlands (1,350), with the largest growth of 3,010 households in the North West. This latter increase represented a rise of 20 per cent over 2002/03, and gave the North West the second highest number of homeless households in England after London (18,030 and 30,080 respectively). Scotland had nearly as many homeless households as London with 29,590 in 2003/04.

The proportion of people made homeless as a result of mortgage arrears remained unchanged from 2002/03 to 2003/04 in the majority of regions and countries. In Yorkshire and the Humber, the East Midlands and the West Midlands there were slight falls of 1 percentage point since 2002/03. Homelessness due to rent arrears also fell during the same period, with the largest reduction of 5 per cent recorded in the South West. The North West and Scotland were the only areas with slight increases (1 per cent) in homelessness due to rent arrears.

An increasing proportion of people cited 'no longer willing to live with parents, relatives or friends' as the reason for their homelessness. The East Midlands, with an increase of 6 percentage points from 2002/03 to 33 per cent in 2003/04, had the largest increase. There were falls across the UK in homelessness caused by a breakdown of relationship with a partner. The largest drop was in the West Midlands where the 2002/03 figure of 27 per cent fell to 23 per cent in 2003/04. (Table 6.12)

Sales and transfers of local authority dwellings

Between 2002/03 and 2003/04 local authorities in England sold a further 7,000 dwellings through the Right to Buy scheme, mainly in the north of England. Since the start of the scheme in 1979 local authorities in the South East have sold or transferred two-thirds of their housing stock, leaving a total of 206 thousand dwellings in 2004. By comparison, at the end of the same period the North East retained a stock of 190 thousand dwellings, equating to half the original regional total. (Web: H1)

Table 6.1   Stock of dwellings[1]

Thousands and percentages

	Thousands			Percentage increase
	1994	1999	2004[2]	1994-2004
United Kingdom	24,135	25,097	25,953	*7.5*
North East	1,086	1,108	1,126	*3.7*
North West	2,838	2,920	2,989	*5.3*
Yorkshire and the Humber	2,060	2,132	2,190	*6.3*
East Midlands	1,682	1,764	1,843	*9.6*
West Midlands	2,124	2,197	2,259	*6.4*
East	2,159	2,270	2,361	*9.4*
London	2,972	3,059	3,146	*5.9*
South East	3,188	3,338	3,466	*8.7*
South West	2,029	2,139	2,236	*10.2*
England	20,139	20,927	21,613	*7.3*
Wales	1,214	1,259	1,296	*6.8*
Scotland[2]	2,193	2,285	2,366	*7.9*
Northern Ireland	590	626	679	*11.5*

1 On 1 April each year, except for Scotland and Northern Ireland (up to 2001)
   where the figure is the one for 31 December the previous year. The figure shown
   for the United Kingdom is the sum of the component countries for these periods.
   See Notes and Definitions.
2 Scotland figure is for 2003 and is provisional.

Source: *Office of the Deputy Prime Minister; National Assembly for Wales;*
Scottish Executive; Department for Social Development, Northern
Ireland

Table 6.2   Housebuilding: permanent dwellings completed: by tenure

Thousands

	Private enterprise[1]		Registered Social Landlords		Local authorities[2]	
	1994/95	2004/05	1994/95	2004/05	1994/95	2004/05
United Kingdom	156.5	183.1	37.7	22.7	3.0	0.1
North East	6.0	6.6	1.3	0.5	0.0	-
North West	16.5	17.2	4.5	0.6	0.1	-
Yorkshire and the Humber	12.0	13.8	2.9	0.4	0.0	-
East Midlands	14.0	14.6	2.7	0.8	0.0	-
West Midlands	13.3	13.0	3.6	1.2	0.2	-
East	18.6	17.8	3.2	2.1	0.1	-
London	9.5	17.7	5.4	6.1	0.2	-
South East	22.0	22.2	4.8	3.4	0.1	0.1
South West	13.8	14.7	2.8	1.5	0.1	-
England	125.7	137.7	31.4	16.6	0.9	0.1
Wales[3]	7.3	7.9	2.9	0.5	0.1	-
Scotland	18.2	22.1	2.8	4.8	1.1	-
Northern Ireland	5.4	14.9	0.5	0.8	0.9	-

1 Includes private landlords (people or companies) and owner-occupiers.
2 Northern Ireland Housing Executive in Northern Ireland.
3 2004/05 figures for Wales are provisional.

Source: *Office of the Deputy Prime Minister; National Assembly for Wales; Scottish Executive; Department for Social Development, Northern Ireland*

Table **6.3**   Tenure of dwellings[1]

Percentages

	Owner-occupied			Rented from local authority[2]			Rented from Registered Social Landlord			Rented from private owners or with job or business		
	1994	1999	2004[3]	1994	1999	2004[3]	1994	1999	2004[3]	1994	1999	2004[3]
North East	60	62	65	29	26	17	4	4	9	7	7	9
North West	68	69	72	19	17	10	5	6	10	8	8	8
Yorkshire and the Humber	64	67	70	22	20	15	3	3	5	11	10	10
East Midlands	70	72	75	18	16	12	2	3	5	10	8	8
West Midlands	67	70	72	22	17	11	3	6	10	8	7	8
East	72	73	75	15	13	10	3	5	6	10	10	9
London	56	57	59	22	19	15	6	8	9	16	16	17
South East	75	75	75	11	8	6	4	6	7	10	11	12
South West	73	74	74	13	9	6	2	5	7	12	12	13
England[2]	67	69	71	18	15	11	4	6	8	11	10	11
Wales	71	72	74	18	16	13	3	4	5	8	9	9
Scotland[3]	57	62	66	33	25	16	4	6	11	7	7	8
Northern Ireland[4]	69	72	77	26	21	14	2	3	3	4	5	5

1 On 1 April each year, except for Scotland and Northern Ireland (up to 2000) where the figure is on 31 December the previous year. From 2002 the figures for Northern Ireland are for 31 March. See Notes and Definitions.
2 Data for 1994 and 1999 have been adjusted to match the Census 2001 estimates.
3 Latest data relate to 2003 and are provisional. Estimates from 2003 will reflect change of tenure of stock transfers which took place for Dumfries and Galloway, Glasgow and Scottish Borders.
4 Northern Ireland figures cover only occupied dwellings.

Source: Office of the Deputy Prime Minister; National Assembly for Wales; Scottish Executive; Department for Social Development, Northern Ireland

Table **6.4**   Households: by type of dwelling, 2002/03

Percentages

	Detached house	Semi-detached house	Terraced house	Purpose-built flat or maisonette	Other[1]
United Kingdom	22	31	27	16	4
North East	13	40	36	9	2
North West	19	40	32	7	2
Yorkshire and the Humber	20	39	32	7	2
East Midlands	30	39	23	6	2
West Midlands	22	43	22	10	2
East	31	31	24	11	3
London	5	21	31	30	13
South East	30	29	26	11	4
South West	28	29	28	10	5
England	22	34	28	12	4
Wales	26	38	23	9	4
Scotland	20	26	17	33	4
Northern Ireland	37	25	31	6	2

1 Includes conversion flats which are particularly common in London.

Source: Survey of English Housing, Office of the Deputy Prime Minister; General Household Survey, Office for National Statistics; Continuous Household Survey, Northern Ireland Statistics and Research Agency

Table **6.5** Households: by length of time at current address, 2002/03

Percentages

	Less than 12 months	12 months, less than 5 years	5 years, less than 10 years	10 years, less than 20 years	20 years or more
United Kingdom	11	25	17	21	26
North East	10	21	15	23	31
North West	9	25	16	21	29
Yorkshire and the Humber	11	26	16	22	25
East Midlands	10	27	14	22	27
West Midlands	9	23	16	21	30
East	10	28	18	19	25
London	13	28	16	20	23
South East	10	27	17	22	24
South West	11	27	18	21	23
England	11	26	16	21	26
Wales	10	27	16	17	29
Scotland	10	27	18	22	24
Northern Ireland	7	22	18	23	31

Source: Survey of English Housing, Office of the Deputy Prime Minister; General Household Survey, Office for National Statistics; Continuous Household Survey, Northern Ireland Statistics and Research Agency

Table **6.6** Selected housing costs of owner-occupiers,[1,2] 2003/04

£ per week

	Type of housing costs				
	Mortgages	Endowment policies	Structural insurance	Service payments[3]	All owner-occupier[4]
Great Britain	57	23	6	9	44
North East	39	16	5	3	32
North West	45	18	5	2	35
Yorkshire and the Humber	42	17	5	2	34
East Midlands	50	19	5	8	37
West Midlands	51	21	5	7	38
East	67	24	6	9	49
London	84	28	7	17	67
South East	78	35	6	11	60
South West	61	21	5	10	43
England	60	23	6	9	46
Wales	40	17	5	6	28
Scotland	43	20	5	6	38
Northern Ireland	42	18	5	..	34

1 Those who did not make any payments within one of the categories are excluded. This table is therefore not directly comparable with data published in editions of Regional Trends before 2001 which included all owner-occupiers. See Notes and Definitions.
2 These figures do not include part own, part rent properties.
3 Northern Ireland service payments data not supplied as figures are not comparable with the rest of the UK.
4 Relates to both householders with a mortgage and those who own their house outright.

Source: Family Resources Survey, Department for Work and Pensions; Family Expenditure Survey, Northern Ireland Statistics and Research Agency

Table **6.7**   Average dwelling prices,[1] 2004

£ thousands and percentages

	Average sale price (£ thousands)				All dwellings		
	Detached houses	Semi-detached houses	Terraced houses	Flats/ maisonettes	Average price (£ thousands) 2003	Average price (£ thousands) 2004	Percentage increase 2003-2004
England and Wales	282	169	140	171	164	183	11.8
North East	215	121	89	104	103	122	17.9
North West	248	138	87	129	113	133	17.5
Yorkshire and the Humber	230	128	95	127	114	134	17.0
East Midlands	223	130	109	115	134	152	13.4
West Midlands	258	144	116	121	140	157	12.5
East	285	185	159	136	178	197	10.5
London	561	318	279	241	259	275	6.1
South East	371	215	179	152	209	228	9.0
South West	294	183	160	145	176	199	13.0
England	287	171	143	172	167	186	11.2
Wales	204	125	99	127	113	139	22.4

1 Excludes those bought at non-market prices. Averages are taken from the last quarter of each year. See Notes and Definitions.

Source: Land Registry

Table **6.8**   Mortgage advances, income and age of borrowers[1], 2004

	First-time buyers			Previous owner-occupiers		
	Average percentage of price advanced	Average recorded income[2] (£ per annum)	Average age of borrowers (years)	Average percentage of price advanced	Average recorded income[2] (£ per annum)	Average age of borrowers (years)
United Kingdom	78.0	32,437	33	63.9	40,734	39
North East	76.7	24,385	35	65.4	33,870	38
North West	79.0	26,143	33	66.6	36,648	38
Yorkshire and the Humber	79.3	27,029	33	65.4	35,705	38
East Midlands	80.4	30,062	32	64.1	36,736	38
West Midlands	78.3	29,009	33	64.5	37,533	38
East	78.8	34,715	32	61.4	42,304	39
London	76.3	44,244	34	64.7	60,091	38
South East	77.0	37,500	32	61.0	47,279	39
South West	77.7	34,268	32	58.8	39,319	40
England	78.0	33,691	33	63.3	42,128	39
Wales	78.0	26,769	34	64.7	34,743	38
Scotland	76.0	24,280	34	68.8	34,138	39
Northern Ireland	82.1	24,103	33	66.0	33,099	38

1 Figures in this table are taken from the Survey of Mortgage Lenders, a survey of mortgages at completion stage. First-time buyers include sitting tenant purchases. See Notes and Definitions.
2 The income of borrowers is the total recorded income taken into account when the mortgage is granted.

Source: Office of the Deputy Prime Minister

Table **6.9** Average weekly rents: by tenure, 2003/04

£ per week

	Average weekly rents by sector[1]		
	Private	Local authorities	Registered Social Landlords
United Kingdom	121	56	68
North East	75	48	57
North West	95	52	64
Yorkshire and the Humber	102	48	58
East Midlands	96	52	64
West Midlands	80	54	61
East	114	58	69
London	182	75	87
South East	132	66	77
South West	101	57	66
England	126	58	70
Wales	79	53	58
Scotland	83	46	53
Northern Ireland	78	49	56

1 Excludes rent-free accommodation and squats. See Notes and Definitions.

Source: Family Resources Survey, Department for Work and Pensions; Northern Ireland Housing Executive; Department for Social Development, Northern Ireland

Table **6.10** Dwellings in council tax bands, 2004/05[1]

Percentages

	Council tax bands[2]							
	A	B	C	D	E	F	G	H
North East	57.8	14.0	14.1	7.5	3.8	1.7	1.0	0.1
North West	43.2	19.0	17.3	9.8	5.8	2.8	1.9	0.2
Yorkshire and the Humber	45.2	19.5	16.3	9.0	5.7	2.7	1.6	0.1
East Midlands	38.3	22.3	17.8	10.5	6.2	3.0	1.7	0.2
West Midlands	32.0	24.9	19.1	10.9	6.9	3.7	2.3	0.2
East	14.4	21.2	26.3	17.4	10.6	5.8	3.9	0.5
London	3.4	13.5	26.7	25.4	15.3	7.7	6.2	1.7
South East	8.7	16.4	25.8	20.0	13.5	8.1	6.5	0.9
South West	17.2	24.4	23.1	15.8	10.6	5.4	3.1	0.3
England	25.4	19.3	21.6	15.1	9.5	5.0	3.6	0.6

1 Based on the number of dwellings on the valuation list on 29 March 2005.
2 For council tax band definitions see Notes and Definitions.

Source: Valuation Office Agency of HM Revenue & Customs.

Table 6.11 County Court mortgage possession orders[1]

Thousands

	1991			2001			2004		
	Actions entered	Suspended orders	Orders made	Actions entered	Suspended orders	Orders made	Actions entered	Suspended orders	Orders made
England and Wales	186.6	69.1	73.9	67.4	29.1	18.7	77.9	26.1	20.3
North East	6.0	2.9	1.9	3.5	1.7	1.2	3.5	1.2	0.9
North West	22.3	8.6	7.5	12.4	5.5	3.8	10.7	3.7	2.7
Yorkshire and the Humber	14.1	5.1	5.7	7.2	3.4	2.3	6.6	2.4	1.7
East Midlands	13.5	4.5	5.2	5.3	2.4	1.6	5.8	2.1	1.6
West Midlands	17.7	6.5	6.9	7.8	3.6	2.2	8.6	3.1	2.2
East	18.6	6.0	8.4	5.7	2.3	1.4	7.9	2.6	2.0
London	35.3	13.1	14.4	7.7	2.7	1.9	13.5	3.9	3.8
South East	32.2	13.2	13.2	8.6	3.4	2.0	11.5	3.8	2.9
South West	16.7	5.8	6.5	4.5	1.9	1.1	5.4	1.8	1.4
England	176.4	65.6	69.9	62.8	27.0	17.3	73.5	24.6	19.2
Wales	10.2	3.5	4.0	4.7	2.1	1.4	4.4	1.5	1.1
Northern Ireland[2]	3.1	..	..	1.6	0.2	0.7	2.2	0.5	1.2

1 Local authority and private. See Notes and Definitions.
2 Mortgage possession actions are heard in Chancery Division of Northern Ireland High Court.

Source: The Court Service; Northern Ireland Court Service

Table 6.12 Households accepted as homeless[1]: by reason, 2003/04

Percentages and numbers

	Reasons for homelessness							
	No longer willing or able to remain with:			Break-down of relation-ship with partner	Mortgage arrears	Rent arrears or other reason for loss of rented or tied accomm-odation	Other reasons[2]	Total[3] (=100%) (numbers)
	Parents	Relatives or friends	Parents, relatives or friends					
England and Wales	22	15	37	20	2	20	21	144,580
North East	25	10	35	29	2	17	17	8,350
North West	17	10	27	26	2	18	28	18,030
Yorkshire and the Humber	17	13	30	24	1	16	29	16,190
East Midlands	22	11	33	26	1	20	20	9,590
West Midlands	22	14	36	23	2	19	21	15,600
East	25	13	39	20	2	24	16	11,190
London	24	27	51	10	1	18	21	30,080
South East	26	15	41	17	1	26	16	15,150
South West	22	11	33	19	1	27	20	11,230
England	22	15	37	20	2	20	21	135,430
Wales[2]	20	8	28	24	2	22	24	9,150
Scotland[4]	18	14	32	22	1	12	32	29,590
Northern Ireland[2]	-	-	21	11	1	10	56	8,600

1 See Notes and Definitions for further details of homelessness.
2 A large proportion of the Northern Ireland total is classified as 'Other reasons' owing to differences in the definitions used. For Wales 'Other reasons' includes Violence/harassment 3 per cent and In institution/care 8 per cent.
3 The totals may not equal the sum of components because of rounding.
4 In Scotland, the basis of these figures is households assessed by the local authorities as unintentionally homeless, or potentially homeless, and in priority need, as defined in section 24 of the Housing (Scotland) Act 1987. The figures for Scotland relate to the financial year 2002/03.

Source: Office of the Deputy Prime Minister; National Assembly for Wales; Scottish Executive; Department for Social Development, Northern Ireland

Chapter 7 Health and Care

Organisation

From 1 April 2002 Primary Care Trusts (PCTs) and Care Groups have been the main providers of NHS (National Health Service) services in England and Wales. Twenty-eight Strategic Health Authorities oversee the work of the PCTs. Table 7.1 gives background information for these authorities.

Of the Strategic Health Authorities, Trent is responsible for services to most people, with 2.7 million living within its boundaries. However, Greater Manchester had the highest number of children, with more than half a million under 16-year-olds, with Surrey and Sussex providing services to more than 550 thousand people of retirement age.

Infant and perinatal mortality

Birmingham and Black Country Strategic Health Authority had the highest perinatal mortality rate (still births and deaths of babies under one week old) in England in 2003, 12.2 per 1,000 live and still births, and only Bridgend and Torfaen in Wales were higher (12.8 and 13.2 per 1,000 live and still births respectively). (Table 7.1)

There has been continued improvement in the survival rates of babies and young children over the last 20 years. Infant mortality has declined in all areas of the United Kingdom during this period from an average of 11.2 in 1981. However, between 2003 and 2004 the rate increased in a few areas, most notably in Wales from 4.1 to 5.1 and in the South West from 4.0 to 4.7 deaths of children under one year per 1,000 live births. The South East now has the lowest infant mortality rate of 3.9 in 2004, with the highest – 6.8 deaths per 1,000 live births – being in the West Midlands, which was considerably above the UK average rate of 5.1.

Of the regions of England, London continues to have the highest rate of stillbirths (6.2 per 1,000 live and stillbirths). The rate of stillbirths continued to show a downward trend, although there were slight increases in several areas such as Wales, Scotland, the East, South East and North East in 2004 compared with rates in 2003.

Perinatal mortality averaged 8.2 still births and deaths of infants under one week of age per 1,000 live and still births in the UK in 2004, compared with 12.0 in 1981. The improvement was most marked in Wales, with rates declining from 14.1 to 7.9 over the 23-year period. West Midlands continued to have high rates of perinatal mortality and was the highest in 2004 at 9.5 deaths per 1,000 births. (Table 7.2)

Mortality rates

The Age-standardised Mortality Ratio (SMR) makes allowance for differences in the age structure of the population over time and sex. Scotland had the highest SMR of 1,089 in 2003, whereas the lowest ratio was 849 in the South West; the South East and the East of England also had low SMRs of 852 and 865 respectively. Age-Standardised Mortality Ratios were higher for females than for males in each of these areas.

Circulatory disease was the largest single cause of death in 2003, averaging 356 deaths per 100,000 people for the UK as a whole. Cancer was the next most common cause, with a Standardised Mortality Ratio of 246 overall. Regional differences were slightly more marked in respect of circulatory disease than for cancer.

Scotland had the highest mortality ratios for both males and females for each of these diseases. Deaths from cancer and circulatory diseases in southern and eastern regions were below the national average in 2003. Over the two years between 2001 and 2003, all regions have shown a decrease in the death rates from circulatory and heart disease. The largest reduction was in Northern Ireland, down by 39 deaths per 100,000 population. Generally speaking, the northern parts of the UK showed the greatest improvements.

There were also reductions in the death rates from cancer in most areas; the greatest improvement between 2001 and 2003 was in the West Midlands.

On the other hand, the death rate from respiratory disease has been on the increase in all areas, and increases were particularly marked amongst the female population, with increases in rate ranging from 5 per 100,000 population in Northern Ireland to 19 in the South West between 2001 and 2003. Except for Wales and Scotland where increase in rates were much the same for males and females, the increases in death rates for females were more than twice those for males in each region during the same time period.

Scotland had the highest incidence of suicides and open verdicts as to cause of death for both males and females (23 and 8 per 100,000 population respectively); this compared with rates in the East of England of 12 and 4 respectively. Rates of suicides and open verdicts are three times higher for males than females overall. (Table 7.4)

Incidence of TB

London had by far the highest notification rate of tuberculosis (TB) in 2004 with 34.8 notifications per 100,000 population; more than twice the second highest rate of 16.4 in the West Midlands. However, the rate in London continues to show small declines since peaks of around 40 per 100,000 people in years 2000 and 2001. The lowest incidence of reported TB was in Northern Ireland at 4.3 per 100,000 population in 2004.

The incidence of TB showed a rise in the South West to 5.3 per 100,000 population in 2004, after being fairly stable for the previous decade. Similarly, in the South East there has been a steady increase in the rate of notification to 7.5 over a number of years since 1999. (Table 7.3)

Cervical and breast screening

The proportion of women screened for cervical cancer has declined slightly over the last few years to just over four-fifths of the target population in 2004. The decline in proportion screened is more marked in the younger age groups. Northern Ireland, Wales and London had appreciably lower proportions of women in the lowest age band (to 34 years) participating in cervical screening in 2004 (67.8, 69.3 and 70.6 per cent respectively), despite screening commencing five years earlier in Wales than elsewhere.

Although over 85 per cent of women in Scotland in the 20 to 60 age group were screened in 2004, the area had one of the highest age-standardised death rates from cervical cancer. This rate of 5.6 per 100,000 women was equalled by the North West. The death rate from cervical cancer was lowest in the East of England at 3.3.

Women aged 53 to 64 in London had the lowest breast cancer screening rate, 64 per cent, 15 percentage points below the East Midlands where almost four-fifths of women aged 50 to 64 participated in the breast screening programme in 2004.

Age-standardised death rates from breast cancer had declined slightly in most regions in the last few years; the largest improvement was in the North East which now has the lowest death rate of 44.5 per 100,000 women aged 20 or over. Unfortunately, Wales, Scotland and Northern Ireland all showed increases in the age-standardised death rates from breast cancer in 2004 compared to 2003. (Table 7.6)

Cancer

Figure 7.5 clearly shows the regional variation in registrations of cancers for selected sites in the body; these variations exist after allowance has been made for age differences in the regional population. For example, the standardised ratio for melanoma of the skin was highest in the South West, one and half times the UK average and more than twice the lowest ratio in London (156 registrations compared with 61 for males and 143 compared with 55 for females).

Inclusion of melanoma means that the South West had the highest standardised registration ratio for females over all types of cancers at 115 (England = 100), and second highest for males with a standardised ratio of 114. If melanomas are excluded from the standardised registration ratios for all cancers, rates in the South West declined significantly, leaving the North East with the highest rates for both males and females of all the English regions in 2003, with 117 and 112 respectively.

Breast cancer continues to be the most common type in England, with 143.5 registrations per 100,000 females, approximately one-quarter of the total cancer registrations. The highest registration rate was in the South West with 173.8 per 100,000 population, almost one-third of all female cancers in that region. Regional differences for breast and prostate cancers were much narrower than for melanoma, ranging from 91 per cent of the UK average in Northern Ireland to 107 per cent in the South West for breast cancer in 2003. The South West also had the highest rate of registrations for prostate cancer with 149.5 per 100,000 males, 14 percentage points above the UK average compared with Scotland which had the lowest, 17 percentage points below the average.

The total incidence of cancer has changed little over the last ten years in England. Registration rates for males have reduced slightly to 389 per 100,000 population in 2003, whereas the rate for females has increased by 5 per cent to 340. These overall rates mask increases and decreases in the incidence of various cancers and also changes in regional patterns. Direct comparison at individual regional level is not possible owing to changes in the areas for which data are collected. Some general patterns can be seen by grouping regions together.

By 2003, registrations of people suffering from stomach cancer have declined to just over two-thirds of the rates in 1994 for England overall. Similar improvements are evident in lung cancer among males. However, there has been very little change in the rate of registration of females with lung cancer for England. In some areas, particularly northern regions (Northern, Yorkshire and the North West Health Regions in 1994 compared with the North East, the North West and Yorkshire and the Humber in 2003), there have been increases in the incidence rate of lung cancer among females.

Between 1994 and 2003, registration rates for some cancers such as skin melanoma and colorectal for both sexes and prostate cancer for males have also shown increases. The rise in the latter was particularly marked in the late 1990s.

Incidence of HIV

The number of patients diagnosed with HIV increased by 17 per cent between 2002 and 2003 and a further 14 per cent between 2003 and 2004 in the UK overall. There are now in excess of 42 thousand infected patients. Sexual activity accounted for about 90 per cent of probable routes of infection in most regions, with the exception of Scotland where injecting drugs probably caused about one-fifth. There was considerable increase in sex between men and women as the probable cause of infection. In 2004 this was the probable cause of 36 per cent of HIV infection in the North West, ranging up to 67 per cent in the East.

While other causes of HIV infection increased, the number of people probably infected by blood products showed a slight decline between 2002 and 2004. Numbers from this source remained small, ranging from 0.4 per cent in Northern Ireland to 4.6 per cent in Wales in 2004. (Table 7.7)

Cigarette smoking

People smoke less in London than in other parts of Great Britain. For both males and females, London had the highest percentages of people aged 16 or over who had never or only occasionally smoked in 2003/04 – 51 and 64 per cent respectively. London also had the highest proportion (11 per cent) of males who smoked less than ten cigarettes per day and one of the lowest percentages, together with males in the South East (8 per cent), of people who smoked 20 or more per day.

In Scotland, 16 per cent of males and 10 per cent of females smoked 20 or more cigarettes per day, in each case the highest proportions of any area. Over the last few years the proportion of males in Scotland smoking 20 or more cigarettes a day has steadily increased, whereas in many other areas there have been little change or slight reductions in high consumption.

Throughout the United Kingdom the proportion of males who had given up smoking was higher than females. Overall, approximately one-fifth of females claimed to be ex-regular smokers, ranging from 16 per cent in London to 30 per cent in Northern Ireland. (Table 7.8)

Alcohol consumption

Two-fifths of males and almost three-fifths of females in Northern Ireland drank nothing in the week leading up to being surveyed in 2003/04. London had the next highest proportions, one-third (for males) and one-half (for females). However, Northern Ireland also had the highest percentage of males (29 per cent) who drank more than the recommended daily maximum of eight units, 6 percentage points above the UK average.

Within England, Yorkshire and the Humber and the North West had the highest proportions of both males and females consuming above their recommended maxima (28 and 13 per cent respectively). By contrast, London had the lowest proportions, 18 per cent of males and only 5 per cent of females, who drank to excess in the review period in 2003/04.

In many areas there was a reduction in the proportion of females who drank more than six units per day in the two years up to 2003/04. In other areas the proportion stayed the same or increased only very slightly. In contrast, over the same period the only areas showing a reduction in the proportions of males drinking in excess of eight units per day were the North East, London and Scotland. There were appreciable increases in the proportion of males drinking above the recommended daily maximum – 6 percentage points in both the East and West Midlands. (Table 7.9)

Illegal drugs

More than a quarter of young people in England and Wales aged 16 to 29 years used illegal drugs in 2003/04, according to the British Crime Survey. By far the greatest increase in use was in Wales, where the proportion more than doubled in the two years to 29.7 per cent. There were increases in the use of hallucinants and cannabis in many areas over this period. Wales has now the highest proportion of young people using cannabis of any area.

Although one-quarter of young people used cannabis in the South East in 2003/04, the region showed the greatest decrease of nearly 6 percentage points since the previous year.

Ecstasy is used by approximately 5 per cent of 16- to 29-year-olds overall, and between 2002/03 and 2003/04 the proportions have increased in many areas particularly in the North East, Yorkshire and the Humber and the West Midlands. The proportion of young people using opiates has also increased in northern regions as well as in London and the East. (Figure 7.10)

Prescriptions

On average in England over £162 was spent per person on prescription drugs in 2004, an increase of approximately 16 per cent from 2002 figures. Other countries of the United Kingdom spent considerably more than this, with Northern Ireland the highest at £214 per head. This represented an increase of 28 per cent over the two-year period.

Wales continued to have the highest number of prescription items dispensed, 18.4 per person, compared with London where the average was 10.5 per person, although the average net ingredient cost in Wales was one of the lowest at £10.70 per item prescribed. The highest net ingredient cost was in Northern Ireland at £13.40 per item, an increase of £1.60 per item in two years and more than twice the rise in most other regions.

There was a continued increase in the number of prescriptions dispensed, which in 2004 was approaching the 900 thousand mark. The greatest increase in number was in the East which showed a 13 per cent growth between 2002 and 2004. The proportion of prescriptions dispensed on behalf of children declined in all regions, again reflecting our ageing population. Between 84 per cent of prescriptions in the South East and 94 per cent in Northern Ireland were exempt from charge. (Table 7.11)

Hospital activity

There were reductions in the number of available NHS beds per 1,000 population in all areas except South West London, the South West Peninsular and Trent in the East Midlands, where increases of 5.7, 5.6 and 2.9 per cent respectively were seen between 2002/03 and 2003/04. Admissions per available bed were also lower than in 2002/03, except in a few areas where increases of up to 5.4 per cent per available bed were seen as in North West London. Other areas in the East and South (for example Essex, Bedfordshire and Hertfordshire, Avon, Gloucestershire and Wiltshire, Surrey and Sussex, South East London) and Greater Manchester, Scotland and Northern Ireland showed an increase in admissions per available bed.

With the exception of the North West which showed a decline of 2.1 per cent, the regions of England had increases in the number of day cases handled between 2003 and 2004. The largest increase of over 16 per cent was in Northern Ireland, which contrasted with a reduction of nearly 20 per cent in Wales and over 7 per cent in Scotland. Shropshire and Staffordshire had the largest increase of day cases within England of 11.3 per cent.

The equivalent of about one-third of the population attended accident and emergency departments in 2003/04. In Cheshire and Merseyside and North Central London the rates were as high as 47.2 and 48.6 per cent of the population. Overall in London, the number of people visiting accident and emergency during 2003/04 was equivalent to over 40 per cent of the population if they each used accident and emergency only once. In all areas except Scotland, the South East and London there were increases in accident and emergency attendances between 2002/03 and 2003/04. The increase in attendance at these clinics was substantial in many areas, the Strategic Health Authority of North Central London having the greatest increase of over 46 per cent in a year, while Cheshire and Merseyside with 42 per cent, Hampshire and the Isle of Wight (38 per cent) and South West London with 37 per cent, were not far behind.

The number of finished consultant episodes increased by more than 4 per cent over-all in England in 2003/04 compared with 2002/03. The greatest increase, of nearly 11 per cent, was in Surrey and Sussex. Shropshire and Staffordshire and South East London with around 10 per cent each were next. Decreases in the number of finished consultant episodes were most noticeable in Kent and Medway, down by nearly 3 per cent between the two years. (Table 7.12)

Number of GPs

The proportion of female general practitioners (GPs) continued to rise to almost two fifths in England and Scotland by September 2004. The proportions were slightly lower in Wales and Northern Ireland at 33 and 35 per cent respectively. In North West and South West London, 48 per cent of GPs were female. London was also the region with the highest proportion of practices operated by a single GP at 31 per cent overall.

Each GP on average looked after 1,666 patients in England in September 2004, and the figures were similar for Wales and Northern Ireland (1,674 and 1,652 respectively). In Scotland, the number of patients for each GP was considerably lower, probably reflecting the greater distances over which people resided. List sizes continued to decrease in most areas in between 2003 and 2004 despite increases in a few areas the previous year. General practitioners in London looked after the largest number of patients, averaging 1,765 across the capital, with doctors in the North West area of the city having the highest average list size at 1,882 patients.

The proportion of the population registered with an NHS dentist showed a decline in most areas in the year to September 2004 compared with 12 months previously. Only Birmingham and the Black Country and a couple of areas in London (North East and South East) had an increased proportion of the population registered with a dentist. (Table 7.13)

Council supported residents

There has been a decline in all regions in the overall number of residents supported by local authorities between 2002 and 2004. The proportions looked after in independent nursing homes and council staffed establishments have shown the largest reduction. The South West was the only region with an increase in the number of people supported in staffed care homes.

In the East of England over 70 per cent of residents who were supported by the local council were looked after in independent residential care homes. This was 10 percentage points higher than any other region of England. The proportion of supported people in independent residential homes increased slightly in all regions except the West Midlands and the South East between 2002 and 2004. In the North East the proportion increased by 4.2 percentage points.

London had by far the highest proportion (33 per cent) of council supported residents who were aged 18 to 64 years old in March 2004, whereas in the North East only 16 per cent were younger than 65 years. Of those under 65 in registered care homes in London, over half were people with learning disabilities (amounting to 18 per cent of all people accommodated in homes). This compared with 8 per cent of the total looked after with learning disabilities in the North East. London also had the highest proportion (almost 9 per cent) being looked after because of mental health problems. (Table 7.14)

Children looked after by local authorities

Scotland had the highest proportion of children in local authority care, with an average of 106 out of 10,000 young people under 18, and the next highest was London with 75 for the year ending March 2004. The average for England was 55, with the lowest rate of 42 in the East Midlands and the South East. Scotland also had the highest rate of new children entering care, equivalent to 42 per 10,000 under 18s in the year to March 2004, whereas new admissions in the South East were the lowest at 16 per 10,000 children.

Compared with 2002, there were 1,400 more young people in care throughout England at the end of March 2004. London accounted for 750 of this increase. There were also reasonably large increases in Wales (675) and Scotland (435). Relative to the size of the under-18 population, Wales showed the largest increase.

Except in Scotland, foster homes continued to be the most common form of accommodation, accounting for almost 70 per cent of children in care in England and Wales. In Scotland less than one-third of the young people under 18 were cared for in this way and in Northern Ireland the figure was 60 per cent in 2004.

London had the highest proportion of young people being cared for in children's homes and hostels at 14 per cent, followed by Scotland with 13 per cent, more than twice the proportion in Wales, where local authorities cared for 6 per cent in homes. (Table 7.15)

Table 7.1 Population and vital statistics for NHS Strategic Health Authorities[1]

Thousands and rates

	Mid-2004 population estimates (thousands)				Birth rate[3] 2003	Total fertility rate[4] 2003	SMR[5] 2003	Perinatal mortality rate[6] 2003	Infant mortality rate[7] 2003
	Total All ages	Children aged 0 to 15	Working age: 16 to pension age[2]	Pension age or over[2]					
North East	**2,545.1**	**479.9**	**1,570.5**	**494.7**	**10.6**	**1.66**	**110**	**7.8**	**4.9**
County Durham and Tees Valley	1,148.7	223.5	705.9	219.2	10.9	1.73	110	8.2	5.3
Northumberland, Tyne and Wear	1,396.4	256.4	864.5	275.4	10.4	1.60	110	7.6	4.6
North West	**6,827.2**	**1,349.9**	**4,198.1**	**1,279.2**	**11.4**	**1.73**	**109**	**9.0**	**5.9**
Cheshire and Merseyside	2,358.5	459.6	1,443.7	455.2	10.9	1.68	108	8.1	5.2
Cumbria and Lancashire	1,929.7	376.4	1,166.8	386.4	10.9	1.79	105	9.3	6.3
Greater Manchester	2,539.0	513.9	1,587.6	437.6	12.3	1.75	113	9.5	6.1
Yorkshire and the Humber	**5,038.8**	**990.7**	**3,102.1**	**946.1**	**11.6**	**1.76**	**101**	**9.0**	**5.7**
North and East Yorkshire and Northern Lincolnshire	1,652.4	310.6	1,002.8	339.0	10.2	1.70	98	7.0	3.9
South Yorkshire	1,278.4	247.7	789.7	241.1	11.4	1.72	105	9.1	5.6
West Yorkshire	2,108.0	432.4	1,309.6	366.0	12.8	1.81	101	10.1	6.9
East Midlands	**4,279.7**	**827.0**	**2,642.5**	**810.2**	**11.0**	**1.70**	**100**	**9.5**	**5.9**
Leicestershire, Northamptonshire and Rutland	1,592.2	319.8	995.3	277.1	12.1	1.81	98	9.0	6.1
Trent	2,687.5	507.2	1,647.2	533.1	10.4	1.64	101	9.9	5.9
West Midlands	**5,334.0**	**1,072.0**	**3,254.3**	**1,007.7**	**12.0**	**1.84**	**101**	**10.2**	**7.4**
Birmingham and the Black Country	2,275.0	485.9	1,377.5	411.6	13.7	1.97	104	12.2	8.6
Shropshire and Staffordshire	1,499.6	288.5	919.8	291.3	10.7	1.69	98	7.3	5.5
West Midlands South[8]	1,559.5	297.6	957.0	304.9	10.7	1.76	103	9.4	7.0
East of England	**5,491.3**	**1,078.1**	**3,346.3**	**1,066.9**	**11.5**	**1.77**	**94**	**7.3**	**4.5**
Bedfordshire and Hertfordshire	1,617.5	336.4	1,003.5	277.7	12.7	1.83	96	7.6	3.9
Essex	1,635.6	323.3	989.8	322.5	11.3	1.78	95	7.2	4.8
Norfolk, Suffolk and Cambridgeshire	2,238.2	418.4	1,353.0	466.7	10.7	1.71	92	7.2	4.7
London	**7,429.2**	**1,442.7**	**4,953.4**	**1,033.1**	**14.9**	**1.71**	**97**	**9.5**	**5.4**
North Central London	1,228.0	232.7	829.1	166.1	14.7	1.63	96	8.5	6.7
North East London	1,531.4	333.4	991.1	206.9	16.6	1.99	105	10.8	5.5
North West London	1,834.7	329.8	1,250.8	254.1	14.3	1.59	87	8.3	4.2
South East London	1,514.1	299.4	996.8	217.9	15.1	1.79	100	11.7	6.5
South West London	1,321.0	247.4	885.6	188.1	14.0	1.57	95	7.6	4.0
South East	**8,110.2**	**1,583.3**	**4,976.3**	**1,550.7**	**11.4**	**1.71**	**91**	**7.0**	**4.2**
Hampshire and Isle of Wight	1,801.4	341.5	1,112.9	347.0	10.7	1.63	91	6.5	3.2
Kent and Medway	1,610.3	327.2	972.1	311.0	11.4	1.81	97	7.9	5.1
Surrey and Sussex	2,577.6	484.2	1,541.0	552.5	10.9	1.69	89	6.4	3.7
Thames Valley	2,120.9	430.5	1,350.2	340.2	12.5	1.74	89	7.3	4.8
South West	**5,038.2**	**931.1**	**3,015.7**	**1,091.4**	**10.3**	**1.70**	**91**	**7.0**	**4.1**
Avon, Gloucestershire and Wiltshire	2,206.2	423.6	1,361.9	420.8	11.3	1.70	92	6.2	4.4
Dorset and Somerset	1,212.9	219.3	699.7	293.9	9.6	1.72	88	6.9	3.6
South West Peninsula	1,619.1	288.2	954.2	376.7	9.4	1.70	91	8.4	4.1
England	50,093.8	9,754.8	31,059.1	9,279.9	11.8	1.73	98	8.5	5.3
Wales	2,952.5	572.5	1,777.8	602.2	10.7	1.71	103	7.5	4.3
Scotland	5,078.4	935.5	3,229.5	913.5	10.4	1.54	116	8.0	5.1
Northern Ireland	1,710.3	383.3	1,051.7	275.2	12.7	1.81	100	8.0	5.2

1 Strategic Health Authorities were introduced by the NHS in England on 1 April 2002. See Maps section and Notes and Definitions.
2 Currently pension age is 65 or over for males and 60 or over for females.
3 Births per 1,000 population.
4 Number of children who would be born to a woman if current patterns of fertility persisted throughout her child-bearing life.
5 Standardised Mortality Ratio (SMR) is the ratio of observed deaths to those expected by applying a standard death rate to the regional population. See Notes and Definitions.
6 Still births (i.e. those born dead after 24 weeks or more gestation) and deaths of infants under one week of age per 1,000 live and still births.
7 Deaths of infants under one year of age per 1,000 live births.
8 Formerly known as Coventry, Warwickshire, Herefordshire and Worcestershire Strategic Health Authority.

Source: Office for National Statistics

Table 7.2   Still births, perinatal mortality and infant mortality[1]

Rates

	Still births[2,3]		Still births[2,3]			Perinatal mortality[3,4]		Perinatal mortality[3,4]			Infant mortality[5]			
	1981	1993	1993	2003	2004	1981	1993	1993	2003	2004	1981	1993	2003	2004
United Kingdom	6.6	4.4	5.7	5.7	5.5	12.0	7.6	9.0	8.5	8.2	11.2	6.3	5.3	5.1
North East	7.5	4.6	5.9	5.5	5.6	12.6	7.9	9.2	7.7	7.7	10.4	6.7	4.7	4.9
North West	7.0	4.5	5.8	6.0	5.5	12.7	7.7	9.0	9.1	8.2	11.3	6.5	5.9	5.4
Yorkshire and the Humber	7.8	4.6	5.9	6.0	5.7	13.5	8.0	9.4	9.0	8.7	12.1	7.3	5.8	5.5
East Midlands	6.2	3.9	5.4	6.1	5.5	11.4	7.2	8.7	9.4	8.2	11.0	6.6	5.9	5.1
West Midlands	7.0	4.4	6.0	6.0	5.5	12.9	8.4	9.9	10.1	9.5	11.7	7.1	7.3	6.8
East	5.5	3.9	5.2	4.9	5.2	10.0	6.8	8.1	7.3	7.5	9.7	5.4	4.5	4.2
London	6.3	4.9	6.1	6.8	6.2	10.3	8.2	9.5	9.5	8.9	10.7	6.5	5.4	5.2
South East	5.8	4.0	5.4	4.8	4.9	10.5	7.0	8.3	6.9	7.0	10.3	5.3	4.3	3.9
South West	6.3	4.0	5.0	5.0	4.7	10.8	6.9	7.9	7.0	7.2	10.4	5.8	4.0	4.7
England	6.5	4.3	5.7	5.7	5.5	11.7	7.6	8.9	8.5	8.1	10.9	6.3	5.3	5.1
Wales	7.3	4.5	5.8	5.1	5.5	14.1	7.0	8.3	7.5	7.9	12.6	5.5	4.1	5.1
Scotland	6.3	4.8	6.4	5.6	5.8	11.6	8.0	9.6	8.0	8.1	11.3	6.5	5.1	4.9
Northern Ireland	8.8	4.1	5.2	5.0	5.0	15.3	7.7	8.8	8.1	8.1	13.2	7.1	5.3	5.5

1 See Notes and Definitions for the Population chapter.
2 Rate per 1,000 live and still births.
3 On 1 October 1992 the legal definition of a still birth was altered from a baby born dead after 28 completed weeks gestation or more to one born dead after 24
    weeks gestation or more. Figures are given on both the old and new definitions for continuity.
4 Still births and deaths of infants under one week of age per 1,000 live and still births.
5 Deaths of infants under one year of age per 1,000 live births.

Source: Office for National Statistics; General Register Office for Scotland; Northern Ireland Statistics and Research Agency

Table 7.3   Notification rates of tuberculosis

Rates per 100,000 population

	1994	1995	1996	1997	1998	1999	2000	2001	2002	2003	2004[1]
United Kingdom	10.8	10.7	10.7	10.9	11.3	11.5	12.1	12.3	12.2	11.5	12.1
North East	6.5	6.9	6.6	7.0	6.6	5.9	5.7	7.7	6.4	6.1	6.8
North West	9.8	9.5	8.8	9.3	10.2	10.7	10.0	10.0	9.4	9.0	9.3
Yorkshire and the Humber	10.1	12.0	11.6	11.7	12.0	11.5	12.1	12.3	10.8	11.4	12.3
East Midlands	9.9	10.1	10.6	9.3	10.4	10.7	10.6	11.1	11.9	7.9	9.9
West Midlands	13.9	12.4	12.5	11.6	12.8	13.5	13.7	13.1	14.9	15.0	16.4
East	4.7	5.1	5.0	4.4	5.1	4.3	4.7	6.0	6.1	6.2	7.6
London	30.3	29.8	31.7	34.8	35.1	35.4	39.9	40.2	38.6	37.2	34.8
South East	5.3	5.5	5.3	5.4	5.5	5.3	6.1	6.6	7.3	7.4	7.5
South West	4.3	4.2	4.2	4.4	4.4	4.3	4.6	4.0	4.8	4.5	5.3
England	11.2	11.2	11.3	11.7	12.2	12.2	13.0	13.4	13.4	12.8	13.2
Wales	6.3	6.2	5.6	6.7	5.9	7.1	6.7	4.9	4.3	4.6	6.1
Scotland	10.7	9.4	10.0	8.5	9.0	9.8	9.3	9.3	8.3	6.1	7.0
Northern Ireland	5.7	5.5	4.5	4.5	3.6	3.6	3.5	2.8	4.0	2.2	4.3

1 Provisional data based on 2003 population figures.

Source: Public Health Laboratory Service, Communicable Disease Surveillance Centre; Scottish Centre for Infection and Environmental Health;
         Department of Health, Social Services and Public Safety, Northern Ireland

Table **7.4**   Age-standardised mortality rates:[1] by cause[2] and sex, 2003

Rates per 100,000 population

	All circulatory diseases			All respiratory diseases			All injuries and poisonings				
	Total	Ischaemic heart disease	Cerebro-vascular disease	Total	Bronchitis and allied conditions	Cancer[3]	Total	Road traffic accidents	Suicides and open verdicts	All other causes	All causes[4]
Males											
United Kingdom	328	188	72	110	46	247	41	10	15	144	870
North East	366	216	83	123	57	285	45	8	18	152	970
North West	365	214	82	125	54	262	44	8	14	150	947
Yorkshire and the Humber	332	198	75	115	51	261	39	11	13	143	890
East Midlands	325	188	67	114	47	244	41	11	14	141	865
West Midlands	337	191	79	111	48	250	42	11	14	155	894
East	288	160	59	93	38	227	37	11	12	128	773
London	314	174	65	118	48	236	36	6	12	147	851
South East	288	160	62	94	37	226	35	9	13	127	769
South West	291	162	67	89	37	223	37	10	13	126	766
England	319	182	70	108	45	242	39	9	13	140	847
Wales	357	206	78	114	52	253	50	11	19	137	911
Scotland	384	231	88	125	55	287	57	11	23	189	1,041
Northern Ireland	328	196	74	118	46	248	46	11	14	143	883
Females											
United Kingdom	377	160	124	142	44	238	24	3	5	218	999
North East	406	189	124	160	65	263	25	2	4	239	1,093
North West	414	180	136	167	58	251	28	3	5	226	1,086
Yorkshire and the Humber	379	171	125	149	52	241	19	3	4	223	1,010
East Midlands	367	155	119	141	39	231	26	4	4	230	995
West Midlands	386	158	131	140	42	233	27	3	4	228	1,013
East	344	139	111	128	33	222	23	4	4	215	933
London	357	146	110	151	41	233	21	3	5	205	967
South East	345	134	115	127	33	219	22	4	4	201	914
South West	346	144	120	116	31	223	21	3	4	202	908
England	369	155	121	141	42	233	24	3	4	216	982
Wales	401	175	128	146	50	239	25	3	5	215	1,025
Scotland	431	193	150	149	57	275	33	4	8	239	1,126
Northern Ireland	382	174	126	153	41	238	22	3	4	193	988
All people											
United Kingdom	356	177	99	128	46	246	33	6	10	182	945
North East	390	205	105	143	62	277	34	5	11	197	1,041
North West	394	199	110	148	57	259	36	5	9	189	1,025
Yorkshire and the Humber	360	187	101	134	52	254	29	7	8	184	960
East Midlands	352	175	94	130	44	242	34	7	9	186	944
West Midlands	366	177	107	128	46	245	34	7	9	192	965
East	321	153	86	113	36	229	30	7	8	172	865
London	339	162	88	137	46	237	28	5	9	177	918
South East	321	150	89	112	36	226	28	6	8	165	852
South West	323	156	94	105	35	227	29	6	9	165	849
England	348	171	96	126	45	241	31	6	9	179	926
Wales	384	193	104	132	52	249	37	7	12	177	979
Scotland	410	213	120	138	57	282	44	7	15	214	1,089
Northern Ireland	357	186	101	137	44	245	34	7	9	169	943

1 Based on deaths registered in 2003. Rates standardised to the mid-1991 United Kingdom population for males and females separately. See Notes and Definitions.
2 Deaths at ages under 28 days occurring in England and Wales are not assigned an underlying cause.
3 Malignant neoplasms only.
4 Including deaths at ages under 28 days.

Source: Office for National Statistics; General Register Office for Scotland; Northern Ireland Statistics and Research Agency

Figure **7.5** Standardised[1] cancer registrations 2001-2003[2]

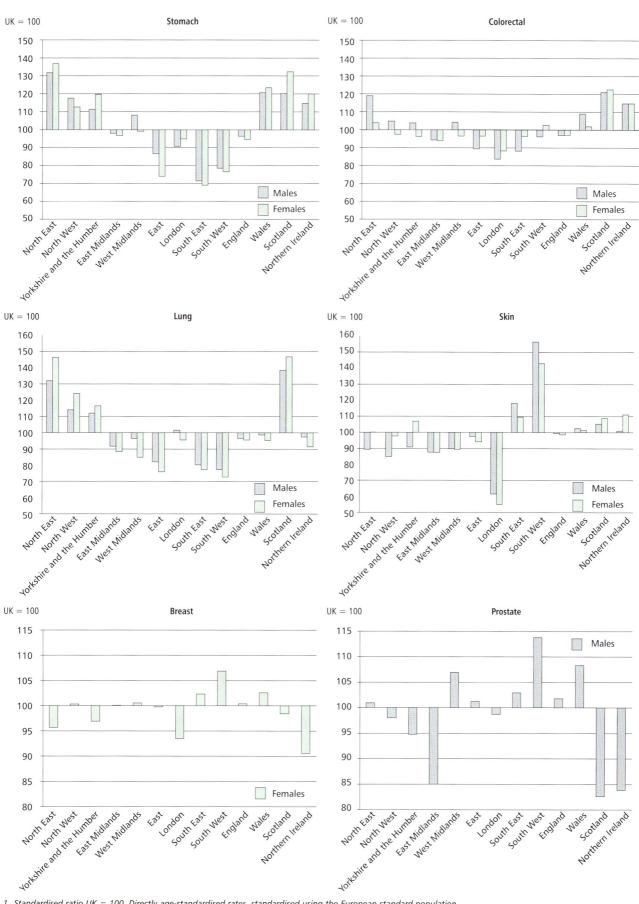

1 Standardised ratio UK = 100. Directly age-standardised rates, standardised using the European standard population.
2 Three-year averages; Scotland 2000-2002.

Source: Office for National Statistics

Table **7.6** Cervical and breast cancer: screening and age-standardised death rates

| | Cervical screening programme at 31 March 2004 | | | | | | Breast screening programme at 31 March 2004 | | | | | |
| | Percentage of target population screened: women aged[1] | | | | | Per-centage recalled early[4,5] 2003/04 | Percentage of target population screened: women aged[6] | | | | Age-standardised death rates,[8] 2002 | |
	25 to 34[2,3]	35 to 44	45 to 54	55 to 64[3]	All aged 25 to 64[2,3]		53 to 54[7]	55 to 59	60 to 64	All aged 53 to 64[7]	Cervical cancer	Breast cancer
United Kingdom	76.1	83.5	83.4	79.5	80.6	..	74.6	74.7	73.9	74.4	4.6	52.3
North East	79.9	84.5	83.4	79.7	82.1	6.3	75.2	73.5	73.0	73.6	3.9	44.5
North West	78.8	83.0	81.9	77.8	80.6	6.8	75.1	76.1	75.5	75.7	5.6	51.2
Yorkshire and the Humber	78.9	84.8	84.4	80.7	82.3	4.4	76.4	77.1	75.9	76.6	5.3	49.2
East Midlands	81.1	86.4	85.3	81.4	83.7	5.1	79.6	80.0	79.4	79.7	4.9	52.5
West Midlands	76.8	83.6	83.2	79.3	80.8	6.7	77.4	77.8	77.0	77.4	4.4	53.4
East	77.5	83.4	83.3	80.2	81.2	5.9	78.3	79.0	78.5	78.7	3.3	54.3
London	70.6	78.7	80.3	76.8	75.7	6.9	63.6	64.5	63.5	64.0	4.5	54.4
South East	77.9	84.7	84.3	81.3	82.1	5.4	76.7	77.4	77.1	77.2	3.9	52.5
South West	78.0	83.5	83.3	79.8	81.3	5.6	71.7	71.9	71.3	71.6	4.5	52.1
England	76.7	83.2	83.1	79.6	80.6	6.0	74.7	75.3	74.6	74.9	4.5	52.0
Wales	69.3	82.5	81.6	77.3	76.8	6.6	68.4	68.9	68.6	68.7	4.6	54.6
Scotland	77.9	90.1	90.9	87.7	85.5	..	76.0	73.0	72.0	74.0	5.6	54.2
Northern Ireland	67.8	74.7	73.7	66.3	71.2	..	73.6	72.3	69.0	71.8	5.1	48.0

1 For England the target population relates to women aged 25 to 64, for Wales to women 20 to 64 and for Scotland to women 20 to 60 years, screened in the previous five years (five and a half years in Scotland). Medically ineligible women (women who for example, as a result of surgery, do not require screening) in the target population are excluded from the figures, except in Northern Ireland.
2 For Wales the age groups are 20 to 34 and 20 to 64 respectively.
3 For Scotland the age groups are 20 to 34, 55 to 59 and 20 to 60 respectively.
4 Percentages recalled early relate to the year 2003/04.
5 Women whose screening test results are borderline or show mild dyskaryosis are recalled for a repeat smear in approximately six months instead of the routine five years; if the condition persists they are referred to a gynaecologist.
6 For England and Wales the target population relates to women aged 53 to 64, for Scotland and Northern Ireland to women 50 to 64, screened in the previous three years. Medically ineligible women (women who for example, as a result of surgery, do not require screening) in the target population are excluded from the figures, except in Scotland. See Notes and Definitions.
7 For Scotland and Northern Ireland the age groups are 50 to 54 and 50 to 64 respectively.
8 Deaths registered in 2004 per 100,000 women aged 20 or over. Standardised to mid-2003 UK population. See Notes and Definitions.

Source: Office for National Statistics; Department of Health; National Assembly for Wales; General Register Office for Scotland; Information and Statistics Division, NHS in Scotland; Northern Ireland Statistics and Research Agency; Department of Health, Social Services and Public Safety, Northern Ireland

Table **7.7** Diagnosed HIV-infected patients: by probable route of HIV infection and region of residence when last seen for care, 2004[1]

Numbers

	Sex between men	Injecting drug use	Sex between men and women	Blood/blood products	Mother to infant[2]	Other/not known	Total
United Kingdom[3]	17,932	1,340	19,904	495	1,463	1,048	42,182
North East	248	14	339	15	19	15	650
North West	1,869	89	1,202	64	86	58	3,368
Yorkshire and the Humber	502	31	1,027	41	67	18	1,686
East Midlands	417	54	1,014	31	85	50	1,651
West Midlands	723	27	1209	30	108	92	2189
East	618	64	1,654	27	76	23	2,462
London	9,523	483	9,198	120	788	562	20,674
South East	1882	114	2270	65	136	67	4534
South West	754	50	641	18	41	51	1,555
England[4]	16,555	926	18,564	411	1,406	937	38,799
Wales	338	19	258	31	20	11	677
Scotland	699	366	751	41	9	51	1917
Northern Ireland	124	5	99	1	8	2	239
Not known	186	23	181	5	20	45	460
Other/abroad	30	1	51	6	0	2	90

1 Patients who were seen for statutory medical HIV-related care at services in the United Kingdom in 2004.
2 Includes 540 children born to HIV-infected mothers in 2004 whose HIV infection status had not yet been confirmed, but of whom 95% are likely to be uninfected: 42 resident in Yorkshire and Humberside, 9 in North East, 43 in East Midlands, 55 in West Midlands, 39 in North West, 23 in Eastern, 259 in London, 48 in South East, nine in South West, six in Wales, three in N Ireland, and four where region was not reported.
3 United Kingdom total includes those reported to be resident abroad or whose country of residence was not reported.
4 Includes 30 patients whose region of residence within England was not known.

Source: Health Protection Agency Centre for Infections; Institute of Child Health (London); Scottish Centre for Infection and Environmental Health

Table **7.8** Cigarette smoking among people aged 16 or over: by sex, 2003/04[1]

Percentages

	Males					Females				
	Cigarettes smoked per day					Cigarettes smoked per day				
	less than 10	10, less than 20	20 or more	Ex-regular smoker	Never or only occasionally smoked	less than 10	10, less than 20	20 or more	Ex-regular smoker	Never or only occasionally smoked
United Kingdom	7	11	10	27	45	7	10	7	21	55
North East	7	9	13	31	40	8	11	8	22	51
North West	6	12	12	28	42	8	12	10	20	50
Yorkshire and the Humber	6	9	10	29	46	7	10	7	21	55
East Midlands	8	13	10	26	43	6	12	6	19	58
West Midlands	5	12	9	27	47	7	10	7	23	53
East	8	10	10	29	43	7	9	6	22	56
London	11	9	8	21	51	8	8	4	16	64
South East	8	9	8	29	47	8	9	5	23	55
South West	6	10	10	29	46	9	8	5	23	55
England	7	10	10	27	46	8	10	6	21	55
Wales	5	15	9	29	43	8	10	8	18	56
Scotland	7	12	16	23	42	6	12	10	19	53
Northern Ireland[1]	6	10	11	33	41	5	10	10	30	44

1 Northern Ireland figures relate to 2002/03.

Source: General Household Survey, Office for National Statistics; Continuous Household Survey, Northern Ireland Statistics and Research Agency

Table **7.9** Alcohol consumption[1] among people aged 16 and over: by sex, 2003/04

Percentages

	Maximum daily amount							
	Males				Females			
	Drank nothing last week	Drank up to 4 units[2]	Drank more than 4 and up to 8 units[2]	Drank more than 8 units[2]	Drank nothing last week	Drank up to 3 units[2]	Drank more than 3 and up to 6 units[2]	Drank more than 6 units[2]
United Kingdom	26	34	17	23	41	37	13	9
North East	26	27	22	25	39	36	17	9
North West	26	29	17	28	38	36	13	13
Yorkshire and the Humber	23	30	19	28	37	38	13	13
East Midlands	22	33	18	27	38	36	16	9
West Midlands	23	35	19	23	45	34	12	9
East	30	36	15	20	43	40	11	6
London	33	35	15	18	50	35	10	5
South East	23	42	17	18	36	42	14	9
South West	22	41	15	22	32	44	15	9
England	25	35	17	23	40	38	13	9
Wales	25	36	16	23	45	33	12	10
Scotland	27	29	17	26	41	32	16	10
Northern Ireland[3]	40	17	14	29	57	20	11	11

1 Comparative consumption levels are different for males and females. See Notes and Definitions.
2 On the heaviest drinking day in the week preceding interview.
3 Northern Ireland figures relate to 2002/03.

Source: General Household Survey, Office for National Statistics; Continuous Household Survey, Northern Ireland Statistics and Research Agency

Figure **7.10** Drug use among 16- to 29-year-olds,[1] 2002/03 and 2003/04[2]

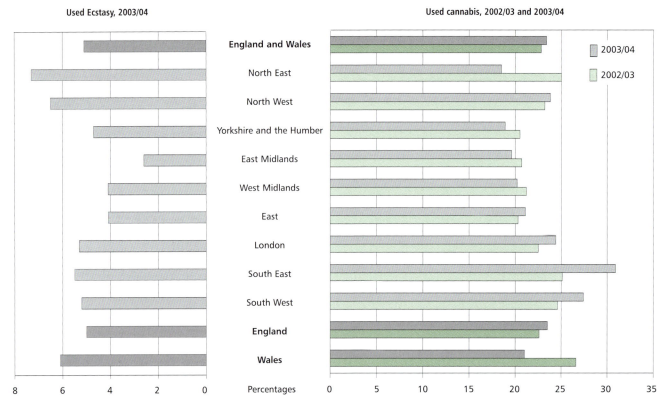

Used Ecstasy, 2003/04

Used cannabis, 2002/03 and 2003/04

1 See Notes and Definitions.
2 Interviews were conducted on a rolling basis throughout the financial year, asking about drug use in the previous 12 months.

Source: British Crime Survey, Home Office

Table **7.11** Prescriptions dispensed, 2004

	Prescription items dispensed (millions)[1]	Percentage of prescription items exempt from charge[2,3]	Percentage of prescription items[2,4] that were for:		Number of prescription items per person	Net ingredient cost (£ million)[5]	Average net ingredient cost[5]	
			Children	People aged 60 or over			£ per person	£ per prescription item
North East	40.9	88.5	5.5	58.2	16.1	450.9	177.6	11.0
North West	112.5	88.0	5.8	57.9	16.5	1,292.3	189.9	11.5
Yorkshire and the Humber	78.4	87.3	5.8	58.7	15.7	841.8	168.0	10.7
East Midlands	59.2	85.5	5.5	59.8	13.9	654.3	153.9	11.1
West Midlands	75.0	87.4	6.9	57.8	14.1	898.0	168.8	12.0
East	73.3	84.6	5.8	59.7	13.4	903.8	165.4	12.3
London	77.9	87.4	8.8	51.5	10.5	992.2	134.3	12.7
South East	98.9	84.3	5.9	60.0	12.2	1,263.1	156.3	12.8
South West	70.0	86.5	5.0	63.3	14.0	783.3	156.7	11.2
England	686.1	86.5	6.1	58.5	13.8	8,079.6	162.1	11.8
Wales	54.0	91.6	..	..	18.4	577.6	196.6	10.7
Scotland	74.7	92.3	..	..	14.8	948.2	187.5	12.7
Northern Ireland	27.3	94.2	..	..	16.0	365.3	213.6	13.4

1 Figures relate to NHS prescription items dispensed by community pharmacies, appliance contractors (appliance suppliers in Scotland and in Northern Ireland), and dispensing doctors, and prescriptions submitted by prescribing doctors for items personally administered, known as stock orders in Scotland and Northern Ireland.
2 For England figures relate to items dispensed by community pharmacists, dispensing doctors and appliance contractors. Personally administered items are free of charge and are therefore excluded. For Scotland, figures relate to items dispensed by community pharmacists and appliance contractors only.
3 Figures for the English regions, England and Wales exclude prescriptions for which prepayment certificates have been purchased. For Scotland and Northern Ireland they are included. Owing to this, and the issues mentioned in footnote 2, comparisons across the four areas should not be made.
4 The data for England for 'people aged 60 or over' and 'children' (children aged 15 or under and young adults aged 16 to 18 who are in full-time education) are estimates based in a 1 in 20 sample of prescription items dispensed by community pharmacists, appliance contractors and dispensing doctors. The data for Wales for 'people aged 60 or over' and 'children' (people aged under 25) and are calculated from a 100 per cent sample of prescriptions. Age-specific data are not available in Scotland and Northern Ireland.
5 Net ingredient cost is the cost of medicines before any discounts and does not include any dispensing costs or fees. This is known as gross ingredient cost in Scotland and ingredient cost in Northern Ireland.

Source: Department of Health; National Assembly for Wales; Information and Statistics Division, NHS in Scotland; Central Services Agency, Northern Ireland

Table **7.12** NHS hospital activity:[1] by region and NHS Strategic Health Authority, 2003/04[2]

| | In-patients (all specialties) | | | | | | Total accident & emergency attendances ('000s) | Consultant out-patient attendances | |
	Average daily available beds[3] per 1,000 population	Admissions[3] treated per available bed[4]	Admissions[4] per 1,000 population	Finished consultants episodes[5] ('000s)	Average length of stay[4] (days)	Day cases ('000s)		Total ('000s)	Of which: new[6] outpatients (percentages)
North East	4.7	40	186	812	7.6	256	863	2,753	32.6
County Durham and Tees Valley	4.3	43	183	342	7.2	95	361	1,028	30.7
Northumberland, Tyne and Wear	5.1	37	189	470	7.9	161	502	1,725	33.7
North West	4.1	43	178	1,995	7.3	520	2,749	7,113	28.4
Cheshire and Merseyside	4.1	44	184	708	7.1	157	1,113	2,676	28.2
Cumbria and Lancashire	3.9	39	152	498	7.6	144	594	1,470	30.9
Greater Manchester	4.2	46	194	789	7.3	219	1,041	2,967	27.4
Yorkshire and the Humber	3.9	43	167	1,439	7.1	439	1,801	4,796	28.0
North and East Yorkshire and Northern Lincolnshire	3.2	45	143	406	7.2	124	509	1,188	29.2
South Yorkshire	4.6	41	190	434	7.4	143	526	1,637	29.9
West Yorkshire	4.1	42	173	599	6.8	171	766	1,972	25.8
East Midlands	3.5	38	131	1,003	7.7	311	1,011	3,155	28.0
Leicestershire, Northamptonshire and Rutland	3.4	41	138	375	7.1	116	334	1,202	27.6
Trent	3.5	36	127	628	8.1	195	677	1,953	28.3
West Midlands	3.6	42	151	1,386	7.7	430	1,765	4,885	29.0
Birmingham and the Black Country	4.0	43	176	679	8.2	201	839	2,618	26.8
Shropshire and Staffordshire	3.3	43	140	382	7.3	140	432	1,092	32.0
West Midlands South	3.1	41	127	324	7.2	89	494	1,175	31.1
East	3.2	40	129	1,289	7.6	391	1,392	4,211	30.9
Bedfordshire and Hertfordshire	2.6	41	107	286	6.9	83	398	1,161	30.9
Essex	2.9	40	116	338	7.8	111	447	1,213	30.6
Norfolk, Suffolk and Cambridgeshire	3.8	40	154	664	7.9	197	548	1,836	31.1
London	3.9	38	149	1,843	8.3	542	3,079	8,168	29.2
North Central London	4.8	36	174	357	8.3	110	597	1,940	28.2
North East London	4.0	35	138	365	9.1	106	613	1,508	30.8
North West London	3.7	39	144	424	8.0	118	741	1,808	27.6
South East London	3.8	42	163	403	7.5	116	557	1,564	31.0
South West London	3.7	36	130	293	9.1	93	571	1,348	29.1
South East	3.2	41	129	1,706	7.8	471	2,240	6,136	31.1
Hampshire and Isle of Wight	3.2	41	131	403	9.0	99	419	1,284	31.3
Kent and Medway	3.0	41	121	313	7.0	83	504	1,214	29.2
Surrey and Sussex	3.5	38	132	557	7.6	175	787	2,018	30.5
Thames Valley	2.9	45	131	433	7.3	114	530	1,620	33.2
South West	3.8	41	154	1,407	7.5	428	1,618	3,904	32.4
Avon, Gloucestershire and Wiltshire	3.7	41	152	610	7.6	191	752	1,740	31.2
Dorset and Somerset	4.0	36	142	321	8.5	106	328	900	35.8
South West Peninsula	3.8	44	166	476	6.8	130	538	1,264	31.7
England	3.7	42	154	12,880	7.6	3,787	16,517	45,120	29.8
Wales	4.8	35	171	503	7.1	107	1,036	2,868	25.8
Scotland	5.9	33	192	971	6.9	389	1,559	4,599	28.6
Northern Ireland[6]	4.9	40	195	332	6.5	151	679	1,482	27.6

1 See Notes and Definitions.
2 Data for Wales, Scotland and Northern Ireland relate to 2002/03.
3 Excluding cots for healthy new-born babies except in Northern Ireland.
4 Admissions and length of stay exclude day cases.
5 Finished consultant episodes in England and discharges and deaths in Wales. Data for Scotland relate to discharges and deaths and transfers to other specialities and hospitals. Data for Northern Ireland relate to discharges and deaths and transfers to another hospital. Healthy new-born babies are included for Northern Ireland but excluded for the other countries.
6 In Northern Ireland data refer to GP referrals, not first attendances.

Source: Department of Health; National Assembly for Wales; Information and Statistics Division, NHS Scotland; Department of Health, Social Services and Public Safety, Northern Ireland

Table **7.13** **General practitioners and dentists:[1] by region and NHS Strategic Health Authority, 30 September 2004**

Numbers and percentages

			General medical services									General dental services[1,2]		
	Number of prac-tices	Of which: practices with one GP (percent-ages)	Number of general medical practition-ers (GPs)[1]	Percent-age who were female GPs	Percentages aged: Under 35	Percentages aged: 65 or over	Part-time GPs (percent ages)[3]	Average list size per GP[4]	Number of prac-tice staff (wte)[5]	Percentage who were direct care practice staff[5,6]	Number of dentists	People registered with a dentist as a percent-age of the pop-ulation[7]	Average registra-tions per dentist
North East	406	19	1,678	38	17	2	25	1,553	4,364	26	980	56	1,452
County Durham and Tees Valley	169	17	739	34	16	1	21	1,594	2,280	30	421	57	1,560
Northumberland, Tyne and Wear	237	20	939	42	18	2	27	1,522	2,083	23	559	55	1,370
North West	1,327	28	4,214	37	13	2	24	1,689	9,721	22	2,726	53	1,327
Cheshire and Merseyside	426	21	1,536	39	14	2	26	1,601	3,355	21	1,002	57	1,339
Cumbria and Lancashire	356	30	1,168	33	10	2	23	1,687	2,707	25	731	49	1,288
Greater Manchester	545	32	1,510	38	13	3	22	1,780	3,659	21	993	52	1,345
Yorkshire and the Humber	836	21	3,234	38	12	3	26	1,618	7,550	27	1,893	53	1,390
North and East Yorkshire and Northern Lincolnshire	253	21	1,024	33	9	2	22	1,650	2,580	28	615	49	1,318
South Yorkshire	219	20	821	40	12	3	28	1,607	1,950	25	485	58	1,518
West Yorkshire	364	22	1,389	41	15	3	27	1,602	3,021	26	793	52	1,368
East Midlands	635	17	2,493	36	13	1	26	1,721	6,346	34	1,499	53	1,487
Leicestershire, Northamptonshire and Rutland	223	20	889	34	12	1	25	1,781	2,070	30	539	54	1,524
Trent	412	16	1,604	37	13	1	27	1,689	4,276	35	960	53	1,466
West Midlands	996	29	3,216	35	11	3	23	1,736	7,296	25	2,092	49	1,251
Birmingham and the Black Country	507	38	1,382	35	11	5	22	1,785	3,176	21	864	52	1,356
Shropshire and Staffordshire	255	27	875	32	11	1	22	1,737	1,909	26	553	45	1,228
West Midlands South	234	14	959	38	12	2	27	1,664	2,210	29	675	49	1,134
East	804	20	3,385	37	10	2	21	1,680	8,246	29	2,305	49	1,176
Bedfordshire and Hertfordshire	231	20	998	41	11	2	22	1,741	2,255	22	823	48	950
Essex	273	32	915	33	8	4	19	1,830	2,371	27	607	48	1,285
Norfolk, Suffolk and Cambridgeshire	300	10	1,472	36	9	1	22	1,544	3,619	35	875	51	1,312
London	1,607	31	4,695	45	13	6	23	1,765	10,242	22	3,862	41	779
North Central London	291	38	793	46	11	6	21	1,769	1,303	22	717	42	711
North East London	349	34	892	38	10	8	21	1,882	2,486	21	660	40	918
North West London	441	31	1,158	48	14	5	21	1,789	2,656	24	1,085	42	697
South East London	294	29	1,004	44	12	5	26	1,702	2,128	23	702	42	905
South West London	232	17	848	48	15	4	29	1,677	1,671	21	698	38	718
South East	1,180	17	4,988	41	11	1	27	1,709	11,070	24	3,832	42	890
Hampshire and Isle of Wight	232	8	1,124	43	9	0	27	1,645	2,669	25	753	42	1,012
Kent and Medway	290	34	906	32	8	3	21	1,835	2,208	20	646	43	1,065
Surrey and Sussex	367	15	1,625	42	14	1	28	1,663	3,361	23	1,365	45	842
Thames Valley	291	11	1,333	43	11	1	30	1,733	2,832	26	1,068	38	760
South West	751	9	3,620	39	11	0	34	1,437	7,171	30	2,191	47	1,064
Avon, Gloucestershire and Wiltshire	323	10	1,604	45	13	0	34	1,431	2,864	29	960	45	1,032
Dorset and Somerset	176	6	867	36	9	0	39	1,438	1,861	34	522	52	1,204
South West Peninsula	252	10	1,149	33	9	1	30	1,445	2,446	27	709	45	1,005
England	8,542	23	31,523	39	14	3	25	1,666	72,006	26	19,754	48	1,214
Wales	501	5	1,816	33	10	2	21	1,674	4,171	22	1,024	46	1,400
Scotland	1,056	16	3,782	40	11	1	20	1,421	..	..	2,082	52	1,260
Northern Ireland	366	20	1,085	35	9	1	18	1,652	..	..	766	53	1,230

1 Figures for GPs (excluding retainers and registrars) include contracted GPs, GMS others and PMS others. For Wales, GP figures include all practitioners excluding GP registrars, GP retainers and locums; figures are not, therefore, comparable with previously published data. For Scotland, figures comprise performers (formerly known as unrestricted and restricted principals in GMS and PMS practices). For Northern Ireland, figures comprise unrestricted principals, PMS contracted GPs and PMS salaried GPs. Figures for general dental practitioners for all countries include principals, assistants and vocational dental practitioners. Salaried dentists, Hospital Dental Services and Community Dental Services are excluded.

2 Dentists are assigned to the region where they carry out their main work. Some dentists may have contracts in more than one PCT or Scottish Health Authority (SHA). In this case, duplication may occur, and SHA with an open GDS and PDS contract. However, the total number of dentists given England does not include duplication.

3 For Northern Ireland, due to new GMS Contract GP working type is no longer recorded. This figure has been calculated with the available data but working type of 28 GPs in 2004 was unknown.

4 For Wales, average list size is per 'all practitioners'.

5 Whole-time equivalents, excluding GPs, retainers and registrars in England, excluding GPs in Wales. For Scotland under the terms of the new GP contract (introduced on 1 April 2004) these data are no longer available.

6 Figures relate to practice nurses, physiotherapists, chiropodists, counsellors, dispensers and complementary therapists.

7 Registrations with dentists practising in each region.

Source: Department of Health; National Assembly for Wales; Information and Statistics Division, NHS in Scotland; Central Services Agency, Northern Ireland

Table **7.14** Council supported residents,[1] 31 March 2004

| | Percentage cared for in type of registered care home | | | | Total of all supported residents (=100%) ('000s) | Percentage aged 18 to 64 in registered care homes | | | | | All ages in staffed care homes[5] (=100%) ('000s) |
| | | | | | | Physically/ sensorily disabled | People with learning disabilities | People with mental health problems | Others | Percentage aged 65 and over | |
	Council staffed	Independent residential[2]	Independent nursing[3]	Unstaffed and other[4]							
North East	9.1	61.4	26.7	2.9	18	3.2	8.5	3.7	0.8	83.9	18
North West	12.0	56.5	30.7	0.8	43	4.2	7.4	4.6	0.5	83.3	43
Yorkshire and the Humber	12.7	56.4	29.2	1.7	32	3.8	9.7	3.5	0.4	82.6	31
East Midlands	14.7	58.6	25.9	0.9	25	4.1	12.7	4.1	0.5	78.6	25
West Midlands	15.5	51.1	31.0	2.3	28	3.5	13.5	4.2	0.5	78.2	28
East	9.6	71.5	18.4	0.5	27	3.8	13.6	3.6	0.4	78.7	27
London	8.8	58.5	27.5	5.2	34	4.7	17.9	8.7	1.7	67.0	32
South East	11.1	61.1	25.7	2.1	40	4.3	15.9	3.9	0.5	75.4	39
South West	9.5	60.4	28.2	1.9	30	3.6	14.3	3.6	0.3	78.2	30
England	11.5	59.3	27.3	2.0	278	3.9	12.9	4.5	0.6	78.0	272

1 Aged 18 and over and includes clients formerly in receipt of preserved rights income support.
2 Voluntary and private residential care homes.
3 Includes general and mental nursing homes.
4 Includes supported residents in homes with less than four residential care places.
5 Local authority-supported residents in councils with social services responsibilities (CSSR) and registered staffed care homes and other accommodation.

Source: Department of Health

Table **7.15** Children looked after by local authorities, year ending 31 March 2004

| | Total children looked after per 10,000 resident population[1] | | | Manner of accommodation (percentages) | | | Number of children looked after[5] (=100%) |
	Children admitted[2]	Ceased to be looked after[2]	Looked after	Foster homes	Children's homes and hostels[3]	Other[4]	
North East	26	27	60	70	11	19	3,300
North West	23	24	65	65	12	23	10,060
Yorkshire and the Humber	21	21	58	67	11	22	6,620
East Midlands	18	20	42	69	10	21	3,940
West Midlands	21	24	56	69	11	20	6,890
East	19	18	47	71	10	19	5,760
London	33	32	75	66	14	20	12,150
South East	16	17	42	69	10	21	7,510
South West	23	25	46	72	8	20	4,900
England	22	23	55	68	11	21	61,100
Wales	26	48	66	71	6	22	4,315
Scotland	42	37	106	30	13	57	11,675
Northern Ireland	25	23	57	61	13	26	2,510

1 Rates are based on mid-2003 estimates of population aged under 18.
2 For Wales, where a child had separate periods of care only the latest period is counted. For Northern Ireland, figures refer to actual numbers of admissions and discharges and not the numbers of children admitted to or discharged from being looked after. For England, only the first occasion on which a child started or ceased to be looked after in the year has been counted.
3 In England, includes homes and hostels both subject, and not subject, to Children's Homes Regulation and also includes Secure Units. In Wales includes local authority homes, private and voluntary registered homes only; and in Scotland relates to residential care homes for children.
4 Includes children looked after at home and children looked after through being under a supervision requirement made by the Scottish Children's Hearings System.
5 England, Wales and Scotland, figures exclude children looked after under an agreed series of short-term placements.

Source: Department for Education and Skills; National Assembly for Wales; Scottish Executive Education Department; Department of Health, Social Services and Public Safety, Northern Ireland

Chapter 8 Income and Lifestyles

Household income

The average gross weekly household income in the UK was £554 during the period 2001 to 2004. The main source of household income was wages and salaries, which accounted for 68 per cent on average of the total. In London, households earned 71 per cent of their average gross weekly income from wages and salaries compared with the South West, where the proportion was lowest at 62 per cent.

Households in London continued to have the highest average gross weekly income at £740, over £80 per week more than the next highest region, the South East. Households in the North East had the lowest income of £458 per week, just over three-fifths (62 per cent) of the London figure. The South West had the highest proportion of income from investments (5 per cent) with a further 9 per cent from annuities and pensions. In contrast, households in London had the lowest income from annuities and pensions at 4 per cent and also received the lowest proportion of their income (8 per cent) from social security benefits in 2001 to 2004.

Northern Ireland had one of the lowest household incomes in the United Kingdom of £461 per week, with almost one-fifth of this coming from social security benefits. Weekly household incomes in the East, London and South East were all considerably above the UK average by £40, £186 and £104 respectively. (Table 8.1)

During the period 2001 to 2004, the average gross weekly income per person in the UK was £234, with 30 per cent of households having under £250 each week. Scotland had the highest percentage, at 8 per cent, of households with a weekly income of less than £100 and also average gross weekly income per person of £214, £20 below the UK average. London had an income per person of £296 per week in the period 2001 to 2004 which was more than 26 per cent above the UK average and over 70 per cent more than the average person in Northern Ireland. Individuals in Northern Ireland earned the lowest gross weekly income of £173, £60 per week below the UK average.

More households in the North East than elsewhere (37 per cent) had a weekly income of less than £250, while the South East had the lowest proportion (21 per cent) with income under £250 a week.

In London, 37 per cent of households had an average gross weekly income of £750 or more, which was the highest proportion of any region and 6 percentage points above the next highest, the South East. (Table 8.2)

Income distribution and savings

The North East had the lowest percentages of individuals with an annual net income ranked in the top fifth in 2003/04, both before and after taking account of housing costs.

Half the individuals in Wales had annual incomes in the lowest two-fifths of the range before taking account of housing costs. However, after taking account of housing costs the country had the greatest increase, of 2 percentage points, of individuals with net incomes ranked in the top fifth. London, together with the South East, had the highest percentage of individuals with a net income ranked in the top fifth before and after housing costs, although there was a reduction of 3 percentage points of individuals in the top fifth after taking account of housing costs.

The cost of housing has the greatest impact in London; the region has the highest percentage in Great Britain of individuals (27 per cent) with an income ranked in the bottom fifth of the distribution after taking account of housing costs. The effect of housing costs has increased the proportion of individuals with a net income in the bottom fifth of the rankings by 5 percentage points. (Table 8.3)

Two-fifths of households in the South East had at least one ISA account in 2003/04, more than twice the proportion in Northern Ireland of 19 per cent.

The proportion of households in the South East with stocks and shares was also the highest, almost three times the proportion in Northern Ireland. Almost one-third of households in the South East held premium bonds in 2003/04, five times the rate in Northern Ireland. (Table 8.4)

Income and tax

In 2002/03, there were a total of 28.9 million individuals in the UK who had an income above the personal allowance threshold of £4,615 and were therefore liable to pay income tax. Overall, more than one-fifth of taxpayers were in the £10,000 to under £15,000 income range. In Northern Ireland, fewer than 630 thousand individuals had incomes above the personal allowance margin, which represented 2 per cent of the UK total.

London had the highest percentage of individuals (47 per cent) with an income liable to tax assessment of £20,000 or over, compared with Northern Ireland where just under 30 per cent of taxpayers were in this income range. The North East had the lowest percentage (11 per cent) of taxpayers with an income of £30,000 or over. (Table 8.5)

The average total income for males was £25,500 in 2002/03, compared with £16,300 for females for the UK overall. This earnings gap shows that males had an average income over 50 per cent greater than their female counterparts. In the South East, the gap of £13,000 was twice as much as between males and females in Northern Ireland.

Males in London had the highest average income of over £34,000 in 2002/03. This was over £12,500 more than the average for females in London and two-thirds more than the average for males in Wales. Despite incomes less than their male counterparts, females in London had incomes on average one and a half times more than females in the North East. (Table 8.6)

Receipt of benefit

Nearly 70 per cent of households in the UK were receiving state benefit in 2003/04. Retirement pension and child benefit were the most common, with 30 and 28 per cent respectively of households benefiting.

In Northern Ireland 78 per cent of households received some kind of benefit, with more than one-third (36 per cent) receiving child benefit; these were the highest percentages of any area in 2003/04. In contrast, about a quarter of households in the South West received child benefit, which was the lowest proportion. The South West had the highest percentage of households (34 per cent) receiving pensions, compared with London and Northern Ireland with the lowest proportions, 22 and 27 per cent of households respectively. (Table 8.8)

Expenditure

Total household expenditure in London was almost 20 per cent above the UK average of £406 per week over the period 2001 to 2004 whereas the figure for the North East was the lowest of all regions at £336. (Tables 8.9 and 8.11)

During the period 2001 to 2004, the UK average expenditure per person was £171.50 per week, ranging from £141.50 in the North East up to £203.70 per week for individuals in the South East.

Households in Northern Ireland spent the most on food and non-alcohol beverages at £46.70 per week and were also the highest spenders on clothing and footwear at £30.90 per week. This compared with families in Wales which averaged 60 per cent of this – £18.50 per week on clothing and footwear. One factor may be the larger household size in Northern Ireland; an average of 2.65 people compared with 2.34 in England in 2001.

In the South East, households spent almost £7 on health compared with Northern Ireland, the North East and Wales, where spending was less than half of this amount per week (£3.10). Spending on health in Scotland at £3.60 per week was also low at two-thirds of the UK average of £4.80. However, spending on alcohol and tobacco was highest in Scotland where households averaged £14.10 per week compared with a UK average of £11.40. Households in London spent almost £60 a week on housing, water, electricity, gas and other fuels which was the highest of all areas. (Table 8.11)

On average, children in Scotland spent the most money in Great Britain, just under £16 per week between 2001 and 2004. Children in the East of England spent only 56 per cent as much as those in Scotland, averaging a little more than £9 per week. (Figure 8.10)

The average spent on food and drink was £22.67 per person, with a further £10.93 on eating out per person per week in the period 2003 to 2004 in the UK overall. Londoners spent the most on eating out at £13.48 per person per week, which was 40 per cent more than households in Scotland (£9.59).

Households in the East spent the highest amount on fish (£1.18), vegetables (jointly with the South East – £3.07 each) and cheese (£0.71) per person per week. This compared with households in the North East who spent £2.44 per week on vegetables in 2003/04, three-quarters of the level in the East and South East, and less than two-thirds of what the South East spent on fruit (£1.24 per week per household in 2003/04). (Table 8.12)

Consumption

Individuals in London consumed the least milk and cream and also meat (1.7 kg and 0.9 kg per week respectively) of all the areas in 2003/04. Consumption of vegetables was lowest in Scotland at 1.7 kg per person per week compared with a UK average of 1.9 kg. (Table 8.13)

Consumer goods

The proportion of households with access to a mobile phone continued to grow and reached an average of 70 per cent across the UK during 2001 to 2004, more than twice the proportion with a dishwasher (30 per cent of households). In the North East, almost a fifth of households had a dishwasher, half the proportion found in the South East.

Almost 60 per cent of households in both the East and West Midlands had a tumble dryer, compared with 45 per cent of households in London. (Table 8.14)

The proportion of households with access to the Internet continued to show substantial increases in all regions. By 2001 to 2004, the proportion of households in London had reached 52 per cent, the highest in the UK, followed by the South East at 51 per cent. In Northern Ireland and Wales just over one-third of households (35 per cent) had access, two of the lowest proportions. (Table 8.15)

Tourism

During the period 2001 to 2004, people in the South East spent the most on holidays at nearly 20 per cent more than the UK average, followed by the East with 11 per cent above the average. (Table 8.16)

UK residents made 20.5 million trips and spent £4,103 million visiting the South West, the most popular destination in 2004. In the same year, overseas residents made 13.4 million trips to London and spent £6,439 million in 90.2 million nights in that region. Overall, UK residents spent £24 billion on holidays in the UK in 2004, almost twice the amount spent by overseas visitors. Both overseas and UK residents made the fewest visits to Northern Ireland and consequently spent the least time and money there. (Table 8.17)

Library resources and use

In general, more books were issued to children than adults, with the UK average of eight books issued to children in 2003/04 and over ten books issued to children in the East of England.

Londoners made the most visits to libraries, 7.1 visits on average per head of population, and £180 million is spent on libraries in this region. (Table 8.18)

National Lottery

Households in the North East and the East spent the most on the National Lottery during the 2001 to 2004 period, averaging £4.70 per week, and the region also had the highest proportion of households participating (63 per cent). London had the lowest number of households participating (39 per cent), well below the UK average of 51 per cent. However, households in London spent on average £4.60 compared with the UK average of £4.40. (Table 8.19)

Overall, the number of grants awarded and the total value of awards have increased over the years to 2004. There was almost an 80 per cent increase in the number of grants awarded from 2001 to 2004.

London continued to be awarded the highest number of grants and largest total value from 2001 to 2004, compared with Northern Ireland which received the least.

There have continued to be increases year on year, for all regions and overseas, in the number of grants issued and their total value, although the percentage increases have declined over time. (Web: IL2)

Table **8.1**   Household income: by source, 2001/02-2003/04[1]

Percentages and £

	Wages and salaries	Self-employ-ment	Invest-ments	Annuities and pensions[2]	Social security benefits[3]	Other income	Average gross weekly household income[3] (=100%) (£)
United Kingdom	68	8	3	7	12	1	554
North East	68	4	2	6	18	1	458
North West	67	7	2	8	15	1	489
Yorkshire and the Humber	66	6	3	8	15	1	474
East Midlands	69	8	3	7	12	1	532
West Midlands	68	8	3	6	14	1	505
East	69	8	3	7	11	1	594
London	71	12	4	4	8	1	740
South East	68	10	4	8	9	1	658
South West	62	9	5	9	14	1	517
England	68	9	4	7	12	1	568
Wales	64	6	2	10	17	1	461
Scotland	69	5	2	7	14	2	500
Northern Ireland	65	8	2	5	19	1	461

1 Combined data from the 2001/02, 2002/03 and 2003/04 Expenditure and Food Surveys. See Notes and Definitions.
2 Other than social security benefits.
3 Excluding Housing Benefit and Council Tax Benefit (rates rebate in Northern Ireland).

Source: Expenditure and Food Survey, Office for National Statistics; Northern Ireland Statistics and Research Agency

Table **8.2**   Distribution of household income, 2001/02-2003/04[1]

Percentages and £

	Under £100	£100 but under £150	£150 but under £250	£250 but under £350	£350 but under £450	£450 but under £600	£600 but under £750	£750 or over	Average gross weekly income[2] per person (£)
United Kingdom	6	9	15	12	11	14	11	24	234
North East	7	12	18	12	10	14	10	16	193
North West	7	11	15	12	11	14	11	20	208
Yorkshire and the Humber	5	11	18	14	11	14	9	18	207
East Midlands	5	8	15	12	12	16	12	21	223
West Midlands	6	10	16	12	11	13	10	22	206
East	4	8	14	11	11	13	12	27	251
London	6	8	12	8	8	10	10	37	296
South East	4	7	10	11	10	14	12	31	283
South West	5	9	16	13	11	14	11	21	231
England	6	9	14	12	10	13	11	25	240
Wales	6	9	18	13	12	13	11	16	197
Scotland	8	9	16	13	10	15	9	20	214
Northern Ireland[3]	7	10	17	13	11	15	10	17	173

1 Combined data from the 2001/02, 2002/03 and 2003/04 surveys. Data are for adults only. See Notes and Definitions.
2 Excluding Housing Benefit and Council Tax Benefit (rates rebate in Northern Ireland).
3 Northern Ireland data are calculated from an enhanced sample, but the United Kingdom figures are calculated from the main Expenditure and Food Survey sample.

Source: Expenditure and Food Survey, Office for National Statistics; Northern Ireland Statistics and Research Agency

Table **8.3**   Income distribution of individuals, 2003/04[1,2]

Percentages

| | Quintile groups of individuals ranked by net equivalised household income | | | | | | | | | |
| | Before housing costs | | | | | After housing costs[3] | | | | |
	Bottom fifth	Next fifth	Middle fifth	Next fifth	Top fifth	Bottom fifth	Next fifth	Middle fifth	Next fifth	Top fifth
Great Britain	20	20	20	20	20	20	20	20	20	20
North East	23	25	21	20	11	20	24	24	20	12
North West	21	23	20	20	16	20	22	21	21	17
Yorkshire and the Humber	23	23	21	19	14	21	24	20	20	15
East Midlands	20	21	21	20	17	19	21	22	21	18
West Midlands	24	22	20	19	16	21	22	21	20	16
East	18	19	20	20	24	18	19	21	19	23
London	22	14	15	18	31	27	15	14	17	28
South East	13	16	20	23	28	16	16	19	22	28
South West	18	22	23	20	17	18	23	22	20	17
England	20	20	20	20	21	20	20	20	20	20
Wales	24	26	21	17	12	21	26	22	17	14
Scotland	20	18	23	21	18	19	18	22	22	19

1 Total income of all members of the household after deductions of income tax and other contributions. See Notes and Definitions.
2 Figures for this year include the self employed.
3 This includes rent, water rates, mortgage interest payments (net of tax relief), structural insurance premiums, ground rent and service charges.

Source: Households Below Average Income, Department for Work and Pensions

Table **8.4**   Households[1] with different types of saving, 2003/04

Percentages[2]

| | Accounts | | | | | | Other savings | | | | | | | |
	Current[3]	Post Office	TESSA	ISA	Basic account[4]	Other bank/ building society[5]	Gilts or unit trusts	Stocks and shares[6]	National Savings	Save As You Earn	Premium bonds	Equity bonds[7]	PEPs	Profit share/ company share option plan
United Kingdom	89	6	7	33	3	54	5	22	4	1	23	-	8	4
North East	87	5	6	27	3	46	3	14	3	-	17	-	4	2
North West	89	5	7	34	5	48	4	21	4	-	20	-	6	5
Yorkshire and the Humber	87	6	7	35	3	51	4	21	3	-	22	-	8	4
East Midlands	86	5	7	32	2	54	5	21	4	1	23	-	7	4
West Midlands	87	7	8	34	3	54	4	19	4	-	22	1	7	4
East	93	7	8	37	2	60	6	27	5	1	30	-	9	5
London	88	6	8	29	2	53	5	24	4	1	20	-	7	4
South East	94	8	9	40	1	65	7	32	5	1	32	-	11	7
South West	95	8	8	38	1	61	8	25	5	1	31	1	10	4
England	90	7	8	35	3	55	5	24	4	1	25	-	8	5
Wales	91	8	6	30	2	48	4	15	3	1	21	-	5	3
Scotland	86	4	5	29	3	46	5	17	2	1	13	-	6	4
Northern Ireland	81	4	6	19	2	37	2	12	2	-	6	-	4	2

1 Households in which at least one member has an account. See Notes and Definitions.
2 As a percentage of all households.
3 A current account may be either a bank account or a building society account.
4 This account has been introduced to allow those who do not have a current account to receive money through direct payment. These include bank or building society basic bank accounts and Post Office card accounts.
5 All bank/building society accounts excluding current accounts and TESSAs and ISAs plus other accounts yielding interest.
6 Includes membership of a share club.
7 Guaranteed equity bonds is a lump sum, fixed-term investment.

Source: Family Resources Survey, Department for Work and Pensions

Table **8.5**   Distribution of income liable to assessment for tax, 2002/03[1]

Percentages and thousands

	| Percentage of taxpayers in each annual income range								Individuals with incomes of £4,615 or more (=100%) (thousands)
	£4,615 to £4,999	£5,000 to £7,499	£7,500 to £9,999	£10,000 to £14,999	£15,000 to £19,999	£20,000 to £29,999	£30,000 to £49,999	£50,000 and over	
United Kingdom[2]	1.5	11.1	12.3	22.0	17.0	19.7	11.4	4.9	28,900
North East	1.7	12.4	14.0	24.5	17.0	19.6	8.5	2.3	1,190
North West	1.6	12.0	13.4	23.6	17.7	18.4	9.9	3.5	3,210
Yorkshire and the Humber	1.8	12.7	13.3	23.6	17.5	18.5	9.4	3.2	2,360
East Midlands	1.5	10.9	12.9	23.9	17.6	19.1	10.4	3.8	2,090
West Midlands	1.6	11.6	12.6	23.1	18.0	19.8	9.7	3.6	2,500
East	1.4	10.1	11.0	20.4	16.9	20.5	13.5	6.2	2,780
London	1.4	9.2	10.1	17.3	15.3	22.4	15.6	8.6	3,420
South East	1.3	9.7	10.6	19.7	16.5	20.2	14.1	7.8	4,140
South West	1.5	11.5	13.1	23.0	17.4	19.2	10.3	3.9	2,570
England	1.5	10.9	12.0	21.6	17.0	19.9	11.8	5.2	24,300
Wales	1.7	12.4	14.2	24.2	17.6	18.6	8.9	2.4	1,360
Scotland	1.5	11.7	12.9	23.3	17.2	19.7	10.0	3.7	2,490
Northern Ireland	1.8	12.2	13.2	26.4	17.4	17.6	8.5	2.9	629

1 Includes taxpayers only and not those above the personal allowance threshold as shown in previous years. See Notes and Definitions.
2 Figures for United Kingdom include members of HM forces and others who are liable to some UK tax but reside overseas on a long-term basis. In addition, the United Kingdom total includes a very small number of individuals who could not be allocated to a region.

Source: Survey of Personal Incomes, Board of HM Revenue & Customs

Figure **8.6**   Average total income[1] by sex, and income gap between males and females, 2002/03

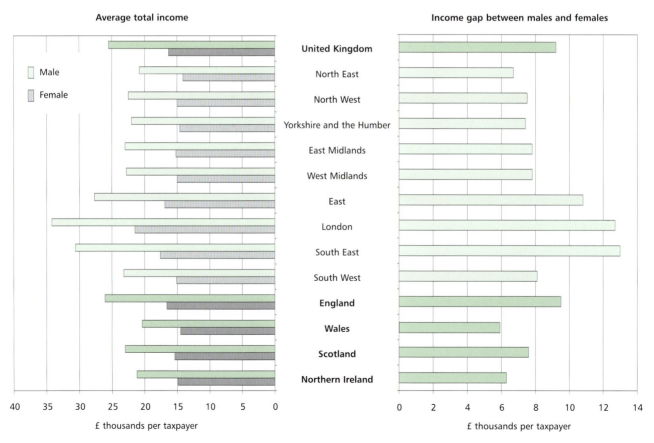

1 Figures are based on individuals with total income above the single person's allowance. See Notes and Definitions.
Source: Survey of Personal Incomes, Board of Inland Revenue

Map 8.7   **Percentage of the population of working age claiming a key social security benefit:[1] by local authority, May 2005**

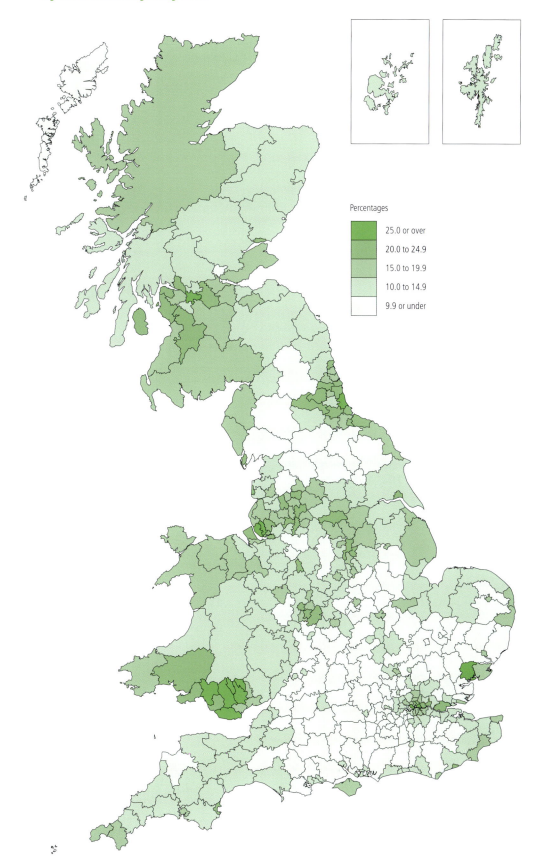

Percentages

- 25.0 or over
- 20.0 to 24.9
- 15.0 to 19.9
- 10.0 to 14.9
- 9.9 or under

1 *Key benefits include claimants of one or more of Jobseeker's Allowance (JSA), Income Support (IS), Incapacity Benefit (IB), Severe Disablement Allowance (SDA), Disability Living Allowance (DLA), Carer's Allowance (CA) and Bereavement Benefit (BB)/Widow's Benefit (WB) for working age claimants (including Pension Credit for males aged 60 to 64).*

Source: DWP Information Directorate (IFD), Work and Pensions Longitudinal (WPLS) 100% data

Table **8.8** Households in receipt of benefit:[1] by type of benefit, 2003/04

Percentages[2]

	MIG/PC or Income Support[3]	Tax Credits[4]	Housing Benefit	Council Tax Benefit[5]	Jobseeker's Allowance	Retirement Pension	Incapacity or disablement benefits[6]	Child Benefit	Any benefit
United Kingdom	12	15	15	19	2	30	16	28	69
North East	18	16	22	28	4	32	24	28	76
North West	15	17	16	22	2	31	21	29	72
Yorkshire and the Humber	13	17	16	21	3	30	17	28	72
East Midlands	11	16	13	18	2	30	16	27	68
West Midlands	13	16	13	20	3	31	16	29	70
East	9	14	11	15	2	31	13	28	68
London	13	9	18	21	3	22	11	26	60
South East	8	12	9	12	2	31	10	28	67
South West	10	15	11	16	1	34	14	26	69
England	12	14	14	19	2	30	15	28	68
Wales	14	17	15	21	3	32	23	28	73
Scotland	15	15	19	24	3	30	20	26	71
Northern Ireland	19	19	18	.	5	27	24	36	78

1 Households in which at least one member is in receipt of benefit. See Notes and Definitions.
2 As a percentage of all households.
3 Pension Credit (PC) was introduced in October 2003 as an alternative to Minimum Income Guarantee (MIG). However, some MIG recipients remain.
4 In April 2003, Working Families Tax Credit (WFTC) and Disabled Person's Tax Credit (DPTC) were replaced by Working Tax Credit (WTC) and/or Child Tax Credit (CTC).
5 A rates system operates in Northern Ireland, which is different from council tax in Great Britain.
6 Incapacity Benefit, Disability Living Allowance (Care and Mobility components), Severe Disablement Allowance, Disabled Person's Tax Credit, Industrial Injuries Disablement Benefit, War Disablement Pension and Attendance Allowance. In October 1999 Disability Working Allowance was replaced by Disabled Person's Tax Credits.

Source: Family Resources Survey, Department for Work and Pensions

Figure **8.9** Total household expenditure in relation to the UK average, 2001/02-2003/4[1]

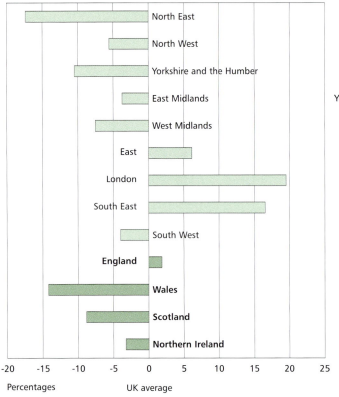
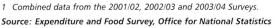

1 Combined data from the 2001/02, 2002/03 and 2003/04 Surveys.
Source: Expenditure and Food Survey, Office for National Statistics

Figure **8.10** Children's spending,[1] 2001/02-2003/04[2]

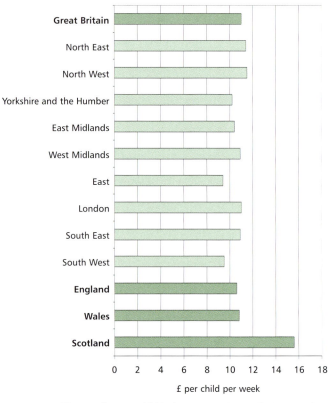

1 Average weekly expenditure per child in the age range 7 to 15. See Notes and Definitions.
2 Combined data from the 2001/2, 2002/03 and 2003/04 surveys.
Source: Expenditure and Food Survey, Office for National Statistics

Table **8.11**   Household expenditure:[1] by commodity and service, 2001/02-2003/04

£ per week and percentages[2]

	Food and non-alcoholic beverages		Alcoholic beverages and tobacco		Clothing and footwear		Housing, water electricity gas and other fuels		Furnishings, household equipment and routine maintenance of the house		Health		Transport	
	(£)	(%)[2]	(£)	(%)[2]	(£)	(%)[2]	(£)	(%)[2]	(£)	(%)[2]	(£)	(%)[2]	(£)	(%)[2]
United Kingdom	42.60	10	11.40	3	22.60	6	37.30	9	30.40	7	4.80	1	59.10	15
North East	38.50	11	10.90	3	19.50	6	28.60	9	24.70	7	3.10	1	48.40	14
North West	40.80	11	12.50	3	22.50	6	33.20	9	28.20	7	3.40	1	55.80	15
Yorkshire and the Humber	38.10	10	11.60	3	19.40	5	32.30	9	27.70	8	4.10	1	54.10	15
East Midlands	42.70	11	11.40	3	20.00	5	31.60	8	30.20	8	3.80	1	60.60	15
West Midlands	41.40	11	11.10	3	21.80	6	32.30	9	29.20	8	4.20	1	54.30	14
East	45.70	11	10.10	2	22.40	5	37.80	9	32.90	8	6.70	2	68.50	16
London	44.60	9	10.50	2	27.50	6	57.00	12	34.30	7	6.20	1	61.30	13
South East	45.30	10	10.90	2	24.90	5	41.90	9	34.20	7	6.80	1	73.30	15
South West	42.70	11	10.90	3	18.70	5	36.40	9	29.80	8	5.10	1	57.80	15
England	42.60	10	11.10	3	22.40	5	38.20	9	30.80	7	5.10	1	60.80	15
Wales	40.60	12	10.90	3	18.50	5	33.40	10	27.20	8	3.10	1	47.30	14
Scotland	42.80	12	14.10	4	24.10	7	32.40	9	28.10	8	3.60	1	50.90	14
Northern Ireland	46.70	12	13.80	4	30.90	8	31.00	8	32.20	8	3.10	1	54.10	14

	Communication		Recreation and culture		Education		Restaurants and hotels		Miscellaneous goods and services		Other expenditure		Average household expenditure	Average expenditure per person
	(£)	(%)[2]	(£)	(%)[2]	(£)	(%)[2]	(£)	(%)[2]	(£)	(%)[2]	(£)	(%)[2]	(£)	(£)
United Kingdom	10.70	3	55.80	14	5.30	1	34.40	8	32.40	8	59.40	15	406.20	171.50
North East	9.30	3	50.70	15	3.30	1	30.70	9	24.60	7	43.30	13	335.70	141.50
North West	9.60	2	57.10	15	4.50	1	33.00	9	32.00	8	51.10	13	383.60	163.30
Yorkshire and the Humber	9.20	3	52.60	14	4.20	1	34.00	9	27.40	8	49.00	13	363.70	158.90
East Midlands	10.00	3	55.80	14	3.90	1	35.40	9	30.60	8	55.00	14	391.10	164.00
West Midlands	10.30	3	53.60	14	2.80	1	31.60	8	29.70	8	53.30	14	375.60	153.60
East	11.00	3	59.10	14	5.40	1	33.40	8	34.30	8	63.70	15	431.20	182.00
London	14.80	3	57.00	12	10.20	2	44.00	9	39.00	8	79.20	16	485.50	194.30
South East	11.60	2	64.30	14	7.40	2	36.40	8	39.40	8	76.90	16	473.40	203.70
South West	9.90	3	52.70	14	5.30	1	30.40	8	32.10	8	58.20	15	390.10	174.10
England	10.90	3	56.80	14	5.60	1	34.90	8	33.30	8	61.40	15	413.80	175.00
Wales	8.80	3	53.10	15	2.90	1	30.30	9	26.10	8	46.30	13	348.60	149.10
Scotland	9.90	3	50.10	14	4.10	1	31.00	8	27.90	8	51.30	14	370.30	158.30
Northern Ireland	10.90	3	48.10	12	3.80	1	36.80	9	33.20	8	48.60	12	393.00	147.40

1 Combined data from the 2001/02, 2002/03 and the 2003/04 surveys. See Notes and Definitions.
2 As a percentage of average weekly household expenditure.

Source: Expenditure and Food Survey, Office for National Statistics

Table **8.12** Expenditure on selected foods bought for household consumption and expenditure on eating out, 2003/04[1]

£ per person per week

	Liquid and processed milk and cream	Cheese	Uncooked carcass meat and poultry	Other meat and meat products	Fish	Vegetables and vegetable products[2]	Fresh and other fruit	Bread	Cereals other than bread	Drinks and confec-tionery	Total house-hold food and drink	Eating out[3]
United Kingdom	1.54	0.59	1.80	3.13	0.94	2.79	1.63	0.90	2.78	4.29	22.67	10.93
North East	1.45	0.46	1.44	3.17	0.89	2.44	1.24	1.00	2.62	3.71	20.16	9.66
North West	1.53	0.57	1.87	3.30	0.88	2.64	1.40	1.01	2.75	4.80	21.69	11.37
Yorkshire and the Humber	1.52	0.53	1.62	2.98	1.03	2.61	1.51	0.87	2.72	4.13	20.77	11.09
East Midlands	1.63	0.57	1.67	3.11	0.92	2.76	1.58	0.89	2.82	4.54	21.99	11.16
West Midlands	1.45	0.58	1.85	2.98	0.82	2.76	1.48	0.89	2.51	3.85	20.59	9.72
East	1.61	0.71	1.88	3.35	1.18	3.07	1.81	0.94	2.93	4.20	23.14	9.87
London	1.37	0.53	1.81	2.77	1.01	2.95	1.86	0.80	2.90	3.89	21.90	13.48
South East	1.65	0.67	1.89	3.05	1.04	3.07	1.93	0.82	2.81	4.38	23.15	11.22
South West	1.70	0.69	1.95	2.98	0.85	2.89	1.88	0.80	2.81	4.61	23.01	10.52
England	1.55	0.60	1.81	3.06	0.97	2.84	1.67	0.88	2.78	4.26	22.12	11.10
Wales	1.47	0.51	1.75	3.33	0.74	2.52	1.39	0.86	2.54	4.12	21.28	9.99
Scotland	1.46	0.55	1.70	3.52	0.86	2.53	1.39	0.99	2.84	4.82	22.64	9.59
Northern Ireland	1.63	0.43	1.97	3.46	0.73	2.82	1.35	1.14	3.13	3.78	21.54	11.69

1 See Notes and Definitions.
2 Including tomatoes, fresh potatoes and potato products.
3 Individual expenditure on all food and drink consumed outside the home.

Source: Expenditure and Food Survey, Department for Environment, Food and Rural Affairs

Table **8.13** Household consumption of selected foods, 2003/04[1]

Kilogrammes per person per week[2]

	Liquid and processed milk and cream	Meat and meat products	Fish	Vegetables and vegetable products[3]	Fresh and other fruit	Cereals including bread
United Kingdom	2.0	1.1	0.2	1.9	1.2	1.6
North East	2.1	1.2	0.2	1.9	1.0	1.7
North West	2.1	1.2	0.2	1.9	1.1	1.7
Yorkshire and the Humber	2.1	1.1	0.2	2.0	1.2	1.6
East Midlands	2.2	1.1	0.2	2.1	1.3	1.6
West Midlands	2.0	1.1	0.1	2.1	1.1	1.6
East	2.1	1.1	0.2	2.0	1.4	1.7
London	1.7	0.9	0.2	1.8	1.2	1.5
South East	2.1	1.0	0.2	2.0	1.3	1.5
South West	2.2	1.1	0.1	2.0	1.3	1.7
England	2.0	1.1	0.2	2.0	1.2	1.6
Wales	2.0	1.1	0.1	2.0	1.1	1.6
Scotland	2.0	1.1	0.1	1.7	1.0	1.6
Northern Ireland	2.2	1.0	0.1	2.1	1.0	1.8

1 Data collected through the Expenditure and Food Survey in which 7,500 households in the United Kingdom keep a record of the type, quantity and costs of foods entering the home during a two-week period. Nutritional intakes are estimated from the survey data. See Notes and Definitions.
2 Except equivalent litres of milk and cream.
3 Including tomatoes, fresh potatoes and potato products.

Source: Expenditure and Food Survey, Department for Environment, Food and Rural Affairs

Table **8.14** **Households with selected durable goods, 2001/02-2003/04[1]**

Percentages

	Micro-wave oven	Washing machine	Dish-washer	Fridge-freezer or deep freezer	Tumble drier	Video recorder	Compact-disc player	Satellite receiver	Mobile phone
United Kingdom	87	94	29	96	56	90	83	46	70
North East	92	95	19	97	56	92	82	49	68
North West	90	92	24	95	57	90	83	48	68
Yorkshire and the Humber	90	94	23	95	54	90	80	44	73
East Midlands	90	96	29	97	59	92	84	47	73
West Midlands	89	94	26	96	59	91	81	44	73
East	86	95	35	96	56	92	85	45	71
London	81	91	29	95	45	86	82	45	69
South East	87	94	39	97	58	92	87	45	77
South West	85	93	31	95	55	88	81	40	68
England	87	94	29	96	55	90	83	45	71
Wales	91	94	24	97	57	90	81	56	65
Scotland	89	96	26	94	57	91	86	47	69
Northern Ireland	87	95	33	92	52	87	73	46	51

1 Combined data from the 2001/02, 2002/03 and 2003/04 surveys. See Notes and Definitions.

Source: Expenditure and Food Survey, Office for National Statistics

Figure **8.15** **Households with Internet access, 1998/99[1] and 2001/02-2003/04[2]**

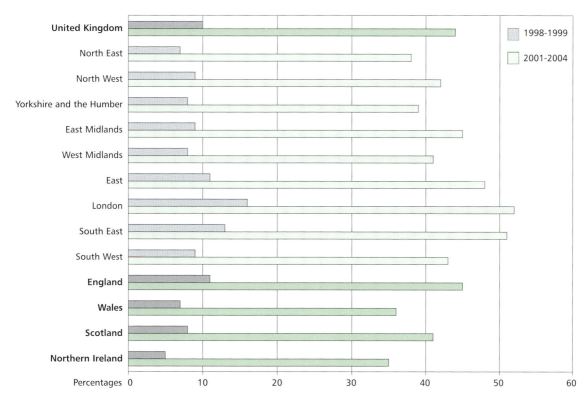

1 Data from 1998/99 Family Expenditure Survey.

2 Combined data from the 2001/02, 2002/03 and 2003/04 surveys. See Notes and Definitions.

Source: Expenditure and Food Survey, Office for National Statistics

Figure **8.16** Household expenditure on holidays in relation to the UK average, 2001/02-2003/04[1]

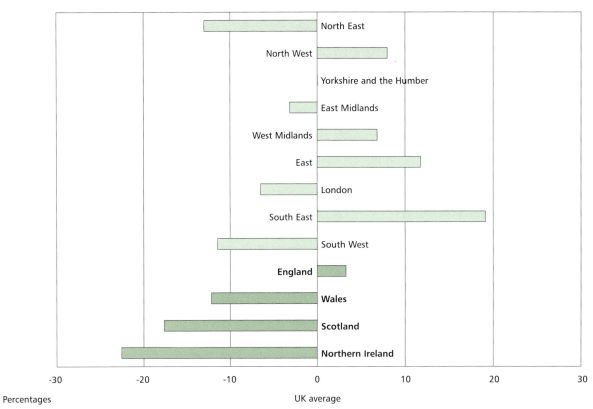

Percentages   UK average

1 Combined data from the 2001/02, 2002/03 and 2003/04 surveys.

Source: Expenditure and Food Survey, Office for National Statistics

Table **8.17** Tourism,[1] 2004

Millions and £ million

	UK residents[1,2]			Overseas residents[3]		
	Number of trips (millions)	Number of nights (millions)	Expenditure (£ million)	Number of visits (millions)	Number of nights (millions)	Expenditure (£ million)
Area visited						
United Kingdom	126.6	408.9	24,357	27.8	227.4	12,930
North East	3.8	10.4	700	0.5	4.3	194
North West	12.9	38.9	2,337	1.8	12.8	558
Yorkshire and the Humber	10.0	26.9	1,584	1.1	8.8	346
East Midlands	8.0	24.1	1,201	1.0	9.1	440
West Midlands	8.6	21.2	1,447	1.7	10.9	552
East	10.0	31.9	1,641	1.9	14.5	609
London	12.8	29.7	2,759	13.4	90.2	6,439
South East	16.6	48.5	3,006	3.9	31.3	1,467
South West	20.5	80.1	4,103	2.0	16.7	714
England	101.4	314.0	18,960	23.6	199.4	11,343
Wales	8.9	31.5	1,492	1.0	6.9	311
Scotland	..	..	..	1.9	19.0	994
Northern Ireland	1.1	3.3	114	0.3	1.6	129

1 The United Kingdom and England figures include the value of tourism in the Channel Islands, the Isle of Man and a small amount where the region was unknown. The United Kingdom figures also include an amount that cannot be allocated to an individual country.
2 The United Kingdom Tourism Survey is moving to a new methodology for measuring the volume and value of domestic overnight trips. In the meantime, caution in using and interpreting the 2004 data is advised as data may not be a truly representative sample of the UK population.
3 The expenditure in this table excludes spending of overseas visitors departing directly from the Channel Islands and that of nil night transit visitors.

Source: United Kingdom Tourism Survey, sponsored by the National Tourist Boards; International Passenger Survey, Office for National Statistics

Table 8.18   Library resources and use, 2003/04

	Library books issues per head of population to:		Number of visits to libraries per head of population	Expenditure (£ millions)	Expenditure per head of population (£)	Stock of books (thousands)	Stock of books per head of population	Resident population per library
	Adults	Children[1]						
United Kingdom	5.2	8.0	5.7	1,060.5	17.80	110,133	1.9	12,884
North East	5.9	6.9	5.8	45.8	18.04	4,737	1.9	11,138
North West	5.8	7.6	6.0	120.9	17.77	12,859	1.9	13,609
Yorkshire and the Humber	4.4	5.5	4.6	83.4	16.64	8,270	1.7	12,129
East Midlands	5.2	8.0	4.8	67.0	15.76	6,515	1.5	12,325
West Midlands	4.8	6.9	5.0	88.0	16.55	9,795	1.8	15,601
East	6.1	10.5	5.9	92.0	16.84	8,307	1.5	14,491
London	4.6	8.9	7.1	180.0	24.36	15,536	2.1	18,703
South East	5.4	9.2	5.8	129.9	16.08	12,861	1.6	15,189
South west	5.6	8.7	5.6	72.3	14.48	7,960	1.6	12,715
England	5.3	8.2	5.7	879.4	17.64	86,841	1.7	14,147
Wales	5.3	5.9	4.9	43.8	14.91	6,388	2.2	8,667
Scotland	5.5	7.3	5.9	106.9	21.04	12,635	2.5	8,411
Northern Ireland	3.2	6.2	4.1	30.4	17.84	4,270	2.5	10,845

1 Children aged 14 and under.

Source: LISU, Loughborough University

Table 8.19   Participation in the National Lottery,[1] 2001/02-2003/04[2]

Percentages and £ per household per week

	Percentage of households participating	Average household expenditure[3] (£)
United Kingdom	51	4.40
North East	63	4.70
North West	57	4.20
Yorkshire and the Humber	55	4.60
East Midlands	54	4.30
West Midlands	53	4.60
East	49	4.70
London	39	4.60
South East	47	4.30
South West	45	4.20
England	50	4.50
Wales	54	4.30
Scotland	56	4.20
Northern Ireland	48	4.10

1 In the two-week diary-keeping period following interview; including scratch-cards.
2 Combined data from the 2001/02, 2002/03 and 2003/04 surveys. See Notes and Definitions.
3 Average weekly expenditure of participating households.

Source: Expenditure and Food Survey, Office for National Statistics

Chapter 9 **Crime and Justice**

Recorded crimes

London had the highest rate of recorded crime at 13,900 crimes per 100,000 population in 2004/05. Although this represents a reduction of 1,300 crimes since 2002/03, it was still more than 2,000 crimes above the next highest region, Yorkshire and the Humber. The rate of recorded crime was lowest in the East of England with 8,800 per 100,000 population in 2004/05.

London had the highest number of offences recorded per head of population in each category except for burglary and criminal damage. The North East had the highest rate for criminal damage at 2,890 offences per 100,000 population in 2004/05, and Yorkshire and the Humber showed the highest rate of burglaries at 1,740. The rate of burglaries in Scotland was less than half the level in Yorkshire and the Humber during the same period, and Scotland had the lowest rate overall at 688 per 100,000 population, although this comparison may be affected by differing criminal justice and policing systems.

The lowest rate of criminal damage was 1,840 in London at 60 per cent of the UK average. The recording of violent crimes against the person was lowest in the East of England at 1,590 per 100,000 population, while the highest rate was in London at 2,750.

Theft and handling stolen goods accounted for approximately one-third of the overall recorded crime in all regions. The rate of theft was lowest in Northern Ireland at 1,820 per 100,000 population in 2004/05; less than half the average rate for England and Wales. (Table 9.1)

Violent offences against the person

Four per cent of people in London, the North West and West Midlands were victims of violent crimes at least once in 2004/05. These rates were the highest in England and Wales, although the percentages of those victimised showed reductions from the previous year in most areas. More than half of these crimes were common assault. (Table CJ1)

Offences committed against households

People's experiences of offences committed against the household were higher in the North West than in other areas of the country with 3,500 crimes per 10,000 households in 2004/05. The lowest rate was in the East with 2,500 crimes per 10,000 households.

Yorkshire and the Humber had the largest drop in household offences from 4,300 in 2003/04 to 3,100 per 10,000 households in 2004/05, a reduction of more than one-quarter.

The North West had the highest proportion of households victimised at least once at 21 per cent in 2004/05, whereas the lowest proportion was in the East with 15 per cent. The North West also had the highest rates of vandalism at 9 per cent. Vehicle theft was the highest in London, where 12 per cent of households were affected, and lowest in the East at 6 per cent of households. (Table 9.2)

Recorded crimes detected

Crimes involving criminal damage and burglary had the lowest clear-up rates for all areas, averaging 14 per cent and 13 per cent respectively across England and Wales. Detection rates appear higher in Scotland, but this may be due to differences in recording practices and the legal system. London had the lowest detection rates of 21 per cent of recorded crime being cleared up by the police in 2004/05. In Wales more than a third of crimes (36 per cent) were resolved. (Table 9.3)

Firearms

London has consistently had a higher number of offences recorded by the police in which firearms were reported to have been used than elsewhere, generally accounting for one-fifth of the overall total for the UK. In 2003/04 this was 5,100 offences compared with 4,300 in the next highest region, the North West. Of the regions of England, the North East has had the lowest number of crimes involving firearms for most of the last six years, except in 1998/99 and 2003/04 when the South West was the lowest with 628 and 1,108 offences respectively.

The number of operations in which firearms were issued to police was highest in London at 3,900 in 2003/04. This was nearly five times the number in the South West, the lowest English region (at 840) and ten times more than in Scotland at 400. Except in 2000/01 when the highest number of operations was in the North West, London has had the highest number of operations in which firearms were issued to the police every year between 1998/99 and 2003/04. (Table 9.4)

Seizures of controlled drugs

London had the highest number of seizures of all class A drugs in 2003, totalling 8,600. For class B and C drugs the greatest number of seizures was in Scotland with 18,500 and 1,500 respectively, compared with 14,700 and 230 seizures of B and C class drugs in London. In 2002, London also had the highest numbers of seizures in classes A and B at 6,200 and 22,400 respectively.

Seizures of class B drugs dropped in total in 2003 compared with 2002, falling by 3,600 to 104,000. Although seizures of drugs in 2003 dropped in many areas, the largest proportionate drop in the number of seizures was related to class B drugs in London, down from 22,400 in 2002 to 14,700 in 2003. (Table 9.5)

Police service strength

The number of police officers on ordinary duty was highest of all in London with just under 32 thousand in March 2005, more than four times the number in North East, the region with the smallest number (7,500 officers). However when the population in each area is taken into account, the North East had 340 people per officer and in London the ratio was 230 people per officer. The East had the lowest relative police strength with 500 people per officer in March 2005.

In 2003, 7 per cent or almost one in 12 police officers in London were from minority ethnic backgrounds, higher than any other region; the West Midlands with 4.5 per cent had the next highest proportion. In Northern Ireland the proportion of minority ethnic officers was the lowest at 0.2 per cent of officers on ordinary duty.

Nearly one-quarter (24 per cent) of ordinary officers in the West Midlands were women compared with just over one-sixth (17 per cent) in Northern Ireland, which had the lowest proportion of any area. The South West had proportionally more special constables than elsewhere, 141 for every 1,000 officers, more than six times the rate in London.

London had the highest number of community support officers (CSOs) at 2,161, which is considerably higher than Wales and the North East which had only 268 and 270 respectively. Traffic wardens were also more numerous in London than elsewhere with 449 in 2005; this was nearly ten times the number in the North East, the region with the fewest (51). However numbers have reduced in all regions over the years since 2003 and the largest fall was for London where the 2005 figure was only two-thirds of the 2003 level of 687 wardens. Although numbers are much smaller in the East, in 2005 there were 56 traffic wardens, one-third of the 2003 level. (Table 9.6)

People found guilty of offences

Among 10- to 17-year-old males, the 2003 rate for conviction for offences of burglary, robbery and theft was highest in the North East with 1,132 found guilty per 100,000 population in that age group. The lowest rate of males found guilty of all categories of indictable offences for this age group was in the South West with 1,057 per 100,000 population in 2003. This was half the highest rate of 2,353 offences, again in the North East. The South West also had the lowest rate of females aged 10 to 17 found guilty, with 243 offences per 100,000 population compared with the highest rate, again in the North East, of 404 in 2003. (Table 9.7)

A fine was by far the most common punishment for people aged 18 or over who were found guilty of an offence in 2004, ranging from 64 per cent of males in the North East to 82 per cent of females in Wales and in London. In each region, except Scotland, a higher proportion of females found guilty of offences were fined compared with males. The largest differences were in Wales and London (82 per cent of females compared with 75 per cent of males in each region in 2004). The North East and North West also showed differences of 7 percentage points between males and females. Conversely, the proportion of males who were given an immediate custodial sentence was highest in Scotland at 13 per cent, more than twice as high as the proportion of females (5 per cent). (Table 9.8)

Imprisonment

Four-fifths (80 per cent) of females given an immediate sentence were imprisoned for one year or less in 2004, ranging in England from 75 per cent in the South East to 85 per cent in the South West. In all regions, males were more likely than females to be sentenced to imprisonment for longer periods, of one year or more. (Table 9.9)

ASBOs (anti-social behaviour orders)[1]

The West Midlands, at 90, had the highest number of ASBOs issued in 2001. In the period since 2002 however, the North West has issued the largest number of orders for anti-social behaviour, rising from 139 in 2002 to 612 in 2004.

The number of ASBOs issued have risen substantially in all areas since 2002. In 2001, the total number issued in England and Wales was 323 (with a further 57 issued in Scotland), while by 2004 the number had increased seven-fold to nearly 2,800 for Great Britain as a whole. (Table 9.10)

1 Anti-social behaviour orders are civil orders that exist to protect the public from behaviour that causes or is likely to cause harassment, alarm or distress. An order contains conditions prohibiting the offender from specific anti-social acts or entering defined areas and is effective for a minimum of two years. The orders are not criminal penalties and are not intended to punish the offender.

Fear of crime and feelings of insecurity

In all regions females were more apprehensive about crimes and professed more to feelings of insecurity than their male counterparts. Only for crimes relating to theft from cars were the proportions of males feeling worried greater, or the same, as for females. In 2004/05 the percentages of females who felt very worried about muggings were twice as high as for males in each region. A quarter of females in London are very worried about rape; this is more than four times the proportion of males. The proportion was even higher in Northern Ireland (27 per cent).

Females aged 60 or over were on average twice as likely to feel very unsafe when walking alone at night as those aged 16 to 59. In the older age group, 35 per cent of females in London felt 'very unsafe' compared with 17 per cent in the South West. (Table 9.11)

Table 9.1 Recorded crimes:[1] by offence group, 2004/05

Rates per 100,000 population

	Violence against the person	Sexual offences	Burglary	Robbery	Theft and handling stolen goods	Of which: Theft of vehicles	Of which: Theft from vehicles	Fraud and forgery	Criminal damage	Drug offences	Other[3]	Total
England and Wales	1,955	115	1,284	168	3,830	458	941	527	2,239	270	121	10,508
North East	1,636	106	1,301	89	3,432	429	818	314	2,889	282	120	10,168
North West	2,113	115	1,506	168	3,864	549	981	443	2,845	274	137	11,464
Yorkshire and the Humber	2,038	114	1,740	98	4,157	602	1,124	450	2,812	248	119	11,776
East Midlands	1,876	124	1,571	124	3,870	419	1,011	525	2,299	213	132	10,733
West Midlands	1,946	120	1,323	199	3,378	481	866	551	2,098	258	152	10,024
East	1,586	93	955	83	3,264	330	790	460	1,965	182	98	8,822
London	2,747	148	1,380	529	5,644	651	1,195	963	1,841	459	148	13,858
South East	1,646	113	1,004	72	3,349	316	797	473	2,016	215	94	8,983
South West	1,722	105	1,082	75	3,277	307	838	445	1,896	219	93	8,914
England	1,963	117	1,301	176	3,864	459	944	539	2,242	267	121	10,590
Wales	1,816	88	997	37	3,241	442	887	314	2,190	313	115	9,110
Scotland[2]	342	100	688	74	2,982	308	550	414	2,532	824	672	8,627
Northern Ireland[3]	1,715	99	783	87	1,818	261	314	304	1,838	153	110	6,907

1 Recorded crime statistics broadly cover the more serious offences. See Notes and Definitions.
2 Figures for Scotland are not comparable with those for England and Wales because of the differences in the legal systems, recording practices and classifications.
3 The Northern Ireland figure includes offences against the state.

Source: Home Office; Scottish Executive; Police Service of Northern Ireland

Table 9.2 Offences committed against households,[1] 2004/05[2]

Rates per 10,000 households and percentages

	Offences per 10,000 households[3] Vandalism	Offences per 10,000 households[3] Burglary[4]	Offences per 10,000 households[3] Vehicle thefts[5]	Offences per 10,000 households[3] All household offences[6]	Percentage of households victimised at least once Vandalism	Percentage of households victimised at least once Burglary[4]	Percentage of households victimised at least once Vehicle thefts[5]	Percentage of households victimised at least once All household offences[6]
England and Wales	1,125	331	1,068	2,978	7.1	2.7	8.2	18.4
North East	900	317	928	2,560	6.5	2.2	7.2	16.5
North West	1,400	404	1,263	3,481	8.8	3.3	9.6	20.6
Yorkshire and the Humber	820	404	1,313	3,120	5.9	3.5	9.7	20.2
East Midlands	1,166	332	906	2,863	6.6	2.6	7.1	16.9
West Midlands	1,185	336	1,061	2,971	7.1	2.5	8.0	18.0
East	1,057	227	798	2,527	6.6	1.9	6.1	15.4
London	1,007	426	1,691	3,184	6.4	3.7	12.3	20.2
South East	1,306	283	842	3,015	8.4	2.3	7.0	19.0
South West	1,099	278	871	2,830	6.9	2.1	6.8	17.1
England	1,134	337	1,078	3,001	7.2	2.7	8.3	18.5
Wales	969	239	905	2,608	6.3	2.0	7.5	16.4
Scotland[2]	1,656	397	..	3,309	9.6	2.9	..	18.3
Northern Ireland[2]	1,215	313	865	2,764	7.1	2.4	6.6	16.1

1 See Notes and Definitions for details of surveys.
2 Data for Scotland relate to 2002. Data for Northern Ireland relate to the period August 2003 to April 2004 and the recall periods referred to the 12 full months prior to interview (excluding the month of interview).
3 The vehicle theft risks are based on vehicle-owning households only.
4 The term used in Scotland is housebreaking. The figures include attempts at burglary/housebreaking.
5 Comprises theft of vehicles, thefts from vehicles and associated attempts.
6 Comprises the three individual categories plus thefts of bicycles and other household thefts.

Source: British Crime Survey, Home Office; Scottish Crime Survey, Scottish Executive; Northern Ireland Crime Survey, Northern Ireland Office

Table **9.3**   Recorded crimes detected[1] by the police: by offence group, 2004/05[2]

Percentages

	Violence against the person	Sexual offences	Burglary	Robbery	Theft and handling stolen goods	Fraud and forgery	Criminal damage	Drugs	Other[3]	Total[3]
England and Wales	53	34	13	20	16	26	14	95	70	26
North East	56	42	13	21	22	49	13	97	79	28
North West	58	35	13	22	18	27	13	93	71	26
Yorkshire and the Humber	53	33	14	29	18	33	12	91	73	25
East Midlands	52	38	10	21	17	29	14	98	76	25
West Midlands	56	33	12	22	18	24	14	94	70	27
East	61	35	15	25	18	27	15	94	73	28
London	43	35	13	15	10	13	13	97	61	21
South East	51	30	13	24	17	33	15	96	69	26
South West	45	28	13	20	17	32	14	96	64	24
England	52	34	13	20	16	26	14	95	69	26
Wales	72	44	19	41	23	46	20	97	86	36
Scotland[4]	77	72	25	39	34	80	21	97	95	45
Northern Ireland[3]	53	46	15	17	17	36	14	74	55	28

1 See Notes and Definitions.
2 Some offences cleared up may have been recorded initially in an earlier year.
3 The Northern Ireland figure includes offences against the state.
4 Figures for Scotland are not comparable with those for England and Wales, because of the differences in the legal systems, recording practices and classifications.

Source: Home Office; Scottish Executive; Police Service of Northern Ireland

Table **9.4**   Firearms 1998/99 to 2003/04

Numbers

	Offences recorded[1] by the police in which firearms were reported[2] to have been used						Operations in which firearms were issued to the police[3,4]					
	1998/99	1999/ 2000	2000/01	2001/02	2002/03	2003/04	1998/99	1999/ 2000	2000/01	2001/02	2002/03	2003/04
United Kingdom[4]	15,859	18,665	19,597	24,622	26,312	26,078	11,184	11,056	11,183	14,154	15,127	17,055
North East	727	783	791	1,008	943	1,116	832	655	776	1,566	1,528	1,749
North West	2,308	2,619	2,983	3,940	4,119	4,267	1,611	1,390	1,999	2,322	1,912	2,045
Yorkshire and the Humber	2,079	2,206	2,541	3,039	3,360	3,239	1,183	1,304	1,179	1,404	1,354	1,389
East Midlands	1,407	1,619	1,440	1,731	2,251	2,084	736	867	1,011	1,479	1,651	1,657
West Midlands	1,092	1,375	1,563	2,301	2,262	2,374	935	840	957	1,301	1,423	1,993
East	761	996	1,052	1,333	1,734	1,749	1,327	1,239	1,288	1,124	1,312	1,445
London	3,005	4,123	4,264	5,680	5,535	5,135	2,889	2,987	1,865	2,487	3,330	3,927
South East	1,276	1,579	1,562	1,658	1,788	2,102	562	626	924	985	917	1,093
South West	628	934	887	1,055	1,140	1,108	294	305	504	690	794	844
England	13,283	16,234	17,083	21,745	23,132	23,174	10,292	10,213	10,503	13,358	14,221	16,142
Wales	591	712	614	655	938	920	636	702	606	633	606	515
Scotland	1,066	982	970	1,029	1,050	972	256	141	150	163	300	398
Northern Ireland	919	737	930	1,193	1,192	1,012	.	.	.	.	.	.

1 See Notes and Definitions for information on coverage of offences.
2 'Alleged' in Scotland.
3 In England and Wales, firearms were discharged by police in seven incidents in both 1998/99 and 1999/2000, nine in 2000/01, 11 in 2001/02, ten in 2002/03 and four in 2003/04. In Scotland, police shots were fired in eight operations in 1998/99, three in 1999/2000, four in 2000/01, seven in 2001/02, six in 2002/03 and five in 2003/04.
4 In Northern Ireland, police officers are armed at all times. Figures relating to operation with firearms are for Great Britain only.

Source: Home Office; Her Majesty's Inspectorate of Constabulary; Scottish Executive Justice Department; Police Service of Northern Ireland

Table **9.5** Seizures of controlled drugs:[1] by type of drug, 2003

Number of seizures

	Class A drugs						Class B drugs			
	Heroin	Cocaine	Crack	LSD	Ecstasy type	All class A drugs[2]	Cannabis	Ampheta-mines	All class B drugs[2]	All class C drugs[2,3]
United Kingdom[4]	12,992	7,743	4,810	134	7,610	34,683	97,958	6,962	104,096	2,999
North East	806	504	66	3	640	1,973	4,215	566	4,687	188
North West	1,395	406	274	4	553	2,600	6,876	629	7,417	81
Yorkshire and the Humber	1,098	252	287	7	455	2,061	5,301	572	5,739	147
East Midlands	656	184	128	7	314	1,223	3,478	436	3,804	123
West Midlands	1,783	449	545	26	800	3,477	9,846	475	10,178	48
East	526	356	290	4	273	1,443	5,131	271	5,355	40
London	1,578	2,020	2,407	39	800	8,639	13,837	521	14,737	231
South East	800	832	387	14	559	2,472	9,897	532	10,309	82
South West	991	504	249	8	966	2,749	8,734	781	9,345	101
England	9,633	5,507	4,633	112	5,360	26,637	67,315	4,783	71,571	1,041
Wales	768	176	81	9	638	1,687	6,947	972	7,696	106
Scotland	2,408	764	55	7	1,197	4,307	17,687	988	18,532	1,543
Northern Ireland	24	70	3	-	300	382	1,803	121	1,865	74
National Crime Squad[4]	19	44	3	0	21	82	48	16	57	0
British Transport Police[4]	43	27	10	2	25	110	1,138	21	1,159	4
Customs and Excise[4]	109	1,157	25	4	74	1,478	3,072	72	3,217	231

1 See Notes and Definitions.
2 Since a seizure may involve drugs other than those listed, figures for individual drugs cannot be added together to produce totals.
3 Class C drugs include benzodiazepines (including temazepam) and anabolic steroids.
4 Figures for the National Crime Squad, the British Transport Police and Customs and Excise cannot be split by region or country, but are included in the UK totals.

Source: Home Office

Table **9.6** Police service strength:[1] by type, March 2005

	Police officers on ordinary duty[2]				Special constables and civilian staff rates per 1,000 officers (on ordinary duty)			
		Percentage of which						
	Number	Minority ethnic groups	Women officers	Population per officer[3]	Special con-stables[4]	Police staff	Community support officers (numbers)	Traffic wardens (numbers)
United Kingdom	165,972	..	20.9	359	84	486	.	1,649
North East	7,515	1.4	20.0	338	53	396	270	51
North West	19,510	2.8	21.2	349	65	462	669	119
Yorkshire and the Humber	12,790	2.7	22.3	392	88	524	612	105
East Midlands	9,437	3.4	19.8	451	138	547	366	86
West Midlands	13,854	4.5	23.6	384	131	473	419	79
East	10,902	2.3	22.5	501	139	617	504	56
London	31,954	7.0	19.4	231	23	434	2,161	449
South East	16,676	2.1	23.2	485	94	613	572	107
South West	10,808	1.2	20.6	463	141	592	373	113
England	133,446	3.7	21.3	374	85	507	5,946	1,164
Wales	7,613	1.1	20.4	386	83	472	268	117
Scotland[5]	16,018	1.2	20.1	317	72	388	.	265
Northern Ireland[5,6]	8,895	0.2	17.2	191	104	355	.	103

1 Full-time equivalents for England and Wales and for Scotland. Actual numbers (whether full or part-time) for Northern Ireland.
2 Includes full-time reserves in Northern Ireland.
3 Based on mid-2003 population estimates.
4 Part-time reserves in Northern Ireland.
5 For police staff and traffic wardens, part-time staff are counted as half full-time.
6 The figure for police staff relates to those who work to the Chief Constable and not to those who work to the Police Authority for Northern Ireland.

Source: Home Office; Scottish Executive; Police Service of Northern Ireland

Table **9.7**   People found guilty: by type of offence[1] and age, 2003

Rates per 100,000 population in the relevant age group

	People aged 10 to 17						People aged 18 or over					
	Violence against the person plus common assault[2]	Sexual off-ences	Burglary, robbery and theft[3]	Drugs off-ences	Other indict-able off-ences[4]	All indictable offences plus common assault[2]	Violence against the person plus common assault[2]	Sexual off-ences	Burglary, robbery and theft[3]	Drugs off-ences	Other indict-able off-ences[4]	All indictable offences plus common assault[2]
Males												
England and Wales	367	16	745	172	245	1,544	263	20	528	210	302	1,323
North East	526	20	1,132	357	319	2,353	302	22	682	305	361	1,672
North West	438	19	902	234	328	1,922	301	24	653	253	387	1,619
Yorkshire and the Humber	393	18	917	153	265	1,747	296	21	685	203	370	1,575
East Midlands	365	17	721	75	211	1,389	279	22	562	163	273	1,298
West Midlands	448	22	755	154	293	1,673	329	26	618	207	382	1,562
East	307	8	591	108	175	1,189	207	15	395	124	211	952
London	307	19	753	299	239	1,617	248	18	535	314	342	1,457
South East	308	11	584	115	190	1,208	196	15	360	142	212	925
South West	297	10	478	107	165	1,057	241	16	415	150	204	1,027
England	366	16	737	173	241	1,533	260	19	528	205	301	1,314
Wales	374	13	870	167	316	1,740	310	22	514	303	332	1,481
Females												
England and Wales	94	-	152	12	44	301	28	-	112	23	56	219
North East	128	0	190	24	62	404	32	-	175	43	70	321
North West	113	0	156	13	61	343	35	-	155	24	72	286
Yorkshire and the Humber	107	-	150	8	39	303	29	-	142	25	65	262
East Midlands	90	0	145	6	43	284	31	-	111	20	51	213
West Midlands	112	-	165	13	46	335	34	-	125	19	67	245
East	94	0	144	7	34	279	23	-	87	14	34	158
London	53	1	166	14	32	265	22	-	105	23	81	232
South East	94	0	149	9	43	295	20	-	73	19	36	148
South West	81	0	109	11	41	243	26	-	81	21	34	162
England	95	-	151	11	44	301	27	-	112	22	56	218
Wales	82	0	156	22	45	304	40	-	107	37	55	240
All people												
England and Wales	234	8	456	94	147	939	141	10	312	113	175	751
North East	332	10	672	194	193	1,402	161	11	417	168	209	966
North West	280	10	538	126	198	1,151	162	12	393	133	222	923
Yorkshire and the Humber	253	10	543	82	154	1,042	157	10	402	111	211	891
East Midlands	232	9	441	41	129	853	151	11	330	90	159	740
West Midlands	284	12	468	85	173	1,022	176	13	364	110	220	883
East	203	4	373	58	106	744	112	7	236	67	120	542
London	183	10	467	160	138	958	133	9	315	165	209	831
South East	204	6	373	63	119	766	105	7	211	78	121	523
South West	193	5	299	60	105	663	129	8	241	83	116	577
England	234	8	452	94	145	933	140	10	313	110	174	746
Wales	232	7	523	96	184	1,042	168	10	300	163	187	829

1 See Notes and Definitions for information on coverage of offences.
2 Following the introduction of a charging standard on 31 August 1994, some people who would have been charged with an indictable offence are now charged with
   common assault, a summary offence. Common assaults have therefore been included for comparability with figures in previous editions of Regional Trends.
3 Includes handling stolen goods.
4 Includes criminal damage and fraud and forgery.

Source: Home Office

Table **9.8**   People aged 18 or over found guilty of offences:[1] by sex and type of sentence, 2004[2]

	Result as a percentage of number of people sentenced						All sentenced	
	Absolute or condit-ional discharge	Fine	All community penalties	Fully sus-pended sentence[3]	Immed-iate custodial sentence[4]	Otherwise dealt with	(=100%) (numbers)	Rates[5]
Males								
England and Wales	7	72	10	-	8	3	1,173,928	59
North East	12	64	11	-	7	6	61,145	64
North West	8	71	11	-	8	2	180,302	71
Yorkshire and the Humber	7	68	12	-	9	4	120,815	64
East Midlands	6	74	11	-	7	2	104,437	64
West Midlands	6	72	11	-	9	3	128,961	65
East	6	74	11	-	8	2	100,088	48
London	5	75	9	-	10	1	165,872	58
South East	6	75	10	-	7	2	138,148	45
South West	8	73	9	-	6	3	95,256	50
England	7	72	11	-	8	3	1,095,024	58
Wales	6	75	10	-	7	2	78,904	72
Scotland[2,6]	8	67	10	.	13	1	99,848	53
Northern Ireland[2]	5	68	6	8	9	5	21,645	36
Females								
England and Wales	8	78	8	-	3	2	266,710	12
North East	12	71	8	-	2	6	16,335	16
North West	8	78	9	-	3	1	46,225	17
Yorkshire and the Humber	9	74	10	-	4	3	25,450	13
East Midlands	9	79	8	-	3	2	22,669	13
West Midlands	8	78	9	-	3	2	25,572	12
East	8	77	9	-	4	1	21,741	10
London	6	82	6	-	5	1	35,828	12
South East	8	79	8	-	3	1	30,949	9
South West	11	75	7	-	2	4	21,572	10
England	8	78	8	-	3	2	246,341	12
Wales	7	82	7	-	2	1	20,369	17
Scotland[2,6]	17	64	11	.	5	3	18,822	9
Northern Ireland[2]	10	71	6	6	2	5	3,412	5

1 See Notes and Definitions. The coverage of the table is all offences, including motoring offences. A defendant is recorded only once for each set of court proceedings, against the principal offence.
2 Figures for Scotland and Northern Ireland relate to 2003.
3 Fully suspended sentences are not available to courts in Scotland.
4 Includes custodial sentences imposed following a sentence deferred for good behaviour in Scotland.
5 People aged 18 or over sentenced as a rate per 1,000 population.
6 To improve comparability, this table excludes breaches of probation and community service orders normally included in Scottish figures.

Source: Home Office; Scottish Executive; Northern Ireland Office

Table 9.9 **People aged 18 or over sentenced to immediate imprisonment: by sex and length of sentence imposed for principal[1] offence, 2004**

Percentages and numbers

	Males				Females			
	Length of sentence (percentages)			Total sentenced to immediate imprisonment[2] (=100%) (numbers)	Length of sentence (percentages)			Total sentenced to immediate imprisonment[2] (=100%) (numbers)
	One year or less	Over one year but less than four years	Four years or over		One year or less	Over one year but less than four years	Four years or over	
England and Wales	73	18	8	91,687	80	15	5	8,310
North East	70	22	8	3,976	79	17	4	326
North West	74	18	8	13,697	82	14	4	1,318
Yorkshire and the Humber	69	22	9	10,272	79	18	3	918
East Midlands	73	19	8	7,510	79	17	4	596
West Midlands	75	18	6	11,350	84	12	4	874
East	79	15	7	8,109	84	12	4	840
London	73	16	11	15,858	77	13	9	1,653
South East	71	20	9	9,483	75	17	8	881
South West	76	18	7	6,034	85	12	4	517
England	73	18	8	86,289	80	14	6	7,923
Wales	76	18	6	5,398	78	19	4	387
Scotland[3,4]	87	9	4	13,291	90	8	2	1,014
Northern Ireland[4]	79	15	6	1,983	89	10	2	62

1 Figures for Scotland are for the length of sentence in total and not just for the principal offence. Figures on sentence lengths for principal offences only are not available for Scotland.
2 Figure for Scotland includes sentence length not known. The total for females includes one female who was given a custodial sentence.
3 To improve comparability, this table excludes breaches of probation and community service orders normally included in Scottish figures.
4 Figures for Scotland and Northern Ireland relate to 2003

Source: Home Office; Scottish Executive; Northern Ireland Office

Table 9.10 **Number of anti-social behaviour orders issued by all courts**

Number

	2001	2002	2003	2004
England and Wales	323	404	1,040	2,643
North East	22	29	43	85
North West	43	139	339	612
Yorkshire and the Humber	32	34	124	402
East Midlands	25	6	33	177
West Midlands	90	80	129	296
East	31	26	85	210
London	13	19	95	293
South East	33	49	85	287
South West	29	10	48	193
England	318	392	981	2,555
Wales	5	12	59	88
Scotland[1]	57	68	75	148

1 Data for Scotland are for financial years, so 2004 refers to 2003/04.

Source: Home Office; Scottish Executive

Table **9.11** Fear of crime and feelings of insecurity, 2004/05[1]

Percentages

	Percentage feeling 'very' worried about					Feeling 'very' unsafe when walking alone at night[2]	
	Burglary	Mugging	Theft of car[3]	Theft from car[3]	Rape	Aged 16 to 59	Aged 60 and over
Males							
England and Wales	10	7	12	11	4	2	7
North East	7	4	12	11	4	2	6
North West	12	9	15	13	4	3	8
Yorkshire and the Humber	9	7	12	11	3	3	8
East Midlands	10	7	13	12	5	2	7
West Midlands	10	8	13	12	4	2	7
East	7	4	9	8	3	2	5
London	15	13	17	19	6	3	14
South East	7	6	8	8	3	1	5
South West	7	4	8	8	3	1	3
England	10	7	12	11	4	2	7
Wales	7	4	13	11	3	1	3
Scotland[1]	9	7	9	9	4	4	13
Northern Ireland[1]	16	9	17	11	5	9	10
Females							
England and Wales	14	14	14	11	18	12	25
North East	13	12	15	10	16	12	20
North West	17	18	16	13	22	12	29
Yorkshire and the Humber	14	14	13	10	17	12	25
East Midlands	16	15	16	11	20	11	24
West Midlands	15	15	16	12	19	15	27
East	11	11	9	7	15	11	22
London	21	23	20	17	25	17	35
South East	12	11	11	9	15	12	23
South West	10	10	10	8	13	8	17
England	15	15	14	11	18	12	25
Wales	13	9	14	12	14	8	20
Scotland[1]	15	18	14	11	19	14	28
Northern Ireland[1]	25	22	26	16	27	30	30

1 Data for Scotland relate to 2003, for Northern Ireland relate to 2003/04. See Notes and Definitions.
2 For Northern Ireland the question relates to fear of 'walking in the dark' (i.e. alone or with others); the figures also include those people who never go out.
3 Based on vehicle owners only except in Northern Ireland where it is based on respondents residing in households owning, or with regular use of a vehicle.

Source: British Crime Survey, Home Office; Scottish Crime Survey, Scottish Executive; Northern Ireland Crime Survey, Northern Ireland Office

Chapter 10 **Transport**

Cars

From 1996 to 2003 new car registrations in the United Kingdom increased by 27 per cent to 2,600 cars. The growth took place in most regions except London which showed a steady decline of 18 per cent over the period. After 2002, other regions also showed decreases. The only regions still showing increases were the North East, West Midlands and Yorkshire and the Humber with 4, 6 and 8 per cent increases respectively.

The West Midlands had the highest proportion of new cars as a percentage of all cars licensed (13 per cent in 2003) compared with 8 per cent each in Wales and the South West. There has been a decrease in the proportion of new cars registered to companies in many regions. The decline was greatest in the East where the proportion of company cars against the whole stock had decreased by almost one-third between 1998 and 2003. (Table 10.1)

The proportion of households in Great Britain with no access to a car stayed at 26 per cent in 2001 and 2002. This compared with a decrease of 4 percentage points between 1997 and 2001.

The proportion of households with two or more cars increased in all areas except in the North East and Wales, which decreased by 0.3 and 0.8 percentage points respectively between 2001 and 2002. There were decreases in the percentage of households with one car in every region except Yorkshire and the Humber where the percentage remained the same as in 2001. (Table 10.2)

All regions saw an increase in the percentage of cars less than three years old in the period 1992 to 2004. However in the East Midlands, the South East and the South West the percentages fell between 2002 and 2004. The South West had the lowest percentage of cars less than three years old (26 per cent) and the highest percentage of cars more than six years old (49 per cent). The North East had the highest percentage of cars less than three years old (38 per cent) and the lowest percentage of cars more than six years old (35 per cent). (Web: T1)

The proportion of females holding full driving licences has increased in all regions over the last decade. The largest increase between 1994 and 2003 was 12 percentage points in Scotland closely followed by Wales and the West Midlands at 10 percentage points each. The percentage of males with full driving licences has remained fairly constant over the same period. The largest changes for males were an increase of 5 percentage points in the North East and a decrease of 5 percentage points in London. (Table 10.3)

Travel

In Great Britain the average (mean) time taken to travel to work in 2004 only increased by a minute or two when compared with 2003. In 2004 the regional average time taken to travel to work was highest at 42 minutes in London. This compared with the Former Metropolitan County of the West Midlands which was the next highest at 27 minutes. The quickest journeys to work in 2004 were an average of 19 minutes in the North East (excluding the former Metropolitan County of Tyne and Wear). (Table 10.4)

The average number of miles cycled per person in Great Britain increased slightly

(3 per cent) between 2002 and 2004. Only the West Midlands and the South East experienced reductions of 14 per cent and 15 per cent respectively.

Although the distance travelled by bus remained the same for Great Britain between 2002 and 2004 there were variations at regional level. The North West saw a 12 per cent reduction to 226 miles per year and the East an 11 per cent reduction, whilst the mileage in Scotland increased by 12 per cent to 398 miles and in the South West it increased by 11 per cent.

In the two-year period 2003-2004 there was a 1 per cent decrease (68 miles) in the distance travelled by car in Great Britain when compared with the two-year period 2002-2003. Wales, Scotland and the East were the only areas showing increases. (Table 10.5)

All regions have seen an increase in the percentage of households within a 13 minute walk of an hourly or better bus service in the period since 1992-1994. The Great Britain proportion increased by 13 percentage points and Wales and the South East saw the largest increases at 18 percentage points. However, since the three-year period 1999-2001 several regions have seen decreases, the North West having the largest at 4 per cent closely followed by the South East with a decrease of 3 per cent. The largest increases were in the East Midlands and Wales, at 9 per cent and 8 per cent respectively. (Figure 10.6)

Purpose of travel and commuting

On average males in Great Britain made 980 journeys during the two-year period 2003-2004, 17 fewer than females. The percentage of trips per person for each purpose of travel remained fairly constant averaged over the two-year period 2003-2004 when compared with the two year period 2002-2003. The biggest changes were a reduction of 4 per cent in the average number of journeys for males in Yorkshire and the Humber and an increase of 3 per cent for females in Wales.

The most common purpose for trips was leisure, which accounted for approximately one-third of all journeys. The percentage of trips for commuting purposes for males varied from a low of 15 per cent in the North East to a high of 20 per cent in London. For females the range was 11 per cent in the South West to 14 per cent in London. (Table 10.7)

In London 42 per cent of workers travelled to work by car in 2004. This compared with 83 per cent in Northern Ireland. However between 2003 and 2004 London showed the largest decrease, 1.2 percentage points, in car travel and the North East the greatest increase at 1.8 percentage points.

The proportion of workers travelling to work by bicycle fell in the UK to 2.5 per cent in the period between 2003 and 2004. London, Scotland and Northern Ireland were the only areas which showed slight increases in numbers travelling to work by bicycle. The proportion of workers in London who used trains to travel to work showed a slight increase in the period from 2003 to 2004 to reach 11.3 per cent, and this more than reversed the fall in the period from 2002 to 2003. London had the highest train usage of all the regions, the East being next highest with 7 per cent. (Table 10.8)

Expenditure on travel and roads

Expenditure on motoring can take up to a fifth of the average total weekly expenditure in a household. In the period 2001 to 2004 households in the East Midlands spent the highest proportion of their expenditure on motoring (20 per cent) while households in London spent the lowest proportion, 14 per cent.

After allowing for approximately half the expenditure being spent on vehicle purchase and maintenance in the period 2001 to 2004, fuel costs were the next highest percentage at between 22 per cent in London (£11.91) and 29 per cent in Northern Ireland (£17.21). However the highest actual expenditure on fuel was £17.35 per week in the South East. (Table 10.9)

The expenditure on all roads decreased slightly in England as a whole between 2002/03 and 2003/04. The largest decrease (£107 million) was in Yorkshire and the Humber, which also had the largest percentage decrease, nearly 20 per cent. The largest increase was £45 million in London while the largest percentage increase was 7 per cent in the East. (Table 10.10)

Traffic

The average daily motor vehicle flow on all roads in Great Britain increased slightly between 2003 and 2004. Only two regions showed any reduction in traffic flow during this period. The West Midlands had a decrease of 5.4 per cent in motorway traffic to 75,400 vehicles per day. London had decreases of 1.9 per cent on motorways (to 94,600 vehicles) and 1.0 per cent on major urban roads (to 28,500 vehicles). (Table 10.11)

Viewed over a long period, London had the smallest increase in traffic on major roads (2.1 per cent) between 1993 and 2004. The largest increase in this time period was 28.8 per cent in the East Midlands, closely followed by Wales with 28 per cent. (Table 10.12)

Accidents

The total number of accidents on all roads in Great Britain fell by nearly 7,000 in the period between 2003 and 2004. In the regions, London had the largest reduction of over 3,000 accidents (a decrease of 9.6 per cent) followed by Yorkshire and the Humber with a reduction of just over 1,100 accidents (a decrease of 5.6 per cent).

The only region showing an increase in the number of accidents was the South West with 62 more accidents on all roads (an increase of 0.3 per cent) between 2003 and 2004. The South West had an increase of 15 percentage points in accidents on rural 'A' roads, even though there was a slight decrease in motor vehicle traffic on that class of road. (Table 10.13)

The number of fatal or serious accidents on all roads fell in all regions in the period 2002 to 2004. In Great Britain as a whole they fell by nearly 4,000; 12 per cent down on 2002. London had the largest reduction of one-quarter or 1,300 accidents. Wales and the North East were the only regions experiencing increases in the number of fatal or serious accidents on major roads, of 2.3 per cent and 3.0 per cent respectively.

In the period 1991 to 2004, fatal and serious accidents on all roads fell in each region, ranging from 28 per cent in the East Midlands to 47 per cent in London. (Table 10.14)

The number of road casualties in the United Kingdom decreased by just over 20 thousand (6.7 per cent) between 2003 and 2004 and by nearly 53 thousand (15.9 per cent) between 1999 and 2004. All regions saw reductions between 2003 and 2004, London having the largest at nearly four thousand fewer casualties, followed by Yorkshire and the Humber with a reduction of over 1,300 casualties.

In 2004 car occupants formed the largest single group of road casualties, accounting for approximately two-thirds overall. The exceptions were London where less than half of all road casualties were car occupants and Wales where the figure was approximately three-quarters.

The percentage of casualties split across the age groups 0 to 15, 16 to 59 and 60 or over remained fairly constant between 2003 and 2004 at approximately 8 to 14 per cent, 74 to 78 per cent and 8 to 12 per cent respectively. (Table 10.15)

Airports

Air passenger numbers increased overall at UK airports by over 15 million between 2003 and 2004. Heathrow showed the largest increase of nearly 4 million passengers. Cardiff and Birmingham were the only airports where the number of passengers decreased, by 27,000 and 127,000 passengers respectively.

The amount of freight handled in total by UK airports increased by over 163 thousand tonnes between 2003 and 2004, the majority of which was due to an increase at Heathrow of 102 thousand tonnes, an increase of over 8 per cent. In 2004 Heathrow handled 56 per cent of the freight at UK airports, followed by the East Midlands with 11 per cent and Stansted with 10 per cent. (Table 10.16)

Table **10.1**   Motor cars currently licensed and new registrations[1]

Thousands and percentages

	Currently licensed				Percentage company cars		New registrations		
	1994	1996	1998	2003[2]	1998	2003[2]	1996	1998	2003[2]
United Kingdom[3]	21,708	22,784	23,878	26,240	10	8	2,077	2,366	2,646
North East	745	783	824	948	5	5	74	78	98
North West	2,375	2,501	2,647	2,942	13	10	235	265	322
Yorkshire and the Humber	1,633	1,707	1,808	2,039	9	7	138	157	211
East Midlands	1,532	1,609	1,698	1,965	9	8	140	173	219
West Midlands	2,070	2,183	2,290	2,612	17	17	275	288	339
East	2,168	2,295	2,429	2,711	9	6	200	232	265
London	2,310	2,362	2,369	2,480	11	6	277	270	228
South East	3,295	3,469	3,709	4,162	10	9	292	361	447
South West	1,976	2,109	2,230	2,523	10	8	130	138	190
England	18,104	19,018	20,006	22,382	11	9	1,762	1,961	2,319
Wales	1,012	1,067	1,129	1,305	7	4	73	83	100
Scotland	1,575	1,674	1,775	2,031	9	7	154	175	219
Northern Ireland	515	540	585	..	9	..	55	71	..

1 At 31 December.
2 Figures for 2003 are for Great Britain.
3 Totals for the United Kingdom include motor vehicles where the country of the registered keeper is unknown, that are under disposal or from countries unknown within Great Britain (but not Northern Ireland).

Source: Annual Vehicle Census/Vehicle Information Database, Department for Transport; Department of the Environment, Northern Ireland

Table **10.2**   Households with regular use of a car[1]

Percentages

	1997			2002		
	No car	One car	Two or more cars	No car	One car	Two or more cars
Great Britain	30	45	25	26	44	29
North East	42	41	17	37	43	20
North West	31	44	25	27	45	28
Yorkshire and the Humber	34	44	22	30	46	24
East Midlands	27	45	29	22	45	33
West Midlands	32	41	28	26	43	31
East	23	49	29	19	45	36
London	39	43	19	38	42	20
South East	19	44	36	18	44	38
South West	24	48	28	18	46	36
England	29	44	27	26	44	30
Wales	31	45	24	27	45	27
Scotland	35	46	18	34	45	21
Northern Ireland	30	47	23	..	..	..

1 Includes cars and light vans normally available to the household.

Source: General Household Survey and Expenditure and Food Survey, Office for National Statistics; National Travel Survey, Department for Transport; Continuous Household Survey, Northern Ireland Statistics and Research Agency

Table **10.3** Full car driving licence holders:[1] by sex, 1992-1994[2] and 2002-2003[3]

Percentages

	Males		Females	
	1992-1994[2]	2002-2003[3]	1992-1994[2]	2002-2003[3]
Great Britain	81	81	54	61
North East	68	73	40	46
North West	77	80	49	58
Yorkshire and the Humber	77	79	51	55
East Midlands	84	86	55	64
West Midlands	80	80	51	61
East	88	86	62	65
London	78	73	51	55
South East	88	87	65	70
South West	88	87	61	69
England	82	82	55	61
Wales	83	82	48	58
Scotland	77	77	46	58

1 Aged 17 years and over.
2 Data are averaged over a three-year period. See Notes and Definitions.
3 Data are averaged over a two-year period. See Notes and Definitions.

Source: National Travel Survey, Department for Transport

Table **10.4** Time taken to travel to work: by workplace, autumn 2004

Percentages and minutes

	Percentage of journeys to workplace					
	Up to 20 minutes	21 to 40 minutes	41 to 60 minutes	61 to 80 minutes	Over 80 minutes	Mean time (minutes)
Great Britain	59	24	13	2	3	26
North East	66	23	9	1	1	22
Tyne & Wear[1]	58	27	12	1	1	25
Rest	72	19	7	0	1	19
North West	61	25	11	1	2	24
Greater Manchester[1]	56	26	14	2	2	27
Merseyside[1]	60	28	10	1	2	24
Rest	66	23	9	1	2	22
Yorkshire and the Humber	62	24	11	1	2	24
South Yorkshire[1]	60	27	12	1	1	23
West Yorkshire[1]	58	26	13	1	2	25
Rest	70	19	8	1	2	22
East Midlands	66	23	9	1	2	22
West Midlands	62	23	11	1	2	24
West Midlands[1]	54	26	16	1	2	27
Rest	71	21	7	1	1	20
East	65	23	9	1	2	23
London	30	26	30	5	10	42
South East	63	23	10	1	3	24
South West	66	23	9	1	2	22
England	58	24	13	2	3	26
Wales	70	21	7	0	1	20
Scotland	60	25	12	1	2	25
Northern Ireland	62	27	9	1	1	23

1 Data relate to former metropolitan counties.

Source: Labour Force Survey

Table **10.5** **Distance travelled per person[1] per year: by mode of transport, 2003-2004[2]**

Miles

| | Walk | Pedal cycle | Cars and other private road vehicles | Public transport | | | | All modes of transport |
				Bus	Rail	Taxi and other	All public transport	
Great Britain	194	35	5,682	260	418	210	887	6,798
North East	199	17	4,668	352	218	345	915	5,799
North West	198	35	5,221	226	246	211	684	6,137
Yorkshire and the Humber	183	31	5,462	258	204	216	678	6,355
East Midlands	206	49	6,611	193	217	166	576	7,443
West Midlands	179	24	5,794	273	285	183	740	6,737
East	178	46	6,686	148	566	167	880	7,791
London	211	37	3,164	456	984	194	1,635	5,048
South East	204	41	6,618	145	594	114	853	7,716
South West	194	39	6,999	190	318	179	687	7,919
England	195	37	5,681	245	443	186	875	6,787
Wales	158	15	6,144	240	152	185	578	6,895
Scotland	199	28	5,466	398	319	440	1,157	6,850

1 Within Great Britain only. Figures relate to region of residence of the traveller and include trips undertaken outside this region. They include trips of less than one mile; these were excluded from the table in Regional Trends 32 and earlier editions. See Notes and Definitions.
2 Data are averaged over a two-year period. See Notes and Definitions.

Source: National Travel Survey, Department for Transport

Figure **10.6** **Bus accessibility,[1] 1992-1994[2] and 2002-2003[3]**

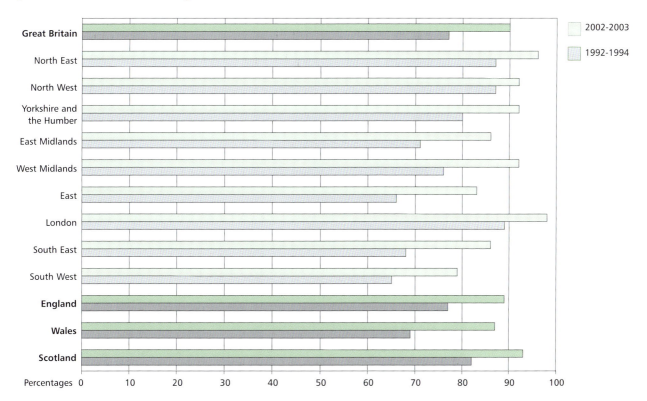

1 Households within 13 minute walk of a bus stop with a service at least once an hour. See Notes and Definitions.
2 Data are averaged over a three-year period. See Notes and Definitions.
3 Data are averaged over a two-year period. See Notes and Definitions.

Source: National Travel Survey, Department for Transport

Table 10.7 Trips per person[1] per year: by purpose, 2003-2004[2]

Percentages and numbers

	Commuting	Business	Education	Shopping	Other personal business	Escort	Leisure	Average number of journeys (=100%)
Males								
Great Britain	18	5	7	18	10	12	31	980
North East	15	3	8	19	9	13	33	977
North West	17	4	7	18	10	12	31	1,011
Yorkshire and the Humber	18	4	7	18	10	12	30	937
East Midlands	16	5	7	17	9	12	34	1,040
West Midlands	18	5	7	17	10	12	30	1,012
East	18	5	7	17	10	14	29	980
London	20	5	10	16	10	10	30	850
South East	18	5	6	18	10	12	30	1,022
South West	17	6	7	17	9	11	32	1,035
England	18	5	7	17	10	12	31	983
Wales	17	5	6	19	10	13	31	966
Scotland	18	4	8	17	10	12	31	962
Females								
Great Britain	12	2	7	21	11	16	30	997
North East	13	2	6	23	10	15	32	989
North West	12	2	6	22	11	16	31	997
Yorkshire and the Humber	12	2	6	22	11	16	31	962
East Midlands	13	2	6	22	10	15	32	1,033
West Midlands	12	2	7	21	10	18	29	1,025
East	12	1	6	21	11	19	29	1,013
London	14	2	9	21	11	16	27	866
South East	12	2	6	21	10	19	30	1,065
South West	11	3	6	21	11	16	33	1,074
England	12	2	7	21	11	17	30	1,001
Wales	12	2	6	22	10	14	33	957
Scotland	14	2	6	21	11	14	31	982
All people								
Great Britain	15	3	7	20	10	14	31	989
North East	14	2	7	21	10	14	32	983
North West	14	3	6	20	11	14	31	1,004
Yorkshire and the Humber	15	3	7	20	11	14	30	950
East Midlands	14	3	6	19	10	14	33	1,037
West Midlands	15	4	7	19	10	15	29	1,019
East	15	3	6	19	11	16	29	997
London	17	3	9	18	11	13	28	858
South East	15	3	6	20	10	16	30	1,044
South West	14	4	6	19	10	14	32	1,056
England	15	3	7	20	10	15	30	992
Wales	14	3	6	20	10	14	32	961
Scotland	16	3	7	19	10	13	31	972

1 Within Great Britain only. Figures relate to region of residence of travellers and include trips undertaken outside of their region. They include trips of less than one mile; these were excluded from the table in Regional Trends 32 and earlier editions. See Notes and Definitions.
2 Data are averaged over a two-year period. See Notes and Definitions.

Source: National Travel Survey, Department for Transport

Table **10.8** Usual method of travel to work,[1] autumn 2004

Percentages

	Car, van, minibus, works van	Motorbike, moped, scooter	Bicycle	Bus, coach, private bus	Rail	Other rail[2,3]	Foot	Other[4]
United Kingdom	71.3	1.0	2.5	7.6	3.9	2.3	10.5	0.8
North East	72.1	1.0	1.7	9.5	0.8	2.2	11.3	1.4
North West	75.6	0.9	1.9	8.0	1.9	0.5	10.3	0.9
Yorkshire and the Humber	72.2	0.7	2.9	9.8	2.0	0.3	11.2	0.8
East Midlands	77.7	1.3	3.0	6.3	0.9	0.1	10.2	0.4
West Midlands	77.5	0.8	1.6	7.8	1.7	0.0	9.9	0.6
East	74.6	1.2	3.4	3.1	7.0	0.6	9.2	0.8
London	41.5	1.3	3.5	15.8	11.3	16.8	8.8	0.7
South East	75.5	0.9	3.0	3.7	5.9	0.2	10.1	0.7
South West	76.3	1.1	3.3	4.3	1.2	0.0	13.3	0.4
England	70.6	1.0	2.8	7.5	4.3	2.7	10.3	0.7
Wales	81.3	0.7	1.4	3.9	1.0	0.1	11.2	0.4
Scotland	69.2	0.5	1.4	11.8	3.0	0.2	12.1	1.8
Northern Ireland	83.3	0.5	0.5	4.0	0.8	..	9.1	1.7

1 Analysis excludes those on government schemes, those who work from home or in the same grounds or building as their home, and those who work in different places using their home as a base. See Notes and Definitions for Chapter 5 also.
2 For some regions, sample sizes are too small to provide a reliable estimate.
3 Underground, light railway and tram.
4 Includes taxi as main method.

Source: Labour Force Survey, Office for National Statistics; Department of Enterprise, Trade and Investment, Northern Ireland

Table **10.9** Household expenditure on transport, 2001/02-2003/04[1]

Average weekly household expenditure (£)

	Motoring costs per car/van						Fares and other travel costs			Total transport expenditure per household	Total expenditure per household
	Cars, vans & motorcycles purchase and repairs	Spares & accessories	Motor vehicle insurance & taxation	Petrol, diesel & other motor oils	Other motoring costs	Total motoring expenditure per car/van	Rail & tube fares	Bus & coach fares	Other travel costs[2]		
United Kingdom	31.83	2.00	10.83	14.80	1.88	61.34	1.84	1.44	4.44	69.06	346.80
North East	24.39	2.68	8.19	12.72	1.19	49.18	1.01	2.02	4.14	56.35	292.40
North West	31.37	1.44	11.42	13.76	1.73	59.71	1.02	1.61	4.75	67.09	332.50
Yorkshire and the Humber	30.95	1.39	10.09	13.09	1.68	57.20	0.95	1.74	4.21	64.10	314.80
East Midlands	34.98	1.97	11.40	15.93	1.80	66.08	0.93	1.32	3.63	71.96	336.10
West Midlands	29.08	1.83	12.09	15.64	1.68	60.32	1.00	1.26	3.78	66.36	322.30
East	36.50	2.52	11.23	16.77	2.37	69.38	3.62	0.92	5.35	79.27	367.50
London	28.77	1.75	10.22	11.91	2.20	54.83	3.88	2.06	5.12	65.89	406.30
South East	41.65	2.88	12.00	17.35	2.24	76.13	2.97	0.93	4.72	84.75	396.50
South West	31.94	2.16	11.29	15.63	2.14	63.15	1.19	1.16	3.62	69.12	331.90
England	32.99	2.06	11.08	14.87	1.96	62.96	2.03	1.41	4.46	70.86	352.50
Wales	24.59	1.59	9.41	14.58	1.66	51.82	0.60	1.07	3.18	56.67	302.30
Scotland	26.29	1.86	8.71	13.53	1.40	51.79	1.21	1.97	4.56	59.53	319.00
Northern Ireland	27.01	1.49	12.94	17.21	1.30	59.95	0.32	1.13	5.66	67.06	344.50

1 Combined data from the 2001/02, 2002/03 and 2003/04 surveys. See Notes and Definitions.
2 Other travel costs include taxis, air and other travel, and bicycles and boats: purchase and repair.

Source: Expenditure and Food Survey, Office for National Statistics

Table 10.10 Public expenditure on roads, 2003/04

£ million

	Motorways and trunk roads[1,2]				Local roads[5]				
	New construction/ improvement and structural maintenance	Current maintenance including routine and winter maintenance[3,4]	Total	Expenditure per 1,000 kilometres	New construction/ improvement for highways lighting, road safety and structural maintenance	Public lighting and routine maintenance[4]	Revenue expenditure on road safety	Total	Expenditure per 1,000 kilometres
North East	34.1	16.4	50.5	101.9	125.2	65.6	5.6	196.4	12.7
North West	116.3	55.7	172.0	117.3	333.8	163.7	23.1	520.6	15.1
Yorkshire and the Humber	76.9	36.8	113.7	106.5	222.5	122.0	12.3	356.8	11.5
East Midlands	96.0	46.0	142.0	100.3	207.9	84.5	14.3	306.7	10.6
West Midlands	118.1	56.6	174.7	137.5	235.5	111.6	13.3	360.4	11.6
East	121.7	58.3	180.0	128.2	283.3	137.6	18.8	439.7	11.8
London	11.6	5.5	17.1	44.4	414.4	238.1	165.6	818.1	58.7
South East	164.2	78.7	242.9	161.0	317.3	181.2	24.8	523.3	11.7
South West	117.4	56.3	173.7	131.0	239.2	125.3	10.8	375.3	7.9
England	856.3	410.5	1,266.8	122.5	2,378.8	1,229.6	288.7	3,897.1	13.7

1 Expenditure on motorway and trunk roads excludes expenditure under Design, Build, Finance & Operate (DBFO) schemes.
2 Figures are now collected on a resource accounting basis and cannot be compared with data prior to 2001/02. In particular, until 2001/02, associated costs of investment (including depreciation and capital costs) were not included within these figures. Apportionment between the Government Office Regions involves an estimation process.
3 Previously this table showed figures for routine and winter maintenance and public lighting. Highways Agency is no longer able separately to identify this expenditure. Figures are now shown under a new heading and cannot be compared with those in versions of this table prior to 2002/03.
4 Includes expenditure on gritting and snow clearing.
5 Local Authority expenditure excludes car parks.

Source: Department for Transport

Table 10.11 Average daily motor vehicle flows:[1] by type of road, 2004

Thousand vehicles per day

	Major roads				Minor roads			
	Motorway	Rural	Urban	All major roads	Rural	Urban	All minor roads	All roads
Great Britain	74.9	10.9	20.3	17.5	0.9	2.4	1.4	3.5
North East	51.0	13.5	21.4	16.8	0.7	2.7	1.7	3.4
North West	74.5	10.7	18.0	22.1	1.0	2.1	1.6	4.2
Yorkshire and the Humber	68.4	12.5	18.9	19.9	1.0	2.0	1.4	3.6
East Midlands	96.1	13.6	19.5	18.5	1.0	2.1	1.4	3.6
West Midlands	75.4	11.5	20.2	20.9	1.0	2.8	1.8	4.1
East	87.3	18.1	18.3	22.5	1.2	2.6	1.6	3.8
London	94.6	29.1	28.5	30.8	1.5	2.7	2.7	6.1
South East	92.4	18.0	19.6	26.7	1.4	2.5	1.9	5.0
South West	67.5	11.0	19.8	15.6	0.7	2.3	1.1	2.6
England	79.5	13.9	20.8	21.4	1.0	2.4	1.6	3.9
Wales	65.3	8.0	17.2	11.0	0.6	2.1	0.9	2.2
Scotland	43.1	4.8	16.7	7.2	0.5	1.9	0.8	2.0

1 Average daily flow is annual traffic divided by road length multiplied by the number of days in the year. See Notes and Definitions.
Source: National Road Traffic Survey, Department for Transport

Figure **10.12** **Traffic[1] increase on major roads[2] between 1993 and 2004**

Percentages 0 5 10 15 20 25 30

1 The volume of traffic is expressed as vehicle kilometres, which is calculated by multiplying the annual average daily flow by the corresponding length of road.
2 Motorways and A roads.

Source: Department for Transport; Department of the Environment

Table **10.13** **Road traffic and distribution of accidents on major[1] roads, 2004**

	Motorway		Urban 'A'		Rural 'A'		All major[1] roads		All roads	
	Motor vehicle traffic on major roads (percentages)	Total accidents on major roads (percentages)	Motor vehicle traffic on major roads (percentages)	Total accidents on major roads (percentages)	Motor vehicle traffic on major roads (percentages)	Total accidents on major roads (percentages)	Motor vehicle traffic (=100%) (billion vehicle kilometres)	Total accidents on major roads (=100%) (numbers)[1]	Motor vehicle traffic (billion vehicle kilometres)	Total accidents (numbers)[2]
Great Britain	30.1	8.8	25.8	56.7	44.0	34.5	320.7	103,501	498.6	207,410
North East	9.7	3.1	34.8	49.3	55.5	47.5	11.2	3,590	19.9	8,113
North West	46.4	12.7	29.4	63.9	24.2	23.4	37.6	13,410	56.6	26,504
Yorkshire and the Humber	34.1	8.8	28.0	57.1	37.9	33.7	26.9	8,331	41.6	18,776
East Midlands	24.9	8.2	18.1	41.1	57.1	50.7	27.4	7,422	40.7	15,200
West Midlands	39.4	10.5	26.9	60.1	33.7	29.3	30.2	9,001	48.6	19,033
East	24.7	11.4	16.1	39.5	59.2	49.1	34.3	9,565	55.1	20,398
London	10.4	1.6	86.4	97.0	3.3	1.4	20.0	18,216	32.7	28,778
South East	38.5	15.1	18.2	44.2	43.3	40.8	57.5	14,648	86.6	29,283
South West	26.8	8.1	16.9	35.2	56.3	56.5	30.1	8,013	47.1	17,944
England	31.7	9.0	26.8	58.9	41.5	32.0	275.1	92,196	428.8	184,029
Wales	19.4	6.0	19.6	36.1	61.0	57.9	17.4	4,640	27.3	9,535
Scotland	21.6	6.9	19.6	40.4	58.8	52.6	28.2	6,665	42.5	13,846

1 Includes accidents on unallocated A roads. See Notes and Definitions for details of road classifications.
2 Includes B,C and unclassified roads. See Notes and Definitions.

Source: Department for Transport

Table 10.14 Fatal and serious road accidents[1]

Numbers and rates

| | Fatal and serious accidents on all roads | | | | | | Fatal and serious accidents on major roads[2] | | | |
| | Numbers | | | Rates per 100,000 population[4] | | | Numbers | | Rates per 100 million vehicle kilometres | |
	1991	1994-1998 average[3]	2004	1991	1994-1998 average[3]	2004	1991	2004	1991	2004
Great Britain	47,931	40,481	29,726	85	71.0	51.1	24,344	15,102	9.4	3.0
North East	1,769	1,295	1,046	68	50.5	41.1	734	476	5.9	2.4
North West	4,914	4,582	3,391	71	67.5	49.7	2,506	1,692	9.6	3.0
Yorkshire and the Humber	4,352	3,521	2,997	87	71.1	59.5	2,084	1,356	10.1	3.3
East Midlands	3,451	3,305	2,470	86	80.6	57.7	1,796	1,242	9.3	3.1
West Midlands	4,447	3,997	2,495	84	76.0	46.8	2,055	1,149	8.5	2.4
East	4,802	4,187	3,300	93	79.9	60.1	2,264	1,526	6.5	2.8
London	7,279	6,082	3,868	105	88.1	52.1	4,399	2,459	23.7	7.5
South East	5,843	5,170	4,036	76	66.2	49.8	2,882	2,023	6.9	2.3
South West	3,793	2,720	2,232	80	56.7	44.3	1,833	1,112	7.1	2.4
England	40,650	34,859	25,835	84	71.0	51.6	20,553	13,035	9.2	3.0
Wales	2,112	1,623	1,302	73	56.0	44.1	1,139	680	8.9	2.5
Scotland	5,169	3,999	2,589	101	78.0	51.0	2,652	1,387	12.1	3.3
Northern Ireland	1,381	1,280	..	86	77.0	..	643	..	9.5	..

1 An accident is defined as one involving personal injury on a public highway in which a road vehicle is involved. See Notes and Definitions.
2 Motorways, A(M) roads and A roads.
3 Used as the baseline for the government targets for reducing road casualties in Great Britain by 40 per cent by the year 2010.
4 Latest population figures available at the time these figures were supplied.

Source: Department for Transport; Police Service of Northern Ireland

Table 10.15 Road casualties:[1] by age and type of road user, 2004

Percentages and numbers

| | Percentage of all road casualties | | | | | | | | All road casualties (=100%) (numbers) | Percentage change compared with 1994-1998 average[4] |
| | Who were aged[2] | | | Type of road user | | | | | | |
	0 to 15	16 to 59	60 or over	Pedestrians	Pedal cyclists	Motor cyclists	Car occupants[3]	Other road users		
United Kingdom										
North East	13.6	76.1	10.2	13.0	5.2	6.1	67.3	8.5	11,458	-5.0
North West	13.1	77.0	9.4	13.5	5.3	6.5	68.1	6.6	37,448	-17.2
Yorkshire and the Humber	12.2	76.0	10.1	12.1	5.0	7.8	67.0	8.1	27,049	-6.1
East Midlands	11.4	75.7	9.5	10.1	5.7	8.9	67.5	7.9	21,293	-7.9
West Midlands	11.5	75.8	8.9	12.4	4.8	7.3	68.9	6.6	25,924	-9.3
East	9.4	77.7	9.9	8.2	6.6	9.8	69.4	6.0	28,069	-7.0
London	8.8	75.7	8.5	18.5	8.6	16.1	47.9	9.1	34,581	-24.5
South East	9.7	77.0	10.5	10.0	6.8	10.4	66.8	6.0	38,869	-13.5
South West	10.2	75.1	11.6	10.5	6.3	10.4	67.9	4.9	24,071	-0.1
England	10.9	76.4	9.8	12.2	6.2	9.6	65.1	7.0	248,762	-12.0
Wales	11.3	77.6	11.1	11.2	3.8	5.7	73.7	5.7	13,687	-7.9
Scotland	13.0	74.6	12.0	16.6	4.2	5.4	64.5	9.3	18,391	-17.5
Northern Ireland[5]	11.9	79.2	8.9	7.8	1.9	4.6	77.6	8.1	10,325	-17.4

1 Casualties in accidents occurring on a public highway in which a road vehicle is involved. See Notes and Definitions.
2 Excludes age not reported.
3 Includes occupants of taxis and minibuses.
4 Used as the baseline for the government targets for reducing road casualties in Great Britain by 40 per cent by the year 2010.
5 Data for Northern Ireland relate to 2003.

Source: Department for Transport; Police Service of Northern Ireland

Table **10.16** Activity at major airports[1]

Thousands and thousand tonnes

	1998					2004[2]				
	Air passengers (thousands)[3]				Freight handled[4] (thousands tonnes)	Air passengers (thousands)[3]				Freight handled[4] (thousands tonnes)
		International					International			
	Domestic[4]	Scheduled	Non-scheduled	Total		Domestic[4]	Scheduled	Non-scheduled	Total	
All UK airports[5]	33,630	89,231	36,135	158,997	2,093	48,515	130,832	36,334	215,681	2,371
Newcastle	872	560	1,489	2,920	1	1,688	1,333	1,686	4,708	1
Manchester	2,634	5,179	9,393	17,206	101	3,271	8,619	9,080	20,969	149
Leeds/Bradford	439	439	521	1,398	-	562	1,273	532	2,368	-
Liverpool	..	..	..	..	..	830	2,146	376	3,352	9
East Midlands	371	411	1,354	2,136	123	812	2,011	1,552	4,375	253
Birmingham	1,187	2,905	2,516	6,608	18	1,336	4,519	2,942	8,797	10
Luton	851	1,886	1,379	4,116	29	1,635	5,015	871	7,520	26
Stansted	1,225	4,085	1,521	6,830	180	2,734	17,056	1,117	20,907	226
Heathrow	7,183	53,061	117	60,360	1,209	6,925	60,085	99	67,109	1,325
Gatwick	2,732	15,403	10,899	29,033	275	3,918	17,405	10,068	31,391	218
London City	..	..	..	..	..	549	1,125	1	1,675	-
Bristol	375	440	999	1,814	-	1,304	2,008	1,291	4,603	-
Cardiff	91	215	924	1,230	-	313	643	918	1,873	3
Aberdeen	1,733	353	566	2,652	5	1,629	535	470	2,634	4
Edinburgh	3,501	764	279	4,545	15	5,838	1,726	428	7,992	27
Glasgow	3,448	896	2,137	6,481	9	4,640	1,633	2,284	8,557	8
Belfast City	1,295	9	10	1,314	1	2,069	21	1	2,091	1
Belfast International	1,809	169	649	2,627	25	3,213	314	876	4,403	32
Other UK airports	3,885	2,457	1,384	7,726	100	5,248	3,365	1,742	10,356	78

1 Airports handling one million passengers or more in 2004. Includes British Government/armed forces on official business and travel to/from oil rigs.
2 Data are not directly comparable with years prior to 2001 because of the exclusion of air taxi operations before this date.
3 Arrivals and departures.
4 Domestic traffic is counted at airports on arrival and departure.
5 Including airports handling fewer than one million passengers.

Source: Civil Aviation Authority

Chapter 11 **Environment**

Rainfall

The average rainfall for winter periods (October to March) was 609 millimetres for the United Kingdom between 1961 and 1990, with an average of 471 millimetres during the summer (April to September). The summer averages across individual countries show greater similarities than those in winter. Of the Environment Agency regions, the South West had the highest winter rainfall and Anglian the lowest, whereas in summer the North West had the highest rainfall, with Anglian having the lowest. Therefore, Anglian was the driest region for the 29 year period. These winter and summer rainfall averages are the baseline against which subsequent annual seasonal rainfall is compared.

Winter rainfall in 2004/05 as a percentage of the 1961 to 1990 winter average has decreased in most areas. Winter periods in previous years show a continual decrease in the United Kingdom overall, with a 13 per cent reduction in 2002/03 compared with 2001/02, and a further 6 per cent between 2002/03 and 2003/04. However, in 2004/05 the United Kingdom winter rainfall increased by 3 per cent, taking it above the recorded average.

In 2004/05, Scotland and Northumbria were the only areas to have winter rainfall above the long-term average, at 17 and 5 per cent above respectively. Both areas showed increases compared with 2003/04. In contrast, the largest decrease was in the Southern region where winter rainfall fell from 10 per cent above the long-term average to 23 per cent below.

Summer rainfall in the United Kingdom presents an inconsistent picture, fluctuating between increases and decreases from 2002 through to 2005. The greatest change was in 2004, when summer rainfall was above average in all areas, with Yorkshire, Anglian and Northumbrian well above (by around 30 per cent), making it the wettest summer over the past four years.

Regional differences in rainfall in summer 2005 were less than previous periods, with rainfall in Scotland at 10 per cent above the average, and both Northumbria and Anglian 7 per cent above. Southern was again the driest region, 20 percentage points below the seasonal average. (Tables 11.1 and 11.2)

Atmospheric pollution/air emissions

Power stations and manufacturing industry are main producers of sulphur dioxide (SO_2) in the United Kingdom. The greatest concentrations of sulphur dioxide are in regions where these industries are more common, for example in the North West and East Midlands. (Map 11.3)

Nitrogen dioxide (NO_2) was highly concentrated in urban areas of the United Kingdom such as Birmingham, Glasgow and Manchester. Central London was the largest area where concentration was high. One of the main sources of nitrogen dioxide is road traffic, hence higher concentrations are found in heavily congested areas or major road networks, for example around the M25 (in particular the Western links section), M1, M6, M60 and M27 motorways. (Map 11.4)

Water consumption

Water and sewerage companies

Water consumption in the area covered by the Severn Trent company was consistently low for unmetered households across all years shown, whereas those with the highest consumption varied over time. Between 2002 and 2004, the Anglian region consistently had the lowest estimated water consumption of all metered households. In 2004/05 people in the Anglian region again consumed the least, at 124.8 litres per head per day, compared with the highest consumption in the Thames region at 152.9 litres per head per day. There was a steady increase in the proportion of households using metered supplies in all regions between 2002/03 and 2004/05. Over this same three year period, the percentages of metered households billed in the Anglian region were over double the England and Wales average. The increase in the percentage of households metered reflects the continuous monitoring and regulation of water use, particularly in those regions where rainfall is low. (Web: E1)

Water-only companies

Water consumption in the area covered by Tendring Hundred was consistently low across all years for unmetered and metered households. The Three Valleys area consumed the highest amount among unmetered households, with the highest for metered households varying between Portsmouth in 2002/03, and the South East in 2003/04 and 2004/05. (Web: E1)

Water abstraction

In England and Wales, the greatest use of abstracted water is for electricity supply. In 2003, this ranged from 1,288 megalitres per day in the Thames Environment Region to 6,970 megalitres per day in the North West. Abstraction of water for public supply is the second most common use overall, accounting for between 23 per cent in the South West and 70 per cent in the Thames region. The South West abstracts least from all surface and groundwaters at 5,545 megalitres per day, 10 per cent of the total, whilst the North West abstracts the most with 9,579 megalitres per day, 16 per cent of the total. (Table 11.5)

Water quality

In 2003, England had a greater percentage of rivers and canals in biological quality category A (38 per cent), with most of those in Wales (48 per cent) and Northern Ireland (41 per cent) in category B. In Northern Ireland there had been a decrease in the biological quality of rivers and canals, with a reduction of 17 percentage points in category A and 2 percentage points in category B between 1990 and 2003. The North West, Yorkshire and the Humber, the East Midlands and the West Midlands are the only areas in England with rivers and canals of 'bad' biological quality in 2003. (Table 11.6)

Most rivers and canals (62 per cent) in England in 2003 were of good chemical quality, which reflects an increase of 18 percentage points from 1990. However, Wales had the greatest proportion (94 per cent) of rivers and canals of good quality.

All regions increased in the proportion of rivers and canals with category A chemical quality, ranging from only 1 per cent in London to 18 per cent in the North West. The greatest improvement in quality was in category B, with an increase of 20 percentage points between 1990 and 2003 in London and East Midlands. The proportion of rivers and canals falling into the lower quality categories (C, D, E and F) decreased, especially in London, East Midlands and the North East. (Table 11.7)

The number of coastal bathing waters in Scotland and Northern Ireland did not change between 1999 and 2004. In England, the South West continues to have the highest number of coastal bathing waters, with increases every year except in 2002.

It was also the only region to have an increase between 2003 and 2004. In Northern Ireland, the percentage of coastal bathing waters complying with the EC Bathing Water Directive fluctuated between 1999 and 2004: for example there was an increase of 6 per cent between 2002 and 2003 followed by a decrease of 12 per cent in 2004. Bathing waters in the Thames region have complied completely between 1999 and 2004. The North West has shown substantial improvement in the quality of its bathing waters from 68 per cent compliance in 1999 to 97 per cent in 2004. However, the proportion complying in other regions remained approximately the same or decreased. (Web: E3)

Pollution incidents (including noise pollution)

In England and Wales most prosecutions for pollution were related to waste. Between 2003 and 2004 there was an increase of 11 per cent in England, and a decrease of 25 per cent in Wales. The greatest regional change was in the Anglian area with an increase of 67 per cent in prosecutions for waste pollution.

Prosecutions for water pollution increased in England between 2003 and 2004 by 15 per cent. Increases were evident in all regions except the Midlands and the South West. The greatest rise was in the Thames region where the number of incidents more than doubled to 21. There was also an increase in the number of incidents in England relating to water abstraction. (Table 11.9)

Offences for noise pollution relating to motor vehicles in England and Wales declined by 59 per cent between 1991 and 2003. Over the same 12-year period, a considerable reduction of 78 per cent was seen in the East, which had the highest number of offences in 1991 and one of the lowest in 2003 at 286. Little change is evident in the North East (9 per cent), but it has had a consistently low number of noise offences over the past 12 years. Between 2002 and 2003, offences in Yorkshire and the Humber, East Midlands and London increased whilst offences in all other regions decreased. In 2003, the East Midlands had most offences reported (489) and the West Midlands had least with 214. (Table 11.8)

Land

In 2003, just over half (51 per cent) of the land in the United Kingdom was used as 'grass and rough grazing', ranging from 36 per cent in England to 73 per cent in Wales and 76 per cent in Northern Ireland. There were similar proportions of 'grass and rough grazing' and 'crops and fallow' in Wales and Northern Ireland, with a greater difference in 'forest and woodland', this type of land being more prevalent in Wales. As a percentage of 'all land' in 2003, 'inland water' was greatest in Northern Ireland (5 per cent) and lowest in England and Wales (0.6 per cent). Scotland had the greatest actual area of 'inland water' (169 thousand hectares). (Table 11.10)

England had the greatest area designated as National Park in 2005 while Wales had the largest proportion, one-fifth of its total area so designated. There are no National Parks in Northern Ireland, but it has the highest percentage (20 per cent) of land area designated as of outstanding natural beauty. At a regional level, Yorkshire and the Humber has the largest area and percentage of region classed as National Park. London and the South East have no National Parks, but taken together 31 per cent is categorised as being of outstanding natural beauty. London also had the highest percentage (22 per cent) of total areas classed as Green Belt land. (Table 11.13)

Of the land changing to residential use between 2001 and 2004, just under a third had previously been agricultural in England. In the regions this ranged from 2 per cent in London to 46 per cent in the South West. However, London had the greatest proportion of previously developed land changing to residential use (90 per cent), with the highest proportion being previously vacant or derelict (43 per cent). The redevelopment of existing residential land was highest in the South East at 28 per cent. The South East had the largest areas changing to residential use (138 hectares). (Table 11.11)

Waste and recycling

Between 2000 and 2004 there was an overall increase in the percentage of household waste recycled in England and Wales. The quantity of household waste stayed more or less constant in most regions. Households in the North West consistently produced the highest amount of waste and London the lowest. As a percentage of waste produced, the North East recycled the least at 12 per cent compared with the South East and East which recycled the most (23 per cent each). (Table 11.14)

Composting was the most common form of recycling in 2003/04, accounting for an average of 64.4 kilogrammes per household per year in England. In regions where the composting of waste was not very common (for example the South West, West Midlands, North East and London), the recycling of paper and card was greatest. In England, the recycling of plastic was least common (0.8 kilogrammes per household per year); however this had increased from 0.6 kilogrammes in 2002/03. (Table 11.15)

Landfill is the most common method for disposal of municipal waste throughout Great Britain. However, this decreased between 2002/03 and 2003/04 with a corresponding increase in recycling and composting. The use of incineration with energy recovery has remained the same. The South East disposed of the most municipal waste (4,529 thousand tonnes) in 2003/04, with the least in the North East (1,637 thousand tonnes). This represents about 0.56 tonnes per head of the population in the South East and 0.65 in the North East. The highest use of incineration with energy recovery was in the West Midlands (31 per cent) whilst the East, South East and South West were the regions with the highest percentages for recycling and composting. (Web: E5)

Table **11.1** Annual rainfall[1,2]

Percentages and millimetres

	Annual rainfall as a percentage of the 1961-1990 average											1961 to 1990 rainfall average (=100%) (millimetres)
	1994	1995	1996	1997	1998	1999	2000	2001	2002	2003	2004	
United Kingdom	110	95	85	95	117	115	124	97	119	83	112	1,080
North West	109	81	78	90	115	109	129	92	118	84	113	1,201
Northumbria	98	91	81	93	120	103	129	104	122	79	117	853
Severn Trent	111	87	80	96	116	121	133	105	120	82	111	754
Yorkshire	106	82	83	92	114	109	135	99	124	81	113	821
Anglian	106	90	78	95	120	115	130	125	120	87	117	596
Thames	108	99	78	89	119	112	140	118	130	82	104	688
Southern	119	96	82	99	111	107	149	115	131	86	98	778
Wessex	119	107	90	101	119	121	140	103	136	86	101	839
South West	123	98	94	100	121	116	131	94	124	80	101	1,173
England	109	90	81	94	116	112	133	105	122	82	108	823
Wales[3]	117	89	86	94	122	117	135	100	120	84	110	1,355
Scotland	108	100	85	95	117	116	113	91	113	84	117	1,436
Northern Ireland	111	102	103	98	119	117	115	85	133	88	103	1,059

1 Monthly rainfall data for all years have been revised since the last edition. The 1961 to 1990 average is unchanged.
2 The regions of England shown in this table correspond to the original nine regions of the National Rivers Authority (NRA); the NRA became part of the Environment Agency upon its creation in April 1996. See Notes and Definitions.
3 The figures in this table relate to the country of Wales; not the Environment Agency Welsh Region.

Source: Met Office; Centre for Ecology and Hydrology, Wallingford

Table **11.2** Seasonal rainfall[1,2]

Millimetres and percentages

	Rainfall average 1961 to 1990		Rainfall as a percentage of the 1961 to 1990 winter and summer averages							
			2001/02		2002/03		2003/04		2004/05	
	Winter	Summer	Winter	Summer	Winter	Summer	Winter	Summer	Winter	Summer[3]
United Kingdom	609	471	118	100	105	80	99	119	102	101
North West	669	534	114	104	98	86	97	123	96	95
Northumbria	456	397	113	97	116	78	99	129	105	107
Severn Trent	397	357	103	95	119	82	96	127	87	92
Yorkshire	441	380	103	108	115	88	93	130	88	101
Anglian	298	298	96	97	136	77	110	129	88	107
Thames	362	327	108	98	138	63	108	107	85	84
Southern	444	335	99	109	127	65	110	106	77	80
Wessex	477	361	106	103	137	73	106	103	85	90
South West	718	456	105	92	115	81	94	104	95	99
England	444	379	105	98	121	77	101	117	88	94
Wales[4]	796	560	116	91	108	87	100	108	95	92
Scotland	836	601	130	100	90	80	98	125	117	110
Northern Ireland	597	462	107	121	118	97	90	112	96	99

1 Winter rainfall is the October to March accumulation; summer rainfall is the April to September accumulation.
2 The regions of England shown in this table correspond to the original nine regions of the National Rivers Authority; the NRA became part of the Environment Agency upon its creation in April 1996. See Notes and Definitions.
3 April to September 2005 data are provisional and subject to revision.
4 The figures in this table relate to the country of Wales; not to the Environment Agency Welsh Region.

Source: Met Office; Centre for Ecology and Hydrology, Wallingford

Map **11.3** Sulphur dioxide concentration[1] across the UK, 2003   Map **11.4** Nitrogen dioxide concentration[1] across the UK, 2003

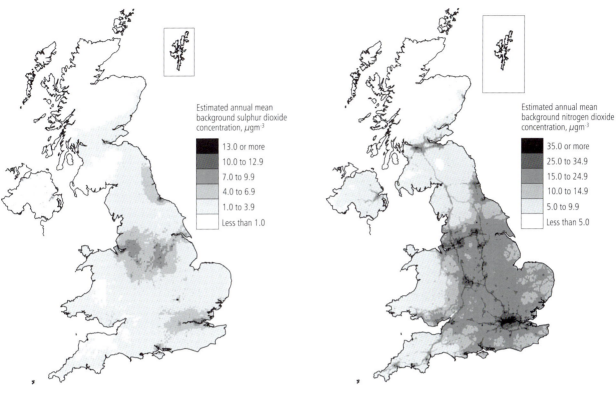

Estimated annual mean background sulphur dioxide concentration, μgm^{-3}

- 13.0 or more
- 10.0 to 12.9
- 7.0 to 9.9
- 4.0 to 6.9
- 1.0 to 3.9
- Less than 1.0

Estimated annual mean background nitrogen dioxide concentration, μgm^{-3}

- 35.0 or more
- 25.0 to 34.9
- 15.0 to 24.9
- 10.0 to 14.9
- 5.0 to 9.9
- Less than 5.0

1 In units of micrograms per cubic metre.

Source: Department for Environment, Food and Rural Affairs

1 In units of micrograms per cubic metre.

Source: Department for Environment, Food and Rural Affairs

Table **11.5** **Estimated abstractions from surface and groundwaters: by purpose, 2003[1]**

Megalitres per day

	Public water supply	Spray irrigation	Agriculture (excluding spray irrigation)	Electricity supply	Other industry[2, 3]	Fish farming, etc	Private water supply[4]	Other[5]	Total
Environment Agency regions[6]									
England and Wales	16,920	315	132	31,378	6,623	3,077	61	86	58,593
North East	2,256	21	11	2,815	947	343	3	3	6,399
North West	1,602	26	7	6,970	851	112	0	10	9,579
Midlands	2,637	64	10	2,530	1,657	16	24	16	6,953
Anglian	2,153	159	16	4,396	1,040	70	4	1	7,838
Thames	4,214	13	15	1,288	216	300	12	5	6,064
Southern	1,303	18	7	4,179	1,054	1,240	2	30	7,834
South West	1,249	8	57	2,982	372	853	3	21	5,545
England	15,414	309	123	25,160	6,137	2,934	48	86	50,212
Wales	1,505	6	8	6,218	486	144	13	-	8,381

1 Some regions report licensed and actual abstractions for financial rather than calendar years. As figures represent an average for the whole year expressed in daily amounts, differences between amounts reported for financial and calendar years are small.
2 Includes mineral washing.
3 From 2003 three licences reassigned to other industry from electricity supply. Hydropower schemes previously estimated, now measured abstractions.
4 Private abstractions for domestic use by individual households.
5 'Other' includes some private domestic water supply wells and boreholes, public water supply transfer licenses and frost protection use.
6 The boundaries of the Environment Agency regions are based on river catchment areas and not county borders. In particular, the figures shown for Wales are for the Environment Agency Welsh Region, the boundary of which does not coincide with the boundary of Wales. Figures for England are derived by adding up figures for the English regions. See Notes and Definitions.

Source: Environment Agency

Table **11.6** Rivers and canals: by biological[1] quality

Percentages and kilometres

	Good A 1990	Good A 2003	Good B 1990	Good B 2003	Fair C 1990	Fair C 2003	Fair D 1990	Fair D 2003	Poor E 1990	Poor E 2003	Bad F 1990	Bad F 2003	Total length surveyed[2] (=100%) (kms) 1990	Total length surveyed[2] (=100%) (kms) 2003
North East	30	44	39	37	15	10	8	6	7	2	2	-	1,990	2,030
North West	12	21	32	32	17	21	9	14	19	11	12	2	3,790	4,690
Yorkshire and the Humber	34	37	22	23	15	20	11	11	9	7	10	1	2,330	3,540
East Midlands	12	25	28	34	41	29	11	8	6	3	2	1	2,830	3,310
West Midlands	22	27	28	27	25	25	16	11	5	7	3	3	2,200	3,540
East	20	44	37	36	31	14	8	4	3	1	1	-	3,050	3,410
London	1	5	10	24	27	24	27	28	28	18	7	-	290	360
South East	31	42	36	34	21	18	7	5	4	1	1	-	3,330	4,230
South West	41	59	40	29	12	8	4	3	2	1	1	-	5,800	6,270
England	26	38	34	31	21	18	9	8	7	4	4	1	26,770	33,460
Wales	37	31	41	48	14	18	5	2	2	1	-	-	3,330	4,570
Scotland[3]	..	..	..	..	..	..	..	..	..	..	..	..	..	..
Northern Ireland[4]	33	16	43	41	19	29	5	12	-	2	0	-	2,190	5,190

1 Based on the River Invertebrate Prediction and Classification System (RIVPACS). See Notes and Definitions.

2 Figures for the English regions will not add to the national figure for England because a small amount of river lengths that are located along the border between England and Wales may be counted in the national figures for both England and Wales.

3 Scottish data are based on a different combined classification scheme involving an assessment of chemical, biological, nutrient and aesthetic measures although predominantly chemical. See Notes and Definitions. In consequence, the figures for Scotland are not shown on this table, but appear in a separate table E2 on the website.

4 1990 data for Northern Ireland relate to 1991.

Source: Environment Agency; Environment and Heritage Service, Northern Ireland

Table **11.7** Rivers and canals: by chemical[1] quality

Percentages and kilometres

	Good A 1990	Good A 2003	Good B 1990	Good B 2003	Fair C 1990	Fair C 2003	Fair D 1990	Fair D 2003	Poor E 1990	Poor E 2003	Bad F 1990	Bad F 2003	Total length surveyed[2] (=100%) (kms) 1990	Total length surveyed[2] (=100%) (kms) 2003
North East	27	31	42	52	16	10	6	3	7	3	2	1	2,030	2,090
North West	17	35	26	26	16	20	14	9	19	8	9	1	4,770	5,430
Yorkshire and the Humber	19	26	32	33	14	22	12	9	19	10	5	1	3,530	4,050
East Midlands	2	15	19	39	37	32	22	9	17	4	2	1	3,410	3,550
West Midlands	6	18	33	38	26	25	18	11	15	8	3	0	3,590	3,920
East	1	6	20	34	38	34	23	16	16	10	2	1	3,530	3,580
London	0	1	13	33	31	14	27	23	28	28	1	1	390	420
South East	8	19	32	40	31	25	14	10	14	6	1	0	4,370	4,440
South West	25	42	36	38	20	14	11	3	6	3	1	0	6,460	6,530
England	14	27	30	35	25	21	15	10	14	6	3	1	30,740	35,860
Wales	54	70	33	24	7	4	4	1	1	1	1	-	3,520	4,780
Scotland[3]	..	..	..	..	..	..	..	..	..	..	..	..	..	..
Northern Ireland[4]	6	10	38	48	41	24	10	11	4	7	1	-	1,680	4,320

1 England, Wales and Northern Ireland data are based on the chemical quality grade of the General Quality Assessment (GQA) scheme. See Notes and Definitions.

2 Figures for the English regions will not add to the national figure for England because a small amount of river lengths that are located along the border between England and Wales may be counted in the national figures for both England and Wales.

3 Scottish data are based on a different combined classification scheme involving an assessment of chemical, biological, nutrient and aesthetic measures although predominantly chemical. In consequence, the figures for Scotland are not shown on this table, but appear in a separate table E2 on the website.

4 1990 data for Northern Ireland relate to 1991.

Source: Environment Agency; Environment and Heritage Service, Northern Ireland

Table **11.8**   Noise offences[1] relating to motor vehicles

Numbers

	1986[2]	1991	1996	2001	2002	2003
England and Wales	11,422	7,676	5,709	3,781	3,356	3,168
North East	683	319	232	373	380	289
North West	1,113	722	597	473	424	381
Yorkshire and the Humber	866	657	380	315	219	290
East Midlands	906	874	563	407	307	489
West Midlands	1,000	498	617	298	265	214
East	1,519	1,318	551	354	384	286
London	1,582	650	634	200	161	256
South East	1,597	1,276	1,069	683	624	427
South West	1,230	790	685	449	373	344
England	10,496	7,104	5,328	3,552	3,137	2,976
Wales	926	572	381	229	219	192

1 Includes written warnings issued for alleged offences, finding of guilt at Magistrates Courts and Fixed Penalty Notices.
2 Fixed Penalties not introduced until October 1986.

Source: Home Office

Table **11.9**   Prosecutions[1] for pollution incidents, 2004

Numbers

	Waste	Water pollution	Integrated pollution control	Radioactive substances	Water abstraction	All
Environment Agency regions[2]						
North East	58	28	0	0	0	86
North West	57	30	1	0	4	92
Midlands	84	12	0	0	3	99
Anglian	40	25	0	1	2	68
Thames	69	21	0	1	4	95
Southern	41	26	0	0	0	67
South West	40	31	0	0	4	75
England	389	173	1	2	17	582
Wales	62	14	0	0	2	78

1 Figures are for the total number of defendants (companies and individuals) prosecuted in 2004 by type of prosecution.
2 In England and Wales. The boundaries of the Environment Agency regions are based on river catchment areas and not county borders. In particular, the figures shown for Wales are for the Environment Agency region for Wales, the boundary of which does not coincide with the boundary of Wales. See Notes and Definitions.

Source: Environment Agency

Table 11.10   Land use, 2003

Percentages and thousand hectares

| | Agricultural land | | | Forest and woodland[3] | Urban land and land not otherwise specified[4] | All land[5,6] (=100%) (thousand hectares) | Inland water[5,6] (thousand hectares) |
	Crops and fallow	Grass and rough grazing[1]	Other[2]				
United Kingdom	19	51	4	12	14	24,251	325
England	29	36	6	9	20	13,028	76
Wales	3	73	1	14	9	2,073	13
Scotland	7	66	2	17	8	7,793	169
Great Britain	19	50	4	12	15	22,894	258
Northern Ireland	4	76	1	6	13	1,358	64

1 Includes sole right and common rough grazing.
2 Set aside and other land on agricultural holdings, e.g. farm roads, yards, buildings, gardens, ponds. Excludes woodland on agricultural holdings which is included in 'Forest and woodland'.
3 Forestry data for Great Britain are compiled by the Forestry Commission and cover both private and state-owned land. Estimates are based on the provisional results of the National Inventory of Woodland and Trees for 1995 to 1999 and extrapolated forward using information about new planting and other changes. Data for Northern Ireland are compiled separately by the Forest Service and also cover both private and state-owned land.
4 Figures are derived by subtracting land used for agricultural and forestry purposes from the land area. Figures include land used for urban and other purposes, e.g. transport and recreation, and non-agricultural, semi-natural environments, e.g. sand dunes, grouse moors and non-agricultural grasslands, and inland waters.
5 At January 2001.
6 Because data come from a number of sources the components do not always add to the totals shown.

Source: Department for Environment, Food, and Rural Affairs; Ordnance Survey; Forestry Commission; Forest Service

Table 11.11   Land changing to residential use: by previous use

Percentages and hectares

| | | Not previously developed uses | | | Previously developed uses | | | | All changes to residential uses (=100%) (hectares)[4] |
	Agriculture	Urban not previously developed uses[1]	Other not previously developed uses[2]	All not previously developed uses	Residential	Vacant and derelict land	Other previously developed uses[3]	All previously developed uses	
North East	38	12	3	53	5	37	5	47	230
North West	27	6	4	37	10	41	13	63	660
Yorkshire and the Humber	30	12	2	44	14	28	14	56	560
East Midlands	43	11	2	56	12	20	12	44	680
West Midlands	24	13	3	41	17	30	13	59	470
East	33	8	3	43	20	18	19	57	760
London	2	5	3	10	22	43	24	90	220
South East	21	10	6	37	28	17	18	63	860
South West	46	4	4	55	21	8	15	45	610
England	31	9	4	43	18	24	15	57	5,050

1 Land in built-up areas which has not been developed previously and is not currently used for agriculture.
2 Includes forestry, open land and water and outdoor recreation.
3 Includes transport and utilities, industry and commerce and community services.
4 Average hectares exclude data from 2004 and are thus the 2001 to 2003 average.

Source: Office of the Deputy Prime Minister

Map **11.12** Protected areas,¹ as at 1 April 2005

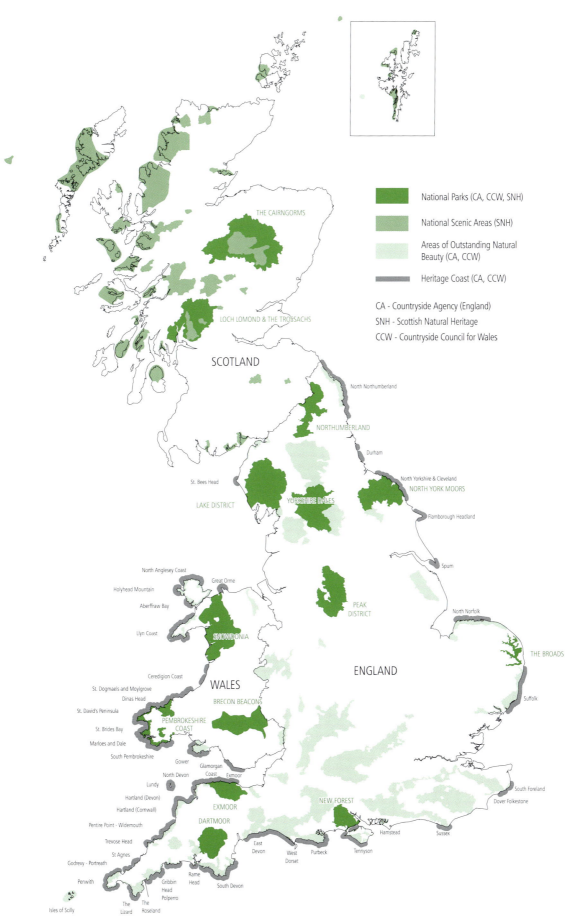

National Parks (CA, CCW, SNH)

National Scenic Areas (SNH)

Areas of Outstanding Natural Beauty (CA, CCW)

Heritage Coast (CA, CCW)

CA - Countryside Agency (England)
SNH - Scottish Natural Heritage
CCW - Countryside Council for Wales

THE CAIRNGORMS

LOCH LOMOND & THE TROSSACHS

SCOTLAND

North Northumberland

NORTHUMBERLAND

Durham

St. Bees Head

North Yorkshire & Cleveland
NORTH YORK MOORS

LAKE DISTRICT

YORKSHIRE DALES

Flamborough Headland

Spurn

North Anglesey Coast

Great Orme

Holyhead Mountain

PEAK DISTRICT

North Norfolk

Aberffraw Bay

Llyn Coast

SNOWDONIA

THE BROADS

Ceredigion Coast

WALES

ENGLAND

St. Dogmaels and Moylgrove

Dinas Head

Suffolk

St. David's Peninsula

BRECON BEACONS

St. Brides Bay

PEMBROKESHIRE COAST

Marloes and Dale

South Pembrokeshire

Gower

Glamorgan Coast

North Devon

Exmoor

South Foreland

Lundy

NEW FOREST

Dover Folkestone

Hartland (Devon)

Hartland (Cornwall)

EXMOOR

Hamstead

Sussex

Pentire Point - Widemouth

DARTMOOR

East Devon

West Dorset

Purbeck

Tennyson

Trevose Head

St Agnes

Godrevy - Portreath

Rame Head

Penwith

Gribbin Head
Polperro

South Devon

Isles of Scilly

The Lizard

The Roseland

1 See Notes and Definitions.

Source: Countryside Agency; Department of Culture, Media and Sport; Centre for Ecology and Hydrology; Office of the Deputy Prime Minister; Countryside Council for Wales; Scottish National Heritage; Department of the Environment, Northern Ireland

Table **11.13**   Designated areas,[1] 2005[2]

	National Parks		Areas of Outstanding Natural Beauty[3]		Green Belt land[2]		Defined Heritage Coasts length (km)
	Area (thousand hectares)	Percentage of total area in region	Area (thousand hectares)	Percentage of total area in region	Area (thousand hectares)	Percentage of total area in region	
United Kingdom	1,972	8	3,377	14	2,032	8	1,568
North East	111	13	143	17	53	6	138
North West	261	18	153	11	252	18	6
Yorkshire and the Humber	315	21	92	6	264	17	80
East Midlands	92	6	52	3	80	5	0
West Midlands	20	2	123	10	267	21	.
East	30	2	110	6	237	12	121
London[3]	..	..	..	..	36	22	
South East[3]	-	-	637	31	356	19	74
South West	165	7	708	30	106	4	638
England	994	7	2,018	16	1,650	13	1,057
Wales	410	20	72	4	.	.	511
Scotland	568	6	1,002	13	155	2	.
Northern Ireland	.	.	285	20	227	16	.

1 See Notes and Definitions.
2 At March 2005, except for Green Belt land which relates to 1 January 1997.
3 National Scenic Areas in Scotland. The South East includes London.

Source: Department for Environment, Food and Rural Affairs

Table **11.14**   Household waste[1] and recycling

Kilogrammes per household per week and percentages

	Household waste				Percentage recycled			
	2000/01	2001/02	2002/03	2003/04	2000/01	2001/02	2002/03	2003/04
North East	22.1	23.2	24.1	24.0	4	5	7	12
North West	25.9	26.0	26.6	25.8	8	9	11	14
Yorkshire and the Humber	22.6	22.8	23.0	22.3	7	9	11	15
East Midlands	23.5	24.2	24.3	24.1	13	14	15	19
West Midlands	23.1	23.6	23.7	23.2	9	10	13	16
East	23.4	23.9	23.8	23.0	15	17	19	23
London	20.9	20.6	20.2	19.7	9	9	11	13
South East	23.9	24.2	24.2	23.7	16	18	20	23
South West	23.2	23.7	23.8	23.2	15	17	19	21
England	23.3	23.6	23.7	23.1	11	13	15	18
Wales	22.8	23.5	23.8	24.1	6	9	12	17

1 Table grossed-up from reported data with estimates for missing values.

Source: Department for Environment, Food, and Rural Affairs; National Assembly for Wales

Table 11.15 Recycling of household waste,[1] 2003/04

Kilogrammes per household per year

	Glass	Paper and card	Total cans	Plastics	Textiles	Scrap metal/ white goods	Compost	Other materials[2]	Total
North East	21.8	53.6	2.5	0.5	2.6	18.4	30.3	24.0	153.6
North West	19.1	52.8	1.1	0.6	2.0	20.3	70.8	24.8	191.3
Yorkshire and the Humber	18.9	44.2	1.0	0.6	1.7	17.4	54.3	31.5	169.4
East Midlands	25.5	56.2	1.7	1.1	2.6	21.6	84.7	48.9	242.3
West Midlands	22.8	65.2	1.6	0.3	2.7	21.2	63.9	12.2	190.0
East	34.9	68.8	3.9	1.2	3.5	24.7	88.6	54.9	280.5
London	20.3	49.9	1.3	0.6	2.4	13.5	22.5	26.9	137.5
South East	36.5	68.2	1.9	0.7	3.8	28.7	84.4	57.6	281.8
South West	39.6	81.4	4.0	1.9	3.3	30.6	72.7	22.9	256.4
England	26.9	60.2	2.0	0.8	2.8	22.0	64.4	34.9	213.9

1 Materials recycled by local authorities through civic amenity and bring/drop-off sites and kerbside collection schemes for household wastes.
2 Other materials includes oils, batteries, aluminium foil, books, shoes and co-mingled collections.

Source: Department for Environment, Food and Rural Affairs

Chapter 12 **Regional Accounts**

Gross value added (GVA)

The United Kingdom's gross value added (GVA) at current basic prices exceeded £1,000 billion for the first time in 2004. The biggest contributors to this were London and the South East, each contributing approximately £160 billion. These two regions together accounted for nearly one-third of UK economic activity in 2004 as measured by GVA.

Northern Ireland continued to have the smallest share with just over 2 per cent (£23 billion) of the UK total. However, this represented a 5 per cent increase in GVA over the previous year. The highest regional growth was in the East Midlands with a rise of 5.3 per cent between 2003 and 2004. (Table 12.1)

GVA per head

London and the South East also had the highest GVA per head of population, £22,200 and £19,500 respectively in 2004. GVA per head was lowest in Wales at just under four-fifths of the UK average of £17,258 in 2004, closely followed by the North East and Northern Ireland.

However, Northern Ireland was one of only five areas for which GVA per head increased in relation to the UK average over the ten years to 2004; the other regions were the East of England, London, the South East and the South West. Northern Ireland, the South West and the East increased by 0.9, 0.6 and 0.3 percentage points respectively, but increases in London and the South East were more marked, 1.5 and 5.4 percentage points respectively. The largest declines in this period were in Wales and Scotland, with a reduction of more than 4 percentage points each. (Table 12.1)

The North East derived the highest proportion (69 per cent) of its GVA from compensation of employees in 2004 (i.e. wages and salaries, insurance and pension contributions etc.). This compared with 61 per cent in the South West, the lowest proportion. In 2001, the North East derived 68 per cent of its GVA from compensation of employees, while Northern Ireland derived 60 per cent. (Table 12.3)

GVA by industry

Manufacturing contributed £146 billion to the GVA total for the UK in 2003. The contribution of this sector has been declining slowly over several years, from nearly 22 per cent in 1996 to 15 per cent of the UK total GVA in 2003. The North West contributed the largest amount of GVA from manufacturing with £18.4 billion in 2003, nearly one-fifth of the total GVA for that region.

A quarter of GVA in the United Kingdom came from real estate, renting and business activities in 2003. This industry group is of great importance – it covers much of the professional services sector, including accountancy, legal and consultancy activities. This amounted to £239 billion, the highest contribution from a single industry group. Nearly one-quarter of the UK GVA from the real estate, renting and business activities sector was generated in London, at almost £57 billion. This sector contributed more than one-third to the total London GVA in 2003.

GVA derived from mining and quarrying of energy-producing materials has been declining steadily over a number of years; accounting for £1,520 million in 2003, it was the lowest contributor of all the industry groups. (This excludes extra-regio which is not allocated to specific regions.) More than half this amount resulted from mining activities in Scotland – £890 million in 2003, greater than all the other UK regions combined. (Table 12.5)

Workplace-based GVA

Regional GVA is calculated on both a residence and a workplace-basis. The estimates referred to so far have been calculated on a residence-basis. In order to calculate workplace figures, adjustments have been made to London, the East of England and the South East as these regions have the largest inter-regional commuting flows. On a workplace basis, London's GVA increased to £185 billion at current basic prices in 2004. This accounted for 18 per cent of the UK's total economy. The South East and East of England accounted for 14 and 9 per cent respectively.

For all other regions, workplace- and resident-based estimates are the same. Accordingly, Wales had the lowest GVA per head of population, around £13,000, compared with London with nearly £25,000 (calculated on a workplace basis) in 2004. London's figure was 49 per cent above the UK average GVA per head; the South East was the only other region with a GVA per head of population above the national average (9 per cent above) with £18,000. The East of England had a GVA per head 3 per cent below the national average with £16,000, while on a residence basis the figure is above the national average, £18,000. (Table 12.6)

Total and gross disposable household income

Total household income has continued to increase over time. The UK figure rose by 4.3 per cent between 2002 and 2003 to nearly £1,149 billion. Within the United Kingdom total, Northern Ireland and the East Midlands had the highest increases, 4.7 per cent each, although Northern Ireland continued to have the lowest household income at £26.6 billion in 2003. London had the lowest increase of 3.8 per cent between 2002 and 2003, but together with the South East continued to have the highest levels of total household income by a substantial margin (£181 billion and £180 billion respectively).

Northern Ireland, together with London, the East, South East and South West, more than doubled its household income in the 12 years since 1991. Northern Ireland had the third largest percentage increase, after London and the South East.

London and the South East also had the highest levels of gross disposable household income per head in 2003, £24,505 and £22,245 respectively. London also had the highest gross disposable income per head (£15,235), nearly half as much again as Northern Ireland with £10,809 per head.

Gross disposable household income per head as a percentage of household income per head averaged 65 per cent for the UK in 2003. For both Northern Ireland and Wales the proportion was over 69 per cent.

The indices of gross disposable household income per head indicate that the relationship between the countries and regions of the United Kingdom has varied little between 1991 and 2003. However, households in the South West moved from just below the UK average to just above early in this period. (Table 12.7)

Table **12.1** Gross value added[1] (GVA) at current basic prices

	1991	1996	1997	1998	1999	2000	2001	2002	2003	2004[2]
£ million										
United Kingdom[3]	523,786	680,477	720,028	763,443	799,387	841,505	883,412	930,796	981,732	1,033,324
North East	19,556	24,208	25,218	26,234	27,005	27,965	29,343	30,801	32,518	34,188
North West	55,695	70,044	73,566	77,479	80,613	83,567	87,914	92,163	97,096	101,996
Yorkshire and the Humber	39,968	50,916	53,773	56,532	58,363	60,535	63,732	67,456	71,553	75,219
East Midlands	34,124	44,270	46,869	49,085	50,879	52,864	55,828	58,908	62,434	65,770
West Midlands	43,047	55,815	59,203	62,491	64,796	67,357	70,556	73,960	77,797	81,745
East	50,181	64,432	68,473	73,273	77,106	81,459	86,179	90,721	95,906	100,307
London	79,358	102,267	110,082	120,692	127,923	133,552	140,366	150,655	159,442	164,961
South East	75,091	100,125	108,039	117,074	123,850	130,430	137,423	144,253	151,814	158,187
South West	38,976	51,135	54,522	57,947	60,795	63,713	67,335	71,095	75,086	78,650
England	435,997	563,211	599,744	640,807	671,329	701,442	738,676	780,012	823,646	861,022
Wales	21,407	27,267	28,432	29,543	30,473	31,735	33,512	35,277	37,359	39,243
Scotland	45,364	58,060	60,755	63,203	65,160	67,399	70,210	74,095	78,504	82,050
Northern Ireland	11,074	15,413	16,283	17,274	18,077	18,918	19,817	20,825	21,952	23,058
United Kingdom less extra-regio[4] and statistical discrepancy	513,841	663,951	705,214	750,827	785,039	819,495	862,214	910,210	961,461	1,005,373
Extra-regio	9,944	16,527	14,815	12,616	14,348	22,010	21,198	20,586	20,271	27,252
Statistical discrepancy	-	-	-	-	-	-	-	-	-	703
As a percentage of United Kingdom[5]										
United Kingdom	100.0	100.0	100.0	100.0	100.0	100.0	100.0	100.0	100.0	100.0
North East	3.8	3.6	3.6	3.5	3.4	3.4	3.4	3.4	3.4	3.4
North West	10.8	10.5	10.4	10.3	10.3	10.2	10.2	10.1	10.1	10.1
Yorkshire and the Humber	7.8	7.7	7.6	7.5	7.4	7.4	7.4	7.4	7.4	7.5
East Midlands	6.6	6.7	6.6	6.5	6.5	6.5	6.5	6.5	6.5	6.5
West Midlands	8.4	8.4	8.4	8.3	8.3	8.2	8.2	8.1	8.1	8.1
East	9.8	9.7	9.7	9.8	9.8	9.9	10.0	10.0	10.0	10.0
London	15.4	15.4	15.6	16.1	16.3	16.3	16.3	16.6	16.6	16.4
South East	14.6	15.1	15.3	15.6	15.8	15.9	15.9	15.8	15.8	15.7
South West	7.6	7.7	7.7	7.7	7.7	7.8	7.8	7.8	7.8	7.8
England	84.9	84.8	85.0	85.3	85.5	85.6	85.7	85.7	85.7	85.6
Wales	4.2	4.1	4.0	3.9	3.9	3.9	3.9	3.9	3.9	3.9
Scotland	8.8	8.7	8.6	8.4	8.3	8.2	8.1	8.1	8.2	8.2
Northern Ireland	2.2	2.3	2.3	2.3	2.3	2.3	2.3	2.3	2.3	2.3
GVA per head (£)										
United Kingdom	9,119	11,699	12,347	13,056	13,622	14,290	14,944	15,691	16,485	17,258
North East	7,560	9,396	9,820	10,244	10,589	10,995	11,552	12,136	12,805	13,433
North West	8,139	10,286	10,827	11,407	11,902	12,336	12,980	13,586	14,269	14,940
Yorkshire and the Humber	8,097	10,263	10,847	11,403	11,776	12,208	12,806	13,510	14,284	14,928
East Midlands	8,507	10,776	11,375	11,877	12,253	12,683	13,325	13,950	14,682	15,368
West Midlands	8,231	10,605	11,250	11,855	12,291	12,782	13,361	13,944	14,624	15,325
East	9,799	12,313	13,001	13,820	14,443	15,155	15,958	16,731	17,556	18,267
London	11,620	14,663	15,693	17,082	17,881	18,455	19,169	20,438	21,582	22,204
South East	9,843	12,836	13,758	14,840	15,569	16,323	17,128	17,933	18,788	19,505
South West	8,314	10,669	11,295	11,949	12,455	12,957	13,621	14,312	15,019	15,611
England	9,107	11,608	12,324	13,126	13,691	14,247	14,938	15,711	16,521	17,188
Wales	7,451	9,431	9,822	10,189	10,506	10,917	11,515	12,067	12,716	13,292
Scotland	8,924	11,402	11,952	12,449	12,847	13,312	13,864	14,658	15,523	16,157
Northern Ireland	6,890	9,275	9,743	10,296	10,766	11,241	11,731	12,274	12,893	13,482
United Kingdom less extra-regio[4]	8,946	11,415	12,093	12,840	13,377	13,917	14,586	15,344	16,144	16,802
GVA per head: indices (UK[5] = 100)										
United Kingdom	100.0	100.0	100.0	100.0	100.0	100.0	100.0	100.0	100.0	100.0
North East	84.5	82.3	81.2	79.8	79.2	79.0	79.2	79.1	79.3	79.9
North West	91.0	90.1	89.5	88.8	89.0	88.6	89.0	88.5	88.4	88.9
Yorkshire and the Humber	90.5	89.9	89.7	88.8	88.0	87.7	87.8	88.0	88.5	88.8
East Midlands	95.1	94.4	94.1	92.5	91.6	91.1	91.4	90.9	90.9	91.5
West Midlands	92.0	92.9	93.0	92.3	91.9	91.8	91.6	90.9	90.6	91.2
East	109.5	107.9	107.5	107.6	108.0	108.9	109.4	109.0	108.7	108.7
London	129.9	128.5	129.8	133.0	133.7	132.6	131.4	133.2	133.7	132.2
South East	110.0	112.4	113.8	115.6	116.4	117.3	117.4	116.9	116.4	116.1
South West	92.9	93.5	93.4	93.1	93.1	93.1	93.4	93.3	93.0	92.9
England	101.8	101.7	101.9	102.2	102.3	102.4	102.4	102.4	102.3	102.3
Wales	83.3	82.6	81.2	79.4	78.5	78.4	78.9	78.6	78.8	79.1
Scotland	99.8	99.9	98.8	97.0	96.0	95.7	95.1	95.5	96.2	96.2
Northern Ireland	77.0	81.3	80.6	80.2	80.5	80.8	80.4	80.0	79.9	80.2

1 Estimates of regional GVA in this table are on a residence basis, where income of commuters is allocated to where they live, rather than their place of work. The data are consistent with the headline series published on 21 December 2005. See Notes and Definitions.

2 Provisional.

3 Components may not sum to totals as a result of rounding.

4 The GVA for extra-regio comprises compensation of employees and gross operating surplus which cannot be assigned to regions.

5 United Kingdom less extra-regio and statistical discrepancy.

Source: Office for National Statistics

Figure **12.2** Gross value added[1] (GVA) per head at current basic prices

GVA per head indices, UK less extra-regio = 100

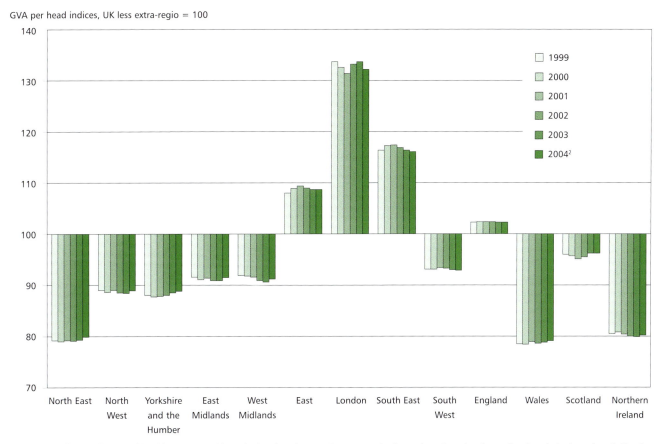

Legend:
- 1999
- 2000
- 2001
- 2002
- 2003
- 2004[2]

1 Estimates of regional GVA in this table are on a residence basis, where income of commuters is allocated to where they live, rather than their place of work. The data are consistent with the headline series published on 21 December 2003. See Notes and Definitions.
2 Provisional.

Source: Office for National Statistics

Table **12.3** Gross value added[1] (GVA) by component of income at current basic prices, 2004[2]

Percentages and £ million

| | Income components as a percentage of total GVA | | Gross value added (=100%) (£ million) |
	Compensation of employees	Operating surplus/ mixed income[3]	
United Kingdom[4]	64	36	1,005,373
North East	69	31	34,188
North West	65	35	101,996
Yorkshire and the Humber	66	34	75,219
East Midlands	64	36	65,770
West Midlands	65	35	81,745
East	64	36	100,307
London	64	36	164,961
South East	62	38	158,187
South West	61	39	78,650
England	64	36	861,022
Wales	65	35	39,243
Scotland	66	34	82,050
Northern Ireland	63	37	23,058
Extra-regio[5]	7	93	27,252

1 Estimates of regional GVA in this table are on a residence basis, where the income of commuters is allocated to where they live, rather than their place of work. See Notes and Definitions.
2 Provisional.
3 Including taxes on production.
4 Excluding GVA for extra-regio and the allowance for statistical discrepancy.
5 The GVA for extra-regio comprises compensation of employees and gross operating surplus which cannot be assigned to regions.

Source: Office for National Statistics

Map **12.4** Gross value added per head at current basic[1] prices, 2004[2]

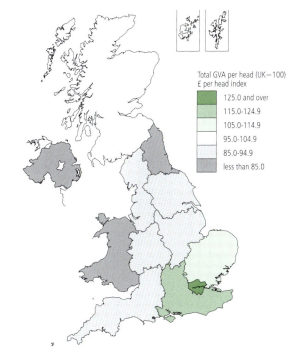

Total GVA per head (UK=100)
£ per head index
- 125.0 and over
- 115.0-124.9
- 105.0-114.9
- 95.0-104.9
- 85.0-94.9
- less than 85.0

1 Consistent with the National Accounts (Blue Book 2005) and with headline series published on 21 December 2005. See Notes and Definitions.
2 Provisional.

Source: Office for National Statistics

219

Table 12.5 Gross value added[1] by industry groups at current basic prices

£ million

	1996	2000	2001	2002	2003[2]	1996	2000	2001	2002	2003[2]
	United Kingdom[3]					North East				
Agriculture, hunting, forestry and fishing	12,032	8,803	8,571	9,213	10,127	241	179	187	188	181
Mining, quarrying of energy-producing materials	2,594	1,982	1,855	1,670	1,540	136	72	48	41	55
Other mining and quarrying	1,599	1,795	1,762	1,474	1,553	83	131	175	104	110
Manufacturing	145,530	152,102	151,098	147,901	146,127	6,819	6,700	6,503	6,390	6,410
Electricity, gas and water supply	16,223	16,112	16,044	16,481	17,113	548	864	676	809	874
Construction	34,715	45,324	50,272	54,784	60,891	1,327	1,691	1,689	2,101	2,238
Wholesale and retail trade (including motor trade)	79,207	103,747	110,873	115,044	121,514	2,506	2,959	3,132	3,501	3,646
Hotels and restaurants	20,515	28,045	29,520	31,191	32,633	657	861	951	1,050	1,085
Transport, storage and communication	53,713	70,263	71,617	74,366	78,332	1,931	1,959	2,127	2,342	2,373
Financial intermediation	41,597	42,650	43,918	63,260	71,499	782	776	811	1,028	1,288
Real estate, renting and business activities	129,413	194,261	211,293	223,600	239,380	3,641	4,523	5,150	5,174	5,581
Public administration and defence[4]	38,750	41,678	43,420	46,017	49,214	1,519	1,658	1,771	1,858	1,996
Education	36,819	47,826	51,592	55,396	59,032	1,646	2,169	2,254	2,437	2,698
Health and social work	43,983	55,960	58,916	62,643	66,656	1,892	2,595	2,756	2,833	2,991
Other services	30,010	42,496	44,955	48,377	51,801	916	1,167	1,372	1,442	1,696
Adjustment for financial services (FISIM[5])	-22,694	-33,581	-33,517	-41,207	-45,921	-366	-456	-447	-513	-677
Total	664,005	819,463	862,189	910,210	961,491	24,279	27,846	29,157	30,785	32,545

	1996	2000	2001	2002	2003[2]	1996	2000	2001	2002	2003[2]
	North West					Yorkshire and the Humber				
Agriculture, hunting, forestry and fishing	894	693	682	730	796	1,122	759	733	772	838
Mining, quarrying of energy-producing materials	28	51	54	29	23	148	170	180	140	170
Other mining and quarrying	99	119	123	83	95	217	95	91	86	90
Manufacturing	19,060	19,173	19,288	19,064	18,414	13,657	13,768	14,460	14,569	14,238
Electricity, gas and water supply	1,717	1,630	1,804	1,839	1,341	1,135	1,065	1,214	1,421	1,150
Construction	3,515	4,368	5,136	5,493	5,763	2,968	3,681	4,095	4,360	5,291
Wholesale and retail trade (including motor trade)	8,868	11,081	11,940	12,117	12,744	6,412	8,068	8,714	9,098	9,757
Hotels and restaurants	2,028	2,780	2,905	3,249	3,500	1,580	1,981	1,984	2,173	2,282
Transport, storage and communication	5,144	6,681	6,804	7,407	8,245	4,012	4,744	5,039	5,544	5,487
Financial intermediation	2,860	3,201	3,259	4,582	5,011	2,241	2,549	2,710	4,036	4,094
Real estate, renting and business activities	11,859	16,177	17,683	19,180	20,746	7,638	10,455	11,199	11,925	13,442
Public administration and defence[4]	3,216	3,792	3,885	4,151	4,298	2,731	3,027	3,243	3,523	3,702
Education	4,194	5,527	5,976	6,615	6,934	2,942	3,895	4,218	4,500	4,823
Health and social work	5,248	6,242	6,524	6,804	7,297	3,614	4,903	4,942	5,274	5,659
Other services	2,604	3,966	3,866	4,270	4,819	1,775	2,810	2,544	2,603	2,946
Adjustment for financial services (FISIM[5])	-1,495	-2,341	-2,254	-2,810	-3,024	-1,144	-1,827	-1,835	-2,448	-2,454
Total	69,840	83,142	87,672	92,802	97,003	51,048	60,142	63,532	67,574	71,517

	1996	2000	2001	2002	2003[2]	1996	2000	2001	2002	2003[2]
	East Midlands					West Midlands				
Agriculture, hunting, forestry and fishing	1,159	856	832	887	986	1,108	804	792	849	937
Mining, quarrying of energy-producing materials	192	97	117	101	84	79	42	42	26	22
Other mining and quarrying	262	262	237	170	172	87	155	113	99	97
Manufacturing	13,448	12,989	13,358	13,302	13,748	16,492	16,643	15,976	15,560	15,089
Electricity, gas and water supply	1,402	968	972	1,013	1,187	1,262	2,145	1,779	1,733	1,861
Construction	2,236	3,217	3,670	4,131	4,307	2,948	3,761	3,925	4,501	5,148
Wholesale and retail trade (including motor trade)	5,882	7,048	7,872	8,112	8,645	7,194	8,817	9,923	10,183	10,617
Hotels and restaurants	1,153	1,525	1,751	1,852	2,046	1,483	2,071	2,216	2,312	2,535
Transport, storage and communication	2,571	3,653	3,755	4,280	4,634	3,906	4,927	5,154	5,237	5,632
Financial intermediation	1,352	1,415	1,480	2,057	2,357	2,347	2,381	2,401	3,326	3,794
Real estate, renting and business activities	6,910	9,619	10,426	11,336	12,453	9,375	13,067	14,535	15,554	16,844
Public administration and defence[4]	1,952	2,184	2,233	2,349	2,575	2,409	2,782	2,768	3,037	3,229
Education	2,299	3,459	3,523	3,967	4,273	3,147	4,164	4,541	5,121	5,196
Health and social work	2,951	3,581	3,954	4,202	4,578	3,317	4,502	4,838	5,145	5,372
Other services	1,524	2,021	2,087	2,223	2,685	1,837	2,782	2,963	3,430	3,399
Adjustment for financial services (FISIM[5])	-587	-829	-798	-1,046	-1,222	-1,210	-1,664	-1,582	-1,903	-2,170
Total	44,707	52,063	55,468	58,936	63,508	55,783	67,380	70,385	74,211	77,603

Table 12.5 Gross value added[1] by industry groups at current basic prices *(continued)*

£ million

	1996	2000	2001	2002	2003[2]	1996	2000	2001	2002	2003[2]
			East					London		
Agriculture, hunting, forestry and fishing	1,623	1,156	1,131	1,210	1,325	62	52	47	40	47
Mining, quarrying of energy-producing materials	240	113	111	110	77	185	171	139	118	87
Other mining and quarrying	90	100	113	121	122	56	47	55	55	72
Manufacturing	12,521	13,226	13,174	12,835	12,860	12,474	14,683	14,530	13,596	13,601
Electricity, gas and water supply	1,259	1,346	1,198	1,164	1,306	1,439	1,667	1,733	1,250	1,393
Construction	3,838	5,409	6,009	6,334	7,045	4,175	5,419	6,040	6,411	7,296
Wholesale and retail trade (including motor trade)	7,719	10,506	11,058	11,859	12,584	12,527	16,322	16,843	16,962	18,170
Hotels and restaurants	1,517	2,310	2,566	2,756	2,973	3,905	5,496	5,378	5,797	5,990
Transport, storage and communication	5,980	7,919	8,029	7,838	8,290	10,846	15,677	15,202	14,845	15,459
Financial intermediation	4,546	4,545	5,260	6,440	6,798	14,004	14,159	14,011	22,205	26,263
Real estate, renting and business activities	13,138	20,825	22,485	23,913	25,422	29,430	48,715	52,148	53,650	56,590
Public administration and defence[4]	3,335	3,716	3,952	4,144	4,554	5,127	4,447	4,669	4,927	5,347
Education	3,428	4,031	4,374	4,530	4,838	4,991	7,123	7,040	7,557	8,322
Health and social work	3,721	4,450	4,778	5,089	5,373	5,643	7,436	7,886	8,392	9,334
Other services	2,849	3,634	4,212	4,382	4,684	7,548	10,806	11,510	12,205	12,466
Adjustment for financial services (FISIM[5])	-1,327	-1,846	-1,788	-2,219	-2,723	-10,464	-15,653	-15,912	-19,344	-21,587
Total	64,478	81,439	86,664	90,506	95,527	101,947	136,567	141,318	148,667	158,850

	1996	2000	2001	2002	2003[2]	1996	2000	2001	2002	2003[2]
			South East					South West		
Agriculture, hunting, forestry and fishing	1,258	928	916	976	1,070	1,737	1,241	1,221	1,270	1,372
Mining, quarrying of energy-producing materials	194	130	111	101	68	38	27	30	22	20
Other mining and quarrying	148	146	159	136	129	293	333	320	308	311
Manufacturing	17,051	18,692	18,329	17,616	17,697	10,494	12,202	11,757	11,647	11,408
Electricity, gas and water supply	2,088	1,927	1,948	2,043	2,885	1,723	1,327	1,768	1,740	1,807
Construction	5,369	6,956	7,916	8,476	9,555	2,611	3,526	4,145	4,528	4,495
Wholesale and retail trade (including motor trade)	12,002	17,777	18,664	19,046	20,018	5,754	7,757	8,493	9,101	9,597
Hotels and restaurants	2,869	4,115	4,353	4,365	4,258	1,732	2,421	2,778	2,872	3,036
Transport, storage and communication	9,507	12,736	12,627	12,832	13,416	3,225	4,075	4,398	4,808	5,013
Financial intermediation	6,199	6,182	6,540	8,984	9,541	2,788	2,796	2,729	3,705	4,376
Real estate, renting and business activities	23,895	38,113	41,398	44,527	46,372	9,173	13,316	14,962	15,879	17,464
Public administration and defence[4]	6,222	7,021	7,141	7,656	7,900	4,435	4,446	4,711	4,883	5,277
Education	4,839	6,067	6,664	6,701	7,451	2,734	3,878	4,485	4,603	4,675
Health and social work	6,269	7,284	7,648	8,378	8,789	3,417	4,790	4,585	4,813	5,147
Other services	4,623	6,516	6,851	7,306	7,657	2,213	3,063	3,257	3,481	3,675
Adjustment for financial services (FISIM[5])	-2,477	-3,845	-3,907	-4,699	-4,756	-1,505	-2,068	-1,936	-2,254	-2,680
Total	100,056	130,748	137,356	144,445	152,049	50,863	63,128	67,701	71,405	74,992

	1996	2000	2001	2002	2003[2]	1996	2000	2001	2002	2003[2]
			England					Wales		
Agriculture, hunting, forestry and fishing	9,204	6,668	6,540	6,923	7,551	568	477	467	507	589
Mining, quarrying of energy-producing materials	1,241	872	831	688	606	103	41	46	39	35
Other mining and quarrying	1,334	1,388	1,387	1,161	1,198	85	135	106	81	94
Manufacturing	122,017	128,076	127,374	124,579	123,463	7,896	7,686	7,407	7,470	7,146
Electricity, gas and water supply	12,573	12,938	13,092	13,012	13,805	924	797	707	1,005	813
Construction	28,987	38,028	42,625	46,334	51,139	1,471	1,702	1,933	2,203	2,495
Wholesale and retail trade (including motor trade)	68,865	90,334	96,638	99,978	105,779	2,617	3,616	3,695	3,878	4,101
Hotels and restaurants	16,925	23,560	24,882	26,427	27,705	925	1,216	1,225	1,282	1,301
Transport, storage and communication	47,123	62,373	63,135	65,135	68,549	1,369	1,767	2,010	2,173	2,449
Financial intermediation	37,120	38,005	39,202	56,362	63,522	932	955	963	1,249	1,426
Real estate, renting and business activities	115,060	174,810	189,986	201,136	214,914	3,796	4,973	5,696	5,964	6,655
Public administration and defence[4]	30,945	33,074	34,372	36,528	38,878	1,911	1,808	1,959	2,106	2,378
Education	30,220	40,312	43,074	46,033	49,210	1,889	2,347	2,605	2,829	2,950
Health and social work	36,071	45,782	47,912	50,930	54,539	2,237	2,905	3,269	3,585	3,749
Other services	25,890	36,764	38,662	41,342	44,028	1,183	1,527	1,681	1,863	2,011
Adjustment for financial services (FISIM[5])	-20,574	-30,529	-30,458	-37,235	-41,293	-408	-564	-542	-613	-723
Total	563,001	702,456	739,253	779,332	823,594	27,498	31,388	33,227	35,620	37,471

Table **12.5** Gross value added[1] by industry groups at current basic prices *(continued)*

£ million

	1996	2000	2001	2002	2003[2]	1996	2000	2001	2002	2003[2]
	Scotland					Northern Ireland				
Agriculture, hunting, forestry and fishing	1,410	1,205	1,144	1,270	1,442	850	452	420	514	544
Mining, quarrying of energy-producing materials	1,241	1,057	967	934	890	9	12	11	10	9
Other mining and quarrying	116	193	182	153	168	64	78	87	79	92
Manufacturing	12,515	12,305	12,444	12,304	11,729	3,101	4,035	3,873	3,547	3,788
Electricity, gas and water supply	2,263	1,995	1,888	2,028	2,021	463	381	357	436	473
Construction	3,402	4,281	4,291	4,734	5,668	855	1,313	1,423	1,513	1,589
Wholesale and retail trade (including motor trade)	6,059	7,465	8,044	8,613	8,884	1,666	2,332	2,496	2,575	2,749
Hotels and restaurants	2,265	2,686	2,779	2,830	2,939	401	583	634	653	689
Transport, storage and communication	4,450	5,041	5,335	5,837	6,106	771	1,082	1,136	1,222	1,228
Financial intermediation	3,031	3,156	3,198	4,870	5,607	514	534	555	780	943
Real estate, renting and business activities	8,907	11,964	12,771	13,470	14,611	1,649	2,515	2,840	3,030	3,200
Public administration and defence[4]	3,898	4,758	5,026	5,233	5,653	1,996	2,039	2,063	2,150	2,305
Education	3,624	3,658	4,388	4,827	5,120	1,086	1,508	1,526	1,707	1,751
Health and social work	4,259	5,475	5,834	6,111	6,220	1,416	1,798	1,902	2,017	2,148
Other services	2,371	3,468	3,740	4,278	4,763	566	736	871	893	1,000
Adjustment for financial services (FISIM[5])	-1,459	-2,149	-2,176	-2,934	-3,374	-253	-338	-340	-424	-531
Total	58,354	66,559	69,855	74,558	78,449	15,153	19,060	19,854	20,701	21,977

1 Estimates of regional GVA in this table are on a residence basis, where the income of commuters is allocated to where they live rather than their place of work. See Notes and Definitions.
2 Provisional.
3 Excludes GVA from extra-regio, which cannot be allocated to any particular region.
4 Public administration, national defence and compulsory social security.
5 Financial intermediation services indirectly measured.

Source: Office for National Statistics

Table **12.6** Workplace-based gross value added[1] (GVA) at current basic prices

	1991	1996	1997	1998	1999	2000	2001	2002	2003	2004[2]
£ million										
United Kingdom	523,786	680,477	720,028	763,443	799,387	841,505	883,412	930,796	981,732	1,033,324
North East	19,556	24,208	25,218	26,234	27,005	27,965	29,343	30,801	32,518	34,188
North West	55,695	70,044	73,566	77,479	80,613	83,567	87,914	92,163	97,096	101,996
Yorkshire and the Humber	39,968	50,916	53,773	56,532	58,363	60,535	63,732	67,456	71,553	75,219
East Midlands	34,124	44,270	46,869	49,085	50,879	52,864	55,828	58,908	62,434	65,770
West Midlands	43,047	55,815	59,203	62,491	64,796	67,357	70,556	73,960	77,797	81,745
East	44,047	57,725	61,241	65,266	68,195	71,452	75,430	79,843	85,028	89,405
London	91,371	116,402	125,572	137,438	145,682	152,634	160,350	170,723	179,672	185,398
South East	69,212	92,697	99,781	108,334	115,002	121,356	128,188	135,062	142,462	148,651
South West	38,976	51,135	54,522	57,947	60,795	63,713	67,335	71,095	75,086	78,650
England	435,997	563,211	599,744	640,807	671,329	701,442	738,676	780,012	823,646	861,022
Wales	21,407	27,267	28,432	29,543	30,473	31,735	33,512	35,277	37,359	39,243
Scotland	45,364	58,060	60,755	63,203	65,160	67,399	70,210	74,095	78,504	82,050
Northern Ireland	11,074	15,413	16,283	17,274	18,077	18,918	19,817	20,825	21,952	23,058
United Kingdom less extra-regio[3] and statistical discrepancy	513,841	663,951	705,214	750,827	785,039	819,495	862,214	910,210	961,461	1,005,373
Extra-regio	9,944	16,527	14,815	12,616	14,348	22,010	21,198	20,586	20,271	27,252
Statistical discrepancy	-	-	-	-	-	-	-	-	-	703
As a percentage of United Kingdom[4]										
United Kingdom	100.0	100.0	100.0	100.0	100.0	100.0	100.0	100.0	100.0	100.0
North East	3.8	3.6	3.6	3.5	3.4	3.4	3.4	3.4	3.4	3.4
North West	10.8	10.5	10.4	10.3	10.3	10.2	10.2	10.1	10.1	10.1
Yorkshire and the Humber	7.8	7.7	7.6	7.5	7.4	7.4	7.4	7.4	7.4	7.5
East Midlands	6.6	6.7	6.6	6.5	6.5	6.5	6.5	6.5	6.5	6.5
West Midlands	8.4	8.4	8.4	8.3	8.3	8.2	8.2	8.1	8.1	8.1
East	8.6	8.7	8.7	8.7	8.7	8.7	8.7	8.8	8.8	8.9
London	17.8	17.5	17.8	18.3	18.6	18.6	18.6	18.8	18.7	18.4
South East	13.5	14.0	14.1	14.4	14.6	14.8	14.9	14.8	14.8	14.8
South West	7.6	7.7	7.7	7.7	7.7	7.8	7.8	7.8	7.8	7.8
England	84.9	84.8	85.0	85.3	85.5	85.6	85.7	85.7	85.7	85.6
Wales	4.2	4.1	4.0	3.9	3.9	3.9	3.9	3.9	3.9	3.9
Scotland	8.8	8.7	8.6	8.4	8.3	8.2	8.1	8.1	8.2	8.2
Northern Ireland	2.2	2.3	2.3	2.3	2.3	2.3	2.3	2.3	2.3	2.3
GVA per head (£)										
United Kingdom	9,119	11,699	12,347	13,056	13,622	14,290	14,944	15,691	16,485	17,258
North East	7,560	9,396	9,820	10,244	10,589	10,995	11,552	12,136	12,805	13,433
North West	8,139	10,286	10,827	11,407	11,902	12,336	12,980	13,586	14,269	14,940
Yorkshire and the Humber	8,097	10,263	10,847	11,403	11,776	12,208	12,806	13,510	14,284	14,928
East Midlands	8,507	10,776	11,375	11,877	12,253	12,683	13,325	13,950	14,682	15,368
West Midlands	8,231	10,605	11,250	11,855	12,291	12,782	13,361	13,944	14,624	15,325
East	8,601	11,031	11,627	12,310	12,774	13,293	13,967	14,725	15,565	16,281
London	13,379	16,690	17,901	19,452	20,364	21,092	21,899	23,161	24,320	24,955
South East	9,072	11,884	12,706	13,733	14,456	15,187	15,977	16,791	17,631	18,329
South West	8,314	10,669	11,295	11,949	12,455	12,957	13,621	14,312	15,019	15,611
England	9,107	11,608	12,324	13,126	13,691	14,247	14,938	15,711	16,521	17,188
Wales	7,451	9,431	9,822	10,189	10,506	10,917	11,515	12,067	12,716	13,292
Scotland	8,924	11,402	11,952	12,449	12,847	13,312	13,864	14,658	15,523	16,157
Northern Ireland	6,890	9,275	9,743	10,296	10,766	11,241	11,731	12,274	12,893	13,482
United Kingdom less extra-regio[3]	8,946	11,415	12,093	12,840	13,377	13,917	14,586	15,344	16,144	16,802
GVA per head: indices (UK[4] = 100)										
United Kingdom	100.0	100.0	100.0	100.0	100.0	100.0	100.0	100.0	100.0	100.0
North East	85.0	82.0	81.0	80.0	79.0	79.0	79.0	79.0	79.0	80.0
North West	91.0	90.0	90.0	89.0	89.0	89.0	89.0	89.0	88.0	89.0
Yorkshire and the Humber	91.0	90.0	90.0	89.0	88.0	88.0	88.0	88.0	88.0	89.0
East Midlands	95.0	94.0	94.0	93.0	92.0	91.0	91.0	91.0	91.0	91.0
West Midlands	92.0	93.0	93.0	92.0	92.0	92.0	92.0	91.0	91.0	91.0
East	96.0	97.0	96.0	96.0	95.0	96.0	96.0	96.0	96.0	97.0
London	150.0	146.0	148.0	151.0	152.0	152.0	150.0	151.0	151.0	149.0
South East	101.0	104.0	105.0	107.0	108.0	109.0	110.0	109.0	109.0	109.0
South West	93.0	93.0	93.0	93.0	93.0	93.0	93.0	93.0	93.0	93.0
England	102.0	102.0	102.0	102.0	102.0	102.0	102.0	102.0	102.0	102.0
Wales	83.0	83.0	81.0	79.0	79.0	78.0	79.0	79.0	79.0	79.0
Scotland	100.0	100.0	99.0	97.0	96.0	96.0	95.0	96.0	96.0	96.0
Northern Ireland	77.0	81.0	81.0	80.0	80.0	81.0	80.0	80.0	80.0	80.0

1 Estimates of workplace-based GVA allocate incomes to the region in which commuters work. The data are consistent with the headline workplace-based series published in December 2005. See Notes and Definitions.
2 Provisional.
3 The GVA for extra-regio comprises compensation of employees and gross operating surplus which cannot be assigned to regions.
4 United Kingdom less extra-regio and statistical discrepancy.

Source: Office for National Statistics

Table 12.7   Household income[1] and gross disposable household income[2]

	1991	1994	1995	1996	1997	1998	1999	2000	2001	2002	2003
Total household income (£ million)											
United Kingdom[3]	574,225	667,658	752,504	796,345	842,507	894,543	937,589	1,010,197	1,067,001	1,101,474	1,148,951
North East	22,847	26,048	28,681	30,236	31,650	33,030	34,077	36,253	37,968	39,163	40,790
North West	64,261	73,328	80,368	84,874	89,284	94,000	97,716	104,515	109,764	113,182	117,997
Yorkshire and the Humber	45,489	52,652	58,235	61,582	64,856	68,395	71,008	75,961	79,841	82,472	86,089
East Midlands	37,368	44,400	49,553	52,340	55,086	58,106	60,530	65,045	68,807	71,329	74,656
West Midlands	47,684	55,989	63,160	66,617	69,991	73,858	76,957	82,539	86,902	89,767	93,673
East	55,708	63,949	73,031	77,387	82,076	87,484	92,141	99,918	106,323	110,219	115,251
London	83,339	96,515	110,424	117,605	126,518	137,440	147,139	160,433	169,938	174,337	181,040
South East	83,958	99,847	115,141	122,350	130,449	139,483	146,724	158,370	167,454	172,451	179,743
South West	45,817	52,403	61,415	65,008	68,795	73,015	76,578	82,647	87,539	90,579	94,696
England	486,471	565,129	640,008	677,999	718,705	764,811	802,870	865,681	914,536	943,499	983,935
Wales	25,059	29,051	32,212	33,861	35,337	36,992	38,501	41,396	43,727	45,353	47,390
Scotland	49,300	57,107	62,609	65,796	68,810	72,070	74,692	80,013	84,324	87,227	91,040
Northern Ireland	12,706	15,795	17,675	18,689	19,655	20,670	21,526	23,107	24,414	25,395	26,586
United Kingdom less extra-regio[4]	573,536	667,082	751,445	795,270	841,427	893,498	936,512	1,009,009	1,065,633	1,099,945	1,147,305
Extra-regio[4]	689	576	1,059	1,075	1,080	1,045	1,077	1,188	1,368	1,529	1,646
Household income (£ per head)											
North East	8,768	9,960	11,105	11,736	12,324	12,898	13,362	14,254	14,948	15,431	16,063
North West	9,326	10,606	11,770	12,464	13,141	13,839	14,427	15,428	16,206	16,685	17,341
Yorkshire and the Humber	9,129	10,472	11,740	12,413	13,082	13,796	14,327	15,319	16,043	16,517	17,186
East Midlands	9,265	10,831	12,111	12,741	13,369	14,060	14,577	15,606	16,423	16,891	17,557
West Midlands	9,050	10,562	12,015	12,657	13,301	14,011	14,597	15,663	16,456	16,924	17,608
East	10,834	12,258	14,029	14,789	15,583	16,500	17,259	18,589	19,688	20,327	21,097
London	12,103	13,863	15,973	16,862	18,036	19,452	20,568	22,169	23,208	23,651	24,505
South East	10,937	12,844	14,832	15,685	16,611	17,681	18,444	19,820	20,871	21,439	22,245
South West	9,716	10,937	12,843	13,563	14,251	15,056	15,689	16,808	17,708	18,234	18,942
England	10,093	11,604	13,228	13,974	14,768	15,666	16,374	17,583	18,494	19,004	19,736
Wales	8,669	9,967	11,152	11,711	12,207	12,758	13,273	14,241	15,025	15,514	16,130
Scotland	9,633	11,108	12,267	12,921	13,536	14,195	14,726	15,804	16,651	17,256	18,001
Northern Ireland	7,918	9,604	10,718	11,247	11,761	12,320	12,821	13,730	14,452	14,968	15,615
United Kingdom less extra-regio[4]	9,920	11,422	12,950	13,673	14,429	15,280	15,958	17,135	18,027	18,542	19,265
Gross disposable household income (£ per head)											
North East	6,111	7,095	7,544	7,958	8,419	8,580	8,918	9,504	10,112	10,414	10,787
North West	6,452	7,536	7,930	8,384	8,910	9,136	9,555	10,207	10,879	11,171	11,559
Yorkshire and the Humber	6,308	7,417	7,937	8,376	8,901	9,151	9,519	10,163	10,791	11,068	11,462
East Midlands	6,284	7,569	7,995	8,420	8,928	9,147	9,522	10,195	10,919	11,213	11,612
West Midlands	6,127	7,391	7,930	8,343	8,839	9,058	9,484	10,169	10,862	11,149	11,552
East	7,312	8,540	9,152	9,661	10,267	10,531	11,048	11,876	12,813	13,225	13,685
London	8,001	9,612	10,280	10,862	11,658	12,058	12,725	13,601	14,484	14,750	15,235
South East	7,292	8,873	9,544	10,165	10,893	11,225	11,752	12,564	13,460	13,803	14,265
South West	6,718	7,767	8,668	9,167	9,716	9,973	10,443	11,159	11,947	12,276	12,704
England	6,842	8,127	8,773	9,276	9,881	10,160	10,649	11,404	12,198	12,517	12,952
Wales	6,169	7,235	7,727	8,089	8,490	8,661	9,056	9,737	10,435	10,759	11,137
Scotland	6,643	7,773	8,158	8,582	9,059	9,228	9,592	10,268	10,970	11,328	11,753
Northern Ireland	5,610	6,959	7,555	7,882	8,277	8,450	8,805	9,424	10,062	10,401	10,809
United Kingdom less extra-regio[4]	6,757	8,019	8,584	9,067	9,643	9,902	10,366	11,097	11,865	12,184	12,610
Gross disposable household income per head, indices (UK less extra-regio=100)											
United Kingdom	100.0	100.0	100.0	100.0	100.0	100.0	100.0	100.0	100.0	100.0	100.0
North East	90.4	88.5	88.0	88.0	87.0	87.0	86.0	86.0	85.0	85.0	86.0
North West	95.5	94.0	92.0	92.0	92.0	92.0	92.0	92.0	92.0	92.0	92.0
Yorkshire and the Humber	93.4	92.5	92.0	92.0	92.0	92.0	92.0	92.0	91.0	91.0	91.0
East Midlands	93.0	94.4	93.0	93.0	93.0	92.0	92.0	92.0	92.0	92.0	92.0
West Midlands	90.7	92.2	92.0	92.0	92.0	91.0	91.0	92.0	92.0	92.0	92.0
East	108.2	106.5	107.0	107.0	106.0	106.0	107.0	107.0	108.0	109.0	109.0
London	118.4	119.9	120.0	120.0	121.0	122.0	123.0	123.0	122.0	121.0	121.0
South East	107.9	110.6	111.0	112.0	113.0	113.0	113.0	113.0	113.0	113.0	113.0
South West	99.4	96.9	101.0	101.0	101.0	101.0	101.0	101.0	101.0	101.0	101.0
England	101.3	101.4	102.0	102.0	102.0	103.0	103.0	103.0	103.0	103.0	103.0
Wales	91.3	90.2	90.0	89.0	88.0	87.0	87.0	88.0	88.0	88.0	88.0
Scotland	98.3	96.9	95.0	95.0	94.0	93.0	93.0	93.0	92.0	93.0	93.0
Northern Ireland	83.0	86.8	88.0	87.0	86.0	85.0	85.0	85.0	85.0	85.0	86.0

1 Household income covers the income received by households and non-profit institutions serving households.
2 Data for 1991 to 1994 are based on Blue Book 2000. Data for 1995 to 2003 are consistent with those published on 29 April 2005.
3 Components may not sum to totals as a result of rounding.
4 Parts of the UK economic territory that cannot be attached to a particular region.

Source: Office for National Statistics

Figure **12.8** Gross disposable income[1] per head

£ per head index, UK[2] less extra-regio[3] = 100

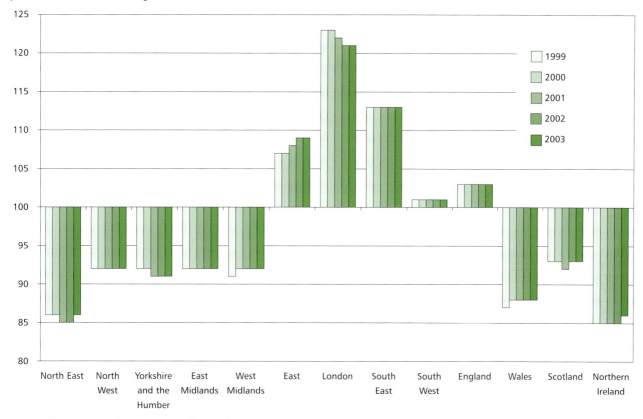

1 Household income covers the income received by households and non-profit institutions serving households.
2 Components may not sum to totals as a result of rounding.
3 Parts of the UK economic territory that cannot be attached to a particular region.

Source: Office for National Statistics

Figure **12.9** Gross disposable household income,[1] 1999 and 2003

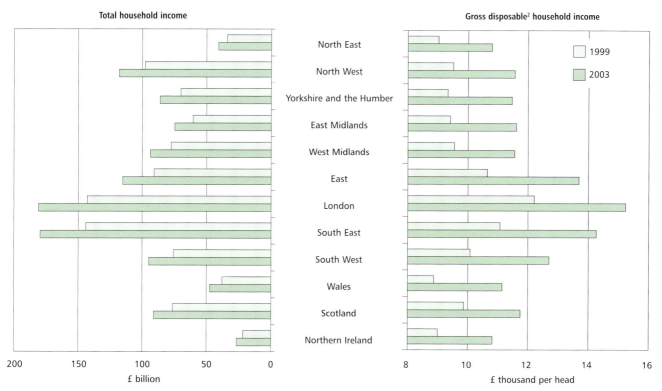

Total household income

Gross disposable[2] household income

1 Household income covers the income received by households and non-profit institutions serving households.
2 Disposable household income adjusted for taxes and certain other outgoings.

Source: Office for National Statistics

Table **12.10**   Sources of household income[1]

£ million and percentages

	Gross operating surplus/mixed Income	Compensation of employees	Property income[2]	Social benefits[3]	Other income[4]	Total income	Disposable income	Disposable income as % of total income
1995								
United Kingdom	84,812	386,422	101,204	149,578	31,956	753,972	499,118	66
North East	2,257	14,980	3,188	6,959	1,296	28,681	19,484	68
North West	8,057	40,953	9,986	17,733	3,641	80,368	54,149	67
Yorkshire and the Humber	5,759	30,045	7,593	12,226	2,611	58,235	39,370	68
East Midlands	5,262	25,630	6,753	9,658	2,251	49,553	32,713	66
West Midlands	6,541	32,913	8,205	12,553	2,947	63,160	41,685	66
East	9,116	37,951	10,164	12,768	3,033	73,031	47,644	65
London	14,048	58,447	15,470	18,643	3,817	110,424	71,064	64
South East	14,647	57,716	16,923	21,284	4,570	115,141	74,089	64
South West	7,810	28,569	8,941	13,344	2,751	61,415	41,450	67
England	73,497	327,204	87,223	125,168	26,917	640,008	421,648	66
Wales	3,442	15,639	3,989	7,618	1,524	32,212	22,319	69
Scotland	5,858	33,467	7,871	12,745	2,670	62,609	41,635	67
Northern Ireland	2,014	8,645	2,124	4,047	845	17,675	12,459	70
Extra-regio[5]	-	1,468	-	-	-	1,468	1,059	-
1999								
United Kingdom	105,761	495,797	119,107	182,057	36,382	939,108	609,428	65
North East	2,564	18,328	3,463	8,254	1,465	34,077	22,744	67
North West	9,455	51,175	11,634	21,336	4,115	97,716	64,717	66
Yorkshire and the Humber	6,711	37,916	8,658	14,757	2,966	71,008	47,179	66
East Midlands	6,201	32,121	7,630	12,001	2,577	60,530	39,538	65
West Midlands	7,836	41,217	9,198	15,384	3,323	76,957	50,002	65
East	11,571	48,785	12,286	16,028	3,466	92,141	58,983	64
London	19,415	81,852	19,831	21,679	4,363	147,139	91,030	62
South East	19,523	75,149	20,654	26,171	5,227	146,724	93,485	64
South West	9,730	36,739	10,372	16,587	3,149	76,578	50,970	67
England	93,006	423,282	103,726	152,197	30,651	802,870	518,648	65
Wales	3,981	19,254	4,181	9,346	1,739	38,501	26,267	68
Scotland	6,372	40,891	8,852	15,567	3,011	74,692	48,652	65
Northern Ireland	2,402	10,848	2,348	4,948	980	21,526	14,784	69
Extra-regio[5]	-	1,519	-	-	-	1,519	1,077	-
2003								
United Kingdom	136,438	614,976	125,059	223,861	50,896	1,151,231	752,592	65
North East	3,157	22,089	3,643	9,872	2,029	40,790	27,393	67
North West	11,725	62,538	11,882	26,152	5,701	117,997	78,652	67
Yorkshire and the Humber	8,421	46,698	8,735	18,107	4,129	86,089	57,415	67
East Midlands	8,376	39,528	7,972	15,130	3,650	74,656	49,377	66
West Midlands	10,338	50,094	9,532	19,046	4,662	93,673	61,455	66
East	15,395	61,364	13,264	20,349	4,878	115,251	74,762	65
London	24,558	102,821	21,588	25,991	6,085	181,040	112,551	62
South East	25,596	93,396	21,546	31,878	7,326	179,743	115,267	64
South West	13,076	46,083	10,769	20,324	4,441	94,696	63,511	67
England	120,642	524,611	108,931	186,849	42,901	983,935	640,383	65
Wales	5,011	23,685	4,439	11,811	2,444	47,390	32,720	69
Scotland	7,639	50,902	9,161	19,167	4,172	91,040	59,439	65
Northern Ireland	3,145	13,495	2,527	6,035	1,383	26,586	18,403	69
Extra-regio[5]	-	2,280	-	-	-	2,280	1,646	-

1 Household income covers the income received by households and non-profit institutions serving households.
2 Property income (resources).
3 Social benefits includes Retirement and Widows' Pensions, Unfunded Social Benefits and Privately Funded Social Benefits.
4 Includes Imputed Social Contributions, Non-Life Insurance Claims and Miscellaneous Current Transfers.
5 Parts of UK economic territory that cannot be attached to any particular region.

Source: Office for National Statistics

Chapter 13 **Industry and Agriculture**

Industry and services

There were over 2.5 million business sites registered for VAT and/or PAYE in the UK in March 2004. The largest number was in the South East with over 390 thousand units, five times more than in the North East which had under 77 thousand. The total number of business sites was up slightly on 2003 for most of the UK, with Wales showing the largest increase of over 2 per cent.

Over one-quarter of the business sites in each region were in the distribution, hotels and catering sector, with the North East having the highest proportion at almost one-third. Northern Ireland had a low number of businesses with around 78 thousand: the province had the highest proportion (22 per cent) of sites engaged in agriculture. (Table 13.3)

Industrial business sites accounted for between 10 and 20 per cent of the total in most areas of the UK in March 2004. The only exception was Inner London where less than 8 per cent of the sites were in the industry sector. The only area to have over a quarter of its sites designated as industrial was Magherafelt, in Northern Ireland.

Over three-quarters of businesses in the UK were in the service sector, with Inner London having the largest proportion at 92 per cent. In London as a whole, there were nine business sites in the service sector for every one in industry. The Orkney Islands in Scotland had the lowest proportion of businesses in the service sector, at 40.7 per cent. (Map 13.2)

Turnover

Manufacturing businesses in the UK had a total turnover of almost £439 billion in 2003, the largest contribution of £59 billion coming from the North West. The North West also had the highest total net capital expenditure of £1.8 billion. When expressed as capital expenditure per employee in manufacturing, Wales had the highest in 2003 with £5,023 per employee. (Table 13.4)

Gross value added (GVA) derived from industry fell in all regions in 2002 compared with the previous year, with less than a quarter of the total GVA for the UK overall from this sector. The region with the highest proportion of its GVA derived from industry was the East Midlands. (Map 13.1)

Businesses

The number of businesses that registered for VAT in the UK during 2004 was 181 thousand; this was 4.1 per cent lower than the total in 2003. Between the two years, the number of deregistrations increased by 7 per cent to 179 thousand in 2004. This resulted in a small net rise of 2,000 in the total stock of VAT registered businesses, making 1.8 million at the end of 2004. Only Wales showed a decrease from 2003 to 2004 in the number of deregistrations.

Business deregistrations in Northern Ireland increased by more than a third from 2003 to 2004 and the region also showed the greatest increase in registrations in the UK. (Table 13.8)

Import and export

Total import trade for the UK increased in 2003 and again in 2004 to reach over £252 billion, a growth of nearly 11 per cent from 2002. Over half of the imports (£133 billion) were from the European Union (EU15). The information in this chapter is based on the composition of the EU prior to May 2004 (when an additional ten Member States joined the EU), in order to allow comparison with previously published data. The South East accounted for a quarter of the import trade from the EU. This region also had the highest number of companies importing from the EU.

The value of total export trade for the UK came to £191 billion in 2004, continuing a slight upward trend from 2002. The UK also showed increases in 2003 and 2004 in the number of companies exporting both to the EU and outside the EU. Only Northern Ireland had more companies exporting to the EU than to countries outside the EU. For the UK as a whole, more than half of the export trade by value went to EU countries, with Wales sending nearly 63 per cent by value of its exports to the EU in 2004. London was the only region where the value of trade to the EU was less than the value going outside the EU.

It should be noted that there is trade carried out that cannot be matched to a specific region of the UK. The commentary above excludes a portion of trade which cannot be allocated to a specific region which is labelled as 'unallocatable trade' on the table. (Table 13.5)

Research and development

The total expenditure on research and development in the UK, including spending by businesses, Government and higher education institutions, came to over £20 billion in 2003, up nearly 11 per cent from 2001. In the North East, research and development increased by two-thirds to £441 million from 2001 to 2003, with the majority of this increase being in the business sector. The region with the greatest expenditure was the South East, with a total of £4.7 billion. This was 20 times the amount spent in Northern Ireland, which spent the lowest amount of £233 million.

Over £13.5 billion was spent by businesses on research and development in the UK, in 2003. Just over half of this was in the East of England and South East combined, where businesses in each region spent nearly £3.5 billion. (Table 13.6)

Agriculture

There were over 307 thousand agricultural holdings in the UK in 2004, the largest number being in Scotland which had more than 50 thousand. This was over 100 times the number in London, which had the smallest number of holdings. (Table 13.12)

The total area used for wheat production in the UK increased by 8 per cent between 2003 and 2004 to almost 2 million hectares in 2004, resulting in an estimated yield of over 15.5 million tonnes of wheat. Over a quarter of both area and yield were located in the East of England. Scotland had the largest area of barley, accounting for nearly one-third of the UK's 1 million hectares. (Table 13.13)

In the UK, there were nearly seven times as many sheep and lambs as pigs in 2004, with over a quarter (27.1 per cent) of them in Wales. Over a quarter of the 5.2 million pigs in the UK were in Yorkshire and the Humber, with almost the same number in the East of England. The East of England was the only region to have more pigs than sheep and lambs. The South West was the region with the most dairy cows, numbering nearly half a million, whereas Scotland has the highest number of beef cows, also with nearly half a million. (Table 13.14)

See also Chapter 2 and Table 2.4 for comparisons in livestock numbers across the EU, which also showed substantial regional variation.

Map 13.1   Percentage of gross value added[1] (GVA) derived from industry and services,[2] 2002

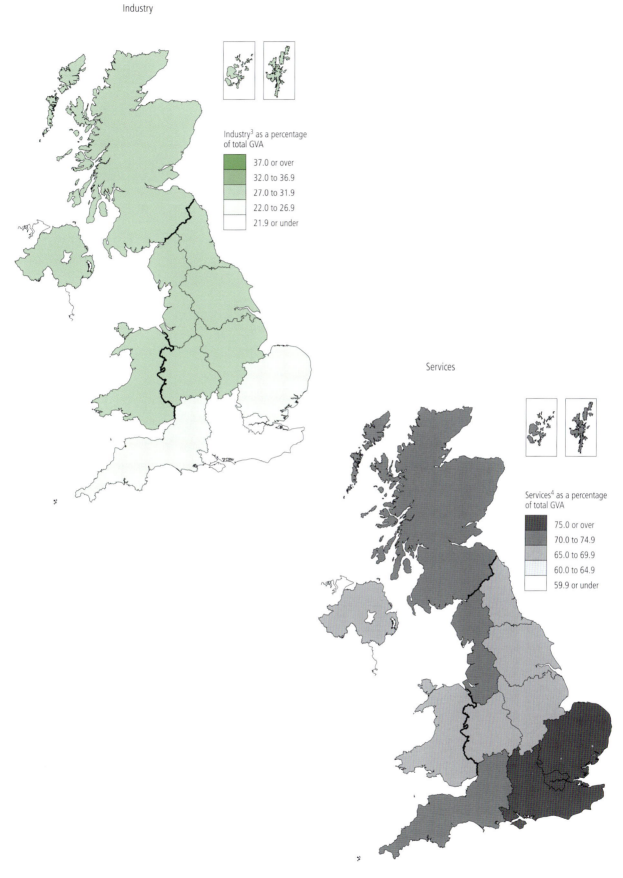

Industry

Industry[3] as a percentage
of total GVA

- 37.0 or over
- 32.0 to 36.9
- 27.0 to 31.9
- 22.0 to 26.9
- 21.9 or under

Services

Services[4] as a percentage
of total GVA

- 75.0 or over
- 70.0 to 74.9
- 65.0 to 69.9
- 60.0 to 64.9
- 59.9 or under

1   Current basic prices. See Notes and Definitions.
2   Standard Industrial Classification sections A and B are excluded.
3   Standard Industrial Classification sections C, D, E, F.
4   Standard Industrial Classification sections G, H, I, J, K, L, M, N, O, P.

Source: Office for National Statistics

Map 13.2 Industry and services[1] as a percentage of total business sites,[2] March 2004[3]

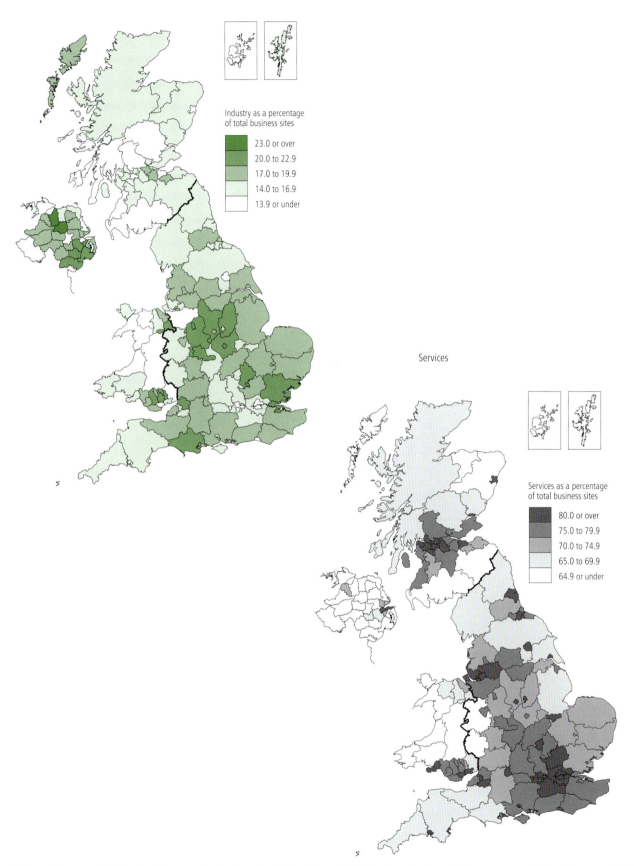

Industry

Services

1 Industry: mining, manufacturing, electricity, gas, water. Services: wholesale, retail, repair, hotels, restaurants, transport, storage, communications, finance, real estate, public administration, education, health, other community. See Notes and Definitions.
2 Registered for VAT and/or PAYE, sites are allocated to countries or regions on local unit basis, e.g. an individual factory or shop.
3 Geographic boundaries relate to the subregions (counties/unitary authorities) in existence on 1 April 1998.

Source: Inter-Departmental Business Register, Office for National Statistics

Table **13.3** Classification[1] of business sites,[2] March 2004

Percentages and thousands

	Agriculture, hunting, forestry & fishing	Mining & quarrying, energy, water supply & manu-facturing	Con-struction	Distrib-ution, hotels & catering; repairs	Transport & com-munication	Financial intermed-iation, real estate, renting & business activities	Education & health	Public admini-stration & other services	Total business sites (=100%) (thousands)
United Kingdom	6.2	7.3	9.0	27.7	4.2	28.1	7.4	10.0	2,573.1
North East	5.4	7.4	8.3	31.9	4.4	22.1	9.6	10.8	76.7
North West	4.8	7.7	8.5	30.6	4.5	26.5	7.9	9.5	257.9
Yorkshire and the Humber	6.3	8.6	9.2	31.0	4.8	22.8	7.7	9.5	192.1
East Midlands	6.8	9.7	10.0	28.6	4.8	23.4	7.8	8.9	175.6
West Midlands	6.0	9.9	9.2	28.8	4.6	25.4	7.3	8.9	213.3
East	5.5	7.8	11.4	26.0	4.8	28.8	6.7	9.1	251.6
London	0.2	5.5	5.6	25.1	3.7	41.2	6.1	12.6	383.1
South East	3.4	6.8	10.0	25.0	3.8	34.0	6.9	10.1	390.9
South West	9.9	7.1	10.1	28.1	3.8	24.8	7.4	8.8	240.8
England	4.8	7.5	9.0	27.6	4.3	29.7	7.2	10.0	2,182.0
Wales	14.6	6.6	9.2	29.2	4.2	19.0	8.0	9.2	116.7
Scotland	10.9	5.9	7.7	29.9	4.3	21.6	8.8	11.0	196.1
Northern Ireland	22.0	6.1	11.3	25.3	4.0	13.1	9.9	8.2	78.3

1 Based on Standard Industrial Classification 2003. See Notes and Definitions.
2 Registered for VAT and/or PAYE, sites are allocated to counties or regions on local unit basis, e.g. an individual factory or shop. See Notes and Definitions.

Source: Inter-Departmental Business Register, Office for National Statistics

Table **13.4** Turnover, expenditure and gross value added in manufacturing,[1] 2003

£ million and £ per person employed

	Total turnover (£ million)	Purchases of goods and services (£ million)	Total employment costs		Net capital expenditure		Gross value added at basic prices	
			£ million	£ per person employed	£ million	£ per person employed	£ million	£ per person employed
United Kingdom	438,906	278,947	82,676	24,004	12,932	3,755	143,161	41,566
North East	21,775	15,128	3,623	23,720	682	4,468	5,859	38,359
North West	58,964	37,215	10,662	24,013	1,839	4,143	18,539	41,751
Yorkshire and the Humber	40,021	26,546	8,003	22,668	1,484	4,203	13,278	37,609
East Midlands	35,568	20,303	7,301	21,851	1,096	3,281	13,450	40,257
West Midlands	46,743	31,508	9,520	22,087	1,206	2,799	14,689	34,079
East	40,021	26,266	7,716	24,862	1,132	3,647	12,707	40,940
London	37,012	22,942	7,166	30,266	807	3,407	13,678	57,769
South East	55,902	34,553	10,305	27,496	1,486	3,965	18,582	49,580
South West	30,931	18,454	6,492	23,374	946	3,408	11,142	40,117
England	366,937	232,913	70,789	24,287	10,680	3,664	121,924	41,831
Wales	26,050	18,503	3,992	21,792	920	5,023	6,127	33,446
Scotland	32,247	20,919	5,958	24,082	976	3,947	11,108	44,896
Northern Ireland	13,672	6,611	1,937	19,568	356	3,593	4,002	40,445

1 Based on Standard Industrial Classification 2003 Section D. See Notes and Definitions.

Source: Annual Business Inquiry, Office for National Statistics

Table 13.5 Export and import trade with EU[1] and non-EU countries,[2] 2004

£ million, percentages and numbers

Exports

	£ million			Percentages		Percentage of UK export trade			Number of companies exporting[3]	
	All export trade	To the EU	To outside the EU	To the EU	To outside the EU	All export trade	To the EU	To outside the EU	To the EU	To outside the EU
United Kingdom	190,548	105,609	84,938	55.4	44.6	100.0	100.0	100.0	20,250	71,607
North East	8,122	5,048	3,074	62.2	37.8	4.3	4.8	3.6	524	1,442
North West	17,838	9,100	8,738	51.0	49.0	9.4	8.6	10.3	2,164	6,609
Yorkshire and the Humber	10,171	5,816	4,354	57.2	42.8	5.3	5.5	5.1	1,595	5,132
East Midlands	13,915	7,575	6,340	54.4	45.6	7.3	7.2	7.5	1,666	5,442
West Midlands	13,724	7,451	6,273	54.3	45.7	7.2	7.1	7.4	2,033	6,853
East	18,029	10,225	7,804	56.7	43.3	9.5	9.7	9.2	2,127	7,852
London	22,454	9,030	13,424	40.2	59.8	11.8	8.5	15.8	2,635	14,145
South East	29,356	15,660	13,696	53.3	46.7	15.4	14.8	16.1	3,402	12,906
South West	9,737	5,840	3,897	60.0	40.0	5.1	5.5	4.6	1,327	5,180
England	143,344	75,745	67,599	52.8	47.2	75.2	71.7	79.6	17,473	65,561
Wales	8,316	5,235	3,082	62.9	37.1	4.4	5.0	3.6	644	1,765
Scotland	11,932	5,969	5,963	50.0	50.0	6.3	5.7	7.0	1,019	3,570
Northern Ireland	4,390	2,626	1,764	59.8	40.2	2.3	2.5	2.1	1,114	711
Unallocatable trade	22,564	16,034	6,530	71.1	28.9	11.8	15.2	7.7	..	..

Imports

	£ million			Percentages		Percentage of UK import trade			Number of companies importing[3]	
	All import trade	From the EU	From outside the EU	From the EU	From outside the EU	All import trade	From the EU	From outside the EU	From the EU	From outside the EU
United Kingdom	252,728	133,051	119,677	52.6	47.4	100.0	100.0	100.0	26,340	106,027
North East	5,685	3,322	2,364	58.4	41.6	2.2	2.5	2.0	629	2,114
North West	18,400	8,458	9,942	46.0	54.0	7.3	6.4	8.3	2,736	9,873
Yorkshire and the Humber	12,321	6,284	6,037	51.0	49.0	4.9	4.7	5.0	2,061	6,988
East Midlands	12,607	6,129	6,478	48.6	51.4	5.0	4.6	5.4	2,260	7,473
West Midlands	17,857	10,286	7,571	57.6	42.4	7.1	7.7	6.3	2,779	9,084
East	33,456	20,581	12,875	61.5	38.5	13.2	15.5	10.8	2,772	10,855
London	39,798	15,591	24,207	39.2	60.8	15.7	11.7	20.2	3,809	23,866
South East	58,488	33,657	24,831	57.5	42.5	23.1	25.3	20.7	4,496	18,205
South West	10,987	4,724	6,263	43.0	57.0	4.3	3.6	5.2	1,672	7,708
England	209,599	109,032	100,567	52.0	48.0	82.9	81.9	84.0	23,214	96,166
Wales	6,289	2,771	3,518	44.1	55.9	2.5	2.1	2.9	734	2,756
Scotland	8,634	2,688	5,947	31.1	68.9	3.4	2.0	5.0	1,155	5,056
Northern Ireland	3,873	2,317	1,556	59.8	40.2	1.5	1.7	1.3	1,237	2,049
Unallocatable trade	24,332	16,242	8,090	66.8	33.2	9.6	12.2	6.8	..	..

1 Data relates to European Union of 15 Member States.
2 EU data are from Intrastat declarations and do not cover all EU trade, see Notes and Definitions.
3 Companies who trade with both EU countries and countries outside the EU will appear more than once in the company count.

Source: HM Revenue and Customs

Table **13.6** Expenditure on research and development, 2002 and 2003

£ million

	2002				2003			
	Expenditure within:				Expenditure within:			
	Businesses[1]	Government[1,2]	Higher education institutions	All R&D sectors[3]	Businesses[1]	Government[1,2]	Higher education institutions	All R&D sectors[3]
United Kingdom	13,110	1,752	4,413	19,275	13,687	2,010	4,457	20,154
North East	128	6	159	293	281	2	158	441
North West	1,661	67	354	2,082	1,559	54	363	1,976
Yorkshire and the Humber	357	62	340	759	382	134	347	863
East Midlands	1,063	65	234	1,362	929	22	223	1,174
West Midlands	695	50	221	966	587	38	228	853
East	2,741	286	402	3,429	3,453	336	412	4,201
London	950	235	1,059	2,244	771	279	1,069	2,119
South East	3,268	459	608	4,335	3,464	583	614	4,661
South West	1,274	228	191	1,693	1,359	231	192	1,782
England	12,138	1,459	3,568	17,165	12,786	1,678	3,606	18,070
Wales	182	41	180	403	264	43	175	482
Scotland	640	238	581	1,459	521	271	575	1,367
Northern Ireland	149	15	84	248	116	17	100	233

1 See Notes and Definitions.
2 Figures include estimates of NHS and local authorities' research and development and estimates for those areas in Central Government not available from the Government Survey and local authorities.
3 Because of the unavailability of regional data, this total does not include expenditure on the private non-profit (PNP) sector.

Source: Office for National Statistics

Table **13.7** Government expenditure on regional preferential assistance to industry

£ million

	1993/94	1994/95	1995/96	1996/97	1997/98	1998/99	1999/2000	2000/01	2001/02	2002/03	2003/04[2]
Great Britain[1,2]	394.4	368.9	343.0	371.1	430.4	393.8	335.0	383.3	357.4	269.7	..
North East	52.7	38.4	46.4	24.3	38.1	22.3	18.1	25.8	36.2	42.5	23.8
North West	40.3	32.4	24.3	23.2	19.4	25.9	25.0	29.5	32.1	26.9	15.8
Yorkshire and the Humber	35.6	23.0	19.7	11.1	12.7	11.9	9.8	9.1	7.7	10.0	14.2
East Midlands	1.9	5.2	7.3	10.5	10.5	7.1	4.0	5.8	7.3	4.1	7.4
West Midlands	14.4	14.7	14.2	25.5	29.8	30.6	20.5	35.8	12.0	10.4	7.8
East	.	0.7	2.1	1.5	2.2	0.7	0.5	0.9	0.9	1.0	2.1
London	.	0.6	1.7	2.9	2.7	3.2	2.3	1.3	1.2	2.0	1.5
South East	.	0.9	4.2	4.1	5.4	3.3	5.0	4.1	4.3	2.5	1.5
South West	9.5	9.4	7.7	7.4	4.5	9.4	4.1	4.0	6.5	3.4	4.0
England[3]	154.4	125.3	127.6	110.5	125.3	114.4	89.3	116.3	108.2	102.8	78.1
Wales[4]	121.2	134.4	117.4	128.2	172.6	153.9	107.8	108.3	122.5	70.0	85.5
Scotland[2]	118.8	109.2	98.0	132.4	132.5	125.5	137.9	158.7	126.7	96.9	..
Northern Ireland	117.6	132.9	131.2	137.1	156.1	153.3	133.0	139.4	130.8	103.7	78.4

1 The system of assistance available in Northern Ireland is not comparable with that operating in Great Britain, and thus UK figures are not produced. See Notes and Definitions.
2 Data for Scotland in respect of 2003/04 are incomplete.
3 Payments for European Regional Incentives, General Consultancy Contracts and Regional Selective Assistance Payments to the European Commission are not included.
4 Welsh statistics do not include data from the Welsh Development Agency from 2002/03 onwards.

Source: Department of Trade and Industry; Department of Economic Development, Northern Ireland

Table 13.8 Business registrations and deregistrations[1]

Thousands and rates

	2003						2004					
	Regist-rations	Deregist-rations	Net change	End-year stock	Regist-ration rates[2]	Deregist-ration rates[2]	Regist-rations	Deregist-rations	Net change	End-year stock	Regist-ration rates[2]	Deregist-ration rates[2]
United Kingdom	189.1	167.6	21.5	1,817.8	40	35	181.4	179.4	2.0	1,819.9	38	37
North East	4.8	4.0	0.8	45.6	23	19	4.3	4.1	0.2	45.8	21	20
North West	18.4	16.0	2.4	172.1	34	29	17.6	16.9	0.8	172.8	32	31
Yorkshire and the Humber	13.7	11.2	2.5	130.3	34	28	12.8	12.2	0.6	130.9	32	30
East Midlands	12.7	10.8	1.9	124.3	37	32	12.2	11.3	0.9	125.2	35	33
West Midlands	15.6	14.4	1.3	152.3	37	34	14.9	15.0	-0.1	152.2	35	35
East	18.5	16.3	2.2	183.6	42	37	17.6	17.5	0.1	183.7	40	40
London	35.9	32.4	3.5	285.7	60	55	35.5	35.9	-0.5	285.3	59	60
South East	30.5	26.9	3.6	287.1	47	41	28.4	28.2	0.1	287.2	43	43
South West	16.4	14.5	1.9	170.4	40	36	15.3	15.0	0.3	170.8	37	36
England	166.5	146.4	20.1	1,551.4	42	37	158.5	156.1	2.4	1,553.8	39	39
Wales	7.1	6.7	0.3	79.8	30	28	6.9	6.7	0.3	80.0	29	28
Scotland	11.8	11.1	0.7	127.3	29	27	11.8	12.0	-0.1	127.1	29	29
Northern Ireland	3.8	3.4	0.4	59.4	29	26	4.1	4.6	-0.5	58.9	31	35

1 Enterprises registered for VAT. See Notes and Definitions.
2 Registrations and deregistrations during the year per 10,000 of the resident adult population. Each year's rate is based on the same year's mid-year population estimate.

Source: Small Business Service

Table 13.9 Business survival rates

Percentages

	Percentage of businesses surviving the stated number of months after year of registration								
	12 months				24 months			36 months	
	1998	1999	2000	2001	1998	1999	2000	1998	1999
United Kingdom	89.6	89.6	90.5	92.2	77.4	77.1	78.9	66.3	66.5
North East	89.4	89.8	90.1	91.4	77.3	76.3	77.3	66.2	65.5
North West	87.9	88.4	90.0	91.5	75.8	75.5	78.1	65.1	64.9
Yorkshire and the Humber	89.9	89.7	90.2	91.5	76.8	77.0	77.4	65.1	66.1
East Midlands	89.2	90.1	89.9	92.1	77.1	77.9	78.7	66.6	67.7
West Midlands	88.8	89.5	90.8	92.1	76.8	76.9	79.4	66.4	66.5
East	91.3	91.4	91.0	92.4	79.8	78.8	79.3	68.8	68.1
London	88.8	88.0	89.6	91.2	75.2	74.5	77.0	62.5	62.8
South East	91.4	91.3	91.6	93.4	80.3	79.7	81.1	69.6	69.7
South West	90.1	90.5	90.8	93.0	78.9	78.3	80.2	68.7	68.0
England	89.7	89.7	90.5	92.1	77.5	77.1	78.8	66.3	66.4
Wales	87.9	89.0	90.0	92.0	76.2	77.5	77.7	66.5	68.0
Scotland	88.8	88.1	90.2	92.5	76.1	75.7	79.1	64.5	65.3
Northern Ireland	90.7	89.6	92.1	94.0	80.9	80.5	82.9	72.4	72.4

Source: Small Business Service

Table **13.10**   Allocation of EU Structural Funds[1]

£ million at 2003 prices

	Objective 1[2]			Objective 2[2]			Objectives 1 and 2		
	2002	2003	2004	2002	2003	2004	2002	2003	2004
United Kingdom	564	628	606	455	504	469	1,019	1,133	1,076
North East	.	.	.	65	75	74	65	75	74
North West	120	135	131	78	84	79	198	219	210
Yorkshire and the Humber	106	119	115	48	54	52	154	173	167
East Midlands	.	.	.	35	39	34	35	39	34
West Midlands	.	.	.	81	89	85	81	89	85
East	.	.	.	15	16	16	15	16	16
London	.	.	.	23	27	28	23	27	28
South East	.	.	.	2	3	3	2	3	3
South West	45	50	50	17	20	17	62	70	67
England	271	304	296	364	407	389	636	711	685
Wales	167	188	183	12	13	11	179	200	194
Scotland	32	35	33	79	84	69	111	120	102
Northern Ireland	93	102	95	..	..	..	93	102	95

1 Only allocations resulting from the Commission's Single Programming Documents are shown. Allocations resulting from Community Initiatives, the value of which is about 8 per cent of the total Objective 1 and 2 allocations, are not included because not all of these can be allocated to the Government Office Regions in the table.
2 See Notes and Definitions for further information.

Source: Department of Trade and Industry

Map **13.11**   Agricultural enterprises as a percentage of total enterprises,[1,2] March 2004

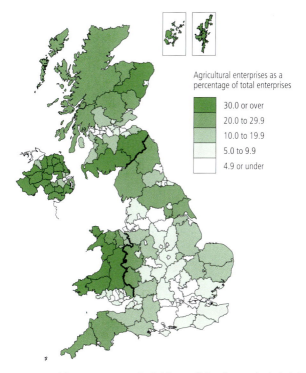

Agricultural enterprises as a
percentage of total enterprises

- 30.0 or over
- 20.0 to 29.9
- 10.0 to 19.9
- 5.0 to 9.9
- 4.9 or under

1 The figures include only those enterprises that are registered for VAT. Some smaller holdings will therefore not be included. See Notes and Definitions.
2 Geographic boundaries relate to the sub-regions (counties/unitary authorities) in existence on 1 April 1998.

Source: Inter-Departmental Business Register, Office for National Statistics

Table **13.12** Agricultural holdings:[1] by area of crops and grass, June 2004

Percentages and numbers

	Area				Total holdings (=100%) (numbers)
	None[2]	Under 10 hectares	10 to 49.9 hectares	50 hectares or over	
United Kingdom	17.4	34.3	25.5	22.8	307,092
North East	19.0	27.0	18.9	35.1	6,503
North West	22.3	32.5	23.2	22.0	22,566
Yorkshire and the Humber	19.0	33.7	21.4	25.8	21,288
East Midlands	18.8	31.6	21.7	27.9	20,361
West Midlands	19.8	35.7	22.6	21.9	25,328
East	18.7	35.3	18.4	27.7	22,629
London	23.0	43.8	19.4	13.8	479
South East	21.3	37.7	21.0	20.1	24,987
South West	21.8	35.1	22.6	20.6	48,683
England	20.4	34.5	21.6	23.5	192,824
Wales	13.0	34.0	31.0	22.0	35,855
Scotland	17.2	40.2	19.7	22.9	50,799
Northern Ireland	2.0	23.0	56.0	19.0	27,614

1 Includes estimates for minor holdings and set-aside land. See Notes and Definitions.
2 These holdings have either a zero farmed area at present or consist only of rough grazing, woodland or other land.

Source: Department for Environment, Food and Rural Affairs; Scottish Executive Rural Affairs Department; Department of Agriculture and Rural Development in Northern Ireland

Table **13.13** Areas and estimated yields of selected crops,[1] 2003 and 2004

Thousand hectares and tonnes per hectare

	Area (thousand hectares)						Estimated yields (tonnes per hectare)					
	Wheat		Barley		Rape (for oilseed)[2]		Wheat		Barley		Rape (for oilseed)[2]	
	2003	2004	2003	2004	2003	2004	2003	2004	2003	2004	2003	2004
United Kingdom	1,837	1,990	1,078	1,010	460	498	7.8	7.8	5.9	5.8	3.3	2.9
North East	66	71	42	39	22	25	8.1	7.7	6.0	6.1	3.6	3.2
North West	28	35	39	40	4	4	7.1	6.9	5.1	5.2	3.6	3.4
Yorkshire and the Humber	233	252	119	109	54	65	8.2	7.6	6.2	6.1	3.9	3.5
East Midlands	353	385	91	78	101	106	7.5	7.7	5.9	6.0	3.5	3.1
West Midlands	150	167	62	53	33	36	7.7	7.6	5.7	5.5	3.6	3.0
East	481	512	164	149	94	91	7.9	7.9	6.1	5.7	3.5	2.7
London[3]	2	2	1	1	-	-	..	..	..	..	..	..
South East[3]	239	249	74	68	74	81	7.7	7.8	5.8	5.9	3.5	3.2
South West	174	191	111	106	40	48	7.4	7.7	5.5	5.3	3.8	2.7
England	1,727	1,865	703	642	422	455	7.8	7.7	5.9	5.8	3.4	3.1
Wales	14	15	25	24	2	3	7.5	7.5	5.3	5.2	..	..
Scotland	88	102	322	316	35	39	8.3	8.6	6.1	5.9	3.4	3.3
Northern Ireland	7	9	28	27	-	-	7.2	7.5	4.9	5.1	..	..

1 Regional figures do not include minor holdings. Therefore they may not add up to the country and UK totals.
2 Excludes crops grown on set-aside scheme land. See Notes and Definitions.
3 Yield data for London included with the South East.

Source: Department for Environment, Food and Rural Affairs; National Assembly for Wales; Scottish Executive Rural Affairs Department; Department of Agriculture and Rural Development for Northern Ireland

Table **13.14** Livestock on agricultural holdings,[1] June 2004

Thousands

	Cattle and calves			Sheep and lambs	Pigs	Poultry		
	Total herd[2]	Dairy cows	Beef cows			Total fowls[3]	Total laying flock[4]	Total poultry
United Kingdom	10,603	2,131	1,739	35,891	5,163	167,858	29,662	181,792
North East	300	21	78	1,984	83	2,210	287	2,292
North West	959	304	91	2,998	163	9,529	2,215	10,450
Yorkshire and the Humber	585	110	84	2,198	1,332	12,248	1,832	14,418
East Midlands	536	105	74	1,301	424	23,382	4,936	24,733
West Midlands	778	205	88	2,336	243	18,580	2,735	19,975
East	228	31	44	344	1,220	23,140	2,062	28,137
London	4	1	1	3	2	317	34	326
South East	488	103	76	1,406	298	13,697	3,750	14,227
South West	1,803	495	195	3,305	473	20,518	5,321	22,140
England	5,679	1,374	730	15,873	4,236	123,622	23,171	136,698
Wales	1,281	271	217	9,737	31	8,351	1,280	8,688
Scotland	1,964	197	496	8,055	472	15,816	2,945	15,897
Northern Ireland	1,678	288	296	2,225	424	20,068	2,266	20,509

1 Regional figures include minor holdings. See Notes and Definitions.
2 Includes bulls, in-calf heifers and fattening cattle and calves.
3 Excludes ducks, geese and turkeys.
4 Excludes growing pullets (from day-old to point of lay).

Source: Department for Environment, Food and Rural Affairs, National Assembly for Wales; Scottish Executive Rural Affairs Department; Department of Agriculture and Rural Development for Northern Ireland

Maps

Sub-regions of England[1]

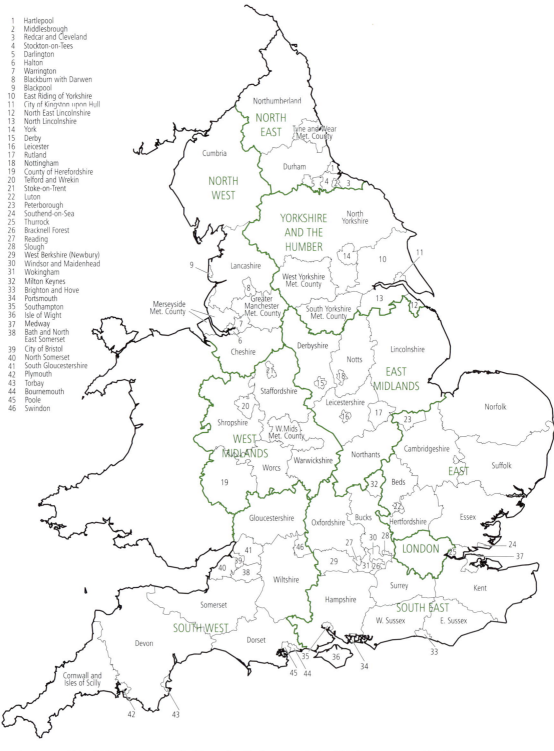

1 Hartlepool
2 Middlesbrough
3 Redcar and Cleveland
4 Stockton-on-Tees
5 Darlington
6 Halton
7 Warrington
8 Blackburn with Darwen
9 Blackpool
10 East Riding of Yorkshire
11 City of Kingston upon Hull
12 North East Lincolnshire
13 North Lincolnshire
14 York
15 Derby
16 Leicester
17 Rutland
18 Nottingham
19 County of Herefordshire
20 Telford and Wrekin
21 Stoke-on-Trent
22 Luton
23 Peterborough
24 Southend-on-Sea
25 Thurrock
26 Bracknell Forest
27 Reading
28 Slough
29 West Berkshire (Newbury)
30 Windsor and Maidenhead
31 Wokingham
32 Milton Keynes
33 Brighton and Hove
34 Portsmouth
35 Southampton
36 Isle of Wight
37 Medway
38 Bath and North East Somerset
39 City of Bristol
40 North Somerset
41 South Gloucestershire
42 Plymouth
43 Torbay
44 Bournemouth
45 Poole
46 Swindon

1 Local government structure as at 1 April 1998. The unitary authorities are listed in the same order in which they are presented in Tables 14.1, 14.2, 14.4, 14.5 and 14.6. See Notes and Definitions.

NUTS levels 1, 2 and 3 in England,[1] 1998

NUTS level 3 areas

1   South Teesside
2   Hartlepool & Stockton
3   Darlington
4   Sunderland
5   Tyneside
6   Halton & Warrington
7   Gt Manchester North
8   Gt Manchester South
9   Blackburn with Darwen
10 Blackpool
11 Sefton
12 Wirral
13 East Merseyside
14 Liverpool
15 East Riding of Yorkshire
16 City of Kingston upon Hull
17 North & North East Lincolnshire
18 York
19 Leeds
20 Bradford
21 Calderdale, Kirklees & Wakefield
22 Sheffield
23 Barnsley, Doncaster & Rotherham
24 Derby
25 South & West Derbyshire
26 East Derbyshire
27 Leicester City
28 Leicestershire CC & Rutland
29 Northamptonshire
30 Nottingham
31 North Nottinghamshire
32 South Nottinghamshire
33 The Wrekin
34 Stoke-on-Trent
35 Staffordshire CC
36 Walsall & Wolverhampton
37 Birmingham
38 Coventry
39 Solihull
40 Dudley & Sandwell
41 Luton
42 Bedfordshire CC
43 Peterborough
44 Southend-on-Sea
45 Thurrock
46 Hertfordshire
47 Inner London - East
48 Inner London - West
49 Outer London - E & NE
50 Outer London - South
51 Outer London - W & NW
52 Milton Keynes
53 Buckinghamshire CC
54 Brighton & Hove
55 Portsmouth
56 Southampton
57 Medway
58 Kent CC
59 N & NE Somerset, South Gloucestershire
60 City of Bristol
61 Plymouth
62 Torbay
63 Bournemouth & Poole
64 Swindon

NUTS level 1 (= GOR)
NUTS level 2
NUTS level 3 (CC = County Council)

1   NUTS (Nomenclature of Units for Territorial Statistics) is a hierarchical classification of areas that provides a breakdown of the EU's economic territory. See Notes and Definitions.

Unitary authorities in Wales

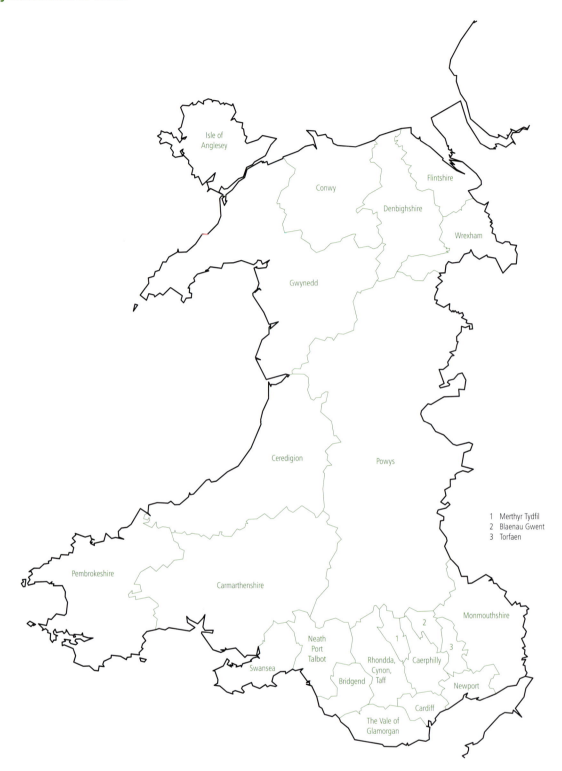

1 Merthyr Tydfil
2 Blaenau Gwent
3 Torfaen

Isle of Anglesey

Conwy

Flintshire

Denbighshire

Wrexham

Gwynedd

Ceredigion

Powys

Pembrokeshire

Carmarthenshire

Monmouthshire

Neath Port Talbot

Rhondda, Cynon, Taff

Caerphilly

Swansea

Bridgend

Newport

Cardiff

The Vale of Glamorgan

NUTS levels 1, 2 and 3 in Wales,[1] 1998

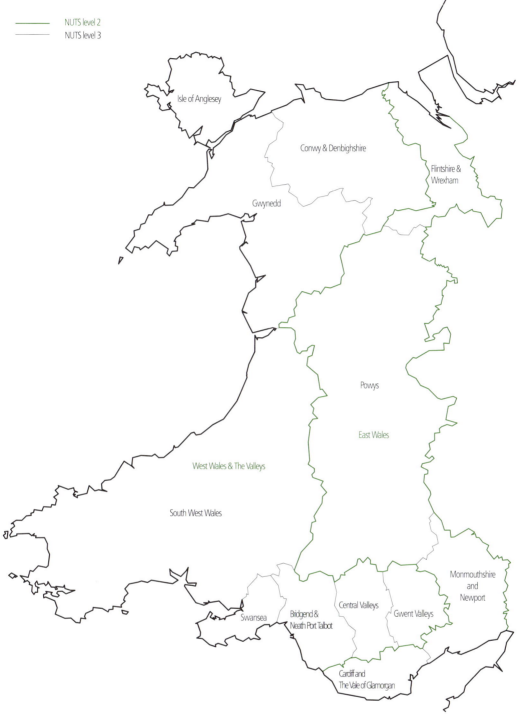

1 NUTS (Nomenclature of Units for Territorial Statistics) is a hierarchical classification of areas that provides a breakdown of the EU's economic territory. The NUTS level 1 area is the whole country. See Notes and Definitions.

Councils in Scotland

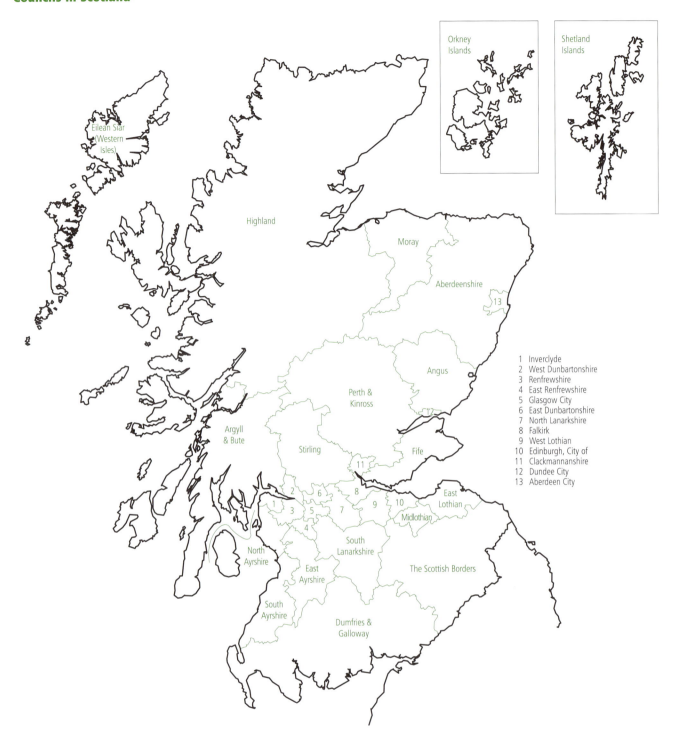

Orkney
Islands

Shetland
Islands

Eilean Siar
(Western
Isles)

Highland

Moray

Aberdeenshire

13

Angus

Perth &
Kinross

Argyll
& Bute

Stirling

Fife

12

11

2   6   8

1   5   7   9   10

3   East
Lothian

4   Midlothian

North
Ayrshire

South
Lanarkshire

East
Ayrshire

The Scottish Borders

South
Ayrshire

Dumfries &
Galloway

1	Inverclyde
2	West Dunbartonshire
3	Renfrewshire
4	East Renfrewshire
5	Glasgow City
6	East Dunbartonshire
7	North Lanarkshire
8	Falkirk
9	West Lothian
10	Edinburgh, City of
11	Clackmannanshire
12	Dundee City
13	Aberdeen City

NUTS levels 1, 2 and 3 in Scotland,[1] 1998

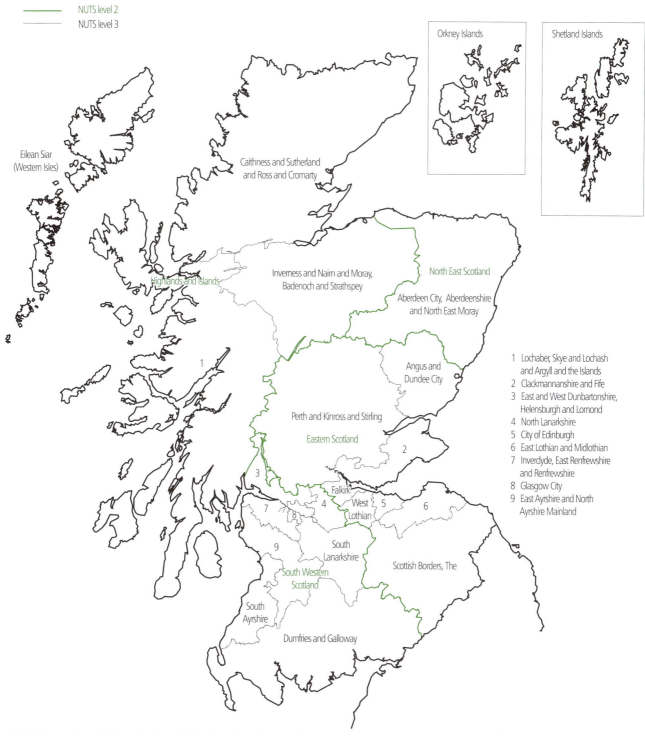

NUTS level 2
NUTS level 3

Orkney Islands

Shetland Islands

Eilean Siar
(Western Isles)

Caithness and Sutherland
and Ross and Cromarty

Highlands and Islands

Inverness and Nairn and Moray,
Badenoch and Strathspey

North East Scotland

Aberdeen City, Aberdeenshire
and North East Moray

Angus and
Dundee City

Perth and Kinross and Stirling

Eastern Scotland

Falkirk

West
Lothian

South
Lanarkshire

South Western
Scotland

South
Ayrshire

Scottish Borders, The

Dumfries and Galloway

1 Lochaber, Skye and Lochash
   and Argyll and the Islands
2 Clackmannanshire and Fife
3 East and West Dunbartonshire,
   Helensburgh and Lomond
4 North Lanarkshire
5 City of Edinburgh
6 East Lothian and Midlothian
7 Inverclyde, East Renfrewshire
   and Renfrewshire
8 Glasgow City
9 East Ayrshire and North
   Ayrshire Mainland

1 NUTS (Nomenclature of Units for Territorial Statistics) is a hierarchical classification of areas that provides a breakdown of the EU's economic territory. The NUTS level 1 area is the whole country. See Notes and Definitions.

Boards and travel-to-work areas in Northern Ireland

Health and Social Services Boards

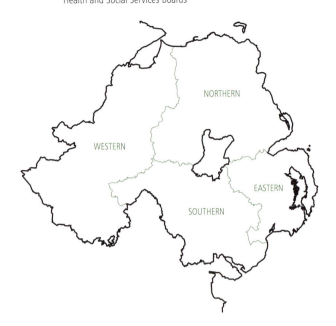

Education and Library Boards

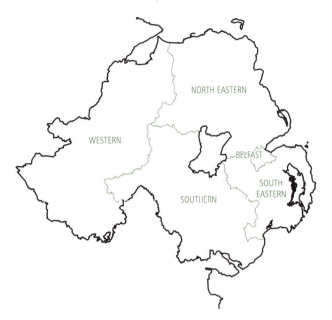

Travel-to-work areas

NUTS levels 1, 2 and 3 in Northern Ireland,[1] 1998

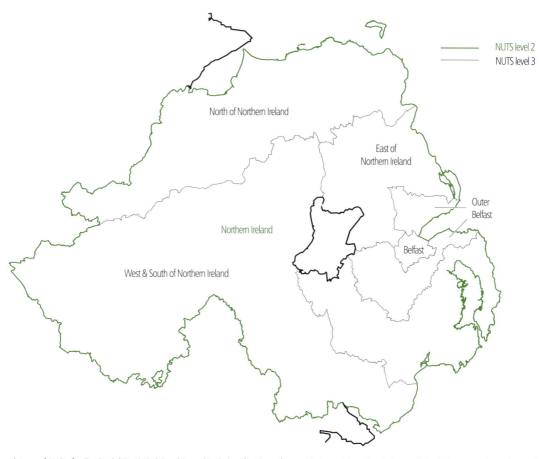

1 NUTS (Nomenclature of Units for Territorial Statistics) is a hierarchical classification of areas that provides a breakdown of the EU's economic territory. The NUTS levels 1 and 2 are represented by the whole country. See Notes and Definitions.

Health areas[1]

1	West Dunbartonshire
2	Inverclyde
3	Renfrewshire
4	East Dunbartonshire
5	Glasgow City
6	East Renfrewshire
7	North Lanarkshire
8	West Lothian
9	Edinburgh, City of
10	Midlothian
11	Clackmannanshire
12	Dundee City

13	Birmingham and the Black Country
14	Neath Port Talbot
15	Rhondda Cynon Taf
16	Merthyr Tydfil
17	Bridgend
18	Blaenau Gwent
19	Caerphilly
20	Cardiff
21	Torfaen
22	Newport

1   Strategic Health Authorities, in England; Welsh Local Health Boards; Scottish Health Boards; Health and Social Services Boards, Northern Ireland.

Source: Office for National Statistics

Police Force areas

Northern

Northern

GREAT BRITAIN

— Police Force area boundary

Northern

Grampian

Tayside

Central

Fife

Strathclyde

Lothian & Borders

Dumfries & Galloway

Northumbria

Northern Ireland

Cumbria

Durham

Cleveland

North Yorkshire

Lancashire

W. Yorks

Humberside

Merseyside

G.M.P.

S. Yorks

Lincolnshire

North Wales

Cheshire

Derbys

Notts

Staffs

Leicester

Norfolk

Dyfed-Powys

West Mercia

W. Mids

Northants

Cambs

Suffolk

Warks

Beds

Gwent

Gloucs

Thames Valley

Herts

Essex

City

South Wales

Wiltshire

Met.

Kent

Avon and Somerset

Surrey

Devon and Cornwall

Dorset

Hampshire

Sussex

Environment Agency regions

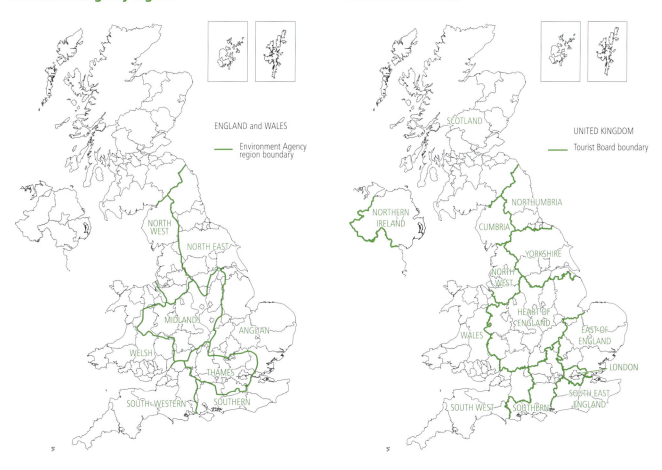

ENGLAND and WALES

— Environment Agency region boundary

NORTH WEST

NORTH EAST

MIDLANDS

ANGLIAN

WELSH

THAMES

SOUTH WESTERN

SOUTHERN

Tourist Board areas

SCOTLAND

UNITED KINGDOM

— Tourist Board boundary

NORTHERN IRELAND

NORTHUMBRIA

CUMBRIA

YORKSHIRE

NORTH WEST

HEART OF ENGLAND

WALES

EAST OF ENGLAND

LONDON

SOUTH WEST

SOUTHERN

SOUTH EAST ENGLAND

Notes and Definitions

*Also included are notes which relate to tables available on the website www.statistics.gov.uk
These are denoted by topic codes commencing with non-numeric characters.*

Government Office Regions within England

Most of the statistics in Regional Trends are on the based on the Government Office Regions (GORs) of England, together with Wales, Scotland and Northern Ireland. Government Offices for the Regions were established across England in 1994. Changes were implemented in order that government departments could work effectively in partnership with local people and organisations to improve the quality of life and prosperity within their area. In 1996, GORs became the primary classification for the presentation of regional statistics. The Government Office for the North West merged with the Government Office for Merseyside in August 1998, so figures for Merseyside are no longer shown separately. In tables, the Government Office for the East of England (formerly the Eastern Region) is referred to as East.

Subregions of England

The implementation of local government re-organisation in England (which took place in four phases on 1 April in each year between 1995 and 1998) is summarised below. The reorganisation involved only the non-metropolitan counties. Unitary authorities (UAs) have replaced the two-tier system of county councils and local authority district councils in parts of some shire counties and, in some instances, across the whole county. For statistical purposes grouping UAs by geography can be helpful.

By legal definition all unitary authorities in England are counties. However, for many purposes the UAs are treated as districts. For the majority of UAs their establishment has been achieved without geographical change. However, for a few unitary authorities, there are some boundary changes at district and ward levels, most notably the County of Herefordshire UA in the West Midlands and Peterborough UA in the East of England.

The local government structure at 1 April 1998 is used throughout the book unless otherwise specified. A wider range of data will be available relating to local authorities via the Regional Snapshot web page:

http://www.statistics.gov.uk/regionalsnapshot

Maps for the various areas referred to in this edition can be found in the previous section.

Unitary Authorities of Wales

On 1 April 1996, the 8 counties and 37 districts of Wales were replaced by 22 unitary authorities. These unitary authorities are usually presented in alphabetical order.

Councils of Scotland

On 1 April 1996, the 10 local authority regions and 56 districts of Scotland were replaced by 32 unitary councils. These councils are usually presented in alphabetical order.

Northern Ireland

The 26 districts of Northern Ireland are presented in the Regional Profiles chapter. For some topics, they are grouped into either the five education and library boards or the four health and social services boards. The districts comprising the education and library boards are as follows:

Board	Districts
Belfast	Belfast
South	Eastern Ards, Castlereagh, Down, Lisburn, North Down
Southern	Armagh, Banbridge, Cookstown, Craigavon, Dungannon, Newry and Mourne
North Eastern	Antrim, Ballymena, Ballymoney, Carrickfergus, Coleraine, Larne, Magherafelt, Moyle, Newtownabbey
Western	Derry, Fermanagh, Limavady, Omagh, Strabane

Health and social services boards are as follows:

Board	Districts
Northern	North Eastern Education and Library Board but including Cookstown
Eastern	South Eastern Education and Library Board but including Belfast
Southern	Southern Education and Library Board but excluding Cookstown
Western	Western Education and Library Board

NUTS (Nomenclature of Territorial Statistics) area classification

NUTS is a hierarchical classification of areas that provides a breakdown of the European Union's economic territory for producing regional statistics that are comparable across the Union. It has been used since 1988 in EU legislation for determining the distribution of the Structural Funds. The NUTS five-tier structure for the UK was reviewed during 1998 as a consequence of the move to using Government Office Regions as the principal classification for English Regions and the local government re-organisation, which took place in the same year. The NUTS structure comprises current national administrative areas, except in Scotland where some NUTS areas comprise whole and /or part local enterprise company areas.

As a result of a European Union-wide NUTS regulation enacted in June 2003 it is now obligatory to use the NUTS geographies in the regulation (including the new codes) and not those in the previous gentleman's agreement. There are only minimal changes for the UK although NUTS levels 4 and 5 no longer have any official status and should now be referred to as LAU (Local Administrative Unit) 1 and 2 respectively.

Other regional classifications

The UK Continental Shelf, now referred to as extra-regio, is treated as a separate region in Chapter 12 (see the Notes and Definitions to Chapter 12, Regional Accounts).

Chapter 3: Population and Migration

Tables 3.1, 3.2 and Maps 3.3, 3.4, 3.5. Also Maps 1.49 and 1.50 in Regional Profiles

The estimated and projected populations are of the resident population of an area, i.e. all those usually resident there, whatever their nationality. Members of HM forces stationed outside the United Kingdom are excluded; members of foreign forces stationed in the United Kingdom are included. Students are taken to be resident at their term-time addresses. Figures for the United Kingdom do not include the population of the Channel Islands or the Isle of Man.

The population estimates for mid-2001 to mid-2004 are based on results from the 2001 Census and have been updated to reflect subsequent births, deaths, net migration and other changes. Details on the calculation of populations estimates for 1992 to 2000 can be found in Population Trends Issue 122 from the following link:
http://www.statistics.gov.uk/StatBase/Product.asp?vlnk=6303&Pos=&ColRank=1&Rank=422

Map 1.50 Projected population

As with population estimates, the projected population of an area includes all those usually resident in the area, whatever their nationality. HM Forces stationed outside the United Kingdom are excluded but foreign forces stationed here are included. Students are taken to be resident at their term-time address.

The projected population change figures for Wales and for England, Scotland and Northern Ireland are not directly comparable with previous editions of Regional Trends as later projections are used. There are changes to the assumptions for fertility, mortality and migration in the preparation of each set of projections.

This table uses 2003-based sub-national projections for England and for Wales, 2004-based projections for Northern Ireland total only and 2002-based for the remaining areas in Northern Ireland.

Table 3.6 Ethnic group

The information for the ethnic group of each respondent is based on the data and categorisation generated from the 2001 Census from ONS, the General Register Office for Scotland and the Northern Ireland Statistics and Research Agency.

In both 1991 and 2001 respondents were asked to which ethnic group they considered themselves to belong. The question asked in 2001 was more extensive than that asked in 1991, so that people could tick 'Mixed' for the first time. This change in answer categories may account for a small part of the observed increase in the minority ethnic population over the period. Different versions of the ethnic group question were asked in England and Wales, in Scotland and in Northern Ireland, to reflect local differences in the requirement for information. However, results are comparable across the UK as a whole.

White includes British, Scottish, Irish and Other British and Other White sub-categories as defined in the 2001 census. Mixed includes the sub-categories White and Black Caribbean, White and Black African, White and Asian and Other mixed.

Tables 3.7, 3.10 and 3.11

Births and deaths

Within England and Wales, births are assigned to areas according to the usual residence of the mother at the date of birth, as stated at registration. If the address of usual residence is outside England and Wales, the birth is included in any aggregate for England and Wales as a whole (and hence in the UK total), but excluded from the figures for any individual region or area.

Birth figures for Scotland include births to both resident and non-resident mothers.

Where sub-national data are given, births have been allocated to the usual residence of the mother if this was in Scotland and to the area of occurrence if the mother's usual residence was outside Scotland.

All figures given for Northern Ireland exclude births to mothers not usually resident in Northern Ireland. However, the UK total includes such births. As with births, within England and Wales a death is normally assigned to the area of usual residence of the deceased. If this is outside England and Wales, the death is included in any aggregate for England and Wales as a whole (and hence in the UK total), but excluded from the figures for any individual region or area.

Death figures for Scotland and Northern Ireland include deaths of both residents and non-residents. Where sub-national data are given, deaths of Scottish or Northern Irish residents have been allocated to the usual area of residence, while deaths of non-residents have been allocated to the area of occurrence.

Table 3.7 Birth and death rates and rate of natural change

Unlike Table 3.8, which relates to population change from mid-year to mid-year, the numbers shown in this table relate to calendar years. Crude birth/death rates and natural change are affected by the age and sex structure of the population. For example, for any given levels of fertility and mortality, a population with a relatively high proportion of persons in the younger age groups will have a higher crude birth rate and consequently a higher rate of natural change than a population with a higher proportion of elderly people.

Table 3.9 Conceptions

The date of conception is estimated using recorded gestation for abortion and stillbirths, and assuming 38 weeks gestation for live births. A woman's age at conception is calculated as the interval in complete years between her date of birth and the estimated date of conception. The postcode of the woman's address is used to determine the area she was living in at the time of the conception.

Table 3.10 Total fertility rate

Age-specific birth rates for the United Kingdom have been calculated on all births registered in the UK, i.e. including births to mothers usually resident outside the UK apart from those to non-residents of Northern Ireland, which are excluded. The England and Wales figures have been calculated on all births registered in England and Wales apart from the non-residents. Data relate to year of occurrence in England and Wales, and year of registration in Scotland and Northern Ireland.

The total fertility rate (TFR) is the average number of children who would be born to a woman if she experiences the current age-specific fertility rates throughout her childbearing years. It is sometimes called the total period fertility rate (TPFR).

Table 3.11 Standardised Mortality Ratio

The Standardised Mortality Ratio (SMR) compares overall mortality in a region with that for the UK. The ratio expresses the actual number of deaths in a region as a percentage of the hypothetical number that would have occurred if the region's population had experienced the sex/age-specific rates of the UK that year.

Tables 3.12 and 3.13 Migration

Inter-regional migration

Estimates for internal population movements are based on the movement of NHS doctors' patients between former Health Authorities (HAs) in England and Wales and Area Health Boards (AHBs) in Scotland and Northern Ireland. These transfers are recorded at the NHS Central Registers (NHSCRs), Southport and Edinburgh, and at the Central Services Agency, Belfast.

The figures have been adjusted to take account of differences in recorded cross-border flows between England and Wales, Scotland and Northern Ireland, and provide a detailed indicator of population movement within the UK. However, they should not be regarded as a perfect measure of migration as there is variation in the delay between a person moving and registering with a new doctor. Additionally, some moves may not result in a re-registration, i.e. individuals may migrate again before registering with a doctor. Conversely, there may be others who move and re-register several times in a year.

International migration

An international migrant is defined as someone who changes his or her country of usual residence for a period of at least a year, so that the country of destination effectively becomes the country of usual residence.

Estimates of international migration are derived from several data sources:

- Migration data from the International Passenger Survey (IPS). This is the principal source that provides data on the number of migrants entering and leaving the country.

- Estimates of migration between the UK and the Irish Republic based on data provided by the Irish Central Statistics Office (CSO).

- Other data sources allow for the estimation of adjustments to the IPS migrant and Irish data. That is, an adjustment for asylum seekers not counted by the IPS (using data from the Home Office (HO)) and adjustments for visitor and migrant switchers (people who change their intentions and, therefore, their migratory status).

The IPS is a continuous voluntary sample survey that provides information on passengers entering and leaving the UK by the principal air, sea and tunnel routes. It excludes routes between the Channel Islands, the Isle of Man and the rest of the world. It has been running since 1961 and is used to collect information on tourism and the balance of payments, as well as on migration. In 2003, the main sample was over a quarter of a million interviews and had an overall response rate of 80%.

The IPS is a sample survey and is, therefore, subject to some uncertainty. Figures obtained from the IPS are subject to both sampling and non-sampling errors. For 2003, the overall standard error for the estimated total inflow of 431,500 migrants was 4.1 per cent and for outflow of 314,000 migrants was 5.2 per cent. As a guide, the standard error for an estimated 1,000 migrants will be in the region of 40 per cent. This reduces to about 10 per cent for an estimate of 40,000 migrants. Thus, generally speaking, the larger the sample supporting a particular estimate, the proportionately smaller its sampling error.

The IPS is based on intentions to migrate and intentions are liable to change. Adjustments are made for visitor switchers (those who intend to stay in the UK or abroad for less than one year but subsequently stay for longer and become migrants) and migrant switchers (those who intend to stay in the UK or abroad for one year or more but then return earlier so are no longer migrants). These adjustments are primarily based on IPS data, but for years prior to 2001, Home Office data on short-term visitors who were subsequently granted an extension of stay for a year or longer for other reasons have been incorporated.

The Irish CSO makes estimates of outflows from the UK to the Irish Republic using data from the Irish Quarterly National Household Survey (QNHS) each April. The QNHS defines in-migrants as those who have arrived in the Irish Republic from the UK since the previous April.

The Irish CSO also provides estimates of migrants from the Irish Republic to the UK. In the QNHS an out-migrant is defined as a person who was usually living in the household in the previous April but is living in the UK at the time of the survey. Given that wholly emigrating households may be under-estimated using this method, estimates of out-migration may be adjusted by CSO in the light of data from other sources including the National Health Service Central Register

(NHSCR), the Census of Population and the Country of Residence Survey.

Home Office provides data on the numbers of applications, refusals, withdrawals, appeals allowed and removals of asylum seekers and their dependants. These data are used to estimate the migration of asylum seekers and their dependants that is not captured by the IPS. HO also provides data on the numbers of asylum seekers and their dependants who are removed from the UK within a year of their application. These data are used to make adjustments to exclude those who were in the UK for less than a year as they do not meet the definition of a migrant.

Data on dependants between 1991 and 2001 were estimates as these data were not collected explicitly during this period. Data from the National Asylum Support Service are used to distribute asylum seeker inflows and outflows between the constituent countries of the UK, and between the government office regions within England.

A consistent methodology has been used to derive international migration estimates for the constituent countries of the UK and Government Office Regions within England. This methodology is currently under review as part of the National Statistics Quality Review of International Migration. Given the small sample size of the IPS for residents of Scotland and Northern Ireland, adjustment of these estimates using data from administrative records is currently made for the purposes of population estimation in Scotland and Northern Ireland.

Table 3.16 Household projections
The household projections are trend-based; they illustrate what would happen if past trends in household formation were to continue into the future. They are therefore not policy-based forecasts of what is expected to happen, but provide a starting point for policy decisions. The projections are heavily dependent on the assumptions involved, particularly international and internal migration, the marital status projections (in England and Wales only) and the continuation of past trends in household formation.

Table PM1 Social class
Based on the Labour Force Survey (see Notes and Definitions to the Labour Market chapter), the table gives percentages of working age people in each socio-economic class based on the National Statistics Socio-economic Classification (NS-SEC). The NS-SEC is an occupationally based classification but has rules to provide coverage of the whole adult population. The information required to create the NS-SEC is occupation coded to the unit groups (OUG) of the Standard Occupational Classification 2000 (SOC2000)

and details of employment status (whether an employer, self-employed or employee; whether a supervisor; and number of employees at the workplace). Similar information was previously required for earlier social classifications: Social Class and Socio-economic Group. The version of the classification which will be used for most analyses (the analytic version), has eight classes, the first of which can be subdivided. The National Statistics Socio-economic Classification Analytic Classes are:

1. Higher managerial and professional occupations

1.1. Large employers and higher managerial occupations

1.2. Higher professional occupations

2. Lower managerial and professional occupations

3. Intermediate occupations

4. Small employers and own account workers

5. Lower supervisory and technical occupations

6. Semi-routine occupations

7. Routine occupations

8. Never worked and long-term unemployed

For complete coverage, the three categories 'Students', 'Occupations not stated or inadequately described' and 'Not classifiable for other reasons' are added as 'Not elsewhere classified' (n.e.c.) included under 8 above.

For those in employment in the reference week of the survey, their occupation was their main job, and for those not in employment, their last occupation if they had done any paid work in the previous eight years.

Chapter 4: Education and Training

Table 4.1 Pupils and teachers by type of school
The pupil–teacher ratio in a school is the ratio of all pupils on the register to all qualified teachers employed within the school during the census week. Part-time teachers and part-time pupils are included on a full-time equivalent basis. The difference in the age at which pupils transfer from primary to secondary school affects the comparison of pupil–teacher ratios between Scotland and the rest of the United Kingdom.

Table 4.2 Class sizes for all classes
Figures for England, Wales and Scotland include classes where more than one teacher may be present. In Northern Ireland a class is defined as a group of pupils normally under

the control of one teacher. Figures previously shown in this publication for England, prior to 1999/2000, related to classes taught by one teacher only. In England, in 2004/05, the average Key Stage 1 class, taught by one teacher, had 25.6 pupils, with 1.2 per cent of classes having 31 or more pupils. Further information, including one-teacher class size data for Key Stage 2, primary and secondary school class sizes can be found in DfES Statistical First Release 42/2005.

Table 4.3 Pupil absence from maintained primary and secondary schools in England

In law, parents of children of compulsory school age (5 to 16) are required to ensure that they receive a suitable education by regular attendance at school or otherwise. Failure to comply with this statutory duty can lead to prosecution. Local Education Authorities (LEAs) are responsible in law for making sure that pupils attend school.

Schools are required to take attendance registers twice a day: once at the beginning of the morning session and once during the afternoon session. In their register, schools are required to distinguish whether pupils are present, engaged in an approved educational activity, or are absent. Where a day pupil of compulsory school age is absent, schools have to indicate in their register whether the absence is authorised by the school or unauthorised.

Authorised absence is absence with permission from a teacher or other authorised representative of the school. This includes instances of absences for which a satisfactory explanation has been provided (for example, illness). Unauthorised absence is absence without permission from a teacher or other authorised representative of the school. This includes all unexplained or unjustified absences.

Tables 4.4 and ET3, and Map 4.5 Examination achievements

The main examination for pupils at the minimum school-leaving age in England, Wales and Northern Ireland is the General Certificate of Secondary Education (GCSE), which is awarded in eight grades, A*-G. GCSE figures relate to achievements by 16-year-olds at the end of the academic year and are shown as percentages of 16-year-olds in school. General Certificate of Education (GCE) A levels are usually taken after a further two years of post-compulsory education, passes being graded from A-E.

In Scotland, National Qualifications (NQs) are offered to students, which include Standard Grades, National Courses and National Units. The Standard Grade is awarded in seven grades, through three levels of study: Credit (1 or 2), General (3 or 4) and Foundation (5

or 6). Students who do not achieve a grade 1-6, but do complete the course, are awarded a grade 7. Standard Grade courses are made up of different parts called 'elements', with an exam at the end.

National Courses are available at Intermediate, Higher and Advanced Higher, and consist of National Units which are assessed by the school/college, plus an external assessment. Grades are awarded on the basis of how well a student does in the external assessment, having passed all of the National Units. Pass grades are awarded at A, B and C. A grade D is awarded to a student who just fails to get a grade C. Intermediate courses can be taken as an alternative to Standard Grade or as a stepping stone to Higher.

Access units are assessed by the school/college, with no exam involved. Groups of units in a particular subject area can be built up at Access 2 and 3 to lead to 'Cluster Awards'.

The relationship between the National Courses and Standard Grades can be seen in the table below.

GCSE figures relate to achievements by 16-year-olds at the end of the academic year and are shown as percentages of 16-year-olds in school. Scottish NQs relate to achievements by pupils in year S4 at the end of the academic year. That is, the achievements of pupils by the end of their last year of compulsory schooling: some may have been passed a year earlier.

The methodology behind the A level data in Table 4.4 has been revised to show the proportion of *candidates* in schools and FE colleges aged 16-18 in England and Northern Ireland (schools only) and aged 17 in Wales (schools only) who achieved GCE A levels, or equivalent. Data for Wales include any examinations taken at an earlier age. The age spread in the examination results figures takes account of those pupils sitting examinations a year early or resitting them.

The post-16 qualifications for pupils in Scotland are Highers and Advanced Highers, therefore it is not possible to show figures for Scotland which are comparable with the rest of the United Kingdom. As a result, United Kingdom figures cannot be calculated.

Average GCE/VCE A/AS points scores are shown in Table 4.4. Points scores are determined by totalling pupils' individual GCE/VCE A/AS results: an A level pass and an AS examination pass are classified at grade E or above. Each grade at AS examination is counted as half that grade at A level. Vocational Certificate of Education (VCE) A level double awards count as 2 A levels. From 2001/02, the number of points assigned to grades within GCE/VCE qualifications in England has changed to reflect the Universities and Colleges Admissions Service (UCAS) Tariff. Data from 2002/03 relate to 16- to 18-year-olds entered for at least one A level or equivalent. This data is not comparable with 2001/02 which refers to those entered for at least two A levels or equivalent. Scores are calculated as shown below:

GCE/VCE AS level:

Grade	UCCA points	UCAS points
A	5	60
B	4	50
C	3	40
D	2	30
E	1	20

GCE/VCE A level

Grade	UCCA points	UCAS points
A	10	120
B	8	100
C	6	80
D	4	60
E	2	40

Standard grades	National courses/units
	Advanced Higher
	Higher
Standard Grade – Credit	Intermediate 2
Standard Grade – General	Intermediate 1
Standard Grade – Foundation	Access 3
	Access 2
	Access 1

VCE A level double award:

Grade	UCAS points
AA	240
AB	220
BB	200
BC	180
CC	160
CD	140
DD	120
DE	100
EE	80

Advanced GNVQ scores are calculated as shown in the table below.

In Wales, at below GCSE standard, the Certificate of Education examination is also available and is widely used by schools. Many pupils take Welsh as a first language at GCSE. In all countries pupils may sit non-GCE/GCSE examinations such as BTEC (SCOTVEC in Scotland), City and Guilds, RSA and Pitman. A proportion of pupils who are recorded as achieving no GCSE, AS or A level qualification will have passes in one or more of these other examinations.

In Table ET3, mathematics figures exclude computing science (England) and computer studies and statistics (Wales) while 'any science' in England and Wales includes double award, single award and individual science subjects. Double award science was introduced with the GCSEs in 1988. Success in double award science means that the pupil has achieved two GCSEs rather than just one pass with single science or the individual sciences of biology, physics and chemistry. The majority of 15-year-olds now attempt GCSE double award science in preference to the single science subjects, although the individual sciences are still popular in the independent sector. There is no equivalent to double award science in the Scottish National Qualifications.

Comparisons of examination results for England, Wales and Northern Ireland with those for Scotland are not straightforward because of the different education and examination systems. However, following the SQA benchmarking analysis, the information below should be used as a guideline:

5 or more GCSEs at grades A*-C = 5 or more Standard Grades at levels 1-3/Intermediate 2 grades A-C/Intermediate 1 grade A only;

1-4 GCSEs at grades A*-C = 1-4 Standard Grades at levels 1-3/ Intermediate 2 grades A-C/ Intermediate 1 grade A only;

GCSEs at grades D-G only = Standard Grades at levels 4-6 only/Intermediate 1 grades B-C only/Access 3 cluster;

See also the National Curriculum notes for Table 4.6

Table 4.6 The National Curriculum: assessments and tests

Under the *Education Reform Act* (1988) a National Curriculum has been progressively introduced into primary and secondary schools in England and Wales. This consists of mathematics, English (or the option of Welsh as a first language in Wales) and science as core subjects, with a modern language, history, geography, information technology, design and technology, music, art and physical education (and Welsh as a second language in Wales) as foundation subjects. The Education Act 2002 extended the National Curriculum for England to include the foundation (i.e. early years education) stage, for suitable areas of learning. Measurable local targets have been defined for four key stages, corresponding to ages 7, 11, 14 and 16.

Pupils are assessed formally at the ages of 7, 11 and 14 by a mixture of teacher assessments and national tests in the core subjects of English, mathematics and science (and in Welsh in Welsh-speaking schools in Wales), though the method varies between subjects and countries. 16-year-olds are assessed by means of the GCSE examination. Statutory authorities have been set up for England and Wales to advise government on the National Curriculum and promote curriculum development generally. Northern Ireland has its own common curriculum, which is similar, but not identical, to the National Curriculum in England and Wales. Assessment arrangements in Northern Ireland became statutory from September 1996, and Key Stage 1 pupils are assessed at the age of 8. Pupils in Northern Ireland are not assessed in science at Key Stages 1 and 2. The National Curriculum does not apply in

Scotland, where school curricula are the responsibility of education authorities and individual head teachers, and in practice almost all 14- to 16-year-olds study mathematics, English, science, a modern foreign language, a social subject, physical education, technology and a creative and aesthetic subject. The Key Stage 1, 2 and 3 figures for England cover all types of school (e.g. maintained and independent). The Government Office Region figures cover LEA maintained schools only.

Tables 4.7 and ET4 Post-compulsory and further (including adult) education

Further education (FE) includes home students on courses of further education (FE) in further education institutions. The FE sector includes all provision outside schools that is below higher education (HE) level. This ranges from courses in independent living skills for students with severe learning difficulties up to GCE A level, and level 3 NVQ/SVQ and other vocational courses. The FE sector also includes many students pursuing recreational courses not leading to a formal qualification. Students in England and Wales are counted once only, irrespective of the number of courses for which a student has enrolled. In Scotland and Northern Ireland, students enrolled on more than one course in unrelated subjects are counted for each of these courses with the exception of those on Standard Grade/GCSE and/or Highers/GCE courses, who are counted once only irrespective of the number of levels/grades. Most FE students are in FE colleges and (in England) sixth form colleges that were formerly maintained by Local Education Authorities (LEAs) but in April 1993 became independent self-governing institutions receiving funding through the Further Education Funding Council (FEFC). However, from April 2001, the Learning and Skills Council (LSC) took over the responsibility for funding the FE sector in England, and the National Council for Education and Training for Wales (part of Education and Learning Wales – ELWa) did so for Wales. The Scottish FEFC (SFEFC) funds FE colleges in Scotland, while the Department for Employment and Learning funds FE colleges in Northern Ireland. There are also a small number of FE students in higher education (HE) institutions, and conversely some HE students in FE institutions.

Students may be of any age from 16 upwards (no minimum age in Scotland), and full- or part-time. Full-time students aged under 19 are exempt from tuition fees and fully funded by the respective further education funding bodies in England, Wales, Scotland and Northern Ireland. Students aged 16 to 18 on FE courses in the Scottish FE colleges are exempt from tuition fees, at the

Grade	Comparable GCE grade	Previous point allocation (12 units)	Previous point allocation (18 units)	UCAS points
Distinction	A/B	18	27	100
Merit	C	12	18	80
Pass	D/E	6	9	60

discretion of the individual colleges. Students are eligible to apply for support (bursary); the policy for eligibility is at the discretion of the colleges. For other students, tuition fees are payable but may be remitted for students in receipt of certain social security benefits. In some cases discretionary grants may be available from LEAs or the colleges themselves. LEAs continue to make some FE provision (often referred to as 'adult education') exclusively part-time and predominantly recreational. The majority of LEAs make part or all of this provision directly themselves, but some pay other organisations (usually FE colleges) to do so on their behalf, i.e. 'contracted out' provision.

Part-time day courses are mainly those organised for students released by their employers either for one or two days a week (or any part of a week in Scotland), or for a period (or periods) of block release.

Sandwich courses are those where periods of full-time study are broken by a period (or periods) of associated industrial training or experience, and where the total period (or periods) of full-time study over the whole course averages more than 19 weeks per academic year (18 weeks in Scotland). Sandwich course students are classed as full-time students.

National Vocational Qualifications (NVQs) and Scottish Vocational Qualifications (SVQs) are occupational qualifications, available at five levels, and are based on up-to-date standards set by employers.

General National Vocational Qualifications (GNVQs) and General Scottish Vocational Qualifications (GSVQs) combine general and vocational education and are available at three levels:

Foundation – broadly equivalent to four GCSEs at grades D-G or four Scottish Standard Grades at levels 4-6.

Intermediate – broadly equivalent to five GCSEs at grades A*-C or five Scottish Standard Grades at levels 1-3.

Advanced – broadly equivalent to two GCE A levels, or three Scottish NQ Higher Grade passes. Advanced GNVQs were redesigned and re-launched as vocational A levels (or, more formally, Advanced Vocational Certificates of Education (VCEs)). They are available as AS levels (three units), A levels (six units) and double awards (twelve units).

Since 1996/97, figures for FE students in England have been extracted from the Individualised Student Record (ISR) – until 1995/96, figures were taken from the Further Education Statistical Record (FESR). Owing to differences in data collection and methodology between the two sources, the ISR figures are not directly comparable with figures derived from the FESR. Since April

2001, the publication of data on further education in England has been the responsibility of the Learning and Skills Council (LSC), which has taken over the funding of further education from the Further Education Funding Council (FEFC).

The participation rates for regions in England in Table 4.7 have been calculated in the following way:

the number of pupils in independent schools *attending* schools in the area;

the number of maintained school pupils *resident* in the area, regardless of where they study;

the number of full-time and part-time further education students *resident* in the area regardless of where they study;

trainees on Government-supported training, according to the area with which their training is contracted;

divided by the estimated total population of the area in January of the latest year shown who were 16 or 17 respectively at the previous 31 August.

Table 4.8 Higher education
Higher education (HE) students are those on courses that are of a standard that is higher than GCE A level, Scottish NQ Higher Grade, GNVQ/NVQ level 3 or the BTEC or SCOTVEC National Certificate or Diploma. Higher education in publicly funded institutions is funded by block grants from the three Higher Education Funding Councils (HEFCs) in Great Britain and the Department for Employment and Learning in Northern Ireland (DELNI). Some HE activity takes place in FE sector institutions, some of which is funded by the HEFCs and some by the FE funding bodies.

The figures for HE students in FE colleges in England and Wales in Table 4.8 have been extracted from the Individualised Student Record (ISR). Figures for England include LSC funded students studying in FE institutions who were undergoing learning at 1 November. Figures for Wales refer to students at 1 December.

Table 4.10 Population of working age by highest qualification
Table 4.10 covers all people of working age (16 to 64 for males, 16 to 59 for females). Please also see notes to Tables 4.4 and ET3.

Degree or equivalent includes higher and first degrees, NVQ level 5 and other degree-evel qualifications such as graduate membership of a professional institute.

Higher education qualification below degree level includes NVQ level 4, higher level BTEC/SCOTVEC, HNC/HND, RSA Higher diploma and nursing and teaching qualifications.

GCE A level or equivalent includes NVQ level 3, GNVQ advanced, BTEC/SCOTVEC National Certificate, RSA Advanced diploma, City and Guilds advanced craft, A/AS levels or equivalent, Scottish Highers, Scottish Certificate of Sixth Year Studies and trade apprenticeships.

GCSE grades A*-C or equivalent includes NVQ level 2, GNVQ intermediate, RSA diploma, City and Guilds craft, BTEC/SCOTVEC First or general diploma, GCSE grades A*-C or equivalent, O level and CSE Grade 1.

Other qualifications at NVQ level 1 or below include GNVQ, GSVO foundation level, GCSE grade D-G, CSE below grade 1, BTEC/SCOTVEC First or general certificate, other RSA and City and Guilds qualifications, Youth Training certificate and any other professional, vocational or foreign qualifications for which the level is unknown.

Table 4.11 Public Service Agreement Targets
Various Spending Review Public Service Agreement (PSA) Targets have now superseded the 2002 National Learning Targets in England. Table 4.11 shows the proportions of people meeting the required qualification levels for some of these PSA Targets. The Targets shown are split into two groups – those for young people and those for adults – and they have been set using the competence-based National Vocational Qualifications (NVQs) and their vocational and academic equivalents. It should be noted that the data in Table 4.11 relate to the regions in which people were resident, and not where they obtained their qualifications. This can lead to some distortion of the regional picture of educational standards.

Spending Review 2004 PSA Objective 3 is for all young people to reach 19 ready for skilled employment or higher education. As part of this Objective, Target 10 includes an aim to increase the proportion of 19-year-olds who achieve at least Level 2 by 3 percentage points between 2004 and 2006, and a further 2 percentage points between 2006 and 2008. PSA Objective 4 is to tackle the adult skills gap, and one of the methods in Target 13 of this Objective is through reducing, by at least 40 per cent, the number of adults in the workforce who lack NVQ 2 or equivalent qualifications by 2010. Working towards this, 1 million adults in the workforce are to achieve level 2 between 2003 and 2006.

The proportion of economically active adults qualified to at least level 3 (Learning and Skills Council Target: By 2004, 52 per cent of adults to achieve level 3) is shown in the table for information.

Table ET2 School meal arrangements
Information is collected for the numbers of

full- and part-time pupils (up to and including and above minimum school leaving age) on each school's register known to be eligible for a free school meal and those who took a free school meal. Prior to 2001, the numbers eligible for a free school meal were those pupils who had, or whose parents had, satisfied the relevant authority that they were receiving Income Support or income-based Jobseeker's Allowance or support provided under Part 6 of the Immigration and Asylum Act 1999. For the 2001 Census, this definition was modified to include only pupils where parents had indicated that they wished their child to have a free meal and had confirmed benefit receipt with the LEA or school.

Chapter 5: Labour Market

Interpretation of the labour market requires a number of different sources of data to be used. There are five main sources: the Labour Force Survey (LFS), the Annual Business Inquiry (ABI), the Northern Ireland Quarterly Employment Survey (QES), the Annual Survey of Hours and Earnings (ASHE) and the claimant count. Problems can arise in drawing together data on the same subject from different sources. For example, the question in the LFS as to whether the respondent is employed produces a measure of employment based on the number of people, whereas a question addressed to employers asking the number of people they employ, as in the ABI, produces a measure of the number of jobs. Thus if someone has a second job he or she will be included twice.

Labour Force Survey (LFS)
LFS estimates are prone to sampling variability. For example, in the March to May 2003 period, unemployment in the United Kingdom according to the ILO definition (seasonally adjusted) stood at 1,474,000. If another sample for the same period were drawn, a different result might be achieved. In theory, many samples could be drawn, each giving a different result. This is because each sample would be made up of different people giving different answers to the questions. The spread of these results is the sampling variability. Sampling variability is determined by a number of factors including the sample size, the variability of the population from which the sample is drawn and the sample design. Once the sampling variability is known, it is possible to calculate a range of values about the sample estimate that represents the expected variation with a given level of assurance. This is called a confidence interval. For a 95 per cent confidence interval, widely used within ONS and elsewhere, we expect that in 95 per cent of the samples (19 times out of 20) the confidence interval will contain the true value that would be obtained by surveying the entire population. For the example given above, we can be 95 per cent confident that the true

value was in the range 1,422,000 to 1,526,000.

In general, the larger the number of people in the sample the smaller the variation between estimates. For this reason estimates based on the LFS for the whole of the UK are more accurate than those for smaller geographical areas or subsets of the population. Generally, the sampling variability around regional estimates is, proportionately, around three times that for national estimates.

Sampling variability also affects changes over time. Changes over time are best viewed using changes in rates rather than levels in order to view them in a wider context of changes in the overall population. Rates are also subject to sampling variability.

The LFS began in 1973. Since 1998 the results have been published 12 times a year, showing on each occasion the average for a three-month period. In this publication, the three-month period used is usually the spring quarter (March to May). Other three-month periods commonly used here and in other publications are the summer (June to August), autumn (September to November) and winter (December to February) quarters.

Labour Force Survey estimates are consistent with 2001 Census UK LFS estimates.

Full details of the reweighting exercise following the 2001 Census can be found at:

http://www.statistics.gov.uk/CCI/article.asp?ID=887&Pos=1&ColRank=2&Rank=224

Glossary of terms

Claimant count
A count, derived from administrative sources, of those people who are claiming unemployment-related benefits at Jobcentre Plus local offices.

Claimant count rate
At a national and regional level, the claimant count rate is normally calculated by expressing the number of people claiming unemployment-related benefits (the numerator) as a percentage of the estimated total workforce (the denominator), which is the sum of claimants, employee jobs, self-employment jobs, HM armed forces and government-supported trainees. At a sub-regional level, a different denominator is used: the resident working-age population of the area. Where national and regional claimant count rates are presented in the same table as sub-regional rates, then the denominator for all the rates is also the resident working-age population of the area.

Economically active/labour force
The labour force (otherwise known as the economically active population) consists of those in employment plus the unemployed.

Economic activity rate
The percentage of the population that is in the labour force.

Economically inactive
People who are neither part of the labour force in employment nor unemployed (according to the ILO definition). For example, all people under 16, those retired or looking after a home, or those permanently unable to work.

Employees (Labour Force Survey)
A household-based measure of people aged 16 or over who regard themselves as paid employees. In this publication, people are counted only once in their main job.

Employee jobs (Employer Survey)
A measure, obtained from surveys of employers, of jobs held by civilians. People with two or more jobs are counted in each job.

Unemployed
An International Labour Organisation (ILO) recommended measure, used in household surveys such as the LFS, which counts as unemployed those aged 16 or over who are without a job, are available to start work in the next two weeks and who have been seeking a job in the last four weeks, or were waiting to start a job already obtained in the next two weeks.

Unemployment rate
The percentage of the economically active who are unemployed.

Labour force in employment (Labour Force Survey)
A household-based measure of employees, self-employed people, participants in government-supported training and employment programmes, and people doing unpaid work for a family business.

Population of working age
Currently, men aged 16 to 64 years and women aged 16 to 59 years.

Self-employed
A household-based measure (from the Labour Force Survey) of people aged 16 or over who regard themselves as self-employed in their main job.

Workforce jobs
A measure of employee jobs (obtained from employer surveys), self-employment jobs (obtained from the Labour Force Survey), all HM Forces, and government-supported trainees (obtained from the Department for Work and Pensions and its Scottish and Welsh counterparts).

Tables 5.1 and 5.2 Labour force
The labour force includes people aged 16 and over who are either in employment (whether

employed, self-employed, on a work-related government-supported employment and training programme or an unpaid family worker) or unemployed. The ILO definition of unemployment counts as unemployed people without a job who were available to start work within two weeks and had either looked for work in the past four weeks or were waiting to start a job they had already obtained in the next two weeks.

Annual Business Inquiry, Short-term Employment Survey and Quarterly Employment Survey

The Annual Business Inquiry (ABI) is a sample survey which ran for the first time in 1998 and replaced the Annual Employment Survey. The ABI is the only source of employment statistics for Great Britain analysed by local area and by detailed industrial classification. The sample is drawn from the Inter-Departmental Business Register (IDBR), and the ABI 1999 sample comprised 78,000 enterprises. An enterprise is roughly defined as a combination of local units (i.e. individual workplaces with PAYE schemes or registered for VAT) under common ownership. These enterprises covered 0.5 million local units and 15 million employees (out of a total population of roughly 25 million in employment). The ABI results are used to benchmark the monthly/quarterly employment surveys (STES) which measure 'movements', by region and industrial group, between the annual survey dates.

The Quarterly Employment Survey (QES) for Northern Ireland is a voluntary survey which covers all employers with at least 25 employees, all public sector employers and a representative sample of smaller firms. Data are collected for both male and female, full-time and part-time employees. Estimates for Northern Ireland are produced on a quarterly basis with unadjusted figures available at the two-digit or division level of the 1992 Standard Industrial Classification and seasonally adjusted figures available at a broad sector level.

Table 5.3 Economic activity rates

The economic activity rate is the percentage of the population in a given age group which is in the labour force.

Table 5.10 Average usual weekly hours

Elementary occupational group covers occupations which require the knowledge and experience necessary to perform mostly routine tasks, often involving the use of simple hand-held tools and, in some cases, requiring a degree of physical effort.

Most occupations in this group do not require formal educational qualifications but will usually have an associated short period of formal experience-related training. All non-managerial agricultural occupations are also

included in this group, primarily because of the difficulty of distinguishing between those occupations that require only a limited knowl-edge of agricultural techniques, animal husbandry, etc., from those that require specific training and experience in these areas.

Table 5.11 Labour disputes

The table shows rates per 1,000 employees of working days lost for all industries and services. The statistics relate only to disputes connected with terms and conditions of employment. Stoppages involving fewer than ten workers or lasting less than one day are excluded except where the aggregate of working days lost is 100 or more. When interpreting the figures the following points should be borne in mind:

a) geographical variations in industrial structure affect overall regional comparisons;

b) a few large stoppages affecting a small number of firms may have a significant effect;

c) the number of working days lost and workers involved relate to people both directly and indirectly involved at the establishments where the disputes occurred;

d) the regional figures involve a greater degree of estimation than the national figures as some large national stoppages cannot be disaggregated to a regional level and are only shown in the figure for the United Kingdom.

Tables 5.12, LM1 and LM2 Gross weekly earnings

This table contains some of the regional results of the Annual Survey of Hours and Earnings, 2005 which has replaced New Earnings Survey. Fuller details of this are given for the Government Office Regions and industry groupings at:

http://www.statistics.gov.uk/StatBase/Product. asp?vlnk=14203

Gross earnings are measured before tax, National Insurance or other deductions. They include overtime pay, bonuses and other additions to basic pay but exclude any payments for earlier periods (for example, back pay), income in kind, tips and gratuities. Results relate to full-time male and female employees on adult rates whose pay for the survey pay-period was not affected by absence. Employees were classified to the region in which they worked (or were based if mobile) in respect of Table 5.12 using postcode information, and to manual or non-manual occupations on the basis of the Standard Occupational Classification 2003 (SOC 2003). Full-time employees are defined as those normally expected to work more than 30 hours per week, excluding overtime

and main meal breaks (but 25 hours or more in the case of teachers) or, if their normal hours were not specified, as those regarded as full-time by the employer.

Median figures have been used in these tables which are less affected by extremes of low and highly paid people. A median is a value where half of the given population earn less than this amount and half earn more. This is a change from previous editions of Regional Trends in which means were used.

Data in Tables LM1 and LM2 relate to full-time employees whose pay was not affected by absence, but they are classified to their region of residence.

Tables 5.13, 5.17 and 5.18 Unemployment

The International Labour Organisation (ILO) definition of unemployment is measured through the Labour Force Survey and covers those people who are looking for work and are available for work (see Glossary of terms). The unemployment rate is the percentage of economically active people who are unemployed.

Counts of claimants of unemployment-related benefits are also published. There are advantages and disadvantages with both, but the two series are complementary. The unemployment rate is the number of people who are unemployed as a proportion of the resident economically active population of the area concerned. The claimant count rate at the national and regional level is the number of people claiming unemployment-related benefits as a proportion of claimants and jobs in each area. This explains why the unemployment rate for London, where inward commuting is an important feature of the local labour market, tends to be significantly higher than the equivalent claimant count rate. The differential is much smaller for a region such as the South East where people commute out of the region into London. At a subregional level, the claimant count rate is the number of claimants in an area as a proportion of the resident working-age population of the area. A fuller description of unemployment and claimant count, and the way they relate to one another, is in the booklet *How exactly is unemployment measured?*, available from the Office for National Statistics or on-line at:

http://www.statistics.gov.uk/statbase/Product. asp?vlnk=2054

Table 5.14, Maps 5.15 and 5.16 Claimant count statistics

From 7 October 1996, a new single benefit, the Jobseeker's Allowance (JSA), replaced Unemployment Benefit and Income Support for unemployed people. People who qualify for JSA through their National Insurance contributions are eligible for a personal allowance (known as contribution-based JSA) for a maximum of six months. People who do not qualify for contribution-based JSA, or whose needs are not met by it, are able to claim a means-tested allowance (known as income-based JSA) for themselves and their dependants for as long as they need it. All those eligible for and claiming JSA, as well as those claiming National Insurance credits, continue to be included in the monthly claimant count.

National and regional claimant count rates are calculated by expressing the number of claimants as a percentage of the estimated total workforce (the sum of claimants, employee jobs, self-employment jobs, HM Armed Forces and government-supported trainees). At a sub-regional level, the claimant count rate is the number of claimants in an area as a proportion of the resident working age population of the area.

Table 5.19 Qualifications
Degree or equivalent includes higher and first degrees, NVQ level 5 and other degree-level qualifications such as graduate membership of a professional institute.

Higher education qualification below degree level includes NVQ level 4, higher level BTEC/SCOTVEC, HNC/HND, RSA Higher diploma and nursing and teaching qualifications.

GCE A level or equivalent includes NVQ level 3, GNVQ advanced, BTEC/SCOTVEC National Certificate, RSA Advanced diploma, City and Guilds advanced craft, A/AS levels or equivalent, Scottish Highers, Scottish Certificate of Sixth Year Studies and trade apprenticeships.

GCSE grades A*-C or equivalent includes NVQ level 2, GNVQ intermediate, RSA diploma, City and Guilds craft, BTEC/SCOTVEC First or general diploma, GCSE grades A*-C or equivalent, O level and CSE Grade 1.

Other qualifications at NVQ level 1 or below include GNVQ, GSVQ foundation level, GCSE grade D-G, CSE below grade 1, BTEC/SCOTVEC First or general certificate, other RSA and City and Guilds qualifications, Youth Training certificate and any other professional, vocational or foreign qualifications for which the level is unknown.

Chapter 6: Housing

Tables 6.1 and 6.3 Dwellings
In the 2001 Census, a dwelling was defined as a self-contained unit of accommodation with all the rooms behind a door that only that household can use. The figures in Table 6.1 include vacant dwellings and temporary dwellings occupied as a normal place of residence. Estimates of the stock in England, Wales and Scotland are based on data from the 2001 Census and projected forward

yearly. Series up to 2001 for England and the regions has been adjusted so that the 2001 estimates match the Census. The figure for 2003 is provisional. In addition, local authority and other public sector landlords' figures supplement the data for Wales and Scotland. Estimates of the dwelling stock by tenure in Table 6.3 are also based on the latest Census for owner-occupied and privately rented dwellings. However, Registered Social Landlords' stock is more accurately taken from the Housing Corporation's own data.

Table 6.2 New dwellings completed
The figures in Table 6.2 relate to new permanent dwellings only, i.e. dwellings with a life expectancy of 60 years or more. A dwelling is counted as completed when it becomes ready for occupation, whether actually occupied or not. The figures for private sector completions in Northern Ireland have been statistically adjusted to correct, as far as possible, the proven under-recording of private sector completions in Northern Ireland. The figures for private sector completions in Scotland include estimates for some local authorities in latter years.

Each local authority district figure includes the full 12 months of NHBC data plus the local authority reported data, which may not cover the full year as returns are not received from all LAs every quarter. Occasionally LAs may only submit partially complete information in their quarterly returns, so four quarters of reported data does not necessarily mean that each tenure-specific breakdown is provided each time. Both the region and county level figures are totals of the appropriate LAs and include estimates for missing or partial LA returns. For this reason regional and county totals may not equal the sum of the districts' figures within those areas.

Table 6.6 Selected housing costs of owner-occupiers
Prior to Regional Trends 36 each category included owner-occupiers who did not make any payments. This group of people has now been excluded from this table.

Mortgage payments: mortgage interest plus any premiums on mortgage protection policies for loans used to purchase the property. For repayment mortgages, interest is calculated using the amount of loan outstanding and the standard interest rate at time of interview.

Endowment policies: premium on endowment policies covering the repayment of mortgages and loans used to purchase the property.

Structural insurance: includes cases where insurance also covers furniture and contents and the structural element cannot be separately identified.

Services: includes payments of ground rent, feu duties (applies in Scotland), chief rent, service charges, compulsory or regular maintenance charges, site rent (caravans), factoring (payments to a land steward) and any other regular payments in connection with the accommodation.

Table 6.7 Average dwelling prices
Average prices in this table are calculated from data collected by the Land Registry. Because of the time lag between the completion of a house purchase and its subsequent lodgement with the Land Registry, data for the final quarter of 2004 are not as complete as those for the final quarter of 2003. The table includes all sales registered up to 31 March 2005.

Table 6.8 Mortgage advances, income and age of borrowers
Figures in this table are taken from the Office of the Deputy Prime Minister's (ODPM) Survey of Mortgage Lenders. This is conducted in partnership with the Council of Mortgage Lenders and has, for most of its 35-year history, involved a variety of mortgage lenders supplying a 5 per cent sample of their completions on a monthly basis. Over the past few years, the number of completions received each month from mortgage lenders has increased significantly with some lenders now supplying all their completions. However, figures in Table 6.8 are taken from the 5 per cent sample.

First-time buyers include sitting tenant purchases.

Table 6.9 Average weekly rents: by tenure
Figures in this table are the average amounts of rent eligible for Housing Benefit paid by a household, calculated before the deduction of any Housing Benefit but after taking off certain expenses such as service charges and council tax. Individual households where the amount is £nil or less than £nil are all treated as £nil, and included in the calculation of the average.

Table 6.10 Dwellings in council tax bands
Council tax bands in Scotland differ from those in England and Wales. The bands are as shown in the table overleaf.

Table 6.11 County Court actions for mortgage possessions
The figures do not indicate how many houses have been repossessed through the courts; not all the orders will have resulted in the issue and execution of warrants of possession. The regional breakdown relates to the location of the court rather than the address of the property.

Actions entered: a claimant begins an action for an order of possession of residential

Council tax bands in Table 6.10 Scotland, England and Wales (at 1 April 1991)

Band	Scotland	England and Wales
Band A	Under £27,000	Under £40,000
Band B	£27,001–£35,000	£40,001–£52,000
Band C	£35,001–£45,000	£52,001–£68,000
Band D	£45,001–£58,000	£68,001–£88,000
Band E	£58,001–£80,000	£88,001–£120,000
Band F	£80,001–£106,000	£120,001–£160,000
Band G	£106,001–£212,000	£160,001–£320,000
Band H	Over £212,000	Over £320,000.

property by way of a summons in a county court.

Orders made: the court, following a judicial hearing, may grant an order for possession immediately. This entitles the claimant to apply for a warrant to have the defendant evicted. However, even where a warrant for possession is issued, the parties can still negotiate a compromise to prevent eviction.

Suspended orders: frequently, the court grants the mortgage lender possession but suspends the operation of the order. Provided defendants comply with the terms of the suspension, which usually require them to pay the current mortgage instalments plus some of the accrued arrears, the possession order cannot be enforced.

Table 6.12 Households accepted as homeless: by reason
In England, the basis for these figures is persons found to be eligible for assistance, unintentionally homeless and falling within a priority need group, and consequently owed a main homelessness duty by a local authority under the homelessness provisions of the Housing Act 1996.

In Wales, the basis for these figures is households accepted for re-housing by local authorities under the homelessness provisions

of Part III of the Housing Act 1985, and Part IV of the Housing Act 1996.

In Scotland the basis of these figures is households assessed by the local authorities as unintentionally homeless or potentially homeless and in priority need, as defined in Section 24 of the Housing (Scotland) Act 1987.

In Northern Ireland, the Housing (Northern Ireland) Order 1988 (Part II) defines the basis under which households (including one-person households) are classified as homeless. The figures relate to priority cases only.

Table H1
Right-to-buy sales were introduced in Great Britain in October 1980.

Table H2 Householders' satisfaction with their area
In the Survey of English Housing, householders were asked to rate their satisfaction with the area in which they lived, while in the Scottish Household Survey, adults were asked to rate their neighbourhood as a place to live. In Table H2, the categories shown are the responses for the Survey of English Housing, and the table below shows how the Scottish responses compare.

Chapter 7: Health and Care
On 1 April 2002 a new organisation was introduced for the National Health Service (NHS) in England, whereby primary care trusts (PCTs) and care groups were created to become the lead NHS organisations in assessing need, planning and securing all health services, and improving health. These care trusts will forge new partnerships with local communities and lead the NHS contribution to joint work with local government and other partners.

In Wales the five health authorities were replaced by 22 local health boards on 1 April 2003. These are responsible for commissioning, securing and delivering health care in partnership with local authorities and the voluntary sector. Their boundaries are conterminous with unitary authorities.

NHS trusts will continue to provide services, working within delivery agreements with PCTs. Trusts will be expected to devolve greater responsibility to clinical teams and to foster and encourage the growth of clinical networks across NHS organisations. High performing Trusts will earn greater freedoms and autonomy in recognition of their achievements. Primary Care Trusts will be able to secure treatment for their patients from a range of providers who are best suited to deliver.

Twenty-eight Strategic Health Authorities (StHA) have replaced the old 95 Health Authorities. These will step back from service planning and commissioning to lead the strategic development of the local health service and performance manage PCTs and NHS Trusts on the basis of local accountability agreements. In February 2004 the Strategic Health Authority of Coventry, Warwickshire, Herefordshire and Worcestershire changed its name to West Midlands South.

The Department of Health will change the way it relates to the NHS, focusing on supporting the delivery of the NHS Plan. Four new Regional Directors of Health and Social Care who will oversee the development of the NHS and provide the link between NHS organisations and the central department have replaced Regional Offices of the Department of Health.

Categories in Table H2 for 2002-2003

Survey of English Housing 2002/03	Scottish Household Survey 2003
Very satisfied	Very good
Fairly satisfied	Fairly good
Neither satisfied nor dissatisfied	No opinion
Slightly dissatisfied	Fairly poor
Very dissatisfied	Very poor

Categories in Table H2 for 2003-2004

Survey of English Housing 2003/04	Scottish Household Survey 2004
As above	As above

Tables 7.1 and HC1 Population and vital statistics for health authorities
Table 7.1 provides basic information relating to the Strategic Health Authorities (StHAs) to aid interpretation of data in the Health and Care Chapter. Table HC1, showing equivalent information for the Regional Health Authorities in existence until March 2002, can be found on the National Statistics website

http://www.statistics.gov.uk/geography/health_geog.asp

Tables 7.1 and 7.4 Age-standardised mortality rates

Mortality rates vary with age so the rates for different areas can be affected by the age structure of their populations. The figures in Tables 7.1 and 7.4 have been adjusted to take into account these differences. The rates have been standardised to the mid-1991 United Kingdom population for males and females separately. This means it is acceptable to compare rates across areas for each sex, but not to compare males with females.

The causes of death included in Table 7.4 correspond to International Classification of Diseases (10th Revision) codes (ICD10) as follows:

all circulatory diseases	I00-I99
ischaemic heart disease	I20-I25
cerebrovascular disease	I60-I69
all respiratory diseases	J00-J99
bronchitis *et al*	J40-J44
cancer (malignant neoplasms)	C00-C97
all injuries and poisoning	V01-Y89
Land Transport	V01-V89
suicides and open verdicts	X60-X84
and	Y10-Y34

The data in these tables relate to registrations in the reference year.

Figure 7.5 Standardised cancer registration rates

Figure 7.5 shows the Standardised Registration Ratios (SRRs) for various cancers in each of the Government Office Regions in England and in Wales, Scotland and Northern Ireland. Registrations are to usual area of residence of the patient and are averages relating to 2001 to 2003, including registrations notified up to July 2003.

For each cancer, the registration rates are taken as standards (with the sexes considered separately). For example, the SRR for cancer of the stomach for the East Midlands was calculated as:

$$SRR = \frac{100 \times \text{No. of registrations of cancer of the stomach in East Midlands}}{\sum_{\text{Age group}} \left[\begin{array}{l}\text{Population in each} \\ \text{age group, East} \\ \text{Midlands GOR x} \\ \text{registration rate for} \\ \text{cancer of the stomach} \\ \text{for that age, England}\end{array} \right]}$$

Incidences of cancer registrations are for malignant neoplasms, classified according to the tenth revision of the International Classification of Diseases (ICD10):

Type of cancer:

Stomach	C16	Malignant neoplasm of stomach
Lung	C33-C34	Malignant neoplasm of trachea, bronchus and lung
Breast	C50	Malignant neoplasm of breast
Prostate	C61	Malignant neoplasm of prostate
Skin	C43	Malignant melanoma of skin
Leukaemia	C91-C95	All leukaemias
Colorectal	C18-C20	Malignant neoplasm of colon and rectum

Three-year average age-standardised registration rates of newly diagnosed cancers per 100,000 population for the United Kingdom and England for 2001-2003 were as shown in the table below.

Table 7.6 Cervical and breast cancer screening

Data from these two cancer screening programmes are snapshots of the coverage of the target population for each programme at 31 March in the stated year.

Figures for the Scottish Breast Screening Programme are derived from the number of women aged 50 to 54, 55 to 59 and 60 to 64 who have attended a routine screening appointment, or a self/GP referral appointment, during this period and a mid-year estimate of the female population in Scotland aged 50 to 64. Medically ineligible women are not excluded from the target population.

Northern Ireland figures for breast screening may include a small number of women who have been counted more than once because of an early recall for screening during the relevant three-year period. The maximum

extent of any such double count can be calculated as less than 0.4 per cent. All population data for Scotland were obtained from the General Register Office for Scotland.

Tables 7.8, 7.9 and HC2 General Household Survey and Continuous Household Survey

The General Household Survey (GHS) and Continuous Household Survey (CHS) are continuous surveys that have been running since 1971 for the GHS and 1983 for the CHS. They are based each year on samples of the general population resident in private (non-institutional) households in Great Britain and Northern Ireland. As multi-purpose surveys, they provide information on aspects of housing, employment, education, health and social services, health-related behaviour, transport, population and social security. Since 1988, GHS fieldwork has been based on a financial rather than calendar year and as a result data were not collected for the first quarter of 1988. From 2000/01, General Household Survey data are weighted to compensate for non-response and to match known population distributions.

Table 7.9 Alcohol consumption

A unit of alcohol is 8 grammes of pure alcohol, approximately equivalent to half a pint of ordinary-strength beer, a glass of wine, or a pub measure of spirits. *Sensible Drinking*, the 1995 inter-departmental review of scientific and medical evidence on the effects of drinking alcohol, concluded that the daily benchmarks were more appropriate than the previously recommended weekly levels. The daily recommendations could help individuals decide how much to drink on single occasions and how to avoid episodes of intoxication with their attendant health and social risks. The report concluded that regular consumption of between three and four units a day for men, and two to three units for women, does not carry a significant health risk. However, consistently drinking

Cancer registrations per 100,000 population, 2001-2003

	United Kingdom		England	
Selected sites	Male	Female	Male	Female
Stomach	16.2	6.5	15.6	6.2
Lung	64.5	34.8	62.2	33.3
Breast		116.5		116.9
Prostate	89.8		91.4	
Skin	10.7	12.4	10.7	12.2
Leukaemia	12.0	7.2	11.8	7.2
Colorectal	53.8	34.0	52.2	33.0

Data obtained from *Cancer Statistics Register 2003*.

more than four units a day for men, or more than three for women, is not advised as a sensible drinking level because of the progressive health risk it carries. The Government's advice on sensible drinking is now based on these daily benchmarks.

Figure 7.10 Drug use

A report written by Aust, R., Sharp, C. and Goulden, C. (2002) *Prevalence of Drug Use: Key findings from the 2001/2002 British Crime Survey* (London: Home Office) may provide useful background information.

Table 7.12 NHS hospital activity

Data for England are based on finished consultant episodes (FCEs). An FCE is a completed period of care of a patient using a NHS hospital bed, under one consultant within one healthcare provider. If a patient is transferred from one consultant to another, even if this is within the same provider unit, the episode ends and another one begins. The transfer of a patient from one hospital to another with the same consultant and within the same NHS Trust does not end the episode. Data for Wales are based on discharges and deaths. Data for Scotland and Northern Ireland are based on a system where transfers between consultants do not count as a discharge. In Scotland figures include patients transferred from one consultant to another within the same hospital – provided there is a change of speciality (or significant facilities e.g. a change of ward) – but transfers from one hospital to another with the same consultant count as a discharge. New-born babies are included for Northern Ireland but excluded from England, Wales and Scotland. Deaths are included in all four.

For Scotland, figures include NHS beds/activity in joint-user and contractual hospitals; these hospitals account for a relatively small proportion of total NHS activity.

A day case is a patient who comes for investigation, treatment or operation under clinical supervision on a planned non-resident basis, who occupies a bed for part or all of that day, and returns home the same day. Scottish figures also include day cases that have been transferred to or from in-patient care.

An outpatient is a non-resident of a hospital seen by a consultant for treatment or advice at a clinical outpatient department. A new outpatient is one whose first attendance (or only attendance) is part of a continuous series for the same course of treatment falling within the period in question. Each outpatient attendance of a series is included in the year the attendance occurred. People attending more than one department are counted in each department.

In Northern Ireland, the outpatient figures are separated into referrals and consultant-

initiated attendances. It is possible for a first attendance to be initiated by a consultant. The number of attendances in 'new attendances' refers to referrals only, and therefore may not include all new attendances. (Referrals can include self-referrals and requests from other consultants or from staff in Accident and Emergency Departments.)

Mean duration of stay is calculated as the total bed-days divided by the number of ordinary admissions (finished consultant episodes in England and Wales, in-patient discharges (including transfers) in Scotland, and deaths and discharges in Northern Ireland). An ordinary admission is one where the patient is expected to remain in hospital for at least one night. Scottish figures exclude patients with learning disabilities and those requiring non-psychiatric specialities. Population figures are based on estimates for 2003 Strategic Health Authorities for people of all ages.

For Northern Ireland, mid-year population estimates for 2000 have been used. It should be noted that where figures are presented to the nearest whole number, this is to facilitate the calculation of rates and the aggregation of age bands. Cases treated per available bed are for ordinary admissions (in-patient discharges including transfers in Scotland) and do not include day case admissions.

Table 7.13 General practitioners and dentists

The figures for general medical practitioners (GPs) include unrestricted principals and equivalents (UPEs), personal medical service (PMS) and general medical services (GMS), contracted GP's and PMS salaried GPs. An unrestricted principal is a practitioner who provides the full range of general medical services and whose list is not limited to any particular group of people. In a few cases, they may be relieved of the liability for emergency out-of-hours calls from patients that are not their own. Most people have an unrestricted principal as their GP. Doctors may also practise in the general medical services as restricted principals, assistants, associated or GP registrars.

A PMS contracted doctor is a practitioner who provides the full range of services through the PMS pilot contract, and like unrestricted principals such doctors have a patient list. A PMS salaried doctor is employed to work in a PMS pilot, provides the full range of services, and has a list of registered patients.

Other types of general medical practitioners include GP retainers, restricted principals, assistants, associates (Scotland only), GP registrars, salaried doctors (para 52 SFA) and PMS other.

For Wales, GP figures include all practitioners excluding GP registrars, GP retainers and

locums. Figures are not, therefore, comparable with previously published data. For Scotland figures comprise performers (formerly known as unrestricted and restricted principals in GMS and PMS practices). For Northern Ireland figures comprise unrestricted principals, PMS contracted GPs and PMS salaried GPs.

The figures for general dental practitioners include principals, assistants and vocational dental practitioners in the general dental service. Salaried dentists are excluded as are Hospital Dental Services and Community Dental Services. Some dentists have contracts in more than one health authority. These dentists have been counted only once in the authority in which they hold their main contract. Neither the hospital dental service nor the community dental services are included. All Scottish data are provisional.

Information on location of GP surgeries can be found under the Access to Services domain of the Neighbourhood Statistics website:

http://neighbourhood.statistics.gov.uk/ dissemination/datasetList.do?Expand17= 1&$ph=60&updateRequired=true&step= 1&CurrentTreeIndex=-1#17

Table 7.14 Council-supported residents

The figures for England relate to the number of residents who are supported (funded) by Councils with Social Services Responsibilities (CSSR) in residential, independent nursing and other unstaffed homes.

Table HC3 NHS hospital waiting lists

The waiting list figures for England are based on the population of the Strategic Health Authority (SHA). That is, they are based on figures received from health authority-based returns and include all patients resident within the SHA boundary plus all patients registered with GPs who are members of a primary care group or trust (PCG/PCT) for which the SHA is responsible, but are resident in another authority. They exclude patients resident in the StHA, but registered with a GP who is a member of a PCG/PCT responsible to a different SHA. Other exclusions are patients living outside England and privately funded patients waiting for treatment in NHS hospitals. However, they do include NHS-funded patients living in England who are waiting for treatment in Scotland, Wales, Northern Ireland, abroad, and at private hospitals who are not included in the corresponding provider-based return.

In Scotland data are collected by trusts for each individual patient waiting for NHS in-patient or day care treatment. Information on Scottish residents waiting outside Scotland is not collected centrally. Average waiting times are calculated from the waiting time associated with each individual patient record.

Figures from Northern Ireland are provider-based. They include all patients waiting for treatment at Northern Ireland Trusts including private patients and patients from outside Northern Ireland.

Mean waiting time. This is an appropriate calculation for the total waiting times of patients still on the list divided by the corresponding number of people waiting.

Median waiting time. The waiting time of 50 per cent of those patients will be less than the median length. This is a better indicator of the 'average' case since it is generally unaffected by abnormally long or short waiting times at the end of the distribution.

Table HC4 NHS Hospital and Community Health Service directly employed staff

General medical practitioners (i.e. family GPs), general dental practitioners, the staff employed by the practitioners, pharmacists in general pharmaceutical services and staff working in other contracted out services are not included in the figures. Medical and dental staff that are included are those holding permanent, paid (whole-time, part-time, sessional) and/or honorary appointments in NHS hospitals and Community Health services. Figures include clinical assistants and hospital practitioners. Bank staff maintain service delivery by covering staffing shortfalls and fluctuating workloads, and as a consequence their input to the service is difficult to measure.

Previously there has been much confusion over non-medical staff groups. To address this issue the health service has now classified the staff into three key areas:

1. Clinical staff – professionally qualified staff treating patients.

2. Support to Clinical Staff – staff providing direct support to clinical staff, often with direct patient care, who free up the time of clinical staff allowing them more time to treat patients.

3. Staff supporting NHS infrastructure – staff essential to the day-to-day running of the organisations.

Unqualified and trainee nurses, health professionals and scientific staff are included under 'Support to clinical staff' as are ambulance staff. Paramedics are categorised as 'Qualified scientific, therapeutic and technical' staff.

Occasional sessional staff in Community Health medical and dental services for whom no whole-time equivalent is collected are not included. Nursing, midwifery and health visiting staff included healthcare assistants, and excluded nurse teachers and students on '1992' courses. Scientific, therapeutic and technical staff comprises scientific and

professional and technical staff incorporating PAMs. Administration and estates are administration and clerical, senior managers and works staff. Other staff are ancillary, ambulance staff and support staff. All direct care staff are in medical and dental; nursing, midwifery and health visiting; and scientific, therapeutic and technical groups.

Chapter 8: Income and Lifestyles

Tables 8.1, 8.2, 8.11, 8.12, 8.13, 8.14 and Figures 8.9, 8.10, 8.15, 8.16 and 8.19 Expenditure and Food Survey

In April 2001 the Expenditure and Food Survey (EFS) replaced the Family Expenditure Survey (FES) and the National Food Survey (NFS). The EFS is being coded to a new set of expenditure codes based on the United Nations and European classification of consumer goods and services, Classification Of Individual Consumption by Purpose (COICOP). The EFS is a continuous survey conducted by the Office for National Statistics. Three-year averages have been used wherever possible to reduce volatility of the data. However, because of changes in coding on the introduction of EFS, some tables may be presented with only one year's data.

In 2003/04, 7,048 households in the United Kingdom participated in the survey, a response rate of 58 per cent in both Great Britain and Northern Ireland.

The Family Expenditure Survey (FES) was a continuous, random sample survey of private households in the United Kingdom and collected information about incomes as well as detailed information on expenditure. All members of the household aged 16 or over and a sample of those aged 7 to 15 kept individual diaries of all spending for two consecutive weeks. Over the three surveys, held between 1998/99 and 2000/01, a combined total of 20,364 households took part. See the FES annual report, Family Spending (http://www.statistics.gov.uk/statbase/Product.asp?vlnk=361), for a description of the concepts used and details of the definitions of expenditure and income.

The National Food Survey (NFS) was a continuous sample survey in which about 6,000 households per year in Great Britain kept a record of the type, quantity and costs of foods entering the home during a one-week period. Nutrient intakes were estimated from the information collected. Data from the NFS have been presented using calendar years. From 1996, about 700 households in Northern Ireland participated in the survey (though figures quoted in this report and elsewhere still generally cover GB for the sake of continuity). From 1994 data were also available on food eaten out in Great Britain (but not Northern Ireland), although these

were not included earlier in the report to maintain continuity. The last NFS data available are for 2000. The 2000/01 figures use NFS data that has been adjusted to match the EFS.

Table 8.3 Measure of income

The measure of income used in compiling Table 8.3 is that used in the Department for Work and Pensions, *Households Below Average Income* series which is derived from the Family Resources Survey. The income of a household, before housing costs, is defined as the total income of all members of the household after the deduction of income tax, National Insurance contributions, contributions to occupational pension schemes, additional voluntary contributions to personal pensions, maintenance/child support payments, parental contributions to students living away from home and Council Tax.

Income includes earnings from employment and self-employment, social security benefits including Housing Benefit and Tax Credits, occupational and private pensions, investment income, maintenance payments, educational grants, scholarships and top-up loans and some in-kind benefits such as the value of free school meals where received. Income after housing costs is derived by deducting a measure of housing costs from the above income.

No adjustment has been made in Table 8.3 for any differences between regions in cost of living, as the necessary data for adjustment are not available. In the analysis of regions it is therefore assumed that there is no difference in the cost of living between regions, although the 'after housing costs' measure will partly take into account differences in housing costs. As this assumption is unlikely to be true, statements have been sensitivity tested where possible against alternative cost of living regimes. Results suggest that estimates of income before housing costs are not sensitive to regional price differentials, but results after housing costs are. In particular, for London and to a lesser extent the South West, living standards may be overstated, and in Wales, the North East, and in Yorkshire and the Humber living standards may be understated.

Income is adjusted for household size and composition by means of the McClements equivalence scale (see below). This reflects the common sense notion that a household of five will need a higher income than a single person living alone in order to enjoy a comparable standard of living. The total equivalised income of a household is used to represent the income level of every individual in that household; all individuals are then ranked according to this level.

McClements equivalence scale

	Before housing costs	After housing costs
Household member:		
First adult (head)	0.61	0.55
Spouse of head	0.39	0.45
Other second adult	0.46	0.45
Third adult	0.42	0.45
Subsequent adults	0.36	0.40
Each dependant aged:		
0 to 1	0.09	0.07
2 to 4	0.18	0.18
5 to 7	0.21	0.21
8 to 10	0.23	0.23
11 to 12	0.25	0.26
13 to 15	0.27	0.28
16 or over	0.36	0.38

Tables 8.4 and 8.8 Family Resources Survey

The Family Resources Survey (FRS) is a continuous survey of around 29,000 private households in the United Kingdom and is sponsored by the Department for Work and Pension (DWP). Results are based on weighted survey data which are adjusted for non-response. The overall response rate was 64 per cent for 2003/04, but varied regionally. In common with other surveys, there is evidence to suggest some problems of misreporting certain types of benefit, such as the under-reporting of Income Support, where respondents have stated that all money received comes from a single benefit e.g. Retirement Pension or Jobseeker's Allowance. 69 per cent of all households are in receipt of at least one type of benefit. This apparently high figure is because of the inclusion of Retirement Pension and Child Benefit which account for 58 per cent of households (30 per cent and 28 per cent respectively).

Table 8.5 and Figure 8.6 Survey of Personal Incomes

The Survey of Personal Incomes uses a sample of around 400,000 cases drawn from all individuals for whom income tax records are held by HM Revenue & Customs (HMRC). Not all cases in the sample are taxpayers – about 15 per cent do not pay tax because the operation of personal allowances and reliefs removes them from liability. The data in Table 8.5 relate to individuals who have a liability to tax by having income greater than the single person's allowance (£4,615 in 2002/03). Below this threshold, coverage of incomes is incomplete in tax records. A more complete description of the survey appears

on the HMRC website (http://www.hmrc.gov.uk/).

Table 8.5 Distribution of income liable to assessment for tax

The income shown is that which is liable to assessment in the tax year. In most cases, this is the amount earned or receivable in that year, but for business profits and professional earnings the assessments are normally based on the amount of income arising in the trading account ending in the previous year. Those types of income that were specifically exempt from tax, e.g. certain social security benefits, are excluded.

Income is allocated throughout the UK according to the place of residence of the recipient, except for the self-employed, where allocation is according to the business address. For many self-employed people their home is their business address.

The table classifies incomes by range of total income. This is defined as gross income, whether earned or unearned, and includes estimates of employees' superannuation contributions after deducting employment expenses, losses, capital allowances, and any expenses allowable as a deduction from gross income from lettings or overseas investment income.

Superannuation contributions have been estimated and distributed among earners in the Survey of Personal Incomes consistently with information about numbers contracted in or out of the State Earnings Related Pension Scheme and the proportion of their earnings contribution. The coverage of unearned income also includes estimates of that part of the investment income (whose liability to tax at basic rate has been satisfied at source) not known to tax offices. Sampling errors should be allowed for when interpreting small differences in income distributions between regions.

Figure 8.6 Average total income and average income tax payable

Income tax is calculated as the liability for the income tax year, regardless of when the tax may have been paid or how it was collected. The income tax liability shown here is calculated from the individual's total income, including tax credits on dividends, and interest received after the deduction of tax grossed up at the appropriate rate. Allowable reliefs etc., and personal allowances are deducted from total income in order to calculate the tax liability. However, relief given at source on mortgage interest is not deducted, as it cannot be estimated with sufficient reliability below a national level. The averages of total incomes for males and females by Government Office Region are based on all individuals with total income in excess of the single person's allowance,

which was £4,615 in 2002/03. The average income tax payable for males and females by Government Office Region is based on those individuals who are liable to tax.

Figures for United Kingdom include members of HM forces and others who are liable to some UK tax but reside overseas on a long-term basis. In addition, the United Kingdom total includes a very small number of individuals who could not be allocated to a region.

Table 8.8 Households in receipt of benefit

Income support is a non-contributory benefit payable to people working less than 16 hours a week, whose incomes are below the levels (called 'applicable amounts') laid down by Parliament. The applicable amounts generally consist of personal allowances for members of the family and premiums for families, lone parents, pensioners, the disabled and carers. Amounts for certain housing costs (mainly mortgage interest) are also included. Local authorities administer housing benefit; people are eligible only if they are liable to pay rent in respect of the dwelling they occupy as their home. Couples are treated as a single benefit unit. The amount of benefit depends on eligible rent, income, deductions in respect of non-dependants and the applicable amount. 'Eligible rent' is the amount of a tenant's rental liability, which can be met by housing benefit. Payments made by owner-occupiers do not count. Deductions are made for service charged on rent that relates to personal needs.

Local authorities also administer council tax benefit. Generally, it mirrors the housing benefit scheme in the calculation of the claimant's applicable amount, resources and deductions in respect of any non-dependants.

Jobseeker's Allowance (JSA) replaced Unemployment Benefit and Income Support for unemployed people on 7 October 1996. It is payable to people under pensionable age who are available for, and actively seeking, work of at least 40 hours per week. Certain groups of people, including carers, are able to restrict their availability to less than 40 hours depending on their circumstances. There are contribution-based and income-based routes of entry to JSA. Both types of JSA are included under the 'Jobseeker's Allowance' column of the table.

Pension Credit (PC) was introduced in October 2003 as an alternative to Minimum Income Guarantee (MIG) and in April 2003, Working Family Tax Credit (WFTC) and Disability Person's Tax Credits (DPTC) were replaced by Working Tax Credit (WTC) and/or Child Tax Credit (CTC).

Retirement pensions are paid to men aged 65 or over and women aged 60 or over who have paid sufficient National Insurance contributions over their working life. A wife who cannot claim a pension in her own right may qualify on the basis of her husband's contributions.

Incapacity Benefit replaced sickness and invalidity benefits from 13 April 1995. It is paid to people who are assessed as being incapable of work and who meet the contribution conditions. The figures do not include expenditure for Statutory Sick Pay (SSP).

Industrial injuries include pensions, gratuities and sundry allowances for disablement and specified deaths arising from industrial causes.

Child Benefit is normally paid in respect of children up to the age of 16. Benefit may continue up to age 19 for children in full-time education up to A level standard; 16- and 17-year-olds are also eligible for a short period after leaving school.

A brief description of the main features of the various benefits paid in Great Britain is set out in *Social Security Statistics* (published annually by Department for Work and Pensions). Detailed information on benefits paid in Northern Ireland is contained in *Northern Ireland Annual Abstract of Statistics* and *Northern Ireland Social Security Statistics*.

Figure 8.10 Children's spending
The data for 2001-2004 were all collected from the Expenditure and Food Survey; however they are not directly comparable with the previous three-year average, which would include data from both the Family Expenditure Survey (2000-2001) and the Expenditure and Food Survey (2001-2003).

The data presented are £ per child per week solely attributable to children aged 7 to 15 years living in responding households. Children were asked to record all purchases made with their own money, including money spent on school dinners, and on fares to and from school. Money spent directly by the parent on these items is excluded.

Figure 8.9, Tables 8.11 and 8.12 Household expenditure
Expenditure excludes savings or investments (e.g. life assurance premiums), income tax payments, National Insurance contributions and the part of rent paid by housing benefit. Housing expenditure of households living in owner-occupied dwellings consists of the payments by these households for council tax (rates in Northern Ireland), water, ground rent, etc., insurance of the structure and mortgage interest payments. Mortgage capital repayments and amounts paid for the outright purchase of the dwelling or for major structural alterations are not included as housing expenditure.

Estimates of household expenditure on a few items are below those that might be expected by comparison with other sources e.g. alcoholic drink, tobacco and, to a lesser extent, confectionery and ice cream.

Table IL1 UK 2000 Time Use Survey
The results in Table IL1 are taken from the UK 2000 Time Use Survey and show the time and participation rates for an average day. The minutes per day are the average time for all people and the participation rates show the proportion of people who actually take part in the activity at some point during their day. The amount of time spent in each activity by just those who participate can be calculated by ((100 + participation rate)/100)*average time for all people.

The results presented are for combined primary and secondary (i.e. where respondents were doing two things at the same time) activities. This has been done because TV viewing, radio and music listening and reading often happen at the same time as another activity (for example reading on the train) and to get a true measure of the time spent in these activities it is sensible to look at the total time. The other activities in this table have almost no secondary time (i.e. they are usually done as a single activity).

Table IL2 The National Lottery grants
From the start of 1995 to the end of 2004, 4,136 National Lottery grants were awarded worth a total of £945 million. These were made throughout the UK apart from 97 grants worth £8.6 million that went to overseas projects.

From 18 May 2002, the National Lottery was also known as Lotto.

Chapter 9: Crime and Justice

Tables 9.1, 9.2, 9.3, 9.7, 9.8 and CJ2 Offences
Figures are compiled from police returns to the Home Office or directly from court computer systems; from police returns to the Scottish Executive Justice Department and from statistics supplied by the Police Service of Northern Ireland.

Recorded crime statistics broadly cover the more serious offences. Up to March 1998 most indictable and triable-either-way offences were included, as well as some summary ones; from April 1998, all indictable and triable-either-way offences were included, plus a few closely related summary ones. Recorded offences are the most readily available measures of the incidence of crime, but do not necessarily indicate the true level of crime. Many less serious offences are not reported to the police and cannot therefore be recorded, while some offences are not recorded because of lack of evidence. Moreover, the propensity of the public to

report offences to the police is influenced by a number of factors and may change over time.

In England, Wales and Northern Ireland, indictable offences cover those offences that must or may be tried by jury in the Crown Court, and include the more serious offences. Summary offences are those for which a defendant would normally be tried at a magistrates' court and are generally less serious; the majority of motoring offences fall into this category. In general, in Northern Ireland non-indictable offences are dealt with at a magistrates' court. Some indictable offences can also be dealt with there.

England and Wales
In England and Wales, Home Office counting rules for recorded crime were revised with effect from 1 April 2002, principally to take account of the National Crime Recording Standard (NCRS) which was produced by the Association of Chief Police Officers (ACPO) in consultation with the Home Office. The Standard aims to promote greater consistency between police forces in recording crime and to take a more victim-oriented approach to crime recording. The national picture for total crime in England and Wales demonstrates an overall NCRS impact of 10 per cent on the recorded crime statistics for 2002/03. Crimes counted in 2002/03 were 10 per cent higher than they would have been under the pre-NCRS recording, reflecting the change in recording practice, rather than a real increase in crime. Estimates of the percentage impact of the NCRS on recorded crime vary considerably between offence types: violence against the person (23 per cent), robbery (3 per cent), all theft (9 per cent), criminal damage (9 per cent).

The revisions will significantly increase the numbers of crimes in the recorded crime count and were introduced across all police forces from April 2002. Some police forces implemented the principles of the standard in advance of this date, and this will have had some effect on the recorded crime statistics reported here. There has also been a more general impetus over recent years both from ACPO and from the Home Office to increase the recording of crimes reported to the police, and this will also have impacted on the recorded crime figures. As with the 1998 counting rule changes, it may take several years for the changes to bed down.

In Scotland the term 'crimes' is generally used for the more serious criminal acts (roughly equivalent to indictable offences); the less serious are termed 'offences'. In general, the Procurator Fiscal makes the decision as to which court a case should be tried in or, for lesser offences, whether alternatives to prosecution such as a fixed penalty might be considered. Certain crimes, such as rape and murder, must be tried by a jury in the High Court; cases can also be tried by jury in the Sheriff Court. The majority of cases (97 per cent) are tried summarily (without a jury), either in the Sheriff Court or in the lay District Court.

Cautions

If a person admits to committing an offence he or she may be given a formal police caution by, or on the instruction of, a senior police officer as an alternative to court proceedings. The figures exclude informal warnings given by the police, written warnings issued for motoring offences and warnings given by non-police bodies, e.g. a department store in the case of shoplifting. Cautions by the police are not available in Scotland, but warnings may be issued on behalf of the Procurator Fiscal.

Tables 9.2 and 9.11 Crime surveys

The British Crime Survey (BCS) was conducted by the Home Office in 1982, 1984, 1988, 1992, 1994, 1996, 1998 and 2000, and annually on a continual basis from 2001. From 2001/02 the survey has measured crimes experienced by respondents in the 12 months prior to their interview, including those not reported to the police. The survey also covers other matters of Home Office interest including fear of crime, contacts with the police, and drug misuse. The 2003/04 survey had a nationally representative sample of 37,213 respondents in England and Wales with an additional 3,318 ethnic boost sample and 2,297 youth boost sample. The sample was drawn from the Small User Postcode Address File – a listing of all postal delivery points. The response rate in the core sample was 74 per cent. The first results from the 2003/04 sweep of the BCS were published in July 2004.

Scotland participated in sweeps of the BCS in 1982 and 1988 and ran its own Scottish Crime Surveys (SCS) in 1993, 1996, 2000 and 2003 based on nationally representative samples of around 5,000 respondents aged 16 or over interviewed in their homes. In addition around 400 young people aged between 12 and 15 completed questionnaires in each of the surveys. The sample was drawn from addresses randomly generated from the Postcode Address file. Both the 1993 and 1996 surveys had response rates of 77 per cent, the 2000 survey had a response rate of 72 per cent and the 2003 survey had a response rate of 68 per cent. The results of the 2003 SCS were published in December 2004.

The Northern Ireland Crime Survey (NICS) was conducted on behalf of the Northern Ireland Office (NIO) in 1994/95, 1998, 2001 and 2003/04. Closely mirroring the format and questions of the BCS, the fieldwork for NICS 2003/04 was conducted between August 2003 and early April 2004, with a recall

period ranging from August 2002 to March 2004. 3,104 people aged 16 years and above participated in the survey. Their addresses were randomly sampled from the Valuation and Lands Agency domestic property database. The response rate was approximately 70 per cent.

In each of the surveys, respondents answered questions about offences against their household (such as theft or damage of household property) and about offences against them personally (such as assault or robbery). However, none of the surveys provides a complete count of crime. Many offence types cannot be covered in a household victim-oriented survey (for example shoplifting, fraud or drug offences). Crime surveys are also prone to various forms of error, mainly to do with the difficulty of ensuring that samples are representative, the frailty of respondents' memories, their reticence to talk about their experiences as victims, and their failure to realise an incident is relevant to the survey.

Table 9.3 Detection rates

In England, Wales and Northern Ireland detected offences recorded by the police include offences for which individuals have been charged, summonsed or cautioned; those admitted and taken into consideration when individuals are tried for other offences, and others where the police can take no action for various reasons. In Scotland a revised definition of 'cleared up' came into effect from 1 April 1996. Under the revised definition a crime or offence is regarded as cleared up where there is sufficient evidence under Scots law to justify consideration of criminal proceedings notwithstanding that a report is not submitted to the Procurator Fiscal because either:

a) by standing agreement with the procurator fiscal, the police warn the accused owing to the minor nature of the offence, or

b) reporting is inappropriate because of the age of the accused, death of the accused or other similar circumstances.

The detection rate is the ratio of offences cleared up in the year to offences recorded in the year. Some offences detected may relate to offences recorded in previous years. There is some variation between police forces in the emphasis placed on certain of the methods listed above and, as some methods are more resource-intensive than others, this can have a significant effect on a force's overall detection rate.

In April 1999, there was a change in the way detections are counted, with some circumstances no longer qualifying as detections. The new instructions provide more precise and rigorous criteria for recording a detection, with

the underlying emphasis on the successful result of a police investigation. The most significant of these criteria is that there must be significant evidence to charge the suspect with a crime (whether or not a charge is actually imposed) so that, if given in court, it would be likely to result in a conviction. Detections obtained by the interview of a convicted prisoner are no longer included, and any detections where no further police action is taken generally have to be approved by a senior police officer or the Crown Prosecution Service. An offence is said to be cleared up in the following circumstances:

- a person has been charged or summonsed for the offence

- a person has been cautioned

- the offence has been taken into consideration (TIC) by the court

- or where no further action is taken and the case is not proceeded with because, for example, the offender is under the age of criminal responsibility, the offender has died, the victim or an essential witness is permanently unable to give evidence, or no useful purpose would be served by proceeding with the charge.

With the effect of the National Crime Recording Standard (NCRS), the detection rate in 2002/03 was 23.5 per cent, slightly higher than the rate in 2001/02 (23.4 per cent). However, the full introduction of the NCRS in April 2002 may have depressed the current detection rate. Precise quantification is not possible, but on a comparable basis to the pre-NCRS crime count, the detection rate in 2002/03 is estimated to have been between 24 and 26 per cent.

Table 9.5 Seizures of controlled drugs

The figures in this table, which are compiled from returns to the Home Office, relate to seizures made by the police and officials of HM Customs and Excise, and to drugs controlled under the *Misuse of Drugs Act 1971*. The Act divides drugs into three main categories according to their harmfulness. A full list of drugs in each category is given in Schedule 2 to the *Misuse of Drugs Act 1971*, as amended by Orders in Council.

Table 9.8 People found guilty of offences

In England, Wales and Northern Ireland the term 'suspended sentence' is known as 'fully suspended sentence' and 'immediate custody' includes unsuspended sentences of imprisonment and sentence to detention in a young offender institution. Fully suspended sentences are not available to Scottish courts.

Tables 9.9 Sentencing

Imprisonment is the custodial sentence for adult offenders. *The Criminal Justice Act*

1991 abolished remission and substantially changed the parole scheme in England and Wales.

Those serving sentences of under four years, imposed on or after 1 October 1992, are subject to automatic conditional release and are released, subject to certain criteria, halfway through their sentence.

Home detention curfews result in selected prisoners in England and Wales being released up to two months early with a tag that monitors their presence during curfew hours. Those serving sentences of four years or longer are considered for discretionary conditional release after having served half their sentence, but are automatically released at the two-thirds point of sentence.

The *Crime (Sentences) Act 1997* implemented on 1 October 1997 included automatic life sentences for people aged 18 and over sentenced in England and Wales for second serious violent or sexual offences unless circumstances are exceptional. All offenders sentenced in England and Wales to a sentence of 12 months or more are supervised in the community until the three-quarter point of sentence.

In Scotland, the release of prisoners sentenced after 1 October 1993 is governed by the *Prisoners and Criminal Proceedings (Scotland) Act 1993*. Under the 1993 Act prisoners serving determinate sentences of less than four years are released unconditionally after having served half of their sentence. Those serving sentences of four years or more (i.e. long-term sentences) are eligible for parole at half sentence. If parole is not granted then they will automatically be released on licence at the two-thirds point of sentence, subject to any additional days for breaches of prison rules. The licence remains in force until the entire period specified in the sentence expires.

In addition, there is provision under the *Crime and Disorder Act 1998* for courts to impose additional post-release supervision (known as an extended sentence) of up to ten years for sex offenders, and five years for violent offenders who have received a long-term sentence. During the period of extended sentence, the offender must comply with licence conditions. Extended sentences can also be imposed for sex offenders who received a short-term custodial sentence. Similarly, the court has a power to impose a supervised release order for those who received a short-term sentence for a violent offence, which ensures social work supervision for a period following release. Where a prisoner released from a long-term sentence fails to comply with the terms of his or her licence, there are options available to the Courts and to Scottish Ministers for dealing with reports of a breach of licence.

One of these is to revoke the licence and order the prisoner's return or recall to custody. This may mean the prisoner being detained until the sentence expiry date. A life sentence prisoner sentenced in Scotland may be released on licence subject to supervision and is always liable to recall.

In Northern Ireland the maximum length of sentence that can be given by a magistrate is 12 months for an indictable offence or 18 months if the person is convicted of more than one indictable offence. Following the enactment of the *Life Sentences (NI) Order 2001*, a court passing a life sentence must state the period which should be served to satisfy the requirements of retribution and deterrence. This is referred to as the 'tariff'. Following the expiry of the tariff a life sentence prisoner may require the Secretary of State to refer his or her case to the Life Sentence Review Commissioners for consideration for release. Prison sentences are rarely served in full. Remission is the cancellation of part of a term of imprisonment and may be granted at up to 50 per cent of the sentence depending upon the circumstances. The Custody Probation Order is unique to Northern Ireland, reflecting the different regime which applies in respect of remission and the general absence of release on licence. It is only available where a period in custody of over 12 months would otherwise be justified. The custodial sentence is followed by a period of supervision by a probation officer for a period between 12 months and three years.

Disposals for mentally disordered offenders: various hospital, community and custodial disposals are available to the courts. In some cases a hospital order, which sends the offender to hospital until such time as treatment is no longer required, may be appropriate.

A hospital order may be combined with a restriction order for offenders who pose a risk to the public, in which case Home Office or Scottish Ministers' consent is needed for release or transfer. A new disposal, the 'hospital direction', was introduced in 1997. The court, when imposing a period of imprisonment, can direct that the offender be sent initially to hospital for treatment. Upon recovery from the mental disorder, the offender is sent to prison to serve the balance of his or her sentence.

Fully suspended sentences may only be passed in exceptional circumstances. In England, Wales and Northern Ireland, sentences of imprisonment of two years or less may be fully suspended. A court should not pass a suspended sentence unless a sentence of imprisonment would be appropriate in the absence of a power to suspend. The result of suspending a sentence is that it will not take effect, unless during

the period specified the offender is convicted of another offence punishable with imprisonment. Suspended sentences are not available in Scotland.

Fines

The *Criminal Justice Act 1993* introduced new arrangements on 20 September 1993 whereby courts are now required to fit an amount for the fine which reflects the seriousness of the offence, but which also takes account of an offender's means. This system replaced the more formal unit fines scheme included in the *Criminal Justice Act 1991*. The Act also introduced the power for courts to arrange deduction of fines from income benefit for those offenders receiving such benefits. The *Law Reform (Miscellaneous Provision) (Scotland) Act 1990* as amended by the *Criminal Procedure (Scotland) Act 1995* provides for the use of supervised attendance orders by selected courts in Scotland. The *Criminal Procedure (Scotland) Act 1995* also makes it easier for courts to impose a supervised attendance order in the event of a default, and enables the court to impose a supervised attendance order in the first instance for 16- and 17-year-olds.

Custody Probation Order: an order introduced uniquely to Northern Ireland by the *Criminal Justice (Northern Ireland) Order 1996*. It reflects the different regime that applies in respect of remission and the general absence of release on licence. The custodial sentence is followed by a period of supervision for a period of between 12 months and three years.

Table 9.10 ASBOs

Anti-social behaviour orders (ASBOs) were introduced by section 1 of the *Crime and Disorder Act 1998* in England and Wales and have been available since April 1999. The powers to impose ASBOs were strengthened and extended by the *Police Reform Act 2002*, which introduced orders made on conviction in criminal proceedings, orders in county court proceedings and interim orders. Orders can now also extend across any defined part of England and Wales.

ASBOs are civil orders that exist to protect the public from behaviour that causes, or is likely to cause, harassment, alarm or distress. An order contains conditions prohibiting the offender from specific anti-social acts or entering defined areas and is effective for a minimum of two years. The orders are not criminal penalties and are not intended to punish the offender. An order should not be viewed as an option of last resort.

Chapter 10: Transport

Table T1 Age of household cars

This refers to the main or only car available to the household, and applies to the vehicle with the greatest annual mileage.

Tables T1, T2, and 10.5 and Figures 10.3, 10.6 and 10.7 National Travel Survey

The National Travel Survey (NTS) is the only comprehensive national source of travel information for Great Britain that links different kinds of travel with the characteristics of travellers and their families. The 1985/86 survey ran from July 1985 to June 1986 and collected data successfully from 10,266 households.

There were no National Travel Surveys held between July 1986 and July 1988.

Since July 1988, the NTS has been conducted on a small-scale continuous basis with an annual sample about one-third the size of the 1985/86 survey. Data from the continuous survey are normally aggregated into three-year blocks for publication. From about 3,400 households in Great Britain each year, every member provides personal information (for example, age, sex, working status, driving licence, season ticket) and details of journeys carried out in a sample week, including purpose of journey, method of travel, time of day, length, duration and cost of any tickets bought.

The time periods for presenting NTS data are as follows:

At national level	Calendar year
At regional level	Up to 2001 because of small sample sizes the data were averaged over a three-year period.
	From 2002 because the sample size has increased but is still relatively small the data are averaged over a two-year period.

Travel included in the NTS covers all journeys by British residents (living in private households) within Great Britain for personal reasons, including travel in the course of work, for example, a doctor on his or her rounds or a business executive travelling to a meeting. It does not include journeys made by people whose work is to travel (such as bus drivers, post deliverers and delivery workers).

Most personal travel over 50 yards is included, including walking. However, to reduce the burden on respondents, short walks of less than a mile are only recorded on the last day of the diary. These walks are grossed up by a factor of 7 when publishing data.

In the NTS a trip is defined as a one-way course of travel having a single main purpose. It is the basic unit of personal travel in the survey. A round journey is split into two trips, with the first ending at a convenient point about halfway round as a notional stopping point for the outward destination. A stage is that portion of a journey defined by the use of a specific method of transport or of a specific ticket (a new stage being defined if either the mode or ticket changes).

The purpose of a trip is normally taken to be the activity at the destination, unless that destination is 'home' in which case the purpose is defined by the origin of the trip. The classification of 'trips to work' is also dependent on the origin of the trip. A trip cannot have two separate purposes; subsidiary purposes (such as a stop to buy a newspaper) are disregarded.

The main mode used for trips is that which is used for the longest stage of the trip (by length); the mode is that used for a stage within a trip. The definition of a 'trip' is not the same as a 'journey'.

The following purposes are distinguished:

Commuting
Trips to a usual place of work from home, or from work to home.

Business
Trips in the course of work, including a trip in the course of work which involves returning to work. This includes all work trips by people with no usual place of work (e.g. site workers) and those who work at or from home.

Education
Trips to or from school or college, etc. by full-time students, students on day release and part-time students following vocational courses.

Shopping
All trips to shops or from shops to home, even when there is no intention to buy.

Personal business
Visits to services, for example hairdressers, launderettes, dry-cleaners, betting shops, solicitors, banks, estate agents, libraries, churches; or for medical consultations or treatment, or for eating and drinking unless the main purpose is entertainment or social.

Escorting
Used when the traveller has no purpose of his or her own, other than to escort or accompany another person; for example, taking a child to school.

Leisure
Travel for leisure purposes is normally included. However, journeys that are themselves a form of recreation are not. Travel by foot away from the public highway is excluded unless both the surface is paved or tarred and there is unrestricted access. Thus walks across open countryside on unsurfaced paths are excluded; and so are walks in pedestrian precincts or parks that are closed at night.

Table 10.10 Expenditure
See Tables T2, 10.11, 10.12 and 10.13 for definitions of types of road.

Current maintenance including routine and winter maintenance: Previously this showed figures for 'routine and winter maintenance and public lighting'. The Highways Agency is no longer able to separately identify this expenditure. Figures are now shown under a new heading and cannot be compared with those in earlier versions.

DBFO shadow tolls: Payments to contractors under DBFO (Design, Build, Finance and Operate) schemes.

Tables 10.11 and 10.13; Figure 10.12 Roads
Major roads: motorways and 'A' roads.

Principal roads: important regional or local roads for which local authorities are the highway authorities.

'A' Roads: trunk and principal roads (excluding motorways).

Minor roads: comprise B, C and unclassified roads.

The Department for Transport has introduced an Urban/Rural classification for roads, which replaces the previously used 'Built-up' and 'Non-built-up' categories. This change in definition means that data for 2002 and subsequently can not be compared with earlier years.

Definitions used in Regional Trends 38 and 39:

Urban roads: major and minor roads within an urban area with a population of 10,000 or more.

Rural roads: major roads and minor roads outside urban areas having a population of less than 10,000.

Previous categories:

Built-up roads: all those having a speed limit of 40 mph or less (irrespective of whether there are buildings or not).

Non-built-up roads: all those with a speed limit in excess of 40 mph.

The previous categorisation created difficulties in producing meaningful disaggregated traffic estimates because an increasing number of clearly rural roads were subject to a 40mph speed limit for safety reasons. The urban/rural split of roads is largely determined by whether roads lie within the boundaries of urban areas with a population of 10,000 or more, with adjustments in some cases for major roads at the boundary.

Tables 10.11 and Figure 10.12 Traffic flow

The figures for 1993 to 2004 have been calculated on a different basis from years prior to 1993. Therefore, figures prior to 1993 are not directly comparable with estimates for later years. Estimates on the new basis for 1993 and subsequent years were first published by the Department for Transport in May 2003 in *Traffic in Great Britain Q1 2003SB(03)6*.

Details of the methodology used to compile the road traffic estimates are available at 'How the Road Traffic Estimates are made' at

http://www.dft.gov.uk/stellent/groups/dft_transstats/documents/page/dft_transstats_027415.hcsp

Tables 10.4, 10.6 and 10.8
The Labour Force Survey

The Labour Force Survey (LFS) is a quarterly sample survey of households living at private addresses in Great Britain. The LFS is a large sample survey in which around 10,000 people aged 16 and over are interviewed each week. Its purpose is to provide information on the UK labour market that can then be used to develop, manage, evaluate and report on labour market policies.

The survey seeks information on respondents' personal circumstances and their labour market status during a specific reference period, normally a period of one week or four weeks (depending on the topic) immediately prior to the interview. For further details of the LFS consult notes to Chapter 5.

Tables 10.13, 10.14, 10.15 Road accidents

An accident is one involving personal injury occurring on the public highway (including footways) in which a road vehicle is involved and which becomes known to the police within 30 days. The vehicle need not be moving and it need not be in collision with anything. A fatal accident is one in which injuries were sustained that caused death within 30 days of the incident.

A serious injury is one for which a person is detained in hospital as an in-patient, or sustains any of the following injuries whether or not he or she is detained in hospital: fractures, concussion, internal injuries, crushing, severe cuts and lacerations, severe general shock requiring medical treatment, or injuries causing death 30 days or more after the accident. There are many reasons why accident rates per head of population (for all roads) and per 100 million vehicle kilometres (for major roads) vary from one area to another, including the mix of pedestrian and vehicle traffic and the considerable differences in vehicle ownership. In addition, an area that 'imports' large numbers of visitors or commuters will have a relatively

high proportion of accidents related to vehicles or drivers from outside the area. A rural area of low population density but high road mileage can be expected, other things being equal, to have lower than average accident rates.

Table T3 Seaports

The Coastal regions are defined as:

East Coast: Orkneys to Harwich inclusive

Thames and Kent: Colchester to Folkestone inclusive

South Coast: Newhaven to Lands End

West Coast: Lands End to Stornoway.

Chapter 11: Environment

Tables 11.1, 11.2, 11.5 to 11.9, and E3
The Environment Agency

The Environment Agency for England and Wales was formally created on 8 August 1995 by the *Environment Act 1995*. It took up its statutory duties on 1 April 1996. The Agency brings together the functions previously carried out by the National Rivers Authority, Her Majesty's Inspectorate of Pollution, the waste regulatory functions of 83 local authorities and a small number of units from the then Department of the Environment dealing with the aspects of waste regulation and contaminated land. One of the key reasons for setting up the Agency was to promote a more coherent and integrated approach to environmental management.

Table 11.6, 11.7 and E2 Water quality of rivers and canals

The quality of rivers and canal waters in the United Kingdom is monitored in a series of separate national surveys in England and Wales, Scotland and Northern Ireland. In England and Wales the National Rivers Authority (now superseded by the Environment Agency) developed and introduced the General Quality Assessment (GQA) scheme to provide a rigorous and objective method for assessing the basic chemical quality of rivers and canals based on three determinands: dissolved oxygen, biochemical oxygen demand (BOD) and ammoniacal nitrogen. The GQA scheme classifies stretches of river into six categories (A-F) of chemical quality, and these in turn have been grouped into the broader categories of good (classes A and B), fair (classes C and D), poor (E) and bad (F). In Northern Ireland, the grading of the 1991 and 1995 surveys is also based on the GQA scheme.

The biological quality of river and canal waters in England, Wales and Northern Ireland is assessed by the River Invertebrate Prediction and Classification System (RIVPACS). This is a computer program that measures quality by monitoring the small animals (invertebrates) that live in, or on the beds of, rivers and canals.

In Scotland, the classification system is not directly comparable with either the GQA or RIVPACS; the same numeric quality band boundaries are applied, but resulting bands are differently combined and described. The Scottish River Classification Scheme results in a single classification class outcome which incorporates biological, chemical and aesthetic data. Also reported is the length of 'unclassified' river stretches – which are river stretches that are not routinely monitored because they are remote from significant discharges and expected to be of good quality.

For presentational purposes information for Scotland is given in a separate table (E2).

Table 11.10 Land use

Details of changes in land use are recorded for the Office of the Deputy Prime Minister by Ordnance Survey (OS) as part of its map revision work in England. The data recorded by OS in any one year depend on OS resources and how these are deployed on different types of map revision survey. The main consequence of this is that physical development (e.g. new houses) tends to be recorded relatively sooner than changes between other uses (e.g. between agriculture and forestry), some of which may not be recorded for some years. The statistics are best suited to analyses of changes to urban uses and of the recycling of land already in urban uses.

Table 11.13 Designated areas

National Parks, Areas of Outstanding Natural Beauty, Defined Heritage Coasts and National Scenic Areas in Scotland, are the major areas designated by legislation to protect their landscape importance. Green Belts have been designated in England, Scotland and Northern Ireland to restrict the sprawl of built-up areas onto previously undeveloped land and to preserve the character of historic towns. Other areas, such as Sites (or Areas) of Special Scientific Interest, National Nature Reserves, Special Protection Areas and Marine Nature Reserves, are protected for their value as wildlife habitat. The dates provided for designated areas are updated every year even if the data itself have not been, except in the case of Green Belts which have not been revised since 1997.

Chapter 12: Regional Accounts

Tables 12.1, 12.3, 12.5, 12.6, Figure 12.2, and Map 12.4 Gross value added (GVA)

Regional GVA is measured as the sum of incomes earned from the production of goods and services in the region. Regional estimates are calculated for individual income components: compensation of employees (formerly known as income from employment); gross operating surplus; mixed income; and taxes (less subsidies) on production. The GVA estimates presented here are based on the European System of Accounts 1995 (ESA95). The figures for all United Kingdom NUTS1 areas are consistent with the UK National Accounts (Blue Book) 2005.

The industry definitions used are in accordance with the Standard Industrial Classification Revised 2003 (SIC2003).

Under the European System of Accounts 1995 (ESA95), the term gross value added (GVA) is used to denote estimates that were previously known as gross domestic product (GDP) at basic prices. Under ESA95, the term GDP denotes GVA plus taxes (less subsidies) on products, i.e. at market prices. UK Regional Accounts are currently only published at basic prices so should be referred to as GVA rather than GDP.

Regional GVA is currently calculated both on a workplace and a residence basis. Residence-based GVA allocates the incomes of individuals to their place of residence, whereas workplace GVA allocates their incomes to where they work. The regional GVA estimates are provided on both a residence and workplace basis. These differ from the residence-based estimates only in London, the South East and the East of England.

The methodology and data sources used in compiling regional gross value added were described in a booklet in the Studies in Official Statistics series, No 31, *Regional Accounts* (HMSO) and more recently in a methodological article included in the December 2000 edition of *Economic Trends* (TSO).

GVA data for NUTS levels 2 and 3 areas, and by industry at NUTS1, are currently only available up to 2003. The NUTS levels 2 and 3 GVA estimates are only produced on a workplace basis.

Tables 12.7, 12.10 and Figures 12.8 and 12.9 Household income and gross disposable household income

The household sector covers people living in traditional households as well as those living in institutions. The latter (about 1.5 per cent of the UK population) includes people living in retirement homes, hostels, boarding houses, hotels and prisons. The household sector also includes sole trader enterprises and non-profit institutions serving households (NPISHs) which do not have separate legal status, examples of the latter being charities and most universities.

Total household income is the sum of incomes for the sector, i.e. wages and salaries, pensions and social security benefits. Gross disposable household income (GDHI) is the total income less certain cost items such as tax payments and social security contributions. In essence, this is the value of the resources that the household sector actually has available to spend.

The consumption of fixed capital (i.e. the depreciation in value of property) is not deducted from either form of income at the regional level and both are expressed at current prices.

In addition to these areas an estimate for a pseudo-geography called extra-regio is also included in the regional household sector accounts. Included in this area are the earnings of UK residents employed in UK enclaves in other countries, mainly civil servants, diplomats and armed forces.

Household sector extra-regio income differs from that included in regional GVA. The biggest difference between the two is that the earnings of offshore (North Sea) oil workers are not classified as extra-regio in Household Income, rather it is allocated to mainland UK regions. Regional Household Income is derived using a variety of data sources. The methodology reflects the aims and definitions of ESA95.

The estimates published here are consistent with the national accounts published in the *UK National Accounts (Blue Book) 2004*. Like the GVA estimates, they are based on ESA95.

The methodologies and data sources used in compiling regional household income were described in the August 2001 and May 2002 editions of *Economic Trends*.

Tables RA1 and RA2 Individual consumption expenditure (ICE)

ICE measures spending by households and NPISHs in a region. The estimates are consistent with *UK National Accounts (Blue Book) 2000*, and are also based on ESA95.

Regional estimates of ICE complement Household Income (discussed above); together they complete the current account of that sector. The margins of error on both sets of figures make it unwise to compare the two in practice.

Estimates of ICE are published by category of expenditure using the Classification of Individual Consumption by Purpose (COICOP). The COICOP classification structure is defined by the ESA95 and estimates of ICE are therefore available on a consistent basis across all EU Member States.

The methodologies and data sources used in compiling ICE estimates were also described in the 2000 edition of *Economic Trends*.

Chapter 13: Industry and Agriculture

Maps 13.1 and 13.2, Tables 13.3, IA1, 13.4 and IA5

The regional gross value added (GVA) estimates are consistent with the national accounts published in the *United Kingdom National Accounts 2005*. Under the European system of accounts 1995 (ESA95) the term GVA is used to denote estimates that were

previously known as gross domestic product (GDP) at basic prices.

GVA percentages for industry and services do not sum to exactly 100 per cent owing to the adjustment of data for financial intermediation services indirectly measured (FISIM). FISIM is an indirect measure of the value of the services for which financial intermediaries do not charge explicitly. The total value of FISIM is measured as the total property income receivable by financial intermediaries other than insurance corporations and pension funds less their total interest payable.

Excluding extra-regio
The GVA for extra-regio comprises compensation of employees and gross operating surplus, which cannot be assigned to the regions.

The industrial breakdown used is in accordance with the Standard Industrial Classification Revised 2003 (SIC2003), for data for 2003 onwards. Data before that date is with the Standard Industrial Classification (SIC) Revised 1992. Agriculture, industry and services are broken down as follows:

AGRICULTURE:

Section A	Agriculture, hunting and forestry
Section B	Fishing

INDUSTRY:

Section C	Mining and quarrying
Section D	Manufacturing
Section E	Electricity, gas and water supply
Section F	Construction

SERVICES:

Section G	Wholesale and retail trade; repair of motor vehicles, motorcycles and personal and household goods
Section H	Hotels and restaurants
Section I	Transport, storage and communications
Section J	Financial intermediation
Section K	Real estate, renting and business activities
Section L	Public administration and defence; compulsory social security
Section M	Education
Section N	Health and social work
Section O	Other community, social and personal service activities

Tables 13.3, IA1 and Map 13.11 Inter-Departmental Business Register
The Inter-Departmental Business Register (IDBR) is a structured list of business units

used for the selection, mailing and grossing of statistical inquiries, as well as for analysis. Information is provided at both the enterprise and local unit level. The enterprise is the level at which the business has some control or independence; the local units are the individual sites (or factories, shops etc.) operated by the enterprise. The IDBR covers more than 99 per cent of UK output, and covers around two-thirds of the total stock of enterprises. The register comprises information on companies, partnerships, sole proprietors, public authorities, Central Government departments, local authorities and non-profit bodies. The main administrative sources for the IDBR are HM Revenue and Customs (formed from HM Customs and Excise and Inland Revenue) for VAT information (passed to the ONS under the *Value Added Tax Act 1994*), and Inland Revenue for PAYE information (transferred under the *Finance Act 1969*). Other information is added to the register for ONS statistical purposes.

Tables 13.4 and IA2 Annual Business Inquiry

The Annual Business Inquiry is a sample survey that covers UK businesses including those engaged in the production and construction industries (formerly the Annual Inquiry into Production). Production and construction industries are Sections C to F of the SIC Revised 1992 and SIC Revised 2003.

Businesses often conduct their activities at more than one address (local unit) but it is not usually possible for them to provide the full range of data for each. For this reason, data are usually collected at the enterprise level. Gross value added (GVA) is estimated for each local unit by apportioning the total GVA for the business in proportion to the total employment at each local unit using employment from the IDBR.

GVA at basic prices is defined as:

The value of total sales and work done, adjusted by any changes during the year in work in progress and goods on hand for sale

less: the value of purchases, adjusted by any changes in the stocks of material, stores and fuel etc.

less: payments for industrial services received

less: net duties and levies etc.

less: the cost of non-industrial services, rates and motor vehicle licences.

It includes taxes on production (like business rates) and net subsidies but excludes taxes *less* subsidies on production (for example, VAT and excise duty). GVA per head is derived by dividing the estimated GVA by the total number of people employed. The data include estimates for businesses not responding, or not required to respond, to the inquiry.

Table 13.5 Export and import trade with EU and non-EU countries

Data are sourced from customs declarations submitted in respect of trade with countries outside the European Union and 'Supplementary Declarations' submitted under the Intrastat EU statistical reporting system. While all imports and exports outside the EU are recorded, the Intrastat system is based on returns from registered companies that exceed a set annual threshold in their trading with the EU (set at £233,000 for 2003 and £221,000 for 2004). Trade is regionalised according to the postcode of declarants and adjustments are made to address the distortion caused by head offices reporting on behalf of their group.

Improvements to the regional trade statistics methodology have been carried out during 2003 to ensure that the total trade reported for *Regional Trade Statistics* mirror the trade published for the UK as a whole (the *'UK Overseas Trade Statistics'*). Certain goods, such as North Sea crude oil, ships and aircraft stores, and transactions involving overseas companies with no place of business in the UK, cannot be allocated to a specific area within the UK. This trade is shown as 'unallocatable trade' ('Unknown' region in HM Customs and Excise press release). Because of these improvements, figures relating to years 2003 and 2004 in Table 13.5 are not comparable with those published in editions of Regional Trends prior to number 38.

From May 2004 the EU expanded from 15 to 25 Member States. See Notes and Definitions relating to Chapter 2 for further details. Table 13.5 is produced using data from 15 Member States.

Table 13.6 Expenditure on research and development

On 1 July 2001 the Government research agency, the Defence Evaluation and Research Agency (DERA), was disestablished and two new organisations were created. Around a quarter of DERA remained with the Ministry of Defence (MOD) as a government agency while the remaining three-quarters became a private limited company (PLC). As a PLC its Research and Development (R&D) activities are now classified and included within the business sector.

Table 13.7 Government expenditure on regional preferential assistance to industry

The Department of Trade and Industry is the lead sponsor for the eight Regional Development Agencies in the UK and the London Development Agency. Their activities cover economic development and regeneration, promoting business efficiency, investment and competitiveness, promoting employment and skills development and contributing to the achievement of sustainable development in the UK.

The types of assistance included in this table for Great Britain are: Regional Development Grants prior to 1996/97; Regional Selective Assistance; Regional Enterprise Grants; expenditure on Land and Factories by the English Industrial Estates Corporation (until 1993/94 after which this falls under the province of the Single Regeneration Budget), Scottish Enterprise, the Welsh Development Agency; and expenditure on land and factories and grants by the Development Board for Rural Wales (until 1998/99) and Highlands and Islands Enterprise.

Northern Ireland has a different range of financial incentives available and so the figures have not been aggregated into a UK total. The items included are Industrial Development Board grants and loans; expenditure on land and factories; Standard Capital Grants; and Local Enterprise Development Unit grants and loans.

All figures are gross and include payments to nationalised industries. GB payments relate only to projects situated in the Assisted Areas of Great Britain.

Table 13.8 Business registrations and de-registrations

Annual estimates of registrations and de-registrations are compiled by the Small Business Service, an agency of the Department of Trade and Industry. They are based on VAT information held by the Office for National Statistics (ONS). The estimates are a good indicator of the pattern of business start-ups and closures, although they exclude firms not registered for VAT, either because their main activity is exempt from VAT, or because they have a turnover below the VAT threshold (£55,000 with effect from April 2002, £56,000 from April 2003 and £58,000 from April 2004) and have not registered voluntarily. Large rises in the VAT threshold in 1991 and 1993 affected the extent to which the VAT system covers the small business population. This means that the estimates are not entirely comparable before and after these years.

Table 13.10 EU Structural Funds

Regions may be eligible for funding in one of two categories. 'Objective 1' funds promote the development of regions that are lagging behind the rest of the European Union. To be eligible, regions need to have a per capita GDP of 75 per cent or less of the EU average. In these areas, emphasis is placed on creating a sound infrastructure, modernising transport and communication links, improving energy and water supplies, encouraging research and development, providing training and helping small businesses.

Areas suffering from industrial decline may be designated 'Objective 2'. These areas need help adjusting their economies to new industrial activities; they have high unemployment rates and a high but declining share of industrial activity. EU grants may be provided to help create jobs, encourage new businesses, renovate land and buildings, promote research and development, and foster links between universities and industry.

In addition, rural areas where economic development needs to be encouraged may be designated 'Objective 2'. In these areas the focus is on developing jobs outside agriculture in small businesses and tourism, and improvements to transport and basic services are promoted to prevent rural depopulation.

Grants under Objectives 1 and 2 are disbursed under the terms of Single Programming Documents or their equivalents, which provide a strategic framework relevant to the region concerned.

The other objective under which grants are allocated, Objective 3, which covers long-term unemployment, jobs for young people and modernisation of farms, is not defined geographically. In addition the Structural

Funds provide support for Community-wide initiatives. These initiatives account for 8 per cent of the Structural Funds budget.

Tables 13.12, 13.13, 13.14 Agriculture census

The annual census encompasses the main agricultural holdings in the United Kingdom. Estimates for minor holdings are included in the national totals for England, Wales, Scotland and Northern Ireland. Generally, minor holdings are characterised by a small agricultural area, low economic activity and a small labour input.

Table 13.13 Areas and yields

The figures for specific crops relate to those in the ground on the date of the June census or for which the land is being prepared for sowing at that date. In England and Wales cereal production is estimated from sample surveys held in September, November and April; oilseed rape production is estimated from a sample survey held in August. In Scotland, cereals and oilseed rape yields are estimated mid-September, followed by sample surveys later in the year. The

Department of Agriculture for Northern Ireland estimates cereal and oilseed rape yields from a stratified sample survey of 200 farms carried out in the autumn of each year.

Table IA3 Direct inward investment from overseas: project successes

Data on projects which have attracted inward investment appear in this table. They are based on information provided to UK Trade and Investment (UKTI) by the beneficiary companies at the time of the decision to invest. There is no obligation to notify the department, so the figures relate only to those projects where UKTI or its regional partners were involved or have come to their notice. They also take no account of subsequent developments.

Table IA6 Less favoured areas

Land in the less favoured areas is commonly infertile, unsuitable for cultivation and with limited potential which cannot be increased except at excessive cost. Such land is mainly suitable for extensive livestock farming.

Symbols and conventions

Reference years. Where a choice of years has to be made, the most recent year or a run of recent years is shows, together with the past population census years (1991, 1998, 2001 etc.) and sometimes the mid-points between census years (1996 etc.). Other years may be added if they represent a peak or trough in the series or relate to a specific benchmark or target.

Rounding of figures. In tables where the figures have been rounded to the nearest final digit, there may be an apparent discrepancy between the sum of the constituent items and the total as shown.

Billion. This term is used to represent a thousand million.

Provisional and estimated data. Some data for the latest year (and occasionally for earlier years) are provisional or estimated. To keep footnotes to a minimum, these have not been indicated; source departments will be able to advise if revised data are available.

Survey data. Many of the tables and figures in Regional Trends present the results of household surveys that can be subject to large sampling errors. Care should therefore be taken in drawing conclusions about regional differences, and especially with subnational changes over time.

Non-calendar years. Data covering more than one year, e.g. 1998, 1999 and 2000 are shown as 1998-2000.

Financial years. For example April 2000 to March 2001, and academic years, for example September 2000 to August 2001 is shown as 2000/01.

Units. Figures are shown in italics when they represent percentages.

Symbols. The following symbols have been used throughout Regional Trends:

- .. not available
- . not applicable
- - negligible (less than half the first digit shown)
- 0 nil

Index